Economic Policy

Economic Policy

Theory and Practice

SECOND EDITION

Agnès Bénassy-Quéré, Benoît Cœuré,
Pierre Jacquet, and Jean Pisani-Ferry

OXFORD
UNIVERSITY PRESS

OXFORD
UNIVERSITY PRESS

Oxford University Press is a department of the University of Oxford.
It furthers the University's objective of excellence in research, scholarship, and education by publishing worldwide. Oxford is a registered trademark of Oxford University Press in the UK and in certain other countries

Published in India by
Oxford University Press
2/11 Ground floor, Ansari Road, Daryaganj, New Delhi 110002, India

First Edition published in 2010
Second Edition published in 2019

ISBN-13: 978-0-19-006169-2

Reprinted 2019
Printed in India by Replika Press Pvt. Ltd.

Contents

Foreword

This book is a book I would have loved to write. Indeed, this is a book I long wanted to write. I wanted to do so out of guilt. For a long time, I have felt that my graduate textbook written with Stan Fischer sent the wrong message. We had made the choice to present models and their logic rather than their applications. The justification was a perfectly good one—namely, that we wanted to show the intellectual structure of macroeconomic theory first. But, de facto, the lack of serious empirics sent another message: that theory was largely divorced from practice and from facts. That message is wrong: theory without facts is much too easy and of very little use. I also wanted to write such a book out of a desire to share with students my excitement about moving between theory, facts, and policy. It is traditional to do so in undergraduate textbooks, at least in the United States. Those textbooks are full of discussions about policy debates—about the effects of policy choices on the economy. I thought it would be even more fun to do so with graduate students who have more tools, both theoretical and econometric, at their disposal.

Agnès Bénassy-Quéré, Benoît Cœuré, Pierre Jacquet, and Jean Pisani-Ferry have beaten me to it. I am happy they did so because they have done a better job than I could have hoped to.

To give a sense of what they have achieved, I shall take one example, the creation or reform of fiscal frameworks like the European Stability and

Growth Pact (SGP). To come to an intelligent set of recommendations, think of all the elements you need to put together:

- You need to understand what sustainability means in theory and in practice, what the costs of not abiding by sustainability are, and how to assess sustainability. When does a debt-to-gross domestic product ratio become truly excessive? What happens then? How fast can you reach that threshold? How fast can you move away from it?
- You need to understand the long-term effects of deficits and debt on output and its composition. How do deficits and debt affect output in the medium and long run? How do they affect the interest rate, the net foreign debt position, the capital stock? What is the cost in terms of lost consumption in the future? Which generations gain, which generations lose?
- You need to understand the short-term effects of deficits and how countercyclical fiscal policy can help in the short run. Do deficits affect activity in the same way, whether they come from tax cuts or spending increases? How important are expectation effects? Can the anticipation of large deficits in the future lead to a decrease in consumption and investment and a decrease in output today? When is this more likely to happen?
- You need to understand the macroeconomic costs of decreased policy flexibility. Are constraints on deficits and debt consistent with an appropriate response of fiscal policy to shocks? What explains sustained divergences within the euro area during the first 10 years? Were such divergences avoidable? Then you need to determine whether and to what extent fiscal policy is the right tool to deal with country-specific shocks and to what extent it can (should) substitute for the lack of an independent monetary policy. Finally, you need to figure out how much policy space is left to governments after they have fought the new Great Recession and rescued their banks.
- You need to think about how to define the rules in practice. How should debt be defined? How should implicit liabilities, coming from Social Security and other promises to future generations, be treated? If rules are defined in terms of deficits and debt, what are the most appropriate definitions of the two concepts for the question at hand? How should rules deal with privatization revenues? Should rules apply to gross debt or to net debt? Should the budget be separated between a current account and a capital account? Should the deficit rules apply only to the government current account? Can rules be enforced by politicians, or do we need to set up independent committees?

- You need to think about political-economy issues. Why are rules needed in the first place—to protect people from their governments, or to protect the governments from themselves? How can a particular set of rules be manipulated or distorted by a national government? How will sanctions against a misbehaving government be imposed? Will these sanctions be credible *ex ante*? Is international coordination, such as in the G20 framework, an advantage or a diversion from every government's duties?

To answer these questions, you need many conceptual tools. Among them are a dynamic general equilibrium model with overlapping generations, a model of short-run fluctuations with careful treatment of expectations, political-economy models to think about the case for rules, and agency models to help you think about the design of specific rules. In each case, with guidance from theory, you need to look at the evidence to get a sense of which theoretical arguments are more relevant. This is not easy to do. Courses will typically give you the theoretical tools without much incentive to apply them and leave you to use them on your own without much practical training. This is not what this book does. It motivates you to use tools, gives you the tools, and shows you how they can be employed.

Last, but not least, this book is among the very first that offer students a rigorous and comprehensive treatment of the global financial crisis and the Great Recession that followed. The authors do not try to cast a veil over the conceptual difficulties economists face when they reflect on the causes of the crisis, on the limitations of traditional approaches that the crisis has uncovered, maybe on the excessive faith in theory, and on the need for more theoretical work to better understand the crisis and make sure it does not happen again. But they do not throw the baby out with the bath water and claim that economists have "mistaken beauty for truth," as was suggested by Paul Krugman. On the contrary, they show how existing theories can be used, cross-fertilized, and replaced in a historical context to understand the crisis better. This is the way forward.

In short, this book trains you to be a good macroeconomist—a good economist. It instills the right attitude and gives you the right methodology: to build solidly on theory, to use the theory to look at the data, and then to go back and forth between the two until a coherent picture forms. As I was reading the book, I felt again the excitement that comes with doing research on macroeconomics. I hope this excitement is contagious, and I wish you a very good read.

Olivier Blanchard, C. Fred Bergsten Senior Fellow,
Peterson Institute for International Economics

Preface

This is a book for those who are eager to find out what shapes, or should shape, economic policy: the major stylized facts that capture the messages from history; the theories that help make sense of these facts and analyze the impact of policy decisions; the controversies that surround policy choices; the rules and institutions that contribute to determining them; and, last but not least, the way experience, theories, and institutions interact.

The first edition of this book—in French—dates back to 2004. This is the second English edition. Meanwhile, Italian and Chinese translations were published, and the fourth French edition (prepared in parallel to the English one) was released in late 2017. Each vintage has been noticeably different from the previous one. The original book arose from a seminar designed to build a bridge between the students' theoretical baggage and economic policy-making, which many of them planned to embrace as a profession, and this second English edition follows the same approach. Not only is this new edition more insightful, more precise, and more comprehensive than the previous one, but it also incorporates the new analytical insights and new practical responses developed in response to the major economic policy challenges that arose in the past 15 years and that have revisited the way many issues are looked at and many problems are approached.

Over the past decade, the world has been hit by the global financial crisis and the Great Recession (uppercase letters reflect the trauma it has caused), prompting a rediscovery of finance by an economic profession that had long assumed that the financial plumbing was flawless; Europe's currency area has come through a near-death experience; inflation has almost disappeared, while forgotten deflation concerns have reemerged; public debt has soared, and the threat of sovereign insolvency that was regarded as the sad privilege of developing countries has reached the advanced world; emerging countries have come of age; income inequality has risen to the forefront, first of political controversies and, gradually, of policy discussions; and the nature of labor has structurally changed. New questions have prompted new research and called for new responses rooted in theory and informed by practical experience.

This new edition fully takes this major renewal into account. It provides the reader with an up-to-date overview of economic policy as it is discussed, designed, and implemented. All chapters have been thoroughly reviewed, some have been entirely rewritten. A new chapter on financial stability has been introduced. The result, we believe, is a book like no other.

The Interaction Between Research and Practice

This book stands at the crossroads between theory and practice. Our premise is that the all-too-frequent disconnect between them is detrimental to both good policy and good research. We posit that going back and forth between practice and theory enlightens practice and helps construct better theories.

All four of us are teachers; all of us combine, or have combined, research and policy advice: we have been advisors, experts, members or chairs of consultative bodies, senior officials, central bankers, researchers in think tanks, and commentators at a national, European, or international level. We have been confronted with the reality of economic policy-making in different places—and this has changed the way we understand, teach, and use economic theory.

We have learned from experience that research can be the victim of its own internal logic and ignore important, sometimes even vital, economic insights. We have also learned that ignorance of the lessons of History and neglect of theoretical advances can make policy ineffective, even toxic.

The global financial crisis will have a long-lasting effect on policy-making and economic theory. Some of the mechanisms at play before and during the crisis had been identified and studied in the aftermath of previous crises, while others have been updated or altogether uncovered. In a first step, in order to fight financial disruption, to revitalize the economy, and to design new crisis-prevention schemes, economists tapped knowledge which had been buried deep in economic textbooks, drawing lessons from economic history; they attempted to avoid repeating past mistakes; and they rehabilitated models which had been considered mere theoretical curiosities. In a second step, new research was initiated. Some of it was very theoretical and aimed to identify sources and contagion channels of financial fragility and to renew our approach to risk management; some of it was empirical and aimed to sharpen our understanding of the impact of economic policy or to explore previously overlooked dimensions, such as income inequality or systemic risk. In this book, we survey this research and discuss its contribution to economic policy, in particular in Chapters 4–6 devoted to fiscal policy, monetary policy, and financial stability.

In Europe, the crisis has uncovered specific deficiencies in the way economic thinking and policy-making interact. The creation of a supranational currency was an undertaking (one may say, an experiment) of unprecedented ambition. Many of the pitfalls that were encountered could have been foreseen, at least in part. Heterogeneity within the currency area, inadequate adjustment mechanisms to asymmetric shocks, self-reinforcing price divergence, and weak incentives to fiscal responsibility, to mention but a few, were well-known issues. They had been identified from the outset by academics, and their significance could be inferred from historical experience. Other challenges related to the non-pooling of bank risk or the lack of a lender of last resort to governments had been identified by some but had not been subject to a complete diagnosis. A deeper, more genuine dialogue between researchers and policymakers could have helped anticipate and prevent the euro area crisis. Unfortunately, however, policy complacency set in after the launch of the euro, and, for long, policymakers seemed more interested in the analyses that justified their choices than in those that questioned them. A genuine dialogue intensified only when it appeared that the euro was under mortal threat.

The Responsibility of Economists

The more theory and policy interact, the greater the responsibility of economists. This raises several issues related to their integrity, their intellectual openness, and their ability to debate.

Let's face it: The crisis has cast suspicion on the economic profession. Economists have been blamed for being blind, complacent, or even captured. They have been charged with intellectual conformism, excessive trust in market mechanisms, being too close to the world of finance, and being weak with the powerful. After the euro area crisis, they have been accused of drawing biased conclusions on the costs and benefits of monetary integration (that is, underestimating the former and overestimating the latter). They have been diagnosed with an acute myopia which leads them to take interest only in social interactions with a pecuniary nature, to focus on the accumulation of wealth more than on its distribution, and to ignore the damage caused by growth and the political forces that shape economic institutions. And they have sometimes been blamed for focusing on specialized, "elegant" models at the expense of understanding a complex reality—for mistaking beauty for truth, as cogently expressed by Paul Krugman.

As for integrity, it is fair to acknowledge that professional economists, while lecturing others about the importance of incentives, have for too long turned a blind eye to their own conflicts of interests. Beyond the pecuniary dimension, which should not be overlooked, economists must be aware that being too close to any professional constituency—including politicians and government technocrats—risks blunting their critical sense. After the crisis, their professional ethics have been questioned. This has already prompted greater disclosure, for example in professional journals, an effort which needs to be further advanced. Full transparency on potential conflicts of interest must be ensured.

As for the criticism of being intellectually blind, it is often based on a mistaken preconception. Economic theory is not the Trojan horse of free-market, small government, minimal redistribution mindset some believe it is in liberal circles. Several recent recipients of the Nobel Memorial Prize in Economics have devoted their research to inequalities, poverty, and government intervention, or to the limited rationality of economic agents. Economists do regard the market as an efficient tool to allocate resources, but they are equally concerned with its failures and unequal distributional effects, and they have designed instruments to identify and correct them.

Democracy would benefit if participants in the public debate made a better (and more informed) use of economic analysis. Economists are not ideologues: they devote an increasing part of their time to empirical work and experiments, tapping a rapidly expanding trove of data. Nowadays, unlike a few decades ago, the bulk of research published in top economic journals is empirical. And theory remains essential to identify the key parameters which will make a policy successful and to guide empirical analysis beyond the surface of pure statistical regularities.

Some economists may see themselves more as advocates—of market efficiency, of economic openness, of price stability or of (de)growth—than as scientists or engineers. And when confronted by politicians, civil society actors, or experts of other disciplines, some cautious and balanced researchers may also tend to simplify their points excessively and overplay their social role. Policymakers often make a biased use of the outcome of research, placing an excessive weight on work that merely confirms their priors. In the mid-2000s, scholars of finance or of the euro too often struck a Panglossian tone, while those who struck a note of caution were largely ignored. In such cases, admittedly, the culprit is less research than the relationship between research and policy, and economists share the blame. And methodological arrogance is unwarranted. When it comes to the myopia and apparent irrationality of individuals, economists often hide behind Elinor Ostrom or Richard Thaler (both Nobel-Prize winners) who have endeavored to understand non-monetary interactions, non-pecuniary incentives, and collective action. And they emphasize that concepts such as utility, intertemporal maximization, or social welfare give them all the necessary instruments to build a multifaceted approach to public action, far from the simple religion of growth. This is all true but easily misleading. Economists should be more open to the finding of other social sciences. The strength of their discipline does not come from any inherent superiority of what George Stigler once celebrated as the "imperial science," but from the blend of analytical rigor and empirical relevance that their profession has been able to develop. They should heed Keynes's invitation to model themselves on the humility and competence of dentists.

A Unique Structure

Economic textbooks typically cover economic theory in a given field—macroeconomics, microeconomics, finance, international trade, etc.—and use real-life stories to illustrate theoretical results. Their representation of economic policy instruments and of the decision-making process often remains rudimentary and abstract: the decision-maker is supposed to choose without constraints the interest rate or the level of public spending, whereas in real life such decisions involve complex processes.

Conversely, many excellent essays on economic policy are more concerned with describing the ebb and flow of new ideas and institutions than with discussing their theoretical underpinnings. They are informative but frustrating. Our book aims to fill that gap. We present the main analytical tools—theoretical and empirical instruments, or old and new—that are relevant to addressing real-life policy issues; we explain how these instruments can be used to identify policy trade-offs and guide the policymakers' choices; and we discuss the theoretical uncertainties, blind spots, and controversies that justify cultivating humility and caution when formulating policy advice and that make the job of economists so challenging and rewarding. We hope that this book will provide the reader with the necessary tools to understand and participate in the debates which will develop in the years to come.

There are nine chapters. The first three set out the general framework of economic policy-making. Chapter 1 describes the methodological foundations and toolbox essentials that will be used in the rest of the book. Chapter 2 adds a note of caution: it outlines the limits of government intervention and the political-economy reasons that may render it suboptimal. Chapter 3 introduces the plurality of policy-making within and between sovereign nations. Chapters 4–9 cover six domains of economic policy: fiscal policy (Chapter 4), monetary policy (Chapter 5), financial stability (Chapter 6), international capital integration and foreign exchange policy (Chapter 7), tax policy (Chapter 8), and long-term growth policies (Chapter 9). Chapter 6 is entirely new and benefited from comments by Laurence Boone, Lorenzo Cappiello, Anne Le Lorier, and Peter Praet, whom we would like to thank here. Each of these six chapters is structured in a similar way: the first section outlines stylized facts derived from recent economic history, the second section introduces the theoretical models policymakers should have command (or at least a knowledge) of, and the third section presents the main policy options. There are many cross-references between the six chapters, but they are written in such a way that each of them can be read on its own.

This book is by no means comprehensive. We cover macroeconomics in a broad sense, focusing successively on money, the budget, finance, exchange rate, taxation, and growth. We have chosen not to address, or address only at the margin, a number of otherwise important areas of economic policy, such as competition policy, social protection, labor policies, international trade, or climate change. We have also decided not to write specific chapters on international economic policy, regional (and especially European) integration, or the management of local governments. Chapter 3 summarizes what economic theory has to say on the assignment of policy instruments to different levels of government and on the difficulties of global governance; however, in any policy domain, some levers are global, some are regional, some are national, and some are local, and we have therefore addressed them in conjunction in each of the six thematic chapters.

Economists are often blamed for resorting to technical vocabulary as a way of protecting themselves from inconvenient questions. To help the reader overcome semantic barriers, we have been careful to define all key concepts at least once in the book and to signal these terms with *italics*. The index at the end of the book provides a complete list of keywords with the corresponding pages where they are defined and illustrated.

Additionally, we have parked most mathematical developments in technical boxes. We see mathematics neither as the purpose of economic science nor as the instrument that would allow us to draw a line between truth and ideology. As Paul Romer once noted, mathematics can be used in support of ideology, and, conversely, some seminal theoretical articles mentioned in this book do not show any equations. Mathematics is nevertheless unique in mapping in a coherent and rigorous way a set of assumptions into conclusions. It is also the basis for statistical tools allowing us to confront assumptions with real-world data. As a language, it is, however, fitter to expose a flow of rigorous reasoning than to explain it and present its conclusions. We give examples of how it can be used, but we also make the reasoning explicit in more literary ways.

As "reading assistance," each chapter includes many charts and tables because our approach fundamentally relies on facts. It also includes theoretical and descriptive boxes. Additionally, there are extensive bibliographical references so that the reader can dig further into any of the issues covered.

Conclusion

We express our gratitude to all those who have encouraged us and who have helped make this joint endeavor a reality. We owe a lot to our students, whose questions and criticisms have greatly improved the relevance, accuracy, and legibility of this book. We also thank our colleagues and friends who have commented on previous versions. Writing on economic policy requires us to update data and facts tirelessly. For this last edition, we have benefited from particularly effective assistance by Paul Berenberg-Gossler, Pranav Garg, and Amélie Schurich-Rey. Without them, this book would be less caught up with today's debates.

Paris, Florence, Frankfurt, New Delhi, March 2018

Economic Policy

1

Concepts

> Practical men, who believe themselves to be quite exempt from any intellectual influences, are usually the slaves of some defunct economist. Madmen in authority, who hear voices in the air, are distilling their frenzy from some academic scribbler of a few years back. I am sure that the power of vested interests is vastly exaggerated compared with the gradual encroachment of ideas. Not, indeed, immediately, but after a certain interval; for in the field of economic and political philosophy there are not many who are influenced by new theories after they are twenty-five or thirty years of age, so that the ideas which civil servants and politicians and even agitators apply to current events are not likely to be the newest. But, soon or late, it is ideas, not vested interests, which are dangerous for good or evil.
>
> John Maynard Keynes (1936; chapt. 24, part 5)

The last sentences of *The General Theory of Employment, Interest and Price* by the famous British economist are a fetish quotation for economists who take them as an acknowledgment of their social role. Yet they also express the complexity of the links between theory and economic policy. They suggest that economic expertise can neither be regarded as the servant nor as the master of political decision. It does influence it, but in an indirect way and with delay.[1]

However, Keynes (1931, part V, chapt. 2, last sentence) also expressed detached irony about the economists' pretense to determine the policymakers' choice:

> If economists could manage to get themselves thought of as humble, competent people on a level with dentists, that would be splendid.

The interaction between economic ideas and political motivations was aptly characterized in the classics as *political economy*.[2] This type of interaction between power and knowledge is certainly not specific to the economic discipline. It arises in all fields where public decision relies at least partially on scientific or technical expertise. For reasons we develop later in this chapter and throughout the book, however, it is more pronounced in economics and more general in the social sciences than, say, in geology or biology.

This chapter introduces the main themes of economic policy analysis. We start in Section 1.1 with a discussion of the various approaches to economic policy an economist can adopt. In Section 1.2, we discuss the arguments for and against public intervention, both from a micro- and a macroeconomic standpoint. Finally, Section 1.3 is devoted to the evaluation of economic policy choices and deals with both criteria and instruments.

1.1 A Primer on Economic Policy

1.1.1 The economist and the Prince: Three alternative approaches

An economist can adopt diverse attitudes vis-à-vis policy decisions: she or he can limit herself to studying their effects on the economy (*positive economics*), she can seek to influence them through recommendations that draw on her expertise (*normative economics*), or, finally, she can take them as a topic for research and study their determinants (*political economy* or *political economics*). All three approaches coexist in today's economics.

a) Positive economics

In positive economics, the economist takes the point of view of an outside observer and aims to determine the channels through which public decisions affect private behavior and outcomes. For example, she analyzes the effects of a tightening of monetary policy, an increase in public expenditure, a tax reform, or a new labor market regulation. Economic policy choices are regarded as entirely *exogenous*, meaning that they are not determined within the model that explains the economy and whose variables—such as prices, incomes, output, and the like—they influence.

Positive economics therefore approaches economic policy with the same concepts and methods as those used to study other economic phenomena: for example, there is hardly a difference between studying the effects of a rise in the central bank money lending rate on nonfinancial agents and analyzing the effects of an exogenous rise in the risk premium which banks require for lending to private agents; similarly, the effects of a rise in the minimum wage can be analyzed within the same framework and with the same tools as those of a strengthening of the bargaining power of trade unions.

b) Normative economics

The second approach is called *normative economics*. The economist here adopts the posture of an adviser to a supposedly benevolent Prince—or political master—and examines which set of decisions can best serve explicit public policy purposes, such as reducing unemployment, improving the standard of living, or safeguarding the environment. The public decision-maker is regarded as a social planner and the economist as an engineer who tells him or her how to select adequate means for reaching certain ends, meaning how to design policies and then how to implement them. Economists are certainly not short of policy advice, and they generally do not need a request from the Prince to express their views. In all cases, however, they make explicit or implicit assumptions about social preferences that cannot be derived solely from economic theory.

Normative economics relies on the knowledge base of positive economics to assess the effects of different possible decisions. However, it also requires a metric within which to compare alternative situations. Assume that a government wants to reduce unemployment and suppose that two competing policies may lead to this result but at the price, for the first one, of a lowering of the employees' average wage income and, for the second one, of an increase in wage inequality. Choosing between these two solutions requires assessing the social cost of each of those policies against the social benefit of lowering unemployment. This implies defining a preference order between situations, each characterized by the unemployment rate, the average wage income level, and a measure of inequality. Constructing such a ranking raises considerable conceptual and practical difficulties.

Furthermore, normative economics frequently implies giving up the *first-best solution* that would be reached in the absence of informational, institutional, or political constraints for a *second-best solution*, one that respects those constraints.[3]

Let us take the example of carbon dioxide emissions, which governments have committed to limit to curb global warming. A first-best solution consists in creating a global carbon dioxide tax to incite companies to use less carbon-intensive energy sources. The carbon tax, however, hurts powerful special interests, such as those of car makers or oil-producing companies; requires international coordination and implementation; and is disputed on equity grounds by developing countries. The climate agreement reached in Paris in December 2015 therefore leaves participating countries free to choose the means they intend to rely on to reduce emissions.

Some governments consider making existing government policies "greener," say by restricting public tenders to companies which meet carbon dioxide emission standards. Such a second-best solution, however, bears significant unintended consequences. It distorts economic choices by making the implicit price of carbon dioxide differ across the economy, and, moreover, due to limited competition among providers, taxpayers may ultimately bear the cost of the policy in place of the owners of the companies—who would be better placed to steer their behavior.

Economists involved in public decisions face many such constraints. The question they face is typically not "how can unemployment be reduced?" but "in view of the stance and prejudices of the main players—government departments, majority and opposition in Parliament, and various stakeholders—what is the most cost-effective proposal consistent with the government's overall policy philosophy and commitments already publicly undertaken?" This second question obviously is a very weak version of the first one, but major economic decisions are very often taken this way. Economists may understandably be tempted to abstain from participating in such decisions. But, as Herbert Stein, a chairman of the Council of Economic Advisors under US presidents Richard Nixon and Gerald Ford, used to say, "Economists do not know very much [about economics. But] other people, including the politicians who make economic policy, know even less" (Stein, 1986, p. xi). Returning to the ivory tower may thus be an undesirable option.

Second-best recommendations nevertheless raise important difficulties. The second-best optimum can in fact be inferior to the initial situation in welfare terms. An example of an inferior second-best solution can be found in trade policy: liberalization on a regional basis only can divert trade from an efficient global producer to a less efficient regional partner, which worsens the allocation of resources in comparison to a situation of uniform tariff protection.[4] What is perceived as a small step in the right direction therefore does not necessarily improve upon the status quo; on the contrary, it can reduce welfare.

Beyond this disturbing result, modern public economics emphasizes the equally formidable difficulty associated with the existence of *asymmetric information* between the public decision-maker, the agents in charge of implementing policies, and those who bear the consequences. Not unlike Soviet central planning, the traditional approach of economic policy postulated that the decision-maker had perfect information (in fact, he or she was frequently assumed to know better than private agents) and perfect control over the implementation of his decisions. The reality, of course, is that the decision-maker has both an incomplete knowledge of reality and an imperfect command of policy implementation. Take the regulator in charge of a specific sector (e.g., telecommunications). He gets information on costs, returns on investment, or demand elasticity largely from the companies that he is responsible for controlling. For the latter, this information has strategic value. They have every reason not to be fully transparent or to provide biased information. When dealing with them, the regulator therefore suffers an informational disadvantage even when he supplements the information provided by the regulated companies with indirect indications derived from observing market prices and quantities.

Likewise, government bodies responsible for policy implementation are not flawless transmitters: they often do not pass on adequate information from below or instructions from above. For example, even if teachers from the education ministry have first-hand knowledge of the situation in their classes, the minister in charge may not have accurate overall information, which obviously affects the quality of his or her decisions. Reciprocally, the minister's policy may not be considered adequate by the teachers who have their own views on education policy, and this affects its implementation and effectiveness.

The importance of information asymmetries for private markets was first highlighted in research by 2001 Nobel laureates George Akerlof, Michael Spence, and Joseph Stiglitz, but it was Jean-Jacques Laffont[5] and Jean Tirole who worked out their consequences for public economics. They initiated research on the *design of contracts* that encourage agents to reveal the information which they would otherwise keep for themselves (thereby allowing regulators to take more appropriate decisions). Such contracts are examples of *mechanism design*, meaning the design of optimal institutions or procedures to deliver social outcomes. Mechanism design covers issues ranging from auctions of public assets, voting procedures for public decisions, regulations to curb private behaviors, or contracts between the government and private contractors. All such mechanisms should be designed in a way that delivers the expected outcome while overcoming the government's lack of information.[6] Key to this outcome, as explained by Nobel Prize laureate Eric Maskin, is *incentive compatibility*:

> Because mechanism designers do not generally know which outcomes are optimal in advance, they have to proceed more indirectly than simply prescribing outcomes by fiat; in particular, the mechanisms designed must generate the information needed as they are executed. The problem is exacerbated by the fact that the individuals who do have this critical information—the citizens in the public good case or the buyers in the asset-selling example—have their own objectives and so may not have the incentive to behave in a way that reveals what they know. Thus, the mechanisms must be *incentive compatible.* (Eric Maskin, 2007, p. 3)

c) Political economics

Like positive economics, of which it can be regarded as an extension, the political economy approach refrains from making prescriptions and takes the viewpoint of an external observer. However, instead of considering the political decision-makers' behavior as exogenous, it treats it in the same way it treats private agents' behavior; that is, as *endogenous* (determined by the state of the economy itself). The government is therefore no longer regarded as a *Deus ex machina* that monitors and steers the private economy in the name of the general interest but, instead, as a machine directed by politicians (i.e., by rational players whose behavior follows specific objectives and faces specific constraints). The simplest models of politically motivated behavior often draw on the simplistic assumption that the politicians' only objective is to hang on to power and therefore to maximize their reelection chances. However, more elaborate models also recognize the need to fulfill electoral campaign pledges (which become a constraint after election); partisan preferences; the role of special interest groups, which may dwell on the need to maintain long-term relationships within a social group; and—at the extreme—corruption and bribery. The political economy approach also endeavors to represent the behavior of technocrats within government or of those in charge of public agencies (central banks, independent authorities, international institutions) and to determine how the external and internal governance and the mandate of these institutions influence economic performance.

A political economy approach is evidently essential to the analysis of gun control policy in the United States. But it is also required in fields like trade policy, to explain why protection varies across sectors, or labor market policy, to understand why the employment performance varies considerably across countries.

Political economy does not exclude normative judgments, but it does have implications regarding their scope. James Buchanan, one of the initiators of modern political economics, claims that such judgments are valid only if applied to the framework (often called *policy regime*) that determines economic policy: the constitution and, more largely, all the rules, procedures, and institutions surrounding economic policy decisions. To draw on a distinction introduced by Robert Lucas (see, e.g., Lucas, 1976), the choice of an economic policy regime involves normative considerations, but the actual economic policy decisions are the result of political processes within the framework of this regime. It would therefore be pointless to exercise normative judgment on what must be regarded as endogenous variables. According to Buchanan, "the object of economic research is 'the economy,' which is, by definition, a *social organization*, an interaction among separate choosing entities. . . . [T]here exists no one person, no single chooser, who maximizes *for* the economy, *for* the polity. . . . That which emerges [from the decision-making process] is that which emerges from results, and that is that" (Buchanan, 1975, pp. 225–226). The role of the economist is to study the functioning of these processes and the incentives they create for public decision-makers. It is to discuss whether these incentives create a political bias or help align the outcome of the decision process with the public interest. It is not to give advice to the Prince or his marquis.

During the last decades of the twentieth century, the political economy approach was strengthened by two concomitant developments. First, the theory of *rational expectations*[7] developed in the 1970s (in particular by Robert Lucas) emphasized that private agents do not react to stimuli as automatons, but rather use their reason to anticipate policy decisions. A good example of such behavior is provided by exchange-rate crises. As developed in Chapter 7, such crises can only be understood by considering the strategic interaction between private speculators and official authorities. These crises often occur because private agents know the public decision-makers' preferences and constraints (or at least guess what they are) and therefore can assess the probability of a currency devaluation. While not directly related to the political economy approach, the theory of rational expectations thus challenged the idea that the State dominates and steers the private economy. It resulted in integrating into economic models a representation that makes public decision-makers react endogenously to endogenous events rather than behave exogenously.

The second development of research on political behavior was a reaction to failures of government intervention in areas such as macroeconomic management, employment, or development. While some of these failures could be ascribed to genuine policy mistakes, insufficient knowledge, or simply bad luck, in other cases there was a need to provide explanations for a persistent inability to learn from past mistakes and from international experience. Why are certain regulations maintained even though they obviously lead to outcomes that contradict stated policy objectives? Why have some developed countries returned to full employment more rapidly than others after the 2009 global crisis? If this were simply a matter of identifying appropriate policies and institutions, some form of learning should be at work, and less-successful governments could be expected to learn, even slowly, from successful ones. Since some do not, there is a need for political economy explanations.

The choice of a regime regarding product, capital, and labor market regulations involves *preferences* and trade-offs between, say, efficiency and equity; economic *interests,* which can differ between, say, incumbents and newcomers; and *representations* of how the economy works, on which various players may disagree.[8] From a knowledge perspective, it is therefore important to identify the source and understand the nature of these disagreements. From a policy perspective, recognizing and explicitly considering the intellectual and political environment of public decisions becomes as necessary as determining what is the first-best solution. Political economy then becomes essential both from a positive point of view (to understand why economic policy does not achieve its objectives) and from a normative one (to evaluate the chances of success of various reform strategies).

Positive economics, normative economics, and political economics thus coexist, and the modern approach of economic policy draws on all three methods. Positive economics remains indispensable to the understanding of the likely effects of public decisions. Normative economics brings intellectual discipline to policy choices and helps address the trade-offs they involve. Both, however, face limits and are increasingly complemented by political economics.

Avinash Dixit (1996) once observed that the traditional approach of economic policy envisaged the ultimate policymaker—the Prince—as an omniscient, omnipotent, and benevolent dictator. The economics of imperfect information taught us that he or she was not omniscient. Second-best theory was developed in recognition of the fact that he or she was not omnipotent. Political economy tells us that he or she is not always benevolent. This should not be a cause for policy nihilism—only a motive against policy naïveté.

The remaining sections of this chapter will focus on the traditional approach whose shortcomings are then discussed in Chapter 2.

1.1.2 What do policymakers do?

The main tasks of economic policymakers can be grouped into six categories:

1. *Set and enforce the rules of the economic game.* Market structures and property rights are not preordained. They are social and historical outcomes shaped by power relations between interest groups, and, if left unchecked, they are fraught with abuse and fraud. Economic legislation provides the framework for the decisions of private agents. Enforcement covers the protection of property rights, competition policy, labor law, and the supervision of regulated markets such as banking and insurance. Economic legislation increasingly has an international dimension (through international treaties and agreements)—especially, but not only, in the European Union.
2. *Tax and spend.* Government spending amounts to about one-half of gross domestic product (GDP) in continental European countries and one-third in the United States and Japan. Budgetary decisions affect households' and firms' income and behavior through taxation and social insurance; they affect productivity and long-term growth through infrastructure, research, and education spending; and they affect aggregate demand through changes in spending or overall taxation (including negative taxation such as subsidies).
3. *Issue and manage the currency.* The choice of a monetary and exchange-rate regime is one of the most important single decisions a government can make. Defining and implementing monetary policy is the function of the central bank, an often independent branch of government that is responsible for setting interest rates, maintaining

the value of the currency, and ensuring that the banking system does not fall short of liquidity, even in the case of a crisis (Chapter 5).

4. *Produce goods and services.* This is much less a government responsibility today than it used to be in the first decades after World War II, but most governments are still responsible for providing healthcare or education services, and some still own public enterprises, notably in sectors like transport or energy.
5. *Fix problems or pretend to.* Ministers are frequently held responsible for a vast array of issues, from financial market turmoil to wage negotiations, company mergers, and plant closures and relocations. Many problems are beyond their capacity to solve, but they can still try to influence private decisions—or at least pretend to.
6. *Negotiate with other countries.* Governments negotiate with other countries on trade liberalization and the definition of global rules and objectives (such as the Sustainable Development Goals). They participate in the governance of global and regional institutions (such as the United Nations, the International Monetary Fund (IMF), the World Bank, the World Trade Organization, or the European Union). They also participate in international fora (G7, G20, Organization for Economic Cooperation and Development [OECD], and regional summits) to hold discussions on global problems such as tax compliance, financial stability, development, and global warming and to set directions for future formal negotiations. International coordination occupies a large part of the agenda of heads of state and governments, central bank governors, and finance ministers.

In fact, economic policy debates vary widely across countries. In the United States, the bulk of the policy discussion revolves around interest rate decisions taken by the Federal Reserve Board and discussion in Congress on the President's tax and budget plans and on a limited set of specific issues such as energy security, trade and investment agreements, social security, or healthcare reform. In Western Europe, the so-called *structural reforms*—that is, attempts at changing labor market institutions, competition in product markets, welfare policy, and pensions—have taken center stage. In recent years, reforms of the euro area and assistance to countries in crisis have been at the very top of the European agenda. Throughout the 2000s and 2010s, economic policy in Eastern Europe, China, and other transition economies has focused on the introduction of markets and the privatization of state-owned companies. In India, major policy issues have also included market liberalization, inclusive finance and poverty reduction. Finally, Argentina, Brazil, Turkey, and others have gone through long phases in which the sole obsession of policymakers was to control inflation, allocate credit, and prevent—or cure—financial crises.

Economic policy also means different things at different times. Before the crisis that erupted in 2007–2008, no policymaker thought she would have to design and implement a wholesale bank rescue, a large-scale budgetary stimulus, or a massive expansion of the central banks' balance sheet. Consequently, financial sector reform has gained prominence in the aftermath of the crisis, both locally and globally.

To speak of "economic policy" in general may thus be regarded as presumptuous. However, there are many common features of economic policymaking across various contexts, fields, institutional setups, and time horizons, and they can be apprehended through a simple unified framework.

a) A simple representation of economic policy

We start by distinguishing objectives, instruments, and institutions:

- The *objectives* of economic policy are numerous (and sometimes contradictory): improving the population's standard of living, promoting sustainable growth, achieving full employment, maintaining price stability, reaching a fair distribution of income, alleviating poverty, and the like. They are sometimes explicitly stated in official texts. For example, the US Full Employment and Balanced Growth Act of 1978—known as the Humphrey–Hawkins Act—mandated the federal government to "promote *full employment and production*, increased real income, balanced growth, a balanced Federal budget, adequate productivity growth, proper attention to national priorities, achievement of an improved trade balance . . . and *reasonable price stability* . . . " (emphasis added). In the European Union, Article 3 of the treaty on the European Union[9] states that the Union "shall work for the sustainable development of Europe based on balanced economic growth and price stability, a highly competitive social market economy, aiming at full employment and social progress, and a high level of protection and improvement of the quality of the environment." What is immediately clear from such laundry lists of wishes is that economic policy has more than one objective and is easily given ambitious targets, irrespective of the difficulty or even impossibility of reaching all of them simultaneously.
- As already discussed, *instruments* are also numerous. Traditional ones relate to monetary policy (the setting of official interest rates) and fiscal policy (the choice of the levels of public expenditures and taxes). Economic policy is sometimes presented as a combination of these two instruments only. However, beyond them, it can and must rely on a variety of microeconomic instruments: structure of taxation, subsidies, social security transfers, privatizations, competition policy, trade policy and more.
- Last, *institutions* directly affect market equilibriums and the effectiveness of policy instruments. According to economic historian and

> Nobel Prize Winner Douglass North (1993), "Institutions are the humanly devised constraints that structure human interaction. They are made up of formal constraints (rules, laws, constitutions), informal constraints (norms of behavior, conventions, and self-imposed codes of conduct), and their enforcement characteristics. Together they define the incentive structure of societies and specifically economies." Lasting features of the organization of products, labor, and capital markets (i.e., the bankruptcy code, the rules governing employment contracts, the legislation on takeovers) or of the framework for economic policy decisions (i.e., budgetary procedures, the statute of the central bank, the exchange-rate regime, the rules governing competition, etc.) are regarded as institutions. This definition includes nonpublic institutions such as trade unions, which are private associations but affect the functioning of labor markets.

Within this framework, institutions represent a kind of social capital. They are not eternal, can evolve, be reformed, or disappear, but they have some permanence and can be taken as given for the traditional analysis of most policy choices—until a deep economic crisis prompts a rethinking of their performance.

b) Economic policy as a succession of trade-offs

Consider a government that targets n different economic variables, such as the unemployment rate, the inflation rate, and the current account balance (in this case, $n = 3$), and has a specific objective for each of them. For instance, the government wants an unemployment rate of around 5% of the labor force, an inflation rate of around 2% per year, and a balanced current account. These preferences can be summarized by a *loss function* that depends on the difference between each target variable and its desired value.

Assume now that the government has p independent policy instruments; that is, p variables that it can handle directly (for instance, the fiscal balance and the short-term interest rate, in which case $p = 2$). Economic policy then consists in setting the p policy variables such that the loss function is minimized.

If $p = n$, then the n policy objectives can all be achieved because there is an equal number of instruments (when objectives and instruments are independent and under certain assumptions; see box 1.1). In our example, however, we have $p < n$, and the n objectives cannot be achieved simultaneously, which implies trading off one objective against another one. For instance, the government needs to accept a current account deficit if it wants to lower unemployment to a level close to 5% while keeping inflation close to 2%. More generally, to reach n independent policy objectives, the government needs at least an equal number of independent policy instruments. This is known as the *Tinbergen rule.*[10]

Box 1.1 Trade-Offs Versus Structural Reforms

Consider a government that has n target variables $Y_1, Y_2, \ldots Y_n$, represented by a vector $Y = (Y_1, Y_2, \ldots Y_n)$, and n corresponding objectives. Its preferences can be summarized by a loss function L that measures the welfare loss associated with a divergence between the value taken by the target variables Y_i and their objective values $\tilde{Y}_i$:

$$L\left(Y_1 - \tilde{Y}_1, Y_2 - \tilde{Y}_2, \ldots Y_n - \tilde{Y}_n\right) \quad \text{(B1.1.1)}$$

L is assumed to be a convex, continuously differentiable function with $L(0, 0, \ldots 0) = 0$. Suppose also that the government can use p policy instruments represented by a p-dimensional vector $X = (X_1, X_2 \ldots X_p)$. With I standing for institutional characteristics, one can postulate that there exists a function H, conditional on institutions, that links the state of the economy, Y, to the instrument vector X:

$$Y = H_I(X) \quad \text{(B1.1.2)}$$

Economic policy then consists in selecting X such that L is minimized, under the constraint (B1.1.2).

If $n = p$, then it is usually possible (assuming independent targets and instruments) to invert Equation (B1.1.2) and find the vector X which allows Y to be exactly at its target level.

If $n > p$, this is no longer the case (provided the n target variables are independent), and the government faces a trade-off. In other words, the program leads to choosing values for $(X_1, X_2 \ldots X_p)$ such that, at the margin, it is not possible to improve on any of the targets without welfare deteriorating due to a higher divergence on other targets. Analytically, this corresponds to a situation where:

$$dL = \sum_{i=1}^{n} \frac{\partial L}{\partial Y_i} dY_i = 0 \quad \text{(B1.1.3)}$$

that is, for any pair (i, j) of objective variables,

$$\frac{dY_i}{dY_j} = -\frac{\partial L / \partial Y_j}{\partial L / \partial Y_i} \quad \text{(B1.1.4)}$$

The *marginal rate of substitution* between any two objectives is therefore equal to the inverse ratio of the partial derivatives of the loss function. This formula, formally identical to what is obtained in a consumption maximization program, means that, at the minimum of the loss function, any improvement in an objective is offset by a deterioration in another one in inverse proportion to the effects of these variations on the loss function. In the simple case where there are two objective variables Y_1 and Y_2 with only one instrument X to reach them, X can be substituted along

(B1.1.2), giving an explicit formulation of the trade-off between Y_1 and Y_2, conditional on the institutions I:

$$g_I(Y_1, Y_2) = 0 \tag{B1.1.5}$$

This relationship is represented in figure B1.1.1. The government can trade Y_2 for Y_1 (or vice versa), along the $g_I(Y_1, Y_2)$ schedule, or it can change the set of institutions from I to J in order to improve the trade-off (in which case the schedule shifts to the north-east of the figure).

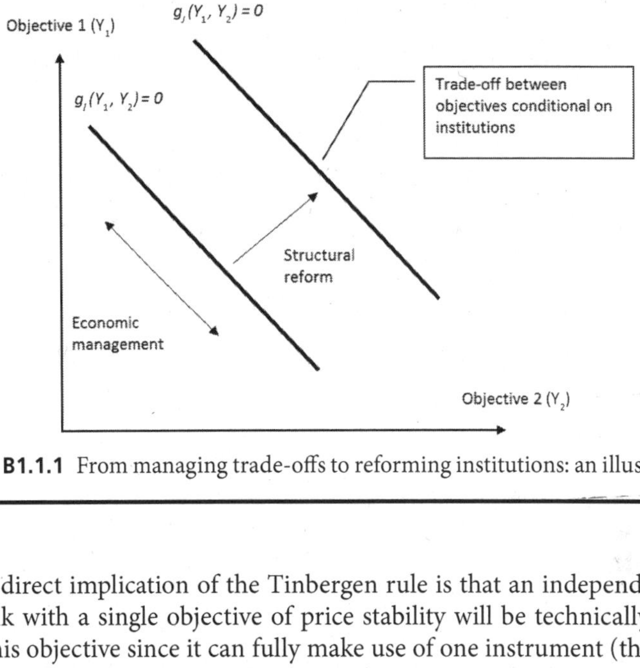

Figure B1.1.1 From managing trade-offs to reforming institutions: an illustration.

One direct implication of the Tinbergen rule is that an independent central bank with a single objective of price stability will be technically able to reach this objective since it can fully make use of one instrument (the official interest rate, assuming that it effectively influences prices). This piece of arithmetic was successfully applied in the 1990s when a large number of central banks around the world became independent and inflation rates decreased dramatically (see Chapter 5).

However, governments generally have many objectives but only a limited number of instruments. Hence, trade-offs are part of a government's everyday life. These trade-offs are conditional on their preferences (for instance, how much more wage inequality they stand ready to accept to reduce the unemployment rate by one percentage point) and also on institutions (for instance, on whether wages are negotiated with unions or set by firms).

In such a setting, divergences in policy prescriptions can be either of a positive or of a normative nature: they can result from different views on the functioning of the economy (the constraint) or from different preferences, as represented by the loss function.

Such a representation was widely used in the 1960s. For instance, A. W. Phillips (1958) evidenced a negative relationship between the unemployment rate and the growth rate of nominal wages for the United Kingdom from 1861 to 1957. This downward-sloping *Phillips curve* led to the idea of a trade-off between unemployment and inflation: according to Phillips's findings, a one percentage point fall in the unemployment rate had to be "paid back" by a 0.8 percentage point rise in the inflation rate. The simultaneous rise of inflation and unemployment in the 1970s challenged this excessively simple representation. The necessity to manage policy trade-offs nonetheless obtains whenever the number of independent instruments is smaller than that of independent policy objectives.

c) Changing the institutions: Structural reform

The trade-offs just described are generally reversible: the central bank raises or cuts the interest rate according to the economic situation, parliament increases or reduces taxes, and the like. However, starting in the 1980s and 1990s, persistent problems in growth and employment in Europe highlighted the limits of such economic management. A good example here is the apparent trade-off between employment and productivity. In some European countries fewer people work, but those who work have a high level of productivity. Other countries achieve much better performances about employment but at the price of weaker productivity. Collectively, the European countries seem confronted with a trade-off described by the negatively sloped AA curve of figure 1.1. Attempts at modifying the position of a country along the AA schedule through various levers such as tax rates and public spending can be characterized as *economic management*.

However, trading off more jobs for less income per worker is unsatisfactory. In a low-employment situation, the true objective of economic policy should be to reach *at the same time* higher employment and higher productivity levels. The right answer would therefore consist in moving the AA schedule outward, thereby simultaneously raising employment and productivity. This requires reshaping institutions: for example, stronger incentives to remain active and take up jobs, more investment in education, an environment that fosters innovation, and the like.

In a more general way, *structural reforms* aim to improve economic policy trade-offs by changing the institutions. The IMF (2004) defines them as entailing "measures that, broadly speaking, change the institutional framework and constraints governing market behavior and outcomes," while the OECD focuses on their ability "to improve long-term material living standards through higher productivity and labor utilization." The mathematical interpretation of policy trade-offs versus structural reforms is detailed in box 1.1.

It is common, but inaccurate, to equate structural policies and supply-side policies. Making the central bank independent, choosing a new currency

Figure 1.1 The employment–productivity trade-off, 2012.
Authors' calculations with OECD data.

regime, or adopting a framework for fiscal policy are true structural reforms because they aim to improve existing trade-offs between various objectives by moving the corresponding schedules outward (see Chapters 4 and 5). Conversely, a change in tax rates, which is mostly a supply-side measure, does not have the character of a structural reform.

However, many of the structural reforms undertaken since the 1980s in advanced economies were admittedly of a supply-side nature. Widespread reform of capital markets through the elimination of credit controls, the scrapping of many deposit regulations, and the liberalization of capital flows had major consequences, both micro- and macroeconomic, with positive as well as negative implications (improved access to finance for firms and households, but also excessive risk-taking which led to the 2007 crisis). Deregulation in product markets, following its initiation in the United States in the 1970s, increased competition and fostered innovation, resulting in productivity gains, especially in sectors such as transport, telecommunications, and energy. In the EU, the gradual introduction starting in the mid-1980s of a *single market*[11] for goods and, to a lesser extent, for services had similar objectives. In developing and emerging countries, and since 2010 in euro area countries hit by the financial crisis, the standard concept has been that of *structural adjustment*—a package of reforms advocated by the IMF and the World Bank (and in Europe by the *Troika* consisting in the European Commission, European Central Bank, and IMF) and enforced on countries requiring financial assistance that encompasses several features of what we call structural reform.

Structural reforms are often viewed as having negative short-term, but positive long-term effects. The most telling example of such effects was, at the end of the twentieth century, the transition of the former planned economies of Central and Eastern Europe and the former USSR to market economies. Figure 1.2 highlights the GDP cost of this transformation: it generally took several years for GDP to return to its pretransition level. Furthermore, some of the most successful posttransition countries where those, like the Baltic States, where the initial fall was the most pronounced.

There is no consensus on whether structural reforms have a negative or positive impact on output in the short run, and it depends much on their nature. On the one hand, reforms aiming to increase productivity exert downward pressure on costs and prices, pushing the *real interest rate* (the gap between the nominal interest rate and the inflation rate) up and weighting on aggregate demand. They may also create anxiety, which favors precautionary savings and wait-and-see attitudes. On the other hand, if individuals and companies spend out of their permanent income, an expected increase in productivity lifts consumption and investment already today. The former, negative impact can moreover be counteracted by a more expansionary monetary policy, except when the country is part of a fixed-exchange-rate regime or a monetary union and when interest rates are already at the lower bound and cannot be lowered any further (Eggertsson, Ferrero, and Raffo, 2014). Some empirical studies have found positive effects to dominate, even in the short run (Bouis et al., 2012), but the issue remains controversial.

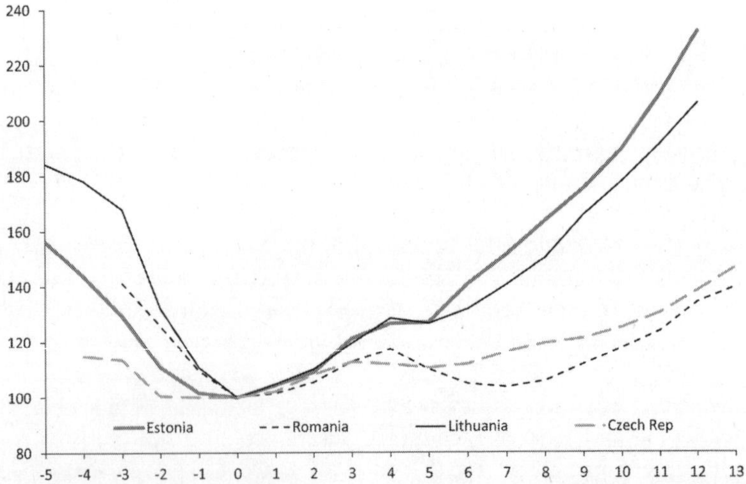

Figure 1.2 GDP impact of the transition to the market economy in the 1990s. Real GDP, trough level = 100. Author's calculations based on the Groningen Growth and Development Center's Global Economic database. The x-axis represents years before or after year 0 when the trough of real GDP was reached.

Such intertemporal effects necessarily raise political economy issues. For a democratic government facing reelection, undertaking reforms that will antagonize voters and only yield benefits after its term expires can be a recipe for failure. How to surmount this political economy constraint (for example, by finding ways to compensate incumbents for the rents they will lose because of the reforms) is a major theme for research.

1.2 The Whys and Hows of Public Intervention

Having presented what policymakers do and how economic policy works, let us move to an upstream question: Why is public intervention needed? What are the objectives of public intervention? Economic theory provides useful and precise answers.

1.2.1 The three functions of economic policy

Musgrave and Musgrave (1989) have distinguished three essential functions of fiscal and, more largely, economic policy:

- *Allocation policies* that intend to optimize the assignment of resources to alternative uses. Allocation policies cover public interventions aiming to affect the quantity or the quality of the factors (capital, unskilled and skilled labor, technology, land, etc.) available for production and their sectoral or regional distribution. Policies providing public goods such as infrastructure or environmental preservation are also included in this category.
- *Stabilization policies* vis-à-vis macroeconomic shocks that move the economy away from internal balance (defined as full employment together with price stability). This calls for policies that aim to bring the economy closer to balance—a role assigned to monetary and fiscal policies.
- *Redistribution policies* between agents or regions. This involves policies designed to correct the primary distribution of income. Progressive taxation policies and social transfers as well as access to education and health are key instruments to this end.

Redistribution clearly has a different scope than either allocation or stabilization since it addresses the distribution of income within society. Allocation and stabilization may seem to pursue similar goals. The distinction between them directly refers to the difference between long-term output growth and short-term fluctuations around the trend: allocation policies aim to increase the maximum level of output that can be reached without creating inflation—generally called *potential output* or *potential GDP*—while stabilization policies aim to minimize the divergence between actual and potential output, known as the *output gap* (figure 1.3 and box 1.2).

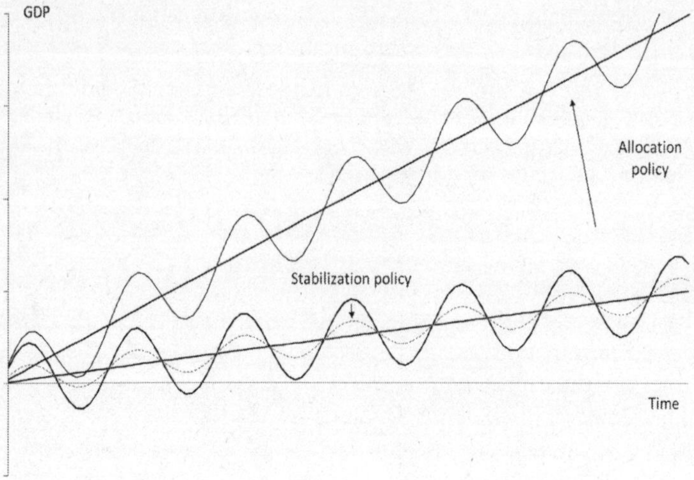

Figure 1.3 Stabilization versus allocation policies.

Box 1.2 Aggregate Supply, Aggregate Demand, and the Output Gap

In a simple model of the supply side of the economy, potential output is determined by the factors of production (mainly labor supply and the capital stock), as well as by the factors affecting productive efficiency. A standard representation is:

$$Y_t = F_t(K_t, N_t) \quad \text{(B1.2.1)}$$

where Y is production, K the capital stock, N employment, and F the production function. K and N depend on time and so does F as improvements in technology allow more to be produced with the same quantity of factors (this simple representation does not consider the quality of labor).

In the short run, K can be considered exogenous, so $K_t = \bar{K}_t$. Let us define $\bar{N}_t$ as the employment level that is reached when unemployment rate is at a level $\bar{u}_t$ consistent with internal balance, called the *equilibrium rate of unemployment*. $\bar{u}_t$ cannot be zero because, at each point in time, a fraction of the labor force is looking for a job. Its level depends on the efficiency of the country's labor market institutions. So, if $\bar{L}_t$ is the labor force,

$$\bar{N}_t = (1 - \bar{u}_t)\bar{L}_t \quad \text{(B1.2.2)}$$

Potential output can thus be defined as:

$$\bar{Y}_t = F_t(\bar{K}_t, \bar{N}_t) \quad \text{(B1.2.3)}$$

It is exogenous in the short term but endogenous in the long term as the capital stock adjusts.

The *output gap* can thus be defined as the difference og_t between the demand-determined output Y_t and the supply-determined potential output $\overline{Y}_t$. It is generally measured as a percentage of the potential output:

$$og_t = \frac{Y_t}{\overline{Y}_t} - 1 \tag{B1.2.4}$$

A negative output gap means that production is below potential, implying nonequilibrium (or involuntary) unemployment. A positive output gap means that production is above potential. This may look strange if one thinks of the capital stock and the available labor force as a physical constraint. However, there are ways to adjust to a higher level of demand. For example, a standard response to excess demand is to have recourse to overtime; or older equipment that was regarded as obsolete but had not been discarded can also be used again; or less-efficient producers, who were hardly able to compete in normal conditions, may increase their supply. However, such responses tend to be costly, implying a rise in the marginal cost of production and therefore a rise in the aggregate price level.

The output gap is a simple notion, but it is hard to measure in practice because the capital stock $\overline{K}_t$, the equilibrium rate of unemployment $\overline{u}_t$, and the production function F are all unobservable (this is less true for the capital stock that could be measured through surveys, but in practice it is generally evaluated on the basis of past investments and assumptions regarding the annual rate of discard of existing equipments). The various available measures, such as those provided by international institutions (such as the IMF, the OECD, and the European Commission) differ significantly and are frequently revised. In addition, Coibion et al. (2017) show that estimates of potential output are sensitive to the cycle and respond not only to supply shocks but also to demand shocks that only affect output transitorily. Because of these difficulties, potential output is sometimes derived from actual output through purely statistical techniques (by applying a filter to the actual series to estimate its trend). However, this ignores the fact that potential output is an economic notion and that its level depends on prices: for example, a higher price of energy reduces potential output because it makes certain energy-intensive production techniques unprofitable.

The difficulty in measuring potential GDP can be illustrated through comparing the United States and the euro area after the global financial crisis. In the United States, the crisis seems to have lowered the level of potential GDP, but not its growth rate (Figure B1.2.1a). In the euro area, both the level and the growth rate seem to have declined (Figure B1.2.1b). Back in 2009, though, it was difficult to anticipate such divergence.

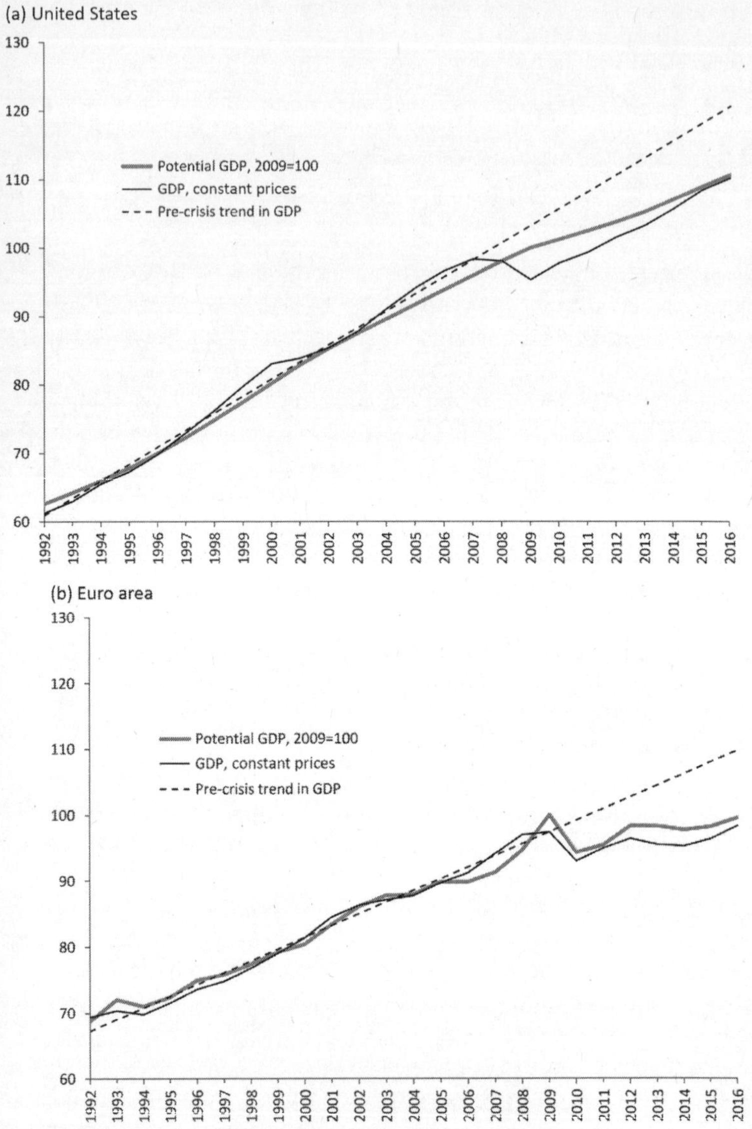

Figure B1.2.1 Potential and actual gross domestic product (GDP), United States and euro area, 2000–2016, 2009 = 100.

The pre-crisis trend is fitted between 1992 and 2007.

IMF, World Economic Outlook Database, April 2017, and authors' own calculations.

This distinction between the three main functions is widely used in policy discussions; it brings some analytical discipline and clarifies the aims of policy decisions. The distinction is followed in this book, of which Chapters 4–7 deal primarily with stabilization, Chapters 8-9 with allocation, and Chapter 8 also with redistribution. As we shall see, however, there are many reasons why these three functions frequently interfere with each other, making economic policy choices less clear-cut than in this simple presentation.

1.2.2 Why intervene?

For economists, public intervention requires justification. This is because the *first theorem of welfare economics* establishes that any competitive equilibrium is a *Pareto optimum*. In other words, it is not possible to improve the welfare of an economic agent without reducing that of another one. The *second theorem of welfare economics* states, conversely, that any Pareto optimal equilibrium can be sustained by a competitive equilibrium, provided that the government can implement initial *lump-sum transfers* (meaning transfers which do not depend on the wealth or income of their recipients).

These are both very powerful and very limited results. They are powerful because if public intervention can improve the fate of some agents only by deteriorating that of others, this immediately raises the question of the moral basis and acceptability of such an intervention. They are, however, limited for three reasons. First, the Pareto criterion does not say anything on the distribution of income and wealth between economic agents. Yet it may be socially desirable, for example, to reduce a wealthy individual's income to improve that of a poor one. Second, Kenneth Arrow and Gérard Debreu (1954) have shown that the first theorem of welfare economics relies on a very demanding set of hypotheses. A true competitive equilibrium requires, *inter alia*, strictly competitive markets, the existence of a complete set of markets that allows the carrying out of transactions on all goods at all periods, and perfect information. Third, implementing lump-sum transfers is politically challenging, and they hardly ever exist in the real world (see Chapter 8). Challenge any one of these assumptions, and there is justification for public intervention (box 1.3).

In fact, these welfare theorems, which were often interpreted as providing the doctrinal basis of laissez-faire, can just as well provide arguments for public intervention (see Stiglitz, 1991, for a discussion). These arguments will tend to be specific to the three functions of economic policy: allocation, stabilization, and redistribution.

a) Allocation

State intervention is justified when it is able to remedy market failures (i.e., to improve the efficiency of resource allocation in comparison to the market outcome). The most frequent reasons for such failures are the presence of monopolies, *externalities*,[12] information asymmetries between agents, market

Box 1.3 Microeconomic Arguments for Public Intervention

Public intervention has microeconomic justification when one of the assumptions of the first theorem of welfare economics is violated.

Competition Is Not Perfect

Rationale. Profit maximization by a company implies equalizing the marginal cost (of producing an additional unit) and the marginal income (from selling an additional unit). Under perfect competition, the marginal income is the market price of the product, and profit maximization leads to a social optimum. If a firm holds a monopoly position or, more generally, has some *market power*,[24] it has to consider the (less than infinite) elasticity of demand for its product and the fact that its marginal income is less than the market price. This is because selling an additional unit when demand is elastic implies lowering the price of all previous units. In comparison with the perfect competition outcome, this leads the firm to reduce quantities sold and to increase the price, to the detriment of the consumer.

Public intervention can aim to restore perfect competition conditions (for example, by blocking mergers leading to, or threatening to lead to, excessive market power). However, it is not always desirable to eliminate monopolies: when production involves high fixed costs or, in general, when there are increasing *returns to scale*,[25] larger firms or even monopolies are more efficient than smaller firms. This is what is meant by *natural monopoly*. For example, it is more efficient to have the railway network managed by a single entity than by several, but this implies regulating its behavior or subjecting it to potential competition (via granting it a fixed-duration contract only) in order to prevent it from exploiting its monopoly power.

Consequences. This argument provides the prime justification of antitrust policy, whose aim is to prevent firms from acquiring a dominant position or from abusing it. In the name of consumer protection, institutions in charge of it, such as the Federal Trade Commission and the Department of Justice in the United States, the Bundeskartellamt in Germany, or the European Commission in the EU, can block mergers and acquisitions if they threaten to create monopolies or fine companies that abuse a dominant position in their market. For example, the European Commission (which is in charge of this policy for cases with a cross-border dimension) regularly blocked merger operations (Olympic Air–Aegean Airlines in 2011, Deutsche Börse–Euronext in 2012, UPS–TNT and Ryan Air–Air Lingus in 2013) that were regarded as a potential threat to competition. It also levied fines on companies whose behavior was regarded as obstructing competition. In 2004, Microsoft was fined €497 million for abusing its market power in the EU. However, the argument also has wider applications: for example, it provides a justification for setting a minimum wage if employers locally hold near-monopoly positions as purchasers of unskilled labor (this is called a *monopsony*).

Economic Activities Have External Effects

Rationale. In the presence of *externalities*, the private cost of a resource or the private profit from production do not coincide with the social cost or the social benefit. For example, a firm that consumes a natural resource such as clean water or whose production technique spoils the environment does not usually take the corresponding social costs into account in its profit maximization. It then tends to overconsume natural resources and to overproduce. The reverse occurs when the externality is positive (i.e., if production has favorable nonmarketable effects). For example, a research and development–intensive firm that establishes a facility in an area tends to exert positive effects on other firms through the development of local suppliers and subcontractors, the creation of a more liquid market for skilled labor, and links with university departments. However, those positive externalities are not considered in the decision by the firm to open a new facility, which leads to a suboptimal number of such facilities. It is also the high negative externalities from a default of large financial institutions that justify rescuing banks in a financial crisis. The risk is that a bank default would make other financial institutions insolvent, thereby triggering a chain reaction.

Consequences. Environmental economics largely rests on this type of argument, both about local pollution (water and air spoilage, waste, etc.) and global pollution (greenhouse effect). The first-best economic response (not necessarily the most frequent one) generally consists in letting agents "internalize" externalities by taxing the negative ones (this is the so-called *polluter–payer principle*) and by subsidizing the positive ones (local governments routinely subsidize investment from nonresident companies or grant them tax exemptions). However, here again, the argument is broader: a company which lays off its employees exerts a negative externality on the community, which bears the cost of unemployment insurance, and the one that hires creates a positive externality. This justifies making a company's contributions to unemployment insurance a function of its hiring and firing behavior, as is the case in the United States. Olivier Blanchard and Jean Tirole (2008) have proposed extending such experience rating (or *bonus-malus system*) to Europe. As for the risks of letting a major financial institution default on its liabilities, the dramatic consequences of the Lehman Brothers bankruptcy in 2008 and the rescue of a series of other US and European banks in the following months illustrate the importance of state intervention.

Information Is Imperfect

Rationale. The optimality of the competitive equilibrium rests on the assumption of perfect information. If information has a strategic character and if agents use it to their profit, the market outcome is no longer necessarily Pareto-optimum. The potency of this argument was recognized with the awarding of the 2001 Nobel Prize to George Akerlof and Joseph Stiglitz who contributed to the development of the economics of imperfect information. Stiglitz and Weiss (1981), for example, showed that when the creditor (say, a bank) has less information than the debtor (say, a company) on the risk incurred in lending, it cannot accurately price the risk in setting the interest rate on the loan. It may then select a price that is too high for good borrowers and will only attract the riskiest ones. To prevent this phenomenon, known as *adverse selection*,[26] it is optimum for the creditor to ration credit, which is socially inefficient (see Chapter 5).

Consequences. Imperfect information is pervasive and it also affects policymakers, who rarely enjoy an undisputed informational advantage. The limits this creates for government intervention are discussed in Chapter 2. Public policy can foster the dissemination of market-relevant information, either in the form of aggregate statistics or through standardizing the disclosure of company-specific information. Accounting and financial reporting standards, for example, are intended to ensure that financial markets benefit from comparable, undistorted information. Governments can also provide public insurance (such as for labor or for health) as a way to overcome adverse selection.

Markets Are Incomplete

Rationale. The optimality of the competitive market equilibrium hinges on the existence of markets for all necessary transactions at all relevant horizons. When such markets are missing, Pareto-optimality is not guaranteed. For example, borrowing to finance one's education is made difficult by the absence of collateral on which the loan can be guaranteed and by the fact that the choice of a professional specialization is hardly reversible. The near-absence of a market for young people to borrow to finance investment in their own human capital tends to limit access to higher education. In the absence of public intervention, private investment in human capital is therefore suboptimal, which harms growth.

Consequences. This argument provides a justification for government to step in where markets are missing. In the preceding example, it gives an economic efficiency motive for providing grants and scholarships to students or to ensure the public provision of education services. However, governments can also contribute to the emergence of new markets, for example, by guaranteeing student loans (Chapman, 2006; Shiller, 2003). In another field, government debt agencies have introduced inflation-indexed bonds which provide private agents with a way to hedge their fixed-income savings against the risk of future inflation.

incompleteness, or agent shortsightedness. These arguments, which have been extensively studied in microeconomics and public economics, traditionally provide solid justifications for regulatory policies, corrective taxation, the public provision of certain goods and services, or public subsidies (box 1.3).

b) Stabilization

While public intervention in the name of allocation aims to alter the long-run market equilibrium, intervention carried out in the name of stabilization is intended to limit short-term deviations from it. The motive remains the search for efficiency, but it is not the possible inefficiency of the equilibrium that matters, but rather the efficiency loss resulting from not reaching it.

Keynes gave two reasons for such intervention. The first one is what he called "animal spirits"; that is, the instability of private behavior under the influence of spontaneous expectations leading to excessive optimism followed by excesses of pessimism:

> Even apart from the instability due to speculation, there is the instability due to the characteristic of human nature that a large proportion of our positive activities depend on spontaneous optimism rather than on a mathematical expectation, whether moral or hedonistic or economic. Most, probably, of our decisions to do something positive, the full consequences of which will be drawn out over many days to come, can only be taken as a result of animal spirits—of a spontaneous urge to action rather than inaction, and not as the outcome of a weighted average of quantitative benefits multiplied by quantitative probabilities. (Keynes, 1936, chapt. 12, part 7)

Second, Keynes argued that *nominal rigidities*[13] of wages and prices prevent the self-correcting market mechanisms from operating and moving the economy back to equilibrium. Especially, nominal wage rigidity implies that the *real wage* (i.e., the nominal wage divided by the price level, which is a measure of the real cost of labor) does not fall in a recession, thus preventing the restoration of full employment.

In the eyes of Keynes, the combination of private instability and ineffective self-correcting mechanisms provided a justification for relying on *countercyclical* monetary and fiscal policies to smooth out economic fluctuations and prevent economic depressions. As illustrated in figure 1.3, such stabilization policies are distinct from allocation policies, which aim to make the economy more efficient and hence to raise the pace of the economy in the long run.

The arguments for stabilization policies have since inception been a matter for theoretical and empirical disputes, especially from the 1970s to the late 1980s, the high noon of the monetarist backlash. Yet economic fluctuations remain a fact of life, and accounting for them while remaining consistent with assumptions of rational behavior has proved to be challenging. The theory of *real business cycles* developed in the 1980s was a conceptually coherent attempt at explaining fluctuations by shocks to the production technology (or *productivity shocks*) and rational responses to them by maximizing agents—thus without relying in any significant way on irrational behavior or nominal rigidities. However, in spite of the considerable literature devoted to this approach, its empirical relevance for the explanation of short-term fluctuations remains disputed.[14]

Of the two explanations offered by Keynes, the first—the notion that economic agents are driven by "animal spirits" rather than by cool-headed rational calculation—was and remains in contradiction with the basic assumptions of economics. Though risk premiums in financial markets do vary over time—and notwithstanding recent developments in experimental economics that indicate that departures from rational behavior are frequent—the animal spirits assumption remains alien to the methodological foundations of the economic profession, which has strived to offer rational explanations of seemingly irrational behaviors (such as financial market bubbles; see Chapter 6). However, as emphasized by scholars of crises such as Kindelberger (1978) and Minsky (1992), and as observed in 2007–2009, the "animal spirits" metaphor seems relevant at least in situations of financial panic.

The argument based on nominal rigidities is theoretically closer to mainstream economics, provided an explanation is given for why and how such rigidities exist and affect economic behavior. As developed in Chapter 5, the standard response long remained the somewhat ad hoc argument that agents enter into contractual arrangements that involve nominal rigidities—for example, wage contracts that specify a nominal compensation and are only renegotiated at discrete intervals. It was only in the 1980s that Keynesian economists provided convincing micro-founded explanations for nominal rigidities by showing that the gain to the microeconomic agent from changing prices in response to a shock can be much smaller than the corresponding macroeconomic benefit.

The standard, contemporary approach is based on a simple aggregate supply-and-demand framework that depicts the relationship between potential output and the product price, on the one hand, and between aggregate product demand

and the product price, on the other. In the short run, aggregate supply depends positively on the product price, as depicted by the aggregate supply curve, because, in the presence of nominal rigidities, a rise in the price level reduces the real wage and makes production more profitable. In the long run, aggregate supply is fixed as unemployment is at its equilibrium level, so the curve is vertical. Aggregate demand depends negatively on the product price through a wealth effect as a rise in price reduces the real value of nominal assets and thereby reduces consumption. The two relationships are depicted by the aggregate supply and aggregate demand curves in figure 1.4 (see box 1.4 for a formal derivation).

In this context, two distinctions need to be made. The first one is between variations of the quantity supplied or demanded in response to a change in the product price (a move along the supply or demand schedules in figure 1.4) and exogenous perturbations (movement of the whole schedule) that are interpreted as *shocks* to the economy. The second one is between shocks to supply and shocks to demand. Supply shocks and demand shocks have become part of every macroeconomic policymaker's toolkit:

- A *supply shock* is an exogenous modification in the relationship between potential output and the product price. For example, at any given level of the wage and the product price, an oil shock (a rise in the price of oil) reduces the level of potential output because it increases prices and reduces the profitability of production: the supply curve shifts to the left.
- A *demand shock* is an exogenous modification in the relationship between product demand and the product price. This can be, for example, a drop in the level of household consumption resulting from a reduction of household wealth: the demand curve shifts to the left.

Although both kinds of shocks may result in either a reduction or a rise in output, they command different policy responses, and it is important to sort out one from the other.

A positive demand shock shifts aggregate demand to the right, resulting in moving from the initial equilibrium E to A′ in the short term on figure 1.4, with both a higher output and a higher price. A positive supply shock, however, shifts aggregate supply to the right, resulting also in higher output but a lower price in the short term (B′). A simple criterion for distinguishing demand from supply shocks therefore is that they result in opposite changes in the price for a similar effect on output.

In the long run, the aggregate supply curve becomes vertical because capital adjusts fully while unemployment is supposed to be at its equilibrium level. The reasoning is the same except that a positive demand shock now exclusively results in a price rise as the equilibrium moves from E to A″. For a supply shock, the result is qualitatively similar to the short-term one as the equilibrium moves from E to B″.

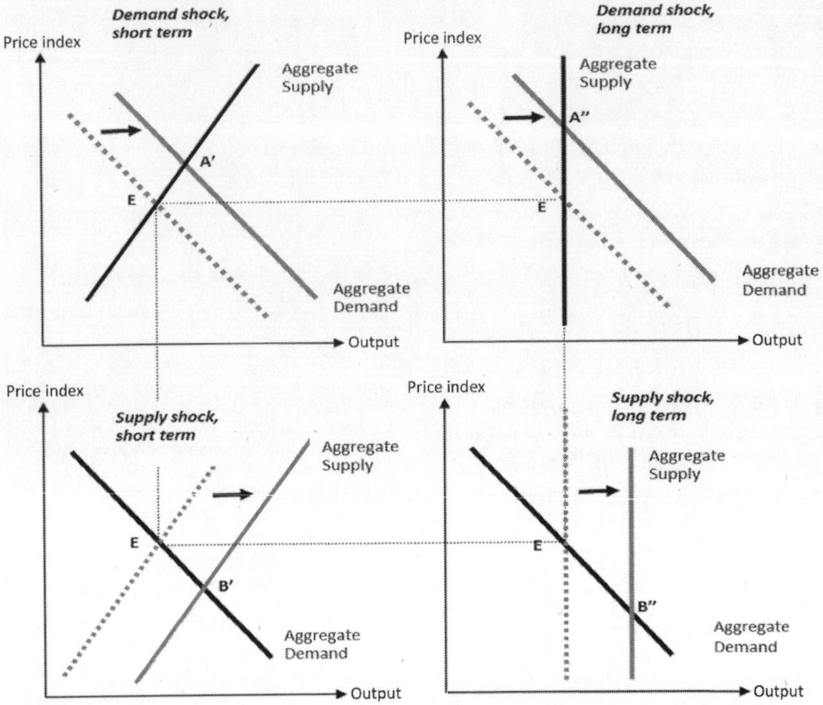

Figure 1.4 Positive supply and demand shocks in an aggregate supply – aggregate demand framework.

The upshot is that a demand shock either does not affect output or moves it in the same direction as price, while a supply shock moves price in the opposite direction to that of output.

This framework helps to explain the role and the limits of stabilization. A fiscal or monetary impulse affects the demand curve and can therefore offset a demand shock. This is, for example, the elementary reasoning behind the response of governments of advanced economies to the depression of 2009: as confidence dropped and household wealth declined, macroeconomic policy aimed to stimulate private demand through lower interest rates and direct transfers to households. However, a fiscal or monetary impulse does not affect the aggregate supply curve so neither is effective in response to a supply shock. If the supply curve shifts to the left in response to a rise in the relative price of oil (which makes other products less profitable and therefore reduces supply), pushing aggregate demand to the right necessarily results in a further increase in the price level and is fully ineffective in the long run. Therefore, *demand policies* are not effective in response to supply shocks. The latter call for *supply policies*.

Box 1.4 Aggregate Supply and Aggregate Demand

Consider a closed economy with a representative household and a firm producing a single consumption good out of homogenous labor. It is natural to suppose that household consumption depends positively on household real wealth. Real wealth in turn depends negatively on the price level since some of the assets, such as cash, bank deposits, and bonds, are denominated in nominal terms. Thus,

$$C = C\left(Y, \frac{\Omega}{P}\right) \quad \text{with} \ \frac{\partial C}{\partial Y} > 0, \ \frac{\partial C}{\partial\left(\frac{\Omega}{P}\right)} > 0 \ \text{and therefore} \ \frac{dC}{dP} < 0 \qquad \text{(B1.4.1)}$$

where C is household consumption, Y is household income, Ω household wealth, and P the product price level.

Constructing the supply curve is slightly more complex. Let us first suppose that labor is the only factor of production and that N, the quantity of it employed in production, is bound by the total available labor force L. Suppose also that the marginal productivity of labor is decreasing because employers start by hiring the best-trained and most productive employees. Let us furthermore specify output as:

$$Y = AN^{\alpha} \quad \text{with } 0 < \alpha < 1 \ \text{ and } \ A > 0 \qquad \text{(B1.4.2)}$$

Potential output is:

$$\bar{Y} = AL^{\alpha} \qquad \text{(B1.4.3)}$$

Suppose that the wage level depends on the price level and the ratio of employment to the labor force, and let P_{-1} be the price level in the previous period:

$$W = \omega P^{\theta} P_{-1}^{1-\theta} \left(\frac{N}{L}\right)^{\gamma} \quad \text{with } 0 \le \theta \le 1, \gamma \ge 0 \ \text{ and } \ \omega > 0 \qquad \text{(B1.4.4)}$$

In the short run, the wage level W is not fully indexed on the price level if $\theta < 1$. This is because wages are set by contracts that are renegotiated at discrete intervals. There is therefore *nominal wage rigidity* and a rise in the price level implies a drop in the real wage W/P. In the long run, however, there is full indexation because the wage adjusts to the price level and the real wage only depends on real factors. The wage level furthermore depends on the degree of tension on the labor market measured by N/L because a rise in employment improves the bargaining power of employees.

Supply is determined by the firm's profit-maximization behavior. The corresponding first-order condition is:

$$\frac{\partial Y}{\partial N} = A\alpha N^{\alpha-1} = \frac{W}{P} \tag{B1.4.5}$$

Combining Equation (B1.4.4) with Equation (B1.4.5) gives:

$$A\alpha N^{\alpha-1} = \omega\left(\frac{P_{-1}}{P}\right)^{1-\theta}\left(\frac{N}{L}\right)^{\gamma} \tag{B1.4.6}$$

which yields a relation between employment and price and therefore between production and price.

In the long run, $P = P_{-1}$, and the solution therefore implies $N = L$, $Y = \overline{Y}$ and $\frac{W}{P} = \omega$. The supply curve is therefore vertical.

In the short run, however, P_{-1} is given and the solution is:

$$Y = HP^{\sigma} \tag{B1.4.7}$$

where H is a positive constant and $\sigma = \frac{\alpha(1-\theta)}{1+\gamma-\alpha} > 0$.

Production depends positively on price because a rise in the price level is only partially translated into a rise in the wage level and therefore reduces the real wage. The supply curve is thus upward sloping, and the price elasticity of supply depends negatively on the degree of short-term indexation of wage over price θ and on its responsiveness to the employment level γ.

As shown in figure 1.4, the effectiveness of demand policies depends on the slope of the short-term supply curve. In an economy with widespread nominal rigidities and a low responsiveness of wages to labor market conditions, the short-run supply curve can be almost flat, which makes demand policies very effective. However, when indexation is fast and wages are responsive to unemployment, the slope of the short-run supply curve can be almost vertical, rendering demand policies close to ineffective. The choice of a proper policy response thus depends both on the identification of shocks and on the underlying properties of the economy.

In real time, however, policymakers are generally unable to identify the nature of the shocks and to evaluate the slopes of the supply and demand curves. For example, they observe a rise in the price level but do not know whether it represents a normal response to shocks to input prices (e.g., oil) or results from a change in agents' behaviors (such as a change in price expectations or indexation mechanisms). We come back to this identification problem in Chapter 2.

Olivier Blanchard and Danny Quah (1989) have proposed an empirical methodology to recognize supply and demand shocks based on their differentiated effects on quantities and prices, as shown in figure 1.4. However, like any econometric estimation, they have to assume that the behavior of private agents stays stable over time. More generally, the ability of governments and central banks to carry out effective countercyclical policies remains an issue of discussion among experts. We come back to this key issue in Chapters 4 and 5.

c) Redistribution

Turning to redistribution, the central argument for intervention is that even if it is Pareto-optimal, the market-determined distribution of income does not necessarily correspond to the social objective nor ensure social justice. The prime motive for intervention here does not stem from a lack of productive efficiency of the market outcome—as for allocation and stabilization—but from a pure equity concern.

A normative criterion is generally required to decide what constitutes an improvement in equity. Which criteria can be used to compare two income distributions is the topic of the next section. What needs to be made clear immediately is that an "improvement" in equity—whatever is meant by that—can take place at constant efficiency, can be traded off against a reduction in efficiency, or can trigger an increase in efficiency.

In the first case, equity concerns can be completely separated from efficiency ones. This happens when the government is able to modify the distribution of income through lump-sum transfers that do not affect economic incentives. Trade policy is a case in point: a classic result from trade theory is that, under fairly general assumptions (and notwithstanding the remark made earlier on the drawbacks of preferential trade agreements), trade opening improves overall efficiency and yields gains to all participating countries. However, the same trade theorems show that there are losers in the process: for example, labor loses and capital wins in a capital-rich country that opens to trade with capital-poor countries. Nevertheless, the overall gain from trade makes it possible for the government to redistribute the benefits from capital to labor in order to ensure that free trade is Pareto-superior to protection (an application of the second theorem of welfare economics mentioned earlier).

In practice, however, lump-sum transfers are almost impossible to implement. Take again the case of trade: to determine whom it should tax and to whom it should redistribute, the government would need to have full *ex ante* information on the effects of liberalization. Furthermore, it would need adequate instruments for redistributing. What it can do concretely is tax income, profit, or consumption and redistribute through targeted assistance programs or means-tested transfers. However, those taxes and transfers change economic incentives and therefore affect the market equilibrium. Equity cannot be separated from efficiency anymore.

This is why redistribution often involves an equity–efficiency trade-off: the more income is redistributed, the higher the efficiency loss because both taxes and transfers reduce the supply of production factors (labor and capital). Keynesian economist Arthur Okun once said that the big trade-off for economic policy was between equality and efficiency (Okun, 1975).

However, redistribution may in some cases *improve* efficiency. For example, public policies ensuring access of the poor to education and healthcare frequently yield efficiency gains through improving the productivity of the labor force. Their justification thus goes beyond their equity effects.

1.3 Economic Policy Evaluation

1.3.1 Decision criteria

To evaluate economic policy choices, and especially to compare alternative policies, precise criteria are necessary. But can a single criterion be used for efficiency, stabilization, and equity? Although this is conceivable in theory, in practice economic policy choices generally imply trade-offs between different objectives.

a) A single objective?

The most encompassing aim that can be assigned to economic policy is the satisfaction of resident individuals or households (in a political economy setup, one would say of voters), or their *utility* as economists call it. In elementary textbooks, the consumer's utility depends on a limited range of items, but nothing precludes broadening it. Determinants of household utility can obviously include the consumption of goods and services, the amount of leisure (and therefore, by difference, the quantity of labor supplied), and the quality of the environment. However, it is also possible to bring into play the variety of goods and services consumed as well as altruistic or moral considerations (for example, the fact that a good was not produced using child labor). Households being suppliers of labor, the maximization of their utility also encompasses their role as producers.

For household i utility in period t can be written, in a very general formulation:

$$U_i^t = \mathrm{U}\left(C_{i1}^t, C_{i2}^t, \ldots, C_{in}^t; N_i^t; E_i^t; \Xi_i^t\right) \tag{1.1}$$

where C_{ik}^t ($k = 1 \ldots n$) is the amount of good k consumed by household i at time t, N_i^t the quantity of labor supplied by household i in period t, E_i^t a vector of variables representing working conditions (intensity of effort, painfulness . . .) and Ξ_i^t a vector of variables representative of the quality of the environment.

Instantaneous utility is, however, insufficient. Based on such a criterion, there would be no reason to invest (since investment increases the quantity of goods and services available for future consumption but reduces current consumption). Nor would there be any reason to prevent future global warming. An intertemporal approach is therefore needed. This requires defining a *discount rate* ρ[15] to aggregate utility over time (assuming households have stable preferences):

$$U_i = \sum_{t=0}^{\infty} \frac{U_i^t}{(1+\rho)^t} \tag{1.2}$$

The *intertemporal utility* U_i of household i thus is the *present value* of its future utilities discounted at rate ρ. The household is supposed to live infinitely, which is a shortcut for stating that parents care about the welfare of their offspring. Although this representation remains very simple—for example, it completely overlooks uncertainty about the future or the possible irreversibility of some decisions—the simple fact that the sequence of all future utility levels can be considered greatly reduces the hedonistic character of the simple utility criterion. U_i indeed brings into play the future availability of goods and services. This criterion can be used to assess the desirability of structural reforms when they entail long-run benefits and short-term costs, as discussed earlier: it allows addressing the trade-off between present and future consumption or intertemporal trade-offs involving the preservation of natural resources whose availability will be valued by future generations. The same approach can be used for assessing the utility cost of policies that fail to keep the economy at long-term balance.

Much depends on the choice of the discount rate ρ: a high discount rate introduces a bias toward the short-term and immediate consumption; a low discount rate brings into play the welfare of future generations. This dimension is important to assess environmental concerns but also for economic policies having an impact on savings, such as tax and pension policies.

This intertemporal utility function, however, remains that of a specific household or of a single, supposedly representative, household. The next step is to aggregate the utilities of heterogeneous individuals. This is fraught with difficulties: Must the utility of all agents be equally weighted? Can the well-being of some be reduced to increase that of others? Those questions have a long history in normative economics.

The *Pareto criterion*—according to which a policy improves upon the status quo if it increases the utility of at least one individual and does not reduce that of any other—only makes it possible to compare a limited set of situations and policies. Figure 1.5, borrowed from Atkinson and Stiglitz (1980), explains why. Let us consider two individuals 1 and 2, represent their respective utilities on the X and Y axes, and suppose that the AF locus gives all possible combinations of their respective utilities. According to the Pareto criterion, C is superior to any situation on AC and E is superior

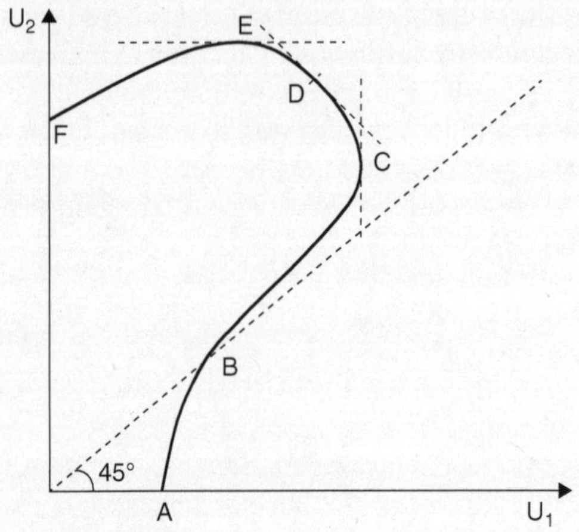

Figure 1.5 Individual utility and social choices: an illustration.
Taken from Atkinson and Stiglitz (1980).

to any situation on *EF* because moving to the North-East improves both utilities simultaneously.

However, there is nothing we can say about the points located on *EC*. Extrapolating to *m* households, choice then requires a *social welfare function* $\Gamma(U_1, U_2, \ldots, U_m)$, where $1 \ldots m$ represent the individuals or households (or, more realistically, categories of households grouped, for example, by income deciles). This makes it possible to compare two income distributions and to decide which one is more desirable. The most usual functions are:

the "Benthamian" function: $\Gamma = U_1 + U_2 + \cdots + U_m$,

and

the "Rawlsian" function: $\Gamma = \text{Min}(U_1, U_2, \ldots, U_m)$.

The first function is named after eighteenth-century philosopher and economist Jeremy Bentham.[16] It assumes that the distribution of utilities across individuals is of no importance and that only the sum of individual utilities matters. With two households, this results in choosing point *D* in figure 1.5 because it corresponds to the maximum aggregate utility (this is where the *AF* locus is tangent to a line of slope –1) even if the corresponding distribution of utility across individuals is definitely uneven as indicated by the distance to the bisector.[17]

Those who value social justice need a more equitable criterion. Strict equalitarianism would result in choosing *B* (intersection between the *AF* locus and the first bisector), which is not optimal according to the Pareto criterion. Starting from *B*, should simultaneous increases in the utility of both agents be rejected only because they would not be equally distributed? A more satisfactory criterion, first proposed by John Rawls,[18] is to seek the maximization of the utility of those who have the least of it. This *maximin* principle leads to choosing *C* where utility U_1 of the least-favored individual is maximum.

It is therefore conceptually possible to assign to economic policy a single objective that includes the three motives for public intervention (allocation, stabilization, redistribution). However, this would require defining very general utility functions and deciding on their aggregation through time and across households. The implication would be a need to decide *ex ante*, for all possible situations, on as complex an issue as the trade-off between intragenerational and intergenerational equity—how much the society stands ready to increase inequality at a certain point in time in exchange for an improvement in the welfare of future generations. It is unlikely that any society would be able to reach consensus on such a function.

b) Specific criteria for allocation, stabilization, and redistribution

In practice, economic policy evaluation generally relies on separate, conceptually different instruments for allocation, stabilization, and redistribution assessments. Social welfare functions of the type just presented are generally used for evaluating allocation policies but most often in a simplified form.

To assess allocation, *partial equilibrium* analyses are the simplest ones as they only consider the sector directly affected by policy decisions and therefore neglect interdependence between sectors arising on the demand side from the economic agents' budget constraints or on the supply side from the limited availability of production factors. For example, the analysis of the effects of reducing the indirect tax rate on a given good or service is limited to the market for that product and therefore overlooks the corresponding change of spending on other products and the overall impact of the implied reallocation of labor and capital that follows the increase in demand. Those are acceptable assumptions only to the extent that the sector considered is small in comparison to the whole economy.

Partial equilibrium analyses can be implemented easily as they only require knowing the price elasticity of supply and demand for the product considered and rely on well-known instruments such as consumer and producer *surplus* (an approximation of the variation of their utility). For example, taxing the consumption of apples harms both consumers and farmers while the government benefits from increased tax revenues. Because a tax distorts behavior, the government, however, gains less than the combined loss of households and farmers. Standard economic theory thus predicts a net loss for the society that corresponds to the (negative) algebraic sum of the three agents' net surpluses (box 1.5). This calculation is valid, however, only if the sector is small because it misses spillovers to other markets and other general equilibrium effects (such as consumers substituting pears for apples or the impact on the economy of the government's improved fiscal position).

Box 1.5 Measuring the Deadweight Loss of Taxation

Suppose that the supply and demand for apples are both linear functions of their price, as in Figure B1.5.1. In the absence of a tax, the equilibrium quantity and price are Q_0 and P_0. Introducing a tax t in dollars per unit drives the consumer price to P^d_1, the producer price to P^s_1, and the quantity produced to Q_1.

How is the surplus changed by the introduction of the tax? In Figure B1.5.1, consumer surplus is measured by the surface comprised between the demand curve and the $P = P_0$ schedule: for any point (P, Q) on the demand curve for which $P > P_0$, there is a surplus because the consumer pays P_0, whereas she would be willing to pay P. The aggregate surplus is the corresponding integral. As a consequence of the tax, this surplus shrinks from A + B + C to A (where letters refer to the corresponding surface on the figure). Producer surplus is measured by the difference between the revenue, $P_0 \times Q_0$, and the cost of production, which is the surface under the supply curve. It shrinks from D + E + F to F. Government surplus is the revenue of the tax $t \times Q_1 = \mathrm{B} + \mathrm{D}$. The change in social surplus is the sum of all three components $(\mathrm{A} + \mathrm{F} + \mathrm{B} + \mathrm{D}) - (\mathrm{A} + \mathrm{B} + \mathrm{C} + \mathrm{D} + \mathrm{E} + \mathrm{F}) = -(\mathrm{C} + \mathrm{E})$.

The corresponding triangle is called a *Harberger triangle* from UCLA professor Arnold Harberger. Its surface measures the deadweight loss of taxation. We come back to these issues in Chapter 8.

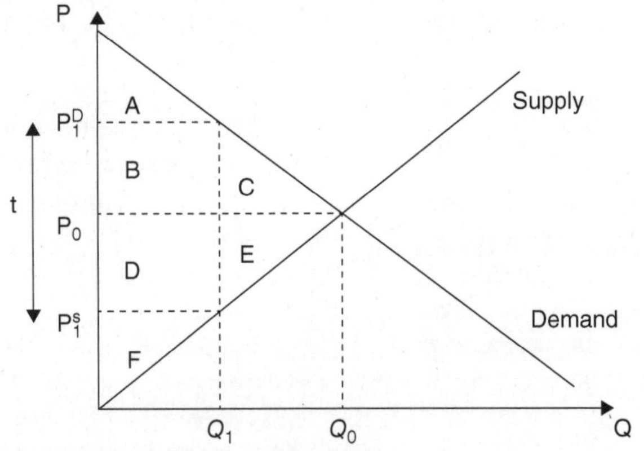

Figure B1.5.1 The welfare impact of a consumption tax in partial equilibrium.

When partial equilibrium analysis is inappropriate, evaluation must rely on a *general equilibrium* approach that takes into account interdependence across sectors and results in a situation where supply balances demand simultaneously on all markets. This can only be done with *simulation models* such as the *Computable General Equilibrium* (CGE) *models*, which are used for assessing the effects of complex trade, structural reform, or tax policy packages (box 1.6).

Box 1.6 Four Categories of Policy Evaluation and Simulation Models

Computable General Equilibrium (CGE) Models

CGE models are based on an extensive representation of the economy with several categories of agents interacting on several markets. These models rely on a detailed description of economic decisions by households and firms that explicitly takes into account budget constraints and other accounting identities, frequently including input–output coefficients. Behavior results from explicit optimization. The corresponding parameters are not estimated on time series (as in macroeconometric models) but are *calibrated*—that is, their values are chosen on the basis of a priori information such as existing studies, and they are adjusted in order for the model to reproduce a given initial situation. This approach is preferred to econometric estimation because the latter is generally impossible due to a very large number of parameters in comparison to available data.

CGE models are widely used today whenever there is a need for evaluating the medium-term consequences of policy decisions affecting several markets or several agents simultaneously. They are the standard instrument for evaluating the outcome of trade negotiations conducted multilaterally within the framework of the World Trade Organization (WTO) or at the regional level (see, for example, Global Trade Analysis Project [GTAP] on www.gtap.agecon.purdue.edu/). They are also the premier instrument for assessing the economic effect of environmental policies—for example, those aiming at reducing greenhouse gas emissions. Other fields of application include development economics (especially for countries where time series on past behavior are unreliable or irrelevant because they have undergone major reforms) and economic history (where CGE techniques can be used to assess the effect of events and decisions). The strength of CGE models rests on their comprehensiveness, their internal consistency, and the fact that they are based on explicit optimizing behavior. Unlike earlier models, those currently in use are frequently dynamic and allow for imperfect competition and the absence of market clearing, like unemployment. They can also be highly disaggregated and therefore take into account differences across sectors or categories of households. Their weakness is that they do not adequately represent short-run effects and rely on weak empirical bases.[a] Major international institutions such as the OECD or the World Bank have developed CGE models or rely on those developed by academic research.

Macroeconomic Models: From Keynesian to DSGE Models

The first macroeconomic models, such as those developed in the 1950s by Jan Tinbergen in the Netherlands and Lawrence Klein at the University of Pennsylvania, were initially derived from Keynesian theory, of which they were intended to provide a formal and quantified representation. They have gradually evolved in line with developments in macroeconomic theory and empirical techniques. They are used both for forecasting and policy simulation purposes.

The main variables in a macroeconomic model (e.g., consumption, investment, employment, price-setting, foreign trade) are taken from national accounts; corresponding behavior is determined by structural equations. The equation parameters are generally *estimated* with econometric techniques[b] or alternatively calibrated.

Initial macroeconomic modeling was essentially empiricist, but it gradually introduced more theoretical discipline, partly in response to a flurry of academic critiques (see Chapter 2). To respond to the criticism that they were assuming very naïve behavior on the part of private agents, model builders introduced model-consistent expectations about the future values of model variables, thereby renouncing the initial (implicit) assumption that they had better knowledge of economic behavior than the agents themselves. Their models were, however, criticized for being based on ad hoc assumptions, for lacking theoretical underpinnings, and for being subject to the so-called *Lucas critique.* The latter argued that supposedly structural parameters in fact reflected behaviors which are impacted by the systematic policy changes that the models were meant to study (see Chapter 2). In response to the criticisms, model builders increasingly developed explicit microeconomic foundations for the estimated equations and adopted more rigorous estimation techniques. At the same time, multinational modeling was developed in order to provide a representation of international interdependence.

Despite having been subjected to scathing critiques, estimated macroeconomic models are still used because they provide readily available instruments for assessing the impacts of shocks or policy decisions. They are, for example, widely used in government administrations, international institutions (OECD, IMF, European Commission), and forecasting institutes (NIESR in the UK, etc.).

A new generation of macroeconomic models called *dynamic stochastic general equilibrium* (*DSGE*) models were developed in the 1990s and 2000s, building on the insights of the real business cycle models of the 1980s but explicitly introducing nominal rigidities in the Keynesian tradition. Thus, consumers maximize intertemporal utility and producers maximize intertemporal profit, but sticky prices prevent markets from clearing.

DSGE models bridge the gap between CGE and macroeconomic models. They include both "deep parameters" (akin to those of general equilibrium models, which are either calibrated or estimated using a priori information on their values) and standard estimated parameters. DSGE models have been adopted by institutions such as the IMF and by most central banks (see Smets and Wouters, 2003, in the European Central Bank's case) in lieu of traditional Keynesian macroeconometric models. They have been criticized, however, in the wake of the global financial crisis for their excessively simple representation of financial intermediation and financial markets. Work has been undertaken to enrich them with financial frictions.[c]

Statistical Models (VAR and Factor Models)

Statistical models depart from the a priori hypotheses about agents' behavior that characterize CGE and macroeconometric models. These models were first developed in the 1980s, in response to dissatisfaction with macroeconometric models (see notably Sims, 1980). Their aim is to empirically determine interdependences between endogenous variables by estimating several equations simultaneously. *Vector autoregressive models* (VARs) are specified in autoregressive form, which implies that each variable depends on its own past values as well as on those of other variables:

$$Y_t = \sum_{k=1}^{K} A_k Y_{t-k} + \varepsilon_t \qquad \text{(B1.6.1)}$$

where Y is a vector of n variables, A_k an (n, n) matrix of estimated coefficients, and ε_t an error term. For example, the effects of monetary policy are assessed through estimating simultaneously the dependence of GDP, inflation, and the short-term interest rate on their past values. Unlike traditional models, VARs do not start from a priori restrictions on the value of the A_k coefficients. This means that systematic policy reactions to shocks—for example, how the central bank responds to a rise in the inflation rate—are estimated in a similar way to the one used for private behavior. VARs have the advantage of embodying the interplay between private and policy players.

The two approaches are not incompatible: the VAR model can be estimated with constraints imposed on the coefficients (they are then called *structural VARs* or *SVARs*). If these constraints are based purely on theoretical consistency, then they are not liable to the Lucas critique. For example, it can be assumed that monetary shocks do not have a long-term impact on output and prices (see Chapter 5). VARs and structural VARs are frequently used for assessing the effects of macroeconomic shocks and policy changes, such as exchange-rate shocks and monetary policy decisions, and they tend to be preferred to larger scale macroeconometric models for such purposes. However, their very aggregate character does not allow them to be used for more detailed policy analyses.

Other examples of statistical models are *factor models*, where the joint dynamics of a large set of short-term economic indicators is assumed to derive from a smaller number of underlying, hidden variables called *factors*. The economic indicators are, for example, industrial output, prices, and household and company survey data, which are typically observed at a monthly frequency. Sargent and Sims (1977) find that two dynamic factors explain more than 80% of the variance of several economic variables, including the rate of unemployment, wholesale price inflation, growth in industrial production, and employment growth. These models are used by central banks and economic institutes to produce forecasts and better anticipate turning points in economic sentiment.

Microsimulation and Agent-Based Models

For the assessment of tax or social policy measures, what is needed is an evaluation that recognizes heterogeneity among households in a much more detailed way than the rough categorization (e.g., rurals–urbans) found in CGE models. This is what *microsimulation models* aim at through explicitly representing a large number of categories of households or individuals.

These models build on the development of large-scale databases providing information on individual agents and can include individual information on tens of thousands of persons, if not more. Equations typically combine optimization (about, for example, labor supply decisions), calibration (about, for example, the evolution of an individual's employment status resulting from the probability of losing one's job or of finding a new one when unemployed), and econometric estimation (about, for example, estimated wage equations determining an individual's wage as resulting from her or his age, gender, and human capital).

Microsimulation models have the great advantage of providing information on the distributional effects of policy changes. However, they do not provide an evaluation of their macroeconomic effects. These models are widely used for assessing the impact of changes in tax and welfare benefit legislation. Examples include the European EUROMOD model based at the University of Essex or the TAXBEN model of the London-based Institute for Fiscal Studies, a simplified version of which is available on the web.

A common feature of *agent-based models* (ABM) and microsimulation models is granularity: both represent a large number of households or firms. In addition to microsimulation models, ABMs assign simple behavioral rules to each agent, which include interaction with and learning from other agents. This enables them, for example, to replicate the herding and panic situations typical of financial markets. ABMs have been used in social sciences and more recently in economics and finance (see Geanakoplos et al., 2012, for an application to the housing market).

[a] See Shoven and Whalley (1984) for an early survey of CGE modeling. A more recent example is given by Dixon and Jorgenson (2013).
[b] In its simplest form, econometric estimation consists in determining the parameters of an equation linking a dependent variable to observed explanatory variables in such a way that the deviation of estimated from actual values of the dependent variable is minimum. A popular technique is the *Ordinary least squares* (OLS) estimation, which consists in finding the parameter values that minimize the sum of square deviations of estimated from actual values of the dependent variable over the estimation period.
[c] See Smets et al. (2010) for a survey of DSGE models at the ECB and Kocherlakota (2010) for a discussion of DSGE models during the financial crisis. A seminal DSGE with financial frictions is presented in Gertler and Karadi (2011).

The effectiveness of stabilization policies is often assessed against an intertemporal utility function like the one presented in Equation (1.2). This relies on the assumption that a single agent's utility suffices to represent the social cost of a departure from equilibrium. A major difficulty, however, arises from measuring the welfare loss from unemployment: in a microeconomic setting, voluntary unemployment increases individual utility because agents value leisure, yet it is difficult to claim that a rise in unemployment generally increases utility. Another difficulty comes from the cost of inflation, which differs widely in the short term and in the long term.[19]

Alternatively, the analysis of stabilization policies often relies on specific *macroeconomic loss functions* such as:

$$L_t = E_t\left(\sum_{s=0}^{T}(1+\rho)^{-s}\sum_{i=1}^{N}\alpha_i\left(y_{t+s}^i - \tilde{y}^i\right)^2\right) \tag{1.3}$$

where $E_t(X)$ stands for the mathematical expectation at date t of variable X, the y^i are the objective variables of economic policy (growth, inflation, fiscal balance, etc.), and $\tilde{y}_i$ their target values; α_i is the weight assigned to variable y^i, and ρ is the *discount factor*. The objective of the government or the monetary authorities is to minimize the value of the loss function. This second representation is closer to the reality of policy debates that concern jobs, growth, or deficits rather than their implications for welfare.

In practice, policymakers never use such functions (most finance ministers would be surprised to see them), but this representation is a fair approximation of reality. Decision-making processes do bring trade-offs into play: for example, between reducing the budget deficit and bolstering GDP growth or between supporting consumption and promoting investment. The inflation–growth trade-off was a key concern in the 1960s and the 1970s, and the desire to avoid being confronted with it again exerted a considerable influence in the choice of an institutional architecture that assigns responsibility for monetary policy to an independent central bank (see Chapter 5). This type of reasoning, moreover, is encouraged by the recourse to models for decision-making. In a way, the representation of economic policy choices in simulation instruments retroacts on economic policy.

The analysis of stabilization policies generally consists in comparing, with the same utility function (Equation (1.2)) or loss function (Equation (1.3)), policy reactions to a given *shock*—an exogenous event such as a fall of world growth or a variation of the investors' appetite for risk. The loss function makes it possible, for example, to determine whether, in response to an adverse shock to private investment, it is preferable to increase public investment, reduce corporate taxation, or lower the interest rate. Results, of course, depend on the macroeconomic model and on the loss function used.

Social welfare functions are almost never used to support concrete decisions on redistribution. Discussions on the redistribution effects of economic policies are almost always based on empirical indicators of inequalities, such as the distribution of income between *deciles* of population, or aggregate indicators such as the *Lorenz curve* and *Gini coefficient* (box 1.7). This is because income

Box 1.7 Measuring Inequality

Inequality is multidimensional, and no single indicator can summarize the entire distribution of income and wealth among individuals or households. A simple and telling measure of income (or wealth) inequality is the *quintile ratio*, defined as the ratio of the income (or wealth) of the top 20% of the population to the bottom 20%. According to the United Nations' Human Development Report, the income quintile ratio ranged from 3.6 in Slovakia to 29.7 in Honduras in 2013, with the United Kingdom standing at 7.2. It is this type of measure that is frequently used in public debate. However, to summarize the whole distribution by the gap between the two extremes overlooks developments affecting 60% of the population.

The *Lorenz curve* provides a graphic representation of the entire distribution. Fractiles of the population ordered by growing income level are plotted on the X axis and the corresponding cumulative share of total income on the Y axis. For an (x, y) point on the curve, y is therefore the share of total income going to the first x% of the population. The bisector corresponds to an equal distribution of income. The greater the distance between the Lorenz curve and the bisector, the larger the inequalities. Figure B1.7.1 gives Lorenz curves for US pre-tax family income in 1980, 1990, 2000, and 2010. It is apparent that income inequality has widened.

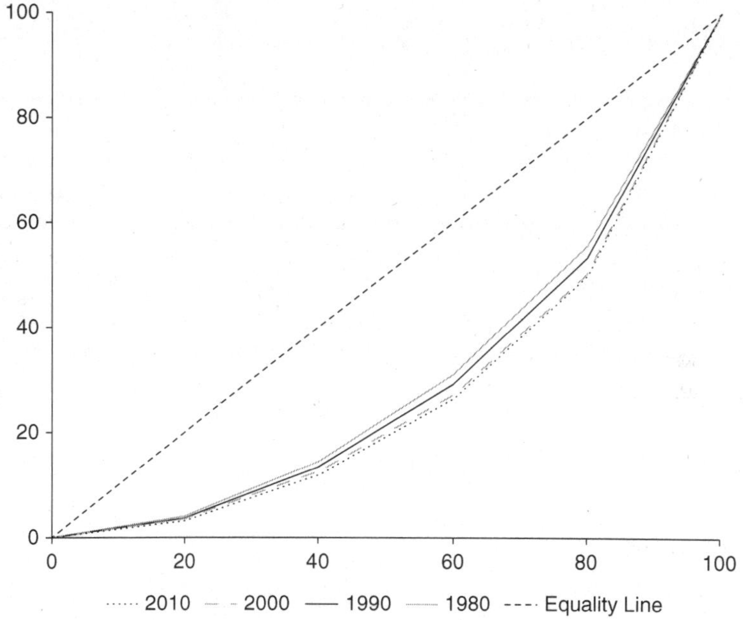

Figure B1.7.1 Lorenz curve, US households 1980–2010.
US Census, retrieved from: http://www.census.gov/hhes/www/income/data/historical/inequality/IE-1.pdf, accessed August 4, 2015.

The *Gini coefficient* provides a synthetic numerical measure of inequality. It is defined as twice the surface of the area between the Lorenz curve and the bisector, which is comprised between 0 (perfectly equal distribution) and 0.5 (maximum inequality). The Gini coefficient therefore varies between zero and 1. Formally, if x_i $(i = 1,\dots n)$ are the limits of the fractiles of the population and y_i the share of each fractile in total income, the Gini coefficient is:

$$G = 1 - \sum_{i=1}^{n} (x_i - x_{i-1})(y_{i-1} - y_i) \qquad \text{(B7.1.1)}$$

In 2013, according to the Human Development Report, the Scandinavian countries and some former Soviet Union countries were those where Gini coefficients were the lowest, starting from 0.25 in Sweden. They were highest in South American and African countries and as high as 0.66 in the Seychelles. Germany stood at 0.28 and the United States at 0.41.

These indicators attempt at providing a summary of the entire distribution. Research pioneered by Thomas Piketty of the Paris School of

Economics has relied on the analysis of the evolution of the share of very high incomes (the top 1% or the top one per thousand) in national income. It provides evidence of a significant rise in the share of top incomes since the 1980s in the United States and the United Kingdom, while the same phenomenon has not been observed in continental Europe. See Atkinson and Piketty (2007) and, for the United States, Piketty and Saez (2003).

levels are better natural references in policy discussions and public debates than utility—although it must also be recognized that relying exclusively on the comparison of income levels can be misleading (for example, for a given distribution of income, an increase of subsidies to social housing is likely to improve the utility of individuals in the bottom deciles while public investment in higher education increases the utility of the top deciles).

1.3.2 Experiments and *ex post* evaluation

Whatever the criterion used, model-based policy evaluation is of an *ex ante* nature as it typically compares the current situation to the one that is expected to result from a given policy. Even when implemented *ex post* to compare the situation after the implementation of a given policy to the one that would have prevailed had this policy not been implemented, the evaluation is based on model parameters previously estimated or calibrated. Therefore, it cannot consider or assess changes in behaviors in relation to the reform (for instance, after a pension reform). There is a need for experimenting the reform (before generalizing its implementation) and carrying out *ex post* evaluation.

a) The pitfalls of evaluation

Successful policy evaluation implies several institutional prerequisites, such as ensuring the independence of the evaluators and their access to data, allowing for open discussion of the assumptions and results, and the like. But it is also faced with analytical pitfalls. A first pitfall has to do with *reverse causality*: for example, observing a negative correlation across individuals between their health expenditures and health status does not imply that healthcare is harmful to health, but rather that individuals with a poor health condition have consumed more healthcare. A second pitfall has to do with *incidence*. The ultimate beneficiary of a policy is not necessarily the targeted one—we'll see many examples of this when we discuss tax policy in Chapter 8. A third pitfall has to do with *omitted variables* (or spurious correlation). Coming back to the healthcare example, it can be observed that high-income individuals enjoy a better health and spend more on their health. This can be mistaken for a direct causality from health expenditures to health condition, whereas both are related to income. Statistical techniques make it possible to work around these issues. The key is to be able to figure out what would have happened if the policy had not been implemented—the *counterfactual.*[20]

b) Making use of experiments

Ex ante evaluation is especially inappropriate when the reform has a structural character and is expected to modify behavior in a way that does not simply replicate experience. It is therefore important to carry out genuine *ex post* policy evaluations. Building on a standard practice in life sciences, corresponding techniques were developed in the 1990s, especially in the field of social policies. They often rest on *natural experiments* that make it possible to compare the behavior of individuals affected by the policy change to that of other individuals whose situation, though similar, has not been affected by it. This is, for example, the case for means-tested transfers: by comparing the behavior of individuals immediately below the threshold to that of those immediately above it—who are therefore very similar in all other relevant dimensions—it is possible to measure precisely the effect of the policy (box 1.8). In certain countries, policymakers also resort to *controlled*

Box 1.8 Evaluating Public Policies Through Natural Experiments

The traditional method for evaluating the response of labor supply to tax changes is to resort to econometric estimates on time series. It is fraught with methodological difficulties, from the identification of labor supply to the lack of experience with relevant tax changes. Also, tax changes may affect only certain categories of the labor force, and aggregate estimates do not allow assessment of the corresponding effects.

The issue would be easy to solve were it possible to resort to controlled experiments—as in the life sciences—with laboratory techniques. This would involve selecting a group of individuals, submitting them to a tax change, and observing their behavior in comparison to a pilot group with comparable characteristics for whom the taxation would have been left unchanged. Such an experiment would make it possible to isolate the pure effect of taxation.

Thanks to the recourse to randomization, experiments of this kind are practiced in certain countries, such as the United States, Canada, or the Netherlands. They are used to evaluate the effectiveness of social policy reforms before they are generalized. However, in other countries, such as France, the practice of controlled experiments was for long held back by constitutional difficulties.

An alternative is to exploit *natural experiments*, as, for example, when two jurisdictions within the same country which previously had similar legislation start implementing differing policies. This closely replicates the conditions of a controlled experiment: comparison of the resulting behavior allows evaluation of the effectiveness of the different policies. This holds even when the two jurisdictions did not have the same policies: the effect of introducing a new policy can be assessed by comparing changes after it has been introduced (this is called the *difference in differences method*). Even within centralized states where legislation is uniform, some events can be regarded as natural experiments. For example, Joshua Angrist and Victor Lavy (1999) were able to make use of the rule that, in Israeli public schools, a class must be divided into two when its size reaches 40. This rule generates exogenous variations in class size which can be used to study the effect of class size on the pupils' performance. Natural experiments are also widely used in development economics (Banerjee and Duflo, 2011).

The econometric techniques in use for analyzing natural experiments were first developed by James Heckman (2000). They aim at eliminating the effect of heterogeneities and selection biases between the target and the control populations. The diffusion of these methods in the 1990s has led to a major advance in the evaluation of social policies.

experiments to assess the potential effect of a policy change under consideration. For example, Canada used this technique to evaluate the employment effect of in-work benefits before they were introduced.[21] MIT economist Esther Duflo received in 2010 the John Bates Clark medal for her work on *randomized control trials* (RCTs), or *randomized experiments*. In RCTs, the policy subject to evaluation is assigned randomly so that there is no selection bias in the constitution of treatment and control groups.

Natural and controlled experiments are used in a variety of fields, from taxation and social transfers to education and punishment of criminals. Though experiments are standard practice in research, their utilization by policymakers remains uneven.

c) Evaluation criteria in practice

In practice, policy evaluation frequently relies on crude criteria for measuring the effect of a decision on, for example, the GDP (i.e., the total value added produced in the economy during a year), or on unemployment, or on various income groups. Some of these criteria lack rigorous economic foundations. This especially applies to GDP: other things equal, an increase in defense expenditure or in spending on security devices in response to a terrorist threat increases GDP but does not increase welfare (in comparison to the situation that prevailed prior to the threat). In a full-employment situation, a reduction in working time (an increase in leisure) may increase welfare but reduces GDP. Even a decline in unemployment does not necessarily improve welfare if, for example, it is obtained at the price of a reduction of the job search period and leads to a deterioration of the matching between labor supply and labor demand. To have more people at work but more of them unhappy and less productive than they could have been had they spent a few more weeks looking for a suitable job can hardly be regarded as an improvement. Alternative criteria have been developed to better measure well-being and happiness (see box 1.9). In 2009, an international commission chaired by Nobel Prize Joseph Stiglitz (Stiglitz, Sen, and Fitoussi, 2009) documented the many faults of GDP and made recommendations to develop indicators that better account for welfare heterogeneity across individuals and for sustainability issues.

One difficulty with the Human Development Index (HDI – see box 1.9) is how to aggregate different items such as GDP per capita and life expectancy.

Box 1.9 Economic Development and Human Development

The economist and philosopher Amartya Sen (1999) pointed out that the life expectancy of African-Americans is lower than that of inhabitants of the Indian state of Kerala. This illustrates how money income can be a misleading indicator of living conditions.

In reaction to the deficiencies of GDP per person, new indices have been developed such as the Human Development Index (HDI) and other composite indices by the Human Development Report office of the United Nations Development Program. Those indicators take into account a number of health, education, and social criteria (nutrition, life expectancy, access to healthcare, etc.). Although initially rather crude, this approach has gradually gained in sophistication, in large part thanks to Sen's research. In the late 1990s, it inspired the definition and adoption by the international community of the *Millennium Development Goals*, which set a number of concrete and measurable social objectives, which have been redefined as 17 *Sustainable Development Goals* in 2015. The HDI is a composite index whose calculation involves life expectancy at birth, knowledge (as a weighted average of adult literacy rate and the combined primary, secondary, and tertiary gross enrollment ratios), and gross national income (GNI) per capita in purchasing power parity US dollars[a] (for a detailed explanation, see Technical note 1 in the United Nations Development Program [2006] Human Development Report).

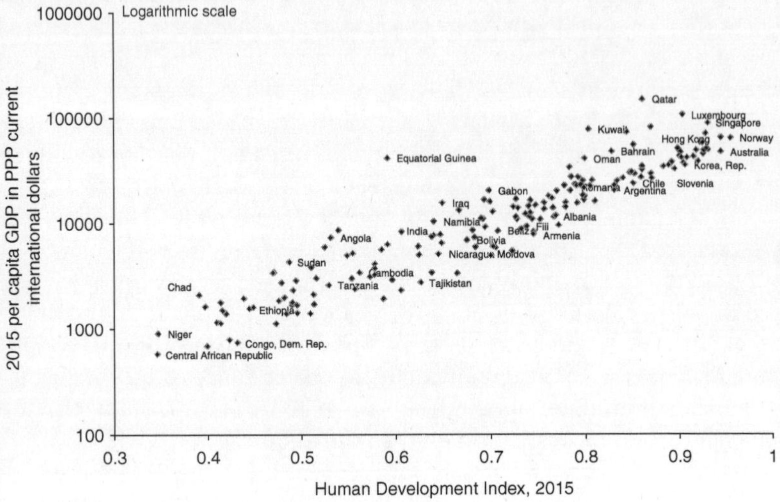

Figure B1.9.1 Gross domestic product (GDP) per capita and Human Development Index in 2015.
2015 per capita GDP in PPP current international dollars (logarithmic scale).
UNDP, Human Development Report 2016.

As shown in Figure B1.9.1, the aggregate HDI is strongly correlated to the economic development level measured by GDP per capita. Nevertheless, significant exceptions do exist: producers of energy and raw material, such as the Gulf States or Equatorial Guinea, exhibit lower HDI ranking than their GDP ranking, which suggests high inequality and insufficient provision of public goods such as health and education; in contrast, some countries such as Georgia, Sri Lanka, or Samoa perform more than 25 ranks better with regards to human development than their national income would indicate.

[a] Purchasing Power Parity (PPP) allows us to compare GDP per capita among different countries if price levels were identical (see Chapters 7 and 9).

An alternative approach is provided by Fleurbaey and Gaulier (2009), who evaluate citizens' implicit willingness to pay for a number of improvements in the quality of life (as compared to a common standard) and then correct the gross national income per capita for the corresponding amounts. They thus produce some sort of a living-standard-income-equivalent that allows comparison of countries. This kind of approach can only be applied to countries of similar standard of living because it relies on marginal effects.

1.3.3 Collateral effects

So far, we have treated the allocation, stabilization, and redistribution functions separately. In reality, an economic policy decision often has effects in more than one dimension. For example, a cut in personal income tax has a permanent allocation effect (it increases labor supply), a temporary stabilization effect (it increases the private agents' income and therefore their demand for goods), and a sustained redistribution effect (it improves the relative income of the agents in the highest income brackets).

It often happens that a policy is adopted for its positive effects on one dimension even though it has adverse effects on others, thus giving rise to trade-offs:

- Redistribution policies frequently introduce undesirable distortions in resource allocation. Means-tested social transfers (such as minimum income) serve a distributive objective but often create *inactivity traps*,[22] and therefore reduce labor supply.
- Trade opening is generally pursued for its allocative effects (the gains from specialization and the corresponding productivity effects, technology spillovers associated with foreign direct investment, etc.) but also has effects on the distribution of income as unskilled jobs are relocated as a consequence of trade with developing countries. The same is true of technical change.
- A reduction in inflation (stabilization policy) can have undesired effects on the distribution of income (redistribution) because it penalizes indebted agents. It can also affect allocation if the unemployment resulting from anti-inflation tightening becomes persistent.

However, a policy adopted for one motive can also have positive effects on other dimensions. For example, a redistribution policy aiming to improve the net pay of unskilled workers (through a workers' tax credit or cuts in social contributions) can have favorable allocation effects through a rise in labor supply.

Finally, the sign of the effect is not always clear. The link between inequalities and growth provides an example (Ostry et al., 2014). Income inequality is sometimes claimed to be positively correlated with growth, either because it allows part of the population to save and accumulate capital or because innovation creates rents which benefit the innovators. The evolution of inequality within China illustrates this relationship. However, inequality is also claimed to be harmful to growth because it does not allow the poorest segments of the population to have access to education and health, and it increases the risk of social and political disruption. The standard example here is Latin America. We return to these issues in Chapter 9.

Table 1.1 summarizes some of these interdependences.

Table 1.1
Direct and indirect effects of three public policies

	Allocation	Stabilization	Redistribution
Reduction in income tax	+ **(Increase in labor supply)**	+ (Increase in demand for goods)	– (Increase in inequalities)
Increase in government expenditures	+/– (Depends on the content of expenditure and on the possibility of crowding out private expenditure)	+ **(By hypothesis)**	+/– (Depends on the content of expenditure)
Increase in social transfers	– (Risk of inactivity trap)	+ (Increase in the demand for goods)	+ **(Reduction in inequalities)**

Direct effects are indicated in boldface.
The initial situation is supposed to be characterized by Keynesian unemployment.

Conclusion

As encapsulated by the famous motto of President Bill Clinton's 1992 election campaign ("it's the economy, stupid"), electoral campaigns are generally fought in a large part on economic matters. So, why is it that reasonable people may disagree on economic policy?

This chapter provides some answers or at least some hints. Politicians can first pursue different social welfare functions: they may, for example, hold contrasting views about the desirable distribution of income. Second, they can respond differently when confronted with trade-offs, for instance, between equality and efficiency. Third, they may discount differently tomorrow's welfare; that is, they may have different time preferences. These three dimensions of genuine policy preferences, attitudes toward trade-offs, and time preferences go a long way toward explaining familiar disputes between left-wing and right-wing parties.

The same type of reasoning provides clues as to why supposedly neutral bodies such as the international institutions are confronted by often-strident opposition from nongovernmental organizations. Ironically indeed, the term "Washington consensus" was coined in 1989 by John Williamson, an economist with the Peterson Institute, to designate a set of policy prescriptions that "more or less everyone in Washington would agree were needed more or less everywhere in Latin America."[23] In the event, it soon came to designate a set of prescriptions many strongly disagreed with.

Ravi Kanbur (2001), a development economist who worked at the World Bank, has shed light on the nature of disagreements on international economic policy choices. He posits that they can arise from differences in the *level of aggregation* adopted, the *time horizon* considered, and assumptions made on *market structure and power*. This especially applies to the debate between proponents and opponents of globalization:

- *Aggregation*: Proponents emphasize the aggregate welfare gains from trade openness because income redistribution can be corrected by fiscal transfers. However, opponents doubt that such corrective policies will actually be implemented, and they fear that the benefits of globalization will accrue to the few and not to the many.
- *Time horizon*: Proponents have a medium-term horizon of five to ten years, and they neglect both the very short term and the very long term; opponents insist on short-term adjustment costs (in particular for the poorest, which relates to the previous point) and on long-term sustainability.
- *Market structure*: Proponents generally suppose that markets are competitive and cleared by prices; opponents underline their imperfection and point out that market openness without government intervention has an adverse impact on income.

The latter item introduces a dimension that has not been addressed in this chapter but will be taken up in Chapter 2: namely, the uncertainty about the structure and functioning of the economy and the resulting policy disagreements. Although advances in economic knowledge have gradually reduced the scope for traditional disputes, new controversies have appeared.

In concluding, however, it is worth recalling that politicians remain free to ignore what economists think is true—or to dismiss its political relevance—and that they often make use of this freedom. Most economists would, for example, say that protracted budget deficits eventually raise long-term interest rates because they increase the supply of Treasury bonds, but Dick Cheney, US Vice President under George W. Bush, reportedly cut short discussions on the matter by saying that "Deficits don't matter. Reagan proved that" (Suskind, 2004, p. 261).

Notes

1. Keynes himself did not escape this rule: his key recommendations were implemented only after World War II.
2. The meaning of this expression has changed over time. In a historical sense (for example, the one Jean-Jacques Rousseau [1755] uses in the "political economy" entry of the *Encyclopaedia* of Diderot and d'Alembert), "political economy" was

equivalent to "general economics" as opposed to "home economics." Jean-Baptiste Say, Adam Smith, David Ricardo, and Karl Marx, among others, used the expression in this way. It kept this meaning in some countries until the end of the twentieth century. In English, however, *political economy* has been replaced by *economics*. In the United States, and later in Europe, a different meaning started to emerge in the 1960s as a strand of research began to explore systematically the political determinants of policy decisions. The corresponding approach was first called *new political economy* but has become known as *political economy* or *political economics*. We follow this usage.

3. This terminology is taken from welfare economics, which is introduced in Section 1.2.2 of this chapter.
4. This classical result of trade policy theory was first established by Jacob Viner (1950). Following Kemp and Wan (1976), many studies have found, however, that preferential trading arrangements can in fact be welfare-improving if they contribute to multilateral liberalization.
5. Jean-Jacques Laffont, a French economist who died prematurely in 2004, initiated the integration of asymmetric information into public economics and applied it to the design of efficient regulation policies. Jean Tirole, his successor at the Toulouse School of Economics, was awarded the Nobel Prize in 2014.
6. For further information on the bidding mechanisms and on the allotment of the 3G telephone licenses, see Klemperer (2004). For a discussion of incentive-compatible contracts in macroeconomic policies, see Cœuré (2012).
7. Expectations are said to be rational when economic agents exploit all available information on the functioning of the economy and the variables relevant for their decisions and form the best possible forecasts. In the framework of a model, the rational expectation of a variable is the forecast that can be made within the model by using all available information on exogenous variables.
8. We return in more detail to the nature of those controversies in Chapter 2.
9. Frequently referred to as the "treaty of Rome," the "Maastricht treaty," or the "Lisbon treaty," the treaty establishing the European Community was signed in Rome in 1957. It was amended several times, most significantly in Maastricht in 1991, to prepare for economic and monetary union; in Nice in 2001, to cope with EU enlargement; and in Lisbon in 2007, to appoint a permanent president of the European Council and give more power to the European Parliament. In what follows, we shall refer to it as the "EU Treaty" or sometimes as the "Maastricht Treaty" when referring specifically to its economic and monetary provisions. Note that the EU treaty in facts consists of two different documents, the "treaty on the European Union," and the "treaty on the functioning of the European Union." Concrete economic and monetary provisions belong to the latter. In 2010–2012, two new treaties were added in response to the euro crisis: the first one created the European Stability Mechanism (ESM), the euro area's financial assistance arm; the second, the Treaty on Stability, Coordination, and Governance (TSCG), strengthened the fiscal discipline and governance provisions.
10. After Jan Tinbergen, the Dutch economist who was awarded the first Nobel Prize in Economics in 1969 for his work on economic policy (Tinbergen, 1952).

11. Within a single market, not only are the customs duties eliminated, but products and factors of production (capital and workers) move without obstacles. Also, there are no obstacles to the cross-border provision of services.
12. An externality, also called an *external effect* or a *spillover*, is the (positive or negative) effect of production or consumption on agents who were not participants in the decision to produce or consume. For example, motor vehicle transportation creates negative externalities through road congestion, noise, and pollution. Positive externalities can, for example, be found in access to social networks such as Twitter or Facebook: their usefulness for any user increases with the number of users connected.
13. Rigidities designate a failure of prices or wages to adjust in response to changes in economic conditions. Economists usually distinguish *nominal rigidities* from *real rigidities*. The former arise from a stickiness in the setting of nominal prices. For example, the wages of employees holding jobs do not change when unemployment varies, or companies do not adjust their price lists when demand falls. Real rigidities are of the same nature but affect real variables such as the real wage, the real interest rate, and the like. For example, nominal wages may change as well as the price of goods without their ratio (the real wage) being affected. Nominal rigidities frequently imply real rigidities, but there can be real rigidities in the absence of nominal rigidities.
14. The real business cycle literature originates in the work of Kydland and Prescott (1982). Galí and Rabanal (2004) provide a skeptical account of its empirical relevance to the US case.
15. The discount rate ρ is the interest rate that should be paid to an agent holding a dollar for him to be indifferent between spending his dollar today and investing it at rate ρ. This is equivalent to saying that the agent is indifferent between receiving 1 dollar in a year and $1/(1+\rho)$ dollars today. $1/(1+\rho)$ is called the discount factor.
16. Jeremy Bentham (1748–1832) was the founder of utilitarianism.
17. It must, however, be pointed out that this social welfare function will exclude extreme income distributions because the marginal utility of income decreases with income: a dollar given to the poor increases their utility more than it reduces that of the rich from whom it was taken.
18. The US philosopher John Rawls (1921–2002) authored *A Theory of Justice* (1971).
19. In a neoclassical framework with rational expectations, the welfare costs of inflation only arise from the costs of individuals holding cash (inflation implies a penalty to holding cash, which necessitates that agents go more often to the bank to withhold cash, in turn requiring larger banks and a greater number of person-hours, etc.) and the costs of changing price tags (i.e., circulating changing information about prices). These two series of costs are respectively called *shoe-leather costs* (as a reference to the premature wear and tear of shoe soles as consumers need to go more often to the bank) and *menu costs*. See Pakko's (1998) review on shoe-leather costs. In the short term, inflation affects individual's welfare because many contracts (such as employment contracts or savings products) are not indexed.
20. See Conseil d'Analyse Economique (2013).

21. Concretely, a sample of potential beneficiaries was randomly selected and divided into two groups. The first one was offered the new in-work benefits, while the second one served as control group. Comparison between the employment behavior of the two groups served to determine the effect of the scheme. See Michalopoulos et al. (2002).
22. An inactivity trap arises when the recipient of a state-dependent or means-tested replacement income (unemployment allowance, welfare transfers) has weak or nonexistent economic incentive to return to work because the loss of social benefits makes the monetary gain from taking up a job too low to compensate for the reduction in leisure.
23. See John Williamson's (2004) account of the history of the Washington consensus.
24. Market power is the possibility for a producer to set a price higher than its marginal production cost (the equilibrium price on a competitive market). This happens when competition is not perfect and the demand for a firm's product is less than infinitely elastic.
25. The return to scale measures the relative increase in production resulting from an increase in the volume of all factors of production (capital, labor, etc.) by a multiplicative factor k. Returns to scale are increasing if production increases by more than k, decreasing if it increases by less than k, constant if it increases by k.
26. Adverse selection takes place when information asymmetry leads to elimination of the most efficient suppliers or buyers from the market. The standard example is that of the market for second-hand cars described by Akerlof (1970): only the sellers know the quality of the vehicles they sell. The competitive selling price corresponds to average quality; therefore, sellers of high-quality vehicles find the price too low and reject selling their car. The result is a fall of average quality and therefore of the price. Eventually, only the lemons may be put on sale. Such adverse selection is obviously not optimal. This problem is common in the insurance business.

References

Akerlof, G. A. (1970), "The Market for 'Lemons': Quality Uncertainty and the Market Mechanism," *Quarterly Journal of Economics*, 84(3), pp. 488–500.

Angrist, J., and V. Lavy (1999), "Using Maimonides' Rule to Estimate the Effect of Class Size on Student Achievement," *Quarterly Journal of Economics*, 114(2), pp. 533–74.

Arrow, K., and G. Debreu (1954), "Existence of an Equilibrium for a Competitive Economy," *Econometrica*, 22(3), pp. 265–90.

Atkinson, A., and T. Piketty (2007), *Top Incomes over the Twentieth Century*, Oxford University Press.

Atkinson, A., and J. Stiglitz (1980), *Lectures on Public Economics*, McGraw Hill.

Banerjee, A., and E. Duflo (2011), *Poor Economics: A Radical Rethinking of the Way to Fight Global Poverty*. PublicAffairs.

Blanchard, O., and D. Quah (1989), "The Dynamic Effects of Aggregate Demand and Supply Disturbances," *American Economic Review*, 79(4), pp. 655–73.

Blanchard, O., and J. Tirole (2008), "The Joint Design of Unemployment Insurance and Employment Protection: A First Pass," *Journal of the European Economic Association*, 6(1), pp. 45–77.

Bouis, R., O. Causa, L. Demmou, R. Duval, and A. Zdzienicka (2012), "The Short-Term Effects of Structural Reforms: An Empirical Analysis," OECD Economics Department Working Papers, No. 949, OECD Publishing.

Buchanan J. (1975), "A Contractarian Paradigm for Applying Economic Policy," *American Economic Review*, 65(2), pp. 225–30.

Chapman, B. (2006), "Income Contingent Loans for Higher Education: International Reforms," in Hanushek, E., and F. Welch, eds., *Handbook of the Economics of Education*, Elsevier/North-Holland, volume 2, chapter 25, pp. 1435–98.

Coibion, O., Y. Gorodnichenko, and M. Ulate (2017), "The Cyclical Sensitivity in Estimates of Potential Output," *NBER Working Paper* 23580, Cambridge, MA: National Bureau of Economic Research.

Cœuré, B. (2012), "Central Banking, Insurance and Incentive," speech at the ECB Conference on Debt, Growth and Macroeconomic Policies, Frankfurt, December 6.

Conseil d'Analyse Economique (2013), "Public Policy Evaluation," *Les notes du conseil d'analyse économique*, No. 1, February.

Dixit, A. (1996), *The Making of Economic Policy*, MIT Press.

Dixon, P. B., and D. W. Jorgenson (2013), eds., *Handbook of Computable General Equilibrium Modeling*, Elsevier.

Eggertsson, G., A. Ferrero, and A. Raffo (2014), "Can Structural Reforms Help Europe?," *Journal of Monetary Economics*, 61, pp. 2–22.

Fleurbaey, M., and G. Gaulier (2009), "International Comparisons of Living Standards by Equivalent Incomes, "*Scandinavian Journal of Economics*, 111(3), pp. 597–624.

Galí, J., and P. Rabanal (2004), "Technology Shocks and Aggregate Fluctuations: How Well Does the RBS Model Fit Postwar US Data?," *NBER Working Papers 10636*, National Bureau of Economic Research, Inc.

Geanakoplos, J., R. Axtell, D. Farmer, P. Howitt, B. Conlee, J. Goldstein, M. Hendrey, N. Palmer, and C. Yang (2012), "Getting at Systemic Risk via an Agent-Based Model of the Housing Market," *American Economic Review: Papers and Proceedings*, 102 (3), pp. 53–58.

Gertler, M., and P. Karadi (2011), "A Model of Unconventional Monetary Policy," *Journal of Monetary Economics*, 58, pp. 17–34.

Heckman J. (2000), "Microdata, Heterogeneity, and the Evaluation of Public Policy," Nobel conference [www.nobel.se].

International Monetary Fund (2004), "GEM: A New International Macroeconomic Model," *IMF Occasional Paper* No. 239.Kanbur, R. (2001), "Economic Policy, Distribution and Poverty: The Nature of Disagreements," *World Development*, 29 (6), pp. 1083–94.

Kemp, M., and H. Wan (1976), "An Elementary Proposition Concerning the Formation of Customs Unions," *Journal of International Economics*, 6, pp. 95–97.

Keynes J. M. (1931), *Essays in Persuasion*, Harcourt, Brace and Company [www.uqac.ca/].

Keynes J. M. (1936), *The General Theory of Employment, Interest and Money*, Macmillan Cambridge University Press.

Kindelberger, C. (1978), *Manias, Panics and Crashes: A History of Financial Crises*, Wiley.

Klemperer, P. (2004), *Auctions: Theory and Practice*, Princeton University Press.

Kocherlakota, N. (2010), "Modern Macroeconomic Models as Tools for Economic Policy," *Banking and Policy Issues Magazine*. Federal Reserve Bank of Minneapolis.

Kydland, F. E., and E. C. Prescott (1982), "Time to Build and Aggregate Fluctuations," *Econometrica*, 50 (6), pp. 1345–70.

Lucas, R. (1976), "Econometric Policy Evaluation: A Critique," *Carnegie-Rochester Conference Series on Public Policy*, 1, pp. 19–46.

Maskin, E. (2007), "Mechanism Design: How to Implement Social Goals," Nobel Prize Lecture, December 8.

Michalopoulos, Ch., D. Tattrie, C. Miller, P. K. Robins, P. Morris, D. Gyarmati, C. Redcross, K. Foley, and R. Ford (2002), "Making Work Pay: Final Report on the Self-Sufficiency Project for Long-Term Welfare Recipients," http://www.mdrc.org/publications/46/abstract.html.

Minsky, H. (1992), "The Financial Instability Hypothesis," *Jerome Levy Economics Institute Working Paper* No. 74, May, http://papers.ssrn.com/sol3/papers.cfm?abstract_id=161024.

Musgrave, R., and P. Musgrave (1989), *Public Finance in Theory and Practice*, McGraw Hill.

North, D. (1993), "Economic Performance Through Time," Nobel Prize lecture, December 9, http://www.nobelprize.org.

Okun, A. (1975), *Equality and Efficiency: The Big Trade-off*, Brookings Institution. New ed., 2015.

Ostry, J. D., A. Berg, and C. G. Tsangarides (2014), "Redistribution, Inequality and Growth," *IMF Staff Discussion Note* SDN/14/02.

Pakko, M. R. (1998), "Shoe-Leather Costs of Inflation and Policy Credibility," *Federal Reserve Bank of St Louis Review*, November/December.

Phillips, A. W. (1958), "The Relation Between Unemployment and the Rate of Change of Money Wage Rates in the United Kingdom: 1861–1957," *Economica*, 25(100), pp. 283–99.

Piketty, T., and E. Saez (2003), "Income Inequality in the United States, 1913–1998," *Quarterly Journal of Economics*, 118(1), pp. 1–39, updated tables available on http://elsa.berkeley.edu/~saez/.

Rawls, J. (1971), *A Theory of Justice*, Belknap Press of Harvard University Press.

Rousseau, J. J. (1755), "Economie," in D. Diderot and J. le Rond d'Alembert, *Encyclopédie*, vol. 5, pp 337–49. English translation: http://quod.lib.umich.edu/d/did/, Scholarly Publishing Office of the University of Michigan Library, 2009.

Sargent, T. J., and C. A. Sims (1977), "Business Cycle Modeling Without Pretending to Have Too Much A-Priori Economic Theory," in C. Sims et al. (eds.), *New Methods in Business Cycle Research: Proceedings From a Conference*, Federal Reserve Bank of Minneapolis, pp. 45–109.

Sen, A. (1999), *Development as Freedom*, Oxford University Press.

Shiller, R. J. (2003), *The New Financial Order: Risk in the 21st Century*, Princeton University Press.

Shoven, J. B., and J. Whalley (1984), "Applied General Equilibrium Models of Taxation and International Trade: An Introduction and Survey," *Journal of Economic Literature*, 22, pp. 1007–51.

Sims, C. (1980), "Macroeconomics and Reality," *Econometrica*, 48, pp. 1–48.

Smets, F., K. Christoffel, G. Coenen, R. Motto, and M. Rostagno (2010), "DSGE Models and Their Use at the ECB," *SERIEs, Journal of the Spanish Economic Association*, 1 (1–2), pp. 51–65.

Smets, F., and R. Wouters (2003), "An Estimated Dynamic Stochastic General Equilibrium Model of the Euro Area," *Journal of the European Economic Association*, 1 (5), 1123–75.

Stein, H. (1986), *Washington Bedtime Stories*, Free Press.

Stiglitz, J. (1991), "The Invisible Hand and Modern Welfare Economics," *National Bureau of Economic Research, Working Paper* No. 3641.

Stiglitz, J., A. Sen, and J. P. Fitoussi (2009), "Report of the Commission on the Measurement of Economic Performance and Social Progress," http://www.ofce.sciences-po.fr/pdf/documents/rapport.pdf.

Stiglitz, J., and A. Weiss (1981), "Credit Rationing in Markets with Imperfect Information," *American Economic Review*, 71(3), pp. 393–410.

Suskind, Ron (2004), *The Price of Loyalty: George W. Bush, the White House, and the Education of Paul O'Neill*, New York: Simon & Schuster.

Tinbergen, J. (1952), *On the Theory of Economic Policy*, North-Holland.

United Nations Development Program (2006), *Human Development Report*, United Nations.

Viner, J. (1950), *The Customs Union Issue, New York*, Carnegie Endowment for International Peace.

Williamson, J. (2004), "A Short History of the Washington Consensus," paper prepared for the Fundación CIDOB conference "From the Washington Consensus Toward a New Global Governance," Barcelona, Spain, September 24–25.

2

Issues

In Chapter 1, economic policy was presented as an engineer's science. A single omniscient, omnipotent, and benevolent policymaker was supposed to engage in optimization, taking social preferences as given and relying for decisions on accurately estimated parameters. It is now time to challenge these assumptions.

Since the 1970s, economic research has systematically explored the deficiencies of the traditional approach to economic policymaking, pointing out severe theoretical and empirical limitations and exploring what remains of the standard prescriptions when these limitations are lifted. As expressed in very similar terms by Avinash Dixit (1996) and Jean-Jacques Laffont (2000*c*), the research program of the past four decades can be read in retrospect as knocking the omniscient, omnipotent, and benevolent policymaker's statue off its pedestal.

The theories developed since the 1970s model the decision-maker as interacting in an imperfect information context with other players who themselves are imperfectly informed but are able to anticipate, compute, and interact strategically and whose behaviors depend on their expectations of the decision-maker's not-always-benevolent actions. Economic policy can still influence the players of that strategic game, but they can no longer be regarded as preprogrammed automatons, and this matters as much for policy implementation as it does for policy design. This representation has deeply influenced the theory as well as, gradually, the practice of economic policy.

Five main limits to the traditional approach to economic policy are investigated in this chapter together with the instruments available to address them. First, the limits of knowledge: governments have imperfect knowledge of the structure of the economy and of the probability laws governing future risks. Second, the limits of representation: firms and households are not akin to ants under a magnifying glass. They devise their own strategies and they react to—and anticipate—economic policy measures. Third, the limits of confidence: policymakers may not be able to convince private agents that they will actually do what they have announced, and this affects the latter's behavior. Fourth, the limits of information: policymakers may have full knowledge of the structure of the economy but lack access to private information and face private actors who make a strategic use of it. Fifth, and finally, there are limits to benevolence: policymakers may not always pursue the general interest.

2.1 The Limits of Knowledge

An important—though implicit—assumption in most of Chapter 1 was that the government has extensive knowledge of the preferences of economic agents and of the structure of the economy. That public and private agents invest in the acquisition of information and use it to make their decisions is certainly a natural assumption, but it faces limits. Here, we review four, non-mutually exclusive propositions:

- The parameters of models used by economists and decision-makers are fraught with uncertainty.

- Decision-makers usually base their decisions on expected outcomes only and seldom consider the full distribution of risks.
- The distribution of risks facing the economy is hardly known, and, in some cases, it cannot even be quantified using traditional probabilistic methods.
- When decisions are irreversible and the environment is uncertain, there are situations in which it is preferable to wait before acting: there is a "precautionary principle" in economic policymaking (that same principle can also conversely justify prompt action when inaction has irreversible consequences).

2.1.1 Model and parameter uncertainty

Let us start from a simple representation of the economy:

$$Y_t = H(X_t, Y_{t-1}, Y_{t-2} \ldots, \theta, \varepsilon_t) \tag{2.1}$$

where X, Y, θ, and ε are multidimensional vectors respectively summarizing government action, the state of the economy, parameters, and exogenous random shocks. X_t can, for example, represent tax rates and public expenditures at time t, while Y_t represents household consumption, and θ the elasticity of consumption with respect to income, wealth, and the interest rate. H represents the accounting and behavioral relations linking all variables, and ε_t is a random vector, the value of which is unknown until period t. Barring unexpected shocks, the state of the economy at time t thus depends on its past evolution and on current government actions. However, the latter's impact depends on θ, which is not directly observable. There are two sources of uncertainty about θ.

- First, *model uncertainty* arising from the choices made by the theorist and the econometrician. Questions here are, for example: Should the interest rate be included in the consumption function? Or are consumption, investment, and export functions linear? Model builders' theoretical assumptions can lead to many different choices for model specification. Policymakers are not always aware that the analyses and recommendations they are presented with rest heavily on those choices.
- Second, for a given model, *parameter uncertainty*, arising from the limited range of observed data points available to the econometrician. What is available for policy analysis is not the true value of θ but an estimate $\hat{\theta}$ extracted from individual or time-series observations with the help of more-or-less-sophisticated econometric techniques (box 2.1). As end-users, policymakers are usually not aware of the extent to which $\hat{\theta}$ is fraught with uncertainty.

For instance, a government facing a recession will feel comfortable undertaking output stimulation through increased public spending if the *Keynesian multiplier* (i.e., the reaction of output to a given increase in public spending) is known to be higher than one. Econometric evidence does suggest that point estimates of the multiplier are on average close to one but, given their distribution, suggests that there are substantial odds that the multiplier could even be lower than zero (see Chapter 4).

Box 2.1 Parameter Uncertainty in Econometric Models

Suppose that the economy is governed by a simpler, linear version of Equation (2.1):

$$Y_t = \theta' X_t + \varepsilon_t \qquad \text{(B2.1.1)}$$

If Y comprises n variables and there are m exogenous variables in X, θ is an $m \times n$ matrix to be estimated based on the observed values of X and Y over, say, the period $t = 1$ to T. θ' is the transposed matrix of θ. The *ordinary least squares* (OLS) estimate of θ, that is, the value of θ that minimizes the sum of squared residuals, is:

$$\hat{\theta} = (\Xi'\Xi)^{-1}\,\Xi'\Psi \qquad \text{(B2.1.2)}$$

Where ψ is a $T \times n$ matrix built by staggering the observed values of Y_t and Ξ is a $T \times m$ matrix built by staggering the observed values of X_t. Ξ' is the transposed matrix of Ξ. Since X and Y are random variables, $\hat{\theta}$ is also random and converges only asymptotically (i.e., when there are a large number of observations) toward the true value θ. The same is true when parameters are observed not only across time but also across individual observations.

The variance–covariance matrix of $\hat{\theta}$ can be computed as a function of ψ and Ξ. For example, if Y includes only one variable (say GDP), if the m variables in X are deterministic and if the variance of the random shock ε is constant over time and equal to σ^2, the variance of $\hat{\theta}$ is a $m \times m$ matrix:

$$Var\,\hat{\theta} = \sigma^2 (\Xi'\Xi)^{-1} \qquad \text{(B2.1.3)}$$

More generally, one can compute the first order approximation of the variance of any well-behaved function g of $\hat{\theta}$ knowing its first derivative $\frac{\partial g}{\partial \theta} = \left(\frac{\partial g}{\partial \theta_1}, \ldots \frac{\partial g}{\partial \theta_m}\right)'$:

$$Var\, g(\hat{\theta}) = \sigma^2 \left(\frac{\partial g}{\partial \theta}\right)' (\Xi'\Xi)^{-1} \frac{\partial g}{\partial \theta} \tag{B2.1.4}$$

This allows building *confidence intervals* for $g(\hat{\theta})$ (i.e., ranges of values for a given confidence level). For instance, suppose that the first variable in X is the logarithm of public spending and the first variable in Y is the logarithm of GDP. Then the top-left element of $\hat{\theta}$ is the point estimate of the Keynesian multiplier, which measures the percentage reaction of GDP to a percentage increase in public spending. Suppose now that this estimate is equal to unity, with a 90% confidence band of [0; 2] and a 95% confidence band of [–0.5; 2.5]. This would mean that there is a 90% probability that the multiplier takes a value between 0 and 2 and a 95% probability that it ranges from –0.5 to 2.5. The larger the band for a given level of confidence (say 95%), the lower the reliability of the point estimate 1. In such an example, it would not possible to say at a 95% confidence level whether the multiplier is positive or negative; that is, whether a fiscal stimulus would lead the economy to expand or to shrink.

2.1.2 Managing risk

In many instances, private companies follow formal decision processes that consider the distribution of risks. The head of marketing who launches a new product and the credit officer who approves a loan to a company do not make their decisions on the sole basis of expected profit. They assess the possibility that the project might fail or that the credit would not be refunded, and they provision for such risk or require the appropriate collateral. A telling and widely used measure of possible loss is *cost at risk* (CaR), which measures how much may be lost at a given confidence level. As an example, if the unit return of an investment project is random and follows a normal law with mean 1 and standard deviation 2,[1] then the expected return of investing €1 million is €1 million, the loss in 10% of cases is more than €1.55 million, and the loss in 30% of cases is more than €50,000. This results from the cumulated distribution of returns, illustrated in figure 2.1.

The same method is used in capital markets to assess the maximum loss of value out of a financial asset or of an asset portfolio at a given time horizon, in which case it is called *value at risk* (VaR). VaR is the cornerstone of modern risk management in and supervision of financial institutions. It requires knowledge of the joint distribution of the returns of all underlying assets (see Chapter 6).

Since von Neumann and Morgenstern (1944), who formalized the seminal work of Daniel Bernoulli (1738), economists have generally assumed that agents know the probability of the various states of nature and maximize their

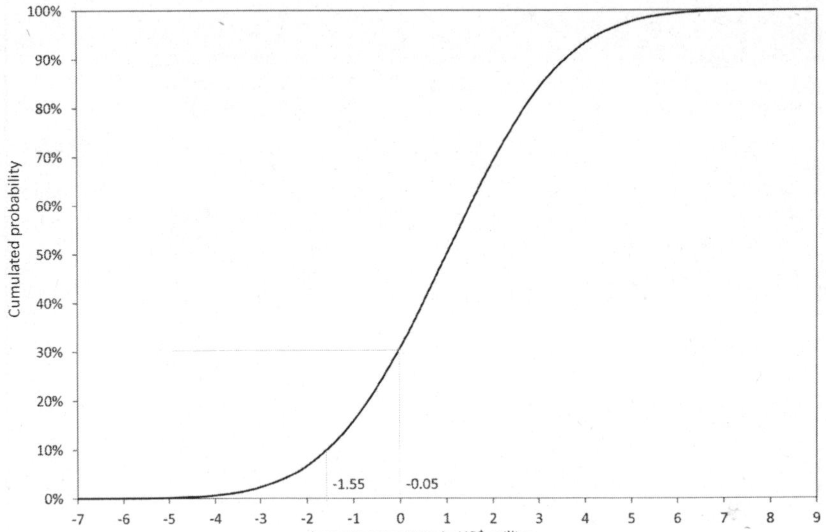

Figure 2.1 Cost at risk: the graph shows the cumulated probability of different returns for a US$1 million investment, based on a normal distribution N(1,2). There is a 30% probability of a return lower than −0.05 million.

expected utility; that is, the expected value of their future utility; that is, the sum of utilities of the gains in each state of nature weighted by their probability. Within this framework, the notion used to model attitudes toward risk is *risk aversion*, which is related to the second derivative of the utility function (box 2.2).

In many economic models, companies are assumed to be risk-neutral (because they have access to financial markets and can use them to insure against all kinds of shocks) and individuals are assumed to be risk-averse (because they have less access to insurance). It is therefore assumed that companies maximize the net present value of their expected future profits, whereas individuals maximize the present value of the *expected utility* of their future consumption. It is assumed that utility is a concave function of consumption, which implies that individuals' welfare decreases when expected future consumption remains constant but its uncertainty increases.

Governments are less used to take risk into account and base most decisions on expected outcomes. In recent time, however, crises like Hurricane Katrina (August 2005) or the demise of Lehman Brothers (October 2008) have forced governments to take risk into account either when they formulate their own decisions or when they regulate private ones. It has become common practice for bank supervisors to gauge the adequacy of bank capital based on *stress tests* simulating "extreme, but plausible circumstances" rather than on expected outcomes (see Chapter 6).

Box 2.2 Risk Aversion

Suppose, in line with the standard assumptions in consumption theory, that the utility of an individual or a representative household increases with consumption but that the marginal utility of consumption is decreasing. In mathematical terms and assuming no savings, this corresponds to $U'(Y) < 0$ and $U''(Y) < 0$ where Y is income and U is utility.

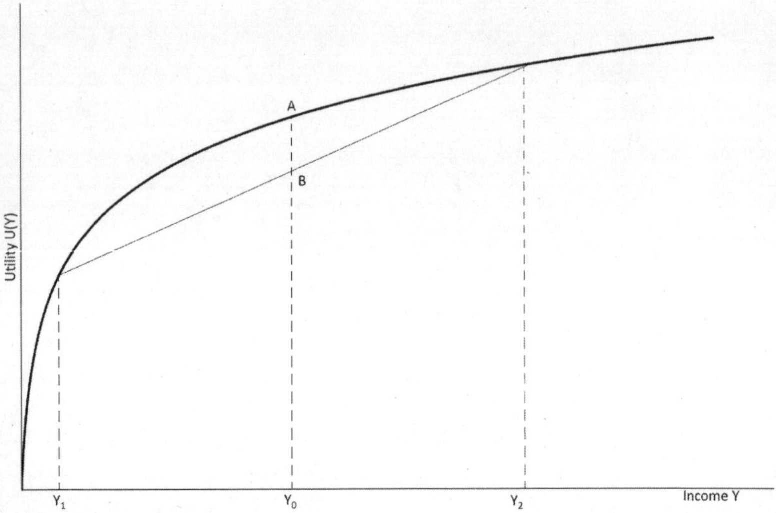

Figure B2.2.1 Income and utility.

Assume that the household is given the choice between receiving with certainty income Y_0 and receiving with a probability of 0.5 either Y_1 or Y_2 such that $Y_0 = (Y_1 + Y_2)/2$. Clearly, expected income is the same in both cases, but since utility is a concave function of income, utility is higher in the first case (corresponding to point A on the graph) than in the latter case (point B). The household prefers certainty to uncertainty. This is called *risk aversion*.

Intuitively, risk aversion depends on the concavity of the curve depicting the relationship between income and utility (i.e., on $U''(Y)$). Two common definitions of risk aversion are used. The first is *absolute risk aversion* (ARA) and the second *relative risk aversion* (RRA). They are also called the *Arrow–Pratt coefficients* and are defined by:

$$ARA = -\frac{U''(Y)}{U'(Y)} \quad \text{(B2.2.1)}$$

and

$$RRA = -\frac{YU''(Y)}{U'(Y)} \tag{B2.2.2}$$

It is usual to use functional forms for utility that exhibit constant absolute risk aversion (CARA) or constant relative risk aversion (CRRA). For example, with logarithmic utility ($U(Y) = \text{Log}\,Y$), the relative risk aversion is constant and equals one. A more general form is:

$$U(Y) = -\frac{Y^{1-\alpha}}{\alpha - 1} \tag{B2.2.3}$$

with $\alpha \neq 1$.

In this case, the relative risk aversion is constant and equals α. Risk aversion is a basic concept in the theory of consumption and savings and has many applications in finance.

Stress testing remains, however, infrequent outside the financial domain. When dealing with risk, policymakers sometimes even ignore expected outcomes (box 2.3).

Recent research in behavioral economics has challenged the expected utility paradigm. Experiments show that individuals do not adhere to rational decision-making behavior, that they frequently rely on rules of thumb rather than complex evaluations, that they try to avoid losses—including sometimes through taking more risk—and that their choices depend on initial conditions and the framing of decisions (for a survey, see the Nobel Prize lecture of Daniel Kahneman, 2002). Behavioral economics has influenced public policy, for example, by suggesting communicating policy advice in a way most likely

Box 2.3 Public Health and Risk

Gollier (2001) reports that, in 2000, the French government had to choose between two new compulsory tests, of which one tested for HIV and hepatitis C in batches of transfusion blood and the other for breast cancer in women over 50 years old. Independent research pointed to an average cost per saved year of life of about €9 million for the former and €1,500 for the latter. However, because of public sensitivity to transfusion-related diseases, the French government wanted to show it was doing its best to prevent blood contamination and chose the former test despite the conclusions of the available cost–benefit analysis.

to influence (or *nudge*) people's decisions.[2] Popular contributions are Thaler and Sunstein (2008) and Kahneman (2011).

2.1.3 Extreme or unquantifiable risks

Most economic models rest on the assumption that shocks are *normally distributed*; that is, that their distribution has the well-known "bell curve" shape, with a given mean and standard error. There are, however, circumstances in which this assumption cannot hold: shocks may be skewed, in which case their median value is not equal to their mean, or their distribution may exhibit *fat tails*, meaning that extreme events are more likely to occur than under a normal distribution. A distribution is said to be fat-tailed, or *leptokurtic*, if its *kurtosis* k is greater than the kurtosis of the normal distribution.[3] As once noticed by mathematician Benoît Mandelbrot, there have been 48 days in the period 1916–2003 when the Dow Jones Industrial Average, a widely used US stock index, moved by more than 7% in a single day. Such an event should occur only every 300,000 years if stock returns were normally distributed with the same mean and standard deviation (Mandelbrot and Hudson, 2004). This observation invalidates the standard assumption of normal returns.

Rare events are all the more important when there are nonlinear mechanisms at play in the economy. For instance, a pronounced recession can throw the economy into a state of deflation in which traditional monetary policy instruments will be inefficient. Protracted recession will furthermore increase the duration of unemployment up to a point where many laid-off workers will lose their skills and will never be hired again. Conversely, a very high inflation rate will trigger wage indexation behavior that will be very difficult to repeal once initiated. The policy conclusion is that central banks can tolerate reasonable fluctuations of inflation around the target value but that they must vigilantly avoid extreme risks (Svensson, 2004). In other words, they should pay special attention to events whose probability is low but whose disruptive effects are high, or *tail risks*.

Diseases such as HIV/AIDS or Ebola are examples of extreme risks that make it very difficult for governments to devise and calibrate a policy response. There are many such examples. To guide decision-making, it is crucial to obtain a consensus on the probabilities of various risks based on independent expertise.[4]

It is difficult to assess the probability of extreme events such as wars, natural disasters, or political regime changes. For example, no available model in physical oceanography makes it possible to quantify the risk that global warming might lead to an inversion of the Gulf Stream, an event which would have far-reaching consequences on both sides of the Atlantic. Frank Knight (1921) distinguished between *risk*, when randomness can be described by a probability measure, and *uncertainty*, when it cannot. A popular way to name Knightian uncertainty is provided by former US Defense Secretary

Donald Rumsfeld's distinction between "known unknowns" and "unknown unknowns." Under uncertainty, traditional economic models are useless since they rely on expected utility. Knightian uncertainty has been applied to financial asset pricing (Epstein and Wang, 1995) and to game theory, but it is not widely used for policy analysis purposes, and most economists still do not make the distinction between "risk" and "uncertainty."

2.1.4 The option value of waiting

A last criticism of the traditional approach to economic policy in an uncertain environment is that it focuses in great detail on the substance of policy decisions, while the major question is often that of their timing. The key concept here is *irreversibility*. If all policy decisions were incremental and reversible, economic policy would be state-contingent: it would adapt at any point in time to the current state of the economy. However, in a world where decisions have irreversible consequences, it can be optimal to wait until new information is available on their costs and benefits.

A well-known result from the theory of investment under uncertainty is that, since the decision to invest is irreversible whereas the decision to defer investment is generally reversible, proper economic calculation implies comparing the value of investing today to the value of investing at any other possible point in the future (Arrow, 1968; McDonald and Siegel, 1986). This implies that, as a rule, investment should be undertaken today only if benefits exceed costs by a certain amount, which is an increasing function of the variance of the project's return. In other words, the possibility of deferring the project has a value, analogous to that of a financial option, described as an *option value* attached to the project (Dixit and Pindyck, 1994).

This concept has a very wide scope and applies to all decisions that involve irreversibility, fixed costs, or discrete (as opposed to continuous) choice in an uncertain environment. Infrastructure investments are a straightforward example, but the same reasoning can also be used at a macroeconomic level, for instance, when considering membership of a monetary union. Sweden, for example, decided not to join the European Union from the outset while preserving the option of joining at a later stage. At the time of writing, this is still its official position.

As noticed early on by Claude Henry (1974), this approach is particularly relevant in assessing projects that cause irreversible damage to the environment, such as building roads through forests, burying nuclear waste below ground, or drilling for oil in a nature reserve. The choice is even more complex when doing nothing may also involve irreversible consequences, as in the case of climate change. Limiting carbon dioxide emissions requires massive investment with an uncertain return and a known opportunity cost, which suggests a policy of waiting. However, annual emissions continue to increase the concentration of carbon dioxide in the Earth's atmosphere (carbon dioxide decays extremely slowly), and there is wide suspicion among scientists that a persistently high concentration may cause large-scale, nonlinear events such as bifurcations in climate dynamics. Inaction thus increases the cost of future stabilization, and doing nothing has a cost of its own. Policy-makers have to make a trade-off between investment irreversibility and environmental irreversibility (Ha-Duong, 1998).

Facing these dilemmas, one may wish to delineate a *precautionary principle* for economic policy, as for environmental problems.[5] There are several pitfalls, however. First, it may not be possible to obtain consensus on a common metrics to gauge costs and benefits, such as increased consumption on the one hand and environmental or human damage on the other. Second, choosing the rate at which future costs and benefits should be discounted raises difficult theoretical and practical issues, especially for very long-time horizons where no market interest rate is available. The general theoretical answer is that long-time-horizon discount rates depend on the shape of the utility function.[6]

How to tackle this problem is at the core of controversies about climate change policies. The Stern Report commissioned by the British government (Stern, 2007) argued that, despite the costs involved in policies that aim at containing climate change, there should be no waiting because not taking immediate action could involve high economic costs in the future. It estimated that the present value of the welfare costs involved in mitigating greenhouse gas emissions equals those of a permanent reduction in the level of world gross domestic product (GDP) by one percentage point, whereas the present value of the welfare costs of inaction would equal that of a permanent reduction of GDP by 5–20 percentage points. On the other hand, its critics claim that Lord Stern did not properly discount future costs (Nordhaus, 2007; Weitzman, 2007) and that he underestimated the potential for reducing the cost of mitigation policies through technical progress and innovation. The first argument raises difficult issues in comparing welfare across generations (box 2.4). The second one builds on the discussion on the option value of waiting.

Box 2.4 Climate Change and the Discount Rate

The evaluation of policy options for climate change mitigation involves assessing costs and benefits over very long-time horizons, typically 50 years or more. The result of such assessments heavily depends on the discount rate used for the computation of present values. For example, the present value of a dollar paid in 50 years' time is 60 cents with a 1% discount rate, but it is only 14 cents with a 4% discount rate. This implies that, in the first case, an optimizing policymaker would be ready to pay 60 cents upfront to prevent 1 dollar of damage in 50 years but that, in the second case, she would only be ready to spend 14 cents.

How to discount the future in presence of uncertainty and the possibility of major damage is a theoretical challenge (Gollier, 2013). As developed by Guesnerie (2003), the intuition that each generation has a responsibility toward the future ones can be justified formally in a model where private consumption of standard goods and the environmental good are only partially substitutable. It leads to choosing a near-zero time discount rate. Consistent with this approach, the Stern report took, on philosophical grounds, the view that the welfare of all generations should have the same weight because there is no reason to value our offspring's welfare less than our own. When computing the present value of the welfare of all future generations', it used a near-zero time discount rate ρ (technically, Stern used $\rho = 0.1$ to take into account the probability of extinction of mankind). The welfare function to maximize was thus:

$$W = \sum_{t=0}^{\infty} \frac{U(C_t)}{(1+\rho)^t} \tag{B2.4.1}$$

where $t = 0, 1, 2 \ldots$ represent generations, C_t is the consumption of generation t, and $U(C_t)$ the corresponding utility. Equation (B2.4.1) can be rewritten in continuous time, which is mathematically more tractable:

$$W = \int_0^{\infty} U(C_t) e^{-\rho t} dt \tag{B2.4.2}$$

Even with $\rho = 0$, however, intertemporal welfare maximization does not imply that all generations' *consumption* should be valued equally. This is because, in the presence of technical progress, future generations will have access to higher levels of consumption. As the marginal utility of income and consumption is decreasing, it remains desirable to trade a lower consumption in the future against a higher consumption today. In concrete terms, the reduction in consumption made necessary by the mitigation of damage to the climate should recognize that development is expected to make future generations better off.

Intertemporal maximization therefore leads to discounting future consumption at a rate that is normally higher than the pure time discount rate ρ. Formally, r, the rate at which future *consumption* should be discounted, equals ρ, the rate at which future *utility* should be discounted, plus the product of the rate of technical progress g, by the elasticity of the marginal utility of consumption with respect to consumption α:

$$r = \rho + g\alpha \tag{B2.4.3}$$

This is known as the *Ramsey equation* (after Frank Ramsey, an early twentieth-century economist who established the mathematical conditions for optimal growth; see Chapter 10).

Stern took $\rho = 0.1\%$, $g = 1.3\%$, and $\alpha = 1$ (which corresponds to a logarithmic utility function), which yields $r = 1.4\%$. This is indeed very low in comparison to discount rates commonly in use for shorter horizons, which are generally around 2%.

This choice of parameters gave rise to a controversy. Nordhaus (2007) claimed that very different results would have been obtained with a discount rate derived from market interest rates or with other intertemporal social welfare functions, such as a Rawlsian one that would maximize the welfare of the poorest generation or one that would aim at maximizing the minimum consumption along the riskiest time path (see Chapter 1).

In response, Stern (2008) criticized the "inappropriate application of a marginal method in a strongly non-marginal context" and pointed out that the solution suggested by his critics—implicitly to invest the money and spend it on solving the climate problem later—ignored potential irreversibility and the fact that in a multigood context, the price of environmental goods will likely have gone up sharply enough to make the standard one-good calculation inadequate.

2.1.5 Implications for policy

Uncertainty and risk have strong potential policy implications. Many errors have been made because governments based policy on wrong parameter estimates or did not properly take risk and uncertainty into account. Policy thinking is increasingly attentive to these issues.

An elementary example, which is telling because it illustrates how easily policy can be wrong even with the simplest dimensions of uncertainty, is provided by fiscal policies. In 1981, President Reagan carried out a fiscal stimulation that was supposed to finance itself through a very positive impact on US output (in 2017, President Trump made a similar gamble). In the early 2010s, the countries of the euro area made severe fiscal adjustments while underestimating their combined effects on output (see Chapter 4).

Central banks deal with uncertainty, too—and they are increasingly describing their role within a decision-under-uncertainty framework. In the United States, the Federal Reserve has become increasingly aware of the existence of tail risks and has altered its policy stance correspondingly. According to Frederic Mishkin, an academic and former Fed Governor, the usual representation of policy based on a linear model and a quadratic loss function (the representation that was introduced in Chapter 1) "may provide a reasonable approximation to how monetary policy should operate under fairly normal circumstances," but, in the presence of tail risks, "optimal monetary policy may also be nonlinear and will tend to focus on risk management" (Mishkin, 2008). Aggressive easing by the Federal Reserve in early 2008 illustrated this philosophy.

2.2 The Limits of Representation

While Keynesianism reigned supreme throughout the 1960s, the past three decades of the twentieth century were marked by a heated debate on the rationale, the methods, and the limitations of public intervention. The discussion was ignited in the early 1970s by a series of sharp criticisms of the goals and methods of economic policy. These criticisms came primarily from economists who objected to the very principle of government intervention. Vindicated by the failure of macroeconomic policies to achieve their primary goals of output stabilization and price stability, especially after the first oil shock—they embarked on a far-reaching project to debunk the inconsistencies of traditional approaches and amend the mechanical approach summarized earlier in Equation (2.1).

2.2.1 Rational expectations

The first challenged came in a technical article by John Muth, published in 1961 in *Econometrica,* which introduced the notion of *rational expectations*. In previously used models, the expectations of households and company managers regarding the future values of economic variables were often disregarded. When they were considered, they were assumed to be extrapolated from the latest trends. Expected future inflation, which matters for consumption, saving, or wage negotiation, was, for example, supposed to depend on inflation observed over the past months or years. Muth argued that this assumption amounted to supposing that agents do not use all information available to them at the time of the decision and are therefore not rational. Rational agents would instead avoid wasting information, and they would form informed predictions that "are essentially the same as the predictions of the relevant economic theory" (Muth, 1961, p. 316). Forecasting errors would result only from events that were not foreseeable within the framework of the existing theory (box 2.5).

Muth's paper had far-reaching consequences in all fields of economic policy. Think of workers preparing for a round of wage negotiations. If they expect consumer prices to increase in the future, they will ask for higher wages to compensate future purchasing power losses. Of course, they cannot anticipate oil shocks or currency depreciations. However, if they know that a government policy is likely to have inflationary effects, they will use this information and build it into their expectations, thereby bringing forward the inflation expected for the future.

As a consequence, governments willing to assess the impact of their decisions have to consider the expected reaction of economic agents. Economic policy is no longer the work of an engineer: it is the art of strategists interacting with other strategists. This is far more demanding.

Box 2.5 Modeling Expectations

The expectation $Z^a_{t,t+1}$ made at time *t* of the value of variable *Z* at time *t* + 1 used to be thought of as a function of its present and past values as well as of other relevant variables *X*:

$$Z^a_{t,t+1} = G(Z_t, Z_{t-1}, Z_{t-2}, \ldots X_t, X_{t-1}, X_{t-2}, \ldots) \qquad \text{(B2.5.1)}$$

This formulation covers several possible specifications. One can suppose that individuals expect economic variables to revert to some long-term equilibrium value or, on the contrary, to amplify past movements.

A convenient specification is *adaptive expectations,* which incorporates new information gradually:

$$Z^a_{t,t+1} = (1-\lambda) Z^a_{t-1,t} + \lambda Z_t \quad 0 < \lambda < 1 \qquad \text{(B2.5.2)}$$

If $\lambda = 1$, then an adaptive expectation simplifies into a *static expectation,* or *naïve expectation,* where the expected value of *Z* is equal to its last observation Z_t: $Z^a_{t,t+1} = Z_t$.

However, the *rational expectation* of *Z* is a different notion and can be written as:

$$Z^a_{t,t+1} = E(Z_{t+1} \mid I_t) \qquad \text{(B2.5.3)}$$

where *E*(.) is the expected value operator and I_t represents the available information at time *t* (i.e., all relevant variables known by economic agents at the time of their decisions).

The difference from the previous formulation is that agents are supposed to make use not only of the observed current and past values of *Z*, but also of the variables that determine future values of *Z*. For example, in a floating exchange rate context they are supposed to know that a depreciation of the exchange rate triggers a rise in domestic inflation and therefore to regard the exchange rate as a leading indicator of future inflation. Or they are likely to expect that a rise in inflation is likely to trigger a rise in the central bank's policy rate.

With rational expectations, forecast errors (i.e., the difference between expected and actual values) are random. They cannot be forecast given the information available because rational expectations are the best expectations that can be formulated given this information. This is especially relevant for foreign exchange and, more generally, for financial markets: One cannot expect to make a profit through making accurate forecasts of exchange rates because the expectations rationally formed by market participants already incorporate available information on the determinants of the exchange rate.

In the special case where Z follows a *random walk*—that is, it is the sum of its latest value and of a random shock with zero average and constant variance (a *white noise*)—we have:

$$Z_{t+1} = Z_t + \varepsilon_{t+1} \qquad \text{(B2.5.4)}$$

Since $E(\varepsilon_{t+1} \mid I_t) = 0$, then $E(Z_{t+1}/I_t) = Z_t$: the rational expectation of Z_t is equal to its naïve expectation. In plain English, this means that the best forecast of Z, given available information, is its last observed value.

a) Are expectations rational?

The rational expectation hypothesis was initially greeted with skepticism. Indeed, even assuming perfect rationality, the assumption that the average economic agent has full knowledge of the functioning of the economy and can correctly anticipate all variables is an extreme one. It overlooks the simple fact that gathering and processing these data requires human capital and involves costs. The notion that households have enough economic culture, information, and computing skills to anticipate the effects of any economic policy on unemployment, inflation, or the public deficit defies intuition.

However, the alternative assumption that individuals do not use any of the information available to them is not attractive either. And the rational expectation hypothesis does not require them to *know* all the laws of the economy, but only to *act* in accordance with them. Economic agents are akin to a character described in Robert Musil's novel *The Man Without Qualities*: industrialist Arnheim does not know the laws of motion of the billiard ball but nevertheless knows how to play it:

> If I wished to state them theoretically, I should have to make use not only of the laws of mathematics and of the mechanics of rigid bodies, but also of the law of elasticity. I should have to know the coefficients of the material and what influence the temperature had. I should need the most delicate methods of measuring the co-ordination and graduation of my motor impulses. . . . My faculty of combination would have to be more rapid and more dependable than a slide-rule. . . . I should need to have all the qualities and to do all the things that I cannot possibly have or do. You are, I am sure, enough of a mathematician yourself to appreciate that it would take one a lifetime even to work out the course of an ordinary cannon-stroke in such a way. This is where our brain simply leaves us in the lurch! And yet I can go up to the billiard-table with a cigarette between my lips and a tune in my head, so to speak with my hat on, and, hardly bothering to survey the situation at all, take my cue to the ball and have the problem solved in a twinkling! (Musil, 1930, 1979).

In the same way, the Zimbabwean employee of the 2000s who anxiously watched the exchange rate to guess future inflation (in a period when the latter was very high) did not necessarily know *why* a depreciation would trigger inflation, but she or he had learned from experience that this was likely to happen. Households usually do not spend much time studying economic variables, but they have to do so when expectation errors would be costly for them—in an hyperinflation context (box 2.6) or when a major policy change is expected, such as a swift fiscal retrenchment or a major tax reform. The same applied in Greece, in 2015, when households anxiously guessed what their bank deposits would be worth in the event of an exit from the euro area.

For some other agents, the rational expectations hypothesis is a natural one. Banks and asset managers who operate in financial markets invest significant resources in economic research, in particular to forecast interest rates and exchange rates. Fed watchers and European Central Bank (ECB) watchers are paid handsomely to gauge the next central bank decisions, and forward interest rates (as observed on future markets) actually track monetary policy decisions quite accurately.

From a methodological standpoint, rational expectations merely impose a consistency constraint on model builders: it cannot be assumed that

Box 2.6 Rational Expectations in Action: The Bulgarian Currency Board

Sofia, Spring 1997. With a monthly inflation rate of 40%, Bulgaria was on the brink of hyperinflation and its currency, the Lev, was in free fall. On April 19, the opposition won the elections. The new government confirmed its will to anchor the currency to the German D-Mark through a currency board (a fixed exchange rate regime; see Chapter 7). On July 1, the currency board was successfully introduced, and inflation began to fall.

In June, just before monetary reform, an opinion poll asked Bulgarians citizens to assess future inflation depending on whether a currency board would be established. On average, their answer was that inflation would be 25% a year if a currency board was established, 50% if not. The prospect of monetary reform had a major impact on expectations.

In the Bulgarian case, two conditions were conducive to such an expectation shift: high inflation meant that any expectation error by an individual agent could induce a significant economic cost, and the introduction of the currency board had been preceded by a national political debate so that everyone knew what was at stake.

Source: Carlson and Valev (2001).

individuals make assumptions that contradict the model. They can also be seen as the limit to which expectations converge when individuals with initially adaptative expectations (box 2.5) learn about the functioning of the economy.[7]

Summing up, rational expectations should be considered as the reference case from which economists can then depart if they have reasons to. One possible departure consists in recognizing that the information available to economic agents and the resources they can invest in its acquisition and treatment are heterogeneous. Another one is to base the modeling of expectations on a detailed study of the way agents form their judgment.

2.2.2 The Lucas critique

Pushing the reasoning further, Chicago economist and future Nobel laureate Robert Lucas showed in a seminal 1976 paper that it is incorrect to use a macroeconometric model like the one presented in box 2.1 to assess the consequences of a significant economic policy change (Lucas, 1976). This is because the model's parameters have been estimated in the context of a certain *policy regime* characterized by a set of rules and the corresponding systematic policy reactions. These reactions—which are in turn incorporated into the agents' expectations and behavior, of which the model is a representation (box 2.7)—cannot be assumed invariant to a change of policy regime or even to economic policy decisions that go beyond a marginal, temporary impulse like a small rise in interest rates or taxation rates.

The *Lucas critique* had a considerable impact on economic policy and shook a dominant and rapidly developing methodology to its foundations. Economic policy could no longer rest on an overly naïve representation of the behavior of economic agents.

2.2.3 Implications for policy

The Lucas critique has contributed to making governments and central banks aware of the pitfalls of quantitative policy evaluations and, more generally, to weakening the technocratic approach to policy choices that prevailed in the 1970s. However, it should not be interpreted as condemning all empirical policy evaluations. Macroeconometric models remain relevant to studying the effects of policy decisions that are nonpermanent or remain within the range of policy changes observed in the past. This, for example, applies to small-scale changes in public expenditures, tax rates, or the interest rate. The Lucas critique implies that to evaluate the effects of a change in policy regime, one should use other instruments such as vector autoregressive models (VARs) or micro-founded models. In practice, policymakers often rely on a menu of models to evaluate the effects of a given policy.

Box 2.7 The Lucas Critique

Let us come back to the standard representation of the economy proposed in box 2.1:

$$Y_t = H(X_t, \theta, \varepsilon_t) \qquad \text{(B2.7.1)}$$

where Y_t is a vector of variables representing the economy at time t, X_t is a vector of policy variables, and ε_t is a vector of random shocks. The model is estimated based on historical time series. Then, a policy evaluation exercise consists in replacing the observed sequence of policies $(X_1 \ldots X_T)$ by an alternative one. For example, a higher sequence of public expenditures can be used to simulate the impact of a fiscal expansion.

In his paper, Lucas (1976) pointed out that this method makes sense only if the function H and the parameter vector θ are stable over time and do not depend in a systematic way on the policy sequence X_t. However, the agents' behavior depends on their expectations of the future values of the variables that affect their environment. H is stable only if the policy change does not affect these expectations. This may not be true if there is a change in the policy regime (e.g., a change in the fiscal rule) or if market expectations react to the new policy (e.g., if private agents anticipate higher taxes in the future following a rise in public spending).

The Lucas critique is not addressed to the choice of the model (i.e., the difference between the chosen model and the "true," unknown functioning of the economy). It is deeper in that it is based on the interaction between economic policy and the behavior of economic agents.

Research has addressed Lucas's objections. First, econometricians have done their best to rely on *micro-founded models*; that is, models where private behaviors (consumption, investment) rely on explicit optimization with rational expectations. In those models, the "deep" parameters that determine the agent's long-term response to policy changes, such as time preference parameters or elasticities of substitution, are calibrated, or, if estimated, they are likely to be independent of the policy regime. Second, they have built on Christopher Sims's suggestion of a constraint-free, purely empirical approach to the relationships between variables (Sims, 1980). This has led to the development of *vector autoregressive* (VAR) models. Recent trends in macroeconometric modeling are described in box 1.6 of Chapter 1.

Beyond policy evaluation, models are devices that help structure, organize, and discipline economists' beliefs. They help identify the key assumptions on which any policy recommendation rests, and they provide an essential framework for general-equilibrium policy analysis. They also encourage the building of new datasets and agreement on appropriate data concepts. General Eisenhower once said "In preparing for battle I have always found that plans are useless, but planning is indispensable." In economic policy, models are sometimes useless, but modeling is indispensable.

2.3 The Limits of Confidence

As explained in the previous section, rational expectations add complexity to the representation of the economy and of its interactions with economic policy. However, their impact goes beyond this mere technical difficulty. They may also directly hamper the effectiveness of public intervention.

2.3.1 Credibility

A compelling example with strong historical relevance deals with inflationary expectations. Assume a situation where unemployment is caused by high real labor costs, wages are negotiated infrequently, and negotiated wages are rigid. If wage earners expect a price increase of 2% and have negotiated their wage increase accordingly, the government may decide to prop up inflation temporarily, say to 4%, so that the real wage (i.e., the nominal wage divided by the price of goods) will be reduced *ex post*. Absent demand constraints, this should encourage job creation and lower unemployment because selling prices rise more than unit labor costs. However, if individuals know in advance the government's plan, they will require a 4% wage increase to protect their purchasing power. The government will end up with a higher inflation (one speaks of an *inflationary bias*) while real wages will remain unchanged. Strategic interaction between government and economic agents will result in inefficiency.

The issue at stake here is not government capture by special interests or partisan politics ahead of the electoral cycle. It is the government's temptation to mislead private agents in the name of the general interest. By announcing that inflation will be 2% and actually delivering 4%, policymakers aim to reduce unemployment. But this seemingly virtuous lie turns out to be self-defeating. The government may want to manipulate private agents, but it is in fact hostage to their expectations.

Thanks to its simplicity, this argument, formalized in 1983 by Robert Barro and David Gordon (the model is explained in Chapter 5), exerted considerable influence on monetary policy thinking in the 1980s and 1990s. It illustrates that when expectations are rational, a government that seeks to optimize social welfare does not necessarily select the best policy. The same line of reasoning can apply to temptations regarding exchange rate policy (announce that you will never devalue, and then take agents by surprise) or to the management of the public debt (issue long-term fixed-rate bonds, and then inflate away the public debt). It can also be extended to taxation. Imagine that a government announces that it will scrap taxes on fixed capital to encourage investment in its country, then reneges on its promise because it is socially optimal *ex post* to finance public goods by taxing capital. If companies anticipate this behavior, they will not invest at all.

In all these examples, the problem arises from the lack of *credibility* of public intervention. The government fails in convincing private agents that it will indeed behave in the way it has committed to. Conversely, a credible policy is all the more effective because it steers expectations. It can thus become subtler. As we shall see in Chapter 5, this is particularly relevant for monetary policy, the effectiveness of which is based to a large extent on the management of expectations (see Woodford, 2001). An economy equipped with a credible central bank can better respond to inflationary shocks triggered by rises in the price of oil and raw materials because agents do not anticipate that these shocks will result in permanently higher inflation. Thanks to its credibility, the central bank can afford to let an oil price shock trigger a one-off increase in the general price level without endangering its medium-term goals. This makes monetary policy more effective (box 2.8). In extreme cases, the expectations channel can actually be the only one to play a role. This confirms Keynes's (1936) intuition that the "state of confidence" is the key variable in an economy prone to instability.

The scholarly concept of credibility has gained a wide audience in the public debate. For the sake of credibility, most countries have made their central banks independent and focused their mandate on fighting inflation. However, political leaders have not lived up to all the consequences of the credibility concept. Unfulfilled promises undermine confidence in economic policy and hamper its effectiveness, such as those of German Chancellor Helmut Kohl, who had famously promised in 1996 to halve unemployment by the year 2000 (it only went down from 8.5% to 7.2%), or of French president Hollande, after his election in 2012, who paid a high political price for failing to deliver on his promise to invert the trend of the unemployment curve.

Box 2.8 Credibly Responsible and Irresponsible Behaviors

For a central bank, a key dimension of credibility is its ability to anchor inflation expectations. If its anti-inflationary stance is credible, short-term developments such as shocks to the price level or its own responses to them do not affect longer term price expectations. This not only helps prevent inflationary spirals, but also gives the central bank more freedom of maneuver in setting interest rates. All modern central banks therefore attach great importance to remaining credible.

Whether a central bank is credible can be assessed from survey data. Many central banks run surveys of professional forecasters, such as the one presented for the European Central Bank (ECB) in figure B2.8.1. The graph shows that five-year expectations were remarkably stable from 1999 to 2016 at a level that corresponded to the stated objective of the ECB ("below but close to 2%") and despite short-run fluctuations of observed and expected inflation rates.

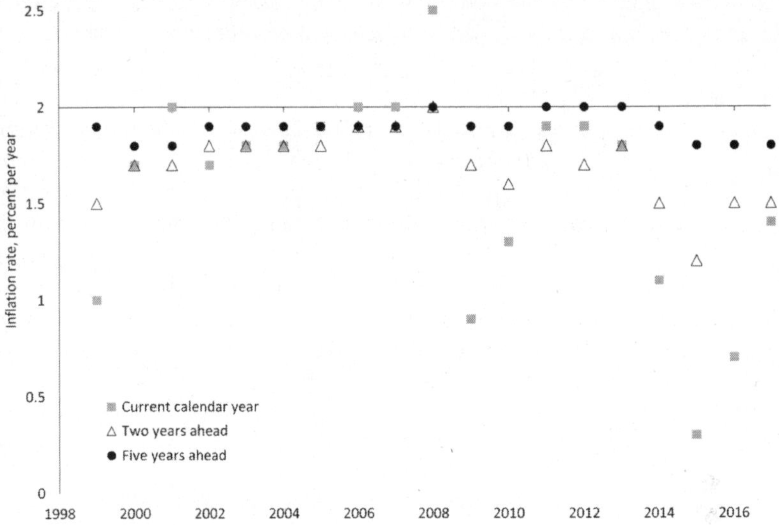

Figure B2.8.1 Inflation expectations in the euro area, 1999–2016.
ECB, Survey of Professional Forecasters, May 2017.

It may sometimes (but more rarely) be important to be *credibly irresponsible.* In the late 1990s, Japan was facing a deflationary crisis. The general level of prices was falling, generating positive real interest rates despite close to zero nominal interest rates. Traditional monetary policy was powerless. A deflationary spiral was looming.

In 1998, Paul Krugman suggested that if the central bank were able to generate positive inflation expectations, expected real interest rates (i.e., nominal interest rates minus expected inflation rates) would decrease, spurring investment and brushing away the risk of a deflationary spiral (Krugman, 1998). He advised the Bank of Japan to "credibly promise to be irresponsible" and to enforce an inflationary policy. Krugman's unconventional proposal was initially regarded with a great deal of skepticism by the Japanese authorities, but they eventually agreed.

In the 2010s, several central banks strongly committed to using the whole range of available conventional and nonconventional policy tools to ward off deflation and reach their inflation target.

2.3.2 Moral hazard

We have seen that when expectations are rational, economic policy can become inefficient if the government misleads private agents. But the problem can be just as serious if it seeks to help them. *Moral hazard* is a well-known problem in insurance theory. By reducing the expected cost of future damages for the insured, insurance induces more risk-taking. Economic policy often provides insurance: directly when the central bank assists banks that face a liquidity shortage or when the government rescues a distressed firm; indirectly when stabilization policy prevents a recession. There is a tension between discouraging excessive risk-taking and helping involuntary victims of an accident.

Moral hazard is no theoretical curiosity. Compensating the victims of floods can encourage construction in areas likely to be flooded. *Ex post*, after the flood has occurred, there are very good reasons for the government to help displaced families. But *ex ante*, it should either prohibit construction in areas susceptible to flooding or credibly claim that those who settle there do so at their own risk. Likewise, central banks generally aim to maintain ambiguity and refrain from saying whether and how they would provide liquidity assistance to distressed banks (see Chapter 5).

A case in point is the Russian financial crisis of 1998. Before it occurred, yields on Russian bonds implied a low-risk premium with respect to US Treasuries although the budget of the Russian federation was in dire straits. This was because the International Monetary Fund (IMF) was widely expected to help Russia repay its private creditors (it had already provided massive assistance to Mexico in 1994 and the Asian countries in 1997). This was a typical instance of moral hazard. But the decision by the IMF was to not add fresh money to the assistance already programmed. On August 17, 1998, the Russian government devalued the ruble and suspended debt repayment. Risk premiums increased sharply, not only on Russian bonds but also on all emerging market economies. For instance, the annual yield spread between Brazilian and US Treasury bonds increased from 7.5% to almost 17% within a few weeks, while the economic situation of Brazil had not changed. The IMF decision on Russia thus acted as a signal.

The dilemma arising from moral hazard often results in inconsistent behavior by policy-makers. On September 14, 2008, the US government refused to bail out the investment bank Lehman Brothers and let it go bust. Only five days later, faced with a major risk of a collapse of the financial system, Treasury Secretary Henry Paulson launched a massive plan to buy distressed assets from banks and other financial institutions. In October 2008, G7 finance ministers and governors pledged not to let any systemically important financial institution fail. One year later, they changed stance once again and mandated the Financial Stability Board to radically revise recovery and resolution policies so that systemic banks should not prove to be "too big to fail" (see Chapter 6).

2.3.3 Time inconsistency

Lack of credibility and moral hazard are examples of what economists call *time inconsistency*: in both cases, the sequence of policy decisions that result from optimizing at each period does not constitute an optimal policy. In other words, *ex post* and *ex ante* optimality do not coincide. In the inflation bias example, it is optimal *ex ante* to announce low inflation, but it is optimal *ex post* to engineer an inflationary shock. In the flood example, it is optimal *ex ante* to announce that victims will not be compensated, but it is optimal *ex post* to minimize the consequences of the flood. In the 2008 Wall Street example, it was optimal *ex ante* to disavow any bank bail-out,[8] but it was indeed also optimal *ex post* to supply liquidities to the banking system to avoid a general banking panic that would have a devastating impact on the economy.

The resulting inefficiency was established in a famous 1977 paper by Finn Kydland and Edward Prescott: they show that, except in specific cases, optimum policies are not consistent over time (box 2.9).

Box 2.9 Time Inconsistency According to Kydland and Prescott (1977)

There are two periods. At each period $t = 1$ and $t = 2$, economic policy consists in choosing the value of the instrument X_t. The value taken by the target variable Y_t depends on the policies followed at the two periods (the fact that Y_1 depends not only on X_1 but also on X_2 reflects the influence of expectations). One has therefore:

$$Y_1 = G(X_1, X_2) \quad \text{and} \quad Y_2 = H(X_1, X_2) \qquad \text{(B2.9.1)}$$

The decision-maker's objective is to maximize $U(Y_1, Y_2, X_1, X_2)$. In period 2, he or she can choose between two policy rules:

- *Ex post optimization*: Select X_2 to maximize U, taking X_1 and Y_1 as given. This implies that:

$$\frac{\partial U}{\partial Y_2}\frac{\partial Y_2}{\partial X_2} + \frac{\partial U}{\partial X_2} = 0 \qquad \text{(B2.9.2)}$$

- *Ex ante optimization*: Select X_2 to maximize U, taking X_1 as given but taking into account the fact that private agents' expectation of X_2 will influence Y_1. This implies:

$$\frac{\partial U}{\partial Y_2}\frac{\partial Y_2}{\partial X_2} + \frac{\partial U}{\partial X_2} + \frac{\partial Y_1}{\partial X_2}\left[\frac{\partial U}{\partial Y_1} + \frac{\partial U}{\partial Y_2}\frac{\partial Y_2}{\partial Y_1}\right] = 0 \qquad \text{(B2.9.3)}$$

Ex post optimization coincides with *ex ante* optimization either if period 2 decisions do not affect the target variable in period 1 ($\partial Y_1 / \partial X_2 = 0$. This happens if private expectations are backward-looking), or if changes in the value of Y_1 do not affect utility. Both assumptions are unlikely to be true under general circumstances. Hence, the government may be tempted to announce X_2 following Equation (B2.9.3) in period 1, but reoptimize X_2 in period 2 following Equation (B2.9.2).

Kydland and Prescott's suggested response to time inconsistency is to banish *discretionary policies* that leave the policymaker free to decide which policy to follow at each point in time. In their view, economic policy should rather follow fixed *policy rules* that leave no or limited discretion to the policymaker, and economic policy evaluation should consist in comparing the performance over time of rules, not of individual decisions. This concept of economic policy as a choice between alternative rules, rather than as a sequence of discretionary decisions, has been immensely influential.

2.3.4 Implications for policy

Criticisms based on credibility and moral hazard emphasize the intertemporal dimension of policy choices and the risks of adverse long-term effects of seemingly optimal short-term decisions. They jointly challenge the traditional discretionary approach to policymaking and its call for leaving considerable latitude to the decision-maker.

Since the challenge began to be recognized in the 1970s, several strands of policy responses have been proposed and implemented. The first response has been rules-based policymaking, an approach introduced in 1979 in the United States when the Federal Reserve endorsed a monetarist strategy focused on preannounced quantitative targets. This mechanistic approach to monetary policy was abandoned in 1987, once inflation had been tamed and it had become clear that monetary aggregates provided poor guidance to monetary policy (see Chapter 5), but it has become increasingly popular in the budgetary field (see Chapter 4).

Second, starting in the 1980s, there has been a general move toward granting independence to central banks to ensure better credibility. This approach has proved successful enough for the independent agency template to be proposed as a remedy to the pitfalls of both discretionary and rules-based fiscal policymaking. Wyplosz (2005) has suggested to delegate the choice of a fiscal stance (though not individual spending and tax decisions) to independent budgetary committees. Although no country has strictly followed this recommendation, many have established budgetary committees to monitor fiscal decisions (see Chapter 4). Finally, central banks themselves have introduced greater transparency in their objectives and decision-making procedures to convince the public that their deeds actually match their words. We shall return to all these techniques in the next chapters.

2.4 The Limits of Information

In the previous sections, we pointed out that governments could face limitations in the knowledge they have of the structure of the economy, but we assumed that they had access to all existing information. However, as already indicated in Chapter 1, the strategic use of information by those who have access to it can give rise to other limitations. The consequences for private and public behavior of such informational asymmetries have long remained underestimated until economic theory started to explore them systematically in the late twentieth century. Joseph Stiglitz (2000) has argued that "the recognition that information is imperfect, that obtaining information can be costly, that there are important asymmetries of information, and that the extent of information asymmetries is affected by actions of firms and individuals is perhaps the most important innovation of 20th century economics." This also applies to economic policy.

These problems are not specific to the public sector. They are pervasive in market economies: for example, in the relationship between producers and consumers or between lenders and borrowers (Stiglitz and Weiss, 1981).

2.4.1 Principal–agent relationship

Asymmetric information is especially important for the contractual relationship between what is generally called a *principal* (say, the shareholder of a firm or the manager within it) and one or several *agents* (say, entrepreneurs or employees). The principal, who delegates a task to the agent, does not have full information about the agent's capabilities and performance, and this generally leads to suboptimal situations (Laffont and Martimort, 2002)—a problem already discussed by Adam Smith (1776) in the case of the relationship between landowners and sharecroppers (or *metayers* in eighteenth-century language).

Agency problems arise at different levels of economic policy-making and implementation: to start with, between the voters and government ministers in charge of policy design; then, between the ministers and the administrative machinery in charge of policy implementation; and, finally, between the machinery and the private agents. As a result, modern economic policy theory makes intensive use of what is called *contract theory*.[9] In the traditional paradigm, government ministers are in command of a flawless administrative apparatus that provides them with accurate information and seamlessly forwards their instructions from the top to the bottom of the bureaucracy—akin to the Soviet "Gosplan" (the central planning commission), which was supposed to determine the smallest details of the functioning of an economy of 300 million inhabitants. The lack of realism of the full-information assumption first emerged in the debate of the 1930s and 1940s between liberals and planners: the impossibility of gathering all information necessary to a centralized decision was turned into a powerful theoretical argument against planning, which Friedrich Hayek put at the heart of his criticism of central planning (Hayek, 1944).

Economists have brought into the picture imperfect information and the strategic behavior of government agencies as well as individual bureaucrats, and they have sobered up their conception of government. Indeed, when public or private agents have privileged information and use it strategically, the central decision-maker is in a situation of inferiority, and her decisions are suboptimal. When reporting to Moscow, Soviet companies met their production targets more easily by systematically overestimating their need for inputs (raw materials and machinery) and underestimating their own productivity. The Gosplan did not have as much information as the company managers and could neither detect nor sanction this behavior. Similar problems arise in a host of situations. A telecommunications regulator may be tasked with controlling prices, but companies know technology and consumption patterns better than the regulator. When local authorities tender water supply contracts to private companies, they de facto grant them exclusiveness of information on the technical state of the network and on water consumption. Health ministers would like to discourage overconsumption of healthcare, but doctors know patients' illnesses better.

2.4.2 Optimal contract design

A solution to this agency problem is to structure a principal–agent contract in a way that aligns the agent's interest with that of the principal and gives him or her incentives to reveal the information he or she has. Driven by expected profit, private agents—notably companies—endeavor to transform their informational advantage into pecuniary revenue. In response, governments design contracts that give them incentives to reveal the information they hold. An example of a bidding mechanism aimed at revealing private information is the design of public procurements. Public contracts should be written in a way that ensures that it is not in the operator's interest to minimize technical problems (which would lower service quality) nor to exaggerate them (which could call for pecuniary compensation). This is generally done by conceding to the operator part of the operating revenue. Box 2.10 presents an example of an optimal procurement contract. The company's compensation can be understood as a (continuous) "menu of contracts" offered to companies: cost-effective companies are ready to assume a larger fraction of their costs, which they know are low, while less-effective companies want their costs to be supported by the contractor. By choosing a given contract, the company reveals otherwise private information on its cost structure. This is an example of *self-selection*.

Another way to deal with information asymmetry is to delegate tasks to those agents that have access to the relevant information. Apprenticeship schemes are an example. The government does not know which skills the economy needs and delegates the task of designing apprenticeships to the social partners, only retaining an oversight role.

Box 2.10 Optimal Public Procurement Under Asymmetric Information

This model is inspired by Laffont and Tirole (1986) and Laffont (2000*b*). We consider a public procurement to a private contractor with unobservable operating costs. The goal is to devise a contract that allows high-cost companies to bid without giving up all profits when the cost is low.

Cost Structure

The government contracts with a single, risk-neutral operator to undertake a project which generates a social surplus. The operating cost of the operator is:

$$C = \beta - e \tag{B2.10.1}$$

β is exogenous and captures the technical characteristics of the company. e measures the cost-reduction effort. On top of the operating cost, there is an upstream cost $\psi(e)$, with $\psi(0) = 0$, $\psi' > 0$, $\psi'' > 0$ and $\psi''' > 0$, which measures the cost of achieving the effort level e through reorganization, training, knowledge management, and the like. The government observes the overall operating cost C *ex post* (for example, by auditing the company), but it does not observe its components β and e and even less the upstream cost $\psi(e)$. The company is refunded the operating cost C plus a flat fee t aimed to encourage the effort e. Public transfers are financed by taxes, and there is an additional opportunity cost for the taxpayer due to the government's own administrative costs and to the distortions induced by taxation. $\lambda > 1$ is thus the "'production cost" of one dollar of government subsidy. The question asked by the government is how to set the flat fee t as a function of the observed cost C.

Surplus Analysis

The surplus of the operator is $S^f = t - \psi(e)$ and that of the government is $S^E = -(1+\lambda)(C+t)$. If Σ denotes the (exogenous) surplus of other agents, the total social surplus generated by the project is:

$$W = \Sigma + S^f + S^E = \Sigma - (1+\lambda)(C + \psi(e)) - \lambda S^f \tag{B2.10.2}$$

The contract between the government and the company is entirely summarized by $t(C)$: Knowing $t(C)$, the company can choose its effort level e so as to maximize S^f.

Optimal Contract Under Imperfect Information

Under perfect information, the government observes *ex ante* β and e. It can at the same time maximize the social surplus W and capture the rent extracted by the company. However, in the general case, the government observes the total cost C but not the effort level e, which itself depends on the characteristics β of the company. Suppose that β is drawn randomly between $\underline{\beta}$ and $\bar{\beta}$ with a probability density f and a distribution function F:

$$F(x) = P(\beta < x) = \int_{\underline{\beta}}^{x} f(u)du \tag{B2.10.3}$$

$e(\beta)$ and $C(\beta)$ depend on the realized value of β and on the nature of function ψ. The contract $t(C)$ has to meet two constraints: The *incentive constraint* $S^f(\beta) = \max_C\{t(C) - \psi(e(\beta))\}$: knowing $t(C)$, the company chooses its effort level (and thus C) to maximize its surplus. A result from maximization theory known as the *envelope theorem* implies that $S^{f\prime}(\beta) = -\psi'(e(\beta)) < 0$ Contracts that induce a higher effort level e make the slope of $S^f(\beta)$ steeper and increase the revenue conceded to low-cost companies. The government faces a trade-off between setting the right incentive and limiting the rent extracted by the operator.

The *participation constraint* is $\forall \beta \in [\underline{\beta}, \bar{\beta}]$, $S^f(\beta) \geq 0$, meaning that the company has to be profitable. Since the revenue S^f is a decreasing function of β and there is an opportunity cost to spending public money, the constraint must be saturated for the highest value of β and can thus be written: $S^f(\bar{\beta}) = 0$.

From these two constraints follows the relationship between the company surplus and its effort level:

$$S^f(\beta) = \int_{\beta}^{\bar{\beta}} \psi'(e(x))dx \tag{B2.10.4}$$

The government maximizes the expected total surplus:

$$\max EW(\beta) = \int_{\underline{\beta}}^{\bar{\beta}} \left[\Sigma - (1+\lambda)(C(\beta) + \psi(e(\beta))) - \lambda S^f(\beta)\right] f(\beta)d\beta \tag{B2.10.5}$$

The first-order condition reads:

$$\psi'(e(\beta)) = 1 - \frac{\lambda}{1+\lambda}\frac{F(\beta)}{f(\beta)}\psi''(e(\beta)) \tag{B2.10.6}$$

which makes it possible to derive the effort function $e(\beta)$, which is decreasing in β, and $t(C)$. The closed-form solution depends on the shapes of the function ψ and distribution f. It can be shown that, in all cases, the optimum contract $t(C)$ is convex and decreasing in C (figure B2.10.1).

There is an intuitive interpretation of this result. In the vicinity of each cost level C, $t(C)$ is similar to a decreasing linear contract $t = a - bC$. The slope b represents the fraction of costs supported by the company. Since $t(C)$ is convex, b decreases the higher the cost level C. Inefficient companies wish a large proportion of their costs to be supported by the government. More-efficient ones are ready to support a larger fraction of costs since they know they are low.

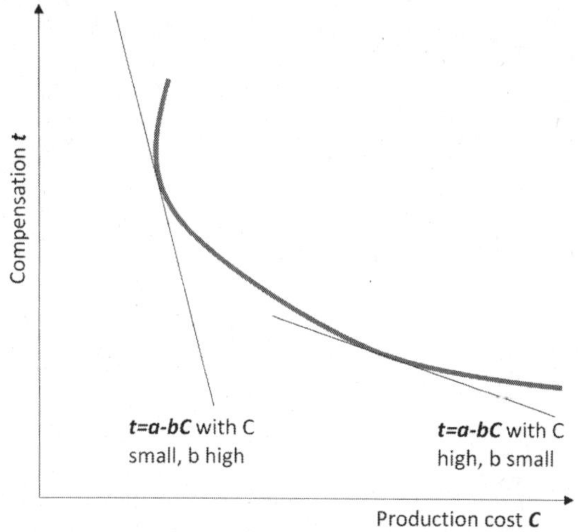

Figure B2.10.1 Optimal contract between the government and the contractor. Based on Laffont and Tirole (1986).

2.4.3 Implications for policy

This method has wide implications for public management in areas such as public service delegation for infrastructure maintenance; waste disposal or water supply; public–private partnerships to build hospitals, schools, or prisons; or the regulation of natural monopolies such as rail infrastructures.

The same approach can be applied *within* the government. Rather than solely betting on the dedication of civil servants, incentive contracts can be devised to incite public employees to better achieve government objectives. This can be done through reallocating to individual units or services part of the benefits from the cost savings they generate. Another famous though seldom-implemented proposal is the so-called *Walsh contract* for central bankers (Walsh, 1995), which makes the wage negatively dependent on the difference between the actual and the target inflation rate (see Chapter 5).

2.5 The Limits of Benevolence

So far, we have not questioned the government's objective of serving the general interest as defined in Chapter 1 through a social welfare function. The previous arguments have underlined the limits to a government's capacity to act in an effective way when private agents behave strategically or in the presence of uncertainty.

The criticism of a government's capacity and willingness to serve the general interest is deeper and of a different nature. Building on earlier insights, modern research has called into question the far too naïve vision of a well-informed and benevolent government that inspired normative economics and, in many countries, still constitutes the intellectual backbone of public service. The famously centralized French system is a case in point. As Jean-Jacques Laffont once commented: "The official and administrative system . . . rests on an idealized vision of political power and democratic life, on a general postulate of benevolence of politicians, the administration and all government officials and assimilated staff."[10] In Laffont's view, the notion that a politician's behavior can be described (as we did in Chapter 1) as the maximization of a social welfare function can be traced back to Jean-Jacques Rousseau, the French eighteenth-century philosopher, and to his vision of the government as a "frictionless device" and a mere "implementation instrument of the people's will," without a proper existence. Today's representative government, which delegates policy implementation to elected officials and then to bureaucrats, departs from this ideal.[11]

2.5.1 Why politicians may depart from the general interest

In addition to the informational dimension discussed in the previous section, five main, non–mutually-exclusive arguments have been mounted against Rousseau's paradigm.

First, politically accountable governments are vulnerable to lack of credibility and time inconsistency because exposure to opinion polls, short mandates, or the threat of losing a majority in parliament render investment in the build-up of a reputation difficult. They may therefore engage in policies that are not optimal from an intertemporal point of view.

Second, governments are exposed to pressures from interest groups. In most countries, the Agriculture Minister is as much the representative of farmers within the government as he or she is the voice of the government vis-à-vis the farmers. The advice he or she provides to the Prime Minister or the President is biased toward the interests of the sector. The Labor Minister is likewise sensitive to the arguments of trade unions and the Defense Minister to those of the military.

The underlying problem is that citizens exhibit heterogeneous preferences. Each of them uses the political system so that the collective decision reflects, as much as possible, his or her own preferences. More than through the majority vote, this can be achieved through *lobbying* politicians and civil servants. Lobbying, which most countries nowadays recognize as a legitimate contribution to policy discussion, is usually intermediated by organizations known as *interest groups*, such as trade unions, consumer or environmental protection associations, industry representatives, community groups, and the like. Lobbying makes increasing use of social networks.

Government money earmarked to special interests (familiarly dubbed *pork barrel* in American English[12]) amounts to a tax levied on all taxpayers to the benefit of the few. Pork-barrel politics is an important dimension of the budgeting process in any country, as it is for the allocation of Europe's structural funds, which finance local infrastructure projects. It notably uses instruments such as campaign financing, media pressure, indoctrination, and corruption. But it can also be more broadly understood as a political process that generates necessary and potentially welfare-improving trade-offs among various interest groups.

The role of interest groups had long been known by sociologists and political scientists before it was acknowledged and modeled by economists. It was not until the early 1970s that George Stigler (1971) spoke of a *regulatory capture* of the regulator by the very interests he or she is responsible for supervising. Ever since, public economics has attempted to better identify this risk and to define how the regulators' mandate and ethical standards (such as mandatory cooling-off periods before they can join the private sector) can be designed and drafted to align their interests with the general interest.[13]

Third, governments are subject to reelection and are naturally motivated by it. The view that politicians are motivated only by the general interest from the first day of their mandate to the start of the next electoral campaign is overly naïve. A government can act in an opportunistic way and seek reelection, for example, by lowering taxes just before a poll (at the risk of having to raise them later), by increasing public expenditures, or by delaying unpopular reforms. This type of behavior gives rise to a *political business cycle*.[14] For example, the six-year electoral cycle affects French local investment, which generally accelerates during the two years before a municipal election and decelerates the year after the election (figure 2.2).[15]

The simple political business cycle model rests on the assumption that citizens are not well-informed enough to decipher the politicians' tactic.

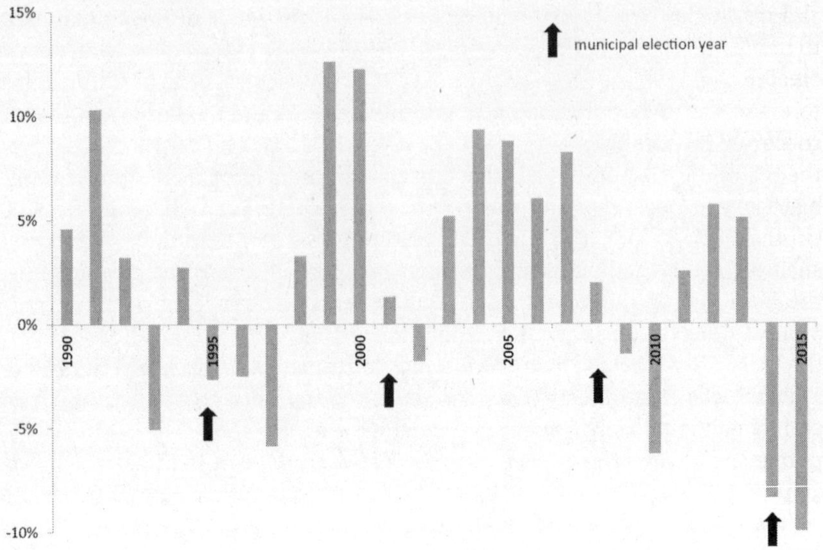

Figure 2.2 The growth rate of local gross capital formation in France (percent per year in volume).
Insee, National accounts.

However, similar biases can also emerge that are detrimental to the interests of the future generations that do not vote. This may concern public finances, pensions, or the environment.

Fourth, governments can be *partisan,* and, rather than serving the general interest, they may take measures that correspond to their prejudices or favor the majority that supports them. A reason for such behavior is that politicians are torn between what Max Weber (1919/1978) called the "ethics of responsibility" and the "ethics of conviction." They are not only accountable to the citizens at large, but also to their supporters and to those who share their beliefs.

Competition compounds the problem. Let us suppose, for example, that one of two competing political parties wishes to direct public investment toward defense and the other one toward social housing. Knowing that if it loses power, priorities will change, the governing party, if doubtful of its reelection, will have a strong incentive to overinvest in its priority area and, at the same time, limit its successor's ability to spend through the legacy of a high public debt. The more the country is divided and the more frequently power shifts between parties, the higher the public debt will be. The problem here comes from each camp's conviction that its policies correspond to the general interest. Under those conditions, ideological division leads to excessive public spending and debt, and it can be confirmed empirically that public debt is positively correlated with the degree of political instability (Persson and Tabellini, 1999, 2000).

Fifth, *divisions between regions*, or *between ethnic or social groups*, may lead to inefficient spending. In such situations (which are often observed in newly created countries but can also arise in developed countries), each faction tries to extort from the government tangible benefits whose corresponding macroeconomic costs (higher public debt or inflation) will be distributed among the whole population. In this case, theory suggests that public spending will be too high, as well as public debt (in the event of debt financing) or inflation (in the event of monetization). There are many examples of such situations, such as the impact of intercommunity tensions in the 1970s and 1980s on the Belgian public debt; the incapacity, in 2000–1, of the Argentine Federal State to get regions to contribute to sound public finance management; or the inflationary behavior of the former Soviet republics in the early 1990s, after the USSR had been dissolved but while the ruble remained. We shall come back to these issues in Chapter 4 by examining the consequences for public finance of "wars of attrition" on the distribution of the costs of a fiscal adjustment.

The combination of informational asymmetries and partisan behavior sometimes results in awkward effects. An observable pattern is for left-wing governments to implement policies that are categorized as right-wing, and vice versa. Cukierman and Tommasini (1998) provided a rationalization for such behavior in an article entitled "When Does It Take a Nixon to Go to China?": imperfectly informed conservative voters would not have endorsed the recognition of communist China by a liberal administration, but the fact that the initiativc came from a conservative president suggested that the move was motivated by national interest, not partisan preferences.

2.5.2 Modeling politicians' behavior

Politicians' behavior has been modeled in several ways.[16] In the simplest theoretical models, politicians have no preferences of their own; their only objective is to be in power. Once elected, they seek to be reelected.

One might think that if politicians are only motivated by (re)election, and voters are well-informed, decisions by politically motivated governments will coincide with the maximization of social welfare or with the decisions the benevolent dictator of Chapter 1 would take. In fact, this is generally not the case.

The reason is the following: majority vote gives a prominent role to the *median voter* (box 2.11). For instance, if left-wing and right-wing parties disagree on the level of government transfers, voters will choose the median level of transfers (i.e., the level at which half of the voters would like it to be lower and half of them would like it to be higher). This is quite a logical outcome in a democracy. However, except under very specific assumptions, this does not coincide with either of the social choice objectives outlined in Chapter 1. The "Benthamian" choice would structure spending to maximize

Box 2.11 The Median Voter

The median voter model was introduced by Black (1948) and builds on the insights of Hotelling's (1929) model of competition. Suppose that voters' preferences can be represented along a single dimension, from "left" to "right," and that the government is elected by simple majority. Suppose furthermore that the competing parties' programs can be represented on the same axis. A voter will choose the party whose preferences are close to his or her own: Voters V_1 to V_4 will, for example, vote for candidate C_1 and voters V_5 to V_9 for candidate C_2 (figure B2.11.1).

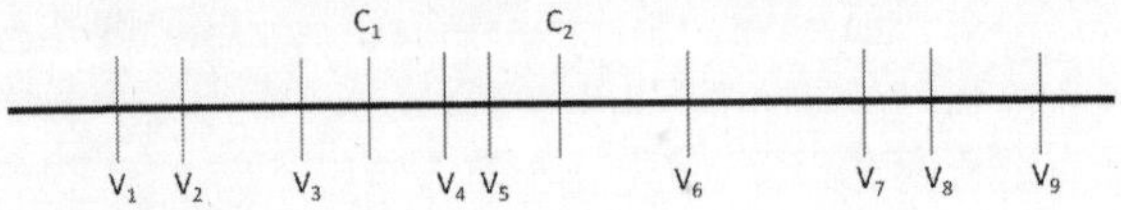

Figure B2.11.1 The median voter.

If there are only two parties, one from the left and one from the right, each party will always capture the more extremist voters. V_1, for example, has no choice but to vote for C_1, even though C_1 is much too centrist to its taste. Clearly, this implies that both parties have an incentive to tilt their programs toward the preferences of the center to capture as many voters as necessary to reach power. This will lead them both to converge on the preference of the median voter V_5. This has two important consequences:

- The program of the winning party is aligned with the preferences of the median voter;
- It is immaterial which party wins the election since both have converged on the same set of policies.

This result, known as the *median voter theorem*, mimics Hotelling's results on product differentiation by monopolistic producers (the famous case of ice cream vendors locating near one another on a stretch of beach, familiar to students of microeconomics). Its empirical relevance should not be taken for granted. In the United States, for example, according to the Pew Research Center,[a] the median Democrat voter was only marginally to the left of the median Republican voter in 1994, which could be regarded as the result of competition to capture the median voter. But, in 2014, the gulf was wide: 92% of Republicans were to the right of the median Democrat and 94% of Democrats were to the left of the median Republican. Increased partisanship had resulted in significant polarization.

There are clearly many simplifying assumptions in this model. Nevertheless, it captures some important features of decision by majority and remains widely used.

[a] http://www.people-press.org/2014/06/12/political-polarization-in-the-american-public/

average welfare, whereas the "Rawlsian" choice would concentrate transfers on the poorest.

The model can also be used to analyze decision-making processes in collegial bodies where each decision is subject to a vote. This is the case in the IMF, the European Union, and monetary policy committees. IMF directors represent groups of countries whose vote is weighted according to their quota in the Fund capital. Voting rights at the EU Council of Ministers are also weighted, as set by the treaty that establishes the ground rules of the European Union, the *Treaty Establishing the European Community.*

The *European Central Bank* (ECB) provides a good example. Its Governing Council comprises six Executive Board members and as many national central bank governors as the number of member countries. Suppose that each national central bank governor favors an interest rate based on his or her own country's rate of inflation.[17] Majority vote among national governors would select the median interest rate, "Benthamian" choice would select the interest rate corresponding to average inflation (this is the behavior expected from the Executive Board members and it corresponds to the mandate of the ECB), and " 'Rawlsian" choice would aim at curbing inflation in the country where it is the highest. All three values would be different. A similar line of reasoning applies to the US Federal Reserve board, albeit with a smaller number of regional representatives.

The situation is worse when there are multiple selection criteria. The *theory of social choice* has shown that, in such situations, the aggregation of individual preferences may result in an impossibility. Even if each voter has a clear ranking among candidates, it is possible that a majority of them prefers A over B, another majority B over C, and a third majority C over A: this is the *Condorcet paradox* (Condorcet, 1784). This observation was formalized by Kenneth Arrow (1951): the *Arrow theorem* establishes that, in the presence of at least three decision criteria, there is only one voting mechanism that does not make the relative ranking of two criteria dependent on the ranking of the other criteria. This mechanism is dictatorship.

More generally, a positive approach that explicitly considers the political process calls for understanding why and how policy outcomes may depart from the optimum. A good example is a parliamentary decision on public spending and taxation. This type of decision is inherently political and results from the aggregation of a variety of preferences that are specific to regions, social groupings, or sectors. Careful analysis of this type of process leads to the conclusion that the budgetary decision may significantly depart from the social optimum (box 2.12). A significant body of recent research has been devoted to understanding how political institutions—for example, a proportional versus a first-past-the-post voting system, or the allocation of agenda-setting powers between government and parliament—affect budgetary outcomes.

Box 2.12 The Political Economy of Public Spending

The level of public spending results from a political process; namely, the vote on the budget in parliament. Depending on their situation and their partisan preferences, citizens hold different views on the budget's level and composition.

Persson (1998) introduced a model where the utility u^{ji} of an individual j belonging to a group i within society (we can think of regions, age groups, or sectors; there are at least three groups) depends on his or her private consumption c^{ji} and on the consumption of a public good g^i that is specific to group i:

$$u^{ji} = c^{ji} + \alpha^{ji} H(g^i) \quad j \in [0,1]; \quad i = 1, \ldots K \qquad \text{(B2.12.1)}$$

α^j is the exogenous weight that individual j of group i assigns to the public good. All individuals receive equal income y, pay group-specific, lump-sum taxes t^i to finance the public good, and consume the remainder:

$$c^{ji} = c^i = y - t^i \qquad \text{(B2.12.2)}$$

First, assume that both taxes and public good provision are group-specific and decided within groups (think about local taxes that finance local infrastructure). Assuming α^j is on average equal to one within each group, then the level of public good provision is identical across groups, as budget constraint and profit maximization lead to:

$$t^i = g^i = H_g^{-1}(1) \quad i = 1, \ldots K \qquad \text{(B2.12.3)}$$

H_g denotes the derivative of H with respect to g.

Alternatively, assume that public good provision is still group-specific but that its financing falls equally on all citizens and that the decision is centralized. In this case, there is a negative externality stemming from the needs to finance other groups' public goods without benefiting from them:

$$c^{ji} = c = y - t = \frac{1}{K}\sum_{i=1}^{K} g^i \quad j = 1, \ldots n; \quad i = 1, \ldots K \qquad \text{(B2.12.4)}$$

If a subset of the groups is somehow able to capture the decision, it can twist it in its favor, which results in excess spending on some public goods. This corresponds to the familiar pork-barrel politics.

The interesting issue is how majority decision on spending affects the outcome. Suppose now that this decision rests with a parliament where each group (in this case locality) has one representative (think of the US senate), and preferences are heterogenous across groups. Each representative tries to maximize the utility for her constituency, which is:

$$u^l = y - \frac{1}{K}\sum_{i=1}^{K} g^i + \alpha^l H\left(g^l\right) \tag{B2.12.5}$$

Finally, suppose that one of the representatives has agenda setting power (i.e., she is able to present a budget to the vote of her fellow members of parliament) and that, in the absence of a positive vote, taxes and public spending are set at zero. The other representatives will approve the budget if it improves the situation in comparison to this default solution. The agenda-setter knows that she needs to assemble a majority of at least half the members of parliament, and she sets itself the goal of maximizing Equation (B2.12.5) subject to this constraint. The outcome is a budget where spending is high in the locality of the agenda-setter, intermediate in the localities whose representatives participate in the coalition, and nil elsewhere. Assuming the agenda-setter builds a coalition at minimum cost for her, this coalition will consist in those representatives whose localities are characterized by the highest α^ls since they are the cheapest to buy off.

This outcome is likely to be socially inefficient because spending is too high in the agenda-setter's locality and too low in localities outside the majority. The model is clearly oversimplified since it does not consider partisan preferences and starts from an excessively rough representation of the decision. Nevertheless, it captures an important insight.

2.5.3 Implications for policy

Taking on board the political dimension should not result in sheer cynicism toward economic policy. It merely acknowledges that political institutions shape economic outcomes and that they should be designed so that the outcome of political processes corresponds to the general interest. In this respect, the political economy approach can help in designing and adopting policy institutions that are conducive to socially desirable outcomes. The process of institutional selection that took place in the 1980s and the 1990s for central banks can therefore to some extent be replicated for budgetary or regulatory institutions.

Furthermore, public decision-makers cannot ignore the risk that government employees themselves have a biased vision of the general interest. Unlike politicians, civil servants are not motivated by the desire to be reelected but by career concern. Civil servants' incentives are thus not aligned with voters' preferences unless their mandate is clear and verifiable. They can also be motivated by the prospect of future employment in the private sector and in some cases by corruption. Most countries have put in place codes of ethics to regulate civil servants' relationships with the private sector. The risk of corruption is even higher in low-income countries, where civil servants are badly paid. The structure of governmental institutions and of the political process are important determinants of corruption (Shleifer and Vishny, 1993).

2.6 The Policy Responses

Now that we are aware of the various limits of economic policymaking and the necessity of creating adequate institutions to address these limits, it is time to examine how economic policy decisions are made in practice.

The last quarter of the twentieth century witnessed the emergence of two major governance technologies: first, the creation and development of specialized agencies equipped with independent policymaking or monitoring power; second, a significantly greater reliance on rules that constrain the behavior of policy authorities.

2.6.1 Delegation to independent agencies

The recourse to independent authorities that act on behalf of the parliament or the government has old roots (see Tucker, 2018, for a full discussion). The Bank of England was created in 1694 (though it was only made independent three centuries later), the US Interstate Commerce Commission was born in 1887, the Securities and Exchange Commission (SEC) was created under Roosevelt in 1934, and, in Germany, the Bundesbank was introduced in 1947 and the federal office for anti-trust (Bundeskartellamt) in 1958. The granting of policy powers to independent agencies has, however, markedly accelerated in the last quarter of the twentieth century, especially in Europe and more recently in emerging countries.[18] Delegation to an independent body has even become the dominant model for central banking, financial services, competition, sector-specific regulation, and drugs regulation.

Delegation does not take place only within countries. The European Union also provides examples of various such authorities (like the ECB or the European Commission in its function as a guardian of competition), and there are international standard-setting committees formed by the regulators themselves (like the Basel Committee for Banking Supervision, see Chapter 6). Private regulatory bodies have also emerged internationally, such as the International Accounting Standards Board, which sets international accounting standards, and the Internet Corporation for Assigned Names and Numbers, a nonprofit body that coordinates the assignment of domain names and IP addresses.

The proliferation of independent authorities has been criticized by politicians from the left as well as from the right. It raises two main questions.

The first question is why and when it is preferable to remove certain fields of public decision from direct political influence. In a democracy, these institutions perform under a mandate given by the legislator, who retains both the responsibility for defining and monitoring the mandate and the option to withdraw its delegation. Yet decisions on a case-by-case basis do escape control by the executive.

The second question is how to conduct economic policy in a system where policy instruments are in the hands of independent bodies that may or may not coordinate with each other. For example, in the United States, responsibility for supervising the financial industry is scattered across the Federal Reserve, the Federal Deposit Insurance Corporation (FDIC), the Office of the Comptroller of the Currency (OCC), the SEC, the Commodity Futures Trade Commission (CFTC), and as many insurance supervisors as there are US states. Banks are supervised by the Fed, FDIC, and OCC while financial markets are supervised by the SEC and CFTC. The 2008 financial crisis led to broadening the remit of the Fed and creating a Financial Stability Oversight Committee chaired by the Secretary of the Treasury. This is an example of the coordination difficulties raised by the delegation model.

When should, in a democracy, a decision be delegated to a technocratic body rather than to a government accountable before parliament? Political science has for a long time been interested in these questions, but it is only since the 1990s that they have received systematic treatment. Contrary to perceptions, economic theory does not recommend an across-the-board delegation of responsibilities to nonelected authorities, nor does it recommend in principle restricting the scope of democratic choice. One can regret, with former Fed Vice Chairman and Princeton Professor Alan Blinder, that the government is "too political"[19] and yet agree with his former colleague Joseph Stiglitz, Chairman of President Clinton's Council of Economic Advisers, that technocratic bodies are not political enough.[20] When appointed President of the European Commission in 2014, Jean-Claude Juncker pledged to make this quintessentially bureaucratic body "more political."[21] Nonelected bodies are subject to failures that are symmetrical to those of governments: behavioral rigidities, insensitivity to the society's changing preferences, inability to trade-off between objectives, and lack of legitimacy to deal with decisions that involve a distributional dimension. As noted by Alesina and Tabellini (2007), foreign policy is also vulnerable to credibility and time inconsistency problems, yet nobody suggests that it should be delegated to an agency, notably because objectives and actions need to be reassessed constantly and cannot be framed within a consistent and stable mandate.

Political and technocratic decisions are thus two imperfect methods of governance. One needs criteria to guide decisions to assign specific responsibilities to technocratic bodies—of course, under a mandate defined and monitored by the legislator. Modeling the technocrat's and the politician's behavior (Alesina and Tabellini, 2007; Maskin and Tirole, 2004) leads to several general insights (cf. box 2.13). Technocratic decision appears preferable when:

1. The matter is very technical;
2. Social preferences are stable and performance criteria are well-defined;

3. The decisions and their effects are not easily observable by voters;
4. The decisions are highly vulnerable to time inconsistency;
5. The decisions have a limited impact on income distribution within generations;
6. The decisions significantly affect the distribution of income between generations;
7. The decisions do not involve trade-offs between incompatible objectives;
8. The decisions entail benefits (or costs) to groups that are likely to be involved in political lobbying.

Box 2.13 Technocrats or Politicians: Who Should Decide?

Eric Maskin and Jean Tirole (2004), on the one hand, and Alberto Alesina and Guido Tabellini (2007), on the other, have studied the choice between two governance regimes—by an independent agency or by political government—in a context of information asymmetry. The choice between a "technocratic" contract and a "political" one depends on the relative performance of the technocrat and the politician, given their respective incentives.

For Maskin and Tirole, the problem lies with the information the electorate has on the stakes involved in economic decisions. They use a two-period model. In each period, two decisions are possible, one of which corresponds to the social optimum. Voters are initially uncertain about which is the better policy. At the end of the initial period, however, they can, with a probability q, discover it (but they remain in uncertainty with probability $1 - q$).

Voters delegate the decision to a policymaker—either an appointed technocrat (a "judge") or an elected officer (a "politician")—who is informed about the likely outcome of alternative policies but who also pursues his own preference, which can differ from that of the voters. For example, voters do not know whether priority should be given to stimulating growth or to fighting inflation. They can delegate this choice but run the risk that their delegate is either too strict or too lax in comparison to their own preferences.

Once named, the *technocrat* chooses the decision that he or she considers good without consideration for the voters' preferences.

The *politician* seeks to be renewed at the end of period 1, which can encourage him or her to behave in a demagogic way: If voters are mistaken about the nature of the good decision, the politician may decide to take the wrong decision in order to please the electorate and ensure his or her reelection. But she or he can also speculate that the electorate will learn what the good decision was and reward him or her for having had the courage to confront opposed public opinion.

Maskin and Tirole find that the technocratic contract is preferable to the political contract when the probability q that the electorate will discover what the good decision was is low. In this case, the politician is unlikely to be rewarded for having taken the good decision and will prefer following the voters in their potential error. On the other hand, if voters acquire information with time, delegation to the elected politician is preferable to delegation to a technocrat (who presents the risk that she or he follows her or his own preferences, which may differ from the social optimum).

This model suggests that one should delegate to technocrats in areas where the electorate is poorly informed and unlikely to acquire information (for example, when the matter is too technical or of insufficient direct importance for citizens to invest in the acquisition of information).

Alesina and Tabellini emphasize motivations. For them, delegation to a technocrat or to a politician are two forms of contract concluded by a sovereign people. They thus follow the line of Laffont-Tirole (see box 2.10). Talents, effort, and outcome are in the two cases connected by a relation:

$$Y = \theta + e + \varepsilon \qquad \text{(B2.13.1)}$$

where Y is the outcome, θ a random variable representing talent, e the effort, and ε a random error term (assumed to be white noise). The question is then to know which contract, technocratic or political, provides the greatest incentive to effort since neither talent nor effort can be directly observed.

The technocrat chooses his or her effort level e to maximize his or her utility function, which is the difference between reward $R^T(e)$ and the cost of effort $\psi(e)$. His or her reward is the expectation of his perceived talent, given the expected outcome Y:

$$R^T(e) = E\left[E(\theta|Y)\right] = E\left[\left(EY - e^a - \varepsilon\right)|Y\right] \qquad \text{(B2.13.2)}$$

where e^a is the effort perceived by the public (at equilibrium $e^a = e$). The politician chooses in the same way his or her effort level, but his or her reward is reelection, which depends on the probability that the result Y exceeds a threshold W:

$$R^P(e) = \Pr\left[Y \geq W\right] = 1 - \Pr\left[\theta \leq W - e - \varepsilon\right] \qquad \text{(B2.13.3)}$$

Each one of these two contracts therefore leads to a level of effort that results from optimization behavior by the agent having received the delegation. The first-order conditions yield the optimum level of effort in each case. Denoting by σ_θ^2 the perceived variance of talent across policymakers and by σ_ε^2 the variance of white noise, we have:

Technocrat:

$$\frac{\partial \Psi(e)}{\partial e} = \frac{\sigma_\theta^2}{\sigma_\theta^2 + \sigma_\varepsilon^2} \tag{B2.13.4}$$

Politician:

$$\frac{\partial \Psi(e)}{\partial e} = \frac{1}{\sqrt{\sigma_\theta^2 + \sigma_\varepsilon^2}\sqrt{\pi}} \tag{B2.13.5}$$

where the marginal cost of effort is an increasing function of effort $(\partial \Psi(e)/\partial e > 0, \partial^2 \Psi(e)/\partial^2 e > 0)$. The main results are:

The presence of noise reduces the level of effort in both cases: the higher the variance of ε, the less clear the relation between effort and performance and the weaker the incentive to effort. Neither contract outperforms the other from this point of view.

The variance of talent raises the technocrat's level of effort, but it reduces that of the politician: When talent is uncertain, the technocratic contract is preferable because the incentive to demonstrate competence is stronger. This suggests that it is preferable to delegate to technocrats the jobs for which the dispersion of unobservable competences is large.

The same model can be used to choose to whom to entrust a responsibility that involves a trade-off between two objectives (or two alternative tasks on which the effort has to be allocated) when there is uncertainty about the preferences of the electorate. In this case, the allocation of the technocrat's efforts is specified *ex ante,* and it is held there because it is the best means of showing competence. On the other hand, the politician shows flexibility and adapts to changes in the electorate's preferences. The political contract is therefore more adapted.

In the same vein, the technocratic contract is shown to be preferable in the event of time inconsistency, while the political contract is found superior when it is necessary to compensate the losers.

Of course, no economic policy issue completely meets the eight criteria, but the latter provide a useful analytical grid. For instance, monetary policy meets all the criteria except the seventh (at least in the short term, raising interest rates will slow down inflation and simultaneously increase unemployment) and the fifth (a decline in interest rates redistributes interest income from *rentiers* to indebted households and firms, and, at the same time, it inflates the value of financial wealth—see Chapter 6). However, the weighting of the objectives can be specified once and for all in the statute of the central bank. As for fiscal policy, it does not satisfy criteria 2, 3, 5, and 7. These are compelling reasons to keep fiscal policy within the realm of political decision-making.

Beyond conventional wisdom and disenchantment with politics, the tendency to assign certain fields of decision to independent agencies can be interpreted as reflecting:

- The increased technical complexity of many decisions, regarding, for example, sectoral or financial regulation and areas (e.g., risk prevention) that call heavily on scientific expertise.
- The legal nature of some decisions, for example, on merger control, the regulation of competition, or the enforcement of sanitary standards.
- The wish to protect policy decisions from trade-offs between conflicting objectives. For example, public opinion does not accept that public health and safety be weakened as a result of any trade-off with economic or financial objectives; similarly, protecting monetary policy, as many countries have done, recognizes that, notwithstanding a short-term trade-off, there is no long-term trade-off between inflation and unemployment.
- The rising importance of intertemporal concerns. In a context of weaker productivity gains and of demographic decline, expectations of future purchasing power depend less on growth prospects and more on inflation. The independence of central banks can thus be interpreted as a guarantee given to savers that the wealth that they accumulate will not be expropriated by inflation.
- An integrated global economy without a global government. In the absence of *ex ante* political legitimacy, international governance tends to rely on technocratic institutions in order to create, through the demonstration of its effectiveness, the conditions of *ex post* legitimacy.

That being said, the choice between political and technocratic governance is less clear-cut than it appears. Intermediate formulas do exist, like those in which elected officials choose the objectives and assign the responsibility for implementation to technocratic bodies that are granted operational independence. The relation between the UK Chancellor of the Exchequer and the governor of the Bank of England with respect to monetary policy provides an example (cf. Chapter 5).

Anyhow, independence does not make politics irrelevant: independent institutions remain formally accountable to parliaments on how they discharge their mandate, and, through their communication, they are accountable to the public at large. Parliaments can repeal the law granting independence to agencies. Even if they do not, constraints do exist: social demand for accountability and transparency has steadily risen over recent decades, forcing independent agencies to formalize their policy rules and operational frameworks, publish the proceedings of their internal discussions, and report their contacts with interest groups.

2.6.2 Policy rules

There has been a long-standing debate over public policy as to whether government decisions should abide by rules or be able to react on a case-by-case, results-based, optimizing basis. Rules are prescriptions for policymakers and other economic agents that are stable across time and therefore commit policymaking and influence private behavior. Their limitation is that they are rigid and may lead to inadequate policy response in situations not previously foreseen. Former European Commission president Romano Prodi famously said that the European fiscal pact was "stupid," and it is true that most rules lack the sophistication that can be found even in animal behavior (Haldane and Madouros, 2012).

The role of rules has notably received much attention in the field of financial regulation. An ongoing trade-off between rules-based and principles-based regulation emerged after the 2001 Enron scandal and was revived in the wake of the 2007–2008 financial crisis. Rules are often complex; as a result, monitoring their implementation is difficult. They also always present loopholes that can be exploited. Conversely, principles-based (risk-focused) regulations allow more discretion and may be less transparent but, under a strong independent regulator, can deliver results that conform better to a set of social objectives embodied in such principles.

In the realm of macroeconomic and especially monetary policy, the debate about rules versus discretion has been of a different nature. Governance by rules originates in the lessons drawn from the literature on economic policy evaluation (see Section 2.1.2) and on time inconsistency (see Section 2.1.3). Robert Lucas's critique of traditional policy evaluation led him to advocate comparing policy *rules* rather than policy *acts*: his main point was that only the results of rules can be rigorously compared (Lucas, 1976). Finn Kydland's and Edward Prescott's preference for rules over discretion rested on a different argument, namely, that "selecting the decision which is best, given the current situation, . . . either results in consistent but suboptimal planning or in economic instability" (Kydland and Prescott, 1977, p. 487).

Rules were first tried—with limited success—with monetary policy. In the late 1970s and the early 1980s, the Federal Reserve briefly endorsed them when it adopted a strategy based on quantitative targets for monetary aggregates. The United Kingdom also implemented a similar strategy. Both experiments, however, were discontinued after a few years.[22] The rules-based approach to policy was revived in the 1990s when a growing number of central banks adopted explicit *inflation targeting* strategies (see Chapter 5). Rules nowadays are, however, less rigid than envisaged in the early monetarist writings, and they aim to combine medium-term discipline with a degree of discretion. This is being done by defining an explicit policy strategy that is followed unless unexpected developments lead to departure from it. In the latter case, policymakers need to explain why they have chosen to do so. This especially has advantages in the presence of Knightian uncertainty as defined in Section 2.1.1 as policymakers in this case need to retain flexibility. In the words of Mervyn King (2004), the Governor of the Bank of England, "the ideal is a framework that will implement what we currently believe to be the optimal monetary-policy strategy and will deviate from that only if collectively we change our view about what that strategy should be." Such an approach is often called *constrained discretion,* and it serves as a reference for several policy institutions, including the US Federal Reserve.[23]

In the budgetary field, rules were introduced later, but nowadays many countries, especially in Europe, have defined policy rules such as the euro area's "Stability and Growth Pact" and the "debt breaks," or balanced budget amendments, adopted by several European countries. Their aim is to enforce responsible fiscal behavior over the medium term, for example, through avoiding excessive debt accumulation or excessive deficits while leaving room for short-term stabilization. Those rules, however, have had limited success, as we shall see in Chapter 4.

There also exist exchange rate policy rules, such as currency boards and crawling pegs (Chapter 7). They were widely used in the 1980s and the 1990s to anchor price expectations and demonstrate a government's commitment to price stability by attaching a highly visible political price to the option of inflating problems away. However, for countries outside a monetary union and without the prospect of joining one, exchange rate regimes have evolved in the direction of increased flexibility.

Conclusion

There have been a few blessed decades, from the immediate aftermath of World War II to the early 1970s, when economic policy could be regarded as dedicated to the public good, conceptually simple, and reasonably easy to implement. When this golden age ended in the 1980s, policymakers and economists were cast out of the Garden of Eden. Since then, they have been living in a much more imperfect world.

The recognition of the limits of standard models should neither lead to underestimating the responsibility of policy nor to putting an excessive faith in the self-regulating virtue of markets.

Notes

1. The assumption that shocks are normally distributed is discussed later in this chapter.
2. The UK government established in 2010 a "Behavioral Insight Unit" to help implement the nudge approach in policymaking. In a Ted Talk in February 2010, Prime Minister David Cameron claimed that "The best way to get someone to cut their electricity bill is to show them their own spending, to show them what their neighbors are spending, and then show what an energy-conscious neighbor is spending." Most economists would nevertheless argue that the best way to have people cut their electricity consumption is to raise the price of electricity.
3. The kurtosis is defined and measured as $k = \mu_4/\sigma^4$, where $\mu_4 = E(X - EX)^4$ is the fourth-order moment of the variable and $\sigma^4 = [E(X - EX)^2]^2$ is the square of its variance. It can be shown that the kurtosis of the normal distribution is equal to 3.
4. On the economics of extreme events, see Posner (2004).
5. The precautionary principle was introduced in 1992 at the United Nations Rio Conference on Environment, and Development. Article 15 of the Rio Declaration states that "where there are threats of serious and irreversible damage, lack of full scientific certainty shall not be used as a reason for postponing cost-effective measures to prevent environmental degradation." The precautionary principle was introduced in the Treaty of Lisbon of the European Union.
6. More specifically, the case for a precautionary principle depends on the relationship between "prudence," defined as the third derivative of the utility function and absolute risk aversion (Gollier, Julien, and Treich, 2000; Gollier, 2002).
7. Bayesian calculus is used to model this learning process; see Evans and Honkapohja (2001).
8. In this discussion, we ignore the collective benefits of insurance schemes. It may be desirable to introduce public insurance schemes in order to encourage risk-taking. For instance, there are guarantee funds for innovating firms and public systems of credit-insurance, notably for exporting firms.
9. See the survey by Holmström and Tirole (1989), and the textbook by Salanié (1997). Laffont and Martimort (2002) is a broader reference on the theory of incentives.
10. Laffont (2000*a*, pp. 118, 124), translated by the authors.
11. Rosanvallon (2000, pp. 12, 23).
12. The term originated in the pre-Civil War period, when slaves were rewarded with salted pork.
13. Recognizing the existence of interest group pressure is not an insult to civil servants' dedication to the general interest. It is only the recognition that it would be inefficient to put them in situations where their personal interests would not be aligned with their professional duty.
14. The expression *political business cycle* was introduced by William Nordhaus (1975). Empirical observations tend to confirm the existence of such a cycle. See, for example, Persson and Tabellini (2001).
15. Municipal investment accounts for 58% of local investment in France.

16. See Persson and Tabellini (1999, 2001) for a survey.
17. This is banned by the ECB Statute, but it is difficult to imagine that the governors do not take account of the preferences of their own home citizens.
18. In the United States, such agencies have existed for a long time, but their field of competence has hardly expanded.
19. Alan Blinder was, successively, a member of the Council of Economic Advisers under the Clinton presidency and then Vice Chairman of the Federal Reserve: "life at the White House is fast-paced, exhilarating, and, of necessity, highly political. Policy discussions may begin with the merits ('Which option is best for the American public?'), but the debate quickly turns to such cosmic questions as whether the chair of the relevant congressional subcommittee would support the policy, which interest groups would be for and against it, what the 'message' would be, and how that message would play in Peoria." He then evokes the Federal Reserve, where, he notes, the reverse occurs; see Blinder (1997, p. 117).
20. "If, as we have argued, there are alternative economic policies, and if these alternatives affect different groups differently, then it matters a great deal who makes decisions, and how those decisions are made. If there is an unemployment/inflation trade-off, and if workers care more about unemployment, while financial markets care more about the erosion of the value of their nominal assets with inflation, then workers and financial markets will see the trade-off in different lights; entrusting the decision about monetary policy to an independent central bank controlled by financial interests, or mandating that the central bank focus only on inflation, makes it more likely that the outcomes will accord with financial interests, rather than the interests of workers" Stiglitz (2003, p. 27).
21. "The Commission is not a technical committee made up of civil servants who implement the instructions of another institution. The Commission is political." Juncker (2014, p. 15).
22. Germany's central bank, the Bundesbank officially followed a monetary target until the changeover to the euro but was widely considered to follow in fact a more pragmatic strategy (Bernanke and Mihov, 1997).
23. Note that Mervyn King speaks of strategies, not individual decisions—otherwise, he would be giving an almost exact definition of time inconsistency.

References

Alesina, A., and G. Tabellini (2007), "Bureaucrats or Politicians? Part I: A Single Policy Task," *American Economic Review*, 97(1), pp. 169–79.

Arrow, K. (1951), *Social Choice and Individual Values*, Wiley.

Arrow, K. (1968), "Optimal Capital Policy with Irreversible Investment," in Wolfe, J. N., ed., *Value, Capital and Growth: Papers in Honor of Sir John Hicks*, Edinburgh University Press, pp. 1–19.

Barro, R., and D. Gordon (1983), "A Positive Theory of Monetary Policy in a Natural Rate Model," *Journal of Political Economy*, 91, pp. 589–610.

Bernanke, B., and I. Mihov (1997), "What Does the Bundesbank Target?" *European Economic Review*, 41(6), pp. 1025–54.

Bernoulli, D. (1738), *Specimen theoriae novae de mensura sortis*, Commentarii Academiae Scientiarum Imperialis Petropolitanae. Translated, Bernoulli, D. (1954), "Exposition of a New Theory on the Measurement of Risk," *Econometrica*, 22, pp. 23–36.

Black, D. (1948), "On the Rationale of Group Decision-Making," *Journal of Political Economy*, 56(1), pp. 23–34.

Blinder, A. (1997), "Is Government Too Political?" *Foreign Affairs*, November–December, p. 126.

Carlson, J., and N. Valev (2001), "Credibility of a New Monetary Regime: The Currency Board in Bulgaria," *Journal of Monetary Economics*, 47, pp. 581–94.

Condorcet, J. A. N. Caritat de (1784/1994), "Assurances (maritimes)," in *Arithmétique politique – textes rares ou inédits* (1767–1789), Paris, Ined, pp. 485–94.

Cukierman, A., and M. Tommasini (1998), "Why Does It Take a Nixon to Go to China?" *The American Economic Review*, 88(1), pp. 180–97.

Dixit, A. (1996), *The Making of Economic Policy: Munich Lectures*, MIT Press.

Dixit, A., and R. Pindyck (1994), *Investment under Uncertainty*, Princeton University Press.

Epstein, L., and T. Wang (1995), "Intertemporal Asset Pricing Under Knightian Uncertainty," *Econometrica*, 62, pp. 283–322.

Evans, G., and S. Honkapohja (2001), *Learning and Expectations in Macroeconomics*, Princeton University Press.

Gollier, C. (2001), "Economie du principe de précaution," in Ewald, F., C. Gollier, and N. de Sadeleer, eds., *Le principe de précaution, Que Sais-Je No. 3596*, Presses Universitaires de France, pp. 104–126.

Gollier, C. (2002), "Time Horizon and the Discount Rate," *Journal of Economic Theory*, 107, pp. 463–73.

Gollier, C. (2013), *Pricing the Planet's Future: The Economics of Discounting in an Uncertain World*, Princeton University Press.

Gollier, C., B. Julien, and N. Treich (2000), "Scientific Progress and Irreversibility: An Economic Interpretation of the 'Precaution Principle,'" *Journal of Public Economics*, 75, pp. 229–53.

Guesnerie, R. (2003), *Kyoto et l'économie de l'effet de serre*, La Documentation française.

Ha-Duong, M. (1998), "Quasi-Option Value and Climate Policy Choices," *Energy Economics*, 20, 599–620.

Haldane, A., and V. Madouros (2012), "The Dog and the Frisbee," in *Proceedings of the Jackson Hole Symposium*, Federal Reserve Bank of Kansas City, pp. 109–59.

Hayek, F. (1944), *The Road to Serfdom*, Routledge.

Henry, C. (1974), "Investment Decisions Under Uncertainty: The Irreversibility Effect," *American Economic Review*, 64, pp. 1006–12.

Holmström, B., and J. Tirole (1989), "The Theory of the Firm," in Schmalensee, R., and R. Willig, eds., *Handbook of Industrial Organization*, vol. 1, Elsevier/North-Holland, pp. 63–133.

Hotelling, H. (1929), "Stability in Competition," *The Economic Journal*, 39, pp. 41–57.
Juncker, J. C. (2014), "Setting Europe in Motion," opening statement in the European Parliament Plenary Session, Strasbourg, 15 July.
Kahneman, D. (2002), "Maps of Bounded Rationality: A Perspective on Intuitive Judgment and Choice," Nobel Prize Lecture, 8 December.
Kahneman, D. (2011), *Thinking, Fast and Slow*, Farrar, Strauss and Giroux.
Keynes, J. M. (1936), *The General Theory of Employment, Interest and Money*. Reprinted in *The Collected Writings of John Maynard Keynes*, vol. VII, 1972, Macmillan.
King, M. (2004), "The Institutions of Monetary Policy," *American Economic Review*, 94, pp. 1–13.
Knight, F. (1921), *Risk, Uncertainty and Profit*, Hart, Schaffner & Marx.
Krugman, P. (1998), "Japan's Trap," available at http://web.mit.edu/krugman/www/japtrap.html.
Kydland, F., and E. Prescott (1977), "Rules Rather than Discretion: The Inconsistency of Optimal Plans," *Journal of Political Economy*, 85, pp. 473–91.
Laffont, J.-J. (2000*a*), "Étapes vers un État moderne: une analyse économique," in *État et gestion publique*, Rapport no. 24 du Conseil d'analyse économique, La Documentation française.
Laffont, J.-J. (2000*b*), *Competition in Telecommunications*, MIT Press.
Laffont, J.-J. (2000*c*), *Incentives and Political Economy*, Clarendon Lectures, Oxford University Press.
Laffont, J.-J., and D. Martimort (2002), *The Theory of Incentives: The Principal-Agent Model*, Princeton University Press.
Laffont, J.-J., and J. Tirole (1986), "Using Cost Observations to Regulate Firms," *Journal of Political Economy*, 94, 614–41.
Lucas, R. (1976), "Econometric Policy Evaluation: A Critique," in Brunner, K., and A. Meltzer, eds., *The Phillips Curve and Labor Markets*, Carnegie-Rochester Conference Series on Public Policy, vol. 1, pp. 19–46.
Mandelbrot, B., and R. L. Hudson (2004), *The (Mis)Behavior of Markets: A Fractal View of Risk, Ruin and Reward*, Basic Books.
Maskin, E., and J. Tirole (2004), "The Politician and the Judge: Accountability in Government," *American Economic Review*, 94, pp. 1034–54.
McDonald, R., and D. Siegel (1986), "The Value of Waiting to Invest," *The Quarterly Journal of Economics*, 101, pp. 707–28.
Mishkin, F. (2008), "Monetary Policy Flexibility, Risk Management, and Financial Disruptions," speech at the Federal Reserve Bank of New York, 11 January.
Musil, R. (1930), *The Man Without Qualities*, translated by E. Wilkins and E. Kaiser, Minerva, 1979.
Muth, J. (1961), "Rational Expectations and the Theory of the Price Movements," *Econometrica*, 29, 315–35.
Nordhaus, W. (1975), "The Political Business Cycle," *The Review of Economic Studies*, 42, pp. 169–90.
Nordhaus, W. (2007), "A Review of the Stern Review on the Economics of Climate Change," *Journal of Economic Literature*, XLV, pp. 686–702.

Persson, T. (1998), "Economic Policy and Special Interest Politics," *The Economic Journal*, 108, pp. 310–27.

Persson, T., and G. Tabellini (1999), "Political Economics and Macroeconomic Policy," in Taylor, J., and M. Woodford, eds., *Handbook of Macroeconomics*, Elsevier/North Holland, chapter 22, pp. 1397–1482.

Persson, T., and G. Tabellini (2000), *Political Economics: Explaining Economic Policy*, MIT Press.

Persson, T., and G. Tabellini (2001), "Political Institutions and Policy Outcomes: What are the Stylized Facts," *CEPR Discussion paper*, No. 2872.

Posner, R. (2004), *Catastrophe: Risk and Response*, Oxford University Press.

Rosanvallon, P. (2000), *La démocratie inachevée, Histoire de la souveraineté du peuple en France*, Gallimard.

Salanié, B. (1997), *The Economics of Contracts: A Primer*, MIT Press.

Shleifer, A., and R. Vishny (1993), "Corruption," *Quarterly Journal of Economics*, 108, pp. 599–617.

Sims, C. (1980), "Macroeconomics and Reality," *Econometrica*, 48, pp. 1–48.

Smith, A. (1776), *An Inquiry into the Nature and Causes of the Wealth of Nations*, Methuen & Co.

Stern, N. (2007), *The Economics of Climate Change*, Cambridge University Press.

Stern, N. (2008), "The Economics of Climate Change," Richard Ely lecture, *American Economic Review*, 98, pp. 1–37.

Stigler, G. (1971), "The Economic Theory of Regulation," *Bell Journal of Economics and Management Science*, 2, 3–21.

Stiglitz, J. (2000), "The Contributions of the Economics of Information to Twentieth Century Economics," *Quarterly Journal of Economics*, 115, pp. 1441–78.

Stiglitz, J. (2003), "Whither Reform? Towards a New Agenda for Latin America," *CEPAL Review*, 80, pp. 7–38.

Stiglitz, J., and A. Weiss (1981), "Credit Rationing in Markets with Imperfect Information," *American Economic Review*, 71(3), pp. 393–410.

Svensson, L. (2004), "Optimal Policy with Low-Probability Extreme Events," *NBER Working Paper*, No. 10196.

Thaler, R., and C. Sunstein (2008), *Nudge: Improving Decisions About Health, Wealth, and Hapiness*, Yale University Press.

Tucker, P. (2018), *Unelected Power*, Princeton University Press.

Von Neumann, J., and O. Morgenstern (1944), *The Theory of Games and Economic Behavior*, Princeton University Press.

Walsh, C. (1995), "Optimal Contracts for Central Bankers," *The American Economic Review*, 85(1), pp. 150–67.

Weber, M. (1919/1978), "Politics as a Vocation," in *Max Weber: Selections in Translation.* Cambridge University Press, chapter 10, pp. 212–25.

Weitzman, M. (2007), "A Review of the Stern Review on the Economics of Climate Change," *Journal of Economic Literature*, XLV, pp. 686–702.

Woodford, M. (2001), "Monetary Policy in the Information Economy," in Hakkio, C., ed., *Economic Policy for the Information Economy*, Federal Reserve Bank of Kansas City, pp. 297–370.

Wyplosz, C. (2005), "Fiscal Policy: Institutions vs. Rules," *National Institute Economic Review*, 191, January.

3

Interdependence

So far, we have assumed that responsibility for policymaking was assigned to one level of government only and that policymakers were fully responsible for decisions with a bearing on their country. We have also assumed that interactions with the rest of the world were small enough to be neglected in the analysis. Over the past decades, however, economic policy has been deeply affected by three secular trends: the rise of international interdependence in the context of globalization; the assignment of policy responsibilities to supranational entities, either at regional level (most notably in Europe, but elsewhere also) or at global level; and the increasing devolution of power to subnational entities such as regions or cities. These transformations have rendered the model of the central government as a single, independent policy player increasingly inadequate.

This raises two important policy questions:

- First, how should individual policymakers behave in a context of significant *horizontal interdependence* between countries? Policy institutions such as governments and central banks are accountable to national citizens, not to citizens in other countries, so they cannot simply opt for the decision that may be optimal from a global standpoint. However, the neglect of interdependence and of the resulting *spillovers* from a country's policy onto its neighbors and economic partners can lead to suboptimal outcomes that are not desirable, even from a strictly selfish policy standpoint. For instance, countries may fail to stimulate their economies through public spending in the event of a global crisis because they expect other countries will do so: they prefer not to increase their public debt while enjoying higher exports to neighboring countries. Conversely, each country may wish to stimulate its economy by lowering the value of its currency, but others will do the same in retaliation and since not all exchange rates can depreciate simultaneously, there is no winner in this zero-sum game. The question, then, is how international cooperation should be structured in order to optimize policy outcomes while respecting political mandates and democratic accountability;[1]

- Second, how should vertical interdependence between different levels of government—say, for example, the municipal, regional, national, European, and global levels—be structured in order to optimize policy outcomes? Specifically, should decision-making powers be devolved to lower levels of government or assigned to higher levels? This is a matter of institutional design and incentives with potentially major consequences for policy effectiveness.

In this chapter, we first discuss if interdependence must (and can) be managed through international coordination (Section 3.1), before moving to the economics of federations and international unions (Section 3.2).

3.1 Interdependence, Spillovers, and Coordination

3.1.1 The rise of interdependence

Interdependence between countries is not equivalent to openness, although the two concepts are related.

a) Openness

Economic openness refers to the degree to which the situation of domestic agents and their decisions are affected by foreign developments. A standard (though not perfect) measure of it is the share of foreign-related flows in total flows (e.g., imports and exports over gross domestic product [GDP]) or the share of foreign-related stocks in total stocks (e.g., the proportion of wealth held abroad). Openness may cover international trade, capital flows, migrations, and other forms of exchanges such as data flows.

Trade openness can be measured through the ratio between international trade and GDP. It is generally calculated as $(X+M)/(2GDP)$, where X and M represent exports and imports, respectively, and GDP is the gross domestic product, all variables being expressed in the same currency (e.g., in current US dollar).

Likewise, *financial openness* can be captured by dividing the stock of cross-border assets A and liabilities L by GDP: $(A+L)/(2GDP)$.[2]

Figure 3.1 compares the evolution of trade and financial openness for advanced economies and for emerging and developing countries over several decades. The average trade openness ratio tripled between the 1960s and the 2010s for both groups of countries. Both globally and for selected countries such as those of Western Europe, trade openness measured by the ratio of imports and exports to GDP now significantly exceeds levels reached in 1913 at the end of the first phase of globalization.[3] A large part of this trade takes place within the framework of *global value chains* that involve a series of suppliers of goods and services from different countries in the production of a final good: in 2009, according to the Organization for Economic Cooperation and Development (OECD, 2013), about a quarter of a typical advanced country's exports consisted in intermediate goods used in third countries' exports, and a quarter of its imports were used in the production of exports.

From the mid-1960s to the mid-2000s, the share of exports (or imports) in G7 countries' GDPs rose from 13% to 25% before stabilizing. In some countries such as China and the former USSR, the transformation from closed to open economies has been dramatic: in 1970, China's external trade in manufactures amounted to 1% of its GDP; in 2005, it had reached 25%.

The aftermath of the global financial crisis saw a slowdown in the growth of world trade relative to global GDP growth without any significant rise of protectionism. Part of the decline of the trade-to-GDP elasticity is attributable to cyclical factors, at least until the incipient trade war in response to tariffs imposed by the U.S. President on steel imports in 2018, but part also has a structural dimension, like the end of the build-up of global value chains (Hoekman, 2015). Nevertheless, trade openness remains high.

As for financial openness, the ratio increased moderately up to the mid-1990s, but then it exploded in advanced economies as capital flows were liberalized, while growing still moderately in emerging and developing countries. Financial openness seems to have picked up in 2007, just before the *global financial crisis.*

The picture is different for labor mobility. According to the International Labor Organization (ILO, 2015), there were 150 million migrant workers[4] in the world in 2013, for a total labor force of 3,338 million. Hence, only 4.5% of workers were migrants. Although significant, this ratio is far below what we have just seen for trade and finance openness. However, labor migrations tend to be concentrated geographically. In the United States, for instance, immigrant workers represented almost 17% of the labor force in 2014, compared to 7% in 1980.[5] In the Arab states of the Middle East, the proportion of migrant workers was as high as 35.6% in 2013, according to ILO. In Europe, economic migration flows increased after the 2008–2009 crisis, even before a dramatic rise in population flows arose in 2015 as a consequence of war and political turmoil in the neighborhood of Europe.

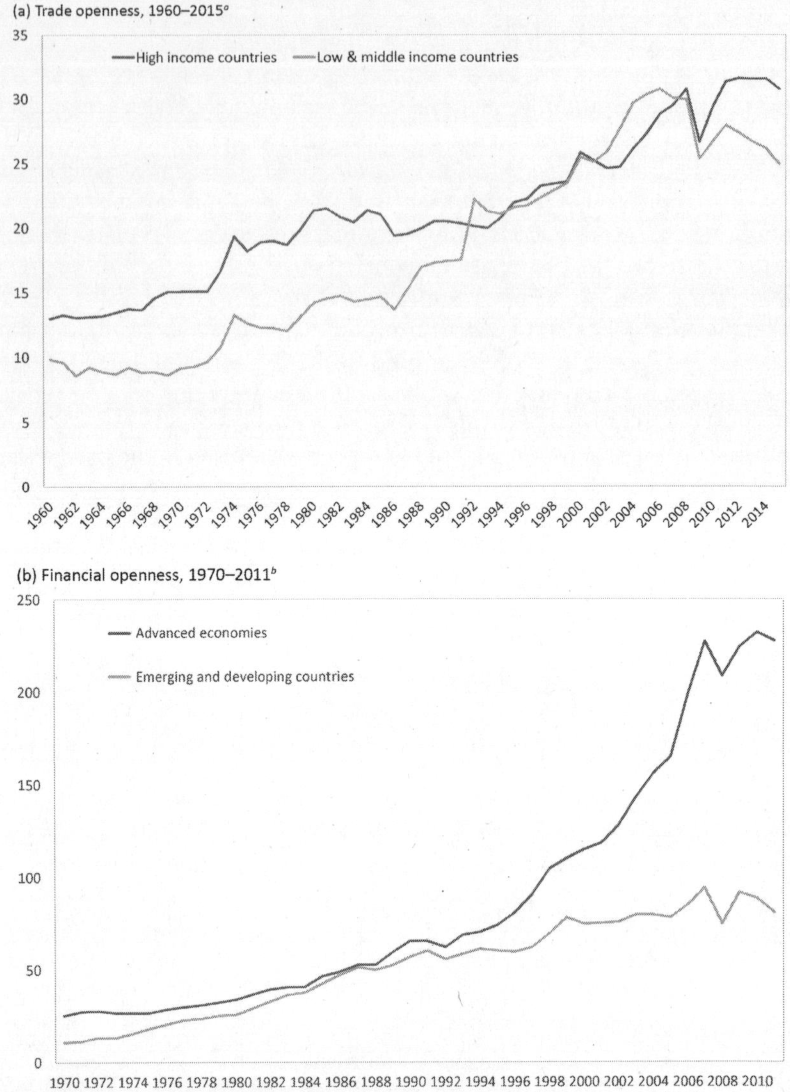

Figure 3.1 Trade and financial openness (% of gross domestic product [GDP]).

[a] Trade openness is measured by $(X+M)/(2^*\text{GDP})$, where X and M denote exports and imports of goods and services, respectively, and GDP is nominal GDP.

[b] Financial openness is measured by $(A+L)/(2^*\text{GDP})$, where A and L represent cross-border assets and liabilities, respectively, and GDP is nominal GDP.

World Bank, and External Wealth of Nations Database (see Lane and Milesi-Ferretti, 2007).

b) Interdependence

Trade, financial openness, and migrations mechanically make countries dependent one on another. For instance, a fiscal expansion in one country will boost the exports of neighboring countries, and a cut in the domestic interest rate may generate positive or negative externalities on other countries through the reaction of capital flows (see Chapter 7).

It would be wrong, however, to assume that the global economy has become fully integrated. Research has consistently pointed out the prevalence of a *border effect*: labor markets, but also product and capital markets, are much less integrated across countries than within countries. This effect was first documented for trade between the United States and Canada, where, despite international integration through the North American Free Trade Area (NAFTA), McCallum (1995) found that trade between a pair of Canadian provinces was typically 22 times larger than trade between a similar Canadian province and a neighboring US state. While qualifying these early findings, more recent work[6] still points to a significant border effect. Even in the EU, where all internal tariffs have been eliminated and all administrative obstacles to trade have been made illegal, two cities or regions trade 10 times more with each other when they belong to the same country than when they belong to different countries (Mayer and Zignago, 2005). The upshot is that eliminating all tariff and regulatory barriers to trade does not suffice to make trade seamless because informational and legal barriers create invisible but powerful obstacles (Chaney, 2014).

Capital flows are also subject to a strong *home bias*: the share of domestic assets in the portfolio of a given country is typically much higher than the share of these assets in the world stock of the corresponding class of assets. For instance, Coeurdacier and Rey (2013) calculated that, in 2008, 77% of the US equity portfolio was invested in domestic equity, whereas US equities represented only 33% of world equity capitalization. Interestingly, the home bias was smaller for individual euro area countries but higher in Australia, Japan, Canada, and emerging countries. Although it has declined since the late 1980s, the home bias remains a pervasive phenomenon.

Conversely, traditional measures of trade and capital openness may not fully reflect *interconnectedness*. For instance, some countries like Belgium, Malaysia, or Singapore display very high trade openness ratios (sometimes exceeding 100%) because trade is recorded on a gross basis whereas GDP is a sum of values added (hence intermediate consumptions are canceled out): import–export activities inflate the numerator but not the denominator. According to OECD-World Trade Organization (WTO) estimates[7] for 2011, 41% of the gross value of exports of Malaysia are made of imported value added (which is incorporated in the exported products). Hence, the share of exports to GDP in terms of value added in 2011 is $0.59 \times 85\% = 50\%$, instead of 85% according to the standard measure.

Likewise, the standard measure of financial openness may not accurately reflect the degree of interconnectedness. For instance, the role of the US dollar as a major funding currency for banks outside the United States induces a global credit cycle that is closely linked to US monetary policy (see Rey, 2013, and the discussion in Chapter 7). To the extent that part of the funding in dollars does not involve inflows from the United States (they may come from other financial centers), the traditional measure of financial openness will underestimate the impact of the United States on global finance. The static measure of financial openness also misses the vulnerability created by financial openness. For instance, a country may suffer a sudden reversal of capital inflows just because another country is experiencing a financial crisis that leads international investors to revise their risk aversion upward.

Finally, interdependence may arise even without any trade, capital, or labor exchange across countries. The most convincing example is climate change: even a completely closed economy contributes to greenhouse gas emissions. Another example is the exchange of ideas that has been stimulated by the Internet without necessarily taking the form of patent trade or talent mobility.

Interdependence calls for cooperation across countries for two reasons. The first is the provision of what has come to be called *global public goods*. The second is the optimization of policy outcomes when a country's decision significantly affects its neighbors or trade and financial partners.

3.1.2 Global public goods

The preservation of climate and biodiversity, but also international financial stability, are nowadays regarded as global public goods—a modern extension of the concept of public good that is standard in the economic analysis of consumption.

To understand what a *public good* is, it is useful to start from two important possible properties of the goods and services offered for consumption: *excludability* and *rivalry*. Excludability means that consumption may be reserved to some individuals or households. Examples include standard private consumption items such as clothing, food, and healthcare, but not clean air, free-to-air TV programs, security, and financial stability (those goods and services are deemed nonexcludable). Rivalry means that one's consumption reduces the availability of the good for others, which is true for fish in a lake but not for public lighting or street safety (those goods are deemed nonrival). A *public good* is a good (or a service) whose consumption is both nonexcludable and nonrival.

The two properties of excludability and rivalry are independent, which implies that all four cases can be found (Table 3.1). Interestingly, goods and services can change category over time: the rise of the sharing economy can be

Table 3.1
Excludability, rivalry, and the definition of public goods

	Excludable	Nonexcludable
Rival	Private good *E.g.: shoes*	Common good *E.g.: a lake's fish resources*
Nonrival	Club good *E.g.: patentable inventions*	Public good *E.g.: street lightening, clean air*

regarded as a move toward less excludable consumption patterns for housing and durable goods such as cars; reciprocally, the rise of pay-per-view channels at the expense of free-to-air TV is a move toward excludability.

The social value of the consumption of a pure private good equals its private value (nobody but I cares about the comfort of my shoes).[8] But this ceases being true for nonrival goods because their supply also creates value for other people without reducing its value for me, which means that the incentive to produce them may be insufficient to ensure adequate supply. If I clean the street in front of my house, this has value for my neighbors, too, and I am therefore tempted to wait until they do so. Excludability can be a solution to the problem (through patenting an invention, one can acquire property rights and can charge others for the use of the invention[9]), but not all goods are excludable. For the *public goods* that are neither rival nor excludable, there is no easy way to ensure adequate supply. Absent government intervention or other institutional arrangements, theory suggests that their production will be suboptimal.[10]

This approach is used to frame the discussion on global governance. Climate preservation, the sustainable management of depletable natural resources, and financial stability, to name but a few, are thus frequently deemed *global public goods.*

In practice, international cooperation in this field involves three major difficulties: First, how to agree on what constitutes an international public good? Second, what are the appropriate instruments or rules to produce it? This is a matter of efficiency. And third, from an equity standpoint, who should contribute to financing it?

Global warming is a case in point where there have been disagreements at all three levels. There is strong scientific evidence that global warming is a fact and that it can be traced back to anthropogenous carbon dioxide emissions, but this evidence is still being disputed, including within the US administration of President Trump. As regards instruments, most economists advocate introducing a global carbon price either through a tax or through a global market for emission permits (see, for example, Gollier and Tirole, 2016) but many governments reject it out of hand as an attack on national sovereignty; others, like the United States, tend to put more emphasis than Europeans on research into new energy sources, clean technologies, and carbon sequestration and storage, even without the driving force of price signals; finally, developing and emerging countries argue that they have not yet significantly contributed to the *stock* of greenhouse gases (which is true, despite the fact that they contribute significantly to the *flow*—as an example, China's emissions have exceeded those of the United States since 2007) and should therefore not be asked to curb their emissions at their current stage of economic development (Bhagwati, 2010). The global agreement reached in Paris in December 2015—later repudiated by US President Trump—indicated that the first obstacle could be overcome and that progress had been made toward overcoming the other two. But there remain serious roadblocks to effective collective action.

Similar issues arise for international development. Failure to address mass poverty in poor countries would in the end reduce the welfare of citizens all around the world, either for reasons of altruism or because underdevelopment penalizes global prosperity and fuels terrorism, crime, the spread of diseases, and mass migration. For this reason, development can be regarded as a global public good. But *overseas development assistance* (ODA) also has a bilateral dimension between donors and receivers.

International cooperation in the production of global public goods is designed and enforced through various means. A particularly effective way is to agree once and for all on common rules and enforce them through a common mechanism. International trade provides an example of such *rules-based coordination* (increasingly questioned by the US administration under President Trump): all the 164 members of the WTO have subscribed to about 60 multilateral agreements and agree to abide by the WTO settlements in case of bilateral disputes.

A less demanding form of cooperation relies on soft, rather than hard law. The 2015 Paris agreement on climate change relies on voluntary pledges by participating countries. These commitments are neither sufficient (full implementation would not suffice to contain the rise in temperature below 2°C) nor binding (there is no enforcement mechanism). However, the agreement includes a review clause, and the hope of its promoters is that it climate action coordination will gradually gain ambition and force.

The coordination of bank supervisors proceeds through common rules (the so-called Basel ratios covering capital and liquidity requirements), yet these guidelines have no legal value until they are translated into national legislation (see Chapter 6). Standards and codes issued by the International Monetary Fund (IMF) and the World Bank, or the OECD's *base erosion and profit shifting (*BEPS) guidelines on taxation, work in the same way. In all these cases, observance essentially relies on transparency and the resulting pressure of peers, private interests, and public opinion.

Likewise, transparency has been used as a way to produce a specific global public good, namely, the ability of governments to tax mobile bases. The BEPS initiative of the OECD includes, for instance, country-by-country reporting requirements for multinational firms. The BEPS guidelines are not binding, but they were endorsed by the G20 in February 2016.

What this description suggests is that there is no single template for global governance, but rather a combination of various approaches and institutional set-ups.

3.1.3 International spillovers

The second motive for international policy coordination arises from cross-border *spillovers* of economic policy. Such bilateral or regional spillovers result from economic interdependence. Three examples provide illustrations:

- In September 2008, the decision by the Irish government to raise the threshold for bank deposits guarantee from €20,000 to €100,000 was quickly followed by European partner countries because they feared that keeping their own guarantees at lower levels would lead depositors to move their accounts to Ireland;
- In Summer 2015, the decision by Germany to open its doors to refugees from the Middle East had major consequences for neighboring Austria since the inflow of people largely came through its territory;
- In December 2015, the decision by the US Federal Reserve to increase the policy rate (and even before, the anticipation of it) caused net capital outflows from emerging and developing countries and the depreciation of fragile currencies (see Chapter 5).

These three cases illustrate that decisions can seriously affect partner countries. Yet spillover effects are normally not taken into account by decision-makers accountable to national constituencies unless formal or informal coordination leads them to take another course.

The pitfalls of such decisions and the essentials of coordination are well-captured by the canonical "prisoner's dilemma" example in which uncoordinated decisions taken by two prisoners can leave each of them worse off (box 3.1). Although hypothetical, it illustrates a game structure that can result from many patterns of interdependence.

There are many examples of interdependence giving rise to international coordination problems. Policy-relevant cases can be found in fields as diverse as public health, energy security, environmental protection, financial stability, and taxation, to name just a few. They are also pervasive in the macroeconomic policy field, where repeated attempts have been made at tackling them through international dialogue (within the G7 and the G20) and institutionalized cooperation, either at multilateral levels (through the IMF) or at regional levels (through, for example, the Eurogroup of Eurozone finance ministers or the Asean+3 Macroeconomic Research Office [AMRO] in East Asia).[11]

Box 3.1 The "Prisoner's Dilemma" and the Shortcomings of Independent Policymaking

The *prisoner's dilemma* was first expounded by the Rand Corporation in 1950 (Tucker, 1950/1980).

After a crime is committed, two suspects are jailed, awaiting judgment. Neither one acknowledges his own culpability. Absent compelling evidence, the judge establishes the following rule: if either one of the two suspects claims his innocence and denounces the other one, he or she will be released and the other suspect will be condemned to a 10-year sentence; if the two suspects accuse each other, they will be considered jointly guilty and will be condemned, but their willingness to cooperate with the judge will be rewarded and they will be condemned to 5 years only; finally, if both of them continue to assert their innocence and do not accuse each other, they will both spend 1 year in prison.

Each prisoner's fate thus depends on his or her own decision as well as on his or her fellow suspect's decision, which gives the problem the structure of a game. The square 2 × 2 matrix of table B3.1 gives the payoffs associated with the two prisoners' decisions in the form of (x,y) where x is the reward to prisoner 1 and y the reward to prisoner 2.

Table B3.1
The prisoner's dilemma decision matrix

	Prisoner 2	
Prisoner 1	Betrayal of other	Cooperation with other
Betrayal of other	(−5, −5)	(0, −10)
Cooperation with other	(−10, 0)	(−1, −1)

To find the optimal strategy for a given prisoner, say 1, the outcome of either decision must be examined depending on the other prisoner's decision. If prisoner 2 betrays prisoner 1 (first column), prisoner 1 will also find it beneficial to betray (because –5 > –10). If prisoner 2 cooperates (second column), prisoner 1 will still find it beneficial to betray (because 0 > –1). So it is individually preferable to denounce the other prisoner. Both prisoners therefore get a 5-year sentence. This is called the *noncooperative equilibrium*, or *Nash equilibrium* (after John Nash, a game theoretician who was awarded the Nobel prize in 1994).

This equilibrium is not optimal: if the two prisoners were able to talk to each other and reach a deal, they would both be better off cooperating and remaining silent, in which case each of them would be sentenced to 1 year only (*cooperative equilibrium*).

This model shows that, in the presence of interdependence, rational decentralized decision-making may not be optimal. It also shows that whereas cooperation is beneficial, it can be difficult to sustain because, once one of the players is convinced that the other will cooperate, he or she may have an incentive to betray. The cooperative equilibrium is unstable, and the noncooperative equilibrium is stable.

Because of its simplicity, this model has been widely used as a reference for analyzing international policy coordination. However, it does not imply that formal cooperation is always necessary. It can be shown (for example, Axelrod, 1984) that such a game leads to a stable cooperative solution when it is played repeatedly over an infinite horizon with the simple retaliation rule that if one of the players betrays, the other responds by not cooperating in the following round ("tit-for-tat" strategy).

More formally, the gain from coordination can be illustrated as follows. There are two symmetric countries,[26] home and foreign (the latter being denoted with an asterisk). As a consequence of interdependence, policy outcomes Y and Y^* not only depend on national policy decisions x and x^* but also on the neighbor's decisions. Hence,

$$Y = H(x, x^*) \quad \text{and} \quad Y^* = H^*(x^*, x) \qquad \text{(B3.1.1)}$$

where Y, Y^* are n-dimensional vectors and x, x^* are scalars (but having more than one policy instrument per country would not affect the result). In each country, the policymaker aims at maximizing a social welfare function $U(Y)$. Because of Equation (B3.1.1), $U(Y)$ can also be written $V(x, x^*)$. When acting in isolation, the national policymaker maximizes V, taking x^* as given. Thus, we have:

$$\max_x V(x, x^*) \quad \text{and} \quad \max_{x^*} V^*(x^*, x) \qquad \text{(B3.1.2)}$$

The first-order conditions give:

$$\frac{\partial V(x, x^*)}{\partial x} = 0 \quad \text{and} \quad \frac{\partial V^*(x^*, x)}{\partial x^*} = 0 \qquad \text{(B3.1.3)}$$

This implies that each country's optimal policy depends on the policy of the neighbor. Formally, solving Equations (B3.1.3) yields two *reaction functions*, each of which represents the optimal reaction of one country to the policy followed by the other one:

$$x = F(x^*) \quad \text{and} \quad x^* = F^*(x) \qquad \text{(B3.1.4)}$$

the intersection of which gives the noncooperative Nash equilibrium. For this equilibrium to be a Pareto optimum, it would have to be a solution to the following equation:

$$\max_{x^*} V^*\left(x^*, x\right) \quad \text{subject to} \, V^*\left(x^*, x\right) \geq V_0^* \qquad \text{(B3.1.5)}$$

where V_0^* corresponds to a given level of utility for the foreign country. The corresponding Lagrangian is:

$$L = V\left(x, x^*\right) + \lambda\left[V^*\left(x^*, x\right) - V_0^*\right] \qquad \text{(B3.1.6)}$$

whose maximization implies:

$$\frac{\partial V}{\partial x} = \lambda \frac{\partial V^*}{\partial x} \quad \text{and} \quad \frac{\partial V}{\partial x^*} = -\lambda \frac{\partial V^*}{\partial x^*} \qquad \text{(B3.1.7)}$$

This condition, which differs from Equation (B3.1.3), in fact corresponds to the maximization, not of V, but of $V + \lambda V^*$. In other words, independent policymaking does not yield an optimal result.

Economic history records several cases of significant spillover effects of monetary and exchange rate policies. In the 1930s, restrictive fiscal and monetary policies in several countries reinforced each other and made the crisis even more severe. A similar coordination failure occurred in the euro area during 2010–2012, when several Member States reduced their fiscal deficits simultaneously, which had negative effect on GDP across the euro area, hence making fiscal adjustments partly ineffective.

Coordination failures also affect exchange rate policies. During the 2010s, the United States was accused by emerging countries such as Brazil of leading a "currency war" through very expansionary monetary policies that tended to weaken the dollar (see Chapter 7).

Two-country models illustrate the economics of policy coordination. A bare-bones example is that of two countries in a fixed exchange rate regime (or a monetary union) that are hit by a common shock and attempt to escape its adverse consequences on their external balance by running a restrictive fiscal policy (box 3.2). As the shock is a common one and both countries react in the same way, this attempt will inevitably prove futile. The only effect of running a more restrictive policy will be to lower output, not to improve the external balance. As in the prisoners' dilemma, both countries lose from pursuing narrow national interest.

Box 3.2 A Bare-Bones Coordination Model

One of the simplest models of coordination is a two-country, symmetric model with an exogenous rest-of-the-world under fixed exchange rates. Countries each have one single instrument at their disposal, namely fiscal policy. Asterisked variables represent the foreign country, nonasterisked ones the home country. Fiscal expansion in each country has an effect on its neighbor so that, if y represents production (measured as the gap between actual production and full employment) and g the fiscal instrument:

$$Y = \phi g + \psi g^* - u \text{ and } Y^* = \phi g^* + \psi g - u \qquad \text{(B3.2.1)}$$

where ϕ, $\psi > 0$, and u represents a symmetric external shock. Let us suppose that both governments care about the external balance b, which is given by:

$$b = \rho\left(g^* - g\right) - u \text{ and } b^* = \rho\left(g - g^*\right) - u \qquad \text{(B3.2.2)}$$

where $\rho > 0$ depends on the demand elasticity of exports and imports. If confronted by a drop in global demand ($u > 0$), each country sees its income and its external balance deteriorate. For this reason, it would wish its partner to embark on a fiscal expansion that would boost its exports. Failing this, it will choose its own fiscal policy in order to minimize a loss function: $L = \omega y^2 + b^2$ (and symmetrically $L^* = \omega^* y^{*2} + b^{*2}$), where ω, $\omega^* > 0$ represent the home and foreign weights of income relative to the external balance in the loss function.

When countries act independently, the optimum policy for the home country is given by:

$$g = \frac{\left(\rho - \omega\phi\psi\right)g^*\left(\omega\phi - \rho\right)u}{\omega\phi^2 + \rho^2} \qquad \text{(B3.2.3)}$$

A symmetrical result holds for g^*.

The reaction of each country to the exogenous fall in external demand ($u > 0$) depends on the relative weights of the internal and external objectives in its loss function (if $\omega < \rho/\phi$, the government reacts to the shock by a fiscal contraction to restore external balance). But this reaction depends on the policy conducted by the other country: there is a *reaction function* that gives each country's optimal policy choice as a function of the other's.

The model being fully symmetrical, both countries will conduct the same policy, $g = g^*$ and therefore, at the Nash equilibrium:

$$g = g^* = \frac{\omega\phi - \rho}{\omega\phi\left(\phi + \psi\right)} \qquad \text{(B3.2.4)}$$

$$y = y^* = -\frac{\rho u}{\omega\phi} \qquad \text{(B3.2.5)}$$

$$b = -u \qquad \text{(B3.2.6)}$$

$$L = \left(1 + \frac{\rho^2}{\omega\phi^2}\right)u^2 \qquad \text{(B3.2.7)}$$

When both countries cooperate by jointly minimizing the sum of the two loss functions, they recognize that trying to rely on restrictive fiscal policy to cushion the impact of the external shock on their external balance is useless. The optimal policy thus is:

$$g = g^* = 0, y = y^* = 0 \text{ and the loss is } L = L^* = (1+\omega)u^2 \qquad \text{(B.3.2.8)}$$

Cooperation makes each government better off if $\rho > \omega\phi$ (meaning that the impact of fiscal policy on the external balance is large enough). In this case, lack of coordination leads to excessively restrictive fiscal policies that reduce output without improving the external balance.

The reasoning is of wider relevance than the model. *Mutatis mutandis*, it remains valid in the case of negative fiscal externalities (which can arise in a monetary union) or of positive and negative monetary externalities (under floating exchange rates), as well as for structural, financial, or tax policies. We come back to it in the thematic chapters that follow.

3.1.4 The shortcomings of international coordination

The prisoners' dilemma may suggest that there is an overwhelming case for coordination. There are, however, strong practical arguments against coordinating national policies, at least in the absence of common institutions able to manage interdependence. Some authors have even argued that simple theories are misleading and that coordination could actually prove harmful.

First, policy spillovers may not always be significant. For instance, it is generally considered that, in normal times, a fiscal expansion by a member of a monetary union will have an ambiguous impact on other member states due to the contradictory effects of positive effects on their exports and negative effects on their investment (through higher interest rates). When monetary policy is constrained, however, or when several countries pursue strong fiscal adjustment at the same time, fiscal spillovers are no longer ambiguous and they may in fact be large (see Chapter 4). This suggests that coordination may be needed in some, though not all circumstances.

Second, governments and other national policy institutions are accountable to their citizens only. It is therefore very hard for them to depart from policy choices dictated by the national interest. US monetary policy may impact growth and inflation in other countries, but the Federal Reserve Act sets objectives for the US economy only. It is true that the game theoretical approach to policy coordination suggests that, as the cooperative equilibrium is superior to the Nash equilibrium, all countries in the end benefit from it.

But many policy decisions are taken assuming that policies in the rest of the world are given.

Third, even if there is agreement to move jointly, governments or other policy players can cheat and refrain from implementing agreed policies. Unilateral departure from a cooperative equilibrium—assuming the partner country sticks to the agreed stance—generally yields first-order gains and is therefore hard to avoid. This is an especially relevant concern when there is imperfect information about the other players' policies. In spite of an extensive monitoring apparatus, European soft coordination processes offer numerous examples of fiscal or reform commitments that are not followed by actual and effective policy decisions.

Fourth, size matters. Spillovers from US policy onto smaller emerging economies may be big, but the opposite does not apply. This is true also of Germany and smaller Eurozone members. In such a context, the smaller countries want the larger one to take their fate into account but cannot commit to reciprocate.

Fifth, assumptions as regards economic mechanisms differ—governments can work on the basis of significantly different models. For example, they may differ from each other about the expected impact of monetary and fiscal policies: one government may regard as contractionary the very same policy that another government considers expansionary. Again, Europe provides a case in point as attitudes toward the impact of fiscal deficits and debts vary. Uncertainty regarding the true model of the economy inevitably complicates coordination. Furthermore, such disagreements can also render it counterproductive (Frankel and Rockett, 1988).[12]

Sixth, coordination can be regarded as a form of collusion that prevents the emergence of adequate policies through a process of policy competition. Martin Feldstein (1988) argued early on that coordinating inadequate economic policies would lead to a result inferior to what could be achieved through noncoordinated but better individual policies. Kenneth Rogoff (1984) has given a formal presentation of this argument in a setting where coordination weakens the commitment of central banks to noninflationary policies.

Seventh and not least, coordination among a subset of players (for example, a few countries or governments only, but not the central banks) can worsen rather than improve the policy outcome (this is a special case of the second-best argument discussed in Chapter 1). For example, in a monetary union, coordination among budgetary authorities that does not involve the central bank can actually result in an inferior performance.

It is such arguments that led two prominent international economic scholars, Maurice Obstfeld and Kenneth Rogoff, to conclude in 2002 that "lack of coordination may not always be a big problem, even in a world with significant economic integration. . . . Continued improvements of monetary policy institutions at the domestic level, coupled with the further broadening of world capital markets, may render [partial coordination] schemes superfluous or even counterproductive" (Obstfeld and Rogoff, 2002, p. 528).

Empirical studies have been conducted to evaluate the concrete benefits from economic policy coordination. The first and still most quoted one was that of Oudiz and Sachs (1984), where the authors evaluated governments' objective functions on the basis of observed past behavior and concluded that, for the major countries, the gains from coordination were of the order of magnitude of half a percentage point of GDP. This was hardly enough to offset the implied limitations to national decision-making.

These results were arguably computed at a time when global trade and financial interdependence was much less intense than it is today. Beyond the mere increase in trade and financial openness discussed in Section 3.1, trade and financial interdependence must increasingly be looked at as taking place within regional and global networks where some countries emerge as global nodes, whereas others play the role of regional gatekeepers (IMF, 2012). This type of representation highlights the global character and asymmetry of international financial interdependence. The highly asymmetric character of global interdependence was especially apparent in 2008 and again in 2011, when US and European financial markets were affected by a severe dry-up of liquidity. On this occasion the Federal Reserve, backed by the US Treasury, extended dollar swap lines to selected partner central banks to make them able to supply dollar liquidity to their own banks (see Chapter 6). More generally, international cooperation is often considered a necessity in case of an acute crisis, whereas in normal times only regular exchanges of information is deemed necessary. However, risks tend to accumulate when the economy is booming, which calls for coordinating supervision in good times.

At global level, systematic coordination of macroeconomic policies has never lasted long, though nonrecurring initiatives have taken place. Historical episodes include the coordinated reflation engineered at the Bonn Summit in 1978, the Plaza Agreement to amplify the depreciation of the dollar in October 1985, and the January 1987 Louvre agreements to stabilize exchange rates. More recently, the G20[13] engineered in 2008–2009 a coordinated stimulus that, for the first time, involved emerging as well as advanced countries and contributed to ward off the risk of an uncontrolled depression. Further initiatives followed with the aim of monitoring and coordinating the pace of monetary and fiscal normalization, but with significantly less success.

These examples do not provide an unambiguous demonstration of the benefits from coordination. The coordinated reflation carried out by Germany and Japan at the time of the 1978 Bonn Summit led to a resumption of inflation and to a current account deterioration in Germany, thus feeding in that country a lasting mistrust of coordination. The 2009 stimulus was more successful (also because the context was deflationary) but, here again, disputes quickly emerged as regards the pace of normalization.

Coordination has been markedly more successful at the technical level, especially among central banks. Reactions to crisis episodes, be it the October 1987 stock market crash, 9/11, the liquidity crisis of August–December 2007, or the shock that followed the bankruptcy of Lehman Brothers in Autumn 2008 were tightly and successfully coordinated between US and European monetary authorities.

3.1.5 Global institutions and governance

The institutional architecture of international coordination displays a high degree of stability. Even before the war ended, two global institutions—the IMF and the World Bank—were created to accompany the reopening of goods markets, provide financial assistance in cases of balance of payment difficulties, and direct capital flows toward reconstruction and development. They still dominate the landscape. Their trade counterpart, the WTO, was created only in 1995, but the secretariat of the General Agreement on Tariffs and Trade (GATT) had been in existence since 1948.[14] The creation of the WTO notably added a dispute settlement body that substantially strengthened the GATT's architecture for addressing disputes between member countries. Other major institutions include the ILO that was created in 1919 and has a standard-setting as well as a consultation role, but its effectiveness is much more limited.; and the OECD, which, in 1961, succeeded the Organization for European Economic Cooperation (OEEC), formed in 1947 to administer American aid to Europe under the Marshall Plan. Sectoral organizations also exist, for example, for health, air transport, telecoms, and (albeit in a fragmented way) the environment.

Because of the global reach of major marketplaces and banks, financial regulation and supervision have been fertile grounds for coordination. The Bank for International Settlements (BIS) was established in 1930 in the context of negotiations over the settlement of war reparations, and it has become the global forum for central banks. Banking regulation is the remit of the *Basel Committee for Banking Supervision*, a specialized BIS committee that has been the workhouse for establishing standardized minimum capital ratios. The latest addition to the landscape, the Financial Stability Board (FSB), is a child of the 2008–2009 financial crisis. It helps setting international rules for financial markets and financial institutions (see Chapter 6).

Global governance, which has gradually emerged as a widely used concept, is a substitute for a world or global government that does not exist. It is organized through the preceding specialized institutions, complemented with two informal subgroups of countries: the Group of Seven (G7) created in 1975,[15] and the Group of Twenty (G20), born in 1999 in the aftermath of the emerging market crises.[16] After the global economic and financial crisis that started in 2007, the G20 was invited to take an increasing role in strengthening international cooperation (the communiqué of the September 2009 Pittsburgh Summit recognized it as the "premier forum" for international economic cooperation). However, its effectiveness quickly declined.

Governance by international institutions borrows from the independent authority model (see Chapter 2): each of them intervenes in a specific area, delimited on the basis of an explicit mandate (cf. table 3.2). Their legitimacy derives less from the process leading to decisions than from their specialization and from their ability to fulfill their mandate (in other words, it rests more on output legitimacy than on process legitimacy).

This system of governance is probably the only one possible since there is no global political authority that has legitimacy to make and enforce choices: in the terms of Chapter 1, there can be no such thing as a world social welfare function in the absence of world representation. The only *legitimate* deliberative body at the world level is the United Nations General Assembly, but the large number and the very heterogeneous sizes of its member states make it quite ineffective for addressing global economic issues. With the unanimous adoption in September 2015 of the 17 Sustainable Development Goals in the aftermath of the earlier 2000-2015 Millennium Development Goals, the United Nations nonetheless emerged as a body capable to set global common objectives and monitor their implementation through its various agencies.

The stability of global institutions should not hide the challenges they are facing. An important one is the rise of regionalism, most apparent in the trade field where multilateral negotiations have stalled while regional agreements have ballooned. Regionalism also regards financial cooperation. Beyond the European Union, which is by far the most advanced regional agreement, a noteworthy development has been the rise of monetary and financial cooperation in Asia. A significant milestone occurred in 2015, with the creation at the initiative of China of the Asian Infrastructure Investment Bank (AIIB), a regional development bank based in Beijing.

Beyond the fact that the policy conducted by a given international organization is a matter for debate, the de facto hierarchy of the existing international institutions can also be criticized for not reflecting the perceived priority of international problems. The power of the IMF and the World Bank and the fact that WTO panels contribute to making international trade law when settling disputes between member states are signs of organizational effectiveness. However, these very strengths also underline the relative inefficiency of the world governance system as regards environment, public health, labor, taxation, and data and they remain dependent on the continuing political commitment of member states.

3.2 Federations and International Unions

Close to 30 countries in the world, representing 40% of the world population, are officially classified as *federations* (or *confederations*) where a large proportion of policy decisions are taken at the subnational level.[17] These are generally large countries such as Brazil, Australia, Germany, India, and the

Table 3.2
Scope, rules, and means of the major international organizations

Sector (institution, creation)	Voting rules	Institutional strength	Legal means	Financial strength
Trade (GATT, 1947 + WTO, 1995)	One country, one vote, simple or qualified majority for the application of the treaties, in practice consensus	Weak, except for dispute settlement	Arbitration and dispute settlement (through the Dispute Settlement Body)	Irrelevant
International monetary cooperation (IMF, 1945)	Constituencies with weighted voting rights, simple or qualified majority; in practice consensus	Strong institutional coherence plus strong G7/G20 support	Limited power to set standards, indirect power on countries under IMF assistance	Major vis-à-vis countries requesting assistance, nil vis-à-vis surplus countries
Development finance (World Bank, 1945)	Like the IMF, with greater role for developing countries	Same as IMF	Almost absent	Declining before the 2007–09 crisis as countries had gained access to financial markets, significantly expanding in the aftermath of the crisis
Central banking cooperation (BIS, 1930)	Weighted voting rights	Via the central banks	Indirect	Indirect
Financial stability (FSB, 2009)	Decision by consensus	Not legally binding, but influential	No	No
Labor (ILO, 1919)	Parity between governments, employers and employees. General Assembly: one country, one vote Board: permanent seats for large countries	Weak	Weak (implementation of agreed standards left to the goodwill of member states)	Weak

Source: Authors.

United States, but smaller ones like Belgium and Switzerland are even more decentralized. The most recent federation is that of Nepal, with the entry into force of its new constitution in January 2018.

Even in unitary states, some decisions are decentralized at the subnational level. Overall, in the OECD, about 30% of total government spending takes place at regional or local levels, whereas central governments account for about 50% (the rest being social security).[18] The degree of decentralization varies greatly from country to country (see Chapter 4).

The transfer of powers to subnational entities has progressed significantly since the 1980s, even in unitary states such as the United Kingdom (with devolution to Scotland of legislative and executive competences in 1998) and France (through small steps, but in an unambiguous direction since the early 1980s).

Federalism is at work at the supranational level also. Although the EU budget is limited to about 1% of GDP, EU Member States are engaged in what specialists call *intergovernmental federalism* and what the former President of the European Commission Jacques Delors called a "federation of Nation States." In the EU, some economic policy competencies, such as trade policy, competition policy, or, for euro area members, monetary policy, have been devolved to the EU. Similar, although less ambitious, attempts at building international unions have been launched in several regions of the world.

For a large proportion of the world population, the reality is therefore one of multilevel government. In such a context, debates about the allocation of competences are often more heated than those over substance. Proponents and opponents of a European tax or social or fiscal policy are involved in constant disputes. Controversies between Catalonia and the Spanish State or between Quebec and the Canadian federation are, or have been, harsh. Last, but not least, Brexit—the decision by Britain to leave the EU—is raising thorny disputes about the divorce settlement and the terms of a possible future partnership.

The *economic theory of federalism* helps clarify these discussions and proposes criteria for the distribution of policy competences within a federation or an international union.

3.2.1 The economics of federations and international unions

The theory of *fiscal federalism* is limited neither to the study of federations—it deals in general with the "vertical" distribution of competencies between administrative and political entities—nor to fiscal matters— all policies are in fact concerned. It aims first at determining the level at which it is relevant to make particular decisions.

The basic rule is *fiscal equivalence* (Olson, 1969), which establishes that the administrative and financing organization of a public policy should coincide with its geographical impact area. The idea goes back in fact to Adam Smith, for whom:

> Those local or provincial expenses of which the benefit is local or provincial (what is laid out, for example, upon the police of a particular town or district) ought to be defrayed by a local or provincial revenue, and ought to be no burden upon the general revenue of the society. It is unjust that the whole society should contribute toward an expense of which the benefit is confined to a part of the society. (A. Smith, 1776, book 5, chapt. 1, conclusion)

In more modern terms, the distribution of competences should be tailored to address positive *externalities* deriving from one locality providing a good (such as an entertainment infrastructure) that also benefits other localities. The same applies to what could be dubbed "internalities"; that is, cases where the impact of a policy is concentrated on a smaller area than that supporting its administration and financing (for instance, the national financing of local transportation systems).

This matching rule between those who pay and those who benefit from public spending does not by itself involve either a centralization or a decentralization bias. It implies that excessive centralization is as ineffective as excessive decentralization and justifies the coexistence of several (possibly overlapping) levels of government in order to adapt the management of the policies to the spatial distribution of their effects. It implies, for example, that river pollution should be addressed by all localities bordering that river, whatever their country, and only by them. This rule is far from being respected in practice: very often, local governments raise taxes to finance infrastructure or services (sport facilities, for example) that benefit residents of neighboring localities. By the same token, expenditures at the national level may benefit the residents of neighboring countries: for example, the French road transport infrastructure benefits Northern European citizens traveling to Southern European beaches.

The design of a fiscal system that preserves the variety of preferences while internalizing externalities raises complex issues. In Switzerland, each level of government has specific competences and sets expenditures and tax levels independently. Cantons whose citizens use the infrastructure of neighboring cities make horizontal payments to compensate them. Furthermore, solidarity transfers take place both within and across cantons. The limit of such an approach is the resulting complexity. However, it sets an important principle.

Regarding the choice between centralization and decentralization, economic motives are only part of the decision criteria. Historically, centralization has often been used to unify countries composed of culturally diverse entities, without regard for the heterogeneity of preferences. But they nevertheless provide important indications. The Oates (1972) decentralization theorem claims that, in the absence of externalities and of economies of scale, decentralization is always preferable. This is because different localities will weigh differently public goods against private ones in their consumption baskets. Hence, local decision will perform better in meeting taxpayers' preferences. To the extent that the public good provided in one locality has no impact on welfare in neighboring ones (no externalities) and that the public good is not provided more efficiently at a centralized level (no economies of scale), this implies that provision at the most decentralized level is preferable.

For certain goods centralization involves gains, either because the benefit from their production cannot be restricted to the residents of one particular country or because it involves increasing returns. This is, for example, the case for defense, research, and environmental policies.

When there are both heterogeneous preferences and externalities across jurisdictions, the allocation of competences involves a trade-off, and the optimal level of decision depends on both the size of the externality and the dissimilarity of preferences. This trade-off is at the core of the theory of international unions formalized by Alesina, Angeloni, and Etro (2005). Their model (box 3.3)

Box 3.3 A Theory of International Unions: The Model of Alesina, Angeloni, and Etro

Alesina, Angeloni, and Etro (2005) formalize the creation of international unions as a response to a trade-off between preference heterogeneity and positive externalities.

A union is made of N countries assumed to be similar in size, which may or may not liaise to cooperate in the provision of a nonrival, but excludable *club good* that benefits all countries involved in producing it jointly (see table 3.1). Each country can also provide it independently, but then it does not benefit from positive externalities deriving from cooperation. Defense or a common energy infrastructure are examples of such club goods.

The cost of participating in the union comes from the fact that the N countries have different relative preferences: some prefer a lower quantity of the club good and a higher disposable income for private consumption. However, while taking part in a union, they opt for a collective choice that will be determined by a vote. They therefore face a trade-off which determines their participation in the union.

The utility function of the representative agent in a "standalone" country i ($i = 1$ to N) is specified as:

$$U_i = Y_i - G_i + \alpha_i H(G_i) \qquad \text{(B3.3.1)}$$

For a country taking part in the union, it is:

$$U_i = Y_i - G_i + \alpha_i H\left(G_i + \beta \sum_{j \neq i} G_j\right) \qquad \text{(B3.3.2)}$$

where Y_i is income in country i; G_i the level of club good provision by country i, financed by taxation so that $Y_i - G_i$ is the disposable income for private consumption; and ΣGj is the club good provision by all other countries of the union. α_i measures for each country i the relative preference for consuming the public good rather than the private one. β (which lies between 0 and 1) measures the externality of other members of the union providing the same club good, and H is an increasing and concave function ($H' > 0$, $H'' < 0$), meaning that more club good provides higher utility to the representative agent, but with a decreasing marginal utility.

When each country chooses its level of production of the club good independently, it neglects the positive externality that this production could have on its partners and therefore chooses a production level below the optimum level that a "social planner" in control of all the G_i would select. This is a typical case of coordination failure. When the N countries take part in the economic union, the level of club good provision is decided by a simple majority. It therefore corresponds to the preferences of the median country (for which the preference α_m lies in the middle of the distribution). The optimal provision of club good for each member of the union then is $\widetilde{G_N}$ such as:

$$\alpha_m H'\left(\widetilde{G_N}\right) = \frac{1}{1+\beta(N-1)} \qquad \text{(B3.3.3)}$$

Since H' is a decreasing function (H is concave), the optimal provision of club good is an increasing function of:

- the number of members N,
- the strength of the externality β, and
- the preference α_m of the median country for the public good.

This is a standard application of the median voter model (box 2.11 in Chapter 2): what matters is not the average preference but the preference of the voter who "makes" the decision. Obviously, this result depends on the voting procedure (simple majority, qualified majority, unanimity). In the event of unanimity (required in the EU for amendments to the treaty and for budgetary decisions), it is the preference of the country least favorable to the club good which determines the decision.

Let us now suppose that the union is already made up of countries 1 to M ($M < N$) with contiguous preferences, ranked so that (without loss of generality) for $1 \leq \ldots k \ldots \leq M$, $\alpha_1 \leq \ldots \alpha_k \ \ldots \ \leq \alpha_M$, and for $j > M$, $\alpha_j \notin [\alpha_1, \alpha_M]$). Upon entering the union, a new member will benefit from the external effects from which it was excluded before. For those that are already members of the union, the arrival of a new member will also cause a positive externality since the newcomer will spend $\widetilde{G}_{M+1}$, but it will also modify the domestic equilibrium by moving the median voter.

Three interesting phenomena arise:

- The inclusion of an additional member whose preference for the club good is low (α small) may nevertheless lead to an increase in the production level $\tilde{G}$, if the externality effect overrides the effect of the displacement of the internal political equilibrium.
- The incumbent members—even possibly a majority of them—may lose from a process of enlargement if it shifts the political balance away from their preferences.
- If M countries with contiguous preferences have already formed a union, the $N - M$ remaining countries may not find it beneficial to join the union because they would lose more from adopting a level of club good production different from their own preferences than they would gain from the benefits derived from other countries' expenditures.

This representation provides a useful framework for thinking about concrete EU issues. Trade policy is a case in point because the European Commission negotiates with third countries on behalf of all Member States on the basis of a mandate given by the Council (of trade ministers from the member countries) by qualified majority. Because it increases the weight of the EU vis-à-vis trade partners, an enlargement improves its bargaining power to the benefit of all members. This is the economies of scale effect. But as trade policy preferences are notoriously diverse within the EU, it also changes the political equilibrium. For this reason, the inclusion of, say, more protectionist new members may result in a loss for the free-trader incumbents (and vice versa).

shows that entities characterized by heterogeneous preferences—for example, on the nature and on the volume of production of public goods—can nevertheless gain from collective action if the welfare benefits from higher efficiency outweigh the welfare costs from the loss of autonomy. Again, national defense provides a simple illustration of their point: few countries can afford a capacity to project their military forces beyond their borders. However, if they join an international cooperative body on foreign security, they can benefit from the expenditures of each member of the union, which they have to balance against the cost of having to agree with partners on the priorities and the practicalities of defense policy.

The same model also indicates that countries can be or perceive themselves to be worse off inside an international union if their preferences strongly depart from medium preferences—a result that sheds light on Brexit. The British decision to leave the EU (following the referendum of June 23, 2016) and the subsequent discussion on the future relationship between the EU and the United Kingdom may be interpreted in the light of this model.

The same point can be made with negative externalities. For instance, suppose that the citizens of country A have a high aversion to income inequalities, whereas those of country B have a low aversion to it. A higher level of redistribution in country A will follow. However, this may induce migration of low-income persons from B to A. Due to budget constraints, country A may have to limit redistribution. Such a "race to the bottom," which is discussed in Chapter 8, may lead governments to depart from their citizens' preferences, hence reducing the benefit of decentralization.

In the EU debate over tax harmonization, proponents argue that the combination of decentralized decision and mobile corporate income tax bases has shifted the burden of taxation onto the immobile middle class, despite the citizens' preferences (a point actually supported by the data, see Egger, Nigai, and Strecker, 2016). Opponents claim that tax harmonization is an infringement on national sovereignty and would ultimately lead to a transfer of the taxation power to an illegitimate supranational authority.

A political argument often used in favor of decentralization is that it provides a guarantee against the confiscatory power of the central government.[19] According to this view, only basic economic functions must therefore be assigned to the central level, while policies likely to have strong distributive effects should be left to the decentralized governmental levels. Competition between decentralized jurisdictions will ensure that none of them will resort to confiscation. Federalism within nations therefore counterbalances the tendency of states to behave like Leviathans and acts as a remedy to the alleged deficiencies of democratic systems. Indeed, following a famous expression introduced by Tiebout (1956), the citizens' ability to "vote with their feet" will force elected officers to respect their preferences. This view—widely held in some federal countries, including the United States—posits that decentralization should be preferred independently from any welfare benefit arising from preference heterogeneity.

3.3.2 The European Union

a) A primer on the EU

The European Union[20] was founded in 1957 as the European Community by six countries (Belgium, France, Germany, Italy, Luxembourg, and the Netherlands) that had previously successfully experienced cooperation among former foes within the framework of the European Coal and Steel Community. The number of Member States increased progressively to 28 in 2013, and it is expected to fall to 27 with the departure of the United Kingdom in 2019.

The European Community was initially created as a customs union complemented by common policies in a few sectors, yet it was from the start equipped with a sophisticated institutional and legal system. Over time, the EU has gradually gained competences over a wide range of policy areas and has morphed into a single market (see box 3.4). In the early 2000s, an attempt

Box 3.4 Various Types of Economic Unions

In a *free trade area*, goods manufactured in the participating countries circulate duty-free, but each state keeps control of its trade policy with third countries. For example, the United States, Canada, and Mexico, associated since 1992 within the North American Free Trade Agreement (NAFTA), do not apply the same customs duties on imports from third countries. The management of a free trade area is complex because these tariff divergences create an incentive to fraud. Rules of origin must be established that specify the conditions for a product to be regarded as actually originating in a country of the area.

In a *customs union*, all imports from the rest of the world carry the same customs duties, whatever their country of entry and of destination. For example, a Korean television set bears the same duties whether it is imported by Antwerp or Barcelona or sold in Prague or in Rome. The management of a customs union is simpler, but it requires that the participating countries adopt a common external tariff, as the Europeans did with the Treaty of Rome of 1957. However, a customs union does not necessitate the removal of internal border controls: up until the 1992 single market, intra-European imports were subject to customs control in order to check that they were in conformity with national legislations.

A *single market* removes obstacles to the mobility of goods, to the freedom to provide services, and to the mobility of workers and capital. It requires the harmonization of regulations, in particular on technical or health standards, whose disparity would hamper trade in goods and services and therefore the adoption of common regulations or the mutual recognition of national regulations. Within the EU, the single market was introduced in 1992. Free provision of services is, however, hard to enforce. Even when not discriminatory, local regulations tend to prevent foreign providers from entering local markets.

A *monetary union* involves the adoption of a common currency, a single monetary policy, and therefore of a common central bank. It also requires policy coordination in several other policy fields, not least fiscal policy. This is what is meant by the Economic and Monetary Union (EMU), which in European parlance refers to the provisions of the treaty that concern the single market, fiscal and economic policy coordination, and the single currency. The EMU started in 1999 with 11 member countries. By 2018, this number had increased to 19, but, for the larger Central and Eastern European Member States such as Poland and Hungary, membership in the Eurozone remained a distant prospect.

In response to the Eurozone crisis of 2010–2012, EMU was complemented with strengthened economic, fiscal, and financial surveillance procedures; a financial assistance arm, the European Stability Mechanism (ESM); and a *banking union* consisting of a unified bank supervision and resolution regime (see Chapter 6).

was made to equip it with a constitution, but the corresponding agreement was rejected in popular referendums in France and the Netherlands. Nevertheless, most of the provisions of the stillborn constitution were made part of a new treaty, the Treaty of Lisbon, which entered into force on December 1, 2009, after ratification by all Member States.

The preference for decentralization is reflected in the EU by principles according to which policies should be assigned to the lowest level of government except when centralization is justified by the need to conduct joint action (see, in particular, the *subsidiarity principle* in box 3.5). However, the formulation of those principles has hardly resulted in a clarification of responsibilities. Since the 1990s, new forms of intergovernmental cooperation have developed, and coordination procedures have been strengthened that further constrain the Member States' autonomy.

Most questions raised by the theory of fiscal federalism are relevant for the study of European integration:

- Even if the Union is a political construct, economic efficiency arguments generally carry a greater weight within the Union than they do within individual Member States in deciding what the Union should do;
- Even though the diversity of preferences has clearly shrunk in some areas (for example, price stability), it remains patent and it has increased with enlargement. In areas (such as social protection) where these preferences differ, diversity calls either for decentralization or for

Box 3.5 European Union Principles

The European Community did not result from an economic project, but from a political ambition: the will "to create, by establishing an economic community, the basis for a broader and deeper community among peoples long divided by bloody conflicts" (European Coal and Steel Community Treaty of 1951). The integration method adopted was intended to pave the way for further, tighter integration. According to the Treaty:

- The process is one of "creating an ever-closer union among the peoples of Europe" (Article 1 of the Treaty on the European Union);
- The *acquis communautaire* makes the transfer of a competence to the higher, central level irreversible and binding for all new members;
- The Union can gain new powers if needed "to attain one of the objectives set out in the Treaties." If "the Treaties have not provided the necessary powers, the Council, acting unanimously on a proposal from the Commission and after obtaining the consent of the European Parliament, shall adopt the appropriate measures" (EU

treaty: Article 352 of the Treaty on the Functioning of the European Union).

Whereas a constitutional approach would have determined *ab initio* the distribution of competences, the European method therefore relies on a combination of small-steps-based pragmatism and powerful lock-in and integration mechanisms.[27]

The Maastricht Treaty of 1993 started to challenge this logic to avoid excessive centralization. The EU treaty includes no less than three principles whose aim is to put a check on excessive centralization: the *principle of conferral* states that "the Union shall act only within the limits of the competences conferred upon it by the member states in the Treaties to attain the objectives set out therein" (Article 5-2); the *principle of subsidiarity* states that "in areas which do not fall within its exclusive competence, the Union shall act only if and insofar as the objectives of the proposed action cannot be sufficiently achieved by the member states" (Article 5-3); and the *principle of proportionality* states that "the content and form of Union action shall not exceed what is necessary to achieve the objectives of the Treaties" (Article 5-4).

In order to justify transferring a competence to the EU, therefore, it is not enough to prove that decentralization is not optimal, but the case must be made that centralization is necessary. This departs from the principles that presided over the creation of the Community.

variable geometry cooperation (or *enhanced cooperation* in the language of EU treaties) between states which exhibit similar preferences.[21]

b) EU competences

Five categories of *competences of the EU* stand out in the current governance structure of the Union:[22]

- *"Exclusive" competences*. Here, "only the Union may legislate" and States can adopt legislation "only if so empowered by the Union or for the implementation of Union acts." This involves primarily trade, competition, and, for euro area members, monetary policy.
- *"Shared" competences for which* the initiative *belongs to the Union*. States "shall exercise their competence to the extent that the Union has not exercised its competence." This primarily involves the management of the internal market, regional environmental policies, the common agricultural policy, consumer protection, transport, and energy.

- The coordination of the economic and employment policies of the Member States.
- The definition and implementation of a Common Foreign and Security Policy.
- Competences to support, coordinate, or supplement the action of the Member States in specified areas such as health, industry, culture, or education.

Two features stand out in this enumeration: first, the truly federal character of the Union since its competences are in some areas higher than those of the Member States; second, the complexity of the European decision system since five categories of competences coexist that are not always easy to distinguish.

From an economic (and nonlegal) perspective, it is possible, however, to give a simplified representation of the distribution of the major competences (cf. table 3.3).[23]

Table 3.3
A simplified outline of competence assignment within the European Union

	Member states	Union
Allocation		
Labor markets	XX	X
Goods markets	X	XX
Markets for services	XX	X
Financial markets	X	XX
Infrastructures, research, education	XX	X
Farm support	X	XX
Foreign trading regime	–	XXX
Climate	X	XX
Stabilization		
Money and exchange rate (euro area)	—	XXX
Financial stability	X	XX
Fiscal policy	XX	X
Redistribution		
Across individuals	XXX	—
Across regions	XX	X
Across countries (within the Union)	—	XXX

Key: By convention, the amount of the X is for each line equal to three. XX in a column indicates that the principal competence belongs at the corresponding level. XXX indicates exclusive competence.

Table 3.3 is schematic, but it has the advantage of revealing the economic logic of European integration. It indicates that the European Union is less centralized than the United States for labor and product markets and fiscal stabilization but that it is as centralized for foreign trade negotiations or climate policy and more centralized as regards state aid control or indirect taxation. This peculiar distribution of competence rests on a number of hypotheses:

1. *Integration within the single market yields significant economic benefits.* This justifies removing regulatory obstacles to trade in goods, services, and capital between EU members. This hypothesis has received scrutiny on the occasion of the 2014 British inquiry into the allocation of competences. Most studies conducted on this occasion concluded that membership in the single market contributes to increasing productivity, output, and income by significant amounts (Emmerson et al., 2016).
2. *Goods and capital are mobile between the countries of the Union, but labor is almost immobile.* This justifies assigning to the Union the regulation of the markets in goods, services, and capital and maintaining the Member States' primary responsibility for labor market regulation and redistribution policies between individuals. Low labor mobility is against the declared ambitions of the European single market (Article 39 of the Treaty states that, within the Union, "freedom of movement for workers shall be secured") but it has long remained a fact of life. Labor mobility increased in the 2000s and the 2010s, but remained limited: in 2015, foreign citizens represented 7.3% of the labor force in the EU, half of whom were from other Member States of the EU28. Migration into the United Kingdom was allegedly one of the motivations for Brexit, but the proportion of foreign workers reached only 6.6% in 2015, against 18.5% in Switzerland (not an EU member, but part of the European Free Trade Area), see figure 3.2.
3. *The management of the single market is a Union responsibility, but states remain in competition for other allocation policies.* The competences of the Union largely derive from the management of the single market. This is the case with international trade (see box 2.5) or with competition, an area where the European Commission was assigned the double role of controlling concentrations and of policing state aid to companies. Member States keep prime responsibility for other allocation policies, in particular for those (infrastructures, research and innovation, education) that are decisive for long-term growth. In these areas, the Union primarily plays a supporting role via its budget.
4. *The single market calls for a single currency.* While the monetary union project partly fulfilled political aims, its economic justification

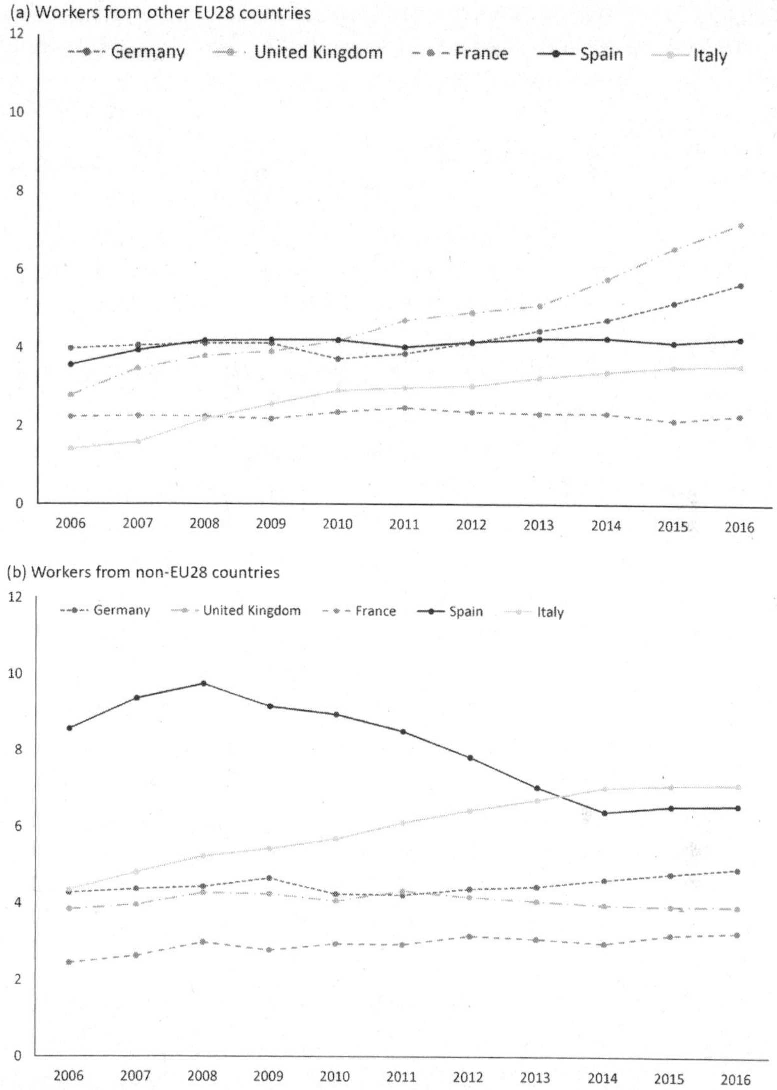

Figure 3.2 Share of foreign workers in employment, 2006–2015 (% of total employment).
Eurostat.

was that full mobility of goods, services and capital within a single market, exchange-rate stability and independent monetary policy were incompatible (Padoa-Schioppa, 1987). To what is known as the "international monetary trilemma" (see Chapter 7), alternative solutions within the single market were to end the fixed exchange rate arrangement or to go for monetary union. At the time, it was perceived that exchange rate flexibility was incompatible with a market where goods circulate without obstacles.

5. *The single currency does not necessarily imply a federal budget but calls for joint surveillance of national fiscal policies.* This point, still the matter of heated debates, involves two separate issues. The first one is whether national fiscal policies must be put under control to prevent unsustainable fiscal behavior from endangering monetary stability. This risk is the justification for the Stability and Growth Pact whose aim is to ensure the avoidance by national fiscal policies of "excessive deficits" (Chapter 4). The second issue is whether a federal budget is needed to provide the stabilization instrument lost because of the absence of national monetary autonomy. In the 1970s, the prevalent view in Europe was that, in the event of monetary union, the EU would need to put in place a federal budget amounting to about 5% of GDP (McDougall, 1977). In fact, the adoption of the euro eventually took place *without any increase* in the EU budget. This budget, which represents a mere 1% of EU GDP, is not designed to perform any macroeconomic stabilization. This puts the onus of stabilization on national fiscal policies and creates the conflict of objectives between discipline and stabilization that is recurrent in the Economic and Monetary Union (EMU). We return to these issues in Chapters 4 and 5.
6. *The Union does not intervene in interpersonal redistribution but fulfils a role of interregional and international redistribution.* In its early years, the Union had almost no redistributive role except toward farmers through the Common Agricultural Policy. Spending on regional development represented just 3% of the EU budget in 1970 and 10% in 1980. In the 1980s, enlargement to include less-advanced countries (Spain, Portugal, Greece, Ireland) and the fear that the single market could lead to a concentration of economic activities in the most prosperous regions led to a significant development of regional policies: Structural Funds and Cohesion Funds. However, enlargement to Central and Eastern Europe did not give rise to a further increase in structural spending in spite of the significant income gap between the old and the new member countries. Redistribution from the former to the latter took place through redeployment of existing programs.

The European model of international union has no equivalent in the world. While there are indeed several hundred regional unions, the vast majority of them are limited to, at best, organizing a free trade area. The North American Free Trade Area (NAFTA), which covers the United States, Canada, and Mexico, does not include any supranational authority nor a common budget. On the whole, integration within the EU, however, falls short of the degree of integration prevailing in existing confederations or federations, such as Switzerland, the United States, or Canada. Those are also based on a single market and a single currency, but they have in addition a common labor market and are endowed with much more important budgets (from 10% to 25% of GDP) that contribute to stabilization and interpersonal redistribution.

c) The future of the EU

Partly because the goal was not (and could not be) defined *ab initio*, there has been considerable path dependency in the history of the EU. The European model took shape through a series of bold initiatives followed by crises and eventually political compromises, occasionally buttressed by economic analyses and recommendations.

The creation of the Common Market in 1957, a combination of customs union and common sectoral policies, came after participating countries had failed in their attempt at creating a European Defense Community. The adoption of the single market was the political outcome of a compromise between the free marketers, who saw in market integration a way to liberalize the markets in goods, services, and capital, and the federalists, who saw in the same liberalization a way to promote European integration.[24] Meanwhile, from an economic perspective, the single market responded to a powerful analytical insight that saw in the constitution of a unified market a means of increasing welfare and of promoting growth (Chapter 10).

The single currency was also the outcome of a political compromise between France, which saw it as a way to escape the domination of the German Bundesbank and as a potential instrument of global European influence, and Germany, which could through the EMU export its own economic policy design: between, therefore, François Mitterrand and Helmut Kohl (Pisani-Ferry, 2013; James, 2014). Its design largely borrowed from the theory of credibility and from arguments in favor of central bank independence (cf. Chapter 5). However, the criteria chosen for constituting the euro area largely ignored the lessons from the theory of optimum currency areas (which could have resulted in excluding some countries) or from the US experience (whose monetary unification took several decades and involved fiscal transfers, cf. Frieden, 2016).

Finally, enlargement in 2004 and 2007, which was the (delayed) result of the dissolution of the Soviet bloc, was widely interpreted as a European reunification of historical significance. Yet, through the anchoring of their economic institutions and the resulting development of trade and foreign direct investment, the expected integration of the new Member States played a major role in their successful economic transition. An illustration of this phenomenon is the comparison between Poland and Ukraine, two former members of the Soviet bloc with similar GDP per capita in 1990 (figure 3.3). Only Poland

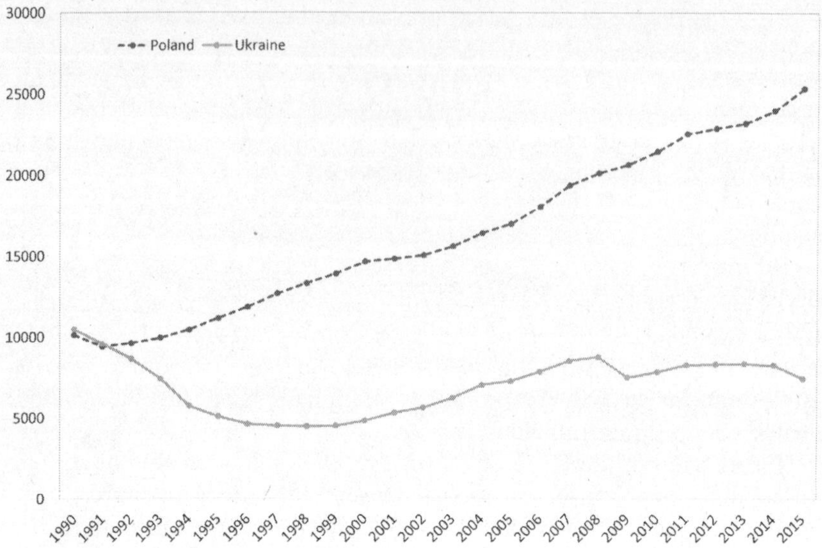

Figure 3.3 Poland and Ukraine: Gross domestic product (GDP) per capita in purchasing power parity dollars of 2011.
World Bank.

joined the EU, in 2004, after a long compliance process. In 2014, GDP per capita was almost three times higher in Poland than in Ukraine in purchasing power parity.[25]

Is the EU model now stable? The rejection of the constitutional project by French and Dutch voters in 2005 was soon followed by the Eurozone crisis (2010–2012) and then by the Brexit vote (i.e., the British referendum in favor of leaving the EU). From 2011 to at least 2015, Greece's participation in the euro remained in the balance, with repeated spells of tension and doubt. In other words, the EU has been living in crisis mode more or less permanently. Meanwhile, however, several major additions were brought to the Eurozone policy system since 2010, and Eurozone membership was gradually enlarged to 19.

The future of the EU elicits as much debate among economists as it does among political scientists, politicians, and the public. Some (Alesina and Wacziarg, 1999) draw from the theory of federalism to claim that Europe has gone too far and intervenes in areas that should remain national prerogatives. Others, on the contrary, call for a deeper economic integration that would ensure a better functioning of the EMU (Van Rompuy et al., 2012; Juncker et al., 2015) and/or for a more democratic political union equipped with stronger and more legitimate political institutions (Habermas, 2015).

The dispute between the antifederalists, who want to decentralize decisions, and the federalists, who want the Union to be assigned new competences, can first be read in light of the discussion on the balance between the diversity of preferences and the potential for economies of scale. The former camp would wish decisions to be better tailored to the heterogeneity of the member countries, whereas the latter would wish them to be centralized so that economies of scale can be exploited in full. It is important to note that both may be right in that the existing distribution of competences may lead to an inefficient outcome in comparison to both a more decentralized and a more centralized solution.

Additionally, there is a debate on the democratic legitimacy of EU decisions. In the words of German political philosopher Jürgen Habermas (2015), "the European Union owes its existence to the efforts of political elites who were able to count on the passive consent of their more or less indifferent populations as long as the peoples could regard the Union as being also in their economic interests. . . . The Union legitimized itself through the results it produced rather than by fulfilling the citizens' political will." In his view, this mode of integration based on *output legitimacy* rather than *process legitimacy* has reached its limits, and the EU must now equip itself with a more democratic and more accountable governance. Opponents object that citizens show little interest for what happens at the European parliament and that Europe's legitimacy continues to rest on the economic outcome it produces.

These debates are both important and somewhat frustrating. Contrary to what the theory of federalism suggests, the European system is characterized by an overlap between national and Union competences. Hence, in the legal texts and in practice, a significant focus has been put on coordination (both among national authorities and between them and the Union authorities). Coordination issues arise in all areas where the Union was conferred a responsibility without the corresponding direct instruments; beyond fiscal policies, for which the problem is well-identified (see Chapter 4), this regards structural policies, a large part of climate change policies, and, increasingly, fields traditionally belonging to the realm of national decision, such as migration. This overlap of responsibilities and the coordination issues that it raises are not specific to the EU, but they are particularly acute in comparison to the situation in federal countries.

Notes

1. Political scientists tend to emphasize the distinction between coordination and cooperation. Here we neglect this difference.
2. The measure of financial openness is further discussed in Chapter 7.
3. See https://ourworldindata.org/international-trade.
4. Migrant workers are workers born in a different country than their current country of residence.

5. Source: http://www.migrationpolicy.org/programs/data-hub/us-immigration-trends#labor
6. Notably by Anderson and van Wincoop (2003), who develop a theoretically consistent model that explains part of the border effect and still find a ratio greater than 10, and Yi (2010), who develops an explanation based on multistage and sequential production and is able to explain away three-eighths of the empirically measured border effect.
7. See the TiVA database, available on OECD.Stat.
8. Unless I produce dust or waste through the use of my shoes, which will have a negative impact on other consumers, see next section on spillovers.
9. See Chapter 8 for more on intellectual property.
10. See Elinor Ostrom (1990), who received the Nobel Prize in 2009 for her work on the diversity of self-organized solutions to manage common pool problems.
11. The ASEAN + 3 group was formed in 1997 by the countries of the Association of South-East Asia Nations (Asean) plus China, Japan, and South Korea.
12. Frankel and Rockett (1988) exploit differences across economic models to show that policy players coordinating on the basis of incoherent models can reach inferior outcomes. Their results are, however, not robust against changes in specification.
13. The main institutions and informal fora of coordination are presented in Section 3.1.4.
14. The creation of an International Trade Organization was envisaged in the Havana Charter of 1948, but it failed to be approved by the US Congress.
15. The G7 was initially created as a G6 in 1975 and included the United States, Japan, Germany, the United Kingdom, France, and Italy. Canada joined in 1976 and Russia in 1998 (until its membership was suspended in 2014). The EU also participates in the G7/G8 summits.
16. The G20 includes the G7 plus Argentina, Australia, Brazil, China, India, Indonesia, South Korea, Mexico, Russia, Saudi Arabia, South Africa, Turkey, and the European Union.
17. The distinction between a federation and a confederation is not a clear-cut one. Confederations are generally established by treaties and are more decentralized. The ultimate power rests with the participant states, whose unanimity is required for important decisions. According to such a distinction, the Swiss Confederation is, in fact, a federation.
18. OECD, Unweighted average of countries. See figure 4.1 in Chapter 4.
19. See Brennan and Buchanan (1980) or Weingast (1995).
20. The EU was initially called the "European Community." It was renamed "European Union" in 1993, when the Treaty of Maastricht added political and foreign policy dimensions to the initial economic dimensions. Here, we refer to the "Union" and use "Community" only when referring to the past.
21. Enhanced cooperation enables a subgroup of at least nine Member States to cooperate within the framework of the Union's nonexclusive competences and, to this end, make use of the Union's institutions. However, this provision, initially introduced in the Maastricht Treaty in a slightly different form, has

only been used twice—for facilitating cross-border divorce and for European patents.

22. As listed in Articles 2 to 6 of the Treaty on the functioning of the European Union.
23. This presentation draws on insights shared by former central banker and minister of Finance Tommaso Padoa-Schioppa.
24. Or, more bluntly, a compromise between UK Prime Minister Margaret Thatcher, a staunch advocate of liberalization and national sovereignty, and EU Commission president Jacques Delors, a former center-left French minister and an adamant federalist.
25. Purchasing power parity is a technique to compare income in different countries while accounting for differences in living costs. See Chapter 7. For a counterfactual analysis of Polish membership of the EU, see Campos, Coricelli, and Moretti (2014).
26. The symmetry assumption is made for simplicity motives only. Removing it does not affect the result.
27. Article 352 could be regarded as an especially powerful instrument for extending the EU's remit, but it does not apply in fields already covered by the treaties and its use has in practice be limited. It was, for example, used to introduce environmental legislation at a time when the field was not covered by the treaty.

References

Alesina, A., I. Angeloni, and F. Etro (2005), "International Unions," *American Economic Review,* 95(3), pp. 602–15.

Alesina, A., and R. Wacziarg (1999), "Is Europe Going too Far?" *Carnegie-Rochester Conference Series on Public Policies,* 51, pp. 1–42.

Anderson, J. E., and E. van Wincoop (2003), "Gravity with Gravitas: A Solution to the Border Puzzle," *American Economic Review,* 93(1), pp.170–92.

Axelrod, R. (1984), *The Evolution of Cooperation*, Basic Books.

Bhagwati, J. (2010), "A New Approach to Tackling Climate Change," *Financial Times,* 22 February. Online at https://www.ft.com/content/c9ee09b0-1fe7-11df-8deb-00144feab49a.

Brennan, G., and J. M. Buchanan (1980), *The Power to Tax: Analytic Foundations of a Fiscal Constitution*, Cambridge University Press.

Campos, N. F., Coricelli, F., and L. Moretti (2014), "Economic Growth and Political Integration: Estimating the Benefits from Membership in the European Union Using the Synthetic Counterfactuals Method," *CEPR Discussion Paper* 9968.

Chaney, T. (2014), "The Network Structure of International Trade," *American Economic Review,* 104(11), pp. 3600–3634.

Coeurdacier, N., and H. Rey (2013), "Home Bias in Open Economy Financial Macroeconomics," *Journal of Economic Literature,* 51(1), pp. 63–115.

Egger, P., S. Nigai, and N. Strecker (2016), "The Taxing Deed of Globalization," *CEPR Discussion Paper* 11259, May.

Emmerson, C., Johnson, P., Mitchell, I., and D. Phillips (2016), *Brexit and the UK's Public Finances*, Institute for Fiscal Studies report, May.

Feldstein, M. (1988), "Distinguished Lecture on Economics in Government: Thinking About International Economic Coordination," *The Journal of Economic Perspectives*, 2(2), pp. 3–13.

Frankel, J., and K. Rocket (1988), "International Macroeconomic Policy Coordination when Policy Makers Do Not Agree on the True Model," *American Economic Review*, 78, pp. 318–40.

Frieden, J. (2016), "Lessons for the Euro from Early American Monetary and Financial History", Bruegel Essays and Lecture Series.

Gollier, C., and J. Tirole (2016), "Negotiating Effective Institutions Against Climate Change," *Economics of Energy & Environmental Policy*, 4(2), pp. 5–27.

Habermas, J. (2015), *The Lure of Technocracy*, Polity Press.

Hoekman, B. (2015), *The Global Trade Slowdown: A New Normal?* Vox-EU eBook.

International Labor Organization (2015), *ILO Global Estimates on Migrant Workers*, December.

International Monetary Fund (2012), *Enhancing Surveillance: Interconnectedness and Clusters*, March.

James, H. (2014), *Making the European Monetary Union*, Harvard University Press.

Juncker, J. C., et al. (2015), *Completing Europe's Economic and Monetary Union* (the Five Presidents' Report), European Commission, June.

Lane, P., and G. M. Milesi Ferretti (2007), "The External Wealth of Nations Mark II," *Journal of International Economics*, 73, pp. 223–50.

Mayer, T., and S. Zignago (2005), "Market Access in Global and Regional Trade," *CEPII Working Paper*, 2005-02.

McCallum, J. (1995), "National Borders Matter: Canada-US Regional Trade Patterns," *American Economic Review*, 85, pp. 615–23.

McDougall, D. (1977), *The Role of Public Finance in European Integration*, mimeo, the European Commission.

Oates, W. (1972), *Fiscal Federalism*, Harcourt Brace Jovanovich.

Obstfeld, M., and K. Rogoff (2002), "Global Implications of Self-Oriented National Monetary Rules," *Quarterly Journal of Economics*, 117, pp. 503–36.

OECD (2013), *Interconnected Economies: Benefitting from Global Value Chains*, May.

Olson, M. (1969), "The Principle of Fiscal Equivalence: The Division of Responsibilities Among Different Levels of Government," *American Economic Review*, 59, pp. 479–87.

Ostrom, E. (1990), *Governing the Commons: The Evolution of Institutions for Collective Action*, Cambridge University Press.

Oudiz, G., and J. Sachs (1984), "Macroeconomic Policy Coordination Among the Industrial Countries," *Brookings Papers on Economic Activity*, 1, pp. 1–64.

Padoa-Schioppa, T. (1987), *Efficiency, Stability, Equity*, Oxford University Press.

Pisani-Ferry, J. (2013), *The Euro Crisis and Its Aftermath*, Oxford University Press.

Rey, H. (2013), "Dilemma not Trilemma: The Global Financial Cycle and Monetary Policy Independence," *Proceedings of the Federal Reserve of Kansas City 2013 Economic Symposium*, pp. 285–333.

Rogoff, K. (1984), "Can International Monetary Policy Coordination be Counterproductive?" *Journal of International Economics*, 18, pp. 199–217.

Smith, Adam (1776), *An Inquiry into the Nature and Causes of the Wealth of Nations*. London: W. Strahan (1st ed.). (Multiple reeditions under the abbreviated title *The Wealth of Nations* in recent re-editions).

Tiebout, C. (1956), "A Pure Theory of Local Expenditures," *Journal of Political Economy*, 64, pp. 416–24.

Tucker, A. (1950/1980), "A Two-Person Dilemma," conference given at Stanford University, later published as "On Jargon: The Prisoner' s Dilemma," *UMAP Journal* (1), p. 101.

Van Rompuy, H., et al. (2012), *Towards a Genuine European Economic and Monetary Union* (the Four Presidents' Report), European Commission, December.

Weingast, B. (1995), "The Economic Role of Political Institutions: Market-preserving Federalism and Economic Development," *Journal of Law, Economics, and Organization*, 11, pp. 1–31.

Yi, K. M. (2010), "Can Multi-Stage Production Explain the Home Bias in Trade," *American Economic Review*, 100, pp. 364–93.

4

Fiscal Policy

The government budget simultaneously fulfills the three functions of allocation, redistribution, and stabilization analyzed in Chapter 1: governments build infrastructure, invest in research, and provide public services such as education; they levy progressive taxes and provide means-related transfers; and they let the budget balance oscillate with the cycle in order to smooth out economic fluctuations.

Even though these functions are intricately intertwined, *fiscal policy* (also called *budgetary policy* in Europe) nowadays mainly refers to stabilization. It consists in all decisions concerning government spending and taxation that are taken in order to influence aggregate demand and to steer the economy toward equilibrium. The decision may be to adjust spending or taxes (in which case we refer to *discretionary fiscal policy*) or to let them evolve automatically depending on growth and inflation (in which case we refer to *automatic stabilizers*).

Fiscal policy is a relative novelty. In the nineteenth and the early twentieth centuries, the primary economic role of a government was to build and maintain roads and other infrastructure, as well as to provide education and postal services (law and order, or defense being arguably not primarily economic functions). Allocation therefore came first.

Redistribution has in a way always been a dimension of fiscal policy because disputes over the distribution of the burden started with the first levies; social policies also emerged early—in Rome, bread consumption started being subsidized in 140 BC. But it is only in the late nineteenth century, with the introduction of the progressive income tax (in 1842 in the United Kingdom and 1862 in the United States) and with the creation of social insurance (in Germany in 1889) that the redistributive state started to take shape.

The idea that management of the government budget can stabilize the economy—that is, that it can help to keep unemployment close to its equilibrium value and avoid the build-up of deflationary or inflationary pressures—was a twentieth-century invention. It owed considerably to John Maynard Keynes and disciples such as Paul Samuelson. In the highly stylized world of macroeconomics, the fiscal decision-maker handles the budget in the same way that the monetary decision-maker handles the interest rate, and their parallel actions make it possible to achieve both low unemployment and price stability.

Stabilization, however, does not only result from decisions. The macroeconomic role of the state owes at least as much to the secular rise of the share of public expenditures in gross domestic product (GDP) that resulted from the generalization of old-age and health insurance, as well as from welfare and publicly funded education programs. In the United States, for example, total government expenditure as a proportion of GDP rose from 2% before World War I to 10% on the eve of World War II, 20% in the 1950s, and 30% in the 1970s. It fluctuated between 30% and 40% until the Great Recession, which made it pass the 40% mark. In Europe, it started from a higher level (about 10% in France and the United Kingdom, and 20% in Germany before World War I) and has reached higher levels (roughly between 45% and 55% of GDP).[1] Within the course of half a century, governments have thus been transformed from irrelevant macroeconomic players into major contributors to aggregate demand.

The consensus on stabilization policy has never been complete. In post-World War II Germany especially, it has almost always been regarded with suspicion. Even in countries where it was more widely accepted, such as the United States or the United Kingdom, empirical and theoretical doubts surfaced in the late twentieth century about the effectiveness of active fiscal policy. The 1970s first witnessed its ineffectiveness in response to an oil shock. Then, the 1980s saw the emergence of theoretical challenges (or the reemergence of old ones). And in the 1990s, experiences with failed fiscal expansions and a few cases of painless consolidations prompted a reassessment of the growth effects of a fiscal stimulus. By 2000, faith in fiscal activism had been shattered: the consensus among policymakers was that, beyond the automatic stabilization provided by the public budget (e.g., by keeping stable expenditures in a downturn), there was not much room for active policies.

A few years later, the global financial crisis brought fiscal policy back to the forefront. In 2009–2010, in response to the fall in GDP, virtually all the largest advanced and emerging countries undertook a major stimulus effort that helped contain the global recession. In the following years, the effectiveness of fiscal policy was positively reassessed in a context of depressed demand, deflationary pressures, and near-zero interest rates. Under such conditions it was found to be both more effective and more necessary.

Already in 2010, however, several sovereign debtors, starting with Ireland and Greece, began having difficulty borrowing on the debt market because of concerns over solvency—an old issue that had come to be regarded as a concern of the past in the advanced world (though not in the emerging and developing world). This triggered renewed discussions on whether fiscal expansions are effective when public debt reaches a high level.

Hence, consensus views about fiscal policy have changed over time and will continue to evolve. It should be noted, however, that structural changes such as the opening up of most economies, the development of financial markets, or different monetary arrangements have also changed the channels and trade-offs of fiscal policy and justified observed evolutions in the making of fiscal policy.

4.1 Issues

4.1.1 What is it all about?

a) Budgets, surpluses, and deficits

A public *budget* is a document that specifies the origin and volume of both income ("receipts") and intended spending over a certain time horizon (usually a year). Receipts consist of income from direct and indirect taxation, social insurance contributions, revenues from public assets, sale of public services, and, possibly, the disposal of public assets. Spending is made on core sovereign activities (such as police, justice, foreign policy, and defense), the provision of public services (education, health care), indirect or direct support to the economy and society (infrastructure, research), social transfers, and interest on public debt.

Budgets are established autonomously by different public entities such as the central government, public agencies, and state and local governments. Budgeting practices are generally broadly similar across subcomponents of government. For international comparison and overall monitoring purposes, statisticians aggregate their account into that of the *general government*.

Although there has been a general trend away from centralization, the degree of fiscal decentralization still varies considerably across countries (see figure 4.1). In 2016, central government spending represented 91% of total spending in the United Kingdom and 28% in Germany. Also, *social insurance*

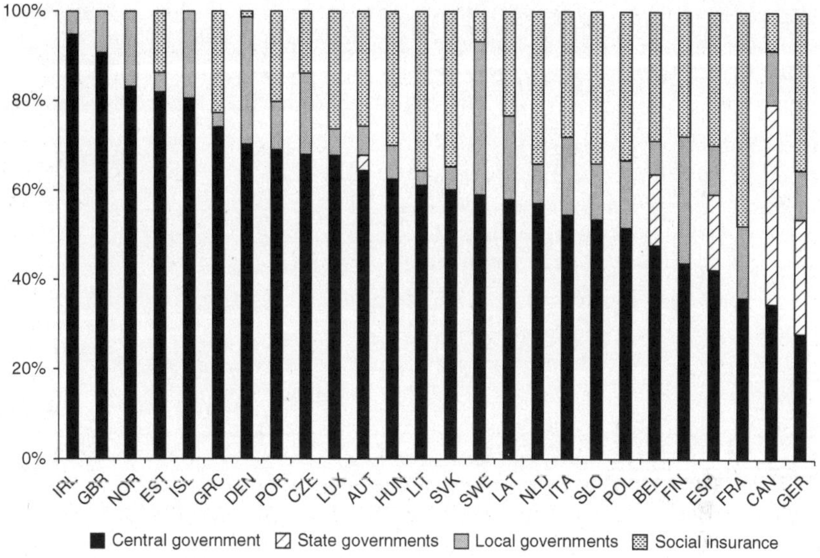

Figure 4.1 Distribution of spending by level of government, 2016 (in percent of total general government spending).
OECD, *Government at a Glance* statistics, 2017.

can either be an integral part of the central (or partially state and local) government or financed separately from specific contributions.[2]

Familiar budget categories include *capital expenditures* (investment on infrastructure and, since recent revisions of national account systems, also spending on research and development) and *current expenditures* (all other items). Interest charges on the public debt depend on the debt level and on long-term interest rates, two variables that, in the short run at least, are beyond the control of the government. Therefore, a useful concept to assess the evolution of spending is that of *primary expenditures* (all spending except interest on public debt). Conditional financial assistance programs negotiated by the International Monetary Fund (IMF) generally specify targets for primary expenditures.

Government accounting rules differ across countries, but the European Union has put in place a harmonized system of public accounts. All accounts are now recorded on an *accrual basis* rather than on a *cash basis* (meaning that transactions are recorded when economic value is created or when claims arise rather than when payments are made). European procedures also distinguish exceptional, or *one-off expenditures,* from *recurring expenditures*.

The preparation of the draft budget, its discussion, and its adoption by parliament are important stages of economic policy decision-making. Organization, procedures, and the time frame vary substantially from country to country. A typical sequence includes the preparation of economic and government receipts forecasts; the setting of expenditure ceilings by sectors; the preparation, by the government departments, of their own draft budgets; cabinet discussions and the consolidation of the whole budget; and discussions and final vote in parliament. The overall process requires at least six months (see the US federal budget process in box 4.1).

The *fiscal (or budgetary) balance*, also called *financial balance* or *net government lending*, is the difference between income and expenditure. There is a *fiscal (or budget) surplus* when the balance is positive and a *fiscal* (*or budget*) *deficit* when the balance is negative. The primary spending concept translates

Box 4.1 The US Federal Budget Process

The federal budget process[a] begins each year with the submission of the President's budget proposal to Congress on the first Monday of February. By early April, the House and Senate budget committees (which may or may not draw on the President's proposal) submit their draft resolutions to the floor for adoption. Differences between the two chambers are resolved by a conference committee.

For the next phase, a distinction is made between *mandatory* and *discretionary spending*. The first refers to spending that is not subject to current congressional approval (for example, it may result from entitlements and other effects from laws enacted in the past—*services votés* to use the telling French expression). Discretionary spending, however, requires an *appropriation bill*. Both chambers work in parallel on 12 categories of spending, each of which is assigned to a different subcommittee. Bills are then passed in each chamber and differences are ironed out in a conference. The appropriation bills are expected to be signed into law by the President, at the latest on October 1. If not, Congress passes a continuing resolution to finance the government on a short-term basis and avoid a shutdown (as happened for example in 2013).

Meanwhile, mandatory spending is reviewed by *authorizing committees* that are also in charge of determining whether additional revenues are needed to finance it. The *budget committee* consolidates the authorizing plans into an omnibus package that is sent to the floor for vote and then to the President for signature.

The parliamentary process therefore takes eight months and often more if it is not concluded by October 1.

[a] See www.cbpp.org/research/policy-basics-introduction-to-the-federal-budget-process, and http://budget.house.gov/budgetprocess/budgettimetable.htm

into a *primary balance* concept, to which we will return because it is useful for determining the dynamics of public debt:

$$\text{Financial balance (net lending)} = \text{primary balance} - \text{interest payments on the debt}$$

Figure 4.2 displays the evolution since 1960 of the financial balance and the primary balance for Italy, a country that has, for a quarter-century, struggled with public debt at or above 100% of GDP. It is apparent that the difference between the two concepts (corresponding to interest payments, represented as bars on the graph) was insignificant in the 1960s and the early 1970s, a period when both public debt ratios and interest rates were low. The gap then gained in importance as a consequence of both high interest rates and recurrent deficits leading up to public debt increases. Primary surpluses only returned in the 1990s, as a consequence of fiscal consolidation and a stronger macroeconomic environment. The peak was reached in 1997, when Italy qualified for the euro by reducing its deficit to 3% of GDP. Interestingly, interest payments also decreased markedly in the second half of the 1990s, again because of both lower interest rates and somewhat lower debt levels.

Fiscal balances tend to rise when economic activity is buoyant and to decline when it is depressed. This is because tax receipts fluctuate in line with

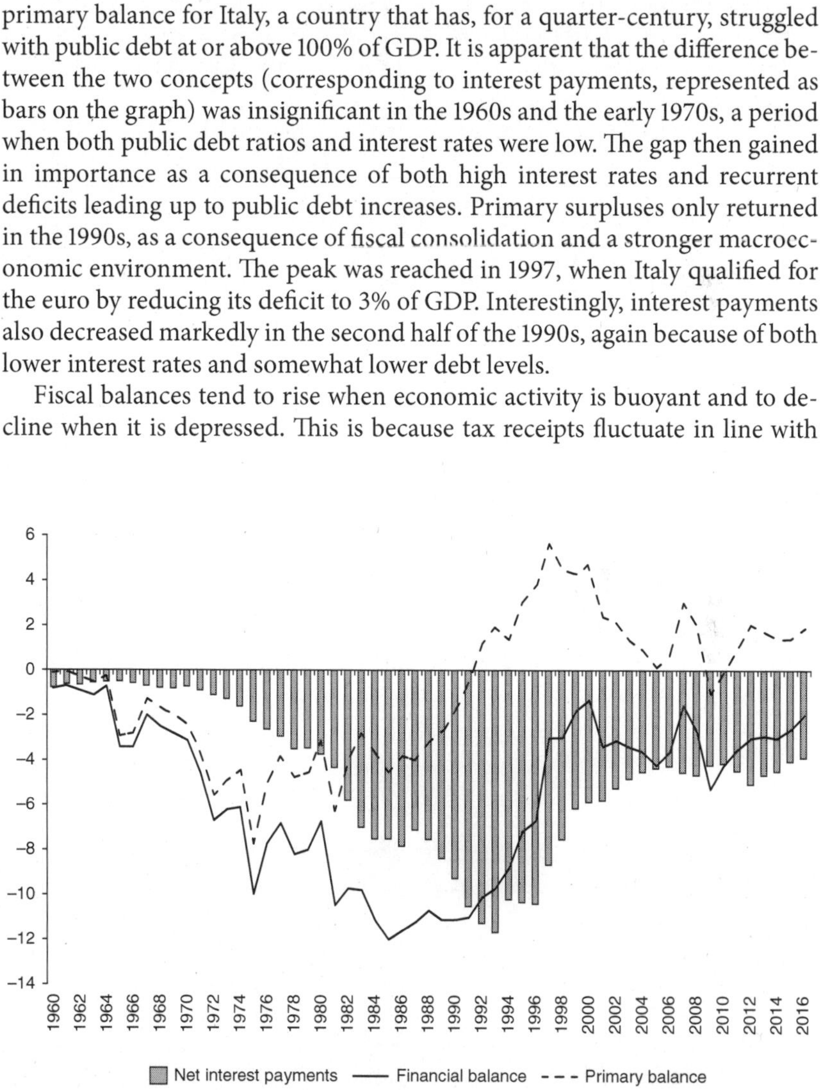

Figure 4.2 Financial and primary balance in percentage of gross domestic product (GDP), Italy, 1960–2016.
Authors' calculations with OECD data.

economic activity (for instance, value-added tax [VAT] revenues depend on household consumption and corporate income tax receipts on corporate profits), whereas public spending does not vary accordingly or, for specific items such as unemployment benefits or transfers, rises in economic downturns. This spontaneous variation of the fiscal balance has a stabilizing effect on aggregate demand and the private sectors' net income (hence the notion of *automatic stabilizers*). For this reason, countries with larger governments tend to exhibit more aggregate macroeconomic stability.[3]

In order to capture changes in fiscal policy, it is useful to calculate a *cyclically adjusted balance* that measures what the financial balance should be, would output be at its potential level (cf. box 4.2). The change in the cyclically adjusted balance from one period to next is traditionally regarded as providing a measure of the *fiscal impulse* or *fiscal stance* because, in contrast to

Box 4.2 Measuring Structural Deficits

The structural (or cyclically adjusted) public balance is usually defined as the public balance that would be obtained, were GDP at its potential level. To calculate it, the first step is to estimate the *output gap*; that is, the percentage difference between actual production and its potential level (see Chapter 1). Then, the average sensitivity of the financial balance s (measured as a percentage of GDP) to a variation of the output gap is estimated. If y is the logarithm of output and $\bar{y}$ that of potential output, this sensitivity is given by:

$$\varepsilon = \frac{ds}{d(y-\bar{y})} > 0 \qquad \text{(B4.2.1)}$$

where d is the differentiation operator. The final step is to subtract the cyclical component $\varepsilon(y-\bar{y})$ from the financial balance s to get the cyclically adjusted, or structural, balance s^*:

$$s^* = s - \varepsilon(y-\bar{y}) \qquad \text{(B4.2.2)}$$

The value of s^* naturally depends on the method used to calculate potential output, and it is affected by the uncertainties surrounding it (cf. Chapter 1). It furthermore depends on the accuracy and stability of the sensitivity parameter ε.

Mourre et al. (2013) review the methodology in use in the EU for measuring ε. They find that its average value in the EU (or euro area) is slightly above 0.5, meaning that a 1 percent deviation of GDP from its potential level results in a 0.5 percentage point deviation of the budget balance. Because of differences in the size of government and the structure of revenues and expenditures, it is higher for some countries (0.65 for Denmark) and lower in others (0.43 for Spain).

Structural balances have shortcomings, which have been highlighted in the turbulent post-2008 environment: potential output is a notoriously fragile notion whose estimates are subject to changes over time and are cyclically sensitive (Coibion, Gorodnichenko, and Ulate, 2017); real-time estimates of both actual and potential growth are often subject to significant revisions (Tereanu, Tuladhar, and Simone, 2014); and the elasticity of tax receipts with respect to variations in the tax base are unstable over time, which results in the instability of the sensitivity parameter. For these reasons, *ex post* estimates of the structural balance may differ markedly from real-time estimates.

Another issue is whether the change in the CAPB correctly measures the fiscal stance. Whereas it is often used for this purpose, the corresponding yearly estimates (generally dubbed *top-down* because they are derived from overall elasticities) may be far from what results from the aggregation of taxation and spending decisions by governments (*bottom-up* approach). Following Romer and Romer (2010), time series based on the aggregation of estimates of individual policy decisions have been built, notably by the IMF (Devries et al., 2011). Because it relies on actual fiscal moves rather than on an *ex post* reconstruction, this *narrative approach* is arguably better suited to measuring discretionary fiscal policy.

The bottom-up measurement of the fiscal effort is, however, not without flaws. It requires relying on an accurate costing of fiscal measures: for example, an evaluation of the budgetary impact of tax reforms. Estimates provided on the occasion of new legislations may be inaccurate, either by mistake or because the government has an incentive to underestimate the budgetary cost of new legislations.

changes resulting from the automatic stabilizers, it is supposed to result from *discretionary fiscal policy* decisions.

The evolution of the financial balance can thus be decomposed into a cyclical component and a discretionary component, equal to the variation of the cyclically adjusted balance:

$$\text{Financial balance (net lending)} = \text{cyclical balance} + \text{cyclically-adjusted balance}$$

The cyclically adjusted balance is often also called the *structural balance*. In the EU fiscal framework, however, there is a slight difference between the two concepts: the structural balance is also purged from one-off receipts or expenditures, such as proceeds from asset sales or bank recapitalizations:

$$\text{Structural balance} = \text{cyclically-adjusted balance} - \text{one-off net receipts}$$

The same decomposition applies to the primary balance, which can therefore be split into a cyclical component and the structural primary balance, also called the *cyclically adjusted primary balance* (CAPB):

$$\text{Primary balance} = \text{cyclical primary balance} + \text{CAPB}$$

A decomposition of the primary budget balance into the structural and cyclical primary balances indicates that the latter accounts for a large part of the short-term fluctuation (figure 4.3). Over the longer term, however, variations of the structural balance are key.

The structural deficit is the main indicator used by international organizations such as the IMF, the Organization for Economic Cooperation and Development (OECD) and the European Commission to monitor budgetary developments and formulate policy recommendations. However, it is not directly observable, and its measurement raises a host of technical difficulties. Two major pitfalls are, first, that the output gap is not measured with accuracy and, second, the instability of the estimated sensitivity of government expenditures and receipts to the level of economic activity (see box 4.2).

As a consequence, estimates of the structural balance vary across institutions and are subject to significant revisions. A particularly striking case is that of Ireland in 2007: it was initially assessed by the European Commission to be in safe structural surplus territory, yet successive revisions led to a reversal of the initial assessment (figure 4.4).

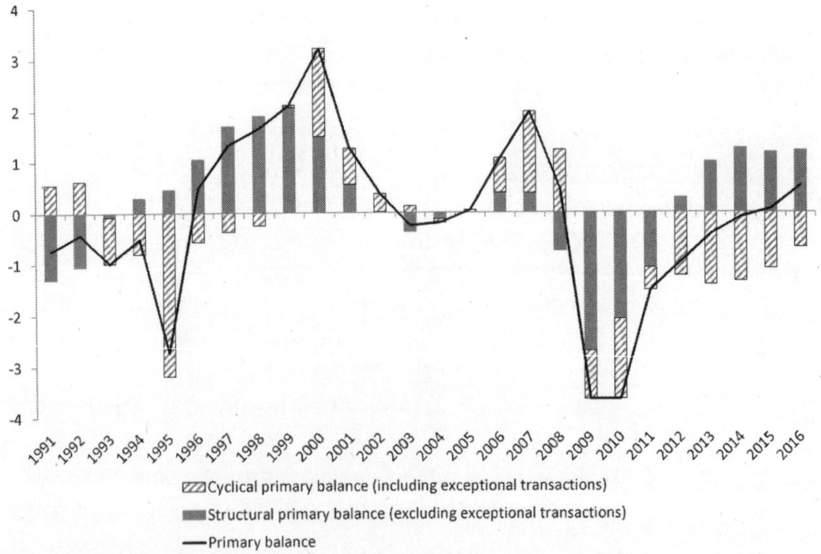

Figure 4.3 Decomposition of the aggregate budget balance of the euro area, 1991–2016 (in percent of potential gross domestic product [GDP]).
Authors' calculations based on OECD *Economic Outlook* data.

Another problem is that whereas the change from one year to the next in the cyclically adjusted balance is meant to represent discretionary policy actions, it often does not match estimates based on actual tax and spending decisions, with the difference being sometimes wide (see box 4.3). The concept of structural balance is therefore both an important one for policy discussions and a far from reliable one for policy decisions. Its use for budgetary surveillance is a cause for concern and a potential matter for disputes.

For 10 years, between 2005 and 2015, the EU gradually increased its emphasis on structural balance indicators (see box 4.3). Especially, the Treaty on Stability, Coordination and Governance (TSCG) of 2013 (also called *fiscal compact*) commits the signatories to keeping structural deficits below 0.5% of GDP over the medium term and mandates the setting of this objective in national laws (Germany introduced such a constitutional rule already in 2009, with a structural deficit limit set at 0.35% of GDP). The resulting fiscal framework has proved perplexing. Since the mid-2010s, doubts have grown in the EU over the wisdom of micromanaging fiscal positions on the basis of unobservable data.

b) Public debt

Receipts, expenditures, and balances are economic *flows*. They are generated in each period. Government assets and liabilities are instead *stocks* that are

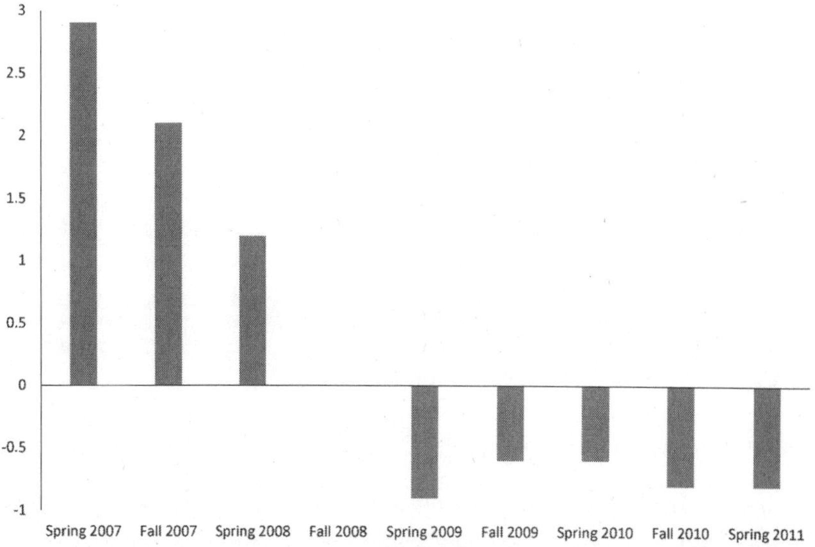

Figure 4.4 Successive evaluations of Ireland's primary structural balance for the year 2007 (in percent of potential gross domestic product [GDP]).
Authors' calculations based on the European Commission's economic forecasts.

Box 4.3 The Use of Cyclically Adjusted Deficits in the EU

The Maastricht Treaty establishing EMU and the initial Stability and Growth Pact (SGP), the secondary legislation that sets out the operational framework for fiscal surveillance, made no room for cyclical corrections. Following the 2005 SGP reform and the decisions taken in the aftermath of the euro area crises, the framework was made more reliant on cyclically adjusted variables. Only the 3% threshold for deciding whether a country is in excessive deficit remained couched in headline terms.

By 2017, there were two main indicators in use.

The Structural Balance

The structural balance is the main indicator used for setting country-specific medium-term objectives under the "preventive arm" of the SGP and for deciding what fiscal adjustment Member States in excessive deficit positions under the "corrective arm" of the SGP should carry out (Mourre et al., 2013).

The Discretionary Fiscal Effort

Changes in the cyclically-adjusted primary balance (CAPB) or the structural deficit provide imprecise measures of the fiscal effort. Building on the action-based approach, the Commission has developed a new bottom-up indicator called the *discretionary fiscal effort*. On the revenue side, the discretionary fiscal effort aggregates the budgetary impact of individual tax decisions. On the expenditure side, the effort is based on the difference between potential output growth and the growth of public spending. Whereas the change in the structural deficit is meant to measure an outcome, the discretionary fiscal effort provides an indicator of the adequacy of the measuress implemented to reduce the structural deficit (Carnot and de Castro, 2015). The discretionary fiscal effort is used in the "corrective arm" of the EU economic governance instituted to monitor national policies.

transmitted from period to period: their value at the beginning of each year equals that at the end of the previous year, as for private assets and liabilities or a capital stock (see Chapter 1). For example, the *public*, or *government debt*—the total financial liabilities of the government—on January 1 equals that on December 31 of the previous year. From one year-end to the next, a deficit increases the debt, while a surplus can be used to pay it down or to buy financial assets.

Public debt accumulation arises because deficits must be financed through borrowing on the bond market or through loans from international organizations.[4] In a simplified setting where the government finances itself by issuing a single type of bond, the relationship between the public deficit and the public debt is:

$$\text{Debt at end of period } (t) = \text{Debt at end of period } (t-1) + \text{Financial deficit of period } (t)$$

Formally, if D represents the deficit and B (for Bonds) the debt:

$$B_t = B_{t-1} + D_t \tag{4.1}$$

Debt therefore increases as long as there are deficits. In this typical stock-flow relationship, debt is measured in nominal terms (disregarding changes in its market valuation) and it is assumed that the government does not sell assets to finance its deficit nor borrow to invest in financial assets. From an accounting standpoint, however, these dimensions should be taken into account. In particular, *gross debt* should be distinguished from the debt net of government assets, which is called *net debt*: for example, the 234% of GDP gross debt government figure for Japan in 2015 is misleading because it neglects the fact that a large part of this debt is held by government agencies; debt net of financial assets is a still high but less frightening 126% of GDP.[5] However, the concept of gross debt is generally used because government assets can be illiquid (see Section 4.1.1.d).

The previous equation can be rewritten, distinguishing the primary deficit and the interest on debt outstanding:

$$\text{Debt at end of period } (t) = \text{Debt at end of period } (t-1) + \text{Interest payment on debt at end of period } (t-1) + \text{Primary deficit of period } (t)$$

Formally, if P is the primary balance (the opposite to the primary deficit) and i the interest on public bonds,

$$B_t = (1+i)B_{t-1} - P_t \tag{4.2}$$

Debt increases if interest payments on the outstanding stock exceed the primary balance. This is why the latter is a key target variable for overindebted countries.

Debt here represents the liabilities of the government or the public sector. Like for the deficits, alternative perimeters can be considered, from the narrow confines of the central government's budgetary functions to the much more broadly encompassing public sector, which includes government agencies, social insurance institutions, local governments, and public entities benefitting from government guarantees. Differences in perimeter matter: in Canada for example, public debt at end 2010 varied from 39% to 67% of GDP depending on the definition chosen.

The old maturing debt securities need to be replaced throughout the year by new ones at prevailing interest rates, while additional debt is issued to finance the deficit. Total securities issuance over the year (i.e., the sum of maturing debts and deficit) is called *gross financing need*. The larger these are, the more difficult it is to tap into the market. If a country loses market access and is forced to rely on official assistance from the IMF and/or the European Stability Mechanism (ESM), the volume of assistance is determined by these needs, which explains the central role of this concept for the design of assistance programs (IMF, 2013):

$$\text{Gross financing needs of } (t) = \text{Maturing debt of period } (t) + \text{Deficit of period } (t)$$

Public debt (also called *sovereign debt* when the borrower is the central government) should not be confused with *external debt*, which represents the liabilities of all domestic agents—public as well as private—vis-à-vis the rest of the world. Of course, both concepts have a common component: government borrowing often results in the accumulation of liabilities vis-à-vis the rest of the world. But some countries, like Italy, exhibit both high levels of public debt and low levels of external debt.

In practice, there are several ways to finance a deficit and therefore several types of financial liabilities. The bulk of them consist in debt securities (long-term bonds and short-term bills) that give the creditors the right to payments in capital and interest, as specified by the associated debt contract (see box 4.4). But governments can also receive loans from banks or international organizations such as the IMF. Or they can incur debt in a hidden form: in situations of stress, they often delay payments to suppliers or even to public employees and pensioners. According to IMF research on a sample of 61 countries, bonds amount to 68% of total debt of the median country, whereas loans represent 22.5% and payables 8.4% (Dippelsman, Dziobek, and Gutiérrez Mangas, 2012).

An alternative to open indebtedness is for the government to finance itself through the national central bank (which amounts to creating money). The counterpart to this *monetization of the deficit* is an increase in the money supply. This practice originates in the capacity (called *seigniorage*, see Chapter 5) of kings to finance expenses by printing money, and it used to be common, particularly to finance wars. Deficit monetization amounts to letting the requirements of the public Treasury, rather than the economy's needs, determine the pace of money creation; when sustained, it has proved

Box 4.4 The Market for Government Debt

In advanced economies, governments fund their financing needs by issuing securities. The amount issued within a given year has to cover the deficit of the year and the reimbursement of debt coming to maturity. This task is performed by ministries of finance or by separate agencies called *debt management offices*. Debt securities can be either short-run (*Treasury bills*, for example with a three-month or a one-year maturity) or long-run (*government bonds,* up to a 50-year maturity). The interest rate paid on debt is usually fixed. It can also be variable: in particular, some countries issue inflation-protected bonds (the return of which is indexed on inflation).

In advanced countries, the average maturity of public borrowing typically lies between 5 and 10 years, but it is somewhat shorter in the United States and longer in the United Kingdom. Governments in advanced countries generally borrow in their domestic currency, while those of emerging countries with less-developed financial markets often borrow in US dollars and, to a lesser extent, in euros. Foreign-currency borrowing may be cheaper but carries an exchange rate risk since the repayment is heavier if the home currency depreciates. Its repayment is also made riskier due to the material impossibility for the central bank to act as a lender of last resort to the government (the central bank only lends its own currency).

Government bonds are traded by investment banks and eventually purchased by institutional investors such as asset managers and pension funds (which manage household savings), insurance companies, central banks, and sovereign wealth funds.

Governments are usually considered more solvent than any private agent, and the interest rate that they pay on their debt is thus considered as the *risk-free interest rate,* on the basis of which all financial securities are valued. However, not all governments are equal, and their borrowing costs depend on their *credit quality*; that is, the likelihood assigned by investors that they will remain able to repay their debt in full. Investors often rely on the assessments provided by *rating agencies*, independent institutions which evaluate the creditworthiness of borrowers.[a] A government's borrowing rate includes a *risk premium* that depends on its rating and compensates the bond holder for the risk incurred.

Central banks typically hold treasury bonds as one of the counterparts of money; they buy (or accept as collateral in repurchase agreements; see Chapter 5) government securities from banks in exchange for providing them with liquidity. This mechanism differs from an outright monetization of the deficit to the extent that the government does not mandate the central bank to buy these securities. Amounts bought by independent central banks derive from monetary rather than fiscal policy considerations.

a The market for ratings is dominated by three agencies: Standard and Poor's, Moody's, and Fitch Ratings.

to be a powerful source of inflation. Hyperinflation episodes are systematically connected to it.

c) Public debt dynamics

Most governments post significant public debt. Few record positive net financial wealth: this mainly applies to countries that hold foreign exchange reserves as an insurance against sudden capital outflows (see Chapter 7) or to countries that produce oil or raw material and intend to spread the benefits from extraction over several generations.[6]

There can be good as well as bad reasons for a government to go into debt. Debt may fluctuate as a consequence of automatic or discretionary stabilization (but this is not a motive for sustained increase as the effects of booms normally offset those of recessions). For a country that must fight a war, ward off catastrophes, or undertake massive public investments, public borrowing is a way to spread the corresponding burden over several generations. In the case of war, it would be morally disputable to require the same generation that pays the price of blood to defend the nation against an aggressor to shoulder the corresponding financial effort. In the same way, a case could be made for partially financing action against climate change through debt: it would be a way to make the future generations pay for the milder climate they will benefit from. But public borrowing that repeatedly finances current expenditures is highly disputable. It is essentially a way to make the future generations pay for the consumption of the current one, and there are no plausible equity arguments to justify such a behavior.

Debt, however, does not need to be repaid entirely because, unlike households, the public sector is not expected to die. Debt can be passed from one generation to the next. Furthermore, debt must be assessed in comparison to the country's national income. It is not the nominal amount of debt that matters, but its size in proportion to GDP as a broad measure of the tax base.

An identical rate of debt accumulation does not have the same consequences in a country whose nominal GDP grows at a fast pace and in a country where it stagnates. Nominal GDP growth resulting from real growth and inflation diminishes the burden of past debt and therefore makes deficits more sustainable. This can be illustrated by a comparison between the United States and three European countries: France, Italy, and Greece over 2007–2014 (figure 4.5). While the increase in nominal debt was higher in the United States than in the three European countries (Greece included!), it was in significant part offset by nominal GDP growth. In contrast, Italy did not record any nominal GDP growth effect, and, in Greece, the decline in nominal GDP was so large that its adverse impact on the debt ratio was almost twice as large as the opposite impact of the 2012 debt restructuring.

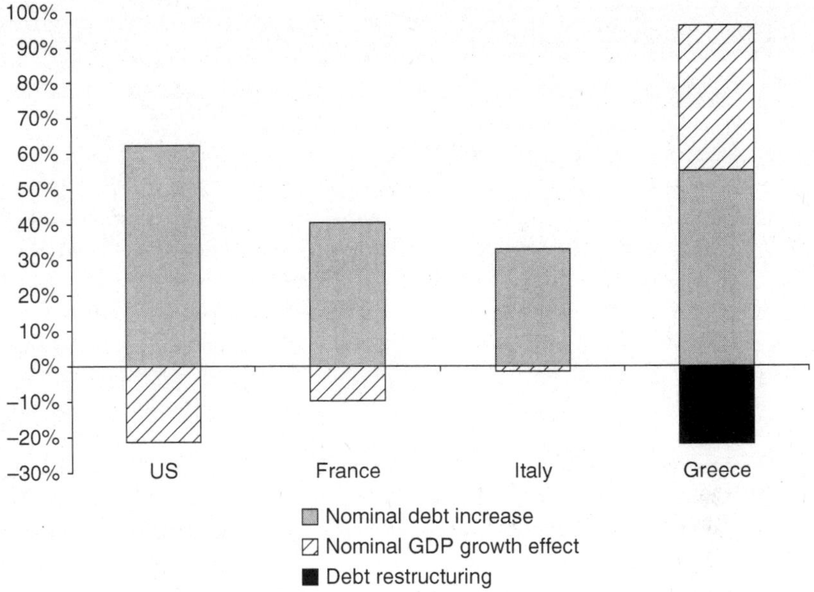

Figure 4.5 Contributions to the change in the public debt ratio, 2007–2014 (in percent of initial gross domestic product [GDP]).

The graph gives a decomposition of the variation of the debt-to-GDP ratio into three effects: (a) the numerator effect resulting from the increase in nominal debt as a consequence of accumulated deficits, (b) the denominator effect resulting from nominal GDP growth, and (c) in the case of Greece, the impact of the 2012 debt restructuring on the 2014 debt stock.

Authors' calculations based on IMF *World Economic Outlook* data.

As explained in more details in box 4.5, the dynamics of the public debt ratio can be described as a horse race between debt accumulation and nominal GDP growth: if the financial deficit remains below a threshold called the *debt-stabilizing deficit*, which is equal to the debt ratio times the nominal grow rate, the debt ratio diminishes; if it is above this threshold, it increases. This sheds light on the debt limit (60% of GDP) and the deficit limit (3% of GDP) set by the European treaty of Maastricht. It was at the time (1992) assumed that countries would grow at 5% annually (3% real growth and 2% inflation), which implied that 3% = 5% × 60% was the corresponding debt-stabilizing deficit.

The financial deficit ratio is, however, not the best variable to assess debt sustainability because it results in part from the interest payments on public debt, which are largelly beyond the control of the current government. It is therefore preferable to write down the debt stabilization condition for the primary balance.

Box 4.5 Public Debt Dynamics

Let Δ be the primary public deficit, B the public debt at year-end, both in euro, and i the nominal interest rate. We neglect cash revenues or disbursements (such as asset sales and purchases) that may affect public debt for a given public deficit. We also suppose that debt is measured at face value and not at current market value, thus ignoring valuation effects. Such assumptions are common but not innocuous: in emerging countries, part of the public debt is US dollar–denominated, and exchange rate movements also influence debt dynamics (see Chapter 7).

The debt dynamics can be written as (with the –1 subscript denoting the end of the previous year):

$$B = (1+i)B_{-1} + \Delta \quad \text{(B4.5.1)}$$

If lowercase letters denote the ratios of the corresponding variables to GDP, n is the nominal growth rate (growth in volume + inflation), g the real growth rate, π the rate of inflation, and r the real *ex post* interest rate, we have:

$$n = g + \pi \quad \text{(B4.5.2)}$$

and

$$i = r + \pi \quad \text{(B4.5.3)}$$

Debt dynamics can thus be expressed as:

$$b = \frac{1+i}{1+n} b_{-1} + \delta \cong (1+i-n)b_{-1} + \delta = (1+r-g)b_{-1} + \delta \quad \text{(B4.5.4)}$$

or, equivalently:

$$b - b_{-1} \cong (i-n)b_{-1} + \delta \quad \text{(B4.5.5)}$$

The debt ratio increases if the interest rate is higher than the nominal GDP growth rate and there is not a sufficient offsetting primary surplus. Equation (B.4.5.5) also gives the primary deficit that stabilizes the debt ratio:

$$\tilde{\delta} = (n-i)b \quad \text{(B4.5.6)}$$

A country whose nominal growth rate exceeds its nominal interest rate can run a primary deficit without seeing its debt-to-GDP ratio increase.

Other things being equal, primary deficits and interest payments on the outstanding stock of public debt increase the debt ratio, whereas primary surpluses and positive nominal GDP growth reduce it. When the nominal GDP growth rate is higher than the interest rate (or, equivalently, when the real GDP growth rate is higher than the real interest rate), a stable debt ratio is compatible with a permanent primary deficit. Conversely, when the interest rate is higher than the growth rate, there must be a primary surplus to stabilize the ratio of debt to GDP, and the larger the (positive) difference between the interest rate and the growth rate, the larger the necessary primary surplus.[7]

The debt dynamics equations help explain why, in the second half of the 1980s, public debt became an issue for advanced countries: the combination of disinflation, lower growth, and higher real interest rates suddenly brought it to the fore after two decades during which governments could afford to overlook debts and deficits. In the same way, the no growth–no inflation environment of the mid-2010s resulted in public debt becoming a serious cause for concern in spite of the record low interest rates.

The approach presented here can be tweaked for assessing the debt situation of developing and emerging countries that are often obliged to borrow in foreign currency. This "original sin" of emerging-country financing adds a currency risk dimension, and, for this reason, it is generally assessed that the limits to their debt are significantly lower than for countries that borrow in their own currency.[8]

d) Shades of liabilities

Government accounts are generally much less comprehensive and sophisticated than the accounts of private companies. Assets are sparsely recorded and part of the liabilities is unrecorded, and there is generally no distinction between different types of debt securities.

Assets are hard to value because many are illiquid. The Japanese government, for example, can sell its shares in the *Japan Post*, but would have more difficulty selling the golden shrine in Kyoto. In Greece, privatization receipts have been miserable during the debt crisis of the 2010s despite suggestions that there would be wealthy buyers for the country's many islands. Net debt ratios are therefore partial images of the government's financial position, and they sometimes give an excessively favorable picture of its financial situation.

Financial liabilities are generally recorded accurately. In the EU, definitions have been standardized and the so-called *Maastricht definition of public debt* includes not only bonds and loans but also *contingent liabilities,* such as the guarantees provided to state-owned companies. Financial debt is generally reported at nominal value. Unlike private companies, governments do not mark their assets and liabilities to market, despite the fact that their debt is being traded and that its value depends on both interest rates and the perceived probability of insolvency.

In addition to financial debt, governments are liable for payments such as pensions to civil servants and other agents entitled to receiving transfers. They also act as insurers in case of major disasters or systemic bank failures. These commitments form what are called *off balance sheet liabilities.*

Off-balance sheet liabilities can be of four sorts, depending on whether they are (i) contractual or implicit and (ii) certain or contingent (table 4.1). For example, civil servants' pensions are both certain and contractual. Bank

Table 4.1
Examples of off balance sheet liabilities

	Certain	Contingent
Contractual	Civil servants' PAYGO pensions	Credit guarantees
Implicit	Old-age dependency costs	Bail-outs of banks
		Natural disasters

Source: Adapted from Polackova (1999).

bail-outs are neither contractual nor certain, but they nevertheless result in huge public finance costs: Argentina in the 1980s, Korea in the late 1990s, and Ireland in the 2010s all suffered fiscal costs amounting to 30–60% of GDP (Laeven and Valencia, 2012).

Several governments produce comprehensive financial statements that provide the public with a more complete image of their financial situation. These comprise a description and valuation of government assets and liabilities and of some off balance sheet claims and liabilities. There are, however, several reasons why governments cannot fully emulate private financial reporting. First, they do not terminate their operations overnight. It is therefore unclear whether their balance sheet should be evaluated on the basis of market or historical prices. Second, many government assets are intangible and difficult to evaluate. Finally, and most importantly, governments can change the very laws under which they operate, blurring the notion of a government "liability." For example, a reform of a pay-as-you-go pension system often amounts to a legal default on previous implicit liabilities. Nevertheless, these nonfinancial liabilities are crucial for evaluating the sustainability of public finances (see Section 4.2). In the United States, for example, accounting for pension provisions increases the gross liabilities of the federal government by nearly 50%.

4.1.2 Lessons from history

a) Public spending: A centennial perspective

As already indicated, the rise of government as an economic player was a major transformation that took place mainly in the second half of the twentieth century. Figure 4.6, which gives the evolution of US federal spending since the end of the nineteenth century, shows the temporary spikes associated with wartime defense spending and the two major steps that led to secular increases in nondefense spending: President Roosevelt's New Deal in the late 1930s and President Johnson's Great Society in the 1960s.

Similar trends can be observed in most other economies, albeit at different times and to different extents (see figures 4.7a and 4.7b). In Europe,

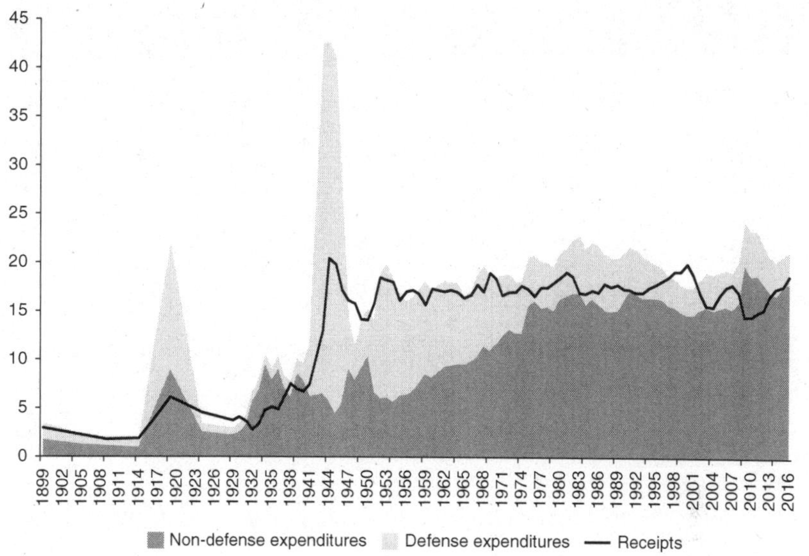

Figure 4.6 US federal government receipts and spending, 1899–2016 (in percent of gross domestic product [GDP]).
Authors' calculations based on US Office of Management and Budget data.

government spending was already higher than in the United States at the beginning of the twentieth century—especially in Germany where Chancellor Bismarck had introduced social security to undercut the socialist movement. Its rise has not been uniform, as indicated by the example of Spain, where it only started after the transition to democracy in 1975. Though government spending as a proportion of GDP is markedly higher in Europe than elsewhere in the world, it has stabilized (or, in the case of Sweden, has decreased after the financial crisis of the early 1990s). In the emerging countries, government spending is lower, but a clear upward trend can be observed.

Most of the increase in public spending has resulted from the rise of social spending—pensions, healthcare, income support, and unemployment insurance. Transfers to individuals and the provision of public health services have increased massively. At the same time, most governments have withdrawn from sectors such as manufacturing, telecoms, postal services, transportation, and, except for the temporary nationalizations of ailing banks in the aftermath of the 2008 crisis, financial services. Overall, global privatization receipts from 1988 to 2014 amounted to nearly 3 trillion US dollars.[9] State subsidies are also on the retreat, although they remain high in energy and agriculture.

A conclusion from these observations is that the conservative revolution launched in the early 1980s by Margaret Thatcher, the British Prime Minister, and US President Ronald Reagan did not succeed in reducing the size of the state, but contributed to redefining its scope: in the advanced and a large

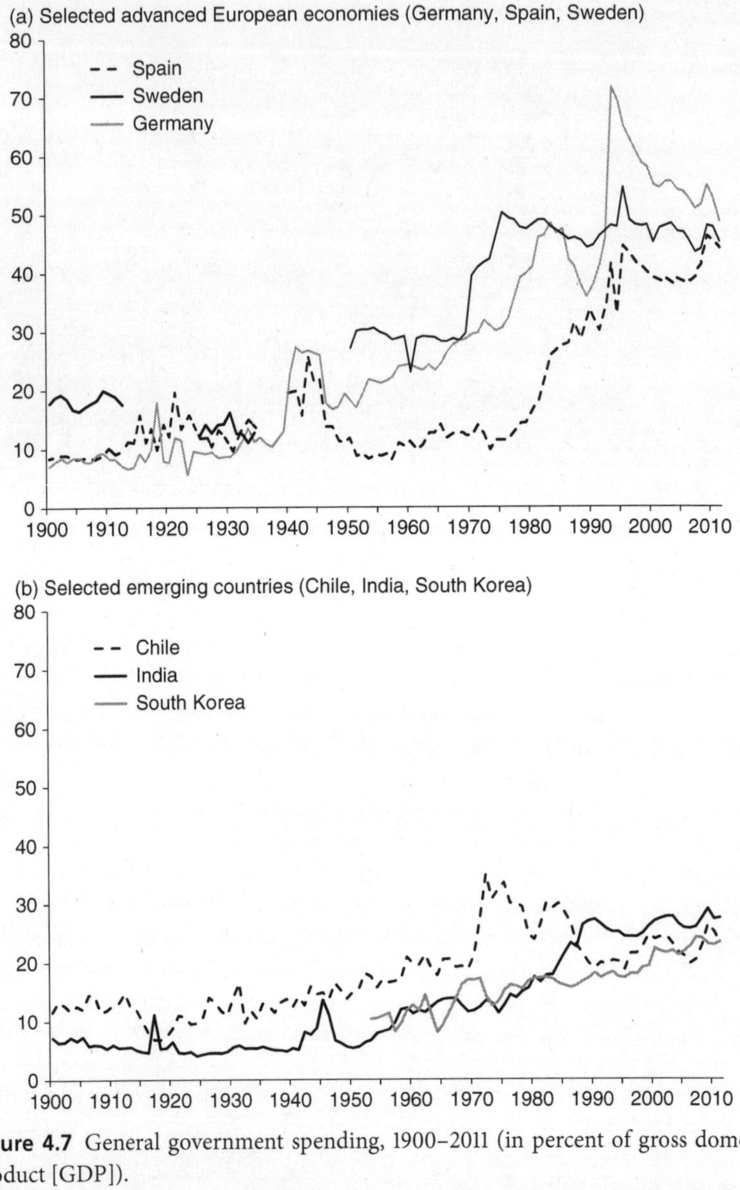

Figure 4.7 General government spending, 1900–2011 (in percent of gross domestic product [GDP]).

Authors' calculations based on IMF *Public Finances in Modern History Dataset*, see Mauro et al. (2013).

part of the emerging and developing countries, governments nowadays are enforcers of the economic rules of the game, providers of universal services, and social insurers, but they are much less manufacturers, bankers, and venture capitalists than they once were. However, this assessment does not apply to China, Russia, or the Gulf countries where state-owned companies are powerful economic players. State capitalism remains a strong force in a world where economic power is shifting.

b) Fiscal policy in practice

There is no fiscal policy to speak of in the absence of a significant budget. But the opposite is not true: a country can record a high government budget and refrain from fiscal activism. Fiscal stabilization policy is a creation of the second half of the twentieth century. It was made official policy under US president John Kennedy in the early 1960s, and its influence gradually extended to Europe (though Germany only briefly endorsed it around 1970). By the late 1970s, it was already subject to controversies: it shared the discredit of policy activism that resulted from inflation and the failure to revive high growth after the oil shocks; it was accused of focusing too much on the demand side, whereas economic difficulties mainly arose from the supply side; its effectiveness was questioned because budgetary decisions must go through a lengthy parliamentary process; it was criticized for being much less nimble than monetary policy, which only requires a decision by the central bank to change the interest rate; and, from a political economy standpoint, it was accused of providing an easy excuse to governments that are politically unable to balance their budget.

Writing at the turn of the century, Stanford professor (and former economic advisor to President George W. Bush) John Taylor (2000) assessed that "empirical evidence suggests that monetary policy has become more responsive to the real economy, suggesting that fiscal policy could afford to become less responsive" (p. 35) and that it seems "best to let fiscal policy have its main countercyclical impact through the automatic stabilizers" (p. 34). Despite these criticisms, though, US presidents never relinquished fiscal policy entirely. It was mainly the political deadlock with Congress over federal spending and federal taxes that made fiscal policy increasingly difficult to rely on.

The fate of fiscal policy should have been more favorable in Europe because, under a fixed exchange rate (until 1998) and monetary union (from 1999 onward), monetary policy was not available at a national level as a stabilization instrument. This should have led governments to rely more on fiscal policy. But failed fiscal reflation attempts after the oil shocks, high levels of public debt and an adverse doctrinal climate made them increasingly cautious. When the monetary union was negotiated in the late 1980s, the focus of Germany was on preventing excessive deficits and a potential monetization of excessive public debts rather than on ensuring that there would be sufficient scope for fiscal stabilization. Its views prevailed, and significant constraints to fiscal activism were introduced in the EU treaty. Most small-country governments had little appetite for it at any rate because, in small open economies, the cost of a stimulus is borne by national taxpayers in the form of higher public debt, whereas a large part of the benefits of higher demand accrue to the country's neighbors. In the end, Europe has remained more reluctant to embrace fiscal activism than the United States.

The one country where fiscal stimulus was lastingly endorsed has been Japan. In the 1990s, the Japanese government launched a series of stimulus packages to counter the effect of its financial crisis and lift off the economy. Partly because the private economy had been severely affected by the crisis and bank restructuring and recapitalization was a condition for the economy to gain momentum, and partly because action lacked decisiveness, the results were disappointing (see box 4.6).

However, fiscal policy was never removed from the policy toolkit. When the global crisis hit in 2008, the Group of Twenty[10] was quick to endorse IMF proposals for a coordinated stimulus. In London in April 2009, the leaders of the G20 committed to "deliver the scale of sustained fiscal effort necessary to restore growth."[11] Data indicate that they actually did deliver. In 2009, the breadth of the concerted stimulus was unprecedented: both emerging and advanced countries participated (see figure 4.8). Already in 2011, however, their stances started to diverge: fiscal policy remained

Box 4.6 Fiscal Policy in Japan in the 1990s

During the 1990s, the Japanese government repeatedly tried to raise the level of GDP growth and inflation through two significant fiscal stimulus programs: one from August 1992 to September 1995, and one from April 1998 to October 2000. In the first round, the fiscal impulse (measured as the change in the cyclically adjusted budget balance) averaged 1.5% of GDP per year, while the second impulse was smaller in magnitude and duration. Both phases of fiscal expansion focused on public investment, mainly infrastructure projects, while most of the remainder was allocated toward purchases of land and to financial and housing loans. The government included a large tax reduction in the first stimulus, with the expectation of compensating the reduction in income taxes with a later rise of value-added tax (VAT) rates. Over the 1990s, government debt doubled as a share of GDP, and the cyclically adjusted budget balance declined from 2% to –6% of potential GDP.

Although it had some positive short-term macroeconomic effects, the fiscal stimulus policy of the 1990s failed to bring back previous growth rates of the Japanese economy (Bayoumi, 2001). Part of the failure can be attributed to factors beyond the immediate control of the authorities (the Asian financial crisis and population aging). But the "lost decade" was also related to the failure of the government to swiftly clean up the banking sector. The resulting "zombie banks" failed to provide credit to stimulate private investment.

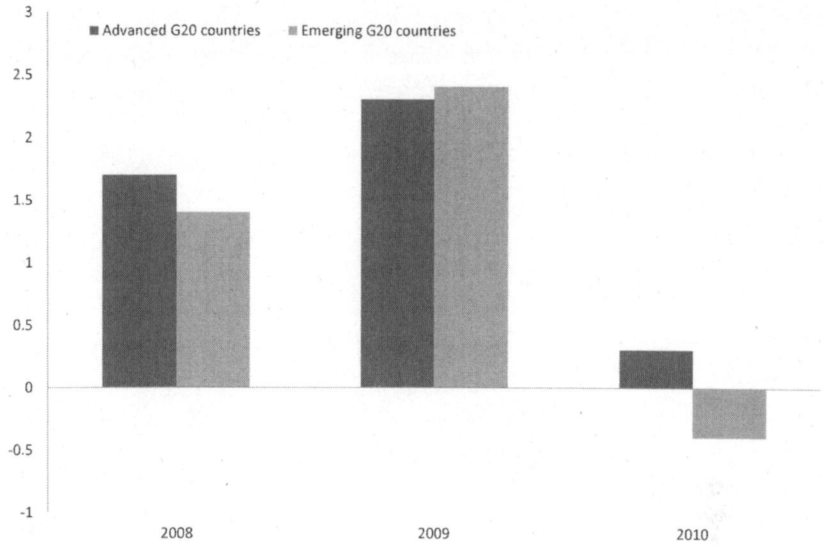

Figure 4.8 The concerted 2009 stimulus (change in the structural primary deficit in percent of potential gross domestic product [GDP]).
Authors' calculations with IMF *Fiscal Monitor* data.

supportive in the United States and China, whereas Europe embarked on an early retrenchment.

c) Sovereign debt, solvency, and debt crises

Historically, sovereign debt has often been the consequence of wars. Figure 4.9, which depicts its evolution since 1800 in the United States and the United Kingdom (two countries for which continuous time series are available), illustrates the point vividly: in both countries, debt peaks correspond to wars (the Napoleonic wars, World Wars I and II for the UK; the Civil War, and World Wars I and II for the US).

Wars, however, are not the only reason why governments incur debt. Peacetime debt also increases, as a result of three types of developments:

- *Protracted public deficits over and above the level corresponding to the stability of the debt ratio* (see box 4.5). This has, for example, been the case of Italy (see figure 4.2), Belgium and France in the last decades of the twentieth century;
- *Major recessions* leading to a collapse of government revenues. In Spain, for example, government revenues dropped suddenly from 40.9% of GDP in 2007 to 34.8% in 2009.[12] This quickly resulted in a significant increase in the debt ratio;

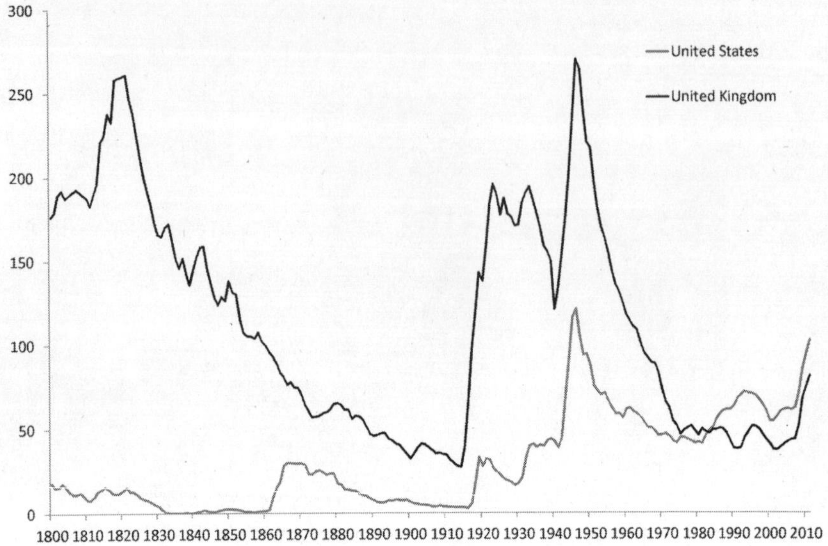

Figure 4.9 Gross public debt-to- gross domestic product (GDP) ratios in the United States and the United Kingdom, 1800–2011 (in percent of GDP)
IMF *Historical Public Finances Dataset*. See Mauro et al. (2013).

- *The materialization of contingent liabilities*. As indicated in table 4.1, the government guarantees depositors (explicitly) and some other creditors of the banks (explicitly or implicitly). Losses in the banking sector translate into public debt if these guarantees are called. This comes on top that of the deep recessions generally triggered by banking crises. Ireland in the 2010s provides a clear case of the potential threat a large banking sector can represent for public finances: in 2007, its debt ratio was 24% of GDP; by 2012 it had reached 122% of GDP, a 98 percentage point increase in five years.[13]

Figure 4.9 may suggest that public debt can reach multiples of GDP without much damage: although its sovereign debt ratio twice exceeded 250% of GDP, the United Kingdom always met its financial commitments, as did the United States, with debt peaking at 121% of GDP in 1946.[14] Comprehensive research by Carmen Reinhart and Kenneth Rogoff (Reinhart and Rogoff, 2014) has shown, however, that these two cases are more the exception than the rule: *debt default*—that is, inability to meet one's debt obligations on time, see box 4.7—has in fact been very common in history. Since 1800, there have been several waves of sovereign default associated with wars and economic crises. In the second half of the twentieth century advanced countries met their obligations, but emerging and developing countries experienced debt crises that ended in *debt restructuring* or at least *rescheduling* (see box 4.7). Overall, the proportion of countries in default each year has often been above one-third (figure 4.10).

Box 4.7 Debt Default, Restructuring, and Rescheduling

A borrower is in *default* vis-à-vis its private creditors as soon as it does not meet a financial commitment enshrined in its debt contracts. It can be in default because it has not repaid the principal on time or because it has not paid interest. A default is a *credit event* (an incident in the payment of debt obligations) that entails two consequences: first, the rating of all tradable debt securities issued by the same borrower is downgraded by rating agencies to D (for *defaulted*) and stop being accepted as collateral by central banks for the provision of liquidity to commercial banks (see Chapter 5); second, after decision by the International Swaps and Derivatives Association (ISDA), the default triggers derivative contracts such as *credit-default swaps* (CDSs), which provide insurance against default risk. For these reasons a default is inevitably a major financial shock.

These provisions apply to relationships to private creditors. Arrears in repayments to official creditors such as the IMF do not have immediate market implications. For example, Greece missed a payment to the IMF in July 2015, but Greek sovereign bonds were not downgraded to D.

Rather than to default, a sovereign borrower can renegotiate its debt with its creditors to obtain a rescheduling of the repayments, a reduction in the interest rate, or an outright reduction of the principal. Negotiations with official creditors take place within the *Paris club* (or, at euro area level, within the Eurogroup of finance ministers). As far as bank loans are concerned, they take place under the auspices of the Institute for International Finance (IIF), the major international banks' association. Negotiations with bondholders are more difficult to organize because they are more dispersed. It is normally incumbent on the borrower to convene a negotiation with its creditors and to ensure that it involves a sufficient proportion of them. An agreement reached with a majority of the bondholders can, however, be challenged in courts by a minority of *holdout creditors* (see Section 4.3.2). For this reason, bond contracts increasingly include *collective action clauses* (CACs) specifying that agreements approved by a qualified majority of the bondholders apply to all.

From an economic viewpoint, an important criterion is whether the renegotiation results in a reduction of the net present value of future payments (of the principal and the interest). There can be such a *debt relief* without a reduction of the principal if the interest rate is reduced or if the borrower is granted a grace period (Greece in the 2010s has benefitted from such a relief on official loans extended by the ESM, see box 4.8). A renegotiation resulting in a postponement of repayments without a change in the present value of future obligations is usually called a *debt rescheduling*. There is *debt restructuring* if the present value is reduced.

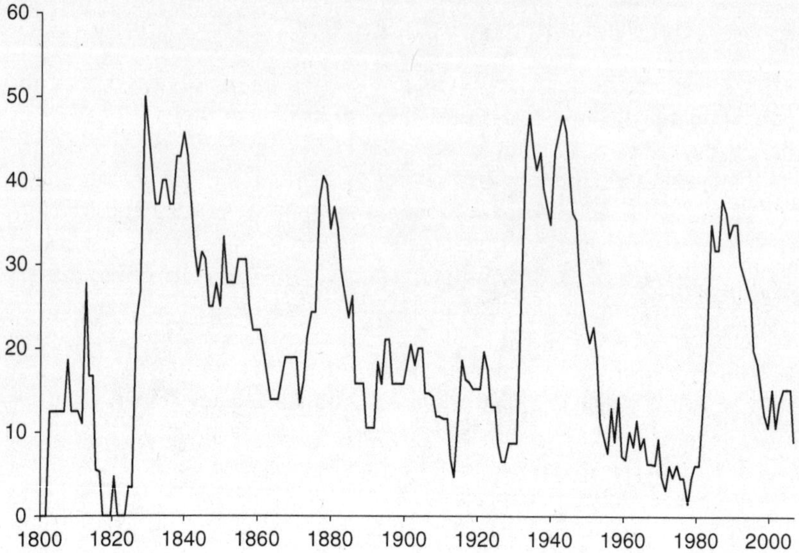

Figure 4.10 Percentage of countries in default on their external debt, 1800–2006. Because of the lack of systematic data on domestic default, only default on external debt is recorded.
Reinhart and Rogoff, 2014.

These facts raise three questions: first, how did the United States, the United Kingdom, and a few other countries succeed in reducing their debt levels? Second, why and how are countries driven into insolvency? Third, what are the consequences of it?

As suggested by Equation (B4.5.5) of box 4.5, there are several ways to exit from excessively high debt. A country can:

a. *Adjust* by recording consistently high primary surpluses;
b. *Inflate* by devaluing nominal debt outstanding through inflation;
c. *Grow out* of debt by recording high real growth rates;
d. *Repress* debt holders by keeping the long-term interest rate artificially low;
e. And finally, *default* on its commitments.

The United States and the United Kingdom after World War II essentially relied on a combination of (b), (c), and (d). In a rather high nominal growth context, maintaining low bond rates through central bank policy helped keep the debt burden low.

Answering the second question is more demanding. It is relatively easy to determine when a household or a private firm is insolvent, but the same does not hold for a government. Unlike households, governments are assumed to have an infinite lifetime, so their debt never requires to be redeemed.[15] To be more precise, expiring debt will be paid off through new borrowing because it is reasonable to think that future generations will be willing, when their turn comes, to continue investing part of their wealth in government securities.

Is there no limit to the state's borrowing capacity? Asking this question amounts to assessing the state's *solvency*; that is, the availability of resources allowing it to meet its commitments. At first sight, the capacity of a state to ensure the service of its debt could appear unlimited since it has the power to raise taxes or, if the central bank is not independent, to monetize the deficit (which is another way of taxing since inflation reduces the real value of money balances and fixed-income securities such as standard bonds). However, there are political limits to the citizens' willingness to pay. As illustrated by many historical episodes, from *Ancien Régime* crises to the Greek crisis of the 2010s, bankruptcy occurs when citizens no longer accept a further reduction of their income and wealth to the profit of the state's creditors. In the words of former senior IMF official John Boorman:

> Debt can almost always be serviced in some abstract sense, through additional taxation and through the diversion of yet more domestic production to exports to generate the revenue and foreign exchange needed to service the debt. But there is a political and social, and perhaps moral, threshold beyond which policies to force these results become unacceptable. (Boorman, 2002, p. 3)

Determining these political, social, and moral thresholds is a daring exercise. The Greek debt saga of the 2010s illustrated this uncertainty vividly: whether or not Greece was able to repay its debt was a matter of constant controversies within and between international institutions (see box 4.8). The political dimension of the issue became even more prominent after the leftist coalition led by Aléxis Tsipras won the general election in January 2015, as this change of majority signaled a seriously diminished tolerance for fiscal adjustment on the part of the Greek citizens.

Solvency characterizes the situation where, at a given moment in time, the government is able to meet all its financial obligations by raising taxes, selling assets, and issuing new debt. If resources exist but cannot be mobilized immediately (for example, in the case of state-owned companies that cannot be sold immediately due to lack of purchasers), or if they are available but can dry up at short notice (in the case of short-term credit extended by foreign banks), there is a risk of a *liquidity crisis* whereby the government is unable to meet the exact schedule of its obligations. Finally, public finance is said to be *unsustainable* if, on the basis of the current economic policy and of available forecasts, the expected development of the public debt leads to a situation of insolvency. Fiscal policy can therefore be unsustainable without solvency problems arising immediately. Nonetheless, this policy will have to be modified in the future.

Public finance sustainability is especially important in a monetary union where the central bank is independent and does not have the mandate to serve

Box 4.8 The Greek Debt Saga

In the 2000s, Greece recorded very large and in part hidden deficits, reaching a 15.5% of GDP deficit and a 127% of GDP debt ratio in 2009. In spite of an exceptionally large fiscal adjustment, estimated by the IMF at 19% of potential GDP between 2009 and 2013 (IMF, 2017); a significant debt reduction negotiated with private creditors in 2012; and favorable borrowing conditions granted by the euro area partners, remaining deficits and the nominal GDP contraction resulted in the public debt reaching 177% of GDP at end-2014. The IMF subsequently assessed that Greek debt was not sustainable unless a primary surplus in excess of 3.5% could be sustained, which was considered politically unrealistic. However, the euro area creditors (partners countries through the European Stability Mechanism (ESM), the financing vehicle set up in 2012 to provide conditional financial assistance to countries in crisis) were willing to provide favorable financing conditions but unwilling to write off nominal debt. Germany, especially, insisted that debt forgiveness was illegal because Article 125 of the European Treaty (known as the *no bail-out clause*) states that "The Community shall not be liable for or assume the commitments of central governments . . . of any Member State." In net present value terms, Greece has benefited from a substantial reduction of its official debt burden, but—at the time of writing at least—in nominal terms there has been no debt relief.

as a *lender of last resort* for sovereigns. This issue has been a matter of lengthy and controversial discussion in the euro area. We return to it in Section 4.3.

Another major difference between a state and a private entity has to do with the consequences of insolvency. When a company goes bankrupt, a competitor buys it up or it is liquidated, in which case its assets are seized by the creditors. A household may similarly lose its assets (e.g., its house). But there is no collateral for sovereign debt. If a state defaults on its commitments, neither domestic nor foreign creditors can seize its assets (unless the latter invade the country).[16] An indebted state's attitude toward its creditors therefore depends on its *willingness to pay* as well as on its *ability to pay*. Default can be the outcome of a rational decision not to repay the creditors (in which case it is called *strategic default*).

This brings us to the third question: What are the benefits and costs of a strategic default? The benefits result from writing off the debt and the corresponding interest burden, while the costs are mainly reputational: the state may be cut off from financial markets or at least pay a higher risk premium on future borrowings because markets will price the risk of another default (see box 4.9). An overindebted country faces a choice: either to strive to meet its obligation and gradually reduce its debt ratio through fiscal adjustment, or to negotiate a debt relief with its creditors. In the first case it preserves its reputation, but, before it succeeds in putting its debt ratio on a convincingly

Box 4.9 The Risk Premium and the Valuation of Public Debt

There are two main reasons why the market valuation of sovereign debt varies over time and across issuers.

First, the value of a fixed-rate government bond on the secondary market depends on the relative level of its interest rate and the current interest rate for assets of the same maturity and risk. Since interest rates vary continuously, bonds carrying different interest rates coexist. Arbitrage by market participants leads the expected return on these bonds to equalize through variation in their value. Assume for example that the government issues a bond carrying a 1% interest rate. Nobody would buy if another bond from the same government carrying 2% can be bought unless the value of the second increases up to the point where both provide the same return. This mechanism is continuously at work on bond markets.

Second, bonds of the same maturity are not equally risky. For riskier ones to be bought, they must carry a higher interest rate. Suppose, for example, that a government issues a \$100 one-year bill and that the *risk-free interest rate* is *i*. If the probability that the government will entirely fail to honor its obligation is π, the expected value of the reimbursement of the principal of nominal value 100, E(*P*), is:[a]

$$E(P) = (1-\pi)\times 100 + \pi \times 0 \qquad \text{(B.4.9.1)}$$

To take this risk, lenders will require to be rewarded with an additional return called *risk premium* ρ such that:

$$(1-\pi i)(1+i)(1+\rho) = (1+i) \qquad \text{(B.4.9.2)}$$

The risk premium corresponding to the insolvency probability π is therefore:

$$\rho = \frac{\pi}{1-\pi} \qquad \text{(B.4.9.3)}$$

It is an increasing function of the probability of default π. As a judgment on debt sustainability fundamentally relies on one's assessment of the willingness of domestic taxpayers to meet their sovereign's obligations, the probability of default envisaged by financial markets is quite volatile. This may generate self-fulfilling crises: if markets suddenly revise the probability of default upward, this increases the risk premium, hence the interest rate on new borrowing, making the debt unsustainable.

a For simplicity, we have assumed that in case of default, the lender does not recover anything. The computation can easily take into account the probability of partial reimbursement.

declining path, it is likely to be facing high borrowing costs; in the second case, its solvency will be improved, but it may suffer lasting reputational damages.

Careful analysis of twentieth-century debt restructuring episodes yields two important lessons. First, reputational damages are limited: markets tend to forgive debt restructurings. More precisely, they do not punish renegotiation or restructuring per se: after an agreement has been reached with the creditors, governments regain market access, and future bonds spreads are correlated to the size of the restructuring (Cruces and Trebesch, 2013). Second, significant debt reliefs are positive for growth, especially when accompanied by reductions in the face value of the debt instead of a mere reduction of the present value (Reinhart and Trebesch, 2016). The upshot is that when a country struggles with unsustainable debt, a debt restructuring may be desirable. The quality of the negotiation process matters, however: markets punish unilateral defaults. Ultimately, the decision will depend on the level of the primary deficit since a defaulting country will be unable to finance its primary deficit in the short term after the credit event. It will also depend on the damage created by a default on the domestic financial sector (since domestic banks may hold large amounts of domestic sovereign debts) and on the dissemination of the debt along domestic households.

Since governments suspected of not being able or willing to repay their debt carry a higher interest rate, there is a risk of vicious circle: as detailed in box 4.5, the higher the interest rate, the higher the required primary surplus for debt stabilization, hence the lower the willingness of domestic taxpayers to continue the fiscal adjustment. Such vicious circles were at the core of the European debt crises of 2010–2012 (figure 4.11): *interest-rate spreads* (or

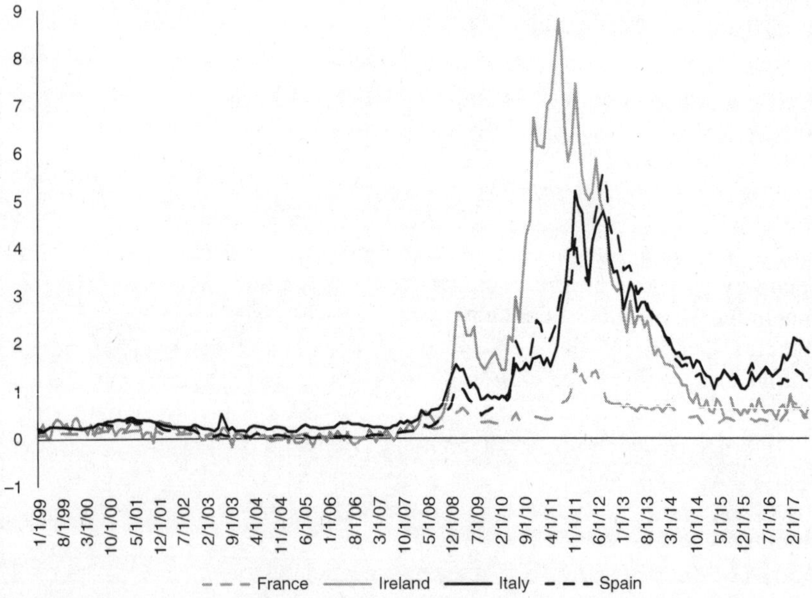

Figure 4.11 Sovereign spreads vis-à-vis Germany, selected euro area countries, 1997–2017 (differences in 10-year sovereign interest rates in percentage points). OECD.

differences) vis-à-vis Germany increased from being negligible to levels that exceeded eight percentage points for Ireland and five for Spain. None of these countries defaulted, but Ireland and Portugal (as well as Spain for the financing of bank rescue) were forced to apply for support from the IMF and the ESM.

What these developments suggest is that the interplay between market expectation of default and actual borrowing conditions is at the core of sovereign debt crises. We return to the issue in the next section to understand how solvency can be more precisely defined.

4.2 Theories

4.2.1 Demand-side effects

a) The basic toolkit

Since its publication in 1936, John Maynard Keynes's *General Theory of Employment, Interest and Money* has provided an essential conceptual framework for analyzing the influence of fiscal policy on aggregate demand. Here, we first briefly sketch the Keynesian theory and the main criticisms it has been subject to.

As indicated in Chapter 1, the standard Keynesian model assumes price stickiness in the short term. The supply of goods and services is supposed to be elastic, and the level of aggregate demand determines output. When demand is insufficient, this results in the underemployment of labor and capital. A fundamental role of macroeconomic policy—be it fiscal or monetary—is to ensure that aggregate demand is such that the economy remains at or close to a level corresponding to equilibrium employment. In response to a negative demand shock, this can be done by increasing public spending or by cutting taxes.

This framework rests on two key assumptions: that because of price stickiness, the macroeconomic balance is not reached through changes in prices and that the response of private spending does not offset the rise in public spending. In the elementary Keynesian model, nominal rigidity and the income–demand relationship are simply postulated. An exogenous increase in aggregate demand (a demand shock) results in an increase in the level of output. The ratio between output variation and the initial exogenous variation of aggregate demand is called the *Keynesian multiplier* (box 4.10).

The Keynesian framework can be represented within the aggregate supply, aggregate demand (AS–AD) model introduced in Chapter 1. The price stickiness assumption implies that the aggregate supply (AS) curve is upward-sloping but not vertical in the short run. In the elementary model, the slope of AS is low, so that production can increase without having a major impact on prices. The aggregate demand curve is downward-sloping due to the negative impact of inflation on demand for goods and services, either through a wealth effect or because of the impact of a rise of the interest rate engineered by the

Box 4.10 A Primer on the Keynesian Multiplier

Suppose that household consumption C is a linear function of current income Y:

$$C = aY + b \quad \text{with } a,b > 0 \qquad \text{(B4.10.1)}$$

The parameter a is the *marginal propensity to consume* (meaning that out of one additional euro of disposable income, the representative household spends a and saves $1 - a$). Let us assume, for example, that $a = 0.8$, so that households consume 80% of any additional unit of income, and that households own companies, so that any profit is treated by them as income.

Suppose that supply is perfectly elastic, so that output adjusts to the level of aggregate demand at constant prices. The closed economy product market equilibrium is given by:

$$Y = C + \bar{I} + \bar{G} \qquad \text{(B4.10.2)}$$

where $\bar{I}$ is aggregate investment and $\bar{G}$ is government demand. Both are assumed to be exogenous.

Suppose the government increases by one unit public spending while keeping taxes constant. This will initially lift output, and thus income distributed to households, by one euro. Out of this additional unit, 80 cents will be consumed and will lift output—thus disposable income—further. At the end of the process, the total increase in output is:

$$1 + a + a^2 + a^3 + \cdots = 1 + 0.8 + 0.8 \times 0.8 + 0.8^3 + \cdots$$
$$= 1/(1-a) = 1/(1-0.8) = 5.$$

The same result can be obtained by solving the two-equation system directly, leading to:

$$\Delta Y = \frac{\Delta \bar{G}}{1-a} \qquad \text{(B4.10.3)}$$

In this example, the multiplier is excessively large, and fiscal policy is therefore implausibly powerful. There are, however, many factors that may lower the multiplier:

First, not all the additional income accrues to consumers because a fraction of it is taxed away by the government. So Equation (B4.10.1) needs to be rewritten $C = a(1-t)Y + b$, where t is the tax rate. The multiplier becomes $1/[1-a(1-t)]$.

Second, in an open economy, an additional euro of disposable income leads households to consume more of both domestic and imported products and firms to import more intermediate goods. Assuming that the marginal propensity to import is m (meaning that an additional unit of income will lead to m units of imports), the Keynesian multiplier becomes $1/\left[1-a(1-t)+m\right]$.

Third, the assumption of complete price rigidity is extreme. If prices adjust upward, part of the increase in demand does not result in an increase of the volume of products consumed but in an increase in their price. This especially applies over time, as prices adjust gradually.

Fourth, the central bank may respond to an increased demand for products by an increase in the interest rate. In this case investment (from firms) declines because firms compare the yield of investment projects with the financing cost or with the return to financial investments. A *crowding-out effect* appears: part of the increase in public demand results in lower private investment (due to the interest rate increase, private investment is crowded out by public demand). Conversely, an interest rate reduction by the central bank in response to a public spending cut partially offsets its negative impact—unless there is no room for cutting the policy rate because it has already reached the "zero lower bound" (see Chapter 5).

All these factors weaken the impact of fiscal expansion on aggregate demand and income.

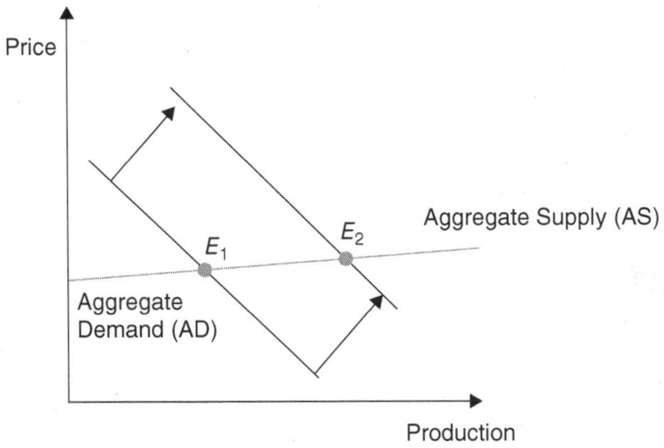

Figure 4.12 Effect of a Keynesian fiscal expansion in an AS-AD framework.

central bank. A fiscal expansion (either a rise in public spending or an exogenous cut in taxes) results in the demand curve moving to the right: production increases. If the slope of the supply curve is low, the adjustment takes place through a variation in the level of output (movement of E_1 to E_2 in figure 4.12).

Here, we have simply postulated the AD curve that summarizes the demand side of the economy. It can be derived from the *IS-LM model* introduced by Hicks (1937) and Hansen (1953) to formalize Keynes's *General Theory*. This model, which has been widely used ever since, consists of two curves that relate output and the interest rate: the IS curve describes the product market

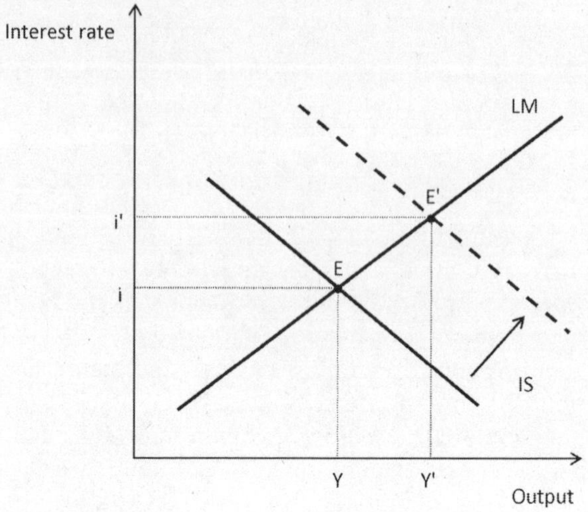

Figure 4.13 Effect of a Keynesian fiscal expansion in an IS-LM framework.

equilibrium and the LM curve the money market equilibrium, both *for a given product price* (figure 4.13):

- The IS curve gives the combination of output and interest rate that results in a product market equilibrium. It is downward-sloping since a higher interest rate results in a lower demand for products;
- For a given money supply, the LM curve gives the combination of output and interest rate that results in money market equilibrium. With a fixed money supply, the positive relationship between output and the interest rate relies on the demand for money, which is supposed to be an increasing function of output (as output grows, more money is needed for transactions) and a decreasing function of the interest rate (as the interest rate grows, private agents prefer to hold interest-bearing assets rather than cash).

In an IS-LM model, a fiscal expansion is represented by a shift of the IS curve to the right (because of the additional demand for goods, output is larger at any given interest rate). This fiscal expansion entails an increase in the interest rate, which reduces the interest-sensitive components of private demand: there is partial *crowding-out* of private demand by public demand.

As we will see in Chapter 5, modern analysis of interest rate formation no longer starts from the assumption that the central bank targets money supply. Rather, the interest rate is supposed to be set by it in response to economic developments in order to ensure price stability (or more generally macroeconomic stability) in the medium run. In other words, most central banks nowadays do not follow a money supply rule, but rather an interest-rate rule. This has led to several reformulations of the IS-LM framework that result in substituting for the LM curve an interest-rate reaction function (Romer, 2000; Bofinger, Mayer, and Wollmerhäuser, 2002). However, such reformulations generally result in representations that make the interest rate dependent on the level of output, as in the LM curve.

Because monetary and fiscal policies are to a certain extent substitutable, the Keynesian approach naturally leads to thinking in terms of *policy mix* (i.e., in terms of the combination of monetary and fiscal policies). Fiscal policy is indeed more effective when supported by monetary policy. At the limit, a perfectly accommodative monetary policy that keeps the interest rate constant in response to a fiscal expansion results in a maximum multiplier effect.[17] This may lead governments to put pressure on the central bank so that it contributes to maximizing fiscal expansion and possibly to submitting monetary policy to *fiscal dominance* (a concept we further explain in Chapter 5). When the central bank is independent, however, it may choose not to accommodate the effects of fiscal policy if it perceives it as potentially inflationary. In figure 4.13, the LM curve does not shift to the right, so the interest rate increases.

This does not imply that an independent central bank always reacts to a fiscal expansion. For example, monetary policy can have hit the "*zero lower bound*" (see Chapter 5) where the policy-determined interest rate remains at or near zero, whereas the economic situation would justify setting it at a significantly negative level. In such a situation, monetary policy does not respond to a fiscal expansion and is therefore fully accommodative without being subject to fiscal dominance. A context of this sort magnifies the impact of fiscal policy because, instead of resulting in a policy-induced increase in the real interest rate, a fiscal expansion results in its lowering (since the nominal interest rate stays constant while price inflation accelerates).[18] Another case where the interest rate may not react to a fiscal expansion can be found within a monetary union, when the country carrying out the fiscal expansion is small enough to have negligible impact on the aggregate inflation rate (see Chapter 7).

b) Intertemporal optimization

The preceding presentation was based on an ad hoc assumption as regards household behavior: they are supposed to set their spending plans on the basis on their current income. This implicitly assumes that households cannot smooth spending over time by resorting to the credit market: when facing a temporary drop in income, they do not borrow from banks to maintain their consumption.

Suppose instead that households have unlimited access to credit. They can maximize their intertemporal utility, which depends both on their present and their future consumption, subject to their intertemporal budget constraint. In this polar case, current consumption does not depend on current income but on the present value of future earnings. If the discount rate equals the interest rate, a temporary income shock does not affect household behavior at all. There is no need for stabilization policy.

Furthermore, fiscal stabilization would be ineffectual under such conditions, as supporting current income through temporarily lower taxes (offset by higher taxes later) has no effect on consumption. The reason is that as the intertemporal budget constraint of the state requires it to raise taxes in the future to repay public debt, a temporary tax cut raises the households' current disposable income, but not their intertemporal disposable income; consumption therefore does not change (box 4.11). Similarly, in the case of an increase in public expenditure, households lower their consumption because expected future taxes reduce their intertemporal income. Assuming again that their discount rate is equal to the interest rate, the decline in private consumption exactly offsets the increase in public spending, so that aggregate demand does not change. There is total crowding-out of private spending by public spending, and output is not affected.

The neutrality of fiscal policy is called *Ricardian equivalence* (see box 4.11) in reference to David Ricardo's classical discussion of the alternative ways to pay for a war (Ricardo, 1820). The intuition for it can be found in earlier statements; for example, in Mirabeau's criticism of the financial policy of King Louis XVI of France (Mirabeau, 1787). It was first formalized by Robert Barro (1974).

Box 4.11 Ricardian Equivalence

Consider an infinitely lived individual who can freely lend and borrow at interest rate r. At each period t, she receives an income Y_t, consumes C_t, and invests (or borrows) $Y_t - C_t$ at rate r. The intertemporal budget constraint, which states that the present value of all earnings equals the present values of all expenditures, can be written as:

$$\sum_{i=0}^{\infty} \frac{Y_{t+i}}{(1+r)^i} = \sum_{i=0}^{\infty} \frac{C_{t+i}}{(1+r)^i} \quad \text{(B4.11.1)}$$

Subject to this constraint, the individual maximizes her intertemporal utility U_t which can be written as the present value of future utility at each period (we assume it separable):

$$U(t) = \sum_{i=0}^{\infty} \frac{u(C_{t+i})}{(1+\rho)^i} \quad \text{(B4.11.2)}$$

Where ρ is the discount rate that measures the individual's preference for the present, and u is a concave function. The first-order condition of this maximization program leads to the following behavior:

$$\frac{u'(C_{t+i})}{u'(C_{t+i-1})} = \left(\frac{1+\rho}{1+r}\right) \quad \text{(B4.11.3)}$$

Knowing that u' (.) is a decreasing function, we can derive the optimal consumption path of the consumer. When the interest rate coincides with the discount rate ($r = \rho$), consumption is kept constant over time; when $r > \rho$, consumption grows over time; when $r < \rho$, it decreases. In all cases, consumption at any point of time depends not on current income, but on intertemporal income as defined in Equation (B4.11.1). A temporary fluctuation of income (a recession, followed by a boom) is smoothed out and does not affect consumption. However, a *permanent* fall of income over the life cycle (for example, due to a productivity shock or a pension reform) reduces consumption even if current income remains unchanged.

Let us now introduce a government that spends G_t and receives lump sum taxes T_t. We assume that the level of public spending does not enter the individual's utility function (the government does not spend on the provision of public services). First, assume that the government maintains fiscal balance $G_t = T_t$ at all times. The intertemporal budget constraint of the individual becomes:

$$\sum_{i=0}^{\infty} \frac{Y_{t+i} - T_{t+i}}{(1+r)^i} = \sum_{i=0}^{\infty} \frac{C_{t+i}}{(1+r)^i} \qquad \text{(B4.11.4)}$$

The first-order condition of the utility maximization program is unchanged: public spending financed by lump-sum taxation does not change the shape of the optimal consumption path of the individual (but the level of consumption at each period falls).

Let us now suppose that the government, while preserving its spending program, decides to reduce taxes at time $t = 0$ by an amount B, and floats securities for this amount B with a maturity of M years at interest rate r. It is further assumed that interest payments on debt B, as well as the repayment of capital, will be financed by lump-sum taxation. The individual's utility maximization program is unchanged: during the initial period, a part B of her income is used to acquire public debt securities, but taxes also fall by B; during the following periods, until $t = M$, additional income rB is received on securities held, but additional taxes rB are paid as a result of the need to finance the government debt service; finally, at period $t = M$, the principal B is repaid to the households, but taxes rise by the same amount. The level of consumption remains unchanged at each period. The variable that changes is savings, the difference between disposable income and consumption.

This result is the Ricardian equivalence theorem. It expresses the idea that debt is deferred taxation. It also suggests that the central government's concern should be to determine the level and nature of public expenditures more so than its financing method (through debt or through taxation).

The assumptions behind the Ricardian equivalence theorem may seem unrealistic: rational expectations, infinitely lived consumers (or, equivalently, full solidarity across generations), the unproductive character of public expenditure (or their lack of impact on consumers' utility or on business productivity), and the absence of credit constraints (households enjoy unlimited access to credit regardless of their debt ratios).

Several of these assumptions are indeed questionable: few households master the complex arithmetic of intertemporal public finances; many have short horizons; a large part of them is constrained by credit; and some public expenditures, notably for research or education, have positive effects on future incomes (see Chapter 9). The joint validity of these assumptions is actually contradicted by empirical evidence (Mankiw, 2000).

However, it is true that as an economy grows, private wealth increases and credit markets develop, and increasingly fewer households are subject to the liquidity constraint postulated by the Keynesian model. In the United States in particular, household can post increases in the value of their property as collateral for credit, which makes them able to turn a capital gain into disposable income. This mechanism, known as "mortgage equity withdrawal," funded 3% of household consumption between 2001 and 2005 (Greenspan and Kennedy, 2007). Even with not fully rational expectations, imperfect access to credit, and finite horizons, part of the households' consumption plans is based on intertemporal calculation, and this affects the Keynesian multiplier. In fact, most empirical tests reject full Ricardian equivalence but confirm partial Ricardian effects that reduce the effectiveness of fiscal policy.[19]

These observations have led to the development of micro-founded models that combine two types of households: unconstrained optimizers and liquidity-constrained *hand-to-mouth consumers*. Macroeconomic consumption results from the aggregation of these two types of behavior (Campbell and Mankiw, 1989; Galí, López-Salido, and Vallés, 2007), possibly in varying proportions. Combined with price rigidity assumptions, such a representation leads to Keynesian properties (hence they are called *new-Keynesian models*). Another technique is to model a household as belonging to overlapping generations, each of which has a finite horizon. If each generation cares about its offspring, the model exhibits Ricardian properties, but if each generation is only interested in its own fate, fiscal policy gains effectiveness as an instrument to smooth out fluctuations in activity (Blanchard, 1985).

Even when the Ricardian equivalence applies, there is a rationale for the government to allow the budget to be in deficit in a recession or as a consequence of outside events such as wars or natural disasters. The reason is that balancing the budget in any circumstance would entail fluctuations in the tax rate that would adversely affect the supply side of the economy. This theory of *tax smoothing* results in a policy recommendation that does not differ markedly from the Keynesian prescription. In both settings, the government should refrain from increasing taxes in a recession or from cutting them in a boom. It should let automatic stabilizers play in full. Where the two approaches differ is as regards the use of discretionary fiscal policy. Stimulating the economy in a recession, over and above the spontaneous impact of automatic stabilizers, is potentially useful in a Keynesian setting but useless in a Ricardian setting.

c) Fiscal controversies

Other arguments have been put forward against the Keynesian approach. The three main ones are:

- *Financial crowding-out*: After a fiscal expansion, the deterioration of the public balance and the corresponding savings shortfall may cause a rise in the long-term interest rate that depresses private demand. This financial crowding-out can arise independently of the central bank's reaction to an increase in public spending, as a consequence of the change in the savings–investment balance. In the AS–AD model, this leads the demand curve not to shift in response to a fiscal shock: only its composition is modified by the substitution of private demand by public demand;
- *Supply rigidity*: The relative price adjustment can be sufficiently quick for the goods–market equilibrium to be supply-determined. If the demand curve moves to the right but the supply curve is very steep, private demand is penalized *ex post* by the rise in prices;
- *Supply-side effects*: In the long run, a permanent increase in public spending must be financed by an equivalent amount of taxes. As such taxes may negatively affect supply (for example, through reducing labor supply in response to taxes on labor income, see Chapter 8), more public spending may pave the way for permanently higher taxes and thereby lower potential output. This may reduce the households' intertemporal income and lead them to cut consumption.

The first argument is in contradiction with the Ricardian critique: it posits that a rise in public spending results in a shortfall of savings and thereby a rise in interest rates, whereas Ricardian equivalence posits that the rise in private savings will offset public dissaving (because households adapt consumption in the expectation of future taxes). Both views are more likely to apply in an economy where public debt is considered not sustainable, hence the probability of defaulting on the debt becomes non-negligible (see Section 4.2.2).

The second argument raises an empirical question: What is the slope of the supply curve? Available estimates suggest that it is upward-sloping but not vertical in the short run, which leaves room for fiscal policy effectiveness. All depends, in fact, on the time horizon: within a period of a few months or quarters, prices are sticky; within a few years, they adjust. Fiscal policy effectiveness (like that of monetary policy, as discussed in Chapter 5) is therefore limited in time.

The third argument about possible negative supply effects cannot be decided upon *in abstracto*. Its validity depends on the nature of public spending (especially on the division between current and capital expenditure) and on the nature of future taxes, which can be more or less distorting (see Chapter 8).

The economic literature has built on these distinctions to highlight the importance of the mix of taxation and spending measures that a fiscal expansion or a fiscal retrenchment relies on (what economists call *composition effects*; see Alesina and Ardagna, 2010). Indeed, the supply-side argument for expenditure-based adjustments is that because they signal lower taxes in the future, they may elicit a positive private-sector response that reduces the adverse effect of the adjustment. It should be noted that the demand-side argument would lead to the opposite conclusion: in a simple Keynesian setting, an expenditure-based adjustment has more direct and immediate effects on demand than a tax-based one whose effects can be smoothed by a reduction in private saving.[20]

d) Empirical methodologies

Given ambiguities and theoretical controversies, the effectiveness of fiscal policy as a stabilization instrument is ultimately an empirical issue. To assess its effects, different types of approaches have been used in the literature. The three main ones are simulations with macroeconomic models, empirical estimates with reduced forms (mainly structural vector autoregressive [VAR] models), and systematic analyses of fiscal action episodes.

Simulations have the advantage of taking into account, within the same model, of a series of transmission channels such as household behavior, firm behavior, and cross-country interactions. They also make it possible to specify the policy impulse precisely (for example, whether it consists of a cut in public expenditure, and of which expenditure, or in an increase in taxes, and which taxes), whether the impulse is permanent or temporary, and the context in which it operates (depending on the response of monetary policy and the cross-country context). Finally, beyond the multiplier, they provide estimates of the impact of fiscal policy on a series of variables such as inflation, the fiscal and external balances, or employment. They have, however, the disadvantage of being model-dependent: they rely on a representation that can be disputed.

Empirical estimates based on reduced forms have the advantage of relying on few *a priori* assumptions and the drawback of being comparatively rough. Blanchard and Perotti (2002) first used structural VAR models to assess fiscal policy in the United States (box 4.12). Similar approaches have been replicated for other countries. The limitation of this method is that it necessarily relies on a limited set of variables (three for Blanchard and Perotti: taxes, public spending, and GDP).

Box 4.12 Vector Autoregressive Empirical Evaluations of Fiscal Policy

Blanchard and Perotti (2002) assess the effects of fiscal policy on the basis of a minimum set of a priori restrictions. They start from a simple VAR model:

$$Y_t = A(L)Y_{t-1} + U_t \tag{B4.12.1}$$

where $Y_t = [T_t, G_t, X_t]'$ is a vector whose three dimensions are taxes (T), public expenditures (G), and GDP (X), all expressed in real per capita terms and in log. A(L) is a polynomial lag operator and $U_t = [t_t, g_t, x_t]'$ is the vector of residuals.

Residuals in U_t are not a priori independent. To account for their correlation and isolate an uncorrelated error vector, one writes:

$$\begin{aligned} t_t &= a_1 x_t + a_2 e_t^g + e_t^t \\ g_t &= b_1 x_t + b_2 e_t^t + e_t^g \\ x_t &= c_1 t_t + c_2 g_t + e_t^x \end{aligned} \tag{B4.12.2}$$

where, for example, a_1 describes the instantaneous impact of GDP on tax revenues and a_2 the instantaneous impact of spending shocks e_t^g on these revenues. This simple structure makes it possible to isolate shocks e_t^t, e_t^g and e_t^x that can be assumed uncorrelated with each other.

To estimate the parameters of the system, Blanchard and Perotti impose a number of restrictions. For example, they assume that fiscal policy reacts only with a lag to changes in GDP (which is reasonable in view of the delays involved in parliamentary decision and the implementation of legislation). This implies that $b_1 = 0$ and that a_1 represents the mechanical effects of changes in GDP on tax revenue, which can be evaluated on the basis of detailed tax elasticities.

These various restrictions result, without imposing significant theoretical priors, in a model whose remaining parameters can be estimated (this is what is called *model identification*). There is no restriction on the sign or the value of the expenditure multiplier.

Once estimated with quarterly data over the period 1960–1997, the model is used to study the response of GDP, public spending, and taxes to an exogenous shock, such as a shock on public spending. In the first period, it reflects the economic impact of the public spending shock on growth. From the second period onward, it also reflects the typical reactions of fiscal policy to the economy.

Blanchard and Perotti find that, in the short term, both public spending and tax multipliers are close to unity: an additional dollar of public spending raises GDP by about a dollar; an additional dollar of taxes reduces it by about a dollar.

The third approach is based on the analysis of significant and lasting fiscal episodes. Building on the case study of large-scale fiscal consolidation episodes (such as those of Denmark and Ireland in the 1980s), Alesina and Ardagna (2010) run a cross-country study in which they retain all years during which the structural primary balance varied by a minimum of ±1.5 percentage point of GDP. The underlying idea is that, unlike what linear models implicitly assume, the multiplier is not constant across fiscal policy initiatives because a major program of debt deleveraging or a sustained expenditure contraction effort will change the expectations and behaviors of private agents.

The *narrative approach* initiated by Romer and Romer (2010) provides the basis for another attempt to disentangle the analysis of fiscal policy from the hypotheses built into structural models without falling into the extreme simplifications of the VAR approach. As explained in box 4.2, action-based fiscal data have the advantage of being independent from unreliable estimates of the structural balance. They can furthermore be used in model-free assessments of the impact of fiscal policy. In the 2010s, the narrative approach has increasingly been used (IMF, 2010; Guajardo, Leigh, and Pescatori, 2014; Alesina et al., 2017).

A variant of the same approach relies on episodes of war, which have the (econometric) advantage of being exogenous and unrelated to prevailing macroeconomic conditions. Analysis of such true fiscal shocks can yield unbiased estimates of the multiplier (though monetary policy may well respond to war-induced changes in government spending).[21] In the same vein, Nakamura and Steinsson (2014) use the differentiated regional impacts of military buildups to evaluate state-level multipliers.

e) The multiplier in practice

Batini et al. (2014) and Mineshima et al. (2014) provide a survey of recent results. The main lessons from research are the following:

1. *The average expenditure multiplier is close to one in large, moderately open economies.* As far as structural models are concerned, Coenen et al. (2012) find that, with similar initial conditions and in response to identical shocks, multipliers are remarkably close: for the United States, they range between 0.9 and 1.3, for example, in the case of a temporary public investment increase with endogenous monetary policy response; they are also around 1 in the case of a coordinated stimulus in Europe, under the same conditions. The VAR approach of Blanchard and Perotti (2002) and the narrative approach of the IMF (2010) yield similar results. This is also the conclusion from the survey of several narrative analyses by Batini et al. (2014).
2. *The characteristics of the economy affect the fiscal multiplier.* It depends on trade openness (negatively) and therefore on the size of the economy (positively), labor market rigidity (positively),

the public debt level (negatively), and exchange rate flexibility (negatively).

3. *The degree of monetary support strongly affects the fiscal multiplier.* Coenen et al. (2012) provide a thorough comparative analysis of seven models in use in central banks or international organizations. They find that, for a two-year temporary fiscal expansion, the multiplier is significantly larger when monetary policy is fully accommodative (no change in nominal policy rate) than when it responds endogenously to fiscal action. In particular, fiscal policy is significantly more effective when monetary policy is constrained by the zero lower bound—a result confirmed by a variety of studies based on different methodologies.[22]
4. *The impact of fiscal policy varies over time depending on the overall economic conditions.* Consistent with the Keynesian approach, Auerbach and Gorodnichenko (2012) find evidence that the US expenditure multiplier varies between zero in boom years and 1.5 in recession years. Consequently, the output cost of fiscal consolidations is higher in bad times and lower in good times.[23]
5. *The short-term impact of a temporary stimulus varies significantly depending on the choice of the fiscal instrument* (figure 4.14). Model simulations consistently indicate that the short-term multiplier is larger for public spending on goods and services than for transfers to households or for tax cuts. They are the lowest for corporate income tax cuts. However, a permanent increase in public spending financed by debt has substantially less favorable short-term effects and has long-term negative effects.
6. *Expenditure-based fiscal consolidations tend to have milder adverse effect on GDP, whereas tax-based consolidations do have a strongly negative impact* (Alesina et al. 2017). The two forms of consolidation differ in their impact on private expectations (hence on private investment) and, in some cases, in the endogenous reaction of monetary policy.
7. *The fiscal multiplier tends to be lower for countries whose fiscal position is weak* (high debt ratio). Consistent with partial Ricardian equivalence, a fiscal expansion that threatens debt sustainability may trigger precautionary saving behavior on the part of private agents. The evidence on the relationship between sustainability and the fiscal multiplier is, however, disputed: Auerbach and Gorodnichenko (2017) find that when economic conditions are weak, fiscal stabilization is effective even for high-debt countries.

Summing up, recent research provides empirical support for using fiscal policy for stabilization purposes, but it also highlights its limitations and the potential for misguided action. The main conclusions is, perhaps, that there is

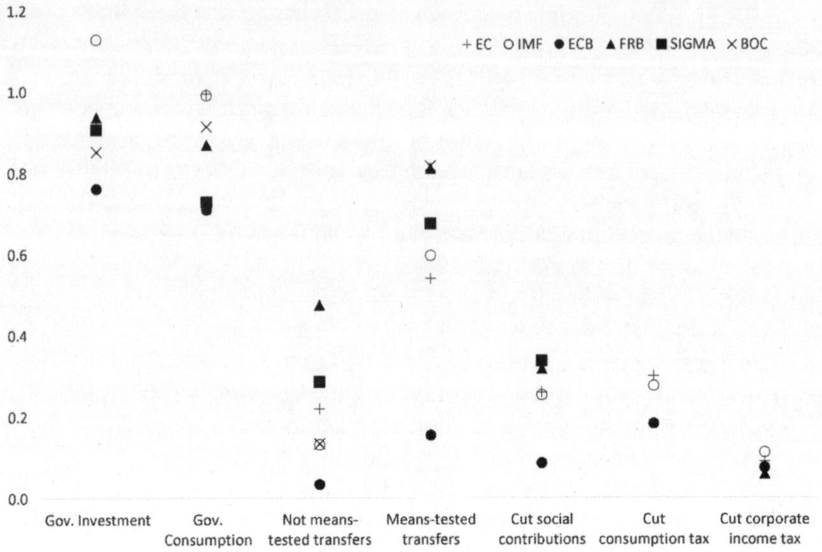

Figure 4.14 Alternative estimates of the impact multiplier (no monetary accommodation).

The stimulus is supposed to last for two years and then be discontinued. The models referred to are those used by major institutions in the United States, the euro area, and Canada. The monetary policy response is endogenously determined by the central bank's reaction function. Each dot corresponds to a particular simulation with a particular model: EC for European Commission, IMF for International Monetary Fund, ECB for European Central Bank, FRB for Federal Reserve Board, SIG for Federal Reserve System SIGMA model (the Board of Governors of the Federal Reserve System uses two models, FRB-US and SIGMA), and BOC for Bank of Canada.

Authors, on the basis of simulations reported in Coenen et al. (2012).

no such thing as a reliable "fiscal instrument" whose impact could be regarded as independent from the context in which it is used and the specific design of fiscal action. We return to these issues in Section 4.3.

4.2.2 Public debt sustainability

There is no universal criterion for assessing public debt sustainability. A first, very rough one relies on the stability of the debt-to-GDP ratio. Consistently, the observed primary balance is compared to the debt-stabilizing benchmark introduced in Section 4.1. This simple exercise has the merit of recalling that, as far as sustainability is concerned, the appropriate level of the fiscal balance depends on the growth rate and the inflation rate (and that the appropriate level of the primary balance depends in addition on the long-term interest rate). The problem with this approach is that the observed debt-to-GDP ratio may not correspond to an optimal, long-run level. If the observed level of debt is too high or possibly too low, targeting its stability provides inadequate guidance to debt sustainability.

a) Concept and indicators

The key to defining sustainability is to allow for a government to remain permanently in debt (because it is infinitely long-lived) while excluding "pushing the debt ahead" as in the speculative chains or *Ponzi games*.[24] The technique has been known for a long time: Lewis Carroll pleasantly illustrates it in *Sylvie and Bruno*:

> "Ah, well, I can soon settle his business," the Professor said to the children, "if you'll just wait a minute. How much is it, this year, my man?" The tailor had come in while he was speaking.
>
> "Well, it's been a doubling so many years, you see," the tailor replied, a little gruffly, "and I think I'd like the money now. It's two thousand pound, it is!"
>
> "Oh, that's nothing!" the Professor carelessly remarked, feeling in his pocket, as if he always carried at least that amount about with him. "But wouldn't you like to wait just another year, and make it four thousand? Just think how rich you'd be! Why, you might be a King, if you liked!"
>
> "I don't know as I'd care about being a King," the man said thoughtfully. "But it does sound a powerful sight o' money! Well, I think I'll wait—"
>
> "Of course you will!" said the Professor. "There's good sense in you, I see. Good-day to you, my man!"
>
> "Will you ever have to pay him that four thousand pounds?" Sylvie asked as the door closed on the departing creditor.
>
> "Never, my child!" the Professor replied emphatically. "He'll go on doubling it, till he dies. You see it's always worthwhile waiting another year, to get twice as much money!" (Carroll, 1889, quoted by Keynes, 1931)

The rigorous definition of *debt sustainability* builds on the intuition that public finances are sustainable if the state meets its *intertemporal budget constraint;* that is, if spending is actually financed—be it today, tomorrow, or the day after tomorrow—because expected future tax receipts cover expected future primary spending and the interest charges on outstanding debt. This can be shown to be equivalent to saying that the present value (at time 0) of the expected debt ratio at time t tends toward zero as t tends toward infinity, a condition known as the *transversality condition* (box 4.13). Intuitively, this means that the future debt can be high but cannot grow faster than the difference between the real interest rate and the real growth rate of the economy. This is also equivalent to saying that the sum of the current debt and the present value of future primary expenditures equals the present value of future receipts.

Box 4.13 Sustainability and the Government's Intertemporal Budget Constraint

Since states do not have a predefined, finite lifetime, there is no need for the net public debt to fall to zero at any given date in the future. Rather, debt sustainability implies that the present value (at time 0) of debt at time *t* tends toward zero as *t* tends toward the infinite. This condition, called the *transversality condition,* is equivalent to the equality between the present value over time of the government's future income and expenditure streams.[a]

We start with the continuous-time equivalent to the debt accumulation equation (B4.5.4) of box 4.5:

$$\frac{db_t}{dt} = (i-n)b_t + \delta_t = (r-g)b_t + \delta_t \qquad \text{(B.4.13.1)}$$

The variation of the debt ratio b_t over time *t* is a function of the interest rate (*i* in nominal terms, *r* in real terms), of the growth rate (*n* in nominal terms, *g* in real terms), and of the primary deficit ratio δ_t. For the sake of simplicity, we assume that the real interest rate and the growth rate are constant. Denoting by b_0 the initial debt ratio, the debt ratio at time *t* can be obtained by integrating Equation (B4.13.1) over time:

$$b_t = b_0 e^{(r-g)t} + \int_0^t \delta_s e^{(r-g)(t-s)} ds \qquad \text{(B.4.13.2)}$$

The present value of b_t at $t = 0$ is obtained by multiplying both sides of this equation by $e^{-(r-g)\,t}$. The discount rate $(r - g)$ allows taking into account the dampening effect of growth on the debt ratio:

$$b_t e^{-(r-g)t} = b_0 + \int_0^t \delta_s e^{-(r-g)s} ds \qquad \text{(B4.13.3)}$$

When *t* tends to infinity, the present value of the debt ratio must tend toward zero, which implies that the right-hand side of the equation also tends toward zero:

$$\lim_{t\to\infty} b_t e^{-(r-g)t} = 0 \text{ implies } b_0 = -\int_0^\infty \delta_s e^{-(r-g)s} ds \qquad \text{(B4.13.4)}$$

The first condition is called the *transversality condition*. If $r > g$, it is necessary and sufficient to fullfil it that the debt ratio increases at a lesser pace than the discount rate $r - g$. If $r < g$, the government can finance the debt service through new borrowing while remaining solvent. This was the situation of the 1970s, a period when public debt problems were benign, and it has become the case again in the 2010s for many countries. But for advanced countries, real interest rates were higher than the growth rates of the economy from the 1980s to the 2000s.

The second condition implies that the present value of future primary surpluses (the opposite of the primary deficits) "repays" the initial debt. Writing $\delta = x + h - \tau$, where x designates expenditure on goods and services, h public transfers, and τ taxes and levies, the condition becomes:

$$b_0 + \int_0^\infty (x+h)_s e^{-(r-g)s} ds = \int_0^\infty \tau_s e^{-(r-g)s} ds \qquad \text{(B4.13.5)}$$

It states that the sum of the initial debt and of the present value of future expenditures must equal the present value of future income. This is the *intertemporal budget constraint* of the government.

Blanchard (1993) takes the sequence of public expenditures and transfers as given in terms of GDP, and calculates the constant tax rate τ^*—which he calls the *sustainable tax rate*—that ensures debt sustainability:

$$\tau^* = (r-g)\left[b_0 + \int_0^\infty (x_s - h_s) e^{-(r-g)s} ds\right] \qquad \text{(B4.13.6)}$$

Taxing income at rate τ is sufficient to service (at rate $r - g$) the sum of the initial debt and of the present value of the future stream of primary expenditures.

The gap between the sustainable tax rate τ^* and the observed tax rate τ, called the *tax gap*, provides an indicator of sustainability. If $\tau < \tau^*$, the long-term sustainability of public debt requires either a rise in taxes or a cut in expenditures.

As a simple finite-horizon benchmark for assessing sustainability, Blanchard also proposes to calculate the constant tax rate necessary to restore the initial level of the ratio of public debt after a given number N of years. However, finite-horizon benchmarks are necessarily more arbitrary.

[a] The layman's version of the transversality condition is a famous remark by Herbert Stein, the former chairman of the Council of Economic Advisers under president Nixon, according to whom "if something cannot go on forever, it will stop."

Consistently, the sustainability of public finance can be assessed by comparing the current tax rate with the *sustainable tax rate* that would ensure debt sustainability if kept constant in the future (box 4.13). The difference between the two is called the *tax gap*. A positive tax gap signals that fiscal policy is unsustainable and that either the level of taxation or the expenditure level will need to be adjusted in the future.

This approach is used in the EU to monitor the fiscal position of member countries. To this end, the European Commission has defined two indicators:[25]

- S1, the *medium-term fiscal sustainability indicator*, gives the improvement in the government structural primary balance that must be carried out over a five-year period to reach, by 2030, a 60% public debt-to-GDP ratio (the EU Treaty reference value), taking into account the financing for any future additional expenditure arising from an aging population. It is a finite-horizon indicator that relies on an *a priori* target for the debt ratio;
- S2, the *long-term fiscal sustainability indicator*, gives the upfront adjustment to the current structural primary balance (assuming it will thereafter be kept at the adjusted value) required to stabilize the debt-to-GDP ratio over the infinite horizon, taking into account the effect of aging on future public spending. Like the tax gap presented in box 4.13, of which it provides an empirical implementation, S2 does not incorporate any specific target for the debt ratio.

This approach, of course, is fragile. First, it relies on long-term projections of growth, interest rates, and public expenditures. Second, it assumes that, provided future revenues match future expenditures, *any* level of public debt can be sustained and financed on the bond market. Third, it provides a global assessment of sustainability but does not specify what the adjustment path should be. Fourth, the sustainable tax rate can vary abruptly ("jump") in response to a change of economic policy scenario—for example, a rise in interest rates or a pension reform that reduces future government spending. Fifth, the long-term sustainability indicator ignores possible short-term financing constraints.[26]

b) Fiscal space

According to the intertemporal budget constraint approach, any level of debt can be sustained provided the adequate primary surplus can be maintained permanently. However, large and sustained primary surpluses amount to making the living generation pay for the fiscal excesses of the previous ones, and they are not sustainable politically. Zheng (2014) finds that, over a 50-year period, only 11 out of 87 countries recorded primary surpluses in excess of 5% of GDP for five years or more. For the assessment of Greek solvency in the 2010s, similar benchmarks were used for determining if there was a high probability that the country would service its debt. When carrying out debt sustainability analyses, the IMF (2013) considers that "closer scrutiny" is called for when a country is projected to maintain a cyclically adjusted primary surplus in excess of 3.5% of GDP over a three-year period.

Building on such observations, Ghosh et al. (2011) depict the fiscal behavior of indebted countries in a stylized graph (figure 4.15). The solid S-shaped line depicts the typical response of the primary balance to variations in the debt ratio. For low debt ratio levels, sustainability is not a concern, and the primary balance does not respond to debt increases. As the debt ratio rises, however, such concerns emerge, resulting in a policy-induced increase in the primary balance.[27] However, when the primary surplus gets large, this response weakens for political economy reasons, and eventually it becomes muted. This response pattern results in the S-shaped policy response curve.

The dashed straight line gives the primary surplus that is required for stabilizing the debt ratio. As discussed previously, its slope is the difference between the real interest rate and the real growth rate. When the S-shaped line is below the dashed line, the debt ratio increases, and vice versa when it is above. To simplify the analysis, we consider the interest rates and growth rates as exogenous.

It is apparent that there are two equilibria for the debt ratio, each of which corresponds to an intersection between the S-shaped and the straight dashed lines. The first d^* corresponds to a stable equilibrium. The second d^{**} is unstable because any increase of the debt level above that threshold results in an unstoppable rise of the debt ratio. For this reason, d^{**} is the maximum possible debt ratio. The *fiscal space* can therefore be defined by the difference $d^{**} - d$ between the maximum and the actual debt level.[28]

The S-curve can be estimated in a panel regression with country fixed effects, resulting in estimates for the difference between the maximum and the current debt ratios. In 2015, the methodology (which has been adopted

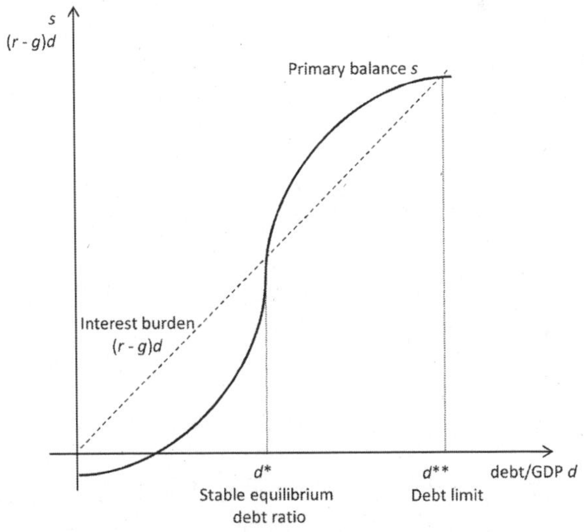

Figure 4.15 Debt sustainability and fiscal space.
From Ghosh et al. (2011).

by Moody's, the rating agency) generally put the maximum debt level in the vicinity of 200–250% of GDP.

As indicated in figure 4.15, the fiscal space depends on $(r - g)$: the higher the difference between the real interest rate and the growth rate, the narrower it is. It is also smaller for countries participating in a monetary union. This is because expectations of insolvency result in a higher interest rate on the public debt r, which in turn pushes d to the left. As shown by Paul De Grauwe (2011), this opens the possibility of self-fulfilling debt crises. This risk can be controlled if the central bank is able to step in and prevent speculation from pushing the sovereign into insolvency. But there are limitations to what the central bank of a monetary union can do. In the euro area, especially, direct financing of governments by the European Central Bank (ECB) or the national central bank is prohibited by treaty, and, although purchase of government bonds on the secondary market is authorized, large-scale central bank intervention on a particular bond market has distributional consequences that may give it a fiscal, rather than monetary character. The euro crisis of 2010–2012 led many to realize that the absence of a lender of last resort for sovereigns results in making individual governments more vulnerable to speculative attacks. ECB interventions on particular markets initiated in 2010 through the Securities Markets Program quickly engendered controversy and led it to create the Outright Monetary Transactions (OMT) program, access to which is conditioned on fiscal adjustment and economic reforms, to be negotiated between the government and the European institutions (see Chapter 5).

c) Sustainability and the effectiveness of fiscal policy

Whether or not fiscal policy is regarded as sustainable is bound to affect its effectiveness. Intuitively, economic agents may spend more in response to a fiscal stimulus if they do not perceive it as endangering the sustainability of public debt, but the same agents may respond by spending less if they expect unsustainability to lead to a policy reversal and the stimulus to be quickly followed by a consolidation.

Sutherland (1997) formalized this intuition in a model that captures the possibility of debt-induced changes in the value of the Keynesian multiplier. The reason is uncertainty regarding the distribution of future taxes across generations. In his overlapping-generations model, presented in box 4.14, consumers have a finite horizon; agents behave in a Keynesian way as long as the public debt remains low enough for the burden of fiscal adjustment to be safely transmitted to future generations; they become increasingly anti-Keynesian (contracting their spending in reaction to a fiscal stimulus) as the likelihood increases that they themselves will have to bear that burden. The same fiscal action can therefore lead to opposite results depending on the level of public debt. Such models rest on somewhat ad hoc assumptions, but they help to describe situations of fiscal crisis during which expectations take a prominent role.

Box 4.14 Public Debt and Fiscal Policy Effectiveness

Sutherland (1997) proposes a simple model where fiscal expansion has the traditional Keynesian effect at moderate public debt levels, but where the multiplier turns negative when debt reaches very high levels.

The representation of households' behavior is based on an overlapping-generation model. At any date, two generations coexist, the "young" and the "old." Fiscal policy is represented by a primary deficit D (per capita) that takes the form of a (non-distortionary) lump-sum transfer to/from the consumers. Denoting r the constant interest rate, the dynamics of the per capita public debt B at time t is given by:

$$dB_t = rB_t dt + D_t \qquad \text{(B4.14.1)}$$

where the deficit D includes a stochastic component. Under these conditions, a series of shocks to the deficit can make the debt explosive.

To fulfill the intertemporal budget constraint, Sutherland imagines a discrete adjustment process: when debt per capita reaches an exogenous ceiling U, a lump-sum tax T is levied on each individual, which reduces the debt to $U - T$; when it reaches an (intuitively negative) floor L, a per capita lump-sum transfer T is paid to each individual, which increases public debt to $L + T$.

Consumers have finite life, with a constant death probability θ. Each individual consumes a quantity c of the same homogeneous good, freely exchanged at a fixed price, and derives from it an instantaneous utility $u(c)$, where u is quadratic. In each period, all individuals receive a fixed income y, plus income $(r + \theta)A$ from their wealth A (wealth is placed with insurance companies that inherit when the individual dies, hence the risk premium θ). The consumer's budget constraint is therefore described by:

$$dA_t = \left[y - c_t + (r + \theta)A_t\right]dt + D_t \qquad \text{(B4.14.2)}$$

The individual maximizes expected utility:

$$E_t \int_t^{\infty} u\left[c_\tau\right] e^{-(r+\theta)(\tau - t)} d\tau \qquad \text{(B4.14.3)}$$

Which results in consumption c_t:

$$c_t = y + (r + \theta)\left[A_t - E_t \int_t^{\infty} \delta_\tau T e^{-(r+\theta)(\tau - t)} d\tau\right] \qquad \text{(B4.14.4)}$$

where δ_τ is equal to 1 when at time τ the debt reaches the ceiling U and a crisis occurs that implies a debt reduction; –1 when debt reaches the floor L and individuals receive a transfer; and zero otherwise.

Individuals therefore consume their income net of the present value (discounted at rate $r + \theta$) of expected future taxes. The results of the model depend on the term:

$$S_t = E_t \int_t^{\infty} \delta_\tau T e^{-(r+\theta)(\tau - t)} d\tau \tag{B4.14.5}$$

Sutherland shows that S is an increasing function of B and that $\partial S/\partial B$ is close to zero when B is low (in absolute value), but larger than unity when B (in absolute value) approaches the thresholds L or U. When B is low, a fiscal expansion (a rise in D in Equation (B4.14.2)) increases consumption in accordance with the traditional Keynesian effect. But when B approaches U, a deficit D triggers expectations of an impending adjustment and causes a *reduction* of consumption in preparation for the upcoming tax increase: the fiscal expansion exhibits an anti-Keynesian effect and leads to a contraction of output.

Empirical investigations confirm that debt sustainability, or the lack thereof, significantly affects the fiscal multiplier. Corsetti et al. (2013) investigate the effectiveness of fiscal policy in a model where the interest rate on public debt depends on the level of government indebtedness. A higher probability of sovereign debt restructuring increases the risk premium demanded by lenders. As long as the central bank does not lose control of the interest rate, it can lower the policy rate to offset the rise on this risk premium. However, when it is constrained by the zero lower bound, it cannot use the same lever anymore, which means that countries at risk of default see that risk magnified by interest rate inertia. The fact that the central bank has hit the zero lower bound therefore both increases the fiscal multiplier (for countries in good shape) and reduces it (for countries in trouble).

4.2.3 Open-economy dimensions

a) The Mundell-Fleming model

The Keynesian approach can easily be extended to the open economy, in particular with the *Mundell-Fleming model*, developed independently by Robert Mundell and Marcus Fleming in the early 1960s.[29] This open-economy extension of the IS–LM model introduces the exchange rate regime as a key determinant of the Keynesian multiplier. In a flexible exchange rate regime, the fiscal multiplier is lowered—even nullified if capital is perfectly mobile across relatively small countries—by the appreciation of the exchange rate that follows a fiscal expansion. Conversely, the multiplier is larger in a fixed exchange rate regime because there is little crowding out (see box 4.15 and Chapter 7 for the definition of exchange rate regimes).

The main results of the Mundell-Fleming model are summarized in table 4.2. Given its simplicity, the model remains a widely used reference by international economy practitioners. For example, it provides a simple framework to think about the consequences of fiscal policy in the euro area. Monetary

Box 4.15 The Mundell-Fleming Model

The canonical Mundell-Fleming model studies macroeconomic policy effectiveness in a small country under *perfect capital mobility* (and under the Keynesian assumption of underemployment of resources). Perfect capital mobility implies that the interest rate cannot deviate from the world interest rate (otherwise capital would flow in or out in search of yield, see Chapters 5 and 7). This is represented by a horizontal interest rate arbitrage condition schedule. At the same time, the internal equilibrium is represented by the IS and LM curves, representing respectively product– and money–market equilibrium. Equilibrium in the model results from the simultaneous fulfilment of three conditions, rather than two in the standard closed economy framework. Which of these conditions endogeneously adjusts to the equilibrium determined by the other two depends on the exchange rate regime.

Floating Exchange Rate

Consider first the case of a *floating exchange rate* regime. Assume that the central bank keeps money supply constant and that the exchange rate is market determined. By shifting the IS curve to the right, a fiscal expansion triggers an increase in output and income, thereby leading to an increase in money demand and—with constant money supply—to an upward pressure on the interest rates. Capital flows in, causing an exchange rate appreciation (a loss of export competitiveness). The IS curve thus shifts back to the left as the demand for the country's products diminishes. Since the open-economy equilibrium is determined by the intersection of LM and the international interest rate arbitrage condition, the only solution is that the exchange rate appreciates up to the point where aggregate demand returns to its original pre–fiscal expansion level (figure B4.15.1). The IS curve and thus fiscal policy play no role in the determination of the output: an increase in public demand simply crowds out the nonresidents' net demand for the country's exports.

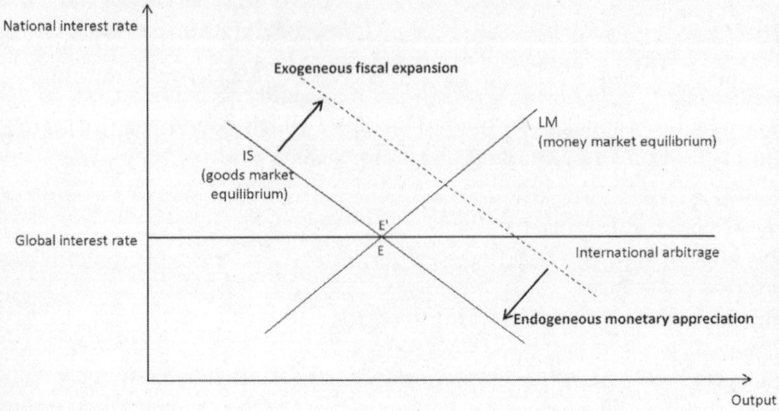

Figure B4.15.1 Fiscal expansion in a floating exchange rate context.

Fixed Exchange Rate

Alternatively, suppose that the exchange rate is *fixed*, meaning that the central bank intervenes on the foreign exchange market through buying and selling foreign currency. Capital inflows consecutive to a fiscal expansion result in the central bank selling the domestic currency for the foreign one, and thereby in an accumulation of foreign exchange reserves by the central bank. If not sterilized (see Chapter 7), this reserve accumulation increases money supply and makes the LM curve move to the right. This endogenous monetary expansion leads to a positive fiscal multiplier (figure B4.15.2). Fiscal policy is powerful and monetary policy is ineffective.

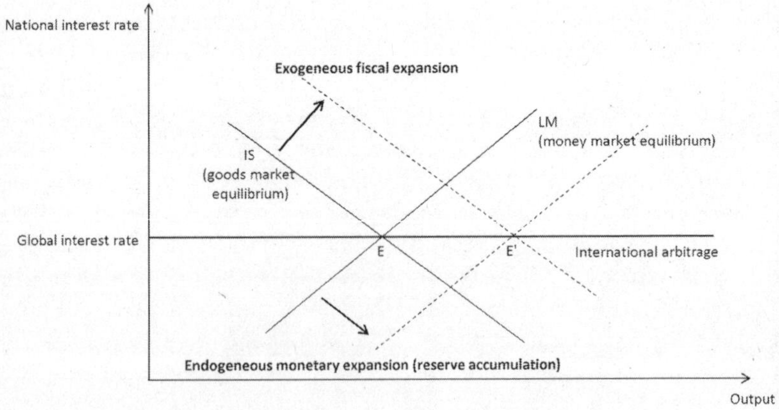

Figure B4.15.2 Fiscal expansion in a fixed exchange rate context.

The Case of No Capital Mobility

When capital is *not mobile*, results are partially reversed: Under a *floating* exchange regime, the deterioration of the current account balance induced by fiscal expansion (because of the increase in import demand) leads to an exchange rate depreciation and to an improvement of export competitiveness, strengthening the initial demand impact of the fiscal expansion. Under *fixed* exchange rates, the current account deterioration results in a reserve loss and in a monetary contraction that counters the initial expansion. Ultimately, the current account must balance—which means that output is determined by what is compatible with the external constraint. Differences in capital mobility and exchange rate regimes thus explain why similar fiscal policies can have contrasting effects on output.

Table 4.2
Short-term effectiveness of fiscal policy in a small open economy: the basic results

	High capital mobility	Low capital mobility
Floating exchange rates	Ineffective	Very effective
Fixed exchange rates	Very effective	Partially effective

union as a whole behaves like a country in a floating exchange rate regime: if capital is fully mobile, fiscal policy is relatively ineffective (unless monetary policy is constrained by the zero lower bound). However, for any given member of the zone, fiscal policy is effective because crowding-out effects are diluted within the zone. Hence, the Mundell-Fleming model suggests that fiscal policy should be used by individual member states hit by asymmetric shocks, but less so as a collective response to a symmetric shock because, in the latter case, the exchange rate adjustment would tend to offset its stabilizing effect (this is only true, however, to the extent that the interest rate responds to the fiscal loosening; at the zero lower bound, this does not hold, implying that fiscal policy can be effective at union level).

Note, however, that the Mundell-Fleming framework does not incorporate two key elements that may strongly modify the impact of a fiscal expansion. First, it is a static model where market expectations play no role. Second, there is no debt, hence no concern over debt sustainability and no risk premium. It is ill-suited to discuss the impact of fiscal policy in a highly indebted country.

b) Fiscal policy spillovers

The reason why fiscal policy is ineffective in a Mundell-Fleming world of high capital mobility and floating exchange rates is that its effects are diluted through the appreciation of the exchange rate: The demand expansion is fully transmitted to the trade partners, leading to what is called a *fiscal spillover effect*.

Spillovers also exist between countries in a fixed exchange rate regime or in a monetary union. In the latter case, the fiscal expansion increases both the demand for goods and the common interest rate, hence the net effect on partner countries is ambiguous: it may be expansionary for some because the trade channel dominates the monetary policy channel and contractionary for others because they are in the opposite situation. Think, for example, of the effects of a Spanish fiscal expansion within the European Monetary Union (EMU): it is likely to benefit significantly Portugal and France, whose exports to Spain are significant, but much less so Austria, Finland, and Estonia because they export little to Spain but are affected by the interest rate increase resulting from the ECB's reaction to a demand-side expansion within the euro area. They could even be hurt. Furthermore, as a fiscal expansion in one country of significant size appreciates the common exchange rate, exports by the monetary union partners may suffer. For this reason, the Mundell-Fleming model indicates that fiscal spillovers within a monetary union are a matter for empirical investigation.

The issue was the matter for heated debates in the context of weak post–euro area crisis recovery in the 2010s. International organizations called upon Germany to support growth through fiscal expansion, but German officials denied that domestic reflation could significantly boost growth in partner countries and, especially, alleviate the woes of peripheral countries. Model-based estimates by the Deutsche Bundesbank (2016) do not find that spillover effects from a German fiscal expansion could be significant: assuming endogenous monetary policy reactions, a 1% of GDP investment boost in Germany would increase German GDP by 0.45% and Dutch GDP by 0.2% after two years, but it would only increase Greek GDP by 0.05% and Spanish GDP by 0.02%. Such normal-times estimates are however disputable because they do not apply in a situation where monetary policy is constrained by the zero lower bound. In the latter situation, a fiscal expansion in the core euro area countries does not result in a rise in the interest rate, and peripheral countries benefit from both higher demand and higher inflation in the core countries. Blanchard, Erceg, and Lindé (2017) find that, under the zero-lower bound, the impact of a core expansion is about half as large in peripheral countries as in core countries.

The upshot is that in the same way the effectiveness of fiscal policy is state-dependent in a single-country context, spillovers onto partner countries are both system-dependent (because they are heavily affected by the exchange rate regime and the degree of capital mobility) and context-dependent (because they depend on whether monetary policy is constrained by the zero lower bound).

4.3 Policies

Fiscal choices everywhere top the policy agenda and are a matter for heated policy debates. Controversies about the proper budgetary stance, fiscal laxity and austerity, debt accumulation, and, in some countries, debt restructuring are the bread and butter of economic policy discussions. Major policy successes or failures are often attributed to fiscal decisions. Doctrines also vary over time: fiscal policy was regarded as the ultimate policy tool in the 1970s, only to fall out of fashion in the 1980s and the 1990s. The global recession of 2009 and the limits encountered by conventional monetary policy in the 2010s have resulted in a significant revival, yet the sovereign debt crises undergone by several European countries have also highlighted the risks involved in testing the limits of the fiscal space.

The debate has been particularly vivid in Europe, where it has focused on the fiscal consequences of forming a monetary union. On the one hand, governments deprived of independent monetary policies are naturally prone to rely more on the fiscal instrument for stabilization purposes. On the other hand, participation in an inflation-adverse monetary union has resulted in the removal of the debt monetization option: as highlighted by the 2010–2012 European sovereign crises, debt has become much riskier after the locking-in of exchange rates. For these reasons, the euro area has provided a rich laboratory for assessing fiscal policy effectiveness, decentralization, and coordination.

Changes in the approach to fiscal policy have not only been a matter of doctrine. Whereas fiscal choices used to be essentially discretionary, they are now increasingly shaped by fiscal rules, such as deficit limits, and by institutions, such as independent fiscal councils. Governments and parliaments remain everywhere in charge of the final decision, but room for discretionary decisions is more limited than in the 1990s. Whether or not such frameworks represent an improvement is a matter for fierce controversies.

We start by presenting and discussing the rules and institutions that constitute the current framework for fiscal policy. Next, we address the resolution of sovereign debt crises. We then analyze the specific case of the euro area. We end with a discussion of the "old" and "new" views of fiscal policy.

4.3.1 Fiscal rules and institutions

As noted already, "fiscal policy" should not be assimilated to "discretionary fiscal policy." In many countries—though not in all—decisions are increasingly shaped by policy rules and institutions that contribute to limiting the scope for discretionary choices. The design of rules and the choice of a mandate for institutions determine a country's fiscal regime and contribute to the quality of its policy.

a) Fiscal rules

In the late 1980s, very few countries were equipped with fiscal rules: according to the IMF (Lledó et al., 2017), only Germany, Indonesia, Japan, Malaysia, Singapore, and, surprisingly, the United States.[30] By 2015, no less than 93 countries had such rules. Many of them had put in place a framework consisting of several guidelines governing the budget balance, the level of expenditure, revenues, or the public debt. The euro area has been at the forefront of this trend toward rules-based fiscal policy, but it is by no means the only region of the world where such a move was apparent.

Fiscal rules are legal provisions that impose constraints on fiscal policy through numerical limits on budgetary aggregates. They can target the deficit, the debt, or public expenditures. They can be couched in nominal terms (such as absolute limits for the financial deficit, the primary deficit, or the saving–investment balance of the public sector), in real terms (such as benchmarks for the real growth rate of public spending), or in structural terms (such as thresholds for and minimum annual improvements of the cyclically adjusted balance). They can apply *ex ante* (to the budget submitted to vote) or *ex post* (to the observed results). They can relate to the general government as a whole or to sub-entities (the federal sector or individual states). They can, as in the EU, result from an international treaty and secondary supranational legislation, as well as be part of the national constitution, or simply national law.

Rules generally aim at correcting distorted incentives that arise from the political economy process and result in overspending and departures from fiscal responsibility. Four main explanations have been put forward to justify them. The first arises from the political business cycle: because voters are ill-informed or perhaps irrational, governments are prone to deficit spending and tend to overstimulate the economy ahead of election years (Nordhaus, 1975); rules help correct the resulting tendency to excessive debt accumulation. The second relies on the consequences of electoral competition: partisanship and disagreements over the allocation of public spending result in a tendency for each camp to overspend on its preferred policies while in power (Tabellini and Alesina, 1990); unlike the previous one, this explanation does not rest on the voters' failure to grasp the consequences of budget deficits but on their division and the strategic use by each camp of the budget deficit. In this setting, a balanced budget rule is socially optimal. The third explanation—developed in Section 4.3.3—is that, in a currency union, national governments do not fully internalize the cost of budget deficits because part of it falls on the partner countries; budget rules help correct this coordination failure. Last but not least, public debt accumulation affects intergenerational equity. The fourth explanation is that because the future generations are not represented in parliament, there is a tendency to transfer the cost of servicing it onto the yet-to-be-born citizens.

Most rules are therefore geared toward fiscal prudence. They could conceptually also help correct excessive caution and a failure to provide adequate fiscal stimulus when needed. There is less of a contradiction than it seems between the two aims: the more governments are prudent in good times, the more aggressively they can pivot to stimulus in bad times.

Research has attempted to account for the spread of fiscal rules. Elbadawi, Schmidt-Hebel, and Soto (2015) find that a higher GDP per capita, democratic institutions, a federal structure, the existence of checks and balances, and political stability all contribute to their adoption. Rules are also more likely in countries characterized by a high old-age dependency ratio, a fixed exchange rate regime or an inflation-targeting regime, and financial openness.

In their landmark article on the design of fiscal frameworks, Kopits and Symansky (1998) identify eight criteria for an "ideal" fiscal rule:

- a clear definition,
- transparent public accounts,
- simplicity,
- flexibility—in particular regarding the capacity to react to exogenous shocks,
- policy relevance in view of the objectives pursued,
- capacity of implementation with possibility of sanctioning nonobservance,
- consistency with the other objectives and rules of public policies,
- accompaniment by other effective policies.

This simple list suggests potentially delicate trade-offs, for example, between simplicity and relevance or between clarity and flexibility. Indeed, rules aim at safeguarding sound government finances in a credible and sustainable way while preserving the contribution of fiscal policy to contra-cyclical output stabilization. However, whether or not they succeed in achieving these objectives is a matter of design and enforcement. Good rules can improve policy, but bad ones can worsen it.

The evolution of the European fiscal framework (see box 4.19 in Section 4.3.3) is a case in point. The original *Stability and Growth Pact* (SGP), the set of fiscal rules and procedures established in the mid-1990s to avoid "excessive deficits", relied exclusively on thresholds and benchmarks for the government financial balance. As such, it did not take cyclical developments into account: a country whose balance had improved because of a cyclical boom was considered compliant with the pact, irrespective of its actual decisions (and a country whose deficit had deteriorated in a recession was considered in breach of the pact, again irrespective of its decisions). A decade later, the SGP was reformed to make room for consideration of the cyclically adjusted deficit, and it was further amended in the wake of the euro crisis so that cyclically adjusted behavior took center stage in the assessment of national policies. It emerged almost immediately, however, that reliance on an unobservable variable was a source of complexity, incoherence over time, and dispute.

Rules that apply to state and local governments play an important role in decentralized systems. They can be part of an overall framework designed to ensure that subnational entities comply with fiscal discipline—especially if state and local governments can apply for support from the center in case of trouble. They can alternatively result from self-imposed discipline. This is the case in the United States, where states are responsible for their own fiscal affairs. The federal constitution grants them a very large degree of fiscal autonomy, and they cannot expect to be bailed out if they lose access to financial markets (see box 4.19 for a historical perspective on the issue). All states but Vermont have enshrined balanced budget requirements in their constitution or their legislation. Rules can mandate an *ex-ante* balance (in which case the state account can exhibit a deficit in case of unfavorable economic developments) or a more stringent *ex-post* balance, often called a *no-carryover provision*. The downside to such provision is that states may be forced to behave pro-cyclically in recessions. This is indeed the case in the United States: although most states have put in place rainy-day funds they can draw on in bad times, there are sharp limitations to what such funds can achieve. In 2009, most US states would have been forced to cut social expenditures in response to the recession, had the stimulus program enacted in 2009 not included federal transfers to state and local governments of the order of magnitude of 0.3% of GDP over a year. More generally, the US policy system assigns the main responsibility for fiscal stabilization to the federal level.

In practice, fiscal rules can be specified in various forms (table 4.3): public debt ceilings, fiscal (financial or primary, headline or structural, overall or on current expenditures) budget balance commitments, rules governing spending targets, and assignment rules for fiscal surpluses. Each has merits and drawbacks.

The balanced budget principle is sometimes expressed as a requirement that current expenditures be financed by current receipts: this is the so-called *golden rule of public finance*. This rule, which was enshrined at the end of the 1960s in the German constitution until it was reformed in 2009, authorizes the use of debt to finance capital expenditures only, unless there is a "disturbance of the macroeconomic equilibrium." The rationale is that debt allows spreading out of the financing of an investment over its lifetime and that, if outstanding government liabilities are matched by (presumably profitable) government assets, this preserves government net wealth. Golden rules have supporters among economists, but they do not prevent debt from becoming unsustainable (if the counterpart of debt accumulation consists in assets of limited marketability and/or low value). Another problem is that the definition of public investment is open to criticism. A narrow definition tends to introduce a disputable bias in favor of brick-and-mortar spending at the expense of investment in human capital, but a broad definition may render the rule ineffective.

Table 4.3
Alternative fiscal rules

Target variable	Pros	Cons
Public debt ratio	Direct link to sustainability Easy to communicate and monitor	Can be pro-cyclical (especially in low-inflation environment) Debt–deficit relation can be affected by one-off developments
Financial balance	Clear operational guidance Easy to communicate and monitor	Often pro-cyclical May lead governments to cut growth-enhancing investment spending
Structural balance	Clear operational guidance Good stabilization properties	Structural deficit is measured with uncertainty Complex to communicate and monitor
Current balance (Golden rule)	Preserves incentive to invest	No direct link to sustainability Often pro-cyclical May favor brick-and-mortar spending
Primary balance	Easy to communicate and monitor in the context of sustainability concerns	Partial link to sustainability Often pro-cyclical
Public expenditure (nominal or real)	Clear operational guidance Easy to communicate and monitor Good stabilization properties	No direct link to sustainability Interferes with allocation decisions May lead governments to substitute tax expenditures to spending

Source: Adapted and expanded from Schaechter et al. (2012) and Fall et al. (2015).

Additionally, the focus on gross rather than net investment is disputable since only net investment benefits future generations.

In 2009, Germany replaced the golden rule by a tighter rule whereby net structural borrowing is limited to 0.35% of GDP per annum for the federal government; the *Länder* will no longer be allowed to run any structural deficit starting in 2020. These limits on structural deficits may be violated only under exceptional events such as natural disasters or severe economic crises, in which case the government is required to provide an amortization plan to parliament. Under the new German rule, the cyclical component of the deficit also falls under close scrutiny, based on the same methodology as for the Stability and Growth Pact. Finally, any implementation deviation is recorded on a control account and must be netted out over time (see Bundesfinanzministerium, 2009).

Countries with a high public debt often choose to target the primary deficit, which is more directly under the control of the government as interest payments on the public debt depend on market-determined interest rates. So did, for example, Belgium, which adopted a primary surplus floor of 6% of GDP at the end of the 1990s. The adjustment programs that the IMF negotiates with countries in financial stress also include primary balance targets.

Standard deficit rules are not adequate for countries facing a high volatility of revenues, such as the commodity producers. For them, the issue is to ensure that temporary revenues arising from exceptional circumstances such as commodity price booms are saved rather than spent. Furthermore, a major policy issue is how to allocate revenues from the exploitation of natural resources: Should they be assigned to the building of infrastructure and human capital, or rather be invested financially so that revenues from the corresponding assets benefit future generations, as Chile (a copper producer) and Norway (an oil producer) have decided (box 4.16)?

Box 4.16 Fiscal Rules in Chile and Norway

Chile and Norway are both commodity producers whose tax revenues are largely determined by the volume of sales and the price of the raw material they are endowed with. For this reason, they have adopted fiscal rules that aim at avoiding pro-cyclicality and at ensuring intergenerational fairness.

The Chilean rule adopted in 2001 specifies that actual government expenditure should be determined by cyclically adjusted revenues net of the target for the cyclically adjusted balance (Schmidt-Hebbel, 2012). There are two adjustments for the cyclicality of revenues: one, based on the output gap, for nonmining revenues, and one, based on the difference between actual and trend mineral prices, for mining revenues. Both are determined by independent committees. The second implies that commodity price windfalls are saved. They jointly imply that government spending is acyclical.

The Norwegian rule, also adopted in 2001, goes further. All revenues from oil extraction are transferred to the government's Oil Fund (officially called "Pension Fund Global"), which is managed by the central bank and invests on global financial markets. The Fund's assets amounted to €850 billion in mid-2017, about twice the Norwegian GDP, and it is one of the largest sovereign funds in the world. The return on invested capital is used to fund the structural, non-oil budget deficit. This is meant, as in Chile, to insulate fiscal policy from fluctuations in oil revenues, to make room for automatic stabilization, but also to ensure intergenerational fairness as oil reserves are expected to be depleted over time. A major concern for the Norwegian authorities was also to avoid the "Dutch Disease" often experienced by countries experiencing commodity booms, when the commodity sector crowds out the other industries.

Experience with the Norwegian rule is regarded as positive: the fiscal rule has given an anchor to policy, it has helped avoid pro-cyclicality, and it has preserved intergenerational fairness. Its application has not been without problems, however: because of the size of the fund and financial market volatility, year-on-year fluctuations of the real return are significant; furthermore, fluctuations in oil prices affect the expected real return path. While the Fund provides a major buffer, it does not fully insulate fiscal policy from the consequences of fluctuations on commodities markets (Norwegian Expert Commission, 2015).

Several countries have adopted expenditure rules, either as a substitute or as a complement to deficit and debt rules. Such rules that limit discretion in the evolution of nominal or real public expenditures have desirable stabilization properties: they prevent governments from increasing spending in response to a temporary surge in revenues and from cutting it in a recession. Whereas expenditure rules do not by themselves take care of ensuring sustainability, they can be coupled coupled with "debt brakes", so that the expenditure target is set at a level that fosters convergence to a certain debt level in the medium term (see Bénassy-Quéré et al., 2018, for an application to the euro area).

b) Fiscal institutions

Many governments, especially in Europe, value the disciplining character of a rule and are convinced that its advantages exceed its disadvantages. Yet all rules have shortcomings. When economic conditions change, sticking to the rule can lead to suboptimal policies: for example, there is no reason why the target for the financial balance should remain unchanged irrespective of lasting variations of the long-term interest rate. But departures from the rules or changes in the rules undermine their credibility. And to make room for particular situations results in complexity (the 2017 *vade mecum* on the EU Stability and Growth Pact is already 224 pages long).

In a landmark article, Wyplosz (2005) observed that the quest for an ideal budgetary rule was reminiscent of the quest for an ideal monetary rule in the 1980s. As far as monetary policy is concerned, this quest proved to be elusive, and the eventual response was to endow well-designed, specific institutions with the responsibility of independently setting interest rates. Building on this precedent, he advocated that an independent fiscal policy committee be in charge of fixing annual fiscal balance targets, leaving to government and parliament full discretion as regards the level and composition of revenues and expenditures. The yearly fiscal balance targets would be set ahead of the budget preparation process so that the committee would be in charge of the macro stance and political government of the micro choices.

The proposal was not taken up by EU governments and is unlikely to be applied any time soon: the choice of a fiscal balance is too political and it involves, indirectly at least, too many distributional choices to be delegated to an independent institution (see box 2.13 of Chapter 2). However, several countries have put in place *independent fiscal councils* that do not have decision-making power but provide real-time assessments of the macroeconomic underpinnings and adequacy of the draft budget. In 1945, the Netherlands was the first country to introduce such an institution. At end-2016, the IMF reckoned that 39 countries were equipped with fiscal councils (Debrun, Zhang, and Lledo, 2017). Their mandates, however, vary widely (Fall et al., 2015): in Austria, for example, the council is in charge of preparing economic and budgetary forecasts, of assessing compliance with fiscal rules, and of providing long-term projections of the public debt; in France its mandate is confined to assessing the realism of the economic forecasts underpinning the budget and the medium-term fiscal plans; whereas in Germany, it includes the assessment of compliance with fiscal rules. In the United States, the Congressional Budget Office is responsible for forecasts, sustainability assessment, and the costing of measures submitted to Congress.

Even when their mandate is narrowly defined, fiscal councils improve the transparency of the budgetary process and help limit the government's tendency to exploit its informational advantage to use budgetary policy for political ends. Broader mandates that include expenditure and revenue forecasts, the costing of policy measures, and debt sustainability assessments further constrain the government's informational advantage while preserving its room for discretionary decisions.

According to Calmfors and Wren-Lewis (2011), fiscal councils are complements rather than substitutes to fiscal rules since they help monitor whether complex rules are actually respected and assess possible deviations. How to combine rules, independent oversight, and democratic decision-making is, however, a delicate issue. The United Kingdom provides a telling example of the subtleties this may imply (box 4.17).

Overall, empirical evidence suggests that fiscal frameworks—whether based on rules, or institutions, or a combination of both—are useful: the adoption of balanced budget rules tends to reduce the deficit, the coexistence of several rules (that target different variables) tends to reduce both the deficit and public spending, and the combination of rules and fiscal councils also has an effect (Fall et al., 2015). However, such estimates do not control for the endogeneity of the fiscal frameworks: it may well be that countries with a preference for fiscal discipline adopt such frameworks more often.[31]

Box 4.18 Fiscal Rules and Institutions in the United Kingdom

Fiscal rules were first introduced in the United Kingdom in 1997 by Gordon Brown, then chancellor of the Exchequer in Prime Minister Tony Blair's first government. The government committed itself to abiding by the *golden rule* of public finances, which required the public sector to borrow only for public investment, and the *sustainable investment rule*, which required the government to ensure that public debt at the end of the economic cycle would not exceed 40% of GDP. The golden rule was met until the global financial crisis, but the sustainable investment rule was arguably only met because the government's own assessments relied on excessively favorable medium-term economic forecasts. It was suspended in the wake of the crisis.

The fiscal framework was reformed in 2010 under PM David Cameron and Chancellor George Osborne in the context of an acute post-crisis worsening of the fiscal situation. The government set two new targets, first to bring the structural deficit below 2% of GDP and, second, to put, by 2020–21, the public debt ratio on a declining path. They also created a new independent institution, the Office for Budget Responsibility (OBR). The OBR has no role in setting the rules, which belong to the remit of the government. But it is in charge of (1) producing the economic and budgetary forecasts that accompany the government's budget statements, (2) assessing whether the government has a greater than 50% chance of meeting its targets, (3) assessing the long-term sustainability of public finances, (4) evaluating fiscal risks, and (5) scrutinizing the government's costing of individual tax and welfare spending measures. To perform these tasks, the OBR has access to government departments and agencies, from whom it may commission specific forecasts. The OBR's work involves significant interaction with the government, both at technical and political levels, but it retains the ultimate responsibility for its published assessments. Its methodologies are made public.

4.3.2 Sovereign debt crises resolution

a) Context

As discussed in the first part of this chapter, sovereign states regularly experience insolvency crises and have to undergo a restructuring of their public debt. For several decades after World War II, such *sovereign debt crises* were deemed a sad privilege of developing countries. In 2011, Lorenzo Bini Smaghi, then a member of the board of the ECB, famously declared that a debt restructuring in Greece would be "like the death penalty which we have abolished."[32] A little more than year later, however, Greece reached agreement with its creditors on a restructuring of its public liabilities that resulted in a debt forgiveness amounting to about €100bn in present value terms, or 50% of the 2012 GDP (Zettelmeyer, Trebesch, and Gulati 2013). Five years later, discussions on a further Greek debt restructuring, this time of the loans from the official sector, were again on the agenda. In the meantime, Ireland, Portugal, and Cyprus had lost and regained market access.

In most countries, a company that is unable to meet a financial obligation enters negotiation with its creditors within the framework of legal provisions that protect the rights of the various stakeholders (essentially creditors, shareholders, and employees) and provide a venue for negotiation, while temporarily ensuring the continuation of operations. Rather than seize the debtor's assets and liquidate the company, it is in the collective interest of creditors to aim at a settlement that preserves as much as possible the value of their claims—which implies that the company is offered a chance to reorganize. Individually, however, each creditor has an interest in being reimbursed as fast as possible. Such a "grab race" is against the creditors' common interest. This contradiction signals a collective action problem that bankruptcy procedures aim at solving.

In the United States, these procedures are governed by what is called "Chapter 11" of the Bankruptcy Code. It permits the debtor to remain in control of its business as a "debtor in possession" under the control of the courts until a settlement is reached. In the meantime, the procedure ensures a standstill on litigations: it prevents "any act to collect, assess, or recover" a claim against the debtor that arose before its commencement. At the end of the procedure, the company may be liquidated, be taken over, or resume normal business operation after reorganization and financial settlement. For example, American Airlines operated under Chapter 11 between end-2011 and end-2013.

The idea of applying bankruptcy principles to sovereign states goes back at least to Adam Smith. But it is since the Mexican crisis of 1982 that a "Chapter 11 for sovereign states" has been a matter for policy discussions.[33] It was first proposed by then-Harvard economist Jeffrey Sachs (1995) and taken up a few years later in a proposal by the IMF (Krueger, 2002). The idea suffered considerable pushback, however, from the financial industry and it failed to be adopted. Agreement was only reached on the inclusion in foreign currency–denominated sovereign bonds of collective action clauses (CACs) that make it possible for bond holders to decide on a settlement with the debtor by qualified majority.

The issue reemerged in the context of the European debt crisis after Chancellor Merkel of Germany and President Sarkozy of France agreed in October 2010 in a meeting in Deauville that financial assistance to euro area members would only be provided to solvent countries. Those deemed insolvent would first need to agree on a restructuring with their creditors. To this end, collective action clauses would be introduced in all new euro-denominated bond contracts from 2013 onward.

The Deauville agreement elicited considerable criticism, first for having acknowledged the possibility of sovereign insolvency in the euro area and, second, for sending a confusing message about future restructuring and the relative treatment of old and new creditors. It was subsequently watered down: the 2012 Treaty establishing the ESM only mentions the need to assess whether the public debt of a country that applies for assistance is sustainable, without spelling out the consequences of this assessment. It largely subcontracts the debt sustainability assessment to the IMF ("Wherever appropriate and possible, such an assessment is expected to be conducted together with the IMF"; Article 13.1.b of the ESM Treaty). This has strong implications because access to Fund lending requires that the country's debt is assessed sustainable "with a high degree of probability." If it is not the case, IMF policy prescribes prior debt restructuring—as it did for Greece in 2015–2017, with the consequence that disagreements between the Fund and European institutions contributed to a protracted impasse in negotiations with the Greek authorities.[34]

b) Issues in the design of sovereign restructuring procedures

There are three main issues that a procedure for sovereign debt restructuring must address. The first is the need to set the incentives right for all parties. Debt restructurings are repeated games: each step in a country's negotiation with its creditors and each decision by a court are carefully scrutinized by other debtors and creditors because they create precedents. It is important that debt restructurings do not violate the creditors' rights, that they are not excessively delayed, and that they do not impose unnecessary hardship to the population. To make restructuring too costly for the debtor country would not only involve welfare costs for the citizens, it could also lead to postponing it excessively and, ultimately, it could reduce the country's ability to repay.[35] But to make it too easy would give an incentive for governments to overborrow, and it would give to creditors an incentive to impose high default risk premia. This is why the institutional set-up should be designed to help find the right balance between conflicting interests (Buchheit et al., 2013).

The second issue arises from the collective action problem created by the multiplicity of lenders. In the 1980s, when lenders were a few international banks, the problem was relatively easily to solve: negotiations could take place with all major banks simultaneously, and authorities such as the IMF and national supervisors could apply moral suasion. From the 1990s onward, the development of disintermediated borrowing made the situation radically different: bonds are now bought by a variety of investment funds and even private individuals; furthermore, they are continuously traded, with the consequence that the identity of creditors changes over time. The problem is meant to be addressed by the introduction of collective action clauses in the bond contracts, but difficulties remain, especially as majority rules only apply to the holders of a particular bond issuance. The combination of separate bonds contracts and a legal obligation to treat all borrowers equally (this is called the *pari passu clause*) involves considerable procedural hardship.

The third issue results from the peculiarities of sovereign borrowing. As discussed already in Section 4.1 of this chapter, sovereign debt is less enforceable than private debt because there is little collateral that can be seized by creditors: most assets are located inside the national borders, and assets held abroad are often protected by sovereign immunity. This makes it possible for a debtor to walk away and suffer little more than reputational damage. At the same time, the fact that states are infinitely long-lived implies that their debts are not easy to get rid of: until a settlement is reached, creditors retain the legal right to insist on repayment. Companies can go bankrupt and their owners can start a new business. But, absent an agreement with its creditors, there is no such thing as a fresh start for a sovereign borrower.

Since the 1990s onward, the problem has been made more acute by the emergence of so-called *holdout funds* that buy sovereign debt at distressed prices on the secondary market and specialize in suing the sovereign to obtain full repayment. Argentina in the 2000s lost its legal battle against holdouts, as a US federal judge (bonds had been issued under US law) prohibited negotiated repayment to the 93% of creditors that had agreed on restructuring unless the holdout creditors were repaid in full. The ruling, which was based on an extreme interpretation of the *pari passu* clause, forced the Argentinean government to agree in 2016 on settling the lawsuit initiated by the holdouts.

Hopes that a statutory solution to these issues could be found through the creation of an international bankruptcy court, or more modestly what the IMF once called a *sovereign debt restructuring mechanism* (SDRM) whose decisions would be binding for all parties involved, were abandoned in the early 2000s and are unlikely to be revived in the context of suspicion for multilateralism that has developed since the mid-2010s.

Initiatives for mitigating the holdout problem have rather been based on provisions ensuring better consistency in the treatment of bond series. With conventional collective action clauses as initially introduced, a debtor seeking a settlement with its creditors needed to obtain the agreement of a qualified majority of them for each bond series. This made it possible for holdouts to concentrate their purchases on the smaller series and block the restructuring. This is why the International Capital Market Association, a self-regulatory body, issued in 2014 model clauses that make decisions by a supermajority of all bondholders binding on the holders of any particular series. The generalization of such "onle-limb" CAC clauses would eventually eliminate the holdout problem (Gelpern, 2014). However, they are not mandatory and will at any rate spread gradually only as their introduction affects new issuances, not the outstanding debt stock.

c) Debt crises resolution in the euro area

The issue of sovereign debt crisis resolution within the euro area arose when Greece proved insolvent. It involves three peculiar features.

First, the bulk of public debt is issued under national law instead of foreign law, as it is the case for emerging countries. This makes it possible for a state to set by itself the terms of the restructuring, as Greece did in 2012: parliament passed a law stating that if holders of two-thirds of the Greek law–governed bonds approved a restructuring, the result would apply to all bondholders (Zettelmeyer et al., 2013). It is to be noted that Greece did not use its legal powers to change unilaterally the value of its sovereign bonds, but rather to make the outcome of the negotiation with a supermajority of the creditors binding on all of them.[36]

Second, public debt is partially held by public entities—the central bank as a consequence of its bond purchase program or the ESM and the IMF as a consequence of their lending. In the case of Greece, by mid-2017, more than two-thirds of government debt was owed to official creditors. For this reason, but also because of the precedent it would set for other countries, restructuring is subject to quasi-statutory procedures. Between 2015 and 2018, the issue of a second Greek restructuring (called for by the deteriorating economic situation and the consequences of domestic deflation on the debt ratio) was the matter for permanent discussions within the Eurogroup of finance ministers. Furthermore, two major official creditors insisted that they should not take part in any restructuring: the IMF because of its preferred status and the ECB because it claimed that this would violate the prohibition of monetary financing.

Third, the importance of sovereign bonds in the balance sheets of the banks makes sovereign restructuring even more delicate: in compliance with the post-crisis regulatory standards, a loss on the banks' sovereign bonds portfolio would have to be borne by their shareholders and creditors. Alternatively, the banks would need to be recapitalized by the defaulting state, as was done in Greece. However, this was one of the channels of the banks-sovereign "doom loop" that threatened stability in the euro area, especially since domestic sovereign bonds were massively used to get refinancing from the Eurosystem, but with varying haircuts (see Chapter 5 and Chapter 6).

Whether or not principles for eventual debt restructuring should be spelled out in the euro area remains a divisive and fiercly debated issue. Part of the policymaking community, especially in France and southern Europe, strongly advocate retaining a significant enough degree of ambiguity to make room for case-by-case, discretionary decisions, and it has rejected academic proposals for a policy framework that would make debt restructuring a possible, if last-resort option (Bénassy-Quéré et al., 2018).

4.3.3 Fiscal policy in the euro area

Many fiscal policy issues are common to all advanced countries. The euro area, however, stands apart: it is the only monetary union that is not equipped with a central (or, equivalently, federal) budget. This has two major consequences. First, in times of financial stress, governments cannot rely on having access to the financing of their national central banks, which strengthens (or at least should strengthen) *ex ante* fiscal discipline but also makes states more fragile *ex post*; although euro area states borrow in their own currency, market constraints resemble those faced by those that borrow in a foreign currency. Second, the absence of both national monetary policies and a common budget puts the burden of stabilization on national fiscal policies. There is therefore a built-in tension between the fiscal prudence inherent to participating in a monetary union and the demand for fiscal activism resulting from the lack of other stabilization instruments. In principle, the solution to this conundrum is to equip the union with credible fiscal rules that provide sufficient room for maneuver in downturns. This was the principle underpinning the Maastricht system, but implementation has proved to be fraught with considerable difficulty.

The problem is best illustrated by a comparison with the United States, where states know that they cannot rely on being bailed-out by the Federal Reserve or the federal government but can abstain from playing a part in macroeconomic stabilization because this role belongs to the remit of the federal government. The US government contributes to cushioning both state-specific shocks (through the automatic operation of taxes and transfers) and country-wide shocks (through automatic stabilizers and discretionary action).

In what follows, we present and discuss in turn fiscal discipline, fiscal federalism, and fiscal policy coordination.

a) Fiscal discipline

The main argument for fiscal discipline in a monetary union is that spillovers from fiscal imprudence are large. When Greece found itself on the verge of bankruptcy in 2010, banks in other member countries that held Greek debt in their portfolio were affected, and states in weak fiscal positions suffered from contagion as market participants started to worry about sovereign risk in the euro area.

It is precisely to prevent such risks that fiscal discipline has been, since its inception, a key tenet of the EMU (see Eichengreen and Wyplosz, 1998). The Maastricht Treaty precludes public securities being directly purchased by central banks on the *primary market* where they are initially issued (which is of little effect as it does not prohibit buying them on the *secondary market* where they are subsequently traded). However, the central bank's policy can be affected even if it does not purchase any bond from sovereigns in trouble. A government that faces difficulty tapping financial markets tends to borrow through short-term instruments (because private investors are reluctant to lend long term for fear of default), and the central bank may soon face a dilemma: either it brings the government to the brink of a failure through a relatively high interest rate, or it departs from its price stability mandate and sets a low interest rate to preserve the government's capacity to pay. The central bank can also be led to intervene in the name of financial stability, as banks that hold debt of a struggling government (most frequently the banks headquartered in the same country) themselves face difficulty accessing the market and are soon forced to rely on ECB liquidity (see Chapter 5).

One of the defining features of the euro area crisis of 2010–2012 was indeed the strong correlation between the risk premia affecting sovereign and banks. It was visible on bond markets as well as in the market for *credit default swaps* where bond holders can get an insurance against a possible default. This correlation, which could not be observed in the United States or other countries when banks were under severe financial stress, was indicative of the fragility of the monetary union (see Chapters 5 and 6).

There are basically two ways to address this problem. One, adopted in the EU, is to monitor and enforce fiscal discipline so that no state finds itself in a situation where its solvency can be put in question. This is the purpose of the "avoidance of excessive deficits" and the possibility of levying fines on states in breach of fiscal rules enshrined in the Maastricht Treaty of 1992, as well as of the secondary legislation built on its basis. Over the years, the EU has put in place an elaborate apparatus of fiscal rules and procedures whose aim is to enforce fiscal discipline while at the same time leaving some room for stabilization action at the national level (see box 4.18).

Box 4.18 Fiscal Rules and Procedures in the Euro Area

During the negotiation of the European Economic and Monetary Union in the early 1990s, it was agreed that Member States must avoid "excessive deficits" (Article 126 of the Treaty on the Functioning of the EU) and should face sanctions if this discipline went unobserved. Reference thresholds of 3% of GDP for the deficit of the general government and 60% of GDP for gross public debt were defined and laid down in the protocol on the excessive deficit procedure annexed to the Treaty. However, the Treaty did not specify the procedure for implementing sanctions.

On the eve of the introduction of the euro, Germany demanded that the fiscal discipline commitments and procedures be detailed. The resulting Stability and Growth Pact includes:

- *A preventive arm.* Each Member State is to adopt a *medium-term objective* for its cyclically adjusted budgetary position that is consistent with the overall objective of being close to balance or in surplus and leaves room for stabilization of normal cyclical fluctuations without breaching the 3% threshold. It prepares a three-year *stability program* that is updated every year and is submitted to the assessment of the Commission and to the approval of the Eurogroup of finance ministers. The program describes the adjustment path toward the medium-term objective, taking as a benchmark a 0.5 percentage point improvement in cyclically adjusted terms per year.
- *A corrective arm.* Except if "exceptional and temporary," the headline (financial, i.e., noncyclically adjusted) fiscal deficits of Member States should never exceed 3% of GDP. When the deficit threatens to reach, or exceeds, the 3% threshold, a specific surveillance procedure (the *excessive deficit procedure*) is set in motion according to a

predetermined timetable of increasing pressures: Steps include early warning, identification of an excessive deficit, recommendation to implement corrective actions, obligation to make a non–interest bearing deposit with the Commission, and conversion of the deposit into a fine. The eventual fine includes a fixed component of 0.2% of GDP and a variable component linked to the size of the deficit, within an annual limit of 0.5%.

Corresponding decisions are made by the *Eurogroup* (i.e., the group of the finance ministers of the euro area), on the basis of recommendations by the European Commission.

After extensive criticism of the SGP, the failure of several member states to comply with it, and a subsequent 2003 decision by the Eurogroup to put the pact "in abeyance" instead of simultaneously stepping up its corrective procedures against France and Germany, a substantial reform of the SGP was adopted in 2005. The goal was to "enhance the economic rationale of the budgetary rules to improve their credibility and ownership."[a] In addition to an emphasis on cyclically adjusted balances instead of headline balances, the medium-term budgetary objective (MTO) of keeping the budget "close to balance or in surplus" was replaced by individual MTOs that recognize the specific economic characteristics of each Member State.

In 2010–2011, the euro area crisis prompted a reexamination of the system of fiscal rules. Neither for Greece (because it had cheated) nor for Ireland or Spain (where the problem came from banks) could the crisis be attributed to a breach of the rules, but the focus was nevertheless on strengthening the fiscal framework. Changes included:

- A new set of legislative provisions (the *six-pack*) that redefined decision procedures, made earlier sanctions possible, introduced a debt reduction criterion alongside the deficit criterion, and mandated the creation of national fiscal councils.[b]
- Another set of legislative provisions (the *two-pack*) that aimed at strengthening the *ex ante* monitoring of budgetary decision. It makes it possible for the Eurogroup to request that a country reconsiders a draft budget deemed in infringement of the rules.
- A new Treaty (the *Treaty on Stability, Coordination, and Governance*-TSCG) that gives stronger legal status to the main provisions of the six-pack and mandates the adoption in each member country of a binding, preferably constitutional balanced budget rule limiting the structural deficit to 0.5% of GDP (unless public debt is below 60% of GDP, in which case the threshold is set at 1% of GDP). The fiscal provisions of the TSCG (or *fiscal compact*) also commit all euro area members to supporting Commission recommendations as regards a

country in breach of the deficit criterion, unless there is a qualified majority to reject them. This provision amounts to changing the voting rule for recommendations from qualified majority to reverse qualified majority. It was meant to introduce a dose of automaticity into the sanction procedure.

In 2015, the European Commission issued a recommendation emphasizing that the existing rules leave room for flexibility in implementation, especially for countries willing to undertake investments or structural reforms (European Commission, 2015).

[a] See the *Presidency Conclusions* of the March 22–23, 2005, European Council, Annex II.
[b] The Six-Pack also introduced a procedure for the prevention and reduction of current account imbalances (it is called the *macroeconomic imbalances procedure*).

The alternative approach is to rely instead on *market discipline*. In this model, states do not behave prudently because they are instructed to behave, but because they know that no one will come to their rescue if they lose market access, hence the interest rate on their debt reflects their fiscal position. Such market discipline requires that the threat of letting a state default be credible, which in turn necessitates that the financial system be protected from the fallout of a state bankruptcy. This is basically the solution adopted in the United States, where, for nearly two centuries, the federal government has consistently refused to bail out insolvent states (box 4.19).

The euro area has gone as far as it could go in the direction of monitoring and directing the individual Member States' fiscal behavior through a set of rules and procedures—short of what former ECB president Jean-Claude Trichet (2013) once called "federalism by exception": direct administration by the EU institutions of a country unwilling to abide by its fiscal commitment and whose behavior threatens the stability of the euro area as a whole. The fiscal framework nevertheless suffers from a series of shortcomings (see, for example, Bénassy-Quéré and Ragot, 2015; Pisani-Ferry, 2015):

- Procedures are excessively complex and ownership by national decision-makers is often lacking;
- Enforcement mechanisms are weak and the credibility of sanctions is questionable;
- The benchmarks of the reformed Stability and Growth Pact are based on unobservable variables, such as the structural deficit, whose measurement is open to controversy;
- The adequacy of the fiscal recommendations that result from the implementation of the rules is questionable from a macroeconomic standpoint;

- The framework does not provide sufficient incentives to investment and growth-enhancing reforms;
- Flexibilities introduced to leave room for intelligent assessment opened the door to undue politicization.

The alternative of relying on market discipline, as in the United States, would, however, raise a host of new issues, if only because the debt of US states, even the largest ones, is an order of magnitude lower than that of the major euro area countries. First, it would require establishing procedures to restructure sovereign debts. Second, it would require national banking systems be

Box 4.19 The States' Fiscal Regime in the United States

The US federal system went through an early test of the fiscal rules of the game in the immediate aftermath of the War for Independence.[a] The war effort had left individual states heavily indebted, and some were effectively bankrupt. A fierce debate on the treatment of the public debt followed, with on one side the Secretary of the Treasury, Alexander Hamilton, who argued that because debt had been incurred for a common purpose it had to be assumed by the newly established federal government, and on the other side Thomas Jefferson, the Secretary of State, who opposed debt mutualization. In the end Hamilton prevailed: the debt was transferred to the federal government and swiftly restructured; states were charged on a per capita basis so that the burden of the revolutionary war would be distributed evenly.

A consequence of this early episode was that a precedent was set, whereby the federal government would bail-out insolvent states. Moral hazard was therefore substantially present, until eight states that had over-borrowed to finance infrastructure defaulted in 1840. British and Dutch creditors, who held the bulk of the debt, argued that the federal government's guarantee, while not explicit, had been implied. In the event of a default, another war with Britain was regarded a possibility. However, Congress rejected the assumption of state debt, thereby establishing a new 'no bail-out' norm.

The norm was upheld in the aftermath of the Civil War, through a wave of local defaults in the 1930s, and again on the occasion of a series of municipal bankruptcies in the 1970s. The only exception regarded the District of Columbia, arguably not an ordinary state, whose government was taken over by Congress in the 1990s.

A consequence of the establishment of a no bail-out norm has been the adoption by individual states of balanced-budget rules: the first wave took place precisely in the 1840s after Congress rejected debt assumption.

[a] This box is based on Henning and Kessler (2012).

protected against the fallout of state insolvency, especially through regulatory incentives to diversify sovereign bond holdings and the creation of a euro area safe asset (see Chapter 6 for details). Third, a fiscal capacity of significant enough firepower to ensure stabilization at the federal level would need to be created (see the discussion in the next section). Proposals along these lines to introduce a modicum of market discipline together with risk-sharing and a fiscal capacity were put forward by French and German academics (Bénassy-Quéré et al., 2018) but they were not endorsed by euro area member states.

b) Fiscal federalism

In federal states, the macroeconomic stabilization function is generally assigned to the federal level, while individual states are often subject, sometimes by their own will, to strict fiscal discipline. In the United States, when a state undergoes a negative income shock, its residents pay lower federal taxes but continue benefiting from federal spending (on public goods, transfers, etc.). The federal budget therefore functions as an automatic shock absorber. An early paper by Sachs and Sala-i-Martín (1992) found that up to 30–40% of economic shocks that affect the states are absorbed by the federal budget. This evaluation has been debated, and the current consensus is rather around 10–30% (European Commission, 2016), which is still non-negligible (see the methodology in Chapter 7, box 7.7). Furthermore, a federal budget tends to encourage labor mobility (through the portability of social entitlements) and capital mobility (through financial integration). In the United States, both channels are more stabilizing than the tax transfer channel (see Chapter 7, box 7.7).

In the euro area, the choice not to supplement the single currency with a federal budget was initially made for political reasons: monetary union was already a significant step toward a European federation, and that was the limit of what governments and public opinion could accept. Furthermore, as public spending is already high, the creation of a federal budget would have required transferring budgetary functions from the national to the European level (rather than the initiation of new functions at the federal level, as was the case in the United States). Whereas the MacDougall report of 1977, an early blueprint for EMU, had envisaged a federal budget of the order of 5–10% of GDP, as indicated in Chapter 3, monetary union was initiated without any federal fiscal leg. It was assumed that fiscally prudent Member States would retain sufficient stabilization power to be able to offset adverse economic developments, either individually in the case of country-specific shocks or jointly in the case of common shocks.

In 2012, the "Four Presidents' Report" prepared jointly by the heads of the main European institutions, including that of the ECB in the aftermath of the sovereign debt crisis mapped out the future of the euro area (Van Rompuy et al., 2012) and floated the idea of a *fiscal capacity* that would "contribute to cushioning the impact of country-specific shocks and help prevent contagion across the euro area and beyond." The notion of a fiscal capacity was voluntarily kept fuzzy: it could mean a proper budget; an insurance fund designed to supplement cyclically sensitive components of national public spending, such as unemployment insurance; or a system of purely macroeconomic cyclical transfers based on relative deviations from potential output.

The key requirements for establishing such a mechanism is that it should have strong enough stabilization properties but no distributional bias. In other words, all countries should be able to receive net transfers in a downturn, but none should benefit from permanent transfers. Meeting these two goals at the same time is not easy: for example, topping up national unemployment insurance with a euro area component would result in permanent net transfers to the countries where structural unemployment is the highest. It would therefore result in subsidies from countries whose educational, labor market, and product market are efficient to countries where the same policies are inefficient. Solutions to address the problem do exist, for example, through the setting up of an unemployment reinsurance scheme that would only cover large, temporary shocks (Bénassy-Quéré et al., 2018), but they raise delicate design issues. Furthermore, any proper euro area budget would need resources and would have to be enshrined in an institutional frameworks that ensures proper democratic accountability to a parliamentary body. The European parliament at present has no taxing power and no euro area chamber has been created within it.

Fears of a "transfer union" that would involve large and permanent transfers from Northern European states to Southern European ones have resulted in considerable caution, especially on the part of Northern Europe countries, toward projects for a fiscal capacity or a euro area budget.

c) Policy coordination

As discussed in Chapter 3, economic literature traditionally identifies two major reasons for nations to coordinate economic policies. The first, already discussed, is the provision of the international public goods that decentralized action will in general fail to produce. The second relates to the suboptimality of uncoordinated decisions in the presence of externalities, even for the pursuit of predominantly national objectives.

These two reasons apply in Europe and especially in the euro area. First, safeguarding financial stability can be viewed as an EU-wide public good. This justifies the prevention of unsustainable budgetary positions unless procedures are in place that protect the banking system against the fallout from sovereign bankruptcy.

Second, as noted in Section 4.2 of this chapter, participation in the monetary union gives rise to specific fiscal policy externalities (box 4.20).

Box 4.20 Fiscal Policy Spillovers Within a Monetary Union

Suppose two identical countries called A and B form a monetary union (U), and let us represent the equilibrium in the Mundell-Fleming diagram as in box 4.15. The three panels in figure B4.20.1 represent, respectively, equilibrium in country A, in country B, and in the monetary union U. The single interest rate is determined by the intersection of the IS and LM curves at the level of the Union (point E). The equilibrium in each country is then determined by the country-specific IS curve, given the single interest rate.

Now let us assume that country A carries out an expansionary fiscal policy, bringing its IS curve to the right. The IS curve of country B also moves (but to a lesser extent) toward the right because it benefits from increased exports to country A. The aggregate IS curve for the whole monetary union also shifts to the right. The common interest rate increases. Country B profits from increased exports, but suffers from a higher interest rate (equilibrium at E″).

If the interest rate externality dominates, country B is likely to react with an expansionary fiscal policy. Output will then increase but at the price of a higher budget deficit, while a fall in the interest rate would have benefited the country's public finance.

Depending on the pair of countries involved, either the interest rate channel or the trade one dominates (see Bénassy-Quéré and Cimadomo, 2012). The externality involved in the latter case is being addressed by the fiscal discipline framework. There is no specific procedure to address the other one. This means that, short of ad hoc policy coordination, each country feels little incentive to implement a stabilizing fiscal expansion.

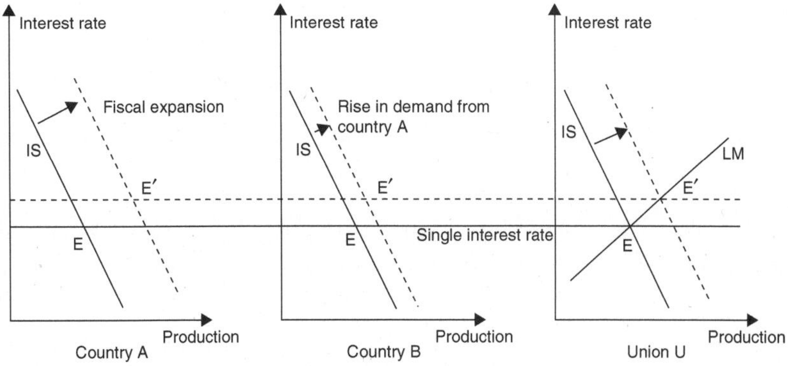

Figure B4.20.1 Impact of a fiscal expansion in a monetary union.

An expansionary fiscal policy in one country creates a positive demand externality for the other members but—if the central bank responds by raising the interest rate—a negative interest-rate externality. This second, different justification for mutual surveillance of national budgetary policies was formalized early on by Beetsma and Bovenberg (1999) and identified as a rationale for common fiscal rules.

Should fiscal policies be coordinated to ensure that the aggregate fiscal stance of the euro area is adequate? As discussed earlier, the Mundell-Fleming model, under flexible exchange rates and perfect capital mobility (these assumptions are normally correct for the euro area as a whole) leads to the conclusion that fiscal policy is ineffective;[37] the task of stabilizing the economy of the euro area accordingly falls primarily on monetary policy and the coordination of fiscal policies to stabilize output appears to be a second-best solution ranking below monetary policy. This conclusion must be questioned when monetary policy is constrained by the zero lower bound: the response to an adverse demand shock relies on fiscal policy, and, absent a coordinated stimulus, the combined policy reactions of individual Member States are bound to be inadequate (Draghi, 2014).

This discussion leads to the following policy assignment rule:

- The common monetary policy should respond to shocks affecting the whole area (symmetric shocks).
- National fiscal policies should respond to country-specific shocks or shocks affecting a group of countries in relation to others within the area (asymmetric shocks);
- Aggregate euro area–level fiscal policy may be called upon to complement monetary policy when the latter proves ineffective or insufficient, especially when the policy rate is at the zero lower bound.

The European institutional framework barely upholds this policy assignment. Whereas fiscal discipline is enshrined in the Stability and Growth Pact, fiscal coordination only rests on an interpretation of the very general clause of Article 121.1 of the Treaty on the functioning of the EU, according to which Member States "regard their economic policies as a matter of common concern and shall coordinate them within the Council." Attempts to monitor the aggregate fiscal stance of the euro area and to strengthen coordination through the so-called *European semester* have been facing a harsh reality: national governments are accountable to national parliaments and, ultimately, national citizens only.

4.3.4 Conclusion: Old and New Views on Fiscal Policy

As noted already, the consensus on the role of fiscal policy has varied markedly in recent decades. From the activism of the 1970s, when President Richard Nixon famously said "We are all Keynesian now" to the nonactivist consensus of the late twentieth century, and then to the post-2008 revival, changes have been wide. Divergences over the role of fiscal policy also have a spatial dimension: for decades, Germany has been the staunch advocate of fiscal discipline, whereas the United States has repeatedly called for making use of the fiscal lever.

The nonactivist consensus of the late twentieth century was well summarized in the already mentioned John Taylor (2000) paper. The core of his argument was that monetary policy dominates fiscal policy for stabilization purposes because its implementation lags are shorter and because it is nimbler (the central bank can change course more easily than a parliamentary chamber). Furthermore, using monetary and fiscal policy in parallel and to the same end would complicate rather than facilitate the task of the central bank, because it would need to figure out what will be the reaction of the fiscal authorities. Further critics such as Martin Feldstein (2002) added that "deliberate 'countercyclical' discretionary fiscal policy has not contributed to economic stability and may have actually been destabilizing at particular times in the past."

Fifteen years later, this view was still largely dominant in Europe, but the US consensus had reverted to activism. Jason Furman (2016), who was Chairman of the Council of US Economic Advisers under President Obama, contrasted the "old view" and the "new view" of the role of fiscal policy (table 4.4).

As developed in this chapter, which view is right at a given moment in time is largely a matter of macroeconomic conditions. The "old" view represented the consensus at a time when aggregate fluctuations were moderate (what Olivier Blanchard and John Simon, 2001, termed "The Great Moderation") and when economic cycles were largely asynchronous, while long-term interest

Table 4.4
"Old" and "new" views on the role of fiscal policy

	"Old" view	"New" view
Effectiveness	Limited by negative side effects (crowding-out of private investment)	Can be very effective (and even crowd in private investment)
Stabilization role	Normally dominated by monetary policy (except at zero lower bound)	Complement to monetary policy (especially at zero lower bound)
Fiscal space	Scarce. Hence, priority should be long-run fiscal balance	Larger than appreciated when real interest rates are low. Stimulus can be combined with long-run consolidation.
International coordination	Generally unnecessary	Can be effective

Source: Adapted from Furman (2016).

rates were positive in real terms. The "new" view represents the consensus of a time when aggregate fluctuations are ample and synchronous, equilibrium real interest rates can be negative, and deflationary pressures weaken the effectiveness of monetary policy while threatening economic stability. If lasting, such changes in economic conditions must affect the prevalent view on economic policy and the institutions that underpin policymaking.

Notes

1. Data mentioned in this paragraph are from the International Monetary Fund's *Public Finances in Modern History Database*. See Mauro et al. (2013).
2. In Europe, collective schemes that provide unemployment, health, and old-age insurance are generally grouped under the heading *social security*, whereas in the United States, social security designates old-age insurance only.
3. This finding holds after controlling for the biases in the estimation arising from the fact that, as argued by Rodrik (1998), countries facing more aggregate fluctuation risks (because of their geographic or sectoral specialization) may have developed an endogenous preference for larger governments. See Galí (1994), Fatás and Mihov (2001), and Debrun, Pisani-Ferry, and Sapir (2010).
4. There are other ways to finance deficits. For example, poor developing countries also finance their deficits through receiving grants. Another possibility, the consequences of which are discussed later and in Chapter 5, is for the government to receive loans from the central bank.
5. Source OECD, Government at a Glance data, 2017.
6. *Sovereign wealth funds* have been established to this end. Examples include Singapore (Government of Singapore Investment Corporation, or GIC) and Norway (where oil income is invested in the Government Pension Fund of Norway). See Box 4.16.
7. As discussed in the following sections, the interest rate cannot be regarded as independent from the debt level. For example, the large primary deficit of Greece in 2009 (8% of GDP) triggered a rise in the risk premium that worsened the outlook of its public finances.
8. The concept of "original sin" was introduced by Eichengreen, Hausman, and Panizza (2005).
9. Source: Privatization Barometer 2013–2014, KPMG and ENI-Enrico Mattei Foundation.
10. The G20 includes the largest economies globally. It began meeting at heads of state and government levels in 2008, in response to the global crisis. It holds annual meetings.
11. See the communiqué of the leaders' meeting on www.g20.utoronto.ca/summits/2009london.html
12. Source: European Commission, AMECO database.
13. Source: European Commission, AMECO database.

14. England however defaulted in the fourteenth century, as did individual U.S. states in the nineteenth century.
15. There are examples of states that wind up and close their books, but legacy debt is then carried over to newly established countries. For instance, Czechoslovakian debt was split between the Czech Republic and Slovakia on January 1, 1993. There are also examples of governments that refuse to pay for their predecessors' debt because they deem it politically illegitimate. This famously happened after the Russian and Chinese revolutions. It has been proposed, as a form of sanction, to formally declare debts incurred by illegitimate dictatorship *odious debt*. But since political regime change cannot usually be foreseen, it is difficult to integrate it into *ex ante* sustainability analysis.
16. To be more precise, they can seize some of its foreign assets but those generally amount to a small fraction of liabilities.
17. On figure 4.14, the IS and LM curves shift simultaneously to the right.
18. For example, Christiano, Eichenbaum and Rebelo (2011) find that in a benchmark, new-Keynesian model, the multiplier is lower than unity in normal conditions but significantly higher than unity at the zero lower bound.
19. On a sample of 21 OECD countries, de Mello et al. (2004) find that a one percentage point drop in public saving results in a one-third to one-half percentage point rise in private saving.
20. The so-called *Haavelmo theorem* (1945) states that in a simple Keynesian setting, a simultaneous reduction of public spending and taxes by a given amount reduces output.
21. The approach was pioneered by Ramey and Shapiro (1998). See also Burnside, Eichenbaum, and Fisher (2004).
22. Chodorow-Reich (2017) surveys the evidence on the value of regional multipliers and concludes that they are consistent with a zero lower bound national multiplier of 1.7 for the United States. Ramey and Zubairy (2017) find that it could be as high as 1.5 at the zero lower bound.
23. The evidence, however, is disputed by Ramey and Zubairy (2017).
24. From the name of a famous Boston crook in the 1920s, who used to entice savers with the promise of high returns, but who would pay them only with the amounts collected from new participants. Ponzi games were played on a large scale in Russia and Albania in the 1990s. The Madoff fraud uncovered in 2008 is another example.
25. The European Commission indicators are published yearly in the Fiscal Sustainability Report prepared by DGECFIN.
26. The European Commission has developed a short-term vulnerability indicator called S0 that relies on a series of ad hoc subcomponents. As for the IMF, it relies on gross financial needs (i.e., on the sum of the financial deficit and of debt redemptions over the year). Gross financial needs in excess of 15–20% of GDP are considered a threat. This alternative approach stresses that the same debt may be sustainable or not depending on its maturity structure.
27. Bohn (1998) provides evidences of such behavior in the US case.
28. In practice, the threshold of unsustainability is in fact lower and the fiscal space is smaller because as d approaches d^{**}, financial markets become aware of the risk of

a shock pushing the debt ratio above that level into the insolvency zone. For this reason they will start pricing the insolvency risk at lower debt levels already.

29. See Mundell (1968) and Fleming (1962).
30. In the United States, the Gramm-Rudman-Hollings Balanced Budget Act of 1985 was temporarily operational.
31. Poterba (1994), however, exploits the fact that budget rules in US states typically date back to the nineteenth century. He finds that their relative stringency had affected state responses to shocks in the 1980s.
32. Interview with the *Financial Times*, May 29, 2011.
33. The Mexican crisis marked the return of sovereign default at the forefront of the international agenda, after three decades with almost no sovereign crises.
34. On the occasion of the Greek case, the IMF introduced a "systemic exemption" so as to be able to lend despite its assessment on the probability that the Greek debt was sustainable. This exemption was removed in January 2016.
35. This was illustrated by the protracted deadlock of the interwar period over German war reparations and later by the Latin American debt crisis of the 1980s, until the Brady plan of 1989 cleared the way for a settlement.
36. The law was challenged in various courts, including the European Court of Human Rights. It was upheld on the ground that the severe financial crisis facing Greece made the restructuring inevitable and that the procedure chosen to implement the restructuring had followed the CAC template adopted by all euro area sovereign issuers.
37. Actually, even under the assumptions of the model, the inefficiency of fiscal policy holds only for a small country, which does not describe the euro area as compared to the rest of the world. For an open economy under flexible exchange rates, however, fiscal stimulus results in stimulating the trading partners' economies.

References

Alesina, A., and S. Ardagna (2010), "Large Changes in Fiscal Policy: Taxes Versus Spending," in J. Brown, ed., *Tax Policy and the Economy* 24, pp. 35–68, Chicago University Press.

Alesina, A., Barbiero, O., Favero, C., Giavazzi, F., and M. Paradisi (2017), "The Effects of Fiscal Consolidations: Theory and Evidence," *NBER Working Paper* 23385.

Auerbach, A., and Y. Gorodnichenko (2012), "Measuring the Output Responses to Fiscal Policy," *American Economic Journal: Ec, Policy,* 4(2), pp. 1–27.

Auerbach, A., and Y. Gorodnichenko (2017), "Fiscal Stimulus and Fiscal Sustainability", *NBER Working Paper*, No 23789, Sep.

Barro, R. (1974), "Are Government Bonds Net Wealth?" *Journal of Political Economy,* 81(6), pp. 1095–1117.

Batini, N., L. Eyraud, L. Forni, and A. Weber (2014), "Fiscal Multipliers: Size, Determinants, and Use in Macroeconomic Projections," *Technical Note*, International Monetary Fund.

Bayoumi, T. (2001), "The Morning After: Explaining the Slowdown in Japanese Growth in the 1990s," *Journal of International Economics* 53(2), pp 241-259.

Beetsma, R., and L. Bovenberg (1999), "Does Monetary Unification Lead to Excessive Debt Accumulation?" *Journal of Public Economics,* 74(3), pp. 299–325.

Bénassy-Quéré, A., and J. Cimadomo (2012), "Changing Patterns of Domestic and Cross-Border Fiscal Policy Multipliers in Europe and the US," *Journal of Macroeconomics,* 34, 845–873.

Bénassy-Quéré, A., and X. Ragot (2015), "A Policy Mix for the Euro Area," *Note of the French Conseil d'analyse économique,* 21 March.

Bénassy-Quéré, A., Ragot, X., and G. Wolff (2016), "Which Fiscal Union for the Euro Area?" *Note of the French Conseil d'analyse économique,* 29 February.

Bénassy-Quéré, A., et al. (2018), "Reconciling risk sharing with market discipline : A constructive approach to Eurozone reform", *Centre for Economic Policy Research Policy Insight* No 91, January.

Blanchard, O. (1985), "Deficits, Debts, and Final Horizons," *Journal of Political Economy,* 93(2), pp. 223–47.

Blanchard, O. (1993), "Suggestions for a New Set of Fiscal Indicators," in H. Vergon and F. van Winden, eds., *The Political Economy of Government Debt,* Elsevier Science Publishers, pp. 307–25.

Blanchard, O., C. Erceg, and J. Linde (2017), "Jump-Starting the Euro Area Recovery: Would a Rise in Core Fiscal Spending Help the Periphery?" *NBER Macroeconomics Annual,* 31(1), pp. 103–82.

Blanchard, O., and R. Perotti (2002), "An Empirical Characterization of the Effects of Changes in Government Spending and Taxes on Output," *Quarterly Journal of Economics,* 117(4), pp. 1329–68.

Blanchard, O., and J. Simon (2001), "The Long and Large Decline in US Output Volatility," *Brookings Papers on Economic Activity,* 1, pp. 135–64.

Bofinger, P., Mayer, E., and T. Wollmershäuser (2002), "The BMW Model: Simple Macroeconomics for Closed and Open Economies: A Requiem for the IS/LM-AS/AD and the Mundell-Fleming Model," *Würzburg Economic Papers* No. 35.

Bohn, H. (1998), "The Behavior of US Public Debt and Deficits," *The Quarterly Journal of Economics,* 113(3), pp. 949–63.

Boorman, J. (2002), "Sovereign Debt Restructuring: Where Stands the Debate?" speech at Cato Institute-The Economist conference, New York, 17 October.

Buchheit, L. C., A. Gelpern, M. Gulati, U. Panizza, B. Weder di Mauro, and J. Zettelmeyer (2013), "Revisiting Sovereign Bankruptcy," Committee on International Economic Policy and Reform, Brookings Institution Report, October.

Bundesfinanzministerium (2009), "Reforming the Constitutional Budget rules in Germany," Public Finance and Economic Affairs Directorate, Deficit Rule Reform Team, August.

Burnside, C., M. Eichenbaum, and J. Fischer (2004), "Fiscal Shocks and their Consequences," *Journal of Economic Theory,* 115(1), pp. 189–17.

Calmfors, L., and S. Wren-Lewis (2011), "What Should Fiscal Councils Do?" *Economic Policy,* 26(68), pp. 649–95.

Campbell, J., and N. G. Mankiw (1989), "Consumption, Income, and Interest Rates: Reinterpreting the Time Series Evidence," in Blanchard, O., and S. Fischer, eds., *NBER Macroeconomics Annual 1989,* MIT Press, pp. 185–216.

Carnot, N., and F. de Castro (2015), "The Discretionary Fiscal Effort: An Assessment of Fiscal Policy and Its Output Effect." *European Economy Economic Papers* 543, European Commission.

Carroll, L. (1889), *Sylvie and Bruno*, Macmillan.

Chodorow-Reich, G. (2017), "Geographic Cross-Sectional Fiscal Spending Multipliers: What Have We Learned?" mimeo, Harvard University, December.

Christiano, L., M. Eichenbaum, and S. Rebelo (2011), "When Is the Government Spending Multiplier Large?" *Journal of Political Economy,* 119(1), pp. 78–121.

Coenen, G., C. J. Erceg, C. Freedman, D. Furceri, M. Kumhof, R. Lalonde, D. Laxton, J. Linde, A. Mourougane, D. Muir, S. Mursula, C. de Resende, J. Roberts, W. Roeger, S. Snudden, M. Trabandt, and J. in't Veld (2012), "Effect of Fiscal Stimulus in Structural Models," *American Economic Journal: Macroeconomics,* 4(1), pp. 22–68.

Coibion, O., Y. Gorodnichenko, and M. Ulate (2017), "The Cyclical Sensitivity in Estimates of Potential Output," *NBER Working Paper* 23580, July.

Corsetti, G., K. Kuester, A. Meier, and G. Müller (2013), "Sovereign Risk, Fiscal Policy and Macroeconomic Stability," *The Economic Journal,* 123, pp. 99–132.

Cruces, J., and C. Trebesch (2013), "Sovereign Defaults: The Price of Haircuts," *American Economic Journal: Macroeconomics*, 5(3), pp. 85–117.

De Grauwe, P. (2011), "Managing a Fragile Eurozone," *CESifo Forum,* 12(2), pp. 40–45.

De Grauwe, P., and Y. Ji (2013), "Self-Fulfilling Crises in the Eurozone: An Empirical Test," *Journal of International Money and Finance*, 34(C), pp. 15–36.

Debrun, X., J. Pisani-Ferry, and A. Sapir (2010), "Government Size and Output Volatility: Should We Forsake Automatic Stabilization," in Buti, M., S. Deroose, V. Gaspar, and J. Nogueira Martins, eds., *The Euro: The First Decade*, Cambridge University Press, pp. 451–506.

Debrun, X., X. Zhang, and V. Lledo (2017), "The Fiscal Council Dataset: A Primer to the 2016 Vintage," International Monetary Fund, March.

de Mello, L., P.-M. Kongsrud, and R. Price (2004), "Savings Behavior and the Effectiveness of Fiscal Policy," *OECD Economics Department Working Paper* 397.

Deutsche Bundesbank (2016), "The International Spillover Effects of an Expansion of Public Investment in Germany," *Monthly Report August 2016*, pp. 13–17.

Devries, P., J. Guajardo, D. Leigh, and A. Pescatori (2011), "A New Action-based Dataset of Fiscal Consolidation," *IMF Working Paper* 11/128.

Dippelsman, R., C. Dziobek, and C. A. Gutiérrez Mangas (2012), "What Lies Beneath: The Statistical Definition of Public Sector Debt," *IMF Staff Discussion Note* 12/09, July.

Draghi, M. (2014), "Unemployment in the Euro Area," speech at the Jackson Hole Central Banking Symposium, 22 August.

Eichengreen, B., R. Hausmann, and U. Panizza (2005), "The Pain of Original Sin," in Eichengreen, B., and R. Hausmann, eds., *Other People's Money: Debt Denomination and Financial Instability in Emerging Market Economics*, University of Chicago Press, pp. 13–47.

Eichengreen, B., and C. Wyplosz (1998), "The Stability Pact: More than a Minor Nuisance?" *Economic Policy*, 13(26), pp. 65–104.

Elbadawi, I., K. Schmidt-Hebbel, and R. Soto (2015), "Why Do Countries Have Fiscal Rules?" in Caballero, R., and K. Schmidt-Hebbel, eds., *Economic Policies in Emerging-Market Economies Festschrift in Honor of Vittorio Corbo*, vol. 21, pp. 155–89, Banco Central de Chile.

European Commission (2016), "Cross-Border Risk Sharing After Asymmetric Shocks: Evidence from the Euro Area and the United States," *Quarterly Report on the Euro Area*, 15(2), Directorate-General ECFIN.

European Commission (2015), "Making the Best Use of the Flexibility within the Existing Rules of the SGP," Communication COM(2015),12 January.

Fall, F., D. Bloch, J.-M. Fournier, and P. Hoeller (2015), "Prudent Debt Targets and Fiscal Frameworks," *OECD Economic Policy Paper* 15.

Fatás, A., and I. Mihov (2001), "Government Size and Automatic Stabilisers: International and Intranational Evidence," *Journal of International Economics*, 55(1), pp. 3–28.

Feldstein, M. (2002), "The Role for Discretionary Fiscal Policy in a Low Interest Rate Environment," *NBER Working Paper* 9203.

Fleming, J. M. (1962), "Domestic Financial Policies Under Fixed and Under Flexible Exchange Rates," *IMF Staff Papers* 9(3), pp. 369–79.

Furman, J. (2016), "The New View of Fiscal Policy and Its Application," speech at the conference *Global Implications of Europe's Redesign*, New York, 5 October.

Galí, J. (1994), "Government Size and Macroeconomic Stability," *European Economic Review*, 38(1), pp. 117–32.

Galí, J., J. D. López-Salido, and J. Vallés (2007), "Understanding the Effects of Government Spending on Consumption," *Journal of the European Economic Association*, 5(1), pp. 227–270.

Gelpern, A. (2014), "A Sensible Step to Mitigate Sovereign Bond Dysfunction," mimeo, Peterson Institute for International Economics, 29 August.

Ghosh, A, Kim, J., Mendoza, E., Ostry, J., and M. Qureshi (2011), "Fiscal Fatigue, Fiscal Space and Debt Sustainability in Advanced Economies," *The Economic Journal* 123(566), pp. 4–30.

Greenspan, A., and J. Kennedy (2007), "Sources and Uses of Equity Extracted from Homes," *Finance and Economics Discussion Series* 2007-20, Federal Reserve Board.

Guajardo, J., Leigh, D., and A. Pescatori (2014), "Expansionary Austerity? International Evidence," *Journal of the European Economic Association* 12(4), pp. 949–968.

Haavelmo, T. (1945), "Multiplier Effects of a Balanced Budget," *Econometrica*, 13(4), pp. 311–18.

Hansen, A. (1953), *A Guide to Keynes*, New York: McGraw Hill.

Henning, R., and M. Kessler (2012), "Fiscal Federalism: US History for Architects of Europe's Fiscal Union," *Bruegel Essays* 6, Bruegel, Brussels.

Hicks, J. (1937), "Mr. Keynes and the 'Classics': A Suggested Interpretation," *Econometrica*, 5(2), pp. 147–59.

International Monetary Fund (2010), "Will It Hurt? Macroeconomic Effects of Fiscal Consolidation," Chapter 3 of *World Economic Outlook*, October, pp. 93–124.

International Monetary Fund (2013), "Staff Guidance Note for the Public Debt Sustainability Analysis in Market-Access Countries," mimeo, 9 May.

International Monetary Fund (2017), *IMF Fiscal Monitor: Achieving More with Less*, April.

Juncker, J.-C., with D. Tusk, J. Dijsselbloem, M. Draghi, and M. Schulz (2015), *Completing Europe's Economic and Monetary Union* (Five Presidents' Report), European Commission, 22 June.

Keynes, J. M. (1931), *Essays in Persuasion*, Harcourt, Brace and Company.

Keynes, J. M. (1936), *The General Theory of Employment, Interest and Money*, Macmillan.

Kopits, G., and S. Symansky (1998), "Fiscal Policy Rules," *IMF Occasional Paper* 162.

Krueger, A. (2002), *A New Approach to Sovereign Debt Restructuring*, International Monetary Fund.

Laeven, L., and F. Valencia (2012), "Systemic Banking Crisis Database: An Update," *IMF Working Paper* 12/63, June.

Lledó, V., Y. Sungwook, F. Xiangming, M. Samba, and Y. Kim (2017), *Fiscal Rules at a Glance*, International Monetary Fund.

MacDougall, D. (1977), *Report of the Study Group on the Role of Public Finance in European Integration*, report to the European Commission.

Mankiw, N. G. (2000), "The Savers-Spenders Theory of Fiscal Policy," *American Economic Review* (Papers and Proceedings), 90(2), pp. 120–25.

Mauro, P., R. Romeu, A. Binder, and A. Zaman (2013), "A Modern History of Fiscal Prudence and Profligacy," *IMF Working Paper 13/5*.

Mineshima, A., M. Poplawski-Ribeiro, and A. Weber (2014), "Fiscal Multipliers," in Cottarelli, C., P. Gerson, and A. Senhadji, eds., *Post-Crisis Fiscal Policy*, MIT Press, pp. 315–372.

Mirabeau H.-G. Riqueti, comte de (1787), *Lettres du comte de Mirabeau sur l'administration de M. Necker*, available on gallica.bnf.fr, French *Bibliothèque nationale*.

Mourre, G., G.-M. Isbasoiu, D. Paternoster, and M. Salto (2013), "The Cyclically-Adjusted Budget Balance Used in the EU Fiscal Framework: An Update," *European Economy*, Economic Paper 478.

Mundell R. (1968), *International Economics*, Macmillan.

Nakamura, E., and J. Steinsson (2014), "Fiscal Policy in a Monetary Union: Evidence from US Regions," *American Economic Review* 104(3), pp. 753–92.

Nordhaus, W. (1975), "The Political Business Cycle," *The Review of Economic Studies*, 42(2), pp. 169–90.

Norwegian Expert Commission (2015), "Fiscal Policy in an Oil Economy: The Application of the Fiscal Rule," *Official Norwegian Reports NOU*, 2015:9, Chapter 1.

Pisani-Ferry J. (2015), "Rebalancing the Governance of the Euro Area," in Dawson, M., H. Enderlein, and C. Jörges, eds., *Beyond the Crisis*, Oxford University Press, pp. 62–82.

Polackova H. (1999), "Contingent Government Liabilities: A Hidden Fiscal Risk," *Finance and Development*, 36(1), pp. 46–49.

Poterba, J. (1994), "State Responses to Fiscal Crises: The Effects of Budgetary Institutions and Politics," *Journal of Political Economy*, 102(4), pp. 799–821.

Ramey, V., and M. D. Shapiro (1998), "Costly Capital Reallocation and the Effects of Government Spending," *Carnegie Rochester Conference Series on Public Policy*, 48, pp. 145–94.

Ramey, V., and S. Zubairy (2017), "Government Spending Multipliers in Good Times and Bad: Evidence from US Historical Data," *Journal of Political Economy*, forthcoming.

Reinhart, C., and K. Rogoff (2014), "This Time Is Different: A Panoramic View of Eight Centuries of Financial Crises," *Annals of Economics and Finance*, 15(2), 1065–1188.

Reinhart, C., and C. Trebesch (2016), "Sovereign Debt Relief and Its Aftermath," *Journal of the European Economic Association*, 14(1), pp. 215–251.

Ricardo, D. (1820), "Essay on the Funding System," in Sraffa, P., ed., *The Works and Correspondence of David Ricardo*, Cambridge University Press, 1951, pp. 143–200.

Rodrik, D. (1998), "Why Do More Open Economies Have Bigger Governments?" *Journal of Political Economy*, 106, pp. 997–1032.

Romer, C., and D. Romer (2010), "The Macroeconomic Effects of Tax Changes: Estimates Based on a New Measure of Fiscal Shocks," *American Economic Review*, 100(3), pp. 763–801.

Romer, D. (2000), "Keynesian Macroeconomics Without the LM Curve," *Journal of Economic Perspectives*, 14(2), pp. 149–69.

Sachs, J. (1995), "Do We Need an International Lender of Last Resort?" Frank D. Graham Lecture, Princeton University, 20 April.

Sachs, J., and X. Sala-i-Martin (1992), "Fiscal Federalism and Optimum Currency Areas: Evidence for Europe from the United States," in Canzoneri, M., V. Grilli, and P. Masson, eds., *Establishing a Central Bank: Issues in Europe and Lessons from the US*. Cambridge University Press, pp. 195–219.

Schaechter, A., T. Kinda, N. Budina, and A. Weber (2012), "Fiscal Rules in Response to the Crisis—Toward the 'Next-Generation' Rules: A New Dataset," *IMF Working Paper* 12/187.

Schmidt-Hebbel, K. (2012), "Fiscal Policy for Commodity-Exporting Countries: Chiles' Experience," *Documento de Trabajo* 415, Banco Central de Chile.

Sutherland, A. (1997), "Fiscal Crises and Aggregate Demand: Can High Public Debt Reverse the Effects of Fiscal Policy?" *Journal of Public Economics*, 65(2), pp. 147–62.

Tabellini, G., and A. Alesina (1990), "Voting on the Budget Deficit," *American Economic Review*, 80(1), pp. 37–49.

Taylor, J. (2000), "Reassessing Discretionary Fiscal Policy," *Journal of Economic Perspectives*, 14(3), pp. 21–36.

Tereanu, E., Tuladhar, A., and A. Simone (2014), "Structural Balance Targeting and Output Gap Uncertainty," *IMF Working Paper* 14/107.

Trichet, J.-C. (2013), "International Policy Coordination in the Euro Area: Toward an Economic and Fiscal Federation By Exception," *Journal of Policy Modeling*, 35(3), pp. 473–81.

Van Rompuy, H., with J.-M. Barroso, J.-C. Juncker, and M. Draghi (2012), *Towards a Genuine Economic and Monetary Union* (Four Presidents' Report), European Council, 5 December.

Wyplosz, C. (2005), "Fiscal Policy: Institutions Versus Rules," *National Institute Economic Review,* 191, pp. 70–84.

Zettelmeyer, J., C. Trebesch, and M. Gulati (2013), "The Greek Debt Restructuring: An Autopsy," *Economic Policy,* 28 (75), pp. 513–63.

Zheng, L. (2014), "Determinants of the Primary Fiscal Balance: Evidence from a Panel of Countries," in Cottarelli, C., P. Gerson, and A. Senhadji, eds., *Post-Crisis Fiscal Policy* MIT Press, pp. 67-96.

5

Monetary Policy

Monetary policy is a demand-side policy just like fiscal policy, but there are two important differences. First, monetary policy is generally delegated to an independent agency—the central bank—with an explicit and narrow mandate, generally price stability. Second, monetary policy affects aggregate demand only indirectly, whereas fiscal authorities purchase goods and services directly. Households and companies take consumption, investment, and savings decisions depending on present and future interest rates on products offered by financial intermediaries (banks, pension funds, etc.). The central bank influences this process indirectly by affecting financing conditions, but it does not lend directly to households and nonfinancial companies, nor does it collect their savings.[1] A key implication is that monetary policy cannot be effective if the financial system is impaired, as was the case during the 2008 financial crisis. Hence, monetary policy cannot be isolated from financial stability (which we address in Chapter 6), and financial crises make the task of central bankers much more difficult.

5.1 Issues

5.1.1 What is monetary policy?

Monetary policy consists in managing the quantity and price of money[2] to achieve one or several objectives depending on the central bank's mandate: price stability, full employment, and, depending on the exchange rate regime (see Chapter 7), exchange rate stability. In the Musgrave and Musgrave taxonomy used in Chapter 1, monetary policy can be classified, like fiscal policy, as a stabilization policy: by affecting interest rates, it alters households' and firms' intertemporal decisions. For instance, a cut in interest rates will reduce the cost of investing, and the subsequent increase in investment will raise aggregate demand.

Monetary policy is designed and implemented by *central banks*, institutions which may have private shareholders but operate under a public mandate written in law or constitution. Central banks operate at the level of a country (such as the US Federal Reserve [Fed]; also the Bank of Japan or the Bank of England) or, in the case of a monetary union, of a group of countries (such as the European Central Bank [ECB] for the euro area[3]). They have the privilege of creating what is called *base money*, or sometimes *high-powered money.*[4] This consists in providing liquidity to individuals in the form of banknotes, and to the financial system in the form of *bank reserves* deposited on accounts at the central bank. This is why the central bank is sometimes called the "bank of the banks." Monetary policy consists primarily in setting the price and quantity of central bank liquidity. By arbitrage, this price determines short-term interest rates paid on the interbank market (where banks lend to each other) and on short-term financial instruments. Depending on market expectations and risks, monetary policy also influences longer term interest rates and a wider range of financial variables in the economy, which in turn influence economic behavior.

Although its purpose is macroeconomic stabilization (and hence intertemporal redistribution), monetary policy also has allocative and distributive consequences. For example, at a given point in time, a lower interest rate reduces the income of savers and benefits debtors. Central bankers consider such distributive consequences limited and balanced over the business cycle, and they see them as means to an end. Politicians and citizens sometimes disagree, which may lead them to challenge the central bank's mandate. Controversies have become more frequent since the global financial crisis, as the scope and magnitude of central bank intervention have increased.

a) Monetary policy in normal times

At any point in time, banks extend credits to households and companies, make payments, and receive deposits from their clients. These operations do not necessarily balance: some banks are more active in providing credit, others manage a large network of branches where customers hold deposit accounts. Banks balance their cash positions by extending very-short-term loans to one another on the *interbank market*. The interbank market is part of the *money market*, a broader concept which encompasses nonbank participants such as corporate treasurers and money market funds. One says that they provide liquidity to each other. However, the aggregate balance between supply and demand for liquidity is not left to the market participants alone: the central bank also intervenes on the market by providing money to and borrowing from banks. This ensures both a smooth functioning of the payment system and a stable price of liquidity. By changing the conditions of liquidity provision, the central bank also affects the price of liquidity and, by extension, the whole range of interest rates and financial asset prices, as we explain later.

In practice, all commercial banks have an account at the central bank on which reserves are deposited (not to be confused with the foreign exchange reserves of the central bank; see Chapter 7). Liquidity is created by the central bank and channeled to a commercial bank by crediting its account (i.e., by increasing its reserves). But central banks do not give money for free, and they seek protection against bank default. Such protection is provided either by purchasing from the bank a corresponding amount of financial instruments (an *outright purchase*) or by requiring it to pledge this amount as *collateral* with the central bank for the duration of the loan. Collateral usually comprises public or private bonds, sometimes other financial assets such as stocks or loans to households and companies. Such collateralized loans are called *refinancing operations*, see table 5.1.[5]

One particular form of collateralized lending is called a *repurchase agreement*, or *repo*, which legally entails a transfer of ownership of the collateral for the duration of the loan. In all cases, if the commercial bank would default, the central bank would end up owning the assets. In a refinancing operation, to account for changes in the market value of the securities used as collateral over the lifetime of the loan, the central bank usually requests an amount of collateral which is larger than the amount of liquidity provided to the commercial bank. The difference is called a *haircut*. It is calibrated based

Table 5.1
Impact of a \$100 bond purchase by the central bank on its own balance sheet and on the balance sheet of a commercial bank

Central bank		Commercial bank	
Assets	Liabilities	Assets	Liabilities
Bonds: \$100	Reserves of the commercial bank: \$100	Reserves at the central bank: \$100 Bonds: −\$100	0

on the risk of default of the issuer of the securities and on how easy it would be to sell it in case of need.[6] For instance, a 10% haircut means that a bank must post securities worth 100 dollars to obtain a loan of 90 dollars from the central bank.

Instead of leaving the money at the central bank, the commercial bank may also use it to buy banknotes for future distribution to its clients.[7] Whether provided through loans, reverse repos, or outright purchases, the liquidity created by the central bank is called *base money*, and liquidity-providing operations are called *open market operations* because all banks can obtain liquidity under the same conditions. These operations aim at transforming assets held by commercial banks into means of payment which can be used to refund private creditors or depositors.

Base money, also called "M0" for reasons explained in box 5.1, is the narrowest concept of money and is strictly limited to money created by the central bank. However, most of money creation is undertaken by commercial banks when they extend credit (box 5.1).

Box 5.1 Money and Monetary Aggregates

One should distinguish between money directly issued by the central bank (banknotes in circulation plus bank reserves, i.e. deposits of commercial banks at the central bank), which is called *M0* and is registered as a liability of the central bank, and money issued by commercial banks for their customers.

Assume that a commercial bank extends a 100 dollar credit to a customer. In the balance sheet of the bank, this results in a 100 dollar loan on the asset side and a 100 dollar deposit on the liability side. On the balance sheet of the customer, this results in a 100 dollar deposit on the asset side and a 100 dollar debt on the liability side, as shown by table B5.1.1. The bank has created 100 dollars of liquidity which the customer can use to purchase goods and services, buy assets, or repay debt. It is both a credit (a loan from the bank) and a means of payment (bank reserves).

Table B5.1.1
Impact of a $100 loan by the central bank on the balance sheets of a commercial bank and of a customer

Commercial bank		Customer	
Assets	Liabilities	Assets	Liabilities
Loan: $100	Customer deposit: $100	Bank deposit: $100	Debt: $100

The sum of base money (M0) and of customer deposits in the commercial banks is called *M1*. By extension, assets that are not means of payments but that can easily be converted into means of payments are sometimes also considered as money in a broad sense: *M2* includes M1 and deposits with a maturity of up to two years, whereas *broad money M3* is the sum of M2 and of money market instruments, which are marketable securities with less than one year to maturity. As shown in table B5.1.2, banknotes and coins in circulation represent less than 10% of M3 in the euro area while overnight deposits account for more than half of it.

Table B5.1.2
Monetary aggregates in the euro area, in billion euros and in % of M3, end-May 2017

	In EUR bn	In % of M3
Currency in circulation	1,092.3	9.4
Overnight deposits	6,344.4	54.9
Total M1	7,436.7	64.3
Deposits with an agreed maturity of up to 2 years	1,279.6	11.1
Deposits redeemable at notice of up to 3 months	2,183.0	18.9
Total M2	10,899.3	94.2
Money market instruments	6667.4	5.8
Total M3	10,566.8	100,0

Source: European Central Bank, Economic Bulletin, June 2017.

Since it enjoys the privilege of creating base money by the stroke of a pen, the central bank does not face any practical limit to the supply of liquidity.[8] It is in reality limited by the need to maintain trust in the currency: If a central bank creates enormous amounts of money, at some point economic players lose confidence and no longer consider it as the safest possible store of value. The privilege of creating base money also raises the temptation to use the central bank to finance public deficits by buying sovereign bonds or directly lending to the Treasury, which is now mostly prohibited. We come back later to this crucial limit to monetary policy.

When drawing liquidity from the central bank, commercial banks pay a fee in the form of a short-term interest rate called the *refinancing rate*. For instance, if the rate applied to a repurchase agreement is 3%, a bank seeking liquidity from the central bank for 5 working days for an amount of 100 million dollars will have to pay for this liquidity service $5 \times (0.03/360) \times 100$ million = 41666.67 dollars.[9] The short-term interest rate can be either positive or negative, in which case the central bank pays a fee to the commercial bank.[10]

The higher the refinancing rate, the lower the demand for liquidity. Hence, by setting a price for its liquidity service, the central bank can influence the demand for it. The short-term interest rate set by the central bank in turn influences all short-term interest rates in the economy and, to a certain extent, long-term interest rates also (see Section 5.1.1.b). In normal times, monetary policy consists in moving policy rates up and down and communicating on their future movements. *Expansionary monetary policy* consists in supporting the demand for liquidity by ensuring low policy rates and/or signaling that they may be low in the future. *Restrictive monetary policy* consists in curbing the demand for liquidity by ensuring high policy rates and/or signaling that they may be high in the future.

Although principles are similar, central banks throughout the world do not all operate in exactly the same way when they provide liquidity to the banking system, as illustrated by the different *modus operandi* of the ECB and the US Federal Reserve (box 5.2).

Box 5.2 Liquidity Provision in the Euro Area and in the United States

In the euro area, liquidity is channeled to the banks mainly through refinancing operations. Banks normally bid for access to central bank liquidity at regular weekly auctions. Historically, the ECB has either allotted liquidity at fixed rate (in which case banks bid for quantities and the ECB sets the interest rate) or at variable rates (in which case banks bid for a quantity and a rate above the minimum rate set by the central bank, and liquidity is allotted in an auction to those offering the higher rates). Variable-rate tenders were used by the ECB between 2000 and 2007 and are considered to better convey the information on liquidity needs in normal time. In 2008, the ECB returned to fixed-rate tenders so that all banks could receive unconstrained liquidity during the financial crisis.

The rate set by the ECB for its weekly operations is called the *main refinancing rate* (also called "rate on the main refinancing operations" or MRO rate). It is complemented with two marginal financing rates that apply to banks willing to deposit (or borrow) liquidity at (from) the ECB on a day-to-day basis. In order to encourage banks to ask for liquidity at the weekly operations rather than on a day-to-day basis, the *marginal deposit-facility rate* it set lower than the main refinancing rate, whereas the *marginal-lending rate* is set higher (figure B5.2.1). At any time, a bank with excess liquidity has the choice between lending to the central bank (at the marginal deposit facility rate) or to another bank (at a rate set on the interbank market); similarly, a bank with a liquidity shortage can borrow either from the central bank (at the marginal lending facility rate) or from another bank (at the money market rate). It follows by arbitrage that the money market rate fluctuates between the two marginal facility rates, at least for those participants who have access to central bank operations. The three rates (main refinancing, marginal lending facility, marginal deposit facility) are sometimes called the *leading interest rates* because they "lead" the market rate. The latter is measured every day by averaging rates contributed by a panel of banks. The average is called the Euro Overnight Interest Average (EONIA). It is the market rate with the shortest maturity.

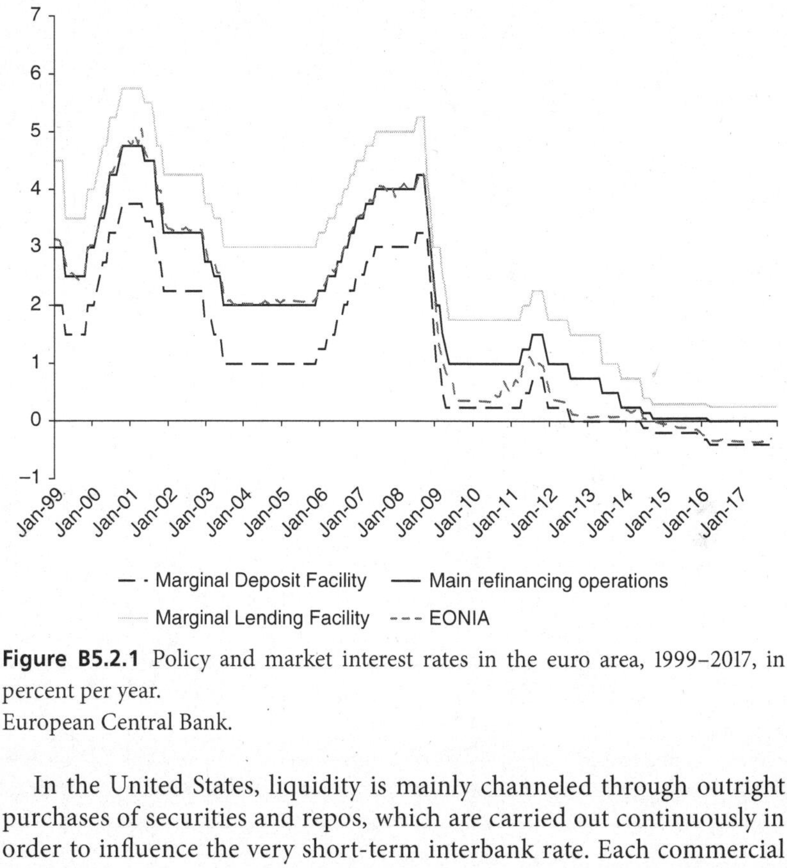

Figure B5.2.1 Policy and market interest rates in the euro area, 1999–2017, in percent per year.
European Central Bank.

In the United States, liquidity is mainly channeled through outright purchases of securities and repos, which are carried out continuously in order to influence the very short-term interbank rate. Each commercial bank holds an account in a regional reserve bank and can lend out of it overnight to other commercial banks at a rate called the effective *Federal fund (or Fed fund) rate*. When the Fed wants the Fed fund rate to fall, it buys securities and credits from banks and credits their accounts: this adds liquidity to the system, which reduces its market price. Symmetrically, selling securities to the banks withdraws liquidity from the banking system. The Fed also sets a floor for the rate on excess reserves deposited by the banks (figure B5.2.2).

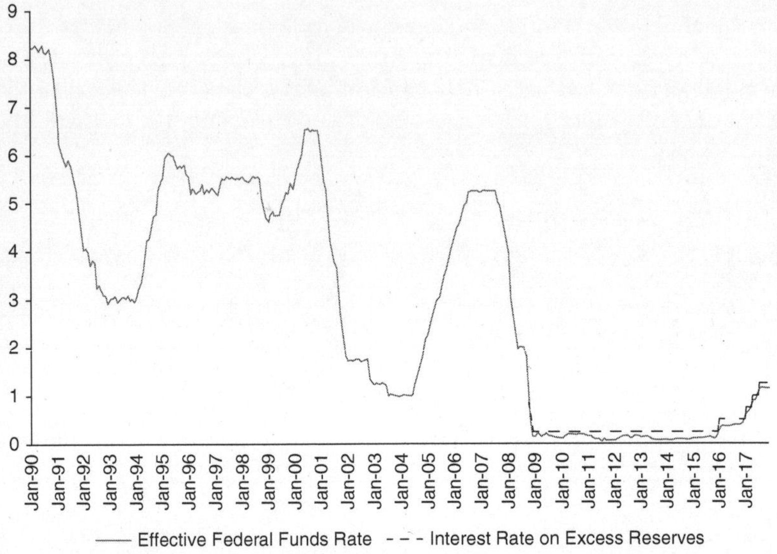

Figure B5.2.2 Policy and market interest rate in the United States, 1999–2017, in percent per year.
Federal Reserve Bank of Saint Louis.

Figure 5.1 reports the evolution of the refinancing rates in the euro area (or Germany before 1999), the United States, and Japan since the 1950s. Four main observations can be made. First, refinancing rates have declined over time in line with trend disinflation and a decline in the natural real rate of interest (see below for a definition), and their volatility has also been reduced. Second, there are cycles of rises and reductions, which correspond to phases of economic expansion and slowdown or contraction. Third, refinancing rates can be kept constant by central banks during several quarters. Fourth, monetary cycles in the three regions synchronized in the 1970s and the 1980s as central banks reacted to the inflation peak caused by the oil shocks, but they have become more autonomous in the 1990s and the 2000s. During the global financial crisis, the Federal Reserve and the ECB brought their interest rates close to zero—a level already reached by the Bank of Japan since the mid-1990s. In December 2015, the Fed was the first to again raise its interest rate.

Aside from changing the price of liquidity, the central bank can also influence banks' lending behavior by requiring them to keep a proportion of

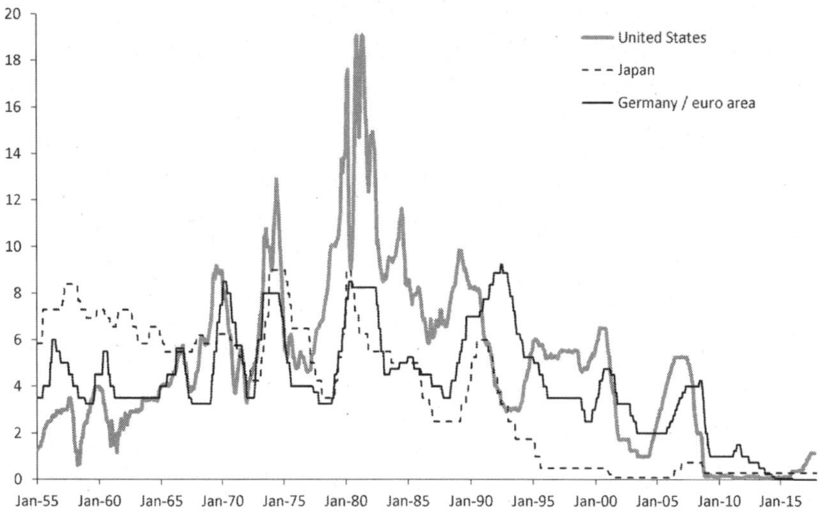

Figure 5.1 Policy interest rates in the United States, the euro area, and Japan, 1955–2017, in percent per year. Central banks.
Germany: discount rate; euro area: main refinancing rate; Japan: official discount rate; United States: effective Fed Fund rate.

the deposits received from the public as a deposit with the central bank. This deposit is called a *reserve requirement*. Not all central banks impose such requirements. Those of the United Kingdom, Canada, and Sweden have eliminated them. The ECB and the Federal Reserve impose a reserve requirement at a low rate (initially 2% for the ECB, reduced to 1% in 2011; 3% above a first threshold and 10% above a second threshold for the Fed).[11] In all these countries, whether or not banks are required to hold reserves does not affect significantly the conduct of monetary policy. In contrast, the Chinese central bank, the People's Bank of China has been using reserve requirements very actively. From 2004, it has raised the reserve requirement ratio several times a year as a complement to interest rates hikes in order to curb credit provision in the country. After 2008, it cut it several times during the global financial crisis, and again after 2015 to address the slowdown in the Chinese economy.

b) From short-term to long-term interest rates

Due to banks' arbitrage between borrowing from other banks or from the central bank, short-term market interest rates always remain close to official rates. Policy rates also influence market rates for longer maturities, albeit in a far less mechanical way.

The *yield curve* (which describes interest rates as a function of their maturity) is primarily shaped by expectations of future monetary policy. This is because investors who want to invest over a long period can either hold long-dated assets or roll short-dated assets over time. If they are not averse to risk (see Chapter 2), the long-term interest rate should be the average of expected future short-term rates. If they are averse to risk, the long-term interest rate also includes a term premium and a liquidity premium (box 5.3). As a result, long-term interest rates are generally higher than short-term ones. Even when no change in short-term interest rates is expected, the yield curve is upward sloping. Inverted yield curves are observed only when investors expect a sharp fall in future interest rates, as was the case in 2006 in the United States (figure 5.2).

Box 5.3 The Yield Curve

Most bonds pay a fixed interest rate. They provide a regular (typically, annual or semi-annual) payment called a *coupon*, and the coupon rate is the ratio of this coupon to the borrowed amount, or *principal*, which is to be refunded at maturity. When issued, bonds are traded on financial markets, and the market interest rate is defined as the ratio between the fixed coupon and the market price. There is a whole range of possible maturities, and hence of interest rates, from overnight to 50 years. The standard theory of the yield curve assumes investors' arbitrage between a long-term investment (paying the long-term rate) and a succession of short-term investments (each paying the short-term interest rate). If investors expect short-term interest rates to increase in the future, they pull out of long-term assets whose price is bound to decline. This pushes long-term interest rates up and steepens the yield curve. If investors expect the short-term interest rate to fall, they will invest in long-term assets, and the yield curve will become flatter or even downward-sloping (or *inverted*). Real-world investors are in fact risk-averse, and investments with a longer maturity have a more uncertain return because of liquidity risk (the risk that the seller will find no buyer for the bond) and market risk (the risk that the market price of the bond lies below its face value). Investors therefore ask for a *liquidity premium* and a *term premium* to accept holding a bond. Through arbitrage, the interest rate for a *N*-year maturity, i_t^N, can thus be expressed as a function of the *N* expected 1-year maturity rates i_{t+i} and an annualized premium ρ_t^N:

$$\left(1+i_t^N\right)^N=\left(1+i_t\right)\left(1+E_t i_{t+1}\right)\cdots\left(1+E_t i_{t+N-1}\right)\left(1+\rho_t^N\right)^N \quad \text{(B5.3.1)}$$

where $E_t i_{t+i}$ is the expectation at time t of the one-year interest rate at time $t+i$. The term premium ρ_t^N increases with *N*. As a consequence, absent expected interest rate variations, the yield curve is normally upward sloping.

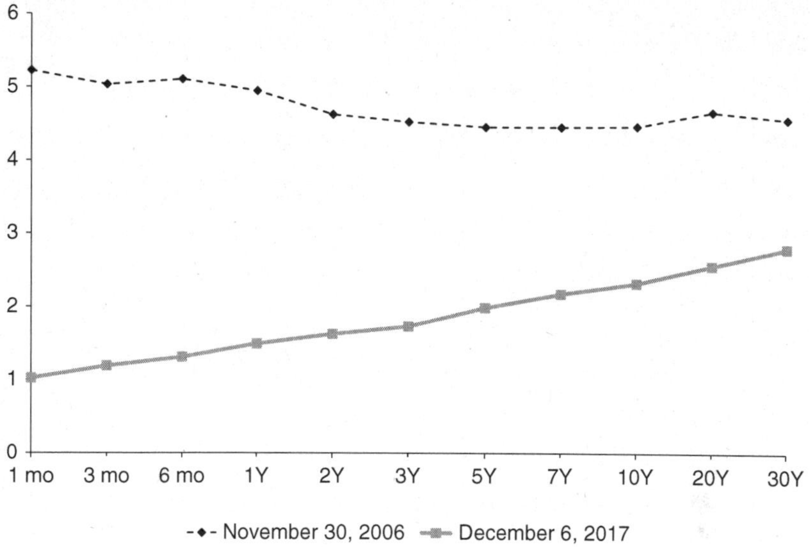

Figure 5.2 Yield curve for US Treasury bonds, in percent per year.
US Department of Treasury.

Because long-term interest rates incorporate expectations about future monetary policy, they can change even when short-term rates are held constant. Central banks can therefore influence long-term interest rates by communicating their intentions through speeches and interviews. As figure 5.3 shows, the successive hikes of the ECB's main refinancing rate in 2006 were well anticipated by market participants and incorporated in advance into longer term interest rates, which increased smoothly throughout the year.

c) Monetary policy at the zero lower bound

During the global financial crisis, central banks in advanced countries reached the limits of monetary policy as described in the previous sections. Policy rates hit zero percent, the so-called *zero lower bound* (ZLB) of monetary policy. This episode evidenced the magnitude of the stimulus needed to fight the global financial crisis, but it may happen more often in the future as a result of the very low level of the *natural rate of interest*, a concept originally introduced by Swedish economist Knut Wicksell (Wicksell, 1898). The natural rate of interest (which economists often label r^*) is the rate which equates savings and investment at a level of output consistent with full employment. It has experienced a trend decline in the 1990s and 2000s for technological and demographic reasons, reaching levels close to zero in advanced economies (see Holston, Laubach, and Williams, 2016).

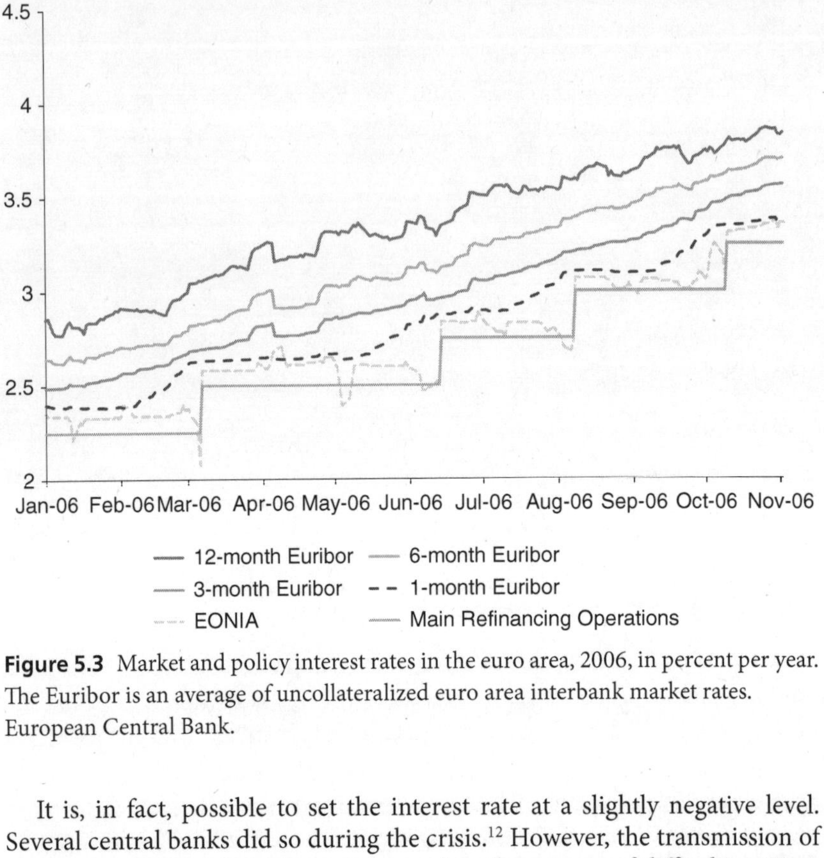

Figure 5.3 Market and policy interest rates in the euro area, 2006, in percent per year. The Euribor is an average of uncollateralized euro area interbank market rates. European Central Bank.

It is, in fact, possible to set the interest rate at a slightly negative level. Several central banks did so during the crisis.[12] However, the transmission of negative interest rates to the economy raises three types of difficulties. First, banks may not be in a position to pass the negative rates on to their loans to households and firms, even though the flattening of the yield curve reduces their interest margin.[13] This is because of the difficulty of charging negative interest rates to retail customers, who interpret them as a tax. Second, negative rates can be interpreted as putting a negative price tag on time and have counterintuitive real-life consequences, such as inciting creditors or even tax collection authorities to reclaim their money later rather than earlier. This criticism assumes a degree of *money illusion* (that is, it assumes that the general public does not fully take into account inflation): after accounting for inflation, real interest rates have often been negative in the past without having such consequences. And third, a negative rate may be avoided by hoarding banknotes, which bear a zero-interest rate:[14] The opportunity cost of hoarding cash (say, the cost of renting a safe or a vault) and the adverse impact of negative rates on banks' interest margins, hence on monetary policy transmission, set a floor to how negative interest rates can be: the effective lower bound may be negative, but it still exists. Some have argued that the effective lower bound could be lowered if banknotes were phased out and replaced by interest-bearing central bank digital currency (Rogoff, 2014).

In such circumstances, three strategies may be combined that all fall under the general heading of *unconventional monetary policies*.[15] The theoretical underpinnings of these policies are discussed in Section 5.2.

First, the central bank may ease the access of commercial banks to central bank liquidity in several ways. It can extend the list of eligible collateral (allowing more loans or securities to be refinanced by the central bank), which the main central banks did at the start of the 2008 financial crisis. Furthermore, the central bank can change the way it provides liquidity. Starting in October 2008, the ECB's refinancing operations were fully allotted at a fixed rate instead of being allotted in limited amount through an auction. The central bank can also provide liquidity at longer horizons in order for banks to feel more secure in an environment of high volatility and liquidity stress. Finally, liquidity can be made conditional to banks lending to the real economy.[16] This first group of actions is labeled *credit easing* because it is meant to enhance the ability of the commercial banks to channel central bank liquidity to nonfinancial borrowers.

Second, the central bank can intervene in a targeted way on specific market segments. The idea here is to mend the transmission channels of monetary policy (i.e., to make sure that monetary policy changes will be reflected by financial conditions across financing instruments). The ECB's Securities Market Program and Outright Monetary Transactions (see Section 5.3), targeted at sovereign bond markets, pertain to this logic, as do the Federal Reserve's and ECB's purchases of securitized loans (mortgages, loans to small- and medium-sized enterprises [SMEs], credit cards) and covered bonds, while the latter also had a credit easing component.

Third, the central bank may aim at flattening the yield curve (i.e., reduce longer term interest rates) through appropriate communication and/or purchases of long-term bonds. In the light of the term structure of interest rates explained earlier, communication aims at lowering expected future short-term rates while purchases aim at lowering term premia. During the global financial crisis, the Federal Reserve was the first to engage in *forward guidance*, a policy aimed at steering market expectations about future policy decisions (box 5.4). The Federal Reserve also bought long-term bonds while selling short-term ones, an operation labelled *Operation Twist*. In 2013, the ECB also introduced forward guidance, expecting "key ECB interest rates to remain at present or lower levels for an extended period of time."[17] Finally, the central bank may deliberately inflate its balance sheet by buying large amounts of assets (typically, sovereign bonds and mortgage-based securities) in the open market. The transmission channels of *quantitative easing* are explained in Section 5.2.3.a.

After the global financial crisis, as a consequence of the policy responses just described, the balance sheets of the main central banks in advanced

Box 5.4 The Federal Reserve's Forward Guidance

December 16, 2008: "Weak economic conditions are likely to warrant exceptionally low levels of the federal funds rate for *some time*." The commitment is repeated in January 2009.

March 18, 2009: The Fed starts saying it expects to hold the fed funds rate near zero "for an *extended period.*"

September 21, 2011: The Fed drops "extended period," opting for specific calendar guidance. It expects to hold rates low "at least through mid-2013."

January 25, 2012: The fed funds rate is likely to stay near zero "at least through late 2014."

September 13, 2012: Officials now expect to hold the fund rate near zero "at least through mid-2015." The Fed also says it expects to hold the rate very low "for a *considerable time* after the economic recovery strengthens." This language is repeated at the October meeting.

December 12, 2012: The Fed says it expects to hold the *Fed funds* rate near zero for "a considerable time after the asset purchase program ends and the economic recovery strengthens" and, in particular, "at least as long as the unemployment rate remains above 6–1/2%, inflation between one and two years ahead is projected to be no more than a half percentage point above the Committee's 2% longer run goal, and longer term inflation expectations continue to be well anchored."

March 19, 2014: The thresholds work for some time, but then officials run into a predicament—the jobless rate is falling much faster than they had forecast, bringing unemployment closer to 6.5% more quickly than anticipated. The Fed then drops the thresholds. In deciding how long to hold rates near zero, it "will assess progress—both realized and expected—toward its objectives of maximum employment and 2% inflation." The Fed repeats that it will wait to raise rates for "a considerable time" after the bond-buying ends. At her first press conference, Chair Yellen says that "considerable time" means roughly six months.

December 17, 2014: The Fed ends its bond-buying program in October, and, in December, it replaces the "considerable time" language with a vow to be "patient" in raising interest rates. The Fed "can be patient in beginning to normalize the stance of monetary policy." The phrase is repeated in the January statement.

March 18, 2015: The keyword "patient" disappears from the press release. "The Committee anticipates that it will be appropriate to raise the target range for the federal funds rate when it has seen further improvement in the labor market and is reasonably confident that inflation will move back to its 2% objective over the medium term."

December 17, 2015: The FOMC "judges that there has been considerable improvement in labor market conditions this year, and it is reasonably confident that inflation will rise, over the medium term, to its 2% objective." It raises the Fed fund rates for the first time since 2008.

Sources: *The Wall Street Journal*, March 17, 2015, and Federal Reserve website.

Figure 5.4 Total assets of major central banks, in percent of gross domestic product (GDP), 2006–2015. Central banks.
Value normalized at 100 in 2006Q2.

economies increased (in percent of gross domestic product [GDP]) up to fourfold in the United States and the United Kingdom (figure 5.4).

5.1.2 The objectives of monetary policy

The objectives that central banks should pursue are specified in their *mandate*. These have varied significantly over time and are still a matter for discussion among politicians and economists. In the 1970s, it was common for central banks to have broad mandates involving difficult trade-offs between alternative targets. One of the lessons drawn from the high inflation of the 1970s and the 1980s has been that central banks ought to be given more precise objectives; price stability emerged as the dominant one. However, not all central banks have a mandate focused on price stability, and even those that do may have to pursue other objectives simultaneously. In addition, the global financial crisis has revived an old discussion on financial stability as a central bank objective, alongside that of price stability.

a) Price stability

Pursuing price stability amounts to safeguarding the real value of money; that is, its *purchasing power* defined as the quantity of goods, services, or assets that one unit of money can buy. More precisely, it amounts to maintaining its internal value (its purchasing power in terms of the domestic consumption basket), which may be different from its external value (the purchasing power in terms of foreign currencies; see Section 5.1.2.c).

There are three reasons why price stability should be central banks' primary mandate: price stability is a desirable objective from a social welfare perspective, central banks are best placed to achieve it, and assigning any other task to them would distract them from accomplishing the former.

The benefits of price stability are rather intuitive, although, as noted by Buiter (2006), deriving them from theory is not straightforward. The most frequently used argument is that inflation distorts economic decisions through the implicit taxation of cash balances and the blurring of relative price signals (not to mention distortions due to taxes being applied to nominal bases). Most central banks aim at keeping the *inflation rate* (i.e., the annual increase in the general level of prices) at a low value. What exactly this low value should be is a delicate question to which we shall return in Section 5.3.

Whether the central bank is best placed to deliver price stability is not obvious. The *monetarist* view is best captured by Milton Friedman's famous sentence "inflation is always and everywhere a monetary phenomenon" (Friedman and Schwartz, 1971), which points to a direct causal relationship between the amount of money in circulation and inflation. This proposition implies that price stability only requires controlling the amount of money in circulation and makes monetary policy the natural instrument for controlling inflation. However, as we shall see later, the relationship between money and prices has broken down in recent times. There must be other justifications for assigning the control of inflation to the central bank. The arguments are both economic and institutional:

- *Economic arguments*: First, contemporary economic models retain an important assumption called the *long-term neutrality of money*—the disconnection, in the long run, between nominal variables (such as the general level of prices, nominal wages, interest rates, the nominal exchange rate, etc.) and real variables (real GDP, employment, real wages, real interest rates, the real exchange rate, etc.). Hence, entrusting the central bank with a narrow mandate of price stability comes at no cost in the long term. In the short term, in an economy faced with aggregate demand shocks, the price stability mandate does not prevent the central bank from stabilizing the economy around its potential growth path since inflation and the output gap are positively correlated.[18]
- *Institutional arguments*: While political institutions face trade-offs with other objectives, an independent institution with a narrow mandate is better equipped to achieve it and more credible to communicate its actions to economic players. Moreover, monetary policy involves less redistribution than say, tax policy. Accordingly, as argued in Chapter 2, there is a stronger case for delegating it to an independent agency. Finally, monetary policy is highly technical, and its success can only be assessed over a long period.

After the inflationary episodes of the 1970s, these arguments have incited most countries to make their central banks independent and focus them on price stability. They were spectacularly successful in reaching this objective until the late 2000s, when low inflation became entrenched in advanced economies. Figure 5.5 shows the distribution of inflation rates in the world in 1980 and in 2014. In 1980, less than 10% of countries had an inflation rate lower than 5%. Central banks had inherited high inflation rates as a result of the two oil shocks experienced in the 1970s, which had been amplified by wage indexation as well as by expansionary policies. At that time, a number of central banks tightened monetary policy either through discretionary policies (as did the Federal Reserve) or by pegging their exchange rate to low-inflation countries (as many European countries did vis-à-vis Germany). Still, some emerging countries registered very high inflation rates in the 1980s. In Israel, for instance, annual inflation exceeded 100% from 1980 to 1986. Some countries even experienced *hyperinflation*, which is usually defined as an inflation rate higher than 50% per month (Cagan, 1956).[19] For instance, prices increased by 20,266% in Argentina between March 1989 and March 1990.

The near disappearance of inflation was a characteristic of the 1990s and the early 2000s, and even the dramatic increase in oil and raw material prices in the mid-2000s did not provoke a major inflationary fever, as had been the case in the 1970s. Japan even experienced *deflation*, that is, a joint fall in output and the price level. This phenomenon had been observed in the interwar period but had become considered a historical curiosity. The Bank of Japan was initially slow to react until it set interest rates to zero and started to aggressively create money, eventually engineering growth and (to some extent) inflation.

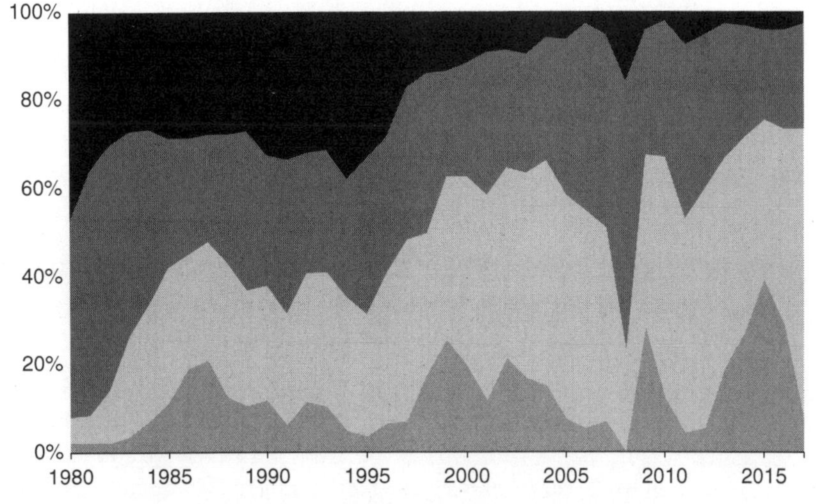

Figure 5.5 World distribution of annual inflation rates, 1980–2016.
Cumulated proportion of countries in each inflation bracket.
Authors' calculations based on IMF data.

In the aftermaths of the global financial crisis, inflation rates fell to close to zero and sporadically became negative in several advanced economies. We come back in Section 5.3 on why such low inflation rate are not appropriate for an economy, especially when indebtedness is high.

How much of the price stability observed in the 1990s and the early 2000s was due to favorable global conditions and how much was due to the quality of monetary policies and institutions is hard to tell. In fact, several explanations are given for the overall reduction of inflation during the recent decades. One is the generalization around the world of the central bank independence model—an institutional development. At least as important, albeit more recent, is globalization and the impact on the global market of the huge production capacity of China and India—a positive global supply shock (box 5.5). A third explanation is weak productivity growth which has weighed on wages in all developed economies.

Box 5.5 How Does Globalization Affect Inflation?

In an influential paper published in 2005, Harvard professor Richard Freeman painted globalization as a huge shock to Western economies with a doubling of the global labor pool as China, India, and the ex-Soviet bloc joined the world economy (Freeman, 2005). This led to wage moderation worldwide until physical capital accumulated sufficiently for the capital–labor ratio to recover. In such environment, any cost push shock was bound to be short-lived because wages were unlikely to spiral up with prices.

The naïve version of the argument is only superficially convincing since it in fact confuses relative prices with the general level of prices: advanced economies could easily sustain higher inflation rates than those of emerging countries if their nominal exchange rate were to depreciate accordingly (see Ball, 2006, for a discussion).

A more rigorous version was offered by K. Rogoff (2003), who argued that increased cross-border integration reduces the power of insiders (those who have a permanent job). This reduces the equilibrium unemployment rate and the incentive for the central bank to inflate the economy. Furthermore, greater competition in product markets may reduce nominal price rigidities. This again reduces the equilibrium inflation rate. The expansion of global value chains, i.e. cross-border trade in intermediate goods and services, is another channel through which global unused capacities can influence domestic inflation (Auer, Borio and Filardo, 2017).

The role of globalization in explaining disinflation should not be overstated. Figure B5.5.1 shows that emerging and developing countries have sustained world inflation over the 1996–2016 period. For an empirical assessment of the global dimension of inflation, see Eickmeier and Pijnenburg (2013) and Forbes (2018).

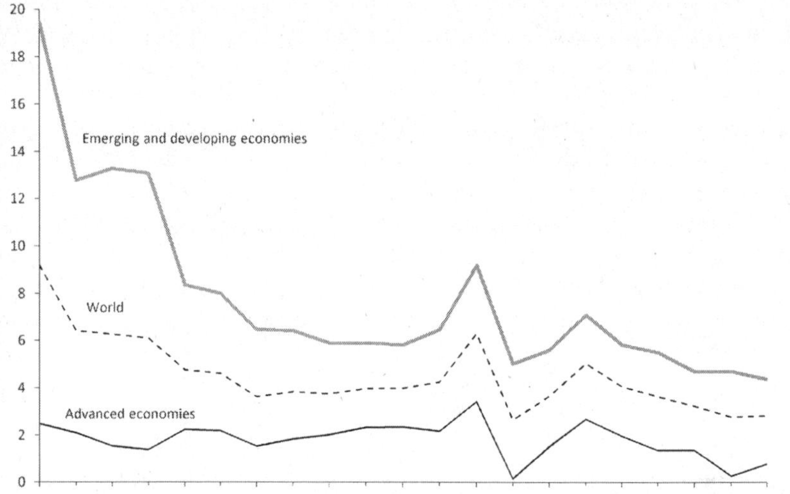

Figure B5.5.1 Consumer price inflation in advanced and in emerging and developing economies, 1996–2016, in percent per year.
IMF, World Economic Outlook database.

b) Output stability

As already mentioned, the strong focus of central banks on price stability does not exclude output stabilization. As a matter of fact, even when output stabilization is not their main objective, central banks behave in practice as if they were aiming at minimizing the output gap on the top of achieving their inflation objective. In 1993, Stanford economist John Taylor showed that the average reaction of the Federal Reserve to US inflation and the output gap could be captured by the following simple equation:

$$i_t = \bar{r} + \pi_t + 0.5(\pi_t - \tilde{\pi}) + 0.5(y_t - \bar{y}_t) \qquad (5.1)$$

where i_t is the short-term nominal interest rate, π_t the inflation rate, $\tilde{\pi}$ the inflation objective, $(y - \bar{y}_t)$ the output gap, and $\bar{r}$ the "neutral" level of the real interest rate.[20] Such behavior was later confirmed for other central banks (see Bernanke and Mihov, 1997, for Germany; and Nelson and Nikolov, 2003, for the United Kingdom). Equation (5.1) is called the *Taylor rule* and has become one of economists' basic tools to assess policy interest rates. It can be calculated using headline inflation or *core inflation* (that is, consumer price inflation excluding its most volatile components related to fresh food and energy).

Although it has no normative content, the Taylor rule is a useful standard for comparing monetary stances over time and across countries. For instance, figure 5.6 compares the evolution of the short-term interest rate of the euro area with that of two interest rates derived from a Taylor rule. The three-month interbank market rate was lower than both measures of the "Taylor rate" during most of the period. It is closer to the Taylor rate based on core inflation than to that based on headline inflation, the latter being more volatile than the former. In 2013–15, the market rate stays in positive territory, whereas declining inflation and a negative output gap would have called for very negative rates had the Taylor rule been applied. To support such a decline in the euribor, however, the ECB resorted to unconventional instruments.[21]

c) Exchange rate stability

Exchange rate stability has been considered historically an intermediate objective of monetary policy. In a country where the central bank is not very credible and money demand is unstable, or when there are doubts on the official inflation figure, pegging the exchange rate to a foreign currency or a basket of foreign currencies provides a transparent anchor to prices. If the national

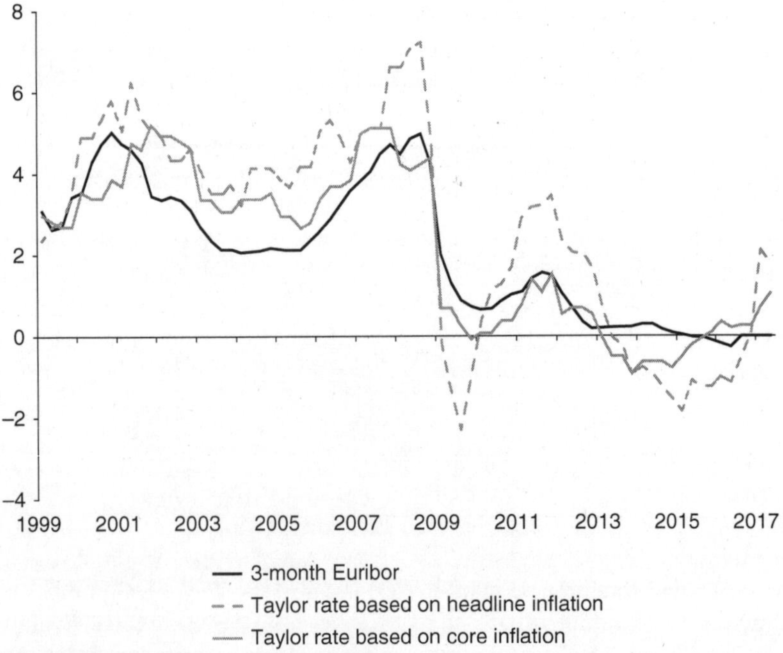

Figure 5.6 The Taylor rule in the euro area, 1999–2017 (percents per year). The neutral real interest rate is assumed to be constant and set at 1%. Authors' calculations based on OECD data.

currency does not depreciate, then economic agents should be careful not to allow wages and prices grow too fast; this discipline curbs inflationary expectations and makes it easier for the central bank to achieve its price stability objective.

Until the 1990s, many Western European countries, as well as Eastern European countries in economic transition after the demise of the Soviet bloc, relied on an external anchor to curb price increases. The attraction of fixed exchange rates has faded with the decline of inflation. Only small countries (such as Bulgaria, Denmark, Ecuador, or Caribbean countries) or oil-exporting countries (such as Saudi Arabia) continue to target the external rather than the internal value of their currency. Switzerland capped the value of its exchange rate against the euro in 2011 but had to remove the cap in January 2015 when the ECB launched its quantitative easing program, pushing the value of the euro down. In small and open economies, the two objectives of internal and external value of the currency are closely related since imported items weigh heavily in the domestic price index. We shall return to the choice of an exchange rate regime in Chapter 7.

d) Financial stability

Financial stability—the proper functioning of financial institutions and financial markets—was always "in the DNA of central banks," as Italian economist and former ECB Executive Board member Tommaso Padoa-Schioppa once said. Keeping the financial system in check was indeed one of the major reasons why central banks were created in the first place (Goodhart, 1988). Financial stability was not a major concern in the context of the highly segmented and regulated post-Great Depression financial systems of the 1960s, but it gained prominence in the wake of the financial liberalization that took place in the 1980s and 1990s and even more so after the global financial crisis.

Financial stability is discussed in detail in Chapter 6. Responsibility for it is generally shared between regulatory agencies that deal with financial institutions and/or markets, the central bank, and the ministry of finance. Some central banks are also banking supervisors (such as in the United States, United Kingdom, and euro area) and/or macroprudential authorities, while some other aren't (such as in China and Japan). Whatever the institutional arrangement in place, monetary policy interacts with financial stability in two ways. First, a well-functioning banking and financial sector is crucial for monetary policy transmission. This is why central banks have a keen interest in financial stability and use their power to create money to provide emergency liquidity to banks, acting as a *lenders of last resort* (Chapter 6).

Second, and symmetrically, monetary policy has a strong influence on financial stability. For instance, low interest rates tend to inflate asset prices (see Section 5.2.2) and induce banks to weaken their lending standards. Likewise, quantitative easing policies also have a large, positive impact on asset prices (see Rogers, Scotti, and Wright, 2015). In the midst of a crisis, these effects help reflate the economy. But they also contribute to building up financial vulnerabilities that need to be monitored and possibly counteracted.

Whether central banks should *lean against the wind* and use interest rates preventively to curb financial excesses (at the risk of interfering with their price stability mandate) or wait and "clean" the economy after these excesses have materialized is heavily debated. Leaning versus cleaning will be discussed later in this chapter and in Section 6.3.3.a) of Chapter 6.

5.1.3 A short history of central banking

The history of central banking officially starts with the creation of the Swedish Riksbank in 1668. The Riksbank is considered the oldest central bank in the world, although the banks of Amsterdam and Hamburg, for example, have been created earlier to provide stable means of payments to merchants (Roberds and Velde, 2014; Ugolini, 2011). It was followed in 1694 by the Bank of England. Both the Riksbank and the Bank of England were private companies, with a mandate to lend to the government (or help the government borrow on the market), but also carrying out fully fledged banking activities. Because other banks held an account with them, they soon became the "banks of the banks," with the ability to clear payments and to act as lenders of last resort. They funded themselves through issuing notes that served as currency and later obtained the monopoly of issuing them. In 1800, the Banque de France was created with similar features, and it obtained the monopoly over banknote issuance as soon as 1803 like the Bank of Japan (1882). In Europe, most central banks were created during the nineteenth century, whereas America waited until the twentieth century to create the Federal Reserve in the United States (1913), followed by the central banks of Colombia, Mexico, Chile, and Canada. Australia and New Zealand also set up their central banks in the twentieth century. Today, central banks are part of government to the extent that they are controlled by the public sector even when their capital is privately owned.

Bordo (2010) divides the history of central banking into four periods: (i) a "golden age" from 1870 to 1914; (ii) a "dark age" during the Great Depression of the interwar period; (iii) decades of government control from the 1930s to the 1950s, followed by a gradual recovery of independence up to the 1970s; and (iv) a renaissance of central banking starting in the 1980s. Whether the global financial crisis has put an end to this latter period is an open question.

The "golden age" of central banking refers to a period when the main concern of central banks was to abide by the gold standard (i.e., the fixed convertibility of their currency in gold) while maintaining financial stability: The central bank needed to channel enough liquidity to the banking system to maintain financial stability, but not too much since excess liquidity would fuel inflation and would endanger the fixed gold parity. The doctrine then was to refinance only "real bills"; that is, bills backed by the real economy (output and trade), as opposed to "speculative bills" or "financial bills." The real bills doctrine was a way to reconcile price stability with financial stability (Goodhart, 2011). Along these lines, purchases of government bonds were prohibited. This doctrine, which relied on a self-stabilizing property of the real economy, collapsed with the Great Depression in the 1930s.

The "dark ages" of the interwar period started with hyperinflation in the early 1920s, followed by a failed attempt to restore the gold standard in 1925. The problem arose not only due to inadequate exchange parities and gold shortage. Current account surplus countries such as France and the United States blocked the "price–specie flow mechanism" that, under the gold standard, was supposed to spontaneously bring their foreign accounts back to equilibrium (Hume, 1742) through internal money creation. Additionally, governments had become more aware of the ups and downs of the real economy—here in the form of rising unemployment. The Federal Reserve awkwardly adhered to the real bills doctrine: after triggering the October 1929 Wall Street crash through monetary tightening, it failed to play its role of a lender of last resort in the face of bank runs (Friedman and Schwarz, 1971). Elsewhere in the world, the central banks also refrained from increasing liquidity provision, fearing that this would force them to exit the gold standard. The latter was eventually abandoned, starting with Britain in 1931.

The next period was dominated by a massive regulation of the banking sector and a domination of ministries of finance over central banks. After World War II, with the exception of Germany, central banks were essentially asked to manage the quantitative restrictions imposed on bank lending as well as international capital controls, whereas treasuries decided on interest rates, maintaining them at a low level in order to stimulate economies and reduce the burden of government debts. Price stability was reached through a combination of controlled money creation and fixed exchange rates under the Bretton Woods system. The system started to go wrong in the 1960s, when the United States expanded its monetary base to finance the Vietnam War. Other countries reacted by hoarding gold rather than dollars, which put downward pressure on the dollar. In August 1971, the convertibility of the dollar into gold was suspended, and, in 1973, the Bretton Woods system was definitely abandoned. The move to floating exchange rates coincided with the first oil shock, which triggered a decade of high inflation. It also gave central banks more freedom to use monetary policy instruments in pursuit of domestic objectives and marked the advent of what we call here monetary policy.

According to Bordo, the "renewed golden age" started in 1979 with the determination of the new president of the Federal Reserve, Paul Volcker, to fight inflation through tight monetary policy. Many countries granted independence to their central banks, with a clear mandate of price stability or even explicit inflation targeting (see Section 5.3). The 1990s and 2000s, which were labeled the "Great Moderation" in reference to low inflation combined with relatively stable real growth, were also an age of financial deregulation, a "triumph of the markets" (Goodhart, 2011). Due to their exclusive focus on consumption price inflation, central banks let asset price bubbles emerge (especially in real estate), while light-touch regulation, combined with the liberalization of international capital flows, allowed commercial banks to increase their leverage and take excessive risks on financial markets. This period ended with the global financial crisis. Unlike in 1929, though, central banks reacted by loosening their monetary stance and played their role of lenders of last resort.

This short history of central banking shows that the balance between price stability and financial stability has always been a major concern. Although much progress has been made on how to manage a financial crisis, the recipe for targeting both price and financial stability with only one instrument (monetary policy) remains to be found. Additionally, the doctrine of central banks concerning the financing of government deficits has changed over time. While in many countries central banks were created in the first place to finance the governments, monetization was prohibited by the gold standard. The modern doctrine allows central banks to purchase government bonds only on secondary markets (where bonds already issued are bought and sold) and only for the purpose of monetary policy (as a tool to increase the monetary base and compress term premiums). Still, market confidence in highly indebted governments may rely on the ability of the central bank to act as a backstop and buy government debt, at least in extreme cases where market participants would start selling debt and push the economy toward a high interest rate equilibrium. Whether this is monetary policy is controversial, as shown by the case brought to the European Court of Justice against the ECB's Outright Monetary Transaction program (European Court of Justice, 2015). We come back to the discussion on fiscal dominance over monetary policy in the next section.

5.2 Theories

Monetary policy theory has been and still is a very active field of research, one where the dialogue between theoreticians and practitioners is vibrant and one where theory has had major influence on the design of policy institutions. In the 1960s and 1970s, the monetarist challenge to conventional Keynesian wisdom emerged from what was initially a critique of monetary policy practices. Similarly, the rational expectation models, which would have a profound impact on macroeconomic thinking and policy (see Chapter 1), were initially developed in that context. The notions of time consistency and credibility, which would make their way into the basic toolkit of policymakers, were also first experimented in the monetary policy field. The contemporary micro-founded neo-Keynesian models embodying price rigidities were developed in response, with the aim of providing sound theoretical foundations to monetary stabilization. The theoretical toolkit appeared inadequate, however, during the 2008 financial crisis, which emphasized the role of the financial sector in transmitting monetary policy, a role largely neglected by the pre-crisis new-Keynesian workhorse.

5.2.1 The basics of monetary policy

a) The long-term neutrality of money

The first question to ask about monetary policy is whether it affects the economy. It is now widely accepted that changes in money supply do not affect real economic variables in the long run, a property known as the *long-term neutrality of money.* This dichotomy between money and real variables, which was first formalized by Scottish philosopher David Hume in 1742, is a consequence of the role of money as a unit of account: in the long run, doubling the quantity of money in circulation or replacing a currency by another one of higher value has no impact on real variables such as GDP, real wages, real interest rates, or the real exchange rate. Only nominal variables (nominal GDP, nominal wages, nominal interest rates, and the nominal exchange rate) are affected.

Hume's *quantity theory of money* is the simplest model consistent with this approach. It states that output is determined by supply and that the value of the transactions that can be carried out with one unit of money during a given period—the *velocity of money*—is exogenous. In this setting, there is a one-to-one relation between money growth and inflation. Controlling money growth allows the central bank to control the inflation rate without incurring any cost in terms of real variables such as real GDP or unemployment (box 5.6).

Box 5.6 The Quantity Theory of Money

Money velocity V is defined as the nominal production allowed by the circulation of one unit of money during one year:

$$PY = MV \tag{B5.6.1}$$

where P denotes the general price level, M money supply, and Y real GDP. Assume that Y grows at a constant rate as a consequence of population and productivity growth. Assume that V is constant or evolves at a constant rate independently of monetary policy. If the central bank controls the growth rate of money supply $\Delta M/M$, then, for a given GDP growth rate $\Delta Y/Y$ and a given evolution of velocity $\Delta V/V$, it also controls inflation $\Delta P/P$:

$$\frac{\Delta P}{P} = \frac{\Delta V}{V} + \frac{\Delta M}{M} - \frac{\Delta Y}{Y} \tag{B.5.6.2}$$

Accordingly, the ECB in 1999 drew on the quantity theory of money and on the German Bundesbank's experience to define the "first pillar" of its monetary strategy. This consisted in targeting M3 growth at 4.5% a year, consistent with a 1.5% inflation rate, a 2.5% real GDP growth in the euro area, and a decrease of velocity by 0.5% a year:

$$1.5\% = -0.5\% + 4.5\% - 2.5\% \qquad \text{(B5.6.3)}$$

In such an approach, the monetary aggregate plays the role of an intermediate objective that is readily observable and more directly under the control of the central bank than the final objective of price stability, yet whose evolution is a good predictor of the final objective. The ECB later downplayed this monetary pillar, notably because money growth had been continuously higher than the target without any major consequence for inflation. The US Fed had had a similar experience and had stopped setting target ranges for M2 growth. However, as shown by figure B5.6.1, the link between money and inflation remains robust in high-inflation countries.

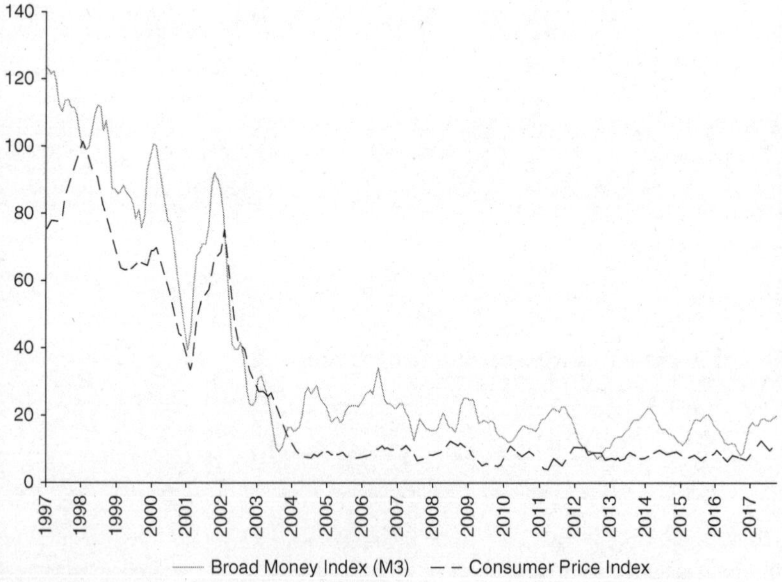

Figure B5.6.1 Money growth and consumer price inflation in Turkey, 1996–2017. OECD, monthly monetary and financial statistics.

As a cross-country, long-run regularity, the link between money growth and inflation—a consequence of money neutrality—raises little discussion. It has been documented in several studies (see, for example, McCandless and Weber, 1995, and Robert Lucas's Nobel lecture, 1996). However, the long-run neutrality of money does not imply that monetary policy has no influence whatsoever on real economic performance.[40] It may affect GDP in the short term due to nominal rigidities (see next section) or high leverage of economic agents (Fisher, 1933). In the long run, high and unstable inflation is widely accepted as having detrimental effects on growth (see, e.g., Barro, 1995).

b) Short-run nominal rigidities

One major explanation for the short-run disconnect between money growth and inflation is the existence of *nominal rigidities*—the fact that, following a shock on money supply, prices and/or nominal wages adjust less than fully in the short run. Accordingly, a rise in money supply increases the real value of monetary holdings, which affects other real variables, lowers the real interest rate and raises real consumption.

In Keynes's *General Theory* (1936), a rise in money supply leads in the short run to a fall in the interest rate. This is because such a fall is the only way to raise money demand if prices do not adjust upward. A lower nominal and real interest rate encourages private agents to hold money balances (which yield no or little return) rather than less liquid assets (yielding the interest rate). The lower interest rate in turn stimulates the demand for goods and services and increases GDP. If there is excess production capacity, GDP rises.[22] In the longer run, however, prices adjust upward, which brings the interest rate and GDP back to their full employment values, consistent with the long-run disconnect between nominal and real variables. In the Keynesian framework, money market equilibrium is achieved in the short run through nominal and real interest rate adjustment rather than through price adjustment. Consistent with this determination, the saving–investment balance is achieved through output adjustment: if saving exceeds investment *ex ante*, total aggregate demand (consumption and investment) lies below aggregate supply and output will decline to meet the level of aggregate demand.

In brief, the short-run impact of monetary policy on real variables such as output or employment relies on partial price adjustment.

In turn, nominal rigidities can be explained by the rational behavior of economic agents (box 5.7). Rigidities are less in a high-inflation environment where indexation mechanisms are more widespread. In the extreme case of hyperinflation, price adjustment is almost instantaneous.

c) Optimal interest rate setting

We have indicated in Section 5.1 that the central banks' main task is to set policy rates. But what should guide this decision? In the 1960s, the response to this question was largely ad hoc and discretionary. In the 1970s and 1980s came the monetarist revolution, which advocated setting interest rates at a

Box 5.7 Why Nominal Rigidities?

Three explanations have been proposed to reconcile nominal rigidities with rational behavior: imperfect information, staggered contracts, and menu costs.

The imperfect information theory of nominal rigidities was developed in parallel by Edmund Phelps (1967) and Robert Lucas (1972). It claims that producers have more information on their own prices than on those of the economy as a whole. Therefore they may confuse a rise of the general price level with a relative price increase of their own product. In such a case, an unexpected monetary expansion initially leads to a rise in output, until producers understand their mistake. The latter is related to incomplete information, not irrationality.

The second explanation, suggested by John Taylor (1980) and Stanley Fischer (1977), notes that multiyear contracts between firms and employees specify wages and possibly the conditions for their increases. The existence of such contracts is justified by the cost of wage negotiation (including strikes) and by the income uncertainty that would result from day-to-day adjustments of wages to market conditions. If only a fraction of wages adjust at each period, then monetary shocks have a short-term impact on output even when they are perfectly anticipated.

The third explanation (Akerlof and Yellen, 1985; Calvo, 1983; Mankiw, 1985) notes that companies generally adjust their prices infrequently (once or twice a year), while the economic conditions they face (including raw material prices, exchange rates, interest rates, etc.) evolve much more quickly. The response of the new Keynesian theory is that such behavior is optimal for each firm in the presence of adjustment costs—called *menu costs* in reference to the printing costs incurred by restaurants when changing their menus. From a macroeconomic standpoint, however, such behavior is suboptimal because each firm fails to take into account that the delay in adjusting its price level temporarily contributes to creating a gap between supply and demand. In the case of a fall in demand, for instance, firms overlook the fact that a fall in the general level of the prices would support demand by raising the purchasing power of the money holdings. This lack of coordination leads the price level to adjust less than required.

Mankiw and Reis (2011) show how these different theories can be introduced in macroeconomic models. Calvo-type rigidities are widely used in dynamic stochastic general equilibrium (DSGE) models (see Chapter 1 and box 5.8).

level consistent with the desired path for the monetary aggregates. However, as already mentioned, the link between money growth and inflation has proved loose, at least in the short run. In addition, financial liberalization and financial innovation have made the control of monetary aggregates difficult. Logically, central banks have started looking for alternative strategies. New models of monetary policy have emerged in which monetary aggregates play a secondary role or are altogether ignored.

This is the case with Richard Clarida, Jordi Galí, and Mark Gertler's (1999) *new-Keynesian*[23] theory of monetary policy, explained in box 5.8. In their model, the central bank sets the short-term interest rate to keep the future inflation rate and the future output gap (the difference between the actual and potential levels of output, see Chapter 1) as close as possible to targets. Different weights can be given to the two objectives depending on the central bank's mandate. These objectives are (i) a zero output gap, which describes full employment, and (ii) constant inflation (assumed to be zero in the model for the sake of simplicity, without impacting the results).

An important feature of the model is the central bank's forward-looking approach. It does not attempt to control the current inflation or output gap, but their expected future values. This is because delays in the monetary transmission mechanism do not allow the central bank to control current variables. This is an important distinction to keep in mind, and one that matters for discussions on monetary strategies.

Since the output gap is negatively related to the real interest rate and positively related to inflation, the two objectives of the central bank are consistent in the presence of demand shocks (which move inflation and the output gap in the same direction) but contradictory in the presence of cost push or supply shocks (which move them in opposite directions). The policy implication of this observation is that the central bank should completely offset demand shocks even if it only cares about inflation, whereas it should only partially offset cost push shocks. In the fall of 2008, the ECB faced such a dilemma with rising inflation (due to oil and food price hikes) and declining expected output (due to the financial crisis). Its initial response was to raise interest rates before engaging in several cuts, in line with the decline of both inflation and GDP growth.

Another implication of the model, which relies on rational expectations combined with autocorrelated shocks, is that the central bank should raise its interest rate by more than 1% when expected inflation increases by one percentage point (Equation (B5.8.9) in box 5.8) in order for the real interest rate to increase and slow down aggregate demand.

Box 5.8 The "New Keynesian" Model of Monetary Policy

The model (Clarida et al., 1999) relies on two equations: an amended IS curve (Equation (B5.8.1)) and an amended Phillips curve (Equation (B5.8.2)):

$$x_t = -\varphi(i_t - E_t \pi_{t+1}) + E_t x_{t+1} + g_t \quad \phi > 0 \qquad \text{(B5.8.1)}$$

$$\pi_t = \lambda x_t + \beta E_t \pi_{t+1} + u_t \qquad \text{(B5.8.2)}$$

x_t denotes the output gap (defined as the log-difference between actual and potential output) at time t, π_t is the inflation rate defined as the percentage variation of prices between $t-1$ and t, i_t is the short-run nominal interest rate, E_t is the expectation operator, g_t is a demand shock, and u_t a cost push (supply) shock. Both shocks are assumed autocorrelated with autocorrelation coefficients equal to μ and ρ, respectively reflecting the persistence of shocks:

$$\mu = Corr(g_t, g_{t-1}); \; \rho = Corr(u_t, u_{t-1}) \quad \text{with } \mu, \rho \in [0, 1]. \qquad \text{(B5.8.3)}$$

Equation (B5.8.1) derives from the optimizing behavior of households with rational expectations. The presence of the expected output gap in this equation comes from consumption smoothing, and the real interest rate has an additional intertemporal substitution effect: when confronted with shocks, households tend to equalize consumption over time but, other things equal, they save more when the real interest rate is higher. Equation (B5.8.2) derives from a staggered nominal price setting by monopolistically competitive firms: because of short-run nominal rigidities, at each period a firm only has a probability less than one of adjusting its price to the level corresponding to profit maximization. The price it chooses then depends on its expectation of future prices and on a discount factor β. More nominal rigidity implies that inflation depends less on the current output gap, that is, λ is low.

Equation (B5.8.2) can be referred to as a Phillips curve because, for a given price expectation, it results in an upward-sloping relationship between inflation and output in the short run or, equivalently, in a downward-sloping relationship between inflation and unemployment—see Chapter 1. In the long run, expectations adjust and the trade-off moderates (technically, it only vanishes entirely if $\beta = 1$, that is if the discount rate equals zero). Iterating Equation (B5.8.2) forward yields:

$$\pi_t = E_t \sum_{\tau=0}^{\infty} \beta^{\tau} \left[\lambda x_{t+\tau} + u_{t+\tau} \right] \qquad \text{(B5.8.4)}$$

Inflation at time t depends on the whole sequence of expected output gaps and cost push shocks from t to infinity. The central bank sets the nominal interest rate so as to minimize a loss function of the type presented in Chapter 1:

$$Min\,L_t = \frac{1}{2}E_t\left[\sum_{\tau=0}^{\infty}\beta^t\left[\alpha x_{t+\tau}^2 + \pi_{t+\tau}^2\right]\right] \text{ with } \alpha > 0 \quad \text{(B5.8.5)}$$

subject to Equations (B5.8.1) and (B5.8.2), where α is the weight given to output stabilization relative to inflation. Equation (B5.8.5) implies that the central bank sets its interest rate at time *t* in order to keep the future output gap and the inflation rate as close as possible to their target level, taking expectations as exogenous.

Since the output gap and inflation at date *t* do not depend on past values but on expected future values, the optimization problem can be solved as a succession of static decisions:

$$Min\,L_t = \frac{1}{2}\left[\alpha x_t^2 + \pi_t^2\right] + F_t \quad \text{(B5.8.6)}$$

subject to:

$$\pi_t = \lambda x_t + f_t \quad \text{(B5.8.7)}$$

with $F_t = \frac{1}{2}E_t\left(\sum_{\tau=1}^{\infty}\beta^\tau\left[\alpha x_{t+\tau}^2 + \pi_{t+\tau}^2\right]\right)$ and $f_t = \beta E_t \pi_{t+1} + u_t$. Since F_t and f_t can be considered exogenous by the central bank, the optimal values for inflation and the output gap are the following:

$$x_t = -\lambda q u_t \text{ and } \pi_t = \alpha q u_t, \text{ with } q = \frac{1}{\lambda^2 + \alpha(1-\beta\rho)} \quad \text{(B5.8.8)}$$

In the case of a demand shock g_t, both the output gap and the inflation rate will remain *ex post* at their target levels because there is no contradiction between the two objectives. In the case of a cost push shock u_t, there is a contradiction between supporting aggregate demand and moderating inflation. Both targets cannot be reached simultaneously unless $\alpha = 0$ (the central bank does not care about the output gap) or $\alpha \to \infty$ (the central bank does not care about inflation).

It follows from Equation (B5.8.8) and from the autoregressive process driving u_t that:

$$E_t \pi_{t+1} = \alpha q \rho u_t \quad \text{(B5.8.9)}$$

Substituting into the IS curve (Equation (B5.8.1)) we obtain the reaction function of the central bank (i.e., optimal interest rate setting):

$$i_t = \gamma_\pi E_t \pi_{t+1} + \frac{1}{\varphi} g_t \text{ with } \gamma_\pi = 1 + \frac{(1-\rho)\lambda}{\rho\varphi\alpha} > 1 \quad \text{(B5.8.10)}$$

The central bank must react to a one percentage point rise in expected inflation by increasing the nominal interest rate by more than one percentage point, so that the real interest rate can increase.

d) Central bank credibility

In an extraordinarily influential paper of 1983, Robert Barro and David Gordon studied the reaction of economic agents when the central bank tries to push output above its natural level. The parable told by Barro and Gordon is a very simple one.[24] It starts from the assumption that equilibrium output is deemed too low by policymakers because it comes with high unemployment. The best way to lower structural unemployment consists in using structural policies such as labor market or tax reforms but there is a temptation to use monetary policy (demand policy can bring workers back to the labor market, but only up to a point). In the model, if the central bank mistakenly targets output to be higher than potential in order to reduce unemployment, the outcome is bound to be higher inflation with no durable unemployment gain. In addition, rational workers and firms who know the parameters of the economy and the central bank's reaction function will rationally expect inflation to be higher and adjust nominal wages accordingly. This will counter the central bank's effort to reduce unemployment below its long-term level, and, in the end, only inflation will remain. There is an *inflationary bias*.

The inflationary bias is also present in the *augmented Phillips curve* theory introduced by Edmund Phelps (1967) and Milton Friedman (1968). As explained in Chapter 1, the Phillips curve depicts a negative relationship between the unemployment rate and the rate of change in nominal wages. However, this only applies for a given expected inflation. Phelps and Friedman argued that, at any unemployment rate, nominal wages would grow faster in response to a rise in the level of the expected consumer price inflation because workers would be eager to defend the purchasing power of their income. This would in turn result in higher inflation. In the long run, with constant labor productivity, it is reasonable to assume that nominal wages and prices grow at the same rate. The implication is that, whatever the inflation rate obtained in the long run, the unemployment rate will return to an equilibrium value called the *nonaccelerating inflation rate of unemployment* (NAIRU). In other words, in the long run, the Phillips curve is vertical. There is no trade-off between inflation and unemployment, and policies aiming at reducing the unemployment rate below the NAIRU only lead to higher inflation. The Barro-Gordon model formalizes inflation bias when the central bank has an optimizing behavior, and Clarida, Galí and Gertler (1999) give it micro-foundations.

The inflation bias disappears if the central bank can commit to a certain inflation target—for instance, because it is independent and endowed with an explicit inflation-targeting mandate or because it is more inflation-averse (or "conservative") than society (see box 5.9). In this case, private agents will no longer anticipate an excess of monetary expansion or a mitigated reaction to cost push shocks. By reducing inflation expectations, such strategy is designed to reduce the need for high interest rates in the short term. This in turn reduces the output cost of fighting inflation. For this to happen, the

Box 5.9 The Inflation Bias and the Conservative Central Banker

Insights from the Barro-Gordon 1983 model can be plugged into the model of box 5.8. Assume that the central bank targets a positive output gap k. The loss function of Equation (B5.8.4) is modified accordingly:

$$Min\ L_t = \frac{1}{2}E_t\left(\sum_{\tau-0}^{\infty}\beta^{\tau}\left[\alpha\left(x_{t+\tau}-k\right)+\pi_{t+\tau}^{2}\right]\right) \qquad \text{(B5.9.1)}$$

Assume for simplicity that $\beta=1$ (no time preference). The optimization program under the constraints of Equations (B5.8.1) and (B5.8.2) yields:

$$\begin{cases} x_t^{k>0} = x_t^{k=0} \\ \pi_t^{k>0} = \pi_t^{k=0} + \dfrac{\alpha}{\lambda}k \end{cases} \qquad \text{(B5.9.2)}$$

where the subscript $k = 0$ refers to the baseline solution of box 5.8 and $k > 0$ to the solution when the central bank targets a positive output gap. From Equation (B5.9.2) it follows that the central bank fails to increase output but does increase inflation. Clearly the loss function is higher than in the baseline case. The inflation bias $\alpha k/\lambda$ positively depends on k, the desired increase in output, and on α, the preference for output stabilization. Appointing a conservative central banker who assigns a lower weight than society to output stabilization reduces the inflation bias (Rogoff, 1985).

central bank needs to be regarded by the public as bound by its mandate or credibly conservative.

Barro and Gordon have made a simple but forceful case for central bank independence. Their paper is part of a broader literature emphasizing central bank *credibility*, defined as its ability to fulfill its own policy announcements. Credibility is undermined by the time-inconsistency problem (Chapter 2): a given announcement may be optimal at date t but no longer at date $t + 1$, which calls for reoptimization by the central bank and hence departure from its initial plans. This is perfectly appropriate if departure is justified by unexpected economic shocks materializing between t and $t + 1$. But the central bank can also be tempted to cheat on citizens (e.g., announce a low-inflation policy to curb nominal wage demands, then renege on it to achieve a lower real wage *ex post*). To the extent that this behavior is understood by agents, they will no longer base their expectations on the central bank's announcement. For this reason, the central bank may need to tie its hands to a *monetary rule*. A popular rule is *inflation targeting*, where the central bank targets the average expected inflation rate over the next one or two years. Another one, especially in developing countries, is a fixed exchange rate regime, where the central bank commits to intervene to keep the nominal exchange rate stable (see Chapter 7).

Another scheme, suggested by New Zealand economist Carl Walsh (1995), consists in designing an incentive contract for the central bank governor that makes his or her compensation a function of the bank's inflation record. Walsh considers delegation of monetary policy responsibility to be a principal–agent issue, where the principal (the government) delegates to the agent (the central bank) the task of attaining a certain objective (low inflation). He shows that the inflation bias will be eliminated if the central banker receives a compensation that negatively depends on money growth (considered as the monetary instrument) or inflation.

5.2.2 Transmission channels of monetary policy

So far, we have posited that monetary policy influences aggregate demand without discussing how. Four *transmission channels* of monetary policy are usually distinguished: the *interest-rate channel, asset-price channel, credit channel,* and *external channel.* All four operate in parallel and contribute to the general equilibrium outcome, but distinguishing them helps us understand how monetary policy works and what determines the magnitude of its impact. It can also be interesting from a policy standpoint, to help in designing monetary policy instruments that specifically address one or several of these channels, especially in case of financial sector impairment.

a) The interest rate channel

The *interest rate channel* is the traditional Keynesian channel: in the presence of nominal rigidities, a monetary expansion leads to a fall in the (nominal and real) interest rate, hence to a revival of investment and durable goods consumption. In the short run, a higher investment has a multiplier effect (see Chapter 4) on the demand for goods and services. The only interest rate which is directly affected by conventional monetary policy is the overnight, nominal interest rate, whereas non conventional measures also affect expected real interest rates at longer term horizons.

The impact of a monetary policy impulse thus depends on the transmission of policy announcements to a range of interest rates and to expected inflation. This in turn depends on the central bank's communication strategy, on the relationship between short-term rates and long-term rates, and on the ability of the banks to pass changes in their refinancing rates to their clients. The impact of monetary policy also varies according to whether banks lend to households at fixed rates, as in Germany or France, in which case, monetary impulses do not impact indebted households until they renegotiate with their bank, or at variable rates indexed on the short-term rate, as in the United Kingdom or Spain, in which case the impact is immediate. All in all, the interest rate channel varies significantly across countries.

b) The asset price channel

The *asset price channel* relies on the negative relationship between asset prices and interest rates (box 5.10): a decrease in the interest rate generally raises the value of financial assets held by households, which, in turn, partially consume this extra wealth. Such wealth effect played an important role in Japan in the early 1990s, when the burst of the asset price bubble had a negative impact on consumption; in 2001, the sharp fall in US stock prices also had a negative impact on consumption, whereas the rise in real estate prices sustained consumption in the United States and in a number of European countries in the run up to the global financial crisis. The asset price channel also affects the

Box 5.10 Interest Rates and the Pricing of Assets

The market price of a bond is inversely related to the interest rate for the following reason. Suppose a perpetual (i.e., never redeemed) bond costs \$1 at time t and yields a 4% annual return; that is, each year forever, the holder of the bond will receive a 4 cents coupon. Suppose that, at time $t + 1$, interest rates have risen from 4% to 5%. This means that new bonds issued in $t + 1$ yield a 5% coupon. Nobody wants to buy the old bond unless it cheapens. Its price adjusts to a new value P such that the bond yields an intrinsic return (coupon/P) of 5% despite paying coupon equal to 4% of the bond face value. This requires that $4\%/P = 5\%$, hence $P = 80$ cents. In this example, a one percentage-point rise in the interest rate triggers a 20% fall in the bond price.

A similar inverse relation between interest rates and asset prices also holds for equities, but in a less mechanical way. The fundamental value of a stock is the price at which the investor is indifferent between, on the one hand, holding the stock and cashing in the dividends attached to it, and, on the other hand, selling it at market value. If investors are risk-neutral, the fundamental value is equal to the net present value of expected future dividends. When the interest rate r is constant and the growth rate of dividends d_t is g, the price p_t of the stock is given by the *Gordon–Shapiro* formula:

$$p_t = \frac{d_t}{r - g} \qquad \text{(B5.10.1)}$$

A more detailed explanation is provided in box 6.4 of Chapter 6. A higher interest rate r discounts more heavily future cash flows and therefore immediately lessens the value of the stock. In addition, the interest rate may affect the dividend through macroeconomic equilibrium. In the short run, a lower r may increase g and magnify the stock price increase.

corporate sector: A rise in stock prices increases the profitability of investment (also known as *Tobin's q*),[25] which supports investment.

The importance of the asset price channel has increased over time as a consequence of increased household participation in financial markets and the general rise in debt- and wealth-to-income ratios. In Anglo-Saxon economies, households using their houses as collateral for consumption loans has played an important role in supporting household consumption in the early 2000s, and in amplifying its fall after the collapse of the housing bubble.

Closely related to the asset price channel is the *risk-taking channel* (Borio and Zhu, 2012). A lower interest rate leads investors and banks to take more risk; that is, not only to lend more to households and firms but also to soften lending standards such as collateral or legal guarantees asked from the borrower (Altunbas, Gambacorta, and Marqués-Ibáñez, 2014; Maddaloni and Peydró Alcade, 2011). One reason is the higher value of the collateral (through the asset price channel). To the extent that banks adjust their leverage in order to keep their risk profile constant, higher asset prices trigger more leverage and more lending (see box 6.10 of Chapter 6). Additionally, lower interest rates are an incentive for asset managers to "search for yield"; that is, to take more risk to reach the return targets set by their principals (see Rajan, 2005). There is a paradox inherent to the risk-taking channel: as noted earlier, what may spur economic recovery by lifting the spirits of households and entrepreneurs may also create moral hazard and sow the seeds of the following financial crisis. Monetary policy may be one of the drivers of the financial cycles observed over long historical periods (Borio, 2014).

c) The credit channel

The *credit channel* works through the impact of the interest rate on the supply of—rather than the demand for—credit. In response to an improvement in their refinancing conditions, banks tend to increase their supply of credit, in addition to reducing their lending rates.

The reason is asymmetric information between borrowers and lenders (Bernanke and Gertler, 1995). It is costly for banks to assess properly the quality of all investment projects for which borrowers—especially SMEs—request loans. Lack of information by banks on the quality of the projects they finance leads them to add to the interest rate a premium compensating for the risk of default. This *agency cost* (named for the principal–agent relationship between the bank and the borrower) penalizes or even dissuades good investment projects whose probability of failure is low. However, risky projects may not be discouraged as borrowers know that their probability of failure is high and accept paying the corresponding premium. The more the bank increases the interest rate, the more it actually discourages good projects and selects bad ones (box 5.11). This *adverse selection* problem, well known in insurance theory, leads the banks to restrict credit rather than reprice risk.[26]

Credit rationing especially affects SMEs since they do not have access to capital markets and rely on bank financing. SMEs in peripheral euro area countries were especially hurt by credit rationing during the 2008 financial crisis and then again during the euro area sovereign debt crisis (see figure 5.7). Although policy rates were brought close to zero percent, SMEs in peripheral countries could not grasp the benefits of expansionary monetary policy because of credit rationing. It is as if the credit supply curve in figure B5.11.1 of box 5.11 had shifted downward, widening the gap with credit demand $D_2(r)$ at any level of interest rate r.

In normal time, a lower interest rate raises the value of the assets used to guarantee the loans and therefore companies' and households' access to credit. Constraints on credit arising from collateral limits are sometimes called "Fisherian" constraints, from Yale economist Irving Fisher's theory of debt deflation, and their systemic consequences are discussed in Chapter 6. In a recession, the value of the collateral is depressed and banks restrict credit supply. This amplifying mechanism is called the *financial accelerator* and counters the transmission of monetary policy impulses.

Box 5.11 Credit Rationing

In a seminal paper of 1981, Joseph Stiglitz and Andrew Weiss consider a bank loan as a contract between the bank and the borrower, defined by its amount, maturity, interest rate, and collateral (i.e., an asset that the bank can take hold of if the borrower is unable to repay the loan).

As a rule, the supply of credit by the bank is an increasing function of the interest rate, whereas the demand for credit is a decreasing function of the interest rate. Hence, both sides will agree on an amount and an interest rate that correspond to the intercept of the two curves. However, Stiglitz and Weiss note that, due to information asymmetry, the supply of credit may not be a monotonic function of the interest rate. Suppose there are two categories of borrowers: the safe (who are likely to repay their debts) and the risky (who are likely to default). The bank cannot observe whether a specific borrower is safe or risky (whereas the borrower knows his own type). Hence, the bank applies the same interest rate to both types of borrowers, which includes a risk premium.

The higher the interest rate, the less inclined are safe borrowers to take a loan because they know they will effectively have to pay the corresponding cost. Hence, a rise in the interest rate does not necessarily increase the expected profit of the bank. The supply of credit $S(r)$ may correspondingly be an increasing function of the interest rate up to a certain threshold but a decreasing function thereafter (figure B5.11.1). A consequence is that the supply curve $S(r)$ may not cross the demand curve $D(r)$. On the figure, this is the case with $D_2(r)$. Then, borrowers are rationed since they will not obtain the amount of credit they need—*for any interest rate*. This situation is called *credit rationing*.

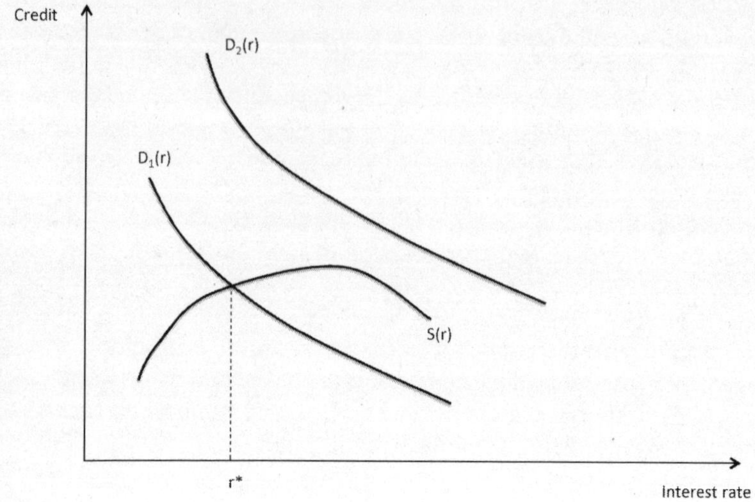

Figure B5.11.1 Credit rationing.

To avoid such situations, banks structure their credit supply to force borrowers to reveal their risk. For instance, the interest rate proposed will be lower the higher the quantity and quality of collateral. This helps banks to assess the level of risk of each borrower and to propose an interest rate with the corresponding risk premium.

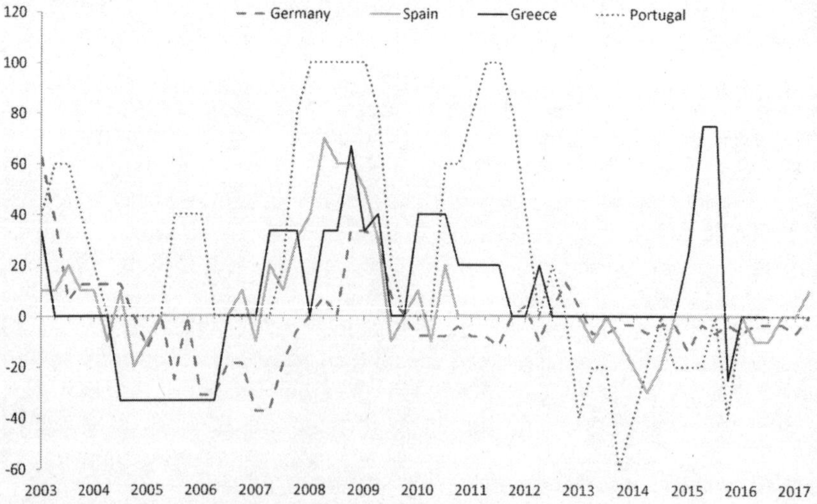

Figure 5.7 Credit standards of loans to small- and medium-size enterprises in the euro area, 2003–2017. Frequency of tightening versus easing, in percent. A positive number means that tightening is more frequent than easing.
ECB Bank Lending Survey, July 2016.

d) The external channel

Monetary policy affects the economy by changing the relative price of present and future consumption and by influencing the relative return of different domestic assets (safe vs. risk-bearing, short-term vs. long-term), but also by changing the relative return of domestic versus foreign assets and domestic versus foreign goods. The latter channel is the *external channel* which materializes as exchange rate variations.

A fall in the domestic interest rate implies a fall in the yield of domestic assets in comparison with foreign ones. To the extent that they are not impeded by capital controls, domestic and foreign asset holders are discouraged from holding domestic assets and encouraged to hold foreign assets. Consistent with the law of supply and demand, the relative price of domestic assets falls. In a floating exchange rate context (see Chapter 7), this amounts to a *depreciation* of the home currency. Conversely, an increase in the domestic interest rate triggers a currency *appreciation*. In turn, the variation of the exchange rate influences: (i) the price level through the implied change in import prices, (ii) aggregate demand through substitutions between traded and nontraded domestic goods and between domestic and foreign traded goods, and (iii) aggregate supply through a change in the price of imported inputs. Through these three mechanisms, the external channel amplifies the effect of monetary policy.

The link between the interest rate and the exchange rate is explained in box 5.12. To the extent that investors' decisions are based on their expectations concerning future economic variables, the exchange rate is affected by announcements about future monetary policy. Conversely, the exchange rate does not react to a change in the interest rate when it was previously announced. Figures 5.8 and 5.9 provide examples of the two cases for the

Box 5.12 The Impact of the Interest Rate on the Exchange Rate

Assuming perfect capital mobility and no risk aversion, an investor will invest his or her wealth in the currency with the highest expected return. Denoting by i the domestic interest rate, each unit of domestic currency invested domestically will be worth $(1 + i)$ units after one year. Similarly, if i^* represents the foreign interest rate, each unit of foreign currency invested abroad today will be worth $(1 + i^*)$ units of foreign currency after one year. However, to invest abroad, the domestic investor needs first to change his or her wealth into foreign currency. Denoting by S the nominal exchange rate (the number of foreign currency units per unit of domestic currency), one unit of domestic currency allows the investor to buy S units of foreign currency, which will be worth $S(1 + i^*)$ after one year. He or she will then be able to convert this amount back at the expected exchange rate S^e. Hence, the repatriated amount in domestic currency is expected to be $S(1 + i^*)/S^e$.

A risk-neutral investor will invest wherever the expected return is higher. This implies at equilibrium:

$$(1+i)=\frac{S(1+i^*)}{S^e} \tag{B5.12.1}$$

This equality is called the *uncovered interest parity* (UIP). It must hold in the absence of capital controls if domestic and foreign assets are perfectly substitutable and if investors are risk-neutral.[a] Considering relatively small interest rates, and with $s = \ln S$ and $s^e = \ln S^e$, the linearized form of the uncovered interest parity is:

$$i = i^* - (s^e - s) = i^* - \Delta s^e \tag{B5.12.2}$$

where Δs^e is the percent of expected appreciation of the domestic currency ($\Delta s^e = s^e - s$). For instance, suppose that the domestic interest rate i is 3% while the foreign interest rate i^* is of 4%. If they do not anticipate any variation of the exchange rate ($\Delta s^e = 0$) *ex ante*, residents will invest abroad; this will make s fall compared to s^e until $s^e - s = \Delta s^e = +1\%$ (i.e., until an appreciation of the domestic currency by 1% is expected). Hence, the relation $s = s^e + i - i^*$ determines the current exchange rate depending on both interest rates and on the expected exchange rate:

$$s = (i - i^*) + s^e \tag{B5.12.3}$$

Assuming rational expectations, the expected exchange rate s^e also fulfills UIP. Introducing time subscripts t and denoting by $x_{t,t+1}^e$ the expectation at time t of variable x ($x = s$ or i) at time t+1, Equation (B5.12.3) can be rewritten as:

$$s_t = (i_t - i_t^*) + s_{t,t+1}^e = (i_t - i_t^*) + (i_t - i_{t,t+1}^{*e}) + s_{t,t+2}^e \tag{B5.12.4}$$

Hence, not only current interest rates, but also interest rates expected for the next period affect the exchange rate. Iterating Equation (B5.12.4) forward until horizon T, we get:

$$s_t = s_{t,t+T}^e + \sum_{\tau=0}^{T-1}\left(i_{t,t+\tau}^e - i_{t,t+\tau}^{*e}\right) \tag{B5.12.5}$$

A variation in the interest rate may have a magnified impact on the exchange rate in the short run depending on: (1) how long the domestic interest rate is expected to differ from the foreign one and (2) what will be the impact of monetary policy on the exchange rate in the long run.

For instance, if the domestic interest rate falls below the foreign one by one percentage point and is expected to stay at this depressed level during three years, the exchange rate immediately depreciates by 3% relative to the expected exchange rate beyond these three years. If the exchange rate is expected to come back to its initial level after three years, then the exchange rate immediately depreciates by 3 × 1 = 3% relative to its initial level, and then appreciates by 1% per year until the initial level is recovered (figure B5.12.1, left panel). Conversely, if the exchange rate is expected to depreciate by, say, 5% in the long run, the initial depreciation is 3 + 5 = 8% relative to the initial level. Then, the exchange rate appreciates by 1% per year until the new long-term level is reached (figure B5.12.1, right panel). In the latter case, the exchange rate is said to *overshoot* its long-term level. Such outcome is consistent with a monetary model of exchange rate determination with sticky prices (Dornbusch, 1976): the expansionary monetary shock involves a depreciation of the nominal exchange rate in the long term; in the short term, price rigidities trigger a fall in the interest rate and an overshooting of the exchange rate.

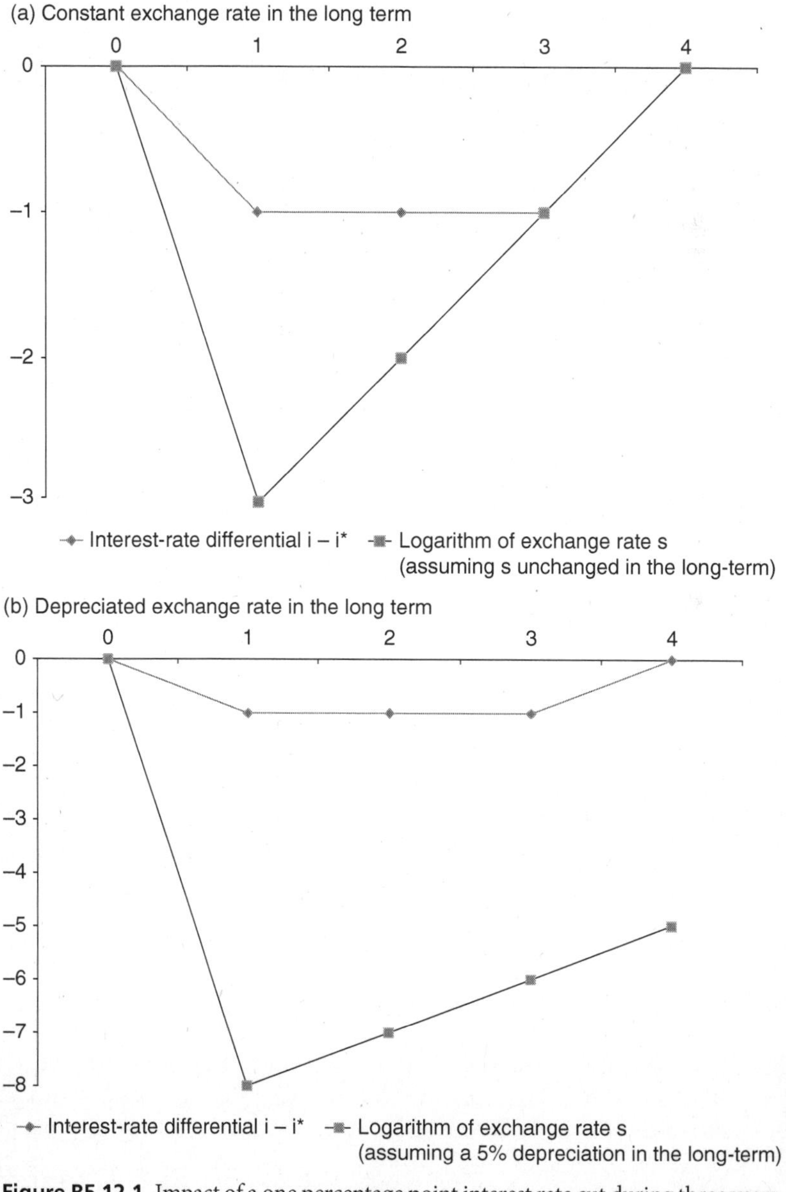

Figure B5.12.1 Impact of a one percentage point interest rate cut during three years.

Such overshooting is consistent with exchange rates generally being much more volatile than interest rates. Indeed, quarterly fluctuations of exchange rates are typically two digits (e.g., +/–10%), whereas quarterly variations in interest rates are single digit (e.g., +/–1 percentage point). Like all asset prices, the exchange rate incorporates all relevant information about future interest rates and their determinants, and this creates a significant volatility. From a policy standpoint, this means that disseminating information concerning future monetary policy (for instance, through speeches) can move the exchange rate even in the absence of immediate monetary action.

[a] The perfect substitutability condition can be violated if the assets do not present the same risk (e.g., if there is a higher probability of default in the foreign country).

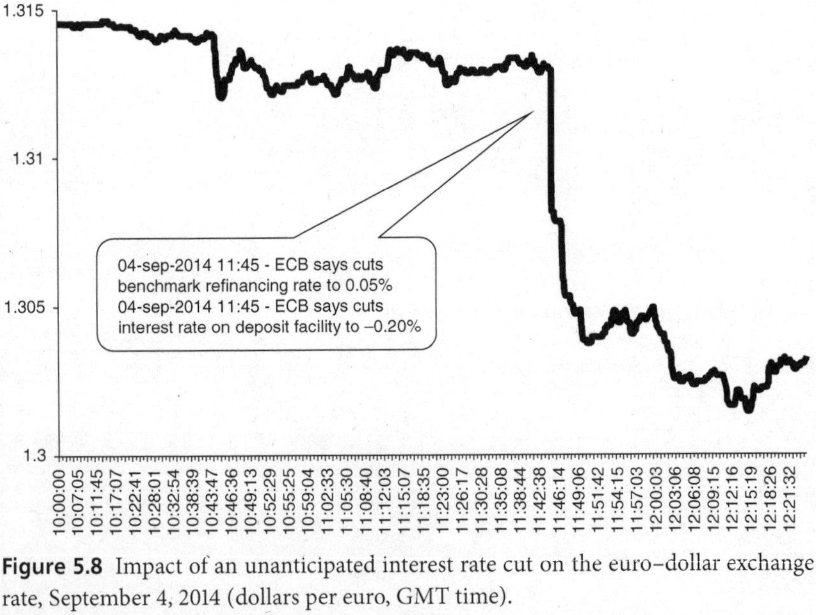

Figure 5.8 Impact of an unanticipated interest rate cut on the euro–dollar exchange rate, September 4, 2014 (dollars per euro, GMT time).
Reuters.

euro–dollar exchange rate. Figure 5.8 shows the impact of an unexpected rate cut by the ECB on September 4, 2014.[27] In the few minutes following the announcement, the euro depreciated by 0.7% against the US dollar. Figure 5.9 shows the case when the president of the ECB announced a future rate hike on

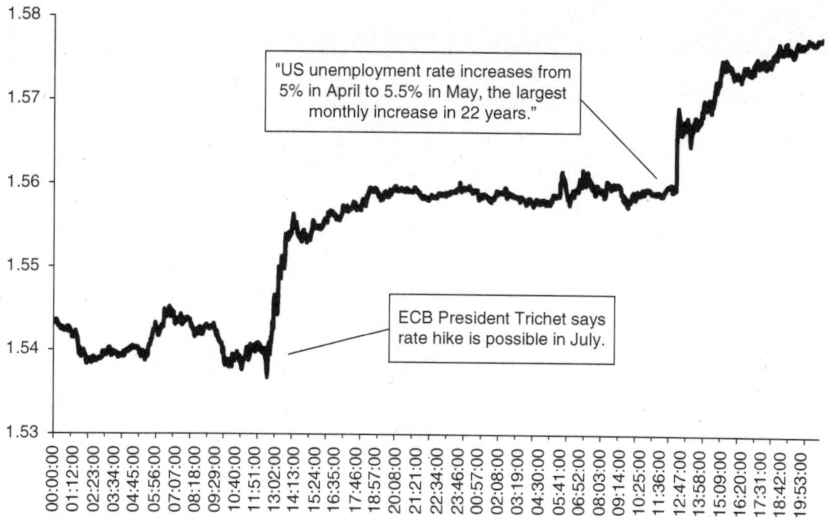

Figure 5.9 Impact of a monetary policy announcement on the euro–dollar exchange rate, June 5–6, 2008 (dollars per euro, GMT time).
Reuters.

June 5, 2008. Although no immediate decision was taken, the euro appreciated immediately by 1% against the dollar. The next day, the US Department of Commerce announced a sharp rise in unemployment. Markets interpreted this announcement as raising the probability that US monetary policy would eventually be relaxed, and the euro appreciated again.

e) Assessing the channels

As explained earlier, the relative importance of the various transmission channels varies from country to country depending on their financial structure. The strength of the interest rate channel depends on the proportion of loans indexed on short-term interest rates; the asset price channel depends on household wealth; the credit channel depends on the share of bank credit; and, quite obviously, the external channel depends on the openness of the economy. Econometric studies have tried to measure the impact of monetary policy in various countries. One popular methodology is vector autoregressive (VAR) analysis, which relies on a few assumptions concerning the functioning of the economy and the transmission channels at work (box 5.13).

Figure 5.10 shows the impact of an increase in the policy interest rate in Turkey, based on a VAR model with five variables (industrial production, producer price index, private credit, exchange rate, and short-term interest rate), estimated with monthly data over 2004–2013. The rate hike triggers a fall in private credit (interest rate and credit channels) and an appreciation of the Turkish lira (external channel). GDP falls. The asset price channel is not shown here.

Box 5.13 Monetary Policy Transmission Channels in Practice

One popular way of studying monetary policy transmission channels is to estimate a dynamic econometric model describing the joint movements of GDP, prices, employment, and of one or more monetary instruments without any theoretical prior. Such a *vector autoregressive* (VAR) model may be written as:

$$X_t = A X_{t-1} + u_t \tag{B5.13.1}$$

where X_t is the vector of the macroeconomic variables under review. For instance, $X_t = (i_t, y_t, p_t)'$ with i_t the nominal interest rate, y_t the logarithm of real output, and p_t the logarithm of the consumer price index. A is a 3×3 matrix of the coefficients to be estimated, u_t is the vector of the three residuals at time t, and V' denotes a transposed vector V. The fact that i_t is exogenous will be reflected by the fact that the first line of A is (1 0 0). This hypothesis can be imposed or tested statistically.

It is then possible to compute the *impulse-response function* that describes how X_t evolves over time following an exogenous shock on the interest rate (first line of the vector u) at time $t = 0$. In the present example, the contemporaneous impact on real output y_t of a *temporary* unitary shock to the interest rate at time $t = 0$ is zero since the shock only affects the interest rate itself. The impact at time $t = 1$ is a_{21}, where a_{ij} is the coefficient on line i and row j of A. At time $t = 2$, the level of y_t is $a_{21} \times a_{11} + a_{22} \times a_{21} + a_{23} \times a_{31}$. In the case of a *permanent* shock to the interest rate, the response of output after τ periods is $y_\tau = \sum_{k=1}^{\tau} \xi_k$ with:

$$\xi_k = (010) A^k (010) \tag{B5.13.2}$$

The coefficients of A can be estimated under constraints based on theoretical priors (such as sign restrictions on the impulse response functions).

It can be noted that none of the transmission channels relies on the direct effect of money growth on inflation postulated by the quantity theory of money.[28]

5.2.3 Monetary policy at the zero-lower bound: Beyond the standard toolkit

The theoretical problem raised by interest rates being close to zero dates back to the *liquidity trap* uncovered by John Maynard Keynes. Monetary policy becomes ineffective because nonfinancial agents are prepared to absorb any increase in money supply for the same interest rate. The interest rate is so

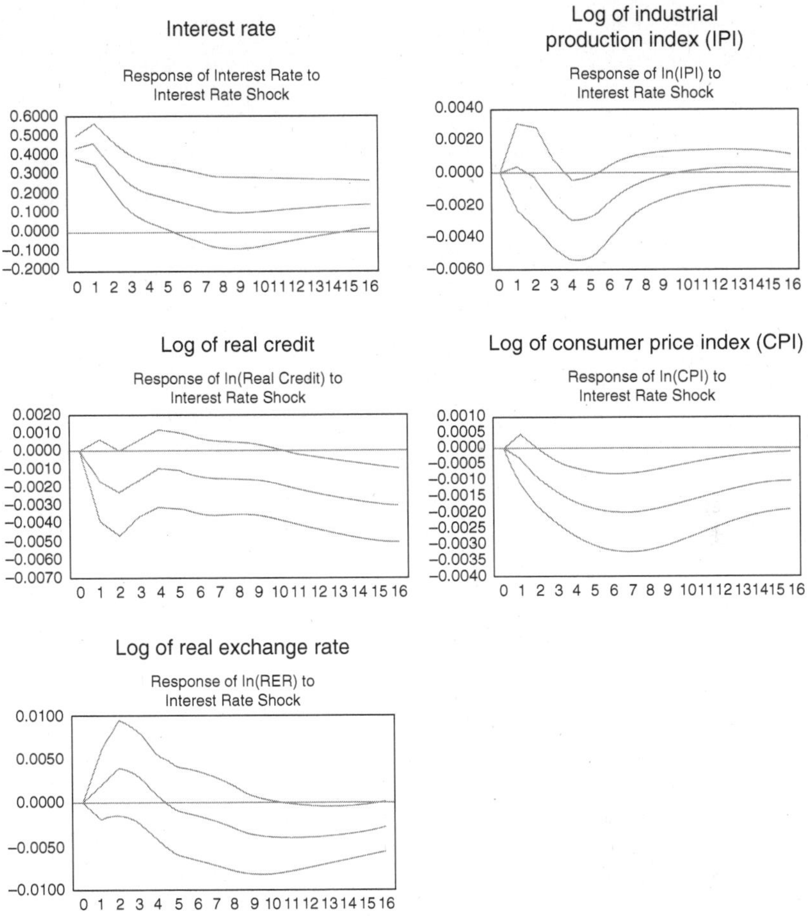

Figure 5.10 Impact of an increase in the short-term interest rate in Turkey. Impulse-response functions, deviations from baseline, in percent, monthly frequency.
Impact of an increase in the short-term interest rate by one standard deviation: mean and confidence band.
Özdemir (2015).

low that there is no longer any arbitrage between money and bonds. In such situations, pouring more money into the system will not lower the interest rate and the economy will remain unaffected. In the IS–LM model, this shows as a non-linear LM curve, as in figure 5.11: when the nominal interest rate i is very low, a monetary expansion (which shifts the LM curve to the right) has no impact on output Y.

The liquidity trap can be compounded with the *debt deflation* mechanism evidenced in 1933 by Irving Fischer: in a situation of high private indebtedness, deflationary pressures increase the real value of debt and weight on households' available income (Eggertsson and Krugman, 2012; see also Chapter 6).[29]

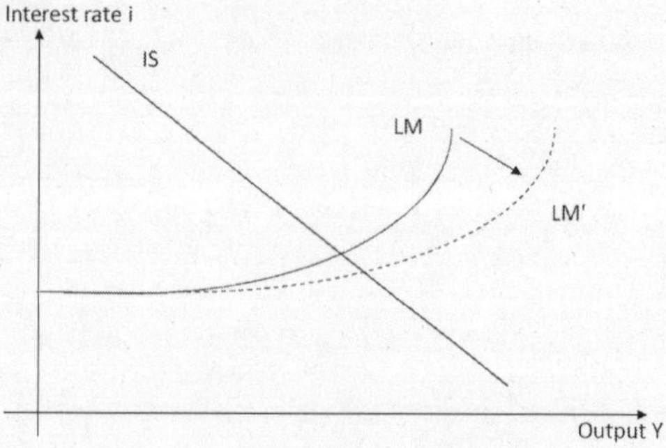

Figure 5.11 The liquidity trap. An expansionary monetary policy shifts the LM curve to the right: a given interest rate *i* is compatible with higher output *Y*. At low interest rates, the LM curve is flat and an expansionary monetary policy has negligible impact on output. The IS-LM model is presented in Chapter 4.

Can the liquidity trap be escaped? In the two decades prior to the 2008 financial crisis, monetary theory had progressively considered money supply as endogenous and mostly irrelevant for monetary policy and money demand as highly unstable. The standard toolkit in the central banks did not assign any role to money supply, nor to banks (see the Clarida-Galí-Gertler model of box 5.8). Although lessons had been drawn from the Japanese crisis (Krugman, 2000; Ito and Mishkin, 2006; Koo, 2009), the crisis found monetary economists largely unequipped to advise central banks as they strayed in the unchartered territory of unconventional monetary policy. The crisis, however, triggered intensive theoretical and empirical work to understand the transmission of quantitative easing, forward guidance, and negative interest rates to the economy (see Beyer, Cœuré, and Mendicino, 2017, for a survey of the relevant models).

a) Quantitative easing

Quantitative easing (QE) consists in a central bank purchasing large amounts of securities on the secondary market in order to increase bank reserves, lower longer term interest rates, and, beyond, inflate a wide range of asset prices. There are three main transmission channels of QE (see Krishnamurthy and Vissing-Jorgensen, 2011, for a review):

- An interest rate channel which, in comparison with conventional monetary policy, influences the yield curve at longer maturities, depending on the assets purchased.[30]

- Portfolio rebalancing: Central bank purchases of risk-free assets depress the return on this class of assets and incentivize investors to switch to more risky assets which, in turn, will see their return decline. Portfolio rebalancing can extend to foreign assets, in which case the domestic currency depreciates, and the external channel is strengthened. QE thus also entails an external transmission channel. Portfolio rebalancing lowers the cost of financing across a broad range of financial instruments, which further support aggregate demand.
- A signaling channel, which also contributes to flattening the yield curve. By loading its balance sheet with a large amount of high-duration securities, the central bank signals a bias against allowing interest rates to go up too early since it would then incur losses. This tends to flatten further the yield curve.

QE can be supplemented with forward guidance on asset purchases. For instance, the ECB announced in 2015 that the bonds purchased would be held to maturity (i.e., it would refrain from selling them before maturity). In 2016, it announced that they would be reinvested: the central bank's balance sheet would start shrinking only long after the end of net purchases. Moreover, forward guidance on rates can be tied to forward guidance on purchases. The ECB has repeatedly said that it would keep rates low or lower until "well past the horizon of is net asset purchases." The theory of forward guidance is discussed in more detail in Section 5.2.3.b.

The portfolio channel of QE has been met with skepticism by monetary theorists. Using a new-Keynesian model where money balances enter households' utility function (because they facilitate transactions), Eggertsson and Woodford (2003) argue that a temporary increase in money supply does not change the path of real GDP over time. QE may increase GDP only to the extent that it changes either fiscal policy (by making government funding easier) or market expectations (e.g. if it is permanent). The reason why QE in itself is irrelevant is that there is a satiation level for money balance holdings corresponding to a zero interest rate. Beyond the satiation level, additional money balances do not provide further liquidity services. The composition of the central bank balance sheet (e.g., the relative weight of government versus private bonds) is also irrelevant. This model, however, disregards financial frictions.

In Cúrdia and Woodford (2011; box 5.14), the central bank provides transaction services to commercial banks rather than directly to households. Because of the satiation level, the *size* of the central bank balance sheet is irrelevant here, too, but its *composition* now matters. Substituting governments bonds for bank reserves has no effect because both are risk-free assets, but substituting private (i.e. risky) bonds for government bonds in the balance sheet of the central bank has a positive impact on bank lending and welfare.

Box 5.14 A Theory of Quantitative Easing

Cúrdia and Woodford (2011) introduce liquidity provision and bank lending in a new-Keynesian model. There is one, single, representative commercial bank. It chooses its lending L and reserves deposited at the central bank m so as to maximize its profit, given the corresponding interest rates i^b and i^m and their spreads on the deposit rate i^d.

Due to imperfect information, when lending one euro to a "good" borrower (that will repay $1+i^b$ in the next period), the bank needs to extend $\chi(L)>0$ euro to "bad" borrowers (that will repay 0). The cost of producing new loans depends positively on the total amount of lending L but negatively on the bank's reserves at the central bank m, below a "satiety" level $\bar{m}(L)$.

At equilibrium, the spread between the different interest rates is the following:

$$\frac{i_t^b - i_t^d}{1+i_t^d} = \omega_t = \Xi(L_t, m_t) + \chi(L_t),\quad \Xi_L > 0,\ \Xi_m < 0,\ \chi_L > 0 \quad \text{(B5.14.1)}$$

$$\Xi(L_t, m_t) = 0 \quad \text{for } m \geq \bar{m}(L)$$

$$\frac{i_t^d - i_t^m}{1+i_t^d} = \delta_t = -\Xi(L_t, m_t) \quad \text{(B5.14.2)}$$

Where Ξ_L and Ξ_m are derivatives with respect to L and m. The central bank controls i^m and it separately sets the supply of reserves m through QE. Up to the satiation level $\bar{m}(L)$, a rise in reserve supply m reduces the cost of financial intermediation Ξ and therefore raises the amount of bank lending L. Above the satiation level, however, QE has no impact on the economy. The story is different when the central bank uses QE to extend loans to the private sector (or buy corporate bonds) rather than buying government bonds. It then by-passes private-sector financial intermediaries that are inefficient due to the information cost χ.

In this line of thinking, the central bank supports aggregate demand by extracting credit risk from the economy. These theoretical controversies have led Ben Bernanke to conclude just before he left the Fed in January 2014 that "the problem with QE is that it works in practice, but it doesn't work in theory."

Empirical evidence is indeed more positive than theory about QE, at least when it comes to its effect on market interest rates and asset prices. In his survey of empirical estimates, Micossi (2015) concludes that, on average, QE carried out in the United States and in the United Kingdom in 2008–09 lowered long-term interest rates by about 100 basis points (one percentage point), a very significant effect. The effect was even larger in the euro area,

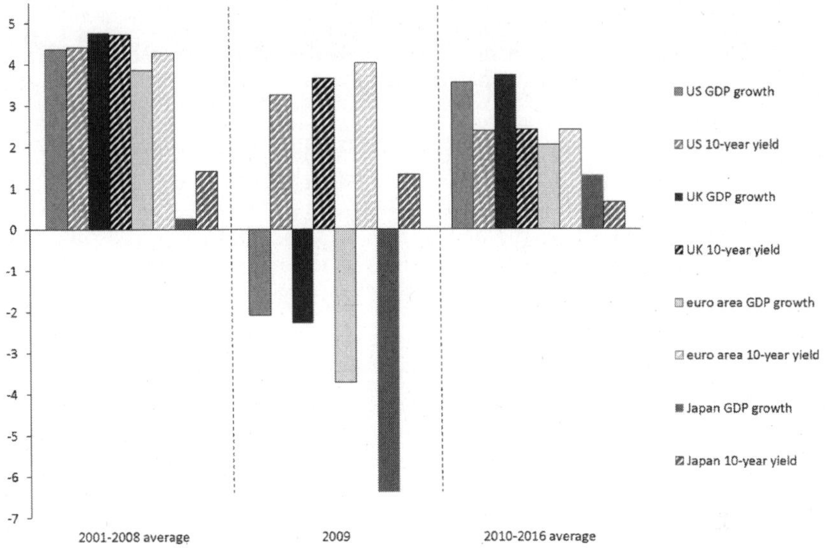

Figure 5.12 Nominal gross domestic product (GDP) growth and 10-year government bond yield, in percent per year.
OECD Economic Outlook database.

especially in those countries initially posting higher long-term rates (Spain, Italy). In these three cases, the effect of QE materialized upon announcement. In contrast, the impact of QE on long-term interest rates in Japan was very limited. The effect of Japanese QE was mainly channeled by the exchange rate (–10%). In the euro area, too, QE resulted in a depreciation of the currency, whereas in the United States, only the first round of QE weakened the dollar.

Empirical evidence is more mixed about the impact of QE on the real economy. The determining factor is whether QE contributes to the deleveraging of the private and the public sectors by pushing nominal growth above the nominal interest rate. Figure 5.12 shows that, from 2010 to 2014, US and UK monetary policies were quite successful in this regard, whereas Japan and the euro area (where QE hadn't started yet) were rather unsuccessful. The fact that growth did not seem to strongly respond to QE is no proof that QE does not work since the effect depends on the counterfactual: deleveraging would have happened anyway, perhaps in a more disruptive way. All in all, it remains difficult to isolate the impact of QE on the real economy.

b) Forward guidance

Forward guidance consists in communicating about future monetary policy in order to guide market expectations. Following Campbell et al. (2012), two types of forward guidance can be distinguished. With "Delphic" forward guidance (a reference to the oracle of ancient Greece's Delphi, Pythia), the central bank discloses its expectation of its own policy course, given its policy rule and its expectation of exogenous variables in the economy. In contrast, "Odyssean" forward guidance (a reference to the episode in the Odyssey when Ulysses ties himself to the mast of his boat to escape the Sirens) is a commitment to a preset course for interest rates, even if it may imply deviating from the policy rule at some point in the future. The forward guidances of the Fed, ECB, and Bank of England after the global financial crisis were "Delphic," without commitment.

Unlike QE, forward guidance fits well in the new-Keynesian model of box 5.8, at least in its Odyssean form. As shown in box 5.15, when the nominal interest rate hits the ZLB, a commitment to let inflation temporarily run above target in the future (as done by the Bank of Japan in 2016) raises inflationary expectations and the output gap in the short run. This result may have created some misunderstanding between academics and policy-makers. The former

Box 5.15 The Theory of Odyssean Forward Guidance

Gauti Eggertsson and Michael Woodford (2003) study forward guidance using a simple, new-Keynesian model of the type presented in box 5.8. The model consists essentially in two equations:

$$x_t = E_t x_{t+1} - \sigma\left(i_t - \mathrm{E}_t \pi_{t+1} - r_t^n\right) \quad \sigma > 0 \qquad \text{(B5.15.1)}$$

$$\pi_t = \kappa x_t + \beta E_t \pi_{t+1} + u_t \quad \kappa > 0,\ 0 < \beta < 1 \qquad \text{(B5.15.2)}$$

where x_t denotes the output gap, π_t the inflation rate, i_t the nominal interest rate, E_t the expectation operator, r_t^{n} the real natural rate of interest (see Section 5.1.1.c), and u_t a cost push shock.

Assume that the central bank is committed to delivering a constant inflation rate π^* (its inflation target). When monetary policy is unconstrained, a necessary condition to fulfill this commitment is to set the nominal interest rate at its natural level:

$$i_t = r_t^n + \pi^* \qquad \text{(B5.15.3)}$$

Assume now that, due to a crisis, the natural real interest rate temporarily falls below zero, down to a level such that $r_t^n < -\pi^*$. Then, the interest rule (Equation (B5.15.3)) implies that the nominal rate should be negative or else the central bank can no longer reach its inflation target. Eggertsson and Woodford show that, in such circumstances, the best interest rate rule is a history-dependent policy whereby the interest rate is set as a function of both current and past economic conditions.

Suppose now that the central bank minimizes the following loss function where the inflation target is set to zero for simplicity:

$$Min\ E_0 \left\{ \sum_{t=0}^{\infty} \left(\pi_t^2 + \lambda x_t^2 \right) \right\} \qquad \text{(B5.15.4)}$$

Then, in the event of a fall in the natural interest rate, the optimal monetary policy consists in committing to running the economy hot once the natural rate comes back to positive territory, even though this will involve positive inflation. Such commitment stimulates the economy in the short term through different channels. First, higher expected inflation immediately lowers the real interest rate, which raises the output gap, as seen in Equation (B5.15.1). Second, the expectation that the interest rate will be kept at a low level also stimulates current spending, which depends on current but also future real interest rates. Finally, the expectation of higher income raises current spending through a permanent income effect. Such policy, however, relies on a moving inflation target that would transitorily rise above its permanent level. The policy is said to be *history-* (or *path-*) *dependent* in the sense that the central bank commits to raise the interest rate more slowly than the increase in the natural interest rate when the latter picks up, as if it were "remembering" the past crisis. A related proposal to let inflation *temporarily* overshoot its target when the economy exits the ZLB has been put forward by Ben Bernanke (2017).

would like to see any forward guidance as Odyssean, while for the latter it can only be Delphic.

Overshooting the inflation target amounts to suggesting that the central bank should (at least partly) target the level of prices rather than their rate of change. *Price-level targeting* resurrects an old suggestion by Wicksell (Hatcher and Minford, 2016). If the inflation rate is 1% during one year while the target is 2%, inflation will need to exceed 2% temporarily in the future in a price-targeting scheme but not in an inflation-targeting one.

Price-level targeting may prove powerful at the ZLB to recreate inflationary expectations. Its main drawback is its lack of transparency since the price-level target is history-dependent. Additionally, it may lead to ill-designed policies when the economy is hit by a permanent cost push shock. Suppose for instance that the price of oil rises permanently by 20% and permanently increases consumer prices by 1%. With a price-level target, the central bank would have to tighten its monetary policy. With an inflation target, it would not react to such a one-off shock. No central bank so far has followed such a radical suggestion (see Cúrdia, 2016, for a discussion).

5.2.4 The interplay between monetary and fiscal policy

Monetary and fiscal policies are both demand policies: they aim at stabilizing aggregate demand at a level close to potential GDP. Both policies can be coordinated to avoid the two instruments acting in opposite directions, hence the concept of a *policy mix*. In the 1980s, however, it was recognized that making the central bank independent from the government, giving it a clear mandate, and prohibiting it to directly finance the budget would better achieve the objective of price stability with limited or no cost in terms of output and employment. The creation of the European monetary union reinforced this conviction since the perimeter of monetary policy (the euro area) would differ from that of fiscal policy (the nineteen Member States).

The Great Recession has shown, however, that one cannot ignore the interplay between monetary and fiscal policy. On the one hand, countries which have retained monetary sovereignty (such as the United States or the United Kingdom) have fared well as borrowers despite rocketing sovereign debts, whereas the ECB's monetary policy was not well transmitted to euro area economies trapped in a sovereign debt crisis. On the other hand, unconventional policies carried out by central banks have important impact on sovereign interest rates, as well as significant distributive consequences, an attribute normally reserved to fiscal policies, to the point where central banks were accused of carrying out "quasi-fiscal" policies. The line between fiscal and monetary policy was blurred, and some have argued that it has been crossed.

a) Seigniorage

When thinking about the relationship between fiscal and monetary policy, it is useful to remember that the power to mint coins was historically reserved for monarchs. Coins appeared around the Aegean Sea about 650 BCE, and a king of Lydia first certified their weight in gold and silver. The idea then soon came to differentiate the face value of the coins from their metallic value, the former being higher than the latter. The difference would then accrue to the king (see Le Rider, 1994). It is also useful to remember that several of the first central banks had a mandate to lend to the government. Before monetary institutions were made independent, it was current practice for governments, especially in wartime, to ask their central banks to extend loans that would not always be repaid. The loans would take the form of overdrafts to the account of the government at the central bank; these funds would then be used to finance war—pure money creation by the central bank.

Modern currencies are no longer backed by precious metals but by the assets of the economy. Like the old kings of Lydia, however, a modern central bank earns an income resulting directly from money issuance since the remuneration of its liabilities is less than that of its assets. This income, called *seigniorage*, is transferred to the government (and as needed to other central bank shareholders). The greater the volume of money creation, the higher the value of seigniorage (see box 5.16)—hence, a natural temptation for the government to press the central bank to create more money.

Box 5.16 The Value of Seigniorage

There are two commonly accepted measures of seigniorage. The first one is the increase in base money ΔM_0 over a given period. The second measure is the opportunity cost of holding base money, iM_0, where i is the short-term nominal interest rate. As detailed here, the two measures are equivalent provided the velocity of base money is constant and the real interest rate is equal to the real growth rate (the golden rule of capital accumulation, see Chapter 9).

Remember the quantity equation of money of box 5.6, $PY = M_0V$ where V is here the velocity of money, P the price level, and Y real GDP. In the long run, if real output growth (as determined by the production function) is g and the velocity of base money is constant, then the growth rate of base money $\Delta M_0/M_0$ is equal to the growth rate of prices ($\pi = \Delta P/P$) plus the growth rate of real output g. We therefore have:

$$\Delta M_0 / M_0 = \pi + g \quad \text{(B5.16.1)}$$

Now, the nominal interest rate i is the sum of the real interest rate r and the inflation rate: $i = r + \pi$. If the real interest rate r is equal to the real growth rate g, then Equation (B5.16.1) can be rewritten:

$$\Delta M_0 / M_0 = i \quad \text{(B5.16.2)}$$

or, equivalently:

$$\Delta M_0 = iM_0 \quad \text{(B5.16.3)}$$

The two measures of seigniorage are then equivalent. For instance, in the euro area, base money represented 16.5% of GDP at end-2014. With a 1% interest rate, this translated into a seigniorage of around 0.17% of GDP. Though not negligible, this was not a game changer for governments. The amount could, however, be inflated in the future by higher interest rates or by an internationalization of the euro. It is thought that approximately 60% of US dollar notes (equivalent to 4% of US GDP) circulate outside the United States. With a 1% interest rate, this translates into an additional seigniorage return of 0.04% of GDP. This amount remains small: the "exorbitant privilege" of the US dollar is not due to the international use of US banknotes but of US dollar-denominated securities (see Chapter 7).

b) Fiscal dominance

In the long run, monetary policy can be independent from fiscal policy only if the latter is sustainable, that is, if the intertemporal budget constraint of the State is met without assuming monetary financing. The impact of unsustainable public finances on monetary policy can materialize directly or indirectly (box 5.17). The fiscal authority can force the central bank to *monetize* debt by purchasing government bonds, or by lending to the government to help it redeem the debt, or by defaulting on debt already held by the central bank (which amounts *ex post* to money creation, see box 5.21). Pressure can also be indirect, for instance, in case the government defaults on private banks which the central bank feels then compelled to support as lender of last resort.

Box 5.17 Monetary Consequences of Deficits: The "Unpleasant Arithmetic" of Sargent and Wallace

Monetary and fiscal policies are normally regarded as mutually independent. Sargent and Wallace (1981) have shown that this is not true in the long run.

The starting point is an overlapping generation model: at each period t, N_t young people and N_{t-1} old ones coexist, with $N_t = (1+n) N_{t-1}$ where $n > 0$ is the growth rate of the population. When he or she is young, each individual receives an endowment and can decide to save part for old-age consumption. Savings are held in the form of money or public bonds. Public bonds bought at t are repaid at $t + 1$ as $(1+R_{t+1})B_t$, where R_t denotes the interest rate. The State levies a tax τ on each young person, consumes P_tG_t, and finances the remaining deficit by debt and/or by monetary creation M_t. P_t is the general price level. The budgetary constraint is:

$$G_t + (1+R_t)B_{t-1} = \tau N_t + B_t + \frac{M_t - M_{t-1}}{P_t} \qquad \text{(B5.17.1)}$$

Consider the steady state where the real amounts per capita ($b = B_t / N_t$, $g = G_t / N_t$ and $m = M_t / N_t$) are constant and where money supply grows at a constant rate $\lambda = M_t / M_{t-1} - 1$. By dividing the preceding formula by N_t, the budgetary constraint becomes:

$$g = \tau + \left(1 - \frac{1+R}{1+n}\right)b + \frac{m}{P}\left(1 - \frac{1}{\lambda}\right) \qquad \text{(B5.17.2)}$$

If the real interest rate R is higher than the growth rate n, then debt dynamics are divergent (see Chapter 4). Either public consumption g has to decline (or the tax burden τ has to increase) or the amount of money per young m has to increase: Monetary policy is subordinated to fiscal policy.

The interplay between monetary policy and fiscal policy does not only run from the latter to the former through debt monetization or monetary financing of governments. Public money can also be needed to recapitalize banks or relieve them of impaired assets and restore the effectiveness of monetary policy, as was done in most advanced economies in 2008–2009 (see Chapter 6).

The fiscal authority can also be tempted to maximize the profit from money creation (i.e., seigniorage) that accrues to the central bank's profit but is partly or entirely handed over to the treasury as dividend. Seigniorage is a tax levied on money holders and sometimes dubbed an *inflationary tax*. There are other components to the inflationary tax, however. To the extent that public debt is not indexed to inflation, unanticipated inflation automatically reduces the debt-to-nominal GDP ratio. This amounts to a transfer from government-debt holders to the government. Also, given that tax receipts are almost fully indexed on inflation, whereas public expenditures are only partially indexed, the government has additional reasons to wish for higher inflation.

The long-run interdependence between fiscal and monetary policy implies that lasting monetary stability is very unlikely if the fiscal authority behaves in an irresponsible way. An example of this type was provided by Argentina prior to the 2002 crisis: although the country was committed by law to maintaining a fixed exchange rate to the US dollar and the currency issued by the central bank was supposed to be fully backed by foreign exchange reserves (a so-called currency board; see Chapter 7), the profligate behavior of the federal and especially subfederal fiscal authorities was never reined in. Ultimately, the government was forced to abandon the dollar peg, triggering a violent currency and financial crisis. The mechanism was different from the closed-economy setting of box 5.17, but the logic was the same.

The policy regime where monetary policy is subordinated to fiscal policy is called *fiscal dominance* (Woodford, 2001). Fiscal policy is "active" and monetary policy is "passive" (Leeper, 1991). This is generally the case in wartime. In the United States, a 1942 agreement committed the Federal Reserve to maintaining "relatively stables prices and yields for government securities." Up until the termination of this agreement in 1951, monetary policy was given the objective of keeping long-term interest rates low, and inflation was stabilized through price controls. Indeed, from 1942 to 1947 and beyond, short- and long-term interest rates barely changed. This helped the United States support the war effort without incurring the corresponding debt costs. The opposite regime where monetary policy is "active" and fiscal policy is "passive" is called *monetary dominance*. The government must meet its intertemporal budget constraint taking as given an independent monetary policy. For this reason, the regime is sometimes called "Ricardian" (Leeper, 1991).

c) Coordinating monetary and fiscal policy

There are also short-term interdependencies between fiscal and monetary policies. Both act on aggregate demand, which means that they are partly substitutes. Without coordination, there is a risk that there is too much or too little of one, of the other, or of both (Beetsma and Uhlig, 1999; Dixit and Lambertini, 2003). Worse, to the extent that they have different objectives, it is perfectly conceivable that they point in opposite directions and end up cancelling each other. This would be the case, for instance, in a situation with high cyclical unemployment and high inflation. Fiscal policy would be expansionary to address unemployment, but monetary policy would be contractionary, all the more so as fiscal policy would expand. The result could be quite dismal: no stabilization of the unemployment rate nor of the inflation rate, and a higher fiscal deficit. In some cases, however, monetary and fiscal policies can be complements, for instance, at the ZLB when the fiscal multiplier is high (that is, when aggregate demand responds strongly to an increase in public spending or a tax cut, see Chapter 4).

In normal times, there is no consensus on the desirability of coordinating monetary and fiscal policies to achieve a policy mix. Skeptics point out that coordination threatens central bank independence or may even be counterproductive (Rogoff, 1984). Furthermore, in a monetary union, it is difficult to coordinate a single monetary policy with many fiscal policies. The EU Treaty foresees rules binding the fiscal policies of participating Member States, but there is no rule binding the aggregate fiscal stance of the Eurozone. In crisis times, however, the case for coordination is more compelling. In 2014, for instance, given the extent of disinflationary pressures in the euro area, the ECB president called for a less contractionary aggregate fiscal policy in the euro area (Draghi, 2014).

d) The distributional effects of monetary policy

Monetary policy is primarily a stabilization policy: the task of the central bank is to ensure price stability, not to promote long-term growth or reduce inequalities. In the long run, money is neutral and monetary policy cannot aim at any objective other than maintaining trust in the currency.

In the short to medium run, however, monetary policy entails various distributional consequences (Nakajima, 2015). First, citizens at the lower end of the income distribution are less protected against upward surprises in inflation (since their income tends not to be indexed, at least in the short term), whereas they suffer more in downturns because low-skilled jobs suffer more than high-skilled ones, and they can't draw on savings to maintain their standard of living. In general, macroeconomic stabilization by itself tends to reduce income inequalities. Second, a rise in the real interest rate transfers resources from borrowers to lenders through both a net income and a net wealth effect, whereas a fall in the real interest rate produces the reverse transfer. Third, nonconventional monetary policy induces specific distributional effects by affecting asset prices. To the extent that financial wealth is concentrated in the top percentiles of the income distribution, this could induce anti-redistributive effects.

All these effects are key transmission channels of monetary policy. They are unavoidable and accepted as means to an end: namely, price stability. However, their distributional effect should be understood and taken into account when designing other policies. Empirically, Carpenter and Rodgers (2004) find that contractionary monetary policies in the United States have more impact on the employment rate of minorities and teenagers relative to the average. Romer and Romer (1999) find that unanticipated inflation tends to narrow the income distribution. Looking at the distribution of assets across Americans, Doepke and Schneider (2006) find that the main losers from inflation are rich, old households, whereas the main winners are young, middle-class households with fixed-rate mortgage debt. Based on US data over the 1980–2008 period, Coibion et al. (2012) conclude that, on balance, a contractionary policy widens inequalities, whereas an expansionary policy reduces them. Claeys et al. (2015) conclude similarly for ultra-loose monetary policy episodes.

The distributional consequences of monetary policy may lead interest groups to challenge decisions of the central bank. In the 2000s, when interest rates were high, the ECB was criticized by French politicians for making the euro too strong and harming jobs in export industries. In the 2010s, when interest rates were zero or negative, the ECB was criticized by German politicians for expropriating savers. In both cases, politicians were speaking on behalf of interest groups which were particularly powerful in their countries and ignoring the general equilibrium consequences of monetary policy. Such criticisms should be ignored by an independent central bank (former ECB president Wim Duisenberg was quoted as saying: "I hear them but I don't listen"), but the complex and potentially large distributive consequences of central banks' nonconventional policies may end up creating a challenge for their independence.

5.3 Policies

In this section, we first analyze how monetary policy is decided by central banks before looking at their key policy choices.

5.3.1 Institutions

Monetary policy is everywhere carried out by central banks.[31] However, this does not imply that they have full responsibility for their decisions. Until the late 1980s, only a few countries—most notably Germany—had a fully independent central bank.

a) Independence

Whichever solution is chosen to counter the inflationary bias (monetary rules, appointing conservative central bankers, incentive contracts, etc.), achieving this goal is facilitated by central bank *independence* from political power. Independence entails appointing central bankers for very long terms and making them immovable except for serious misconduct, prohibiting instructions from governments, and granting the central bank financial independence. There is some empirical evidence (Alesina and Summers, 1993) that, over the long term, inflation is negatively correlated to the degree of independence of the central bank in industrialized countries. In developing countries, however, the effectiveness of central bank independence also depends on the overall quality of institutions (Acemoglu et al., 2008).

In the 1990s and 2000s, an increasing number of countries granted full independence to their monetary institution, as illustrated in figure 5.13. The move toward more independence resulted first and foremost from the better ability of independent central banks to cope with the inflationary pressures of the previous decades: in a competition between two institutional models, central bank independence had won. However, it also benefitted from theoretical breakthroughs, such as Robert Lucas's and Robert Barro's models (see Chapter 1), which show how the trade-off between inflation and unemployment

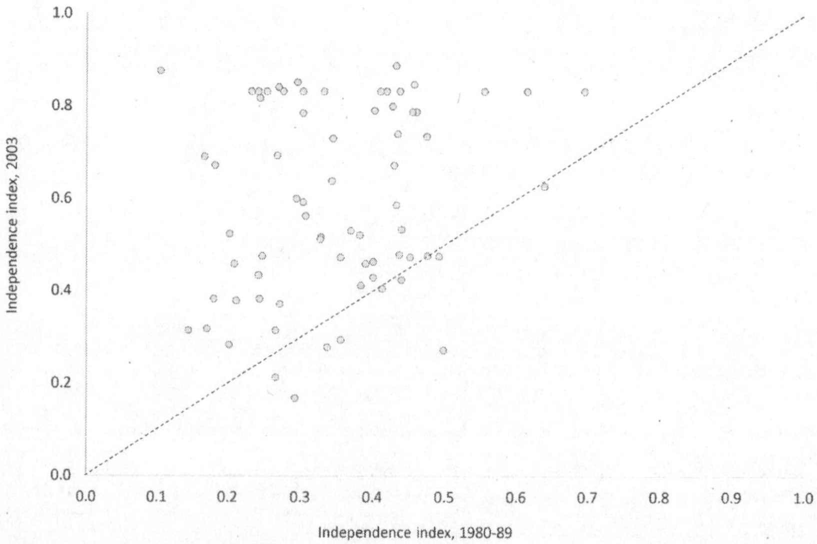

Figure 5.13 Central bank independence in the 1980s and in 2003. The central bank independence index is based on four components related to, respectively, appointment procedures for the head of the central bank, the resolution of conflict between the central bank and the executive branch of the government, the use of an explicit policy target, and rules limiting lending to the government.

Cuckierman et al. (1992); Crowe and Meade (2008).

disappears when expectations are rational, even in the short run. A particularly forceful illustration is the Barro-Gordon model discussed above, where attempts by the central bank to exploit a short-run trade-off are anticipated by private agents, which results in an inefficiently high inflation and no employment gains. This suggested, first, that there was no cost in focusing the central bank on fighting inflation rather than on output stabilization and, second, that there were benefits to making it independent from government.

Another argument in favor of central bank independence is the risk of fiscal dominance outlined in Section 5.2. The institutional setup of the euro area was specifically designed to ensure monetary dominance—a crucial feature in a currency area with one currency but several governments. In practice, however, it is not always easy to draw a line between monetary and fiscal policy (see box 5.18).

Box 5.18 The Tension Between Monetary and Fiscal Policies in the Euro Area

The EU Treaty enshrines a regime of monetary dominance in the Eurozone, with an independent central bank, fiscal rules intended to ensure the solvency of the participating member states, and the prohibition for the central bank of financing governments (Article 123 of the Treaty on the functioning of the EU). The interplay between monetary policy and fiscal policy, directly and through the banking sector, has, however, challenged this principle. The tension was apparent during the euro area crisis in the early 2010s. Commercial banks held large amounts of domestic governments' bonds in their balance sheets and therefore played a central role in government funding. A government default would have triggered bank failures, in which case it was widely expected that the government would step in and recapitalize banks, creating a feedback loop between the risks of default of governments and of banks, a situation called the *bank-sovereign nexus* or the *doom loop* between euro area bank and sovereign credit (see also Chapter 6). This created the risk of multiple equilibria: in one equilibrium, banks and governments were solvent, while in another both were insolvent. In the summer of 2012, countries such as Spain and Portugal were at a clear risk of jumping from the former to the latter. To prevent it, the ECB extended cheap long-term funding to the banks and let national central banks provide Emergency Liquidity Assistance (see chapter 6). In addition, it also announced the possibility of unlimited purchases of government bonds conditional to governments undertaking a structural adjustment (the Outright Monetary Transactions, see box 5.21). These ECB decisions have been considered by some as overstepping the remit of elected governments and infringing the prohibition of monetary financing of the governments, although such claims were later brushed away by the European Court of Justice (European Court of Justice, 2015).

In most countries, central bank independence is guaranteed by law. The US Constitution gives Congress authority over the value of money. Congress can thus change the Fed's mandate by simple majority. The institution's independence is protected by various counterpowers such as financial markets, the press, and its own reputation. In Europe, the ECB is much more independent since its statute and mandate are enshrined in the EU Treaty and have therefore a constitutional value: Only a unanimous decision by the EU Member States, followed by ratification by their parliaments or by popular vote, can take away the ECB's independence.

b) Statutes, mandates, and accountability

There are notable discrepancies among independent central banks' statutes and mandates. Even leaving aside the Fed (which has a broad mandate, as indicated in table 5.2), the Bank of Japan (which is "autonomous" according to the 1997 Bank of Japan Act) and the People's Bank of China (which is not independent), the ECB and the Bank of England differ in several respects. Price stability is legally the main objective for both, and both enjoy full independence in the conduct of monetary policy, but, while the ECB itself sets the quantitative inflation objective (namely, since 2003, inflation being "below but close to 2%"), the Bank of England implements an objective decided by the government (O'Donnell, 2001). Under the 1998 Bank of England Act, the Chancellor of the Exchequer may specify in writing to the central bank "what price stability is to be taken to consist of." Doing it in writing prevents him or her from pushing for a higher inflation without telling the public and for criticizing the Bank for implementing a policy he or she has defined.

To establish its reputation, besides being independent, the central bank must do what it says and say what it does. Hence, its reputation basically relies on (i) its track record and (ii) its communication. A number of schemes have been proposed to help it in doing so:

- *Commitment*: The solution consisting in tying one's hands was adopted in the late 1980s by many European countries, such as France, which anchored their currencies to the German currency, the Deutsche Mark, within the European monetary system. More recently, economies in transition have pegged their currencies to the euro (Baltic countries, Bulgaria) or even dropped their monetary sovereignty altogether by adopting either the dollar (Ecuador, El Salvador) or the euro (Kosovo, Timor Este) as their domestic currency. These strategies are instances of exchange rate regime choices that will be discussed in Chapter 7. Forward guidance can also be a form of commitment (see Section 5.2.3B).
- *Conservative central bankers*: Kenneth Rogoff (1985) suggested eliminating the inflation bias by appointing a "conservative" central

Table 5.2
The mandates of four central banks

	Legal vehicle	Price stability	Exchange rate stability	Output stability	Financial stability
US Fed	Full Employment and Balanced Growth (Humphrey-Hawkins) Act, 1978	Yes	No, but may intervene on exchange markets, alongside the US Treasury	Yes, on an equal footing with price stability	Yes, reinforced in 2011 by Dodd-Franck Act
ECB	EU Treaty and protocol on the statute of the European System of Central Banks	Yes	No, but exchange rates are part of the indicators followed by the ECB, and it has the sole right to conduct foreign-exchange operations.	Yes, but secondary to price stability	Yes, but as secondary competence in support to governments. The ECB also has a macroprudential authority (cf. Chapter 6).
Bank of England	Bank of England Act, 1998	Yes. Price stability is defined by the government	No	Yes, secondary to price stability	Yes
Bank of Japan	Bank of Japan Law, 1997	Yes	No, but may be instructed by the Ministry of Finance to intervene on exchange markets	No, only as a consequence of price stability	Yes

banker (i.e., a governor whose preference for price stability would be higher than the social preference). This proposal has not been implemented *de jure* but *de facto*: one criterion to select central bank governors is their anti-inflationary credentials.

- *Long mandates*: Central bankers' mandates are generally very long: 14 years for Fed governors (even though few of them serve a full term), 8 years for ECB executive board members, 5 years for the members of the Monetary Policy Committee of the Bank of England and the Policy Board of the Bank of Japan. This aims at ensuring that the same individuals are in office when the policy is announced and when its outcome is observed and that they are free from the political cycle.
- *Incentive contracts*: Incentive contracts à la Carl Walsh (1995) are not frequent. In most countries, central bank governors can be dismissed only for crime, misdemeanor, or offense to the bank's reputation, but in New Zealand, the Reserve Bank Act of 1989 stipulates that the central bank governor can be dismissed in case the objectives are not met. A less radical solution, adopted in the United Kingdom, is to compel the governor to justify himself publicly in an open letter when the inflation target set by the government is missed.[32]
- *Transparency:* Central bank transparency is the flip side of its independence. Nonelected, independent technocrats should be held accountable to the public. Transparency can also help the central bank monitor expectations, enhance the effectiveness of its policy, and, at the same time, smooth the impact of its policy decisions by preparing the markets (box 5.19). Transparency works through the disclosure of models, data, forecasts, methodology, voting records, and meeting minutes. Inflation targeting is one way of making monetary policy more transparent. Accordingly, those central banks applying inflation targeting frameworks (Sweden, the United Kingdom, New Zealand, Canada, Australia, Norway, Iceland, Czech Republic, Hungary, Turkey, Israel, South Korea, South Africa, and Thailand; see Hammond, 2012) are considered highly transparent (figure 5.14). Still, despite their more flexible monetary strategies, the Fed and the ECB also fare well thanks to their extensive disclosure policies. Both central banks have a clear and observable 2% inflation objective over the medium term; both publish minutes of their meetings with a delay (and, in the case of the ECB, without individual votes record); and both organize a press conference immediately after the meetings, where the Chair provides a detailed explanation of the policy decisions taken at the meeting and answers questions.[33]

Box 5.19 Central Bank Transparency

Central bank transparency can be defined as "the extent to which central banks disclose information that is related to the policymaking process" (Eijffinger and Geraats, 2006). The authors distinguish between political transparency (which relates to the information on policy objectives), economic transparency (dissemination of the data, forecasts, and models used by the central bank), procedural transparency (the way monetary decisions are taken), policy transparency (explanation of policy decisions, information on policy inclination, release of minutes, and voting records), and operational transparency (information on errors and unexpected events).

There has been a clear trend toward more central bank transparency from 1998 to 2014 (figure B5.19.1). As evidenced by Dincer and Eichengreen (2014), the movement toward more transparency took place essentially from 1998 to 2010, with stabilization afterward.

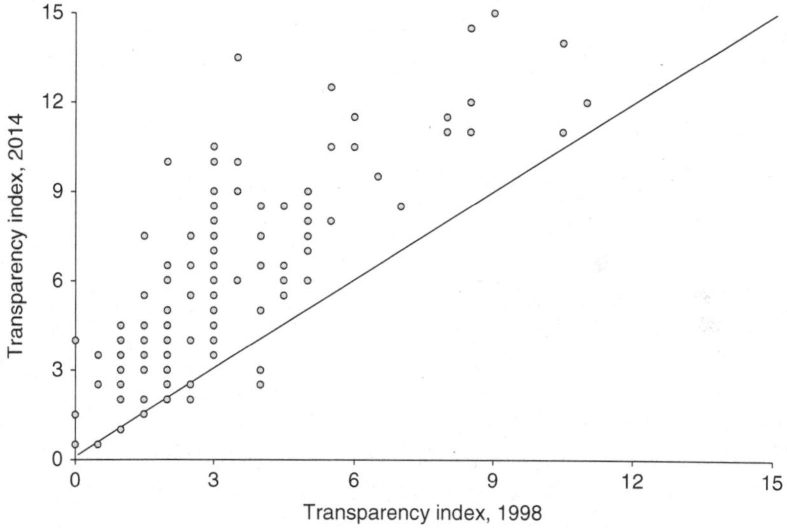

Figure B5.19.1 Transparency index for 110 central banks, 1998 and 2014. The index varies from 0 (no transparency) to 15 (maximum transparency). Dincer and Eichengreen (2014).

According to Dincer and Eichengreen, the rise in central bank transparency may be justified in four different ways. First, it is the key counterpart of central bank independence since more independence requires more accountability to allow for democratic control. Second, central bank transparency participates in a more general movement in favor of government transparency, which is a rising demand from the people.

Third, transparency can be seen as a way to improve the effectiveness of monetary policy since it enables the central bank to more closely monitor market expectations. It can also smooth the effects of policy decisions by preparing the market in advance through speeches and minutes. Fourth, transparency enhances the credibility of central bank commitments. It can also help the central bank deviate from regular policy in exceptional times since the central bank has more room to explain its behavior.

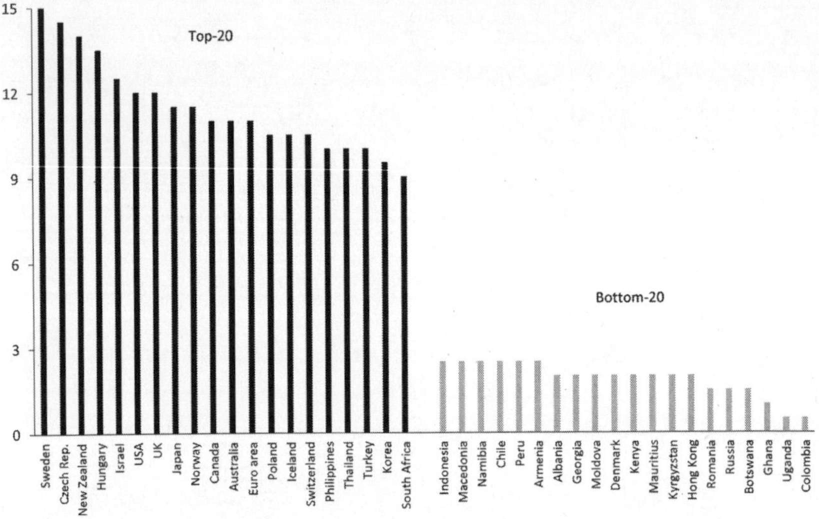

Figure 5.14 Top and bottom 20 central banks in terms of transparency in 2014. The transparency index ranges from 0 (no transparency) to 15 (maximum transparency) and is calculated for 110 central banks.
Dincer and Eichengreen (2014).

Whether or not some of these schemes are in place, the central bank fundamentally derives its legitimacy from its ability to fulfill its targets and from its *accountability*; that is, its exposure to external scrutiny and its answerability vis-à-vis democratic representation (see Chapter 2). In most countries, central bankers regularly appear before parliamentary committees to explain their policy and respond to criticism. In the United States, pursuant to the Humphrey-Hawkins Act, the Federal Reserve reports to Congress annually on its activity and twice-yearly on monetary policy. In the euro area, the President of the ECB testifies quarterly in front of the Economic and Monetary Committee of the European Parliament and appears informally in front of national Parliaments. In the United Kingdom, all members of the Monetary Policy Committee are individually accountable and heard by the House of Commons Treasury Select Committee. All central banks report in detail their analysis of the economy, inflation, and financial stability.

c) Monetary policy committees

A less spectacular evolution of central banking in the 1990s and 2000s has been the move toward collegial decision-making by *monetary policy committees*. In the euro area, monetary policy is decided by the Governing Council of the ECB, which consists of the six members of its Frankfurt-based Executive Board and the central bank governors of the euro area countries.[34] In the United States, the Federal Open Market Committee (FOMC) includes the seven members of the Board of Governors of the Federal Reserve System, the President of the Federal Reserve Bank of New York, and four of the eleven Reserve Bank Presidents who rotate on an annual basis. Since the mid-1990s, a number of countries (e.g., the United Kingdom, Japan, Sweden, Norway, Switzerland, Brazil) have switched from individual policymaking (the governor alone) to monetary committees.[35] Such evolution can be viewed as a by-product of central bank independence. As Blinder (2007, p. 107) puts it: "When the central bank was just following orders communicated by the government, there was not much reason to have a committee on the other end of the phone."

A committee has a higher probability of taking the right decisions than has a single governor. This is what the Condorcet jury theorem states under the following assumptions: (i) costless information, (ii) common preferences across committee members; (iii) sincere voting; (iv) no pre-voting communication. Each of these assumptions can be debated, however. In particular, it has been highlighted that a large committee may not perform better than a single governor because each committee member has a small probability of being pivotal (i.e., able to move the majority), which reduces the incentive to seek information, or because of higher transaction costs when aggregating members' points of view. Social experiments tend to confirm that committees make better decisions than single individuals, although there is no consensus on their optimal size (Blinder and Morgan, 2005; Siebert, 2006). As for pre-voting communication between committee members, it varies from one central bank to another: it is strictly limited in the FOMC but not in the ECB Governing Council.

Another question is the composition of monetary committees and, particularly in federations and in monetary unions, the representation of regional or national governors. A large committee allows a wide representation of regions or countries, which brings additional information. It also allows each committee member to explain common decisions to its constituency. However, regional biases may lead to decisions which do not reflect the interest of the economy as a whole. This risk has been highlighted in the euro area case, where successive enlargements to new countries have increased the weight of national governors in monetary decisions as compared to the six Executive Board members. In 2018, national governors represented 19/25 (76%) of the ECB Governing Council against 11/17 (65%) when the euro was launched in 1999 and 4/12 (33%) for Federal Reserve Banks presidents in the FOMC (assuming that all governors are appointed to the Board). This proportion could theoretically reach 27/32 (82%) if the euro area were enlarged to the 27 Member States of the European Union post-Brexit. If each governor votes based on his or her country's own interest and only the executive board takes the situation of the whole area into account, then there is a risk that the monetary decision does not fulfill the ECB's euro area–wide mandate.[36]

Committee-based decisions raise specific questions concerning communication and transparency. On the one hand, there is a risk that disorganized communication by different committee members confuses economic players. On the other hand, transparency on each governor's reaction function helps explain the decision-making process and better anticipate decisions. In practice, the risk of confusing communication is limited by the publication of the minutes. As a matter of fact, monetary committees are not found systematically less nor more transparent than single policymakers (Blinder, 2007).

d) The central bank–treasury relationship

As explained in Section 5.2, there is no consensus in the literature on the need for coordination between monetary and fiscal policy, at least in normal times. The conventional wisdom is that it is enough for each policy player to keep his or her own house in order within his or her mandate, sticking to stated policy principles. This provides sufficiently clear information for the other players to take their own decisions. Any coordination beyond a mere exchange of information would risk blurring the objectives followed by policymakers without clear benefits in exchange. The Maastricht Treaty, which does not envisage explicit coordination between monetary and fiscal authorities but only exchanges of information, reflects this view. The Commissioner responsible for economic affairs and the President of the group of euro area finance ministers, the Eurogroup, have a statutory right to attend the meetings of the Governing Council of the ECB. In turn, the President of the ECB attends the meetings of the Eurogroup, where finance ministers gather once a month to discuss the economic situation, policy priorities, and crisis situations. This light arrangement was, however, shaken up during the global financial crisis and the euro area crisis. The ECB was closely associated with the management of the crisis, including in its fiscal dimension. For instance, the ECB has participated (alongside with the European Commission and the IMF) in the so-called *Troika* negotiating and monitoring adjustment programs in crisis countries on behalf of finance ministers. This arrangement is specific to the euro area: one does not imagine the Federal Reserve taking an active part in policy discussions about a US state. It allows the Governing Council to benefit from superior information when taking decisions on liquidity provision to banks in these countries, but it also creates potential conflicts of interest and risks hampering the central bank's independence by creating the perception that it overreaches its mandate.

In Japan, the government of Prime Minister Shinzo Abe elected in December 2012 designed a strategy ("Abenomics") to revive growth and fight negative inflation through the combination of three "arrows": an expansionary monetary policy, an expansionary fiscal policy, and a program of structural reforms. In this framework, monetary policy is no longer fully independent but part of a wider macroeconomic strategy. Such close cooperation between monetary and fiscal policy is, however, rare in advanced economies. Interactions between monetary and fiscal authorities were observed in the United States and the United Kingdom during the crisis. However, they were generally limited to the treatment of the banking crisis. In fact, following the terminology of the former President of the ECB Jean-Claude Trichet, central banks tend to reject "*ex ante* co-ordination" for the sake of independence, but they accept "*ex post*" coordination in crises to minimize economic disruption and to the extent that cooperation in fact helps them comply with their mandate.

5.3.2 Key policy choices

a) What inflation objective?

What is the appropriate level of inflation? Edmund Phelps (1973) has characterized the optimal inflation rate as resulting from a trade-off between the distortions stemming from the inflationary tax and those arising from other taxes. In advanced economies, there is no general recommendation. Just like the porridge of *Goldilocks,* which should be neither too hot nor too cold, inflation ought to be neither too high nor too low.[37] This raises statistical (box 5.20) and theoretical issues.

In a full-information, rational-expectation setting, and if price and wages were perfectly flexible, economic agents would be almost completely indifferent to the level of inflation—except for the cost of withdrawing more often from ATMs to avoid holding excessive non–interest bearing cash. However, high inflation erodes all nonindexed income: wages, pensions, and fixed-income revenue. In a high-inflation environment, households are desperate to protect their purchasing power in various ways, such as entering into indexed contracts (e.g., wages being indexed on prices), invoicing in foreign currencies, holding foreign assets, and the like. This was the case in Germany in the 1920s and in many developing countries in the second half of the twentieth century. Inflation therefore generates rigidities which then make it more difficult to reduce it.

Box 5.20 The Pitfalls of Measuring Consumer Prices

Measuring inflation is difficult. Macroeconomics deals with the general level of prices, but, in the real world, only relative prices are observed. Surveys provide prices for individual items, but products change with increasing frequency. From one period to the next, new products appear and quality improvements are brought to existing products. When a smartphone is replaced at an unchanged price by a new model with enhanced functionalities, it is reasonable to conclude that prices of smartphones are *falling*. But by how much? *Hedonic price* methodologies correct for quality improvements by decomposing each product into a bundle of consumer services. However, they are applied to a limited number of goods. In addition, there are other sources of bias in the measurement of inflation, such as the development of new distribution channels or shopping habits.

It is generally considered that official figures tend to overestimate inflation. This is important for monetary policy since it means that central banks seeking very low inflation rates will in fact face a risk of deflation (i.e., a decrease in the general level of prices). In 1996, at the request of the US government, an independent commission chaired by Stanford Professor Michael Boskin concluded that the growth rate of the US Consumer Price Index (CPI) was overestimated by 0.8% to 1.6% a year, the *Boskin effect* (Boskin et al., 1996).

The US government thereafter introduced a yearly revision of the consumption basket. Consistently, a second study performed by the Federal Reserve in 2001 found a measurement bias of only approximately 0.6% (Lebow and Rudd, 2001). Similar measurement biases have been estimated in other countries. The bias could lie between 0.35% and 0.8% per year in the United Kingdom (Cunningham, 1996) and be 0.9% in Japan (Shiratsuka, 1999). Beyond these measurement difficulties, consumers' perception of inflation can differ significantly from the statisticians' measurements. For instance, consumers are more attentive to the prices of those goods they need to purchase frequently (food, gas) than to those they purchase infrequently (insurance, durable goods).

Another argument against inflation is that a high inflation *level* generally comes hand in hand with high inflation *variability*, which creates economic uncertainty and distorts economic decisions since agents may confuse variations in the general level of prices with variations in relative prices. Also, inflation variability results in expectation errors. This can hamper investment and hence long-term GDP growth. Empirically, Bruno and Easterly (1996) find that GDP growth is reduced when inflation is higher than 20–40% a year. Barro (1997) finds that, other things being equal, a rise in the inflation rate by 10 percentage points eventually reduces annual growth by about 0.3 percentage points. However, smaller changes at lower inflation levels (say, inflation moving from 2% to 3% annually) do not appear to affect GDP growth in the long term.

Inflation can also be too low in the light of the risk of a liquidity trap and/or hitting the ZLB of interest rate (see Section 5.2). In a deep crisis, it may be the case that the natural rate of interest becomes negative. Zero or negative inflation imply that the central bank should set its *nominal* policy rate below zero to stabilize the economy, which is possible but difficult for reasons explained earlier in this chapter (Summers, 2014).

Inflation can also be too low to compensate in an effective way the downward rigidity of nominal wages. Labor contracts rarely include the possibility of revising wages downward. This has been documented in the United States by Ackerlof, Dickens, and Perry (1996, 2000) who argue that at near-zero inflation rates the Phillips curve, which relates unemployment to the inflation rate, is not strictly vertical even in the long run: if nominal wages are rigid downward, some inflation is the "oil in the wheels" that allows reducing real wages and hence the unemployment rate. The authors advocate an inflation "band" of 1.5–4% per year in developed countries.[38]

A final argument, largely specific to the euro area, stems from the need to give enough room to relative price adjustment between economies participating in a monetary union (see also Chapter 7). In the absence of nominal exchange rates, the only way to lower the real exchange rate in the face of a negative economic shock is by lowering prices and wages locally, a strategy known as *internal devaluation*. But low average inflation in the monetary union, combined with downward wage rigidity, leaves little room for such adjustment to take place. A higher average rate of inflation makes it easier for countries to adjust to idiosyncratic shocks. This argument is not relevant for countries with floating nominal exchange rates but can also be applied to discuss sectoral adjustment within countries.

On the whole, there is broad agreement that central banks should adopt a low but positive inflation objective. The central banks of the largest advanced economies (the United States, euro area, Japan, and United Kingdom) have all converged toward a 2% objective. It has been argued nevertheless that a higher inflation target would keep the economy more safely away from liquidity traps or deflationary spirals. Blanchard et al. (Blanchard, Dell'Ariccia, and Mauro, 2010) have mentioned a 4% target.

Figure 5.15 shows the inflation targets of various central banks in 2012. Most are centered on 2–4.5% per year. This narrow range can be explained both by the low level of inflation in most countries in the early 2010s and by some convergence in preferences. The width of the inflation band varies considerably across countries. In Sweden or the United Kingdom, only the central figure is communicated by the central bank, whereas in Brazil, Ghana, and Turkey, the inflation target has a 4% width.

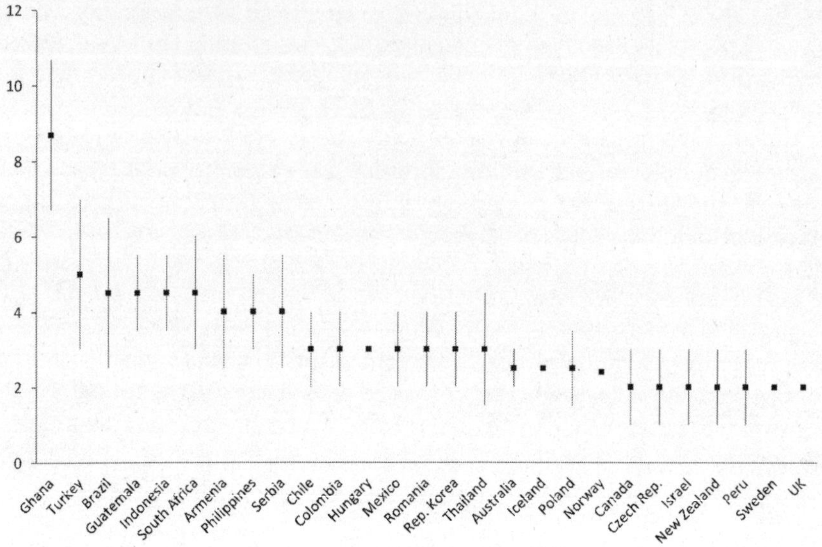

Figure 5.15 Inflation targets in 2012, in annual percent.
Hammond (2014).

b) Which monetary strategy?

A major challenge for monetary policy is that the instrument (e.g., the interest rate) only affects the final objective (e.g., the inflation rate) with "long and variable lags," to quote an expression first introduced by Milton Friedman. The central banker must act as a sailor who changes the course of his ship only gradually and who permanently runs the risk of giving too much or too little impulse. Natural questions relate to the kind of outside information he or she should react to in order to best keep up with the course, what information he or she should neglect; and how he or she should formulate and communicate its strategy in a way that helps agents form expectations about the future course of monetary policy.

Since the 1960s, the debate about monetary strategy has never abated, although it is not any more between the advocates of quantitative (i.e., money supply) and interest rate strategies.

Assume that the central bank aims at keeping inflation at a certain level, say 2%. How should it set the interest rate? Lars Svensson (1999, 2001) proposes distinguishing among three types of rules:

- *Instrument rules* express the instrument(s) as a function of predetermined or forward-looking variables such as inflation or the output gap. The Taylor rule, which relates the interest rate to inflation and the output gap (Section 5.1.2), is an example. It is often used as a benchmark to assess the monetary policy stance, although in practice no central bank follows such a mechanistic rule.

- *Targeting rules* minimize a loss function at a given horizon. The rule specifies the objectives of the central bank and characterizes the trade-offs it possibly faces. Inflation targeting is a well-known example (see later discussion). Targeting rules have the merit of being transparent about the objective and strategy while giving the central bank more discretion than a pure instrument rule.
- *Intermediate-targeting rules* target an intermediate variable which is correlated with the objective but easier to observe and to control. This was the role assigned to monetary aggregates in the strategies of the 1970s, before the relationship between money and inflation broke down. In small open economies, the nominal exchange rate can also be used as an intermediate target (see Chapter 7).

Svensson further distinguishes between explicit rules, where the variables entering the reaction function can be observed—as in a Taylor rule—and implicit rules, where some variables entering the reaction function are anticipated and not directly observable.

The dilemma then is choosing between relevant but not directly observable variables (such as inflation and production 18 months ahead) and directly observable but less relevant variables such as past inflation and output gap.

Money targeting rules of the third type were widespread from the 1960s to the 1980s, and Germany officially targeted money aggregates until 1999, though in a loose way. However, since the wave of financial deregulation and innovations of the late 1980s, the relationship between money and inflation has become looser and looser. Both the Federal Reserve and the Bank of England were quick to play down the importance of monetary aggregates, and it is now admitted that the credibility of the Bundesbank stemmed from its performance rather than from its strategy. Indeed, money growth was rarely close to the preannounced target. When it was established in 1998, the ECB chose to emulate the Bundesbank to "inherit" its credibility. It maintained money targeting but broadened the approach: its monetary strategy was initially based on two "pillars," an objective of 4.5% for the annual growth of M3 (see box 5.6) and a combination of leading indicators of inflation such as output prices, import prices, wage costs, and the like. The M3 objective was replaced in 2003 by a broader analysis of trends in money supply and money demand (i.e., credit to the economy).

Since the early 1990s, central banks have increasingly followed an implicit rule based on medium-run inflation forecasts: *inflation targeting.* New Zealand paved the way in 1990, soon followed by Canada, the United Kingdom, Sweden, Australia, and a large number of emerging economies. Inflation targeting is a subtle exercise. Contrary to what is commonly believed, it does not target the current rate of inflation, but the central bank's own inflation forecast. This forecast is conditional on available information, including the current (and possibly future) monetary stance. The transparency of the rule is ensured through publishing both inflation forecasts and the models and assumptions used to prepare them. This strategy has several advantages. First, it ensures a high degree of transparency and predictability of monetary policy. Second, it is forward-looking, which allows the central bank to look through transient shocks such as a rise in the price of oil. Third, it combines the advantages of a rules-based policy with reliance on a wider set of information that is traditionally associated with the discretionary approach. Furthermore, inflation targeting is almost never strictly focused on price stability and puts some weight on stabilizing the real economy.[39] However, it can only work if the central bank is virtuous and refrains from using its own private information on future inflation for a strategic purpose. This is even more needed when the inflation forecast is not based on a constant interest rate assumption but on a market forecast or on an explicit preannounced path for interest rates (as is the case in New Zealand, Sweden, and Norway). This requires considerable discipline and sophistication. In emerging countries, the credibility of inflation targeting may be undermined by the lack of independence of statistical offices.

Once the monetary policy strategy is decided, another debate has to do with the frequency and speed of interest rate adjustments. Two central banks with the same strategy may react differently to news because they incorporate them at a difference pace and attach a different price to the risk of having to change course. A comparison between the Fed and the ECB illustrates this debate (see figure 5.1). The Fed lowered its interest rates swiftly to address the downturn of 2001–02 and raised them again quickly in 2004–06 when the US economy recovered. The ECB reacted much more sluggishly to the business cycle during the same period. A similar contrast between Fed "activism" and ECB "prudence" was evidenced in 2008 in reaction to the financial crisis. The risk attached to activism is to be forced to change course, upset financial markets, and, due to delays in transmission channels, end up delivering procyclical policies. Conversely, the risk attached to prudence is to fail to exploit the full potential of monetary policy as a countercyclical instrument and increase the burden on fiscal policy (leading to higher public indebtedness), or delay unduly the return of the economy to full employment, with possible longer term effects.

Different speeds of adjustment between the Fed and the ECB have led interest rates on both sides to temporarily diverge in the face of common shocks. According to the uncovered interest parity (see Section 5.2), the exchange rate may magnify macroeconomic stabilization in the most reactive area and hamper it in the other. We come back to this mechanism in Chapter 7.

c) Should the central bank care about asset prices?

A third debate has emerged in the 2000s against the background of ample liquidity creation, asset price inflation, and persistently low inflation. The issue is whether price stability can remain the main, if not single, objective of the central bank when financial stability is under threat due to rocketing asset prices in combination with rising leverage. On the one hand, by influencing all market interest rates, monetary policy may be the most potent instrument to curb asset price inflation and induce more prudent behavior in the financial system: in the words of Harvard economist and former Fed governor Jeremy Stein, it "gets into all the cracks" (Stein, 2013). On the other hand, central bankers have no particular expertise for deciding on whether, for example, stock or housing prices are "too high," and they are wary of the moral hazard created by giving public insurance to private investors, which can lead to excessive risk-taking (Bordo and Jeanne, 2002; Goodhart and Hofmann, 2001). The traditional response by central bankers is therefore to "clean" after bubbles have burst rather than "lean" against their developing (Bernanke and Gertler, 2001; White, 2009). This doctrine is not fully satisfactory, however, since the burst of asset price bubbles may itself push the economy into a liquidity trap where the central bank will find it difficult if not impossible to achieve its mandate. For instance, the delay with which the Fed raised its policy rate after the recovery from the dotcom crisis of 2001 is often mentioned as a key ingredient in the subsequent financial crisis. The Fed was then obliged to use not only conventional, but also unconventional instruments to tackle the economic crisis. The choice between "cleaning" and "leaning" is further discussed in Chapter 6.

d) Challenges to monetary dominance

During the global financial crisis, central banks played their role as lenders of last resort, reduced policy rates to levels close to or below zero, and developed a range of unconventional policies (see Section 5.1). This has had large distributive consequences and blurred the line between monetary and fiscal policy, challenging monetary dominance and raising concerns that central banks may be losing their independence.

How to end exceptional policies

Central banks like to think that liquidity provision in crisis time does not conflict with their price stability mandate. This is certainly true when liquidity is provided to one particular institution, but less so when they engage in large-scale liquidity provision, as they have done in the aftermath of the 2008 crisis. Money creation can in principle be reversed in case of a resurgence of inflation when the demand for liquidity goes back to normal. Refinancing operations have a fixed, relatively short term. In the case of long-term bond purchases, central banks can mop up liquidity by selling the bonds back to the market; by proceeding to liquidity-absorbing, reverse-repo operations (selling securities to the banks for a limited period of time); or by issuing central-bank bills. However, the central bank may be reluctant for financial stability reasons to create a large-scale adjustment in asset prices. It may then be overly cautious when reducing its balance sheet, at the expense of its fight against inflation.

The Fed normalization strategy is an example of this delicate balancing act. In December 2013, the Fed started to gradually phase out the QE program initiated in 2009. It took until October 2014 to stop net asset purchases completely through gradual "*tapering*." As can be seen on figure 5.16, the Fed was left with a stock of more than 3.5 trillion dollars—or 22% of US GDP—in government bonds and mortgage-backed securities. Rather than letting its balance sheet endogenously shrink as the bonds would mature, the Fed announced that it would calibrate reinvestments to fine-tune this reduction consistent with the desired path for interest rates (Dudley, 2014). The next question was how to lift policy rates in an environment of excess liquidity. In December 2015, the Fed announced a rise in the target range for the Fed funds rate from 0–0.25% to 0.25–0.50%, raised the rate paid on excess reserves to 0.50%, and offered to lend bonds to banks through reverse-repo operations, giving them an incentive to park liquidity at the Fed rather than injecting it in the economy. The prudence of the Fed when designing its normalization strategy partly reflects concerns over persistently low US inflation, but also a fear of possible financial disruptions.

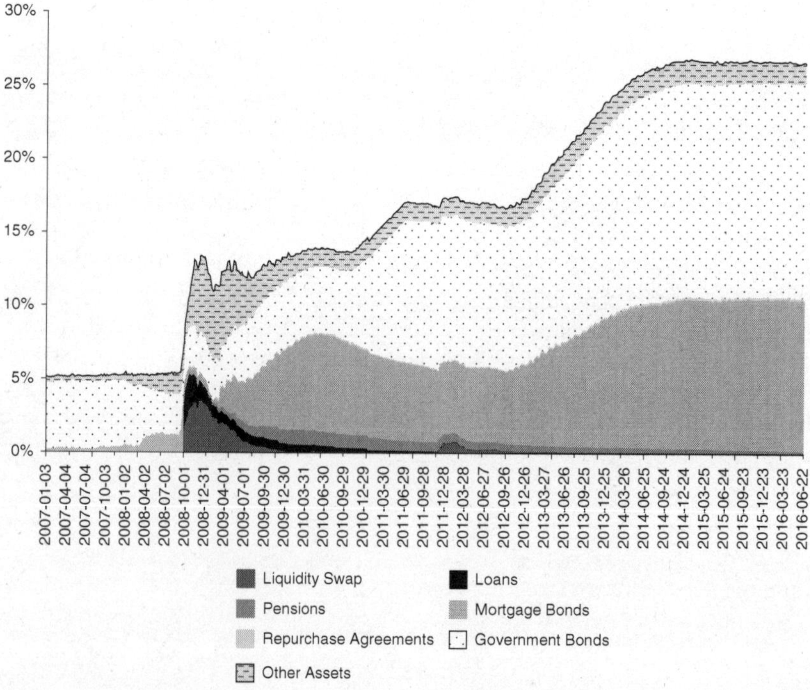

Figure 5.16 Balance sheet of the US Federal Reserve, 2007–2016, in percent of 2013 gross domestic product (GDP).
Federal Reserve Board.

Monetary or fiscal dominance?

Buying government bonds, or accepting them as collateral for refinancing operations, is standard for a central bank, provided that government credit is good enough or appropriate haircuts are applied. This is no longer the case if government debt is unsustainable. In that case, there is a risk that the central bank incurs a loss if the government is incapable to service its debt or if it has to sell the bonds back on the market at a lower price than the price it acquired them. This amounts to monetary financing of the government. Although the central bank cannot do it intentionally, it may happen in practice and it then evidences fiscal dominance (see Section 5.2).

Fiscal dominance being a long-term concept, it is not easy to pass a judgment on whether it happened in the global financial crisis. One indication is the rising share of central bank holdings of government bonds. At mid-2017, the Bank of Japan held half of all Japanese government bonds (figure 5.17). In the euro area, the restructuring of Irish banks Anglo Irish and Nationwide in 2010 and their refinancing in 2012 by the Central Bank of Ireland prompted the ECB to raise serious concerns of monetary financing. The same year, the introduction by the ECB of potentially unlimited purchases of government bonds in specific countries, the *Outright Monetary Transactions*, prompted complaints in Germany about potential violation of the EU Treaty (box 5.21). The two examples show how fragile the separation between monetary and fiscal policy is when financial stability is at stake. This justifies making financial stability a policy objective in its own right and, for this purpose,

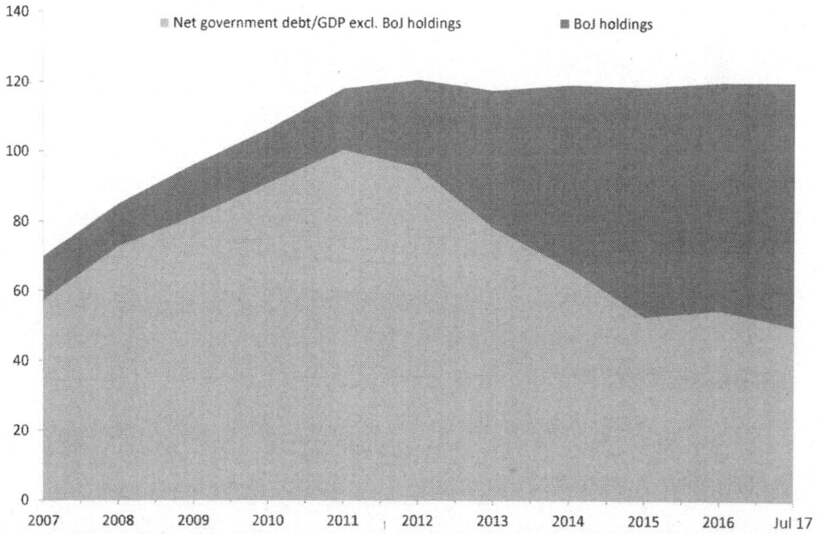

Figure 5.17 Japanese government net debt with and without Bank of Japan holdings, 2007–2017, in percent of gross domestic product (GDP).
Bank of Japan and OECD.

Box 5.21 Monetary Financing of the Fiscal Deficit? Two Case Studies

The Restructuring of Irish Banks

Irish banks had financed the housing boom of the 2000s. In September 2008, after Lehman Brothers' collapse, they found it difficult to refinance on markets. To avoid a panic of both creditors and depositors, the Irish government extended a blanket guarantee on most of the six largest banks' liabilities: during two years, in case one of these banks was unable to reimburse a creditor, the government would substitute for it. Although it was never called on, the guarantee meant that the banks could no longer be "bailed in" (i.e., creditors would not participate financially in any bank restructuring, see box 6.13 of Chapter 6). In September 2010, when the guarantee expired, the banks could still not refinance themselves on the market, which triggered a run on deposits. The banks soon ran out of eligible collateral to obtain liquidity from the ECB. The ECB then authorized the Central Bank of Ireland (CBI) to extend liquidity through the Emergency Liquidity Assistance (ELA) scheme (see Section 5.1). The Irish government recapitalized two banks, Anglo Irish and Nationwide (merging them into a "bad bank" called Irish Bank Resolution Corporation or IBRC) with promissory notes issued by the government. These notes were pledged at the CBI against cash, which was then used to pay the banks' creditors and depositors and repay previous ELA loans. In 2012, the IBRC was unable to reimburse ELA loans and had to be liquidated. The maturities of the promissory notes were extended by up to 40 years and the notes were repossessed by the CBI. As a result of this chain of events, the central bank held long-term government bonds which were not acquired at market conditions and had helped finance the recapitalization of a commercial bank, typically a fiscal responsibility. To avoid an infringement of the EU Treaty, the ECB asked the CBI to rapidly sell the promissory bonds on the market. For more details, see Whelan (2012).

Outright Monetary Transactions (OMT)

On July 26, 2012, in the midst of financial market turmoil in peripheral euro area countries, ECB President Mario Draghi pledged that the central bank would do "whatever it takes, within its mandate" to protect the euro area. In September 2012, the ECB announced that it would stand ready to buy government bonds of euro area crisis countries in unlimited amounts in cases where it identified "redenomination risk"; that is, expectations of a country leaving the euro area pushing up long-term interest rates in a way not related to economic fundamentals. Soon, the German government was sued by German citizens in the country's Constitutional Court and in the European Court of Justice for letting the ECB do what they considered monetary financing of euro area governments. In response, the ECB stressed the conditionality attached to the OMT (through a requirement that countries would subscribe to a financial assistance program of the European Stability Mechanism, which comes with structural adjustment) and that bonds would be purchased on the secondary market, compliant with the ECB mandate. This made the OMT a monetary, not a fiscal tool. The ECB also said that it would be careful not to suppress market functioning and would cap the amounts it would buy. The European Union Court of Justice decided on July 16, 2015, that the OMT "does not exceed the powers of the ECB in relation to monetary policy and does not contravene the prohibition of monetary financing of Member States." For more details, see Cœuré (2013).

identifying policy instruments other than monetary policy—an issue we discuss in Chapter 6.

Notes

1. The proposition that the central bank could directly channel money to households has been discussed after the 2008 financial crisis under the name of "quantitative easing for the people" or "helicopter money".
2. As already noted by Aristotle, money fulfills three functions: unit of account, means of exchange, and reserve of value.
3. On January 1, 2018, there were 19 countries in the euro area: Austria, Belgium, Cyprus, Estonia, Finland, France, Germany, Greece, Ireland, Italy, Latvia, Lithuania, Luxembourg, Malta, the Netherlands, Portugal, Slovakia, Slovenia, and Spain.
4. Some countries have historically experienced free banking, where commercial banks would freely create money. In the United States, from 1836 to 1866, 712 State Banks were permitted to issue banknotes whose relative price, or exchange rate, depended on the signature of the bank. Austrian economist Friedrich Von Hayek was an ardent advocate of a regulation of money supply by the market (Von Hayek, 1978).
5. The range of collateral used in private transactions is much broader. Italian farmers famously pledge wheels of Parmigiano cheese as collateral when they borrow from banks.
6. The liquidity of a security and the liquidity created by the central bank are two different concepts. The different meanings of 'liquidity' are discussed in Chapter 6.
7. Coins are not mentioned here since they are not minted by central banks but by governments.

8. Commercial banks, too, can create money just by extending a new loan and this is the bulk of money creation. However, money creation by the banks is not unlimited and is constrained by reserve requirements as well as by leverage, liquidity, and capital rules applicable to their balance sheets (see box 6.12 and 6.14 in Chapter 6).
9. By tradition, the rate on repos is arithmetic, not geometric.
10. The central banks of the euro area, Denmark, Sweden, Switzerland, and Japan have set refinancing rates or deposit rates to levels below zero. The other large central banks have kept their policy rates above zero.
11. A 1% reserve requirement works the following way. Suppose that a customer has a bank deposit of 100 euros in a bank located within the euro area. Then, the bank must deposit at least 1 euro at the central bank. If the customer uses the 100 euros to repay a debt, then the bank can reduce its reserve accordingly, but the bank of the creditor will raise its reserve deposit by the same amount. As a result, the bank of the depositor can only use 99% of the deposit to extend new loans. In practice, reserve requirements rarely bind quantitatively. Moreover, since the 2008 financial crisis, banking regulation has imposed separate liquidity requirements (Chapter 6).
12. See footnote 10.
13. By borrowing short term and lending long term, banks make a profit if the yield curve is upward-sloping (see Box 5.3). When the yield curve is flat, banks can only make a profit by increasing the price of intermediation (i.e., by not fully transmitting their reduced funding cost).
14. Applying a negative rate on banknotes would necessitate imposing a stamp on each banknote, with a limited validity period. This would be highly burdensome and difficult to implement.
15. For a detailed record of unconventional monetary policy measures taken during the 2008–09 financial crisis, see Fawley and Neely (2013).
16. In December 2011 and February 2012, the ECB conducted very long-term refinancing operations (VLTROs) with a maturity of three years. In June 2014 and March 2016, it launched a series of targeted longer term refinancing operations (TLTROs) with a maturity of up to four years, linking liquidity provision to banks' lending behavior. The TLTROs were similar to Funding for Lending operations carried out by the Bank of England.
17. See the Introductory Statement to the Press Conference following the ECB's Governing Council meeting of July 4, 2013. A similar statement was reiterated in subsequent press conferences.
18. The output gap and its relation to prices are explained in Chapter 1.
19. Fifty percent per month corresponds to 12,875% a year.
20. The "neutral" interest rate can be defined as equal to the growth rate of the economy, which maximizes consumption per capita at the steady state according to the golden rule of growth theory (see Chapter 9). It mainly depends on demography and technological change.
21. Wu and Xia (2016) have proposed a methodology to compute a "shadow policy rate" at the lower bound which captures the impact of unconventional monetary

policies. The ECB has estimated its 2014–2015 credit easing measures to be equivalent to a 100-basis point cut in interest rate in terms of their impact on borrowing costs in the Eurozone (Draghi, 2016).

22. The mechanism was later formalized by John Hicks and Alvin Hansen through the IS–LM model (see Chapter 4).
23. New Keynesian economics refers to the research agenda developed in the 1980s, in particular at the Massachusetts Institute of Technology by Stanley Fischer, Olivier Blanchard, Nobuhiro Kiyotaki, and others, which sought to depart from the flexible prices, perfect markets setup and give micro foundations to price stickiness, labor market rigidities, and coordination failures. It should not be confused with Neo-Keynesian economics, an earlier concept which refers to the post-World War II formalization of Keynes by economists such as John Hicks, Paul Samuelson, and Franco Modigliani, which was not micro founded.
24. For a critical appraisal, see Blinder (1997). Alan Blinder, a professor at Princeton University, was also a vice chairman of the US Federal Reserve.
25. Tobin's q is the ratio of the market value of the companies and the cost of renewal of their stock of physical capital. It is the central variable of the neoclassic theory of investment. When q increases, the market value of the company increases in relation to the replacement cost of the capital; therefore the price of new equipment falls relative to its financing cost by share issue, which leads to a rise in investment. In the absence of adjustment costs of the capital stock, one should permanently have $q = 1$; when the adjustment is not immediate, investment depends positively on q. See, for example, Caballero (1999).
26. It is for the same reason that poor, single-person entrepreneurs are cut off from bank credit. The development of micro-credit can be regarded as a way of overcoming credit restrictions through a system of reciprocal screening and guaranteeing.
27. The unexpected feature of this policy decision can be checked by looking at press releases during the days prior to September 4.
28. This credibility channel is absent from the usual theoretical and empirical models, but it is very much present in central bankers' communication: in January 2016, ECB President Mario Draghi concluded a press conference on monetary policy with a resounding: "*We don't give up* [on our objective to bring inflation back towards 2%]." He was clearly hoping that his statement itself would influence inflation expectations.
29. To the extent that the debt is not indexed on inflation (for instance, because it bears a fixed interest rate), a fall in prices mechanically raises the debt-to-income ratio of agents.
30. The average duration of the government bonds purchased by the ECB under its QE program of 2015–16 was nine years, while its ordinary liquidity tenders had a one-week horizon, and its longest credit operation had a four-year horizon.
31. That is, insofar as the regulation of broad money and interest rates is concerned. Some stores of value and means of exchange are not controlled by the central bank and may at times gain quantitative importance, such as consumer credit provided outside of banks, bitcoins, or frequent flyer mileage. They are, however, not part

of monetary policy insofar as the decision to issue them is not related to macroeconomic stabilization or financial stability objectives.

32. The letters are available on the Bank of England's website. For a description of the Bank of England's remit, see HM Treasury (2001).
33. The communication policies of the Fed and the ECB have largely converged in the early and mid-2010s, with the Fed announcing its inflation objective and initiating press conferences, whereas the ECB started to publish accounts of the meetings of the monetary policy meetings of the Governing Council. The Fed, however, publishes the full transcript of its meetings with a 10-year lag, which the ECB does not.
34. The implementation of monetary policy is decentralized. It involves both the ECB and the national central banks of the euro area: for example, the Irish banks get refinancing from the Central Bank of Ireland and the Dutch ones from De Nederlandsche Bank.
35. A survey by Pollard (2004) indicates that 79 out of 88 central banks surveyed make policy decisions through a committee.
36. To reduce this risk, only 18 national governors can vote, and votes rotate within three groups of countries, depending on their size.
37. In a country where underground activities play a significant role, it can be optimal to create moderate inflation because the inflation tax is paid by all sectors, including the underground economy (where transactions are often carried out in cash).
38. Wyplosz (2001) recommends not going below 1%.
39. For a survey of inflation targeting, see Svensson (2008).
40. Although the level of nominal variables, including the money stock, is generally considered as independent from that of real variables in the long term, in the short and medium term, the rate of change of nominal variables may affect that of real variables: the neutrality of money is widely accepted, but the superneutrality is not.

References

Acemoglu, D., S. Johnson, P. Querubin, and J. A. Robinson (2008), "When Does Policy Reform Work? The Case of Central Bank Independence," *Brookings Papers on Economic Activity*, 1, pp. 351–418.

Akerlof, G., W. Dickens, and G. Perry (1996), "The Macroeconomics of Low Inflation," *Brookings Papers on Economic Activity*, 1, pp. 1–76.

Akerlof, G., W. Dickens, and G. Perry (2000), "Near-Rational Wage and Price Setting and the Long Run Phillips Curve," *Brookings Papers on Economic Activity*, 1, pp. 1–44.

Akerlof, G., and J. Yellen (1985), "A Near-Rational Model of the Business Cycle with Wage and Price Inertia," *Quarterly Journal of Economics*, 100, pp. 823–38.

Alesina, A., and L. Summers (1993), "Central Bank Independence and Macroeconomic Performance: Some Comparative Evidence," *Journal of Money, Credit and Banking*, 25(2), pp. 151–62.

Altunbas Y., L. Gambacorta, and D. Marqués-Ibáñez (2014), "Does Monetary Policy Affect Bank Risk-Taking?" *International Journal of Central Banking*, 10(1), pp. 95–135.

Auer, R., Borio, C., and A. Filardo (2017), "The globalisation of inflation: The growing importance of global value chains," *BIS Working Paper*, 602.

Ball, L. (2006), "Has Globalization Changed Inflation?" *NBER Working Paper*, 12687.

Barro, R. (1995), "Inflation and Economic Growth," *Bank of England Quarterly Bulletin*, May.

Barro, R. (1997), *Determinants of Economic Growth*, MIT Press.

Barro, R., and D. Gordon (1983), "A Positive Theory of Monetary Policy in a Natural Rate Model," *Journal of Political Economy*, 91(4), pp. 589–610.

Beetsma, R., and H. Uhlig (1999), "An Analysis of the Stability and Growth Pact," *Economic Journal*, 109, pp. 546–71.

Bernanke, B. (2017), "Monetary Policy in a New Era," Conference on Rethinking Macroeconomic Policy, Peterson Institute for International Economics, October 12–13.

Bernanke, B., and M. Gertler (1995), "Inside the Black Box: The Credit Channel of Monetary Policy Transmission," *Journal of Economic Perspectives*, 9(4), pp. 27–48.

Bernanke, B., and M. Gertler (2001), "Should Central Banks Respond to Movements in Asset Prices?" *American Economic Review*, 91(2), pp. 253–57.

Bernanke, B., and I. Mihov (1997), "What Does the Bundesbank Target?" *European Economic Review*, 41, pp. 1025–54.

Beyer, A., Cœuré, B., and C. Mendicino (2017), "The Crisis, Ten Years After: Lessons for Monetary and Financial Research," *Economics and Statistics*, 494-495-496, pp. 45–64.

Blanchard, O., G. Dell'Ariccia, and P. Mauro (2010), "Rethinking Macroeconomic Policy," *IMF Staff Position Note*, SPN/10/03.

Blinder, A. (1997), "What Central Bankers Could Learn from Academics, and Vice-versa," *Journal of Economic Perspectives*, 11(2), pp. 3–19.

Blinder, A. (2007), "Monetary Policy by Committee: Why and How?" *European Journal of Political Economy*, 23, 106–23.

Blinder, A., and J. Morgan (2005), "Are Two Heads Better than One? Monetary Policy by Committee," *Journal of Money, Credit, and Banking*, 37, pp. 798–811.

Bordo, M. D. (2010), "Long Term Perspectives on Central Banking," *Norges Bank Occasional Paper* 42, pp. 35–50.

Bordo, M., and O. Jeanne (2002), "Monetary Policy and Asset Prices: Does 'Benign Neglect' Make Sense?" *International Finance*, 5, pp. 139–64.

Borio, C., and H. Zhu (2012), "Capital Regulation, Risk-Taking and Monetary Policy: A Missing Link in the Transmission Channel?" *Journal of Financial Stability*, 8, pp. 236–51.

Borio, C. (2014), "The Financial Cycle and Macroeconomics: What Have We Learnt?" *Journal of Banking and Finance*, 45, pp. 182–98.

Boskin, M., J. Ellen, R. Dulberger, R. Gordon, Z. Griliches, and D. Jorgenson (1996), *Toward a More Accurate Measure of the Cost of Living*, final report to the Senate Finance Committee.

Bruno, M., and W. Easterly (1996), "Inflation and Growth: In Search of a Stable Relationship," *Federal Reserve Bank of Saint Louis Review*, 78, pp. 139–46.

Buiter, W. (2006), "Rethinking Inflation Targeting and Central Bank Independence," inaugural lecture at the London School of Economics.

Caballero, R. (1999), "Aggregate Investment" in Taylor, J., and M. Woodford, eds., *Handbook of Macroeconomics*, Elsevier, pp. 813–862.

Cagan, P. (1956), "The Monetary Dynamics of Hyperinflation," in Friedman, M., ed., *Studies in the Quantity Theory of Money*, University of Chicago Press, pp. 25–117.

Calvo, G. (1983), "Staggered Prices in a Utility Maximizing Framework," *Journal of Monetary Economics*, 12(3), pp. 383–98.

Campbell, J., C. Evans, D. Fiser, and A. Justiniano (2012), "Macroeconomic Effects of Federal Reserve Forward Guidance," *Brookings Papers on Economic Activity*, Spring.

Carpenter, S., and W. Rodgers, III (2004). "The Disparate Labor Market Impacts of Monetary Policy," *Journal of Policy Analysis and Management*, 23(4), p. 813–830.

Claeys, G., Z. Darvas, A. Leandro, and T. Walsh (2015), "The Effect of Ultra-Loose Monetary Policies on Inequality," *Bruegel Policy Contribution*, 2015/09.

Clarida, R., J. Galí, and M. Gertler (1999), "The Science of Monetary Policy: A New Keynesian Perspective," *Journal of Economic Literature*, 37, pp. 1661–707.

Cœuré, B. (2013), "Outright Monetary Transactions, One Year On," CEPR-IFO-KfW conference on "The ECB and its OMT programme," Berlin, September 2.

Coibion, O., Y. Gorodnichenko, K. Kueng, and J. Silvia (2012), "Innocent Bystanders: Monetary Policy and Inequality in the US," *NBER Working Paper*, 18170.

Cunningham, A. (1996), "Measurement Bias in Price Indices: An Application to the UK's RPI," *Bank of England Working Paper*, 47.

Cúrdia, V. (2016), "Is There a Case for Inflation Overshooting?" *Federal Reserve Bank of San Francisco Economic Letter*, 2016-04.

Cúrdia, V., and M. Woodford (2011), "The Central-Bank Balance Sheet as an Instrument of Monetary Policy," *Journal of Monetary Economics*, 58(1), 54–79.

Dincer, N., and B. Eichengreen (2014), "Central Bank Transparency and Independence: Updates and New Measures," *International Journal of Central Banking*, 10(1), pp. 189–253.

Dixit, A., and L. Lambertini (2003), "Interaction of Commitment and Discretion in Monetary and Fiscal Policies," *American Economic Review*, 93, pp. 1522–42.

Doepke, M., and M. Schneider (2006), "Inflation and the Redistribution of Nominal Wealth," *Journal of Political Economy*, 114(6), p. 1069–1097.

Dornbusch, R. (1976), "Expectations and Exchange Rate Dynamics," *Journal of Political Economy*, 84(6), pp. 1161–76.

Draghi, M. (2014), "Unemployment in the Euro Area," Annual Central Bank Symposium in Jackson Hole, August 22.

Draghi, M. (2016), "How Domestic Economic Strength Can Prevail Over Global Weakness," Deutsche Börse Group New Year's reception, Eschborn, January 25.

Dudley, W. C. (2014), "The Economic Outlook and Implications for Monetary Policy," New York Association for Business Economics, New York City, May 20.

Eggertsson, G., and P. Krugman (2012), "Debt, Deleveraging, and the Liquidity Trap: A Fisher-Minsky-Koo Approach," *Quarterly Journal of Economics*, 127(3), pp.1469–513.

Eggertsson, G., and M. Woodford (2003), "The Zero Bound on Interest Rates and Optimal Monetary Policy," *Brookings Papers on Economic Activity*, 1, p. 139–211.

Eickmeier, S., and K. Pijnenburg (2013), "The global dimension of inflation – Evidence from factor-augmented Phillips curves," *Oxford Bulletin of Economics and Statistics*, 75 (1), pp. 103–122.

Eijffinger, C., and P. Geraats (2006), "How Transparent Are Central Banks?" *European Journal of Political Economy*, 22, pp. 1–21.

European Court of Justice (2015), Judgment of the Court (Grand Chamber) in Case C-62/14: Request for a preliminary ruling under Article 267 TFEU from the Bundesverfassungsgericht (Germany) in the proceedings Gauweiler and others vs Deutsche Bundestag, June 16.

Fawley, B., and C. Neely (2013), "Four Stories of Quantitative Easing," *Federal Reserve Bank of St. Louis Review*, 95(1), pp. 51–88.

Fischer, S. (1977), "Long-Term Contracts, Rational Expectations, and the Optimal Money Supply Rule," *Journal of Political Economy*, 85(1), pp. 191–205.

Fisher, I. (1933) "The Debt-Deflation Theory of Great Depressions," *Econometrica*, 1 (4), pp. 337–57.

Forbes, K. (2018), "Has globalization changed the inflation process?," 17th BIS Annual Research Conference, June 22.

Freeman, R. (2005), "What Really Ails Europe (and America): The Doubling of the Global Workforce," *The Globalist*, June 3.

Friedman, M. (1968), "The Role of Monetary Policy," *American Economic Review*, 58(1), pp. 1–17.

Friedman, M., and A. Schwartz (1971), *A Monetary History of the United States, 1867–1960*, Princeton University Press.

Goodhart, C. (1988), *The Evolution of Central Banks*, MIT Press.

Goodhart, C. (2011), "The Changing Role of Central Banks," *Financial History Review*, 18 (2), pp. 135–54.

Goodhart, C., and M. Hofmann (2001), "Asset Prices, Financial Conditions, and the Transmission of Monetary Policy," Conference on Asset Prices, Exchange Rates, and Monetary Policy, Stanford University, March 2–3.

Hammond, G. (2012), *Centre for Central Banking Studies: State of the Art of Inflation Targeting*, Bank of England, Handbook 29.

Hatcher, M., and P. Minford (2016), "Stabilization Policy, Rational Expectations and Price-Level Versus Inflation Targeting: A Survey," *Journal of Economic Surveys*, 30(2), pp. 327–55.

HM Treasury (2001), "The Specification of the Inflation Target," and "The UK Model of Central Bank Independence: An Assessment," in Balls, E., and

G. O'Donnell, eds., *Reforming Britain' s Economic and Financial Policy*, Palgrave, pp. 71–109.

Hume, D. (1742/2007), "Of Interest," "Of Money," and "On the Balance of Payments," in *Essays, Moral, Political, and Literary*, Cosimo Classics.

Ito, T., and F. S. Mishkin (2006), "Two Decades of Japanese Monetary Policy and the Deflation Problem," in *Monetary Policy Under Very Low Inflation in the Pacific Rim*, NBER-EASE, vol. 15, Chicago University Press, pp. 131–93.

Keynes J. M. (1936), *The General Theory of Employment, Interest and Money*, Palgrave Macmillan.

Koo, R. (2009), *The Holy Grail of Macroeconomics: Lessons from Japan's Great Recession*, Wiley.

Krishnamurthy, A., and A. Vissing-Jorgensen, A. (2011), "The Effects of Quantitative Easing on Interest Rates: Channels and Implications For Policy," *Brookings Papers on Economic Activity*, 43(2), 215–287.

Krugman, P. (2000), "Thinking about the Liquidity Trap," *Journal of the Japanese and International Economies*, 14(4), pp. 221–37.

Holston, K., T. Laubach, and J. Williams (2016), "Measuring the Natural Rate of Interest: International Trends and Determinants," *Federal Reserve Bank of San Francisco Working Paper* 2016-11.

Lebow, D., and J. Rudd (2001), "Measurement Error in the Consumer Price Index: Where Do We Stand?" *Journal of Economic Literature*, 41(1), pp. 159–201.

Leeper, E. M. (1991), "Equilibria Under 'Active' and 'Passive' Monetary and Fiscal Policies," *Journal of Monetary Economics*, 27(1), pp. 129–47.

Le Rider, G. (1994), *Leçon Inaugurale*, Collège de France, March 9.

Lucas, R. (1972), "Expectations and the Neutrality of Money," *Journal of Economic Theory*, 4(2), pp. 103–24.

Lucas, R. (1996), "Nobel Lecture: Monetary Neutrality," *Journal of Political Economy*, 104, pp. 661–82.

Maddaloni A., and J.-L. Peydró-Alcalde. (2011), "Bank Risk-Taking, Securitization, Supervision and Low Interest Rates: Evidence from the Euro Area and the US Lending Standards," *Review of Financial Studies*, 24 (6), pp. 2121–65.

Mankiw, N. G. (1985), "Small Menu Costs and Large Business Cycles: A Macroeconomic Model of Monopoly," *Quarterly Journal of Economics*,100, pp. 529–39.

Mankiw, N. G., and R. Reis (2011), "Imperfect Information and Aggregate Supply," in Friedman, B., and M. Woodford, eds., *Handbook of Monetary Economics*, Elsevier, pp. 183–229.

McCandless, G., and W. Weber (1995), "Some Monetary Facts," *Federal Reserve Bank of Minneapolis Quarterly Review*, 19, pp. 2–11.

Micossi, S. (2015), "The Monetary Policy of the European Central Bank (2002–2015)," *CEPS Special Report*, No. 109, May.

Nakajima, M. (2015), "The Redistributive Consequences of Monetary Policy," *Federal Reserve Bank of Philadelphia Business Review*, 98(2), pp. 9–16.

Nelson, E., and K. Nikolov (2003), "UK Inflation in the 1970s and 1980s: The Role of Output Gap Mismeasurement," *Journal of Economics and Business*, 55(4), pp. 353–70.

O'Donnell, G. (2001), "UK Policy Co-ordination: The Importance of Institutional Design," HM Treasury.

Phelps, E. (1967), "Phillips Curves, Expectations of Inflation and Optimal Employment over Time," *Economica*, 34(3), pp. 254–81.

Phelps, E. (1973), "Inflation in the Theory of Public Finance," *Swedish Journal of Economics*, 75(1), pp. 67–82.

Pollard, P. (2004), "Monetary Policy-making around the World: Different Approaches from Different Central Banks," Federal Reserve Bank of Saint Louis.

Roberds, W., and F. Velde (2014), "Early Public Banks," *Federal Reserve Bank of Chicago Working Paper*, 2014-03.

Rajan, R. (2005), "Has financial development made the world riskier ?", Federal Reserve Bank of Kansas City Symposium, "The Greenspan Era : Lessons For the Future", Jackson Hole, August 25–27.

Rogers, J. H., C. Scotti, and J. H. Wright (2015), "Unconventional Monetary Policy and International Risk Premia," 16th Jacques Polak Annual Research Conference, November 5–6.

Rogoff, K. (1984), "Can International Monetary Policy Cooperation be Counterproductive?," *Journal of International Economics*, 18 (3–4), pp. 199–217.

Rogoff, K. (1985), "The Optimal Degree of Commitment to an Intermediate Monetary Target," *Quarterly Journal of Economics*, 100, pp. 1169–90.

Rogoff, K. (2003), "Globalization and Global Disinflation," *Federal Reserve Bank of Kansas City Economic Review*, 4th Quarter, pp. 45–78.

Rogoff, K. (2014), "Costs and Benefits to Phasing Out Paper Currency," *NBER Working Paper*, 20126.

Romer, C. D., and D. H. Romer (1999), "Monetary Policy and the Well-Being of the Poor," *Economic Review, Federal Reserve Bank of Kansas City*, Q I, pp. 21–49.

Sargent, T., and N. Wallace (1981), "Some Unpleasant Monetarist Arithmetic," *Federal Reserve Bank of Minneapolis Quarterly Review*, Autumn, pp. 1–17.

Shiratsuka, S. (1999), "Measurement Errors in the Japanese Consumer Price Index," *Bank of Japan, Monetary and Economic Studies*, 17(3).

Siebert, A. (2006), "Central Banking by Committees," *DNB Working Paper*, 091/2006.

Stein, J. (2013), "Overheating in Credit Markets: Origins, Measurement, and Policy Responses: Restoring Household Financial Stability after the Great Recession: Why Household Balance Sheets Matter," research symposium sponsored by the Federal Reserve Bank of St. Louis, February 7.

Stiglitz, J., and A. Weiss (1981), "Credit Rationing in Markets with Imperfect Information," *American Economic Review*, 71(3), pp. 393–410.

Summers, L. (2014), "US Economic Prospects: Secular Stagnation, Hysteresis, and the Zero Lower Bound," *Business Economics*, 49(2), pp. 65–73.

Svensson, L. (2008), "Inflation Targeting," *The New Palgrave Dictionary of Economics*, 2nd edition, Palgrave Macmillan.

Svensson, L. (1999), "Inflation Targeting as a Monetary Policy Rule," *Journal of Monetary Economics*, 43, pp. 607–54.

Svensson, L. (2001), "Inflation Targeting: Should It Be Modeled as an Instrument Rule or a Targeting Rule?" *European Economic Review*, 46(4/5), pp. 771–80.

Taylor, J. (1980), "Aggregate Dynamics and Staggered Contracts," *Journal of Political Economy*, 88(1), pp. 1–23.

Ugolini, S. (2011), "What do we really know about the long term evolution of central banking? Evidence from the past, insights from the present," *Norges Bank's Bicentenary Project, Working Paper*, 2011/15.

Von Hayek, F. (1978), *Denationalization of Money. The Argument refined*, Institute of Economic Affairs.

Walsh, C. (1995), "Optimum Contracts for Central Bankers," *American Economic Review*, 85, pp. 150–67.

Whelan, K. (2012), "ELA, Promissory Notes and All That: The Fiscal Costs of Anglo Irish Bank," *Economic and Social Review*, 43(4), pp. 653–73.

White, B. (2009), "Should Monetary Policy 'Lean' or 'Clean?'" *Federal Reserve Bank of Dallas, Globalization and Monetary Policy Institute Working Paper*, 34.

Wicksell, K. (1898), *Interest and Prices*, Macmillan.

Woodford, M. (2001), "Fiscal Requirements for Price Stability," *Journal of Money, Credit and Banking*, 33(3), pp. 669–728.

Woodford, M. (2007), "How Important Is Money in the Conduct of Monetary Policy?" *CEPR Discussion Paper*, 6211.

Wu, J. C. and F. D. Xia (2016), "Measuring the Macroeconomic Impact of Monetary Policy at the Zero Lower Bound," *Journal of Money Credit and Banking*, 48 (2-3), pp. 253–91.

Wyplosz, C. (2001), "Do We Know How Low Should Inflation Be?" *CEPR Discussion Paper*, 2722..

6

Financial Stability

> The financial risks that are being created by the system are indeed greater. . . . [I]t's possible that these developments are creating more financial-sector induced procyclicality than in the past. They may also create a greater (albeit still small) probability of a catastrophic meltdown.
>
> IMF Chief Economist R. Rajan at the Federal Reserve Bank of Kansas City Symposium, Jackson Hole, August 27, 2005 (Rajan, 2005)

> I [find] the basic, slightly Luddite premise of the [Rajan] paper slightly misguided. . . . The tendency toward restriction that

runs through the tone of the presentation seems to me to be quite problematic.

Harvard President L. Summers, commenting on Rajan at the Federal Reserve Bank of Kansas City Symposium, Jackson Hole, August 27, 2005.

Few industries are as controversial as finance. In the public, finance isn't seen as an industry providing services to households and firms (on a level, say, with transports or garbage collection) but as a source of risks, extracting excessive rents from the economy. The global financial crisis of the late 2000s uncovered large-scale greed, misconduct, and reckless risk-taking of bankers rescued with taxpayer money. Movies exposing their misdeeds, such as Charles Ferguson's *Inside Job*, Adam McKay's *The Big Short,* or Martin Scorcese's *Wolf of Wall Street* have met with popular success. The financial industry has been held responsible for millions of jobs lost in the crisis, and lashing out at bankers remains commonplace among politicians.

Yet, we use finance every day. We settle our lunch with plastic money, we borrow to buy property and goods, we save for our retirement, and we invest our cash balances. Back in 1911, Joseph Schumpeter deemed finance essential for technological innovation and economic development. For mainstream economists, finance supports the functioning of modern market economies by smoothing income over time, pooling savings and channeling them to productive investment, processing and sharing information, and diversifying risk.[1] The economic profession has often been a cheerleader for finance, as shown by the remarks by Harvard Professor and former Treasury Secretary Larry Summers quoted at the start of this chapter, just two years before the start of global financial crisis. And the empirical literature on finance and development has uncovered a positive relationship across time and economies between financial depth and gross domestic product (GDP) per capita, albeit with qualification (see Section 6.1).

What went wrong with finance? Can policy makers do a better job at encouraging socially useful financial innovation while addressing the risks it poses to society? Given the social value of financial intermediation and the devastating cost of financial crises, the stakes are high. This chapter informs the discussion by exposing the theories underpinning finance and discussing the policies supporting financial stability. The analysis mostly stays in a closed-economy setup, with international savings and investment being discussed in Chapter 7. Cooperation and competition on financial regulatory policies are addressed in the Conclusion.

6.1 Facts

6.1.1 A brief history of finance

The basic functions of finance have existed since early ages, at least since fiat currency was introduced in human societies, and maybe beforehand, as many anthropologists believe that debt has predated money.[2] Interest-bearing loans between individuals secured by collateral are mentioned in the Code of Hammurabi (Babylon, eighteenth century BCE) and in the Old Testament. The temple of Delos, in Greece, extended loans secured by houses, an early example of a residential mortgage. Roman banks collected deposits and extended loans, although demand for financial intermediation was limited in an agrarian society where large savers were landowners and therefore also investors.[3] Cicero described interest rates adjusting to the supply and demand for loans, and his famous speech on the Manilius law explains how financial panic propagated from Asia to Rome in 66 BCE, an early case of what economists would now call "cross-border financial contagion." Tacitus documented how the Roman Treasury bailed out distressed landowners when the price of land collapsed in 33 BCE (Frank, 1935).

Financial intermediation broadened and deepened in Middle Age and Renaissance Europe (Braudel, 1981), particularly in Italy, alongside with the development of pilgrimage and trade which required cross-border loans and money transfers. Pilgrims used exchange letters to deposit money in one city and use it in another. The Medici family in Florence established a branch network with banking partners. Double-entry ledgers, introduced in fourteenth-century Genoa, helped keep track of the clients' claims, liabilities, and net balances. Similar developments occurred in the Islamic world to finance trade around the Mediterranean and later in China with the expansion of the *piaohao* (or "Shanxi Banks") to finance trade and remittances across the empire.

Finance soared from the seventeenth century in England and Holland with the development of trade credit and the introduction of bills of exchange which could themselves be traded, complementing bank-based finance with market-based finance. Cash-strapped governments issued bonds to finance wars. Douglass North and Barry Weingast (1989) have argued that market-based finance would not have emerged without favorable institutional foundations such as strong enforcement of investors rights and the existence of risk-free government bonds, both of which favored England and Holland over France. By the end of the eighteenth century, building on a continuous stream of financial innovation, a dense financial intermediation network had spread through Europe, with banks and capital markets operating across national borders. Advanced risk management techniques such as forward contracts or options were used in some commodities markets, anticipating what would become derivative contracts.[4]

The scope of finance was, however, confined to loans and fixed-income instruments and to the financing of trade and government spending. What radically changed the face of finance (and by way of consequence, of capitalism) was *limited liability*: contracts allowing private investors to finance projects without being personally liable beyond their initial investment. Limited liability had been tested from the twelfth to thirteenth centuries in the *commenda* structure for maritime trade, a limited partnership where outside investors were liable only to the extent of their investment.[5] It became the common way to incorporate joint stock companies only in the nineteenth century. Limited liability encouraged the allocation of previously idle savings to risky projects and created a vast market for corporate equity, allowing companies to grow. Financing opportunities were further expanded by the issuance of corporate debt leveraging the available equity. While government bonds accounted for half the capitalization of the London market in 1860, their share had dropped below 5% by 1914.[6] In the late nineteenth century, the financial landscape as we know it was in place with financial institutions such as banks, asset managers, and pension funds and financial markets trading government bonds, corporate equity, debt, and, in some countries, residential mortgages. This landscape remained largely unchanged for most of the twentieth century. It expanded across national borders through successive waves of financial globalization (see Chapter 7).

The *mix* of financing channels was, however, different across countries (see Section 6.1.2 on financial structures). Governments and banks would play a larger role in Japan and in Europe than in the United States, where firms would rather issue equity and bonds. The lack of deep capital markets in Continental Europe owes partly to collective preference for pay-as-you go pensions over funded pension schemes (except in the Netherlands and Nordic countries), which explains the limited footprint of large asset managers.[7]

Another wave of financial innovation started in the mid-1980s in the United States with the surge of *derivative products* such as swaps, futures, and options, defined as financial contracts with a payoff depending on the performance of an underlying financial asset (stocks, bonds, commodities, etc.) or on the realization of exogenous random events, such as catastrophe bonds (tradable insurance contracts against hurricanes or earthquakes), and *credit-default swaps* (CDS) which indemnify the owner in case a company or government defaults on their debt payments. Derivatives started as contracts signed *over-the-counter* (OTC)—that is, in a bespoke manner between two counterparties—, then gradually became standardized, making it possible to report them to regulators and to trade them on exchanges. They were invented as ways to hedge risk in simple financial assets such as stocks, bonds, or currency rates, but soon they were used for speculative purposes, such as in the case of "naked CDSs" which don't hedge existing claims but merely bet on a risk of default. According to the Bank for International Settlements, the total market value of OTC derivative contracts soared from around US$3 trillion in 1998 to US$35.3 trillion at its peak in 2008 (compared to US$18.9 trillion of international debt securities).[8]

New waves of innovation keep changing the face of the financial industry. Together with the intensive use of big data to collect and process customer information, "FinTech" may once again reshape financial intermediation and allow the emergence of new players (see Section 6.3.1.e)).

6.1.2 Financial structures and instruments

The role of the financial system is to "facilitate the allocation and deployment of economic resources, both spatially and temporally, in an uncertain environment." (Merton, 1995) There are many examples of such deployment. Issuing debt allows future income to fund current expenses. Investing in financial assets allows current income to fund future expenses. Diversifying one's wealth or underwriting insurance contracts allow sustaining one's consumption and investment in the face of adverse income shocks.[9] If I invest in stocks of companies whose activity is sufficiently different from the one I work for, I cash in dividends when my labor income drops, and, in this way I protect my standard of living. Access to finance is often key to escaping poverty: the microcredit pioneered by Muhamad Yunus, a social entrepreneur and banker from Bangladesh who was awarded the Nobel Peace Prize, aims at countering the financial exclusion resulting from the fact that fixed costs and asymmetric information prevent banks from offering small loans to poor entrepreneurs.

As our short history of finance has shown, different *financial structures* have emerged across space and time. Finance can be either *intermediated* (or *bank-based*) or *disintermediated* (or *market-based*, meaning at arm's-length from banks).

Intermediated finance is operated by financial institutions that collect money from individuals and lend to others. Banks take deposits and extend loans, asset managers buy financial or physical assets on behalf of clients, and so forth. These activities create assets and liabilities on the intermediary's balance sheet; the intermediary accompanies the investment or loan over its lifetime and monitors the success or failure of the underlying projects.

Among financial intermediaries, banks are special because they perform *maturity transformation* (i.e., they collect sight deposits and invest in longer term loans and financial assets). Later, we'll show how the maturity mismatch between banks' assets and liabilities is a key source of risk for themselves and for the economy and a key reason why they are heavily regulated, but one should not forget that maturity transformation is at the same time central to their social role. Other financial intermediaries such as money market funds and open-ended investment funds may perform maturity transformation by collecting short-term savings and investing in long-term assets, and they can then be considered as "shadow banks," a concept which we discuss more at length later in this chapter.

Finance is disintermediated when individuals lend directly to one another, underwrite an *IOU* ("I owe you," a document acknowledging one's debt), or buy a promissory note (essentially the same document, but transferrable to a third party who then becomes the creditor). In the case of a company, possible debt contracts are loans, bills, and bonds (transferrable debt instruments which often pay a fixed interest rate, distributed as a *coupon*), or *stocks* (transferrable property rights which pay a time-varying fraction of the company's revenue, distributed as a *dividend*). Stocks can be quoted and exchanged on a public trading venue (a *stock exchange*), or held as *private equity*. In both cases, they are representative of the company's *own funds* or *equity*, that is, its liability to its shareholders.[10] Marketable financial instruments (bills, bonds, and stocks) are also called *securities*.

In arm's-length finance, the role of financial intermediaries is limited to identifying (in financial jargon, *originating*) potential lenders and borrowers, to buying and selling financial assets, and to providing advisory services, remunerated with fees. The key functions of allocating savings, monitoring projects, and exerting corporate control are also performed by capital markets outside the scope of financial intermediaries. Box 6.1 illustrates the case of securitization activity.

Box 6.1 A Primer on Securitization

Securitization, the technique through which bank loans are transformed into marketable securities, was invented in the 1970s when US government-sponsored financial institutions such as Fannie Mae (the Federal National Mortgage Association) started securitizing residential mortgages. Previously, banks held loans on their balance sheets until they matured or were paid off (the *originate-and-hold* model). But, after World War II, depository institutions simply could not keep pace with the rising demand for housing credit and sought ways of increasing the sources of mortgage funding. To attract investors, an investment vehicle was developed that picked mortgage pools, sorted them by credit quality into *tranches*, and sold the tranches, thus allowing banks to reduce their exposure to credit risk and thereby to increase their volume of credit (the *originate-and-distribute* model; see Coval, Jurek, and Stratford, 2009).

The repackaging of claims picked within a homogenous asset class such as residential mortgages, loans, bonds, trade, credit card receivables, and the like, each being small relative to the overall pool, helps diversify idiosyncratic risk. Tranches can then be pledged to back the issuance of *asset-backed securities* (ABS), which are traded on markets and sold to investors. ABS pay a coupon out of the pooled stream of revenue of the underlying assets. The largest class of ABS are backed by real estate claims and called *mortgage-based securities* (MBS).

Imagine now that some homeowners have lost their jobs and stop paying interest on their residential mortgages. The available pool of revenue shrinks, and some ABS suspend coupon payments. The riskiest tranche is the one which first stops paying coupons: it is said to be *junior. Senior* tranches stop paying coupons last and are the safest. It is easy to see that the credit rating of an ABS depends on the seniority of the tranches. The most senior tranches (i.e., the ones which will last stop paying a coupon) achieve the best rating, typically dubbed "AAA" by credit rating agencies, and they offer a lower yield even when the underlying pool includes high-risk assets. More junior tranches are less well-rated ("AA," "A," and so forth) and serve a higher yield to compensate for the higher risk.

Seniority is not specific to securitization. It describes the order in which any firm's liabilities are repaid in case of default; that is, if its assets fall short of providing the necessary revenues. Typically, seniority is a characteristic of a financial instrument. For example, debt is more senior than equity, reflecting the fact that equity holders own the firm, while bondholders are only lenders. Some debt instruments, called *junior debt*, are contractually or statutorily junior to ordinary loans and bonds.

Securitization was too successful. In the United States, the outstanding amount of ABS reached US$2.5 trillion in 2007, almost 20% of US GDP. It gradually became opaque and risky as securitized credits were themselves restructured and repackaged into more complex ones, with several layers of packaging and tranching, making them very difficult to monitor and value. The market collapsed after 2007 (see box 6.9 in section 6.2.3 for a theoretical discussion), and efforts were devoted to creating a new "simple, transparent and comparable" securitization, with simple structures and transparency on the underlying assets (Bank of England and European Central Bank, 2014). Banks which originate securitized products have to retain part of them (typically, 5%) on their balance sheets as an incentive for them to monitor risks.

The US and UK financial sectors are predominantly market-based, with around 80% of households and companies funding themselves on markets and 20% funding themselves through banks. Japan and continental Europe are bank-based, with broadly opposite proportions, although continental Europe is now moving toward a more market-based structure (see Section 6.3). Demirgüç-Kunt and Levine (1999) found financial systems to be generally more developed in richer countries, with relatively larger banks and other financial intermediaries and deeper stock markets (all gauged as shares of local GDP), but institutional factors also matter. Other things being equal, they found countries with French civil law tradition, poor protection of shareholder and creditor rights, poor contract enforcement, high levels of corruption, poor accounting standards, restrictive banking regulations, and high inflation to have less deep financial systems.

As illustrated by figure 6.1, economies tend to be more market-based as they become richer. Moreover, Demirgüç-Kunt and Levine have shown that countries with common law traditions, strong protection of shareholder rights, good accounting regulations, low levels of corruption, and no explicit deposit insurance tend to be market-based rather than bank-based. This

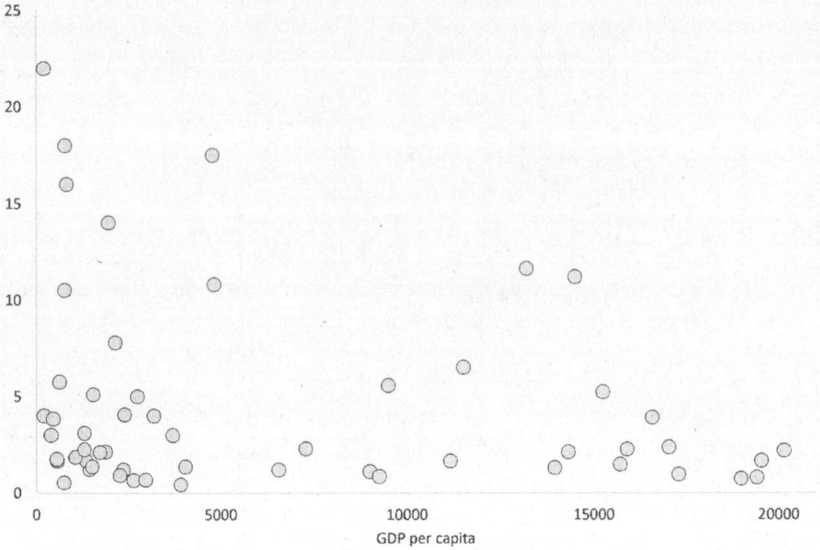

Figure 6.1 Financial structures and economic development: Gross domestic product (GDP) per capita and claims of deposit money banks on the private sector as % of market capitalization, 1990–1995.
Data taken from Demigürç-Kunt and Levine (1999).

finding echoes North and Weingast's remark reported earlier and, generally, the economic literature on "legal origins" discussed in Chapter 9. The "legal origins" approach to financial structures is only one attempt to explain their strong path dependency and dependence on institutional developments.[11] It ignores, for example, that pre-World War I France benefitted from deep bond markets, as well as the role of prefunded pensions in spurring market development.

The social functions of disintermediated and intermediated finance are in principle similar, hence the popular term of *shadow banking,* which describes lending to the economy by non-bank financial intermediaries such as asset managers, money market funds, or insurance companies which operate outside the purview of bank regulation. However, the types of contracts, and hence the way projects are monitored, the incentives of participants, and the regulation they are (or should be) subject to are quite different under different financial structures.[12] They also affect the way monetary policy is transmitted to the economy.

In a broader sense, finance also includes the "plumbing" of the financial system (i.e., the *financial market infrastructures* which allow money and financial assets to be shipped from one place to another). These include *payment systems* such as credit card schemes or the *real-time gross settlement systems* (RTGS) which allow banks to net out millions of payment orders in real time, transfer money, and settle their accounts at the end of the day with central bank money (see Chapter 5). These also include *custodians,* which book securities on behalf of issuers and investors and keep track of their movements, and *clearing houses*, also called *central-clearing counterparts* (CCPs). Clearing houses net out transactions on standardized securities and derivative contracts among a large number of participants, acting as the seller to every buyer and the buyer to every seller, which produces economies of scale in risk management and use of collateral.[13]

In an even broader sense, finance includes third-party providers of information on the creditworthiness of companies and securities, such as producers of market research inside and outside of banks, and *credit-rating agencies* that provide standardized assessments of the solvency of individual private and sovereign borrowers.

Apart from a few financial centers such as Luxembourg or Singapore, the direct contribution of financial activities typically ranges from 5% to 10% of gross value added in advanced economies (figure 6.2). However, measuring the economic weight of finance through the sole lens of national accounting can be misleading. One gets to much larger numbers when including ancillary services such as law, accounting, and related high-value added services, which explains why competition is fierce between financial centers. Competition is global among global market places: London, New York, Tokyo, Hong Kong, Shanghai, and Singapore. Competition is also regional. In 2016, the UK referendum on leaving the European Union triggered a beauty contest among continental market places (Amsterdam, Dublin, Frankfurt, Luxembourg, Milan,

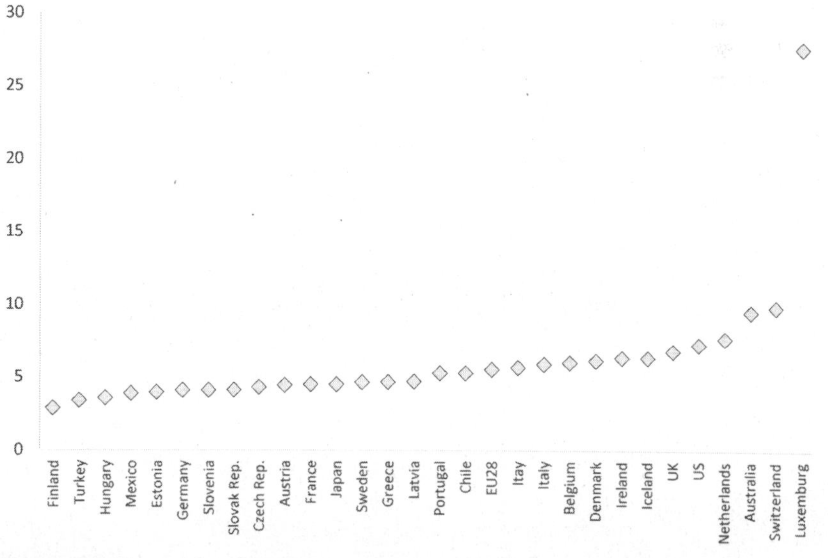

Figure 6.2 Financial and insurance activities in % of gross value added in 2015. OECD data.

Madrid, and Paris) to attract finance out of London. Likewise, competition is fierce among Shanghai, Hong Kong, and Singapore.

Measuring the sole value added created by finance overlooks its raison d'être, that is, allocating savings where they are needed and hedging consumers and companies against risk, which contributes to value added in all other industries. As Larry Summers once noted, one does not measure the importance of electricity by its share in value added.[14]

6.1.3 Financial crises

What makes it so important to regulate and supervise finance is the recurrence of financial crises. Finance was always associated with episodes of excessive risk-taking and asset price bubbles. Such episodes usually end in a crash, causing income and job losses well beyond the financial industry.

Charles Kindleberger told the history of modern financial crises, culminating in the Dutch tulip mania of 1634–1637 (figure 6.3) and the South Sea and Mississippi bubbles of 1719–1720 (Kindleberger and Aliber, 2005; see also Mackay, 1841; Garber, 1990). The US stock market crash of 1929 is another example. A more recent and comprehensive account is provided by Reinhart and Rogoff (2010), who survey two centuries of financial crises. According to them, nearly one-third of the surveyed countries were in a banking crisis each year before World War I and again in the 1990s, while sovereign debt crises (that is, government default or debt restructuring, see Chapter 4) have been even more frequent, nearing half of the countries each year in the 1830s and again in the 1880s, the 1940s, and the 1990s.

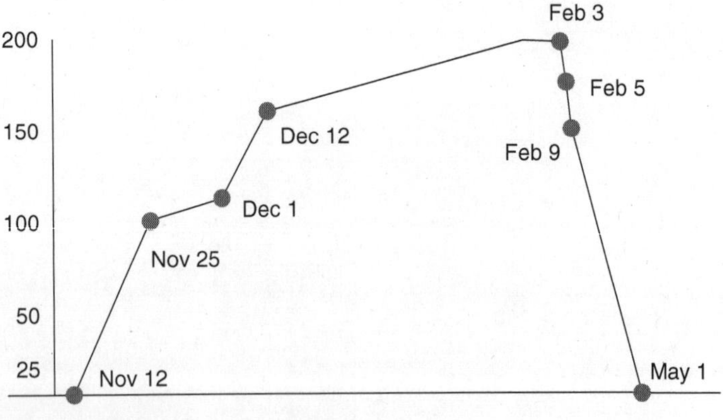

Figure 6.3 Tulip price index, 1636–1637.
The index was built by the author to allow comparisons across tulip varieties. See Van der Veen (2012) for a discussion.
Thompson (2007).

Common features of financial crises are *leverage* (the reliance on debt to finance investment into high-yielding risky assets) and *bubbles* (lasting departures of asset prices from their economic values). Crises are generally preceded by an expansion of the balance sheets of financial intermediaries, sustained by rising debt to finance investments in real estate or financial assets, driving up their prices. Rising asset prices in turn raise the value of collateral that intermediaries can pledge to secure borrowing and thus allow them to borrow even more, creating a positive feedback loop in the financial system (see box 6.10 for a full explanation). Such expansions are often associated with a deterioration of credit standards; that is, complacency in the assessment of risk and lighter guarantees requested from the borrower. At some point in the life of the bubble, prices have risen so much above the level justified by the expectation of future cash flows that market sentiment abruptly shifts, investors start selling, and the bubble bursts. The cliff-like shape of figure 6.3 is typical of such episodes. Financial intermediaries are then left with huge losses, and, absent capital injections, they go bankrupt, with broader negative spillovers to the economy.

Bubbles can be specific to asset classes. Nowadays, tech companies, commercial and residential real estate, or cryptocurrencies come to mind. Bubbles sometimes spread across financial markets, in which case the spillovers to the real economy can be very strong, positively on the way up and negatively on the way down. According to a school of thought led by Yale economist Hyman Minsky, unstable financial cycles fueled by indebtedness are inherent to capitalism, which departs from the neo-classical paradigm in which feedback forces always ensure the return to a long-term equilibrium (Minsky, 1986, 1992). As a tribute to Minsky's financial instability hypothesis, the tipping point when economic agents finally recognize that asset valuation is not matched by future incomes streams is often called the *Minsky moment*. One has in mind the moment in the classic Warner Brothers' Road Runner cartoon when Wile E. Coyote realizes that he is running in thin air—and crashes to the ground.

This leaves the reader wondering about the *fundamental value* of a financial asset. A straightforward answer is the net present value of the expected monetary cash flows accruing to it (we'll see such a model in Section 6.2) or, in the case of a physical asset, the net present value of the opportunity cost of owning it (for instance, owning property avoids paying a rent, hence the fundamental value of property is the net present value of future rents). In the case of nonfinancial assets, value can also be defined as the monetary equivalent of utility flows derived from its ownership, such as the aesthetic pleasure of owning a work of art. The notion of "fundamental" is therefore highly dependent on a theory of expectations.

The externalities created by a financial crisis to the rest of the economy can be severe. *Before the crisis,* they are both positive because financial optimism helps finance risky endeavors that pay off over the long term and negative because of the misallocation of capital invested in the inflated asset, which could be better employed for productive use. Railroads and iron in the nineteenth century and digital innovations in the twenty-first century illustrate the former effect (Ventura and Voth, 2015), while empty office buildings in Thailand post-1997 or empty seaside residences in Spain post-2012 illustrate the latter. *After the crisis,* and unless one is a strong believer in Schumpeter's creative destruction explained in Chapter 9, the externalities are clearly negative. As figure 6.4 illustrates, the reduced value of collateral and the capital losses occurred by individuals, financial intermediaries, and the government weigh on consumption and investment in a deep and lasting way.

The cost of financial crises is typically large, with sharp recessions, slow recoveries, and a very persistent impact on GDP. Reinhart and Rogoff (2009) found the average peak-to-trough impact on GDP to be larger than nine percentage points across a sample of recent banking crises in developed and emerging economies (figure 6.4).[15] The euro area's slow recovery from its double-dip recession of 2008–2009 and 2011–2013 is a sad case of a "lost decade." Only in late 2014 did the region's GDP recover its level from 2008.

Financial crises are even more severe when they are not confined within the domestic financial sector and have balance-of-payments and fiscal ramifications. The balance-of-payments dimension typically materializes in small open economies financed by external borrowing. Lower domestic asset prices trigger capital outflows and a fall in the value of the domestic currency (which raises the domestic burden of foreign currency debt). This happened in 1997–1998 in several East-Asian economies whose currencies had been pegged to the US dollar, and prices of domestic assets (typically, commercial property) had become overvalued. Currency depreciation and

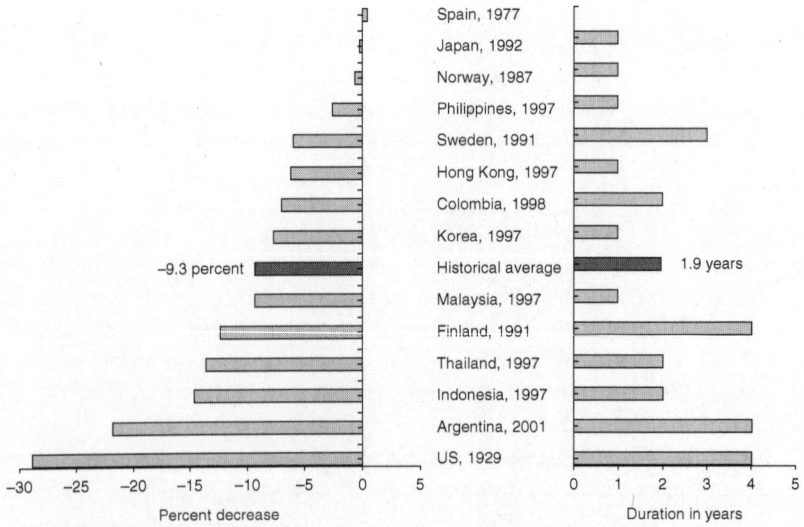

Figure 6.4 The real cost of banking crises: peak-to-trough decline in real gross domestic product (GDP) and years duration of downturn.
Reinhart and Rogoff (2009), figure 4, p. 470.

asset price deflation are mutually reinforcing and deepen the adverse impact of the crisis on the financial sector. One speaks of *twin crises* of the banking system and of the balance of payments (Chapter 7).

The fiscal dimension typically comes from the government having to step in and spend fiscal resources to bail out domestic banks (Chapter 4). Financial crises can impose a considerable burden on public finances. According to International Monetary Fund (IMF) research, over the 1970–2011 period, this fiscal cost exceeded 20% of GDP in every fifth crisis episode (Laeven and Valencia, 2012). In the late 2000s, it reached 40% of GDP in Ireland. Conversely, fiscal crises can trigger financial crises when domestic banks are large holders of government debt at a time when its price is depressed by a higher probability of default. Both combine to create a *doom loop*, or *bank–sovereign nexus*, a two-way link between the risks of default of banks and the sovereign. Corporates also feed the loop since weaker banks restrict their lending volumes and conditions, and lower corporate investment weighs on economic growth and on tax revenues (figure 6.5). The doom loop was one of the key mechanisms of the euro area crisis that started in 2010.[16] A key priority of the post-crisis financial regulatory agenda has been to protect taxpayers from the consequences of banking crises (see section 6.3, in particular box 6.13).

Crises also hit individual financial institutions. *Bank runs* start when depositors lose confidence in the ability of a bank to guarantee the value of their deposits and rush to withdrew them. This is because the bulk of banks' assets are either illiquid, meaning that they cannot be sold or lent in a repurchase

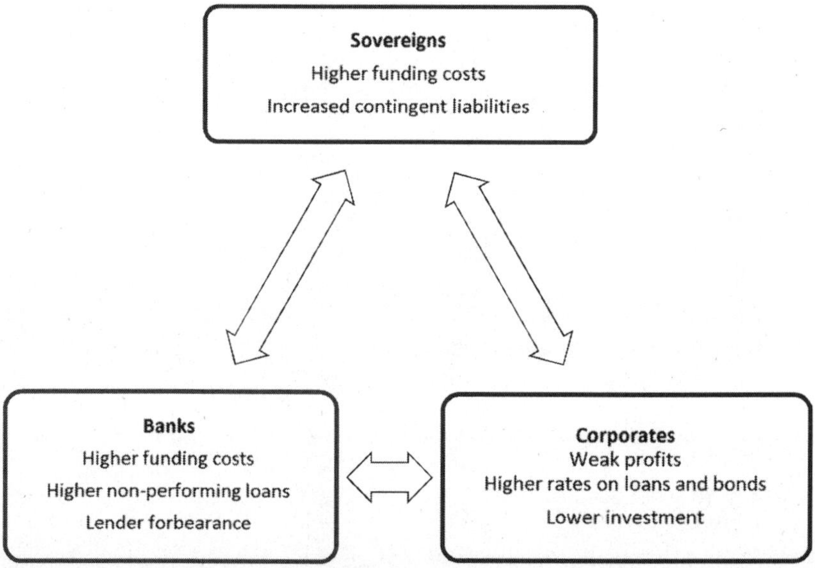

Figure 6.5 The bank–sovereign doom loop.
IMF, Global Financial Stability Report, October 2013.

agreement to generate cash (think of loans to individuals or companies, which are not easy to transfer to another bank), or because selling them would not generate as much cash as previously expected. An early example of a bank run is the Mississippi Crisis of March 1720 in Paris, a run on the Compagnie des Indes Orientales managed by Scottish banker John Law, who was also King Louis XV's finance minister. The bank was funded by issuing shares and short-term commercial paper, initially invested in mining projects in French Louisiana which proved elusive. In the spring of 1720, confidence in the bank gradually deteriorated, then collapsed. Seventeen were killed when depositors ran on the bank's headquarters on July 17, 1720.[17]

There were repeated bank runs in the nineteenth century, such as those on the First National Bank of New York in 1873 and on Overend Gurney in London in 1866. Bank runs do not belong to the past. An iconic image of the global financial crisis is one of British depositors lining up in October 2007 to withdraw their money from local branches of Northern Rock, a building company which had financed real estate investment with client deposits and short-term market borrowing. In June and July 2015, Greek banks were closed for several weeks to prevent a run after the European Central Bank (ECB) announced that it would limit their refinancing if the government would default.

Banks are inherently prone to such accidents because they do maturity transformation. Avoiding liquidity crises is a key objective of banking regulation, as we'll see in Sections 6.2 and 6.3. Insurance companies and pension funds are less prone to runs given the more sluggish nature of their liabilities, which cannot easily be called upon before term, but runs are possible on asset management companies when investors are free to withdraw their funds. Runs also happen in capital markets when financial institutions fund themselves by issuing short-term bills or by lending assets on repo. Investors in short-term securities can lose confidence just as depositors do (see later discussion in Section 6.2.3).

Depending on their size and interconnectedness with the rest of the economy, runs on individual institutions can morph into systemic crises. This happened in the summer of 2007 when the market for commercial paper, a key place for banks to raise short-term funding, suddenly froze because of increasing mistrust in the quality of the mortgages held by banks. The sudden illiquidity of securities that were until then actively traded was a signal that the global financial crisis had started.

6.1.4 Finance and economic performance

We described earlier the link between economic development and financial depth, already identified by Joan Robinson (1952). The causality also runs the other way. A deeper financial system stimulates growth by channeling savings to productivity-enhancing investments and reduces precautionary savings by allowing a better diversification of risk and an easier access to financial instruments. However, an oversized financial sector can be a sign of weak lending standards, excessive leverage, and investment in overpriced non-productive assets, implying lower productivity today and a possible crisis tomorrow. This can come along with misallocation of human capital due to excess wages paid in the financial sector, as illustrated by figure 6.7. PhDs in mathematics or nuclear physics working on trading floors rather than doing fundamental research are individually rational but create a welfare loss for society. To sum up, the relationship between financial depth and economic well-being may follow an inverted U-curve, implying that there may be an optimal size of the financial sector.[18]

Between 1960 and 2010, both financial markets and financial intermediaries grew much faster than nominal GDP. Between 1995 and 2015, global stock market capitalization doubled as a share of global GDP, while credit to the private sector increased only by one-half (figure 6.6). This raises the legitimate question as to whether the financial sector has become oversized (in other words, whether it has passed the peak of the inverted U-curve), at least in advanced economies.

What does the empirical literature say about the link between finance and growth? In the 1990s, a consensus emerged on the positive causality from financial depth to economic development. King and Levine (1993) found the level of financial development to be strongly associated with *future* real per capita GDP growth, physical capital accumulation, and improvements

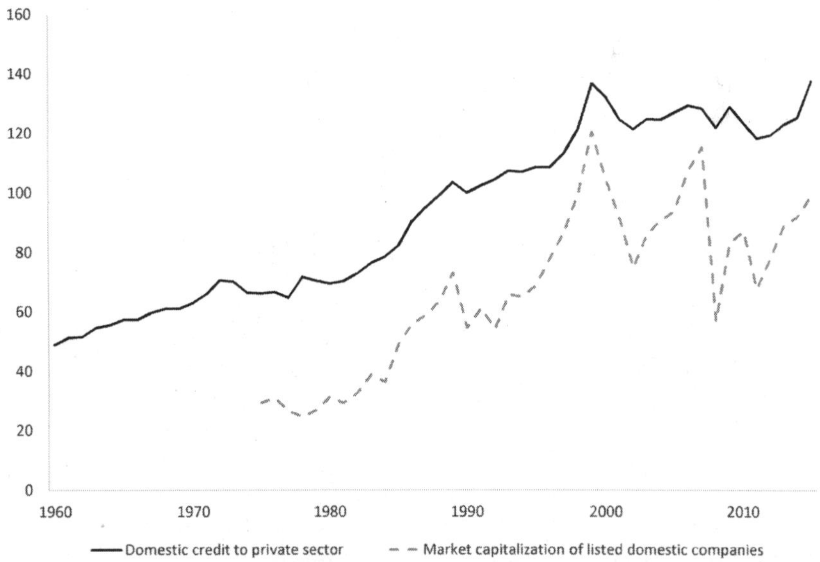

Figure 6.6 The rise of global finance: credit to private sector and market capitalization of listed companies as % of global gross domestic product (GDP), 1960–2015. World Bank, World Development Indicators.

in the efficiency of physical capital. Further studies confirmed the causality (Rousseau and Sylla, 2003).[19] Economists then became more critical. The Asian crisis of the late 1990s, the dot-com bubble of the early 2000s, and the later global financial crisis have exposed the "dark" side of finance and led the economic profession to conclude that the causality may hold in the initial stages of economic development, but not for mature economies (Aghion et al., 2005; Bordo and Rousseau, 2011). Zingales (2015) has noted that economists tend to downplay the rents generated by finance. According to Arcand, Berkes, and Panizza (2012), the marginal effect on growth of extending more credit to the private sector turns negative beyond 110% of GDP, a level reached globally in the early 1990s, as shown by figure 6.6. Likewise, Easterly, Islam, and Stiglitz (2000) found macroeconomic volatility to be higher when credit exceeds 100% of GDP, while at firm level, Cecchetti and Kharoubi (2014) found that an exogenous increase in finance, by disproportionately benefiting high collateral/low productivity projects, reduces total factor productivity growth. Admittedly, these results characterize advanced economies. Emerging and low-income economies are less likely to be on the wrong side of the inverted U-curve.

Finally, a normative question is whether the size of finance is commensurate to its social value. Work by Thomas Philippon and Ariell Reshef on the US financial sector speaks to the opposite. Since the 1990s, finance has poached highly skilled workers out of other industries by paying a substantial premium (as much as 50% more before the global financial crisis for similar education levels; see figure 6.7). High wages in the financial industry have

Figure 6.7 Excess wages in finance in % relative to the non-farm private sector, 1920–2005.
The premium accounts for the skill structure.
Phillippon and Reshef (2012), figure X.B, p. 1591.

accounted for 15–20% of the overall increase in US wage inequality since the 1980s. To put it bluntly, too much talent is allocated to the financial industry. There are too many bankers and too few engineers.[20] At the same time, the unit cost of producing financial services may have increased (Philippon, 2015; Philippon and Reshef, 2012, 2013), questioning the efficiency of the industry.

This section has shown that finance contributes to all three functions of economic policy defined in Chapter 1. First, finance plays an *allocative* role by channeling resources over time and across individuals and economic sectors. A failure to play this role hampers investment in physical and human capital and thus society's ability to lift its standard of living. Second, finance plays a *stabilizing* role by insuring households and firms against economic shocks. A failure to play this role magnifies macroeconomic volatility, as financial crises have shown repeatedly. And third, finance has *distributive* consequences which can be either positive (e.g., when it helps poorer households expand their economic opportunities) or negative (e.g., when inflated financial asset prices make the rich richer). Finance is "a good servant but a bad master" (Brittan, 2011). It provides valuable services to society, but when it has become overextended quantitatively and qualitatively, one can question its allocative, stabilizing, and distributive efficiency.

Policies aimed at developing the financial sector to lift long-term growth and ensure financial inclusion are primarily discussed in Chapter 9. This chapter focuses on prudential policies, which aim at ensuring that incentives of financial sector participants are aligned with public interest and that market failures in the financial system don't create negative externalities for the rest of the economy. These policies can be *microprudential* or *macroprudential*. The former policies are addressed at individuals and financial institutions, considering the rest of the financial system as exogenous (Sections 6.3.1 and 6.3.2). The latter policies are addressed at the financial system as a whole, given common exposures and interconnections (Section 6.3.3). But first, we need to understand better how finance works and the market failures and externalities it faces.

6.2 Theories

Financial theory has been historically fragmented depending on whether it deals with the funding choices of companies (covered by "corporate finance" and by industrial organization) or with the functioning of capital markets ("finance" as an academic discipline) and on whether it takes a microeconomic or a macroeconomic angle (in which case a large part of monetary economics and international macroeconomics is also relevant, see Chapters 5 and 7).

There was a golden era when economists saw the "market for loanable funds" as the place where demand and supply of a single homogenous good, capital, would be cleared by interest rate adjustment. The invisible hand would equalize risk-adjusted returns across financial instruments. Early theories of financial intermediation (Gurley and Shaw, 1960) saw the main role of financial intermediaries as helping both sides meet by providing *risk transformation* services; that is, collecting short-term savings from households and providing long-term funding to companies. Provided that the service was delivered smoothly, macroeconomists could ignore finance altogether—and so they did.

This representation broke down in the 1980s and 1990s. Economists understood that information asymmetry is a source of market failure. Research refocused on *agency problems* between borrowers, lenders, and financial intermediaries; that is, understanding the cost of monitoring borrowers and designing incentive-compatible loan contracts. The same period saw the rise and fall of the *efficient market hypothesis,* according to which all relevant information on a financial asset is conveyed by its market price. This hypothesis has been progressively replaced with a more granular understanding of price formation. More recently, economists have investigated direct and indirect spillovers across the financial system and sought to understand better the nature of systemic risk.

This section starts by exploring the basic functions of finance—financing corporate investment, matching the supply and demand of capital—then focuses on the specific role of banks and the risks they create. We then move to the macroeconomic level and explore the build-up and propagation of systemic risk. Theories of insurance and old-age pensions are not addressed.

6.2.1 Capital structure in the financing of the firm

Firms finance their operations and investment either internally by retaining part or all of their earnings or externally by raising debt or equity. The starting point of corporate finance was the demonstration in 1958 by Franco Modigliani and Merton Miller that, assuming perfect information and frictionless markets, a firm's *capital structure* impacts neither its value nor its average cost of capital (box 6.2). The reason is simple. The market value of the firm is the discounted sum of the stream of future dividends and coupons which share- and bondholders are entitled to receive. Dividends and coupons are paid out of the firm's earnings, which only depend on its assets, not its liabilities. Modigliani and Miller themselves have acknowledged that their *theorem* relies on unrealistic assumptions. It remains a useful benchmark to reflect on capital structures. Fifty years of research on corporate finance have been an exercise in deconstructing the Modigliani-Miller model, relaxing its key assumptions one after another.[21]

The absence of taxes is clearly a strong assumption. In all countries, interest payments are at least partially deductible from the corporate income tax base, which creates a bias toward debt (Langedijk et al., 2015).[22] A further complication arises from the fact that tax rates are different on retained earnings, capital gains, and dividends, which creates a pecking order among these different funding sources.

Box 6.2 The Modigliani-Miller Theorem (1958)

Consider a firm with assets A, producing at each period a cash-flow ρ^A. It can finance its assets either by issuing debt (bonds or loans with value D, serving a fixed risk-free rate i) or equity (stocks with value E, serving a variable rate r^E). The firm's balance sheet is shown in table B6.1.

Table B6.1
A Firm's Simplified Balance Sheet

Assets	Liabilities
Loans and financial assets A	Debt D
	Equity E

The value of the firm's assets A is equal to the value of liabilities which funded them:

$$A = E + D \tag{B.6.2.1}$$

In this simplified setup, financing investment out of retained earnings is equivalent to raising equity. How does the liability structure of the firm (i.e., the mix of D and E) influence its market value and the average cost of capital? Not at all, according to F. Modigliani and M. Miller in their 1958 paper.

Shareholders ask for a premium to compensate for the higher variability of dividend payments, while debt is assumed to be riskless (it is assumed that the firm does not default). The return on equity r^E is thus higher than the return on debt i. One could expect the firm to lose market value when D/E goes up, but it is in fact not the case. To understand why, consider two firms with the same assets A and different capital structures. Firm 1 has no debt ($E_1 = A$), while firm 2 has debt D and equity $E_2 = A - D$. An equity investor endowed with A can either buy firm 1 and claim all future cash flows, ρ^A, on its assets, or buy firm 2, claim what remains of ρ^A after payment of the interests on the debt, and use the remaining money $A - E_2$ to invest in the risk-free asset. Both strategies yield identical cash flows, since $(\rho A - iD_2) + i(A - E_2) = \rho A$. This assumes that investors freely access the market for risk-free debt.

The total return on the firm's assets, ρ, is also the *weighted average cost of capital*:

$$\rho = \frac{E}{A} r^E + \frac{D}{A} i \tag{B6.2.2}$$

Hence our first result: *the weighted average cost of capital does not depend on the capital structure*. This follows from the fact that the cash flow

ρ^A generated at each period by the firm depends only on its assets before being distributed as dividend or as coupon. And now a second result: *the return on equity increases with the debt-to-equity ratio.*

$$r^E = \rho + (\rho - i)\frac{D}{E} \qquad \text{(B6.2.3)}$$

These two results apply to any firm, financial or nonfinancial. In particular, if the theorem's conditions were met, requiring banks to hold more capital should not impact their average cost of financing and thus should not make their loans costlier (see Section 6.2.2 for a discussion).

There are important conditions for the results to hold, which Modigliani and Miller acknowledged. First, there is no transaction cost to raising equity or debt. Second, creditors, shareholders, and firm managers have access to the same information on the firm's future cash flows. Third, there are no taxes. Fourth, investors have access to the same risk-free capital market as the firm does. Fifth, the financing structure does not impact the distribution of cash flows, which assumes in particular that the firm never defaults. Each of these assumptions can be disputed.

Another key assumption is the absence of corporate default. It was relaxed by Robert Merton in his celebrated 1974 article on the valuation of corporate debt which links the value of a firm's debt to its risk of default (box 6.3). Merton paved the way to evaluating complex financial instruments with default risk and to modeling the interest rate differential between risky and riskless debt, the *credit spread.*

The most crucial of all Modigliani-Miller assumptions is perfect information. The equivalence result assumes that creditors, shareholders, and firm managers have access to the same information on the firm's future cash flows. In the real world, firm managers have inside information on the firm's prospects and strategy which bankers and investors do not have, creating a risk that they don't act in the best interest of the latter.[23] A vast literature has studied the *principal–agent relationship* between shareholders and creditors on the one hand and firm managers on the other hand, both from a positive and from a normative perspective.

A first strand of literature has focused on *agency costs*, defined as the cost of monitoring firm managers to make sure that they don't divest money from the purposes agreed by the firm's owners (Jensen and Meckling, 1976). Another strand of literature has used the paradigm of the Spence signaling model (1974) and focused on the signal sent to investors by the firm's financing choices (Myers and Majluf, 1984). Issuing equity dilutes existing shareholders and depresses the price of the firm's stocks, unless it is justified by higher future profits. If equity investors don't have access to information on the firm's prospects, they will see debt as a better option.[24] This produces the *pecking*

Box 6.3 Default Risk and the Value of Debt (Merton, 1974)

Valuing a fixed income instrument such as a fixed-interest rate bond or a loan does not require modeling a sequence of variable cash flows, as would be needed for a stock. However, one needs to pass a judgment on the risk of default: whether the principal will be fully redeemed when the instrument matures.

Consider a firm issuing at date $t = 0$ an amount of debt D with tenor T. Let x_t be the value of the firm's assets at any date t. The firm defaults on its debt at date T if x_T is not enough to pay back D. Creditors are more senior than shareholders and will seize the residual value of the firm's assets up to D. Summing up, the payoffs V_T^D and V_T^E for the creditors and shareholders are given by the following nonlinear formulas, also explained in table B6.3.1:

$$V_T^D = min\left(D, x_T\right) \quad \text{and} \quad V_T^E = min\left(0, x_T - D\right) \qquad \text{(B6.3.1)}$$

Table B6.3.1
Final Payoffs as a Function of the Value of the Firm's Assets

Asset value	Creditor payoff V_T^D	Shareholder payoff V_T^E
$x_T < D$	x_T	0
$x_T > D$	D	$x_T - D$

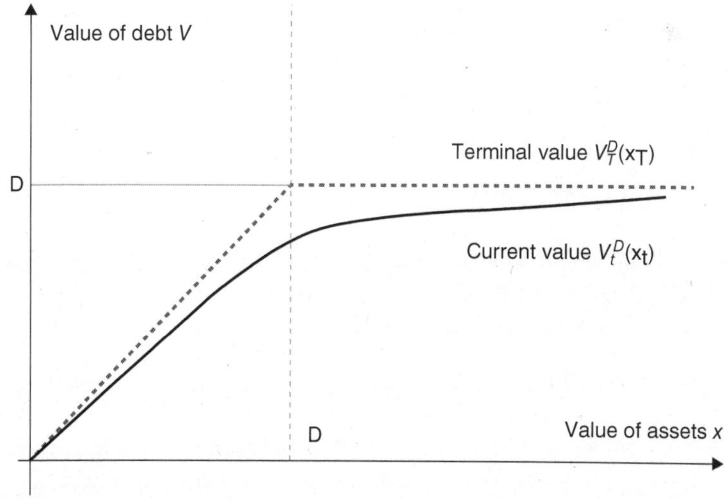

Figure B6.3.1 The value of a firm's debt as a function of the value of its assets.

Equation (B6.3.1) describes options on the value of the firm's assets. In financial parlance, shareholders hold a *call option* on the assets with strike price D (i.e., an option to buy the assets if the price is higher than D), and creditors hold a *put option* (i.e., an option to sell the assets) with the same strike price D. If the stochastic process governing x_t over time has a constant mean and finite variance per unit of time, then the value of the two options can be computed at any time $0 \leq t \leq T$ as a function of x_t using an option valuation formula such as the one found by Black and Scholes in 1973, just before Merton's article was published.

Figure B6.3.1 shows the value of debt as a function of the value of assets, both at the terminal date T (dotted line) and at an earlier date t (plain line). As the value of the assets goes down (moving from the right to the left of the figure), it becomes increasing likely that debt will not be paid back, and its value increasingly departs from D.

The *credit spread*, defined as the difference between the yield on risky debt and the yield on risk-free debt, is the value of the put option. It increases with the maturity of debt and with the riskiness of the firm, defined as the variance of the return on its assets. The empirical performance of structural default models *à la* Merton has been disappointing. Actual corporate credit spreads are wider than implied by the model.[60] The insight, however, remains. The model was improved by Leland (1994) to account for bankruptcy cost and corporate taxes.

order approach to corporate financing: in the presence of information asymmetry, firms will first resort to internal finance, then raise short-term debt, then long-term debt, and, only in last resort, equity.[25]

6.2.2 Capital markets

Capital markets are where financial assets are underwritten and traded. These include stocks, bonds, loans (insofar as the initial contract allows them to be transferred by the lender to another market participant), foreign exchange, and any derivative instrument built on those.

The social role of capital markets is to match the supply and demand for capital. Their effectiveness in doing so crucially depends on their ability to produce prices which reveal the right information about the future stream of cash flows accruing to any asset. A vast literature has developed on efficient asset pricing, first for a single asset, then for portfolios, with the latter capturing the benefits of diversification. The literature then focused on information asymmetry and its impact on price formation under various assumptions on market microstructure.

a) Asset valuation and the efficient market hypothesis

The simplest possible asset pricing model, under rational expectations and a Von Neumann-Morgenstern expected utility paradigm (Chapter 1), is the *discounted cash flow* or present-value method. Consider a risk-neutral investor indifferent between holding a financial asset and investing in a riskless asset. A possible price of the financial asset is the expected value of the cash flows it generates, discounted with the risk-free yield—say, in the case of a stock, the expected discounted value of its future dividends. This is the *fundamental value* of the asset. In case the risk-free interest rate r is constant and cash flows grow at a constant rate g over time, this yields a very simple formula: the asset price today is equal to today's cash flow divided by $r - g$ (Equation (B6.4.6) in box 6.4). Applied to stocks, this is known as the *Gordon-Shapiro formula* or the *Gordon growth model*. If the investor is averse to risk, the formula can be modified using a risk-adjusted discount rate.

Box 6.4 A Basic Model of Financial Asset Pricing and Rational Bubbles

Consider a risk-neutral investor with rational expectations (see Chapter 1) who chooses at the start of period t between investing in a financial asset (say, a company's stock) with stochastic price p_{t+s} at the beginning of each period $t+s$ in the future, and a riskless asset (say, a Treasury bill) yielding a deterministic rate of return r_{t+s}. The stock generates a dividend d_{t+s} distributed at the end of period $t+s$. E_t denotes the mathematical expectation of any variable conditional to information available to the investor at the beginning of period t.

At the beginning of each period $t+s$, the investor is indifferent between investing in the risk-free asset and holding the stock. The latter choice gives her the right, at the end of the period, to receive a dividend and, if she so wishes, to sell the stock with a (positive or negative) capital gain:

$$\left(1+r_{t+s}\right)p_{t+s} = E_{t+s}\left(d_{t+s} + p_{t+s+1}\right) \qquad \text{(B6.4.1)}$$

Assume that:

$$\lim_{s\to\infty}\prod_{k=0}^{s}\left(1+r_{t+k}\right)^{-1} = 0 \qquad \text{(B6.4.2)}$$

The simplest solution to Equation (B6.4.1) identifies the stock price with the present value of future dividends:

$$\hat{p}_t = E_t\sum_{s=0}^{\infty}\left[\prod_{k=0}^{s}\left(1+r_{t+k}\right)^{-1}\right]d_{t+s} \qquad \text{(B6.4.3)}$$

The stock price goes up when future dividends are expected to increase, all the more so as the increase is persistent, and when future discount rates decrease. In the special case where r is constant over time, the solution becomes:

$$\hat{p}_t = E_t \sum_{s=0}^{\infty} (1+r)^{-(s+1)} d_{t+s} \quad \text{(B6.4.4)}$$

Assume now that dividends grow at a constant rate $g < r$ over time:

$$d_{t+s} = (1+g)^s d_t \quad \text{(B6.4.5)}$$

The solution becomes the Gordon formula:

$$\hat{p}_t = \frac{1}{1+r} E_t \sum_{s=0}^{\infty} \left(\frac{1+g}{1+r} \right)^s d_t = \frac{1}{r-g} d_t \quad \text{(B.6.4.6)}$$

$\hat{p}_t$ is the discounted cash-flow, or fundamental value of the stock, but it is not the only possible value. To understand why, let's come back to the short-term relation in Equation (B6.4.1). Any price taking the following form is also a solution of Equation (B6.4.1):

$$\bar{p}_t = \hat{p}_t + b_t \quad \text{(B6.4.7)}$$

provided that b_t satisfies for all $s \geq 0$:

$$(1+r_{t+s}) b_{t+s} = E_{t+s} b_{t+s+1} \quad \text{(B6.4.8)}$$

For example, if r is constant over time, it is enough that b_t grows at a constant rate r:

$$\bar{p}_t = \hat{p}_t + b_0 (1+r)^t \quad \text{(B6.4.9)}$$

where b_0 is constant.

To sum up, the stock price is the sum of a *fundamental value* which depends only on the future stream of dividends and of a *speculative* (or *bubble*) *component* which does not depend on dividends but only on the expectation of future capital gains. The bubble component is fully consistent with rational expectations. Expectations about b_0 can change, and, depending on the mood of investors, the stock price can reverse at any time to its fundamental value or, for that matter, to any other speculative path based on another value of b_0. If the dividend stream cannot be easily expected, investors can confuse the two components. This makes the price vulnerable to shifts in investors' beliefs and requires a learning process.

Discounted cash flows do not yield the only possible price. Even if the fundamental value is known, the same assumptions yield an infinite number of prices, each equal to the discounted cash flows plus a *rational bubble* motivated by the sole perspective of capital gains, which is expected to grow in line with the risk-free interest rate (box 6.4). When the fundamental value is unknown, investors can confuse the two components and believe, for instance, that a higher stock price reflects higher future dividends when it only reflects speculation.

The *efficient market hypothesis* was introduced by Chicago economist Eugene Fama. It is customary to distinguish among three forms of market efficiency depending on which information is incorporated into prices. *Strong efficiency* assumes that prices capture all information available anywhere in the economy, including privately; *semi-strong efficiency* assumes that they capture all publicly available information; and *weak efficiency* assumes that they only capture information on past prices and returns.

Weak efficient market hypothesis implies that one cannot make a profit by forecasting future prices based on their past behaviors, implying that so-called technical analysis based on past regularities (such as stock prices or exchange rates remaining in a given corridor or following known patterns) has no predictive power because all existing information is fully used by traders, which makes *current* prices incorporate all information concerning the future.[26] This assumption is often associated with stock prices following a *random walk*; that is, a sum of serially independent random variables drawn out of a known probability distribution with constant variance and no "memory" (meaning that future movements are independent from past movements).[27] This model dates back to Louis Bachelier's thesis at the Sorbonne in Paris on the behavior of stock prices (Bachelier, 1900). One way to understand why is to see that the price change between today and tomorrow only reflects new information, independent from the price today. The random walk hypothesis has simple implications for the variance of stock returns at a given horizon, which makes it easy to test empirically (box 6.5).

As for the strong efficient market hypothesis, it implies that no trading strategy, whichever information it is based on, can beat the market. If it would hold, then "a blindfolded chimpanzee throwing darts at the *Wall Street Journal* could select a portfolio that would do as well as the experts" (Malkiel, 2003).

Empirical studies have generally rejected the efficient market hypothesis. Critics such as Robert Shiller (2000) have noted that stock prices are too volatile to be generated by rational behavior and that they exhibit *mean reversion* (meaning that stocks with lower price multiples produce higher returns or that successions of price increases relative to a trend are followed by decreases; see Poterba and Summers, 1988) which makes them partially predictable, violating the efficient market hypothesis. Behavioral explanations include investors using rules of thumb rather than attempting at forecasting and discounting future cash flows and overreacting to good or to bad news. These explanations relate more generally to Keynes's famous remark on *animal spirits* (see Chapter 1, p. 25).

On the other hand, empirical studies have found limited scope for profitable trading strategies based on regularities in returns (Malkiel, 2003).

Box 6.5 Testing Market Efficiency

Assume that the time series p_t describing a stock price is a random walk with a deterministic trend μ per unit of time:

$$p_{t+1} = p_t + \mu + \varepsilon_{t+1} \tag{B6.5.1}$$

ε_t is a normally distributed innovation with mean 0 and variance σ^2, uncorrelated over time. N periods ahead, one can write:

$$\mathrm{Var}(p_{t+N} - p_t) = \mathrm{Var}\left(N\mu + \sum_{i=1}^{N} \varepsilon_{t+i}\right) = N\sigma^2 \tag{B6.5.2}$$

$$\frac{1}{N}\frac{\mathrm{Var}(p_{t+N} - p_t)}{\mathrm{Var}(p_{t+1} - p_t)} = 1 \tag{B6.5.3}$$

For example, if a stock price follows a random walk, then the variance of its annual change should be equal to 52 times the variance of its weekly change. If the *variance ratio* of Equation (B6.5.3) is less than one, one says that the stock price is *mean reverting*. If it is larger than one, then the stock price is said to be persistent. Using a version of this test, Lo and MacKinlay (1988) have found US stock prices to be persistent, and they have therefore rejected the random walk hypothesis at different horizons.

Moreover, proponents of the efficient market hypothesis have objected that empirical tests rely on a pricing model; that is, on assumptions on how prices relate to fundamental news about the underlying assets. It may well be the pricing model rather than the efficient market hypothesis itself which is wrong. Investors may have been reacting rationally to changes in asset future cash flows or riskiness that are just not captured by the model.

The debate on the efficient market hypothesis has technical ramifications but it has often been a sideshow for principled (and largely ideological) disagreements on the efficiency of free markets. It bears important regulatory consequences. If markets are efficient, why regulate them? Eugene Fama and Robert Shiller have taken opposite sides in this discussion, and, ironically, they were awarded the Nobel prize together in 2013 (along with econometrician Lars Peter Hansen).

b) Portfolio diversification

One important service provided by financial intermediaries is to diversify risk, which helps consumer and firms insure against shocks to their income. A vast literature has studied the composition of investment portfolios depending on the risk and return of individual securities, following seminal work developed in the early 1950s by Harry Markowitz. The basic approach, the *capital asset pricing model* (CAPM), is explained in box 6.6. It has been generalized as the *arbitrage pricing theory* (APT) (Ross, 1976). These models form the basis of the pricing approaches used by market participants, such as asset managers who invest their clients' long-term savings and pensions.

c) Information asymmetry on financial markets

The strong or semi-strong efficient market hypothesis assumes that private information is fully revealed by prices. It implies that no profitable trading strategy can yield more than the market. This is totally at odds with the existence of a large and active investment industry, drawing on economic

Box 6.6 Portfolio Selection

In the model of box 6.4, every asset is valued individually as a function of its expected cash flows. In portfolio choice models, asset prices are set jointly as a function of the return and risk of all assets. Diversifying risk allows one to maximize the return–risk ratio of a portfolio by exploiting the imperfect correlation between assets. The main assumptions are the following: investors are small enough to be price-takers, they all have the same investment horizon, they care about the mean and standard error of the return on their portfolio, they can borrow and lend without restriction in the same riskless asset, and there is no transaction cost.

The model has two periods. In the first period, an investor invests her wealth W in a market made of N stocks, each of which yields a return R_i, meaning that investing W_i in stock i yields $R_i W_i$ in period 2, with $W = \sum_{i=1}^{N} W_i$. The value of R_i in period 2 is stochastic, and the investor knows its probability distribution. Let $R = {}^t(R_1, \dots R_N)$, where ${}^tX$ is the transposed vector of X. An investment portfolio is a vector $w = {}^t(w_1, \dots w_N)$, with $w_i = W_i / W$ being asset i's share in total wealth W. The total return, on the portfolio w is:

$$R(w) = {}^tRw = \sum_{i=1}^{N} R_i w_i \tag{B6.6.1}$$

The expectation and variance of the portfolio's return are $E[R(w)] = {}^t\bar{R}w$ and $\text{Var}[R(w)] = {}^tw\Omega w$, with $\bar{R}$ and Ω being the mean and covariance matrix of the random vector R. Let us now assume that the investor is risk adverse and minimizes the following quadratic loss function:

$$\min_w \frac{1}{2}\text{Var}[R(w)] - \gamma E[R(w)] \tag{B6.6.2}$$

under the condition: ${}^{t}ew = 1$ with $e = {}^{t}(1,\ldots 1)$. $\gamma > 0$ is inversely related to the investor's risk aversion (see Chapter 1). Assuming that the covariance matrix Ω is invertible, an *efficient portfolio* solves this quadratic program. One can show that the solution $w(\gamma)$ takes the following form:

$$w(\gamma) = (1 - \alpha(\gamma))w_{min} + \alpha(\gamma)w_M \qquad \text{(B6.6.3)}$$

$$\text{with: } \alpha(\gamma) = \gamma\, {}^{t}\bar{R}\Omega^{-1}e, \quad w_{min} = \frac{\Omega^{-1}e}{{}^{t}e\Omega^{-1}e} \text{ and } w_M = \frac{\Omega^{-1}\bar{R}}{{}^{t}e\Omega^{-1}\bar{R}}$$

The investor invests in a combination of two portfolios only, weighted according to her risk aversion γ. w_M is the *market portfolio* and w_{min} is the minimum variance portfolio which the investor picks if she is very risk-adverse. This is Tobin's "two-fund" or "separation" theorem.

Figure B6.6.1 plots the expected return $r(\gamma) = {}^{t}\bar{R}w(\gamma)$ and standard error $\sigma(\gamma) = \sqrt{{}^{t}w(\gamma)\bar{\Omega}w(\gamma)}$) of the portfolio's return when γ moves from 0 to $+\infty$. This hyperbole is called the *efficient frontier*. It describes the combinations of the N stocks maximizing return and minimizing risk in the sense of Equation (B6.6.2). When risk aversion decreases, one travels along the efficient frontier toward the north-east of the figure, where portfolios are riskier and deliver a higher return.

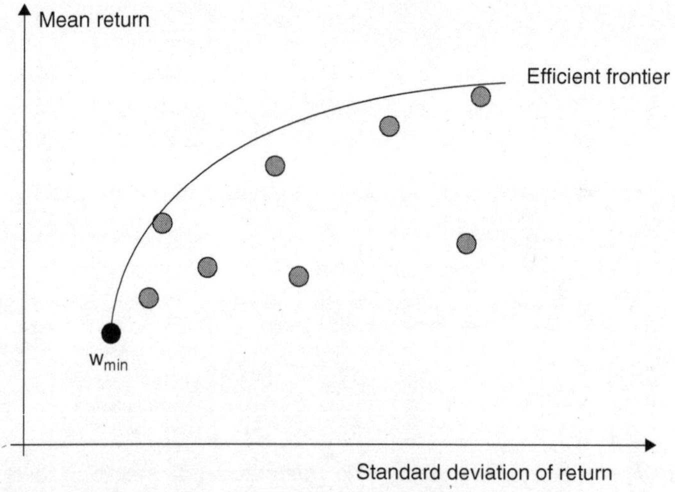

Figure B6.6.1 The efficient frontier with risky assets only.

Let us now add a riskless asset with known return r_f. An investment portfolio is now a vector with $N + 1$ weights ${}^{t}(w_0, {}^{t}w)$, where w_0 is the weight on the riskless asset (which can be negative in case the investor sells the riskless asset to finance a risky portfolio). One can show that the two-fund solution Equation (B6.6.3) becomes:

$$\begin{pmatrix} w_0 \\ w \end{pmatrix} = (1-\beta(\gamma))w_f + \beta(\gamma)w_M \qquad \text{(B6.6.4)}$$

$$\text{with:} \quad w_f = \begin{pmatrix} 1 \\ 0 \end{pmatrix} w_M = \begin{pmatrix} 1 - {}^t e\Omega^{-1}\left(\bar{R} - r_f e\right) \\ \Omega^{-1}\left(\bar{R} - r_f e\right) \end{pmatrix}$$

$\beta(\gamma)$, which is not detailed here, depends on risk aversion and on the assets covariance matrices. Any efficient portfolio is a linear combination of the riskless asset and the market portfolio, as shown by figure B6.6.2. The weights depend on the investor's risk aversion. The set of all efficient portfolios is called the "securities market line." It is tangent to the efficient frontier at point w_M.

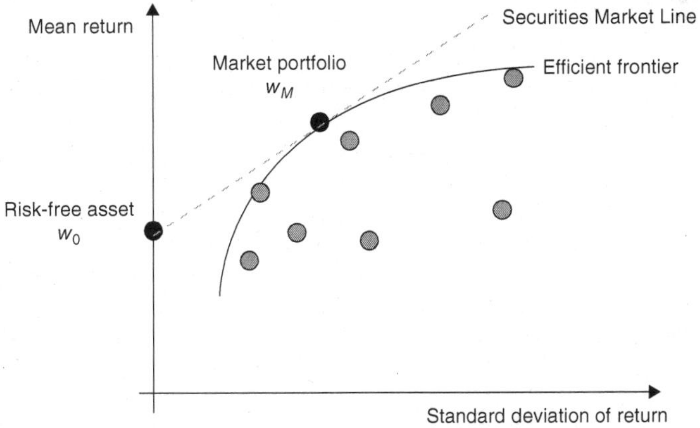

Figure B6.6.2 The efficient frontier and the securities market line with a riskless asset.

Let (r_M, σ_M) be the expected return and risk of the market portfolio. We have:

$$\forall \gamma \geq 0, r(\gamma) = r_f + \frac{(r_M - r_f)}{\sigma_M}\sigma(\gamma) \qquad \text{(B6.6.5)}$$

Along the securities market line, the excess return of an efficient portfolio (defined as the difference between its return and the riskless interest rate) depends on its risk level in a linear way. The slope of the securities market line is called the *price of risk*. Finally, if one considers an asset i $\in$\{1..N\}

located "below" the efficient frontier, if $w_i = {}^t(0\ldots1\ldots0)$ is the portfolio with asset i only, if R_i is the return on asset i, and if $\sigma_{iM} = {}^t w_i \Omega w_M$ is its covariance with the market portfolio, then one can show the following:

$$R_i = r_f + \beta_i\left(r_M - r_f\right) \quad \text{with} \quad \beta_i = \sigma_{iM} / \sigma_M^2 \qquad \text{(B6.6.6)}$$

Equation (B6.6.6) summarizes the *capital asset pricing model* (CAPM). The excess return on an asset depends on the elasticity of its return to fluctuations in the market return, as measured by coefficient beta. Beta being higher than 1 means that the asset's risk and return are higher than the market. An asset's beta can be negative, meaning that it provides a hedge against market fluctuation, and, accordingly, its return can be lower than the riskless interest rate.

and technical analysis, and designing and distributing investment products to retail and institutional investors. Just like corporate finance, finance itself embarked in a revolution in the 1980s when the consequences of asymmetric information were fully understood and integrated in models of price determination.

Rational expectation equilibrium models of price formation assume that rational market participants buy and sell based on whichever (possibly partial) information is available to them on the future cash flows of assets and on the observation of publicly available market prices. Such models rely on assumptions on the motivations of different market participants: Are they proprietary traders buying and selling securities to maximize profit, or are they financing and hedging underlying commercial transactions? They also rely on assumptions on how information on fundamentals is acquired, freely or at a cost. These assumptions jointly describe *market microstructure.*

An important result of this literature is a paradox uncovered in 1980 by Sanford Grossmann and Joseph Stiglitz. Because acquiring information is costly, if prices reflect all available information as assumed by the efficient market hypothesis, then there is no incentive to acquire it; but, in this case, the market price cannot reveal existing information.

> The degree of market inefficiency determines the effort investors are willing to expand to gather and trade on information, hence a non-degenerate market equilibrium will arise only when there are sufficient profit opportunities, i.e., inefficiencies, to compensate investors for the costs of trading and information-gathering. The profits earned by these industrious investors may be viewed as economic rents that accrue to those willing to engage in such activities. (Lo and McKinlay, 1999, pp. 5–6)

An important lesson of this literature is that information disclosure is not only about protecting investors but also about ensuring a good functioning of the market. Models of market microstructure have been used to inform the policy discussion on information disclosure in markets and on market organization, including the choice between decentralized, *over-the-counter (OTC)* markets and centralization of buy and sell orders on an order book.[28] Just as any markets, capital markets need strong legal frameworks to deliver economic benefits.

Models of market microstructure also shed light on events with dire macroeconomic consequences: market crashes. Markets often crash without a clear triggering event. This was famously the case on "Black Monday," October 19, 1987, when the Dow Jones Industrial Average (DJIA) fell by 22.6%, and on most recent occasions such as the "flash crashes" of May 6, 2010, on the US stock market (with the DJIA falling by more than 5% within minutes) and of October 15, 2014, on the US Treasury market.[29] Economists are never short of explanations after the fact, but these may be conflicting. Markus Brunnermeier from Princeton University has grouped the relevant models into four categories[30]:

1. *Bursting bubble models*: A rational bubble develops with investors buying stocks based on the sole expectation of higher future prices, then collapses (see the model developed in box 6.7). This doesn't require any change in fundamentals;
2. *Liquidity shortage models*: The market stops clearing after an unexpected drop in prices which may or may not be driven by fundamental news. This assumes that investors have not built sufficient buffers in good times to absorb losses in bad times and that they are constrained in their ability to buy or retain assets when their prices are low;
3. *Multiple-equilibria and sunspot models*: Information on fundamentals is incomplete and investors coordinate their expectations on an arbitrary price. An exogenous event can trigger a switch to the low-price equilibrium if investors believe, even mistakenly, that this event conveys information on the true price;
4. *"Lumpy" information aggregation models*: Information is incomplete and the disclosure of a new piece of information prompts a reassessment by investors of the fundamental value. If information is revealed in a sequential way, one speaks of "informational cascades" or "informational avalanches." For instance, one single trader selling a stock or a government bond may prompt others to conclude that the prospects of the company or the country are weaker than previously thought and to start selling as well.

6.2.3 Why banks are special, and why they should be regulated

Well-designed financial intermediation can help address the agency problems identified in Section 6.2.1, but every financial structure raises its own issues and calls for different regulatory answers. Here we focus on deposit-taking financial institutions, also called *commercial banks*, in contrast to *investment banks* which do not collect deposits.[31]

The value of banks as financial intermediaries comes primarily from their ability to provide *liquidity, monitoring*, and *maturity-transformation services.*[32]

- On the *asset* side of their balance sheets, banks identify investment and consumption projects, extend medium- to long-term loans, and build long-time relationships with borrowers, enabling them to monitor projects over their lifetime. *Delegated monitoring* by banks on behalf of savers (Diamond, 1984, 1996) reduces information asymmetry and lowers agency costs. The Japanese "main bank" system was long given as an example of such stable relationships until it was liberalized in the end-1980s.[33] Small German banks still pride themselves with playing such a role. This system does not favor transparency or competition but is not without merits: compared to an entirely decentralized structure, pooling a large number of loans on a single balance sheet enables banks to diversify risk and generate economies of scale.
- On the *liability* side, banks provide a liquidity service by pooling a large number of deposits, which enables them to insure depositors against idiosyncratic liquidity shocks.
- Using both sides of their balance sheets, banks perform *maturity transformation* by converting liquid short-term household savings into less liquid long-term loans, an activity which is crucial to finance corporate and durable good investments and which would not happen if households would lend directly to companies.

Irrespective of their social benefits, these activities expose banks to three types of risks: misaligned incentives, adverse selection, and liquidity mismatch.

a) Misaligned incentives

Bankers act as brokers between savers and borrowers, but their interests are not necessarily aligned. Performance-based compensation structures and the possibility to divert free cash flow toward projects chosen by bank managers can lead to excessive risk-taking. This risk of course exists in any company, but it is magnified in banks by a truly extraordinary amount of leverage. In 2009, banks' median *leverage ratio* (i.e., the ratio of assets to equity) was around 10 in the United States and 15 in Europe, against 2.4 and 4.5 for nonfinancial firms (Kalemli-Ozcan, Sorensen, and Yesiltas, 2012). In other words, for every dollar or euro invested by their shareholders, banks borrowed 9 dollars or 14 euros on financial markets. The ratio was even larger for large investment banks; close to 40 for Barclays and around 50 for Deutsche Bank and UBS in 2007. In box 6.7, simple math shows that equally risky assets generate larger returns for equity holders when a bank is more leveraged in normal times but also larger losses in times of crisis. If a bank is leveraged 40 times, as Barclays was in 2007, a 2.5% decrease in the value of its assets wipes out is entire equity.

The structure of a bank's liabilities has consequences for the incentives of its depositors, creditors, and shareholders and therefore for its risk

Box 6.7 Leverage, Return on Equity, and Capital Losses

We use the same notations as in box 6.2. A bank holds assets (loans and securities) A financed by equity E yielding a return on equity r^E and debt D yielding a risk-free nominal interest rate i, with $A = E + D$. Let $\delta = D / E$ be the debt-to-equity ratio. Note that the leverage ratio in the regulatory sense (see Section 6.3) is $E / A = 1/(1+\delta)$. Let ρ be the return on the bank's assets, equal to its weighted average cost of capital:

$$\rho = \frac{E}{A} r^E + \frac{D}{A} i \tag{B6.7.1}$$

As in Equation (B6.2.3) previously, the return on equity of the bank increases with its leverage:

$$r^E = \rho + \delta(\rho - i)$$

For example, if i = 2% and ρ = 3% on an annual basis, and if the bank leverages 15 times its equity (as the median European bank did in 2009), then r^E = 18% annually. If equity is leveraged 40 times (as in Barclays in 2007), then r^E = 43% annually.

Leverage boosts the return on equity, but it magnifies possible losses for equity holders. Assume that the bank incurs a negative return of z% on its assets ($dA/A = -z$) due to an impairment of its loan portfolio or a markdown of the market value of the securities it holds. Assume that debt D is held constant. Keeping in mind that $E = A - D$ and that $A/E = 1 + \delta$, the impact on equity E is:

$$\frac{dE}{E} = \frac{A}{E}\frac{\partial E}{\partial A}\frac{dA}{A} = -(1+\delta)z \tag{B6.7.3}$$

Under the previous assumptions on i and ρ, if the bank's assets register a loss of z = 2% in a given year, equity will be depleted by 32% if it is leveraged 15 times and by 82% if it is leveraged 40 times. In the former case, a 6.25% loss on assets is enough to wipe out the entire equity since 16 × 6.5% > 100%). In the latter case, a 2.5% loss is enough.

profile. This is because different liabilities have different *seniority* when the bank needs to absorb losses. By law, losses are first borne by shareholders, then by the holders of *junior debt* (typically, debt convertible into equity), and finally by holders of senior debt and depositors (beyond levels insured by deposit guarantee schemes). At any point down this waterfall, the government can step in and inject capital in the bank, for instance, in cases when exposing creditors to losses would create broader financial stability risks.

Both shareholders and bondholders exert control on the bank: bank executives are appointed by the former, who vote in shareholder meetings, and the latter can "vote with their feet" by selling their bonds. In contrast, depositors have no interest nor ability to monitor and control large and complex institutions. The impossibility to write down a complete contract between the bank's owners/creditors and managers is the basic reason why the Modigliani and Miller theorem does not apply to banks. The financial structure of a bank and particularly its level of equity do matter (Dewatripont and Tirole, 1994). By the same token, this also justifies regulatory intervention on the capital structure; for example, by imposing capital and liquidity requirements (which will be discussed in Section 6.3).

Shareholders are in the frontline to absorb losses and thus have an incentive to monitor risks taken by the bank—up to a point. They are in fact protected insofar as the government can always step in and bail them out. Moreover, under the limited liability principle, their losses cannot exceed their investment (i.e., equity). This protection can lead shareholders to take excessive risks with adverse consequences for depositors, for other banks (if the bank has borrowed from them and if client deposits are guaranteed by an industry-wide scheme), and for taxpayers (if the government finally steps in). Negative externalities extend to the economy at large if the bank stops lending to households and companies.

The best way to internalize these negative externalities while avoiding direct state intervention is capital regulation. This consists in constraining the capital structure of the bank and forcing it to hold a sufficiently large buffer of liabilities that can be written off when the bank faces large losses. In addition, *bail-in* rules can force creditors to be part of the resolution, thereby protecting depositors and taxpayers (see box 6.13), in contrast with *bail-out,* which consists in tapping outside sources (especially taxpayers) to keep a bank alive.

There always remains a residual risk that depositors are hit. Such risk materialized in March 2013 in Cyprus, when nearly half of uninsured deposits of the country's largest bank, Bank of Cyprus, were converted into equity. The risk is controlled by the existence of *deposit insurance* (or *deposit guarantee*), at least up to a certain amount (deposits are insured up to 100,000 euros in European countries and 200,000 dollars in the US) and assuming that the insurance scheme is funded by the industry (without which taxpayers remain on the hook). Deposit insurance is also motivated by the risk of self-fulfilling liquidity crises, an issue addressed further later.

To sum up, banks are monitored by a diverse group of stakeholders: shareholders, creditors, and the *prudential supervisor* acting on behalf of depositors and taxpayers. A more radical way to protect depositors and shareholders would be to force a separation between commercial and investment banks. We'll come back to this proposal in Section 6.3.

One remaining question is how to align the incentives of bank managers and staff with the interest of shareholders. Performance-based compensation of staff (e.g., bonuses tied to the bank's earnings or stock price, and distributed as bank shares) has long been considered the best answer. The global financial crisis has shown, however, that such compensation practices also create perverse incentives, such as structuring financial products so as to frontload the gains and backload the losses, and lack of recognition of possible future losses.

b) Adverse selection

A bartender can refuse to sell alcohol to drunken clients, but producers of goods and services seldom refuse to sell their products (in fact, this would often be illegal discrimination). Banks are, on the other hand, often accused of not lending to potential borrowers even if they would be willing to pay a high interest rate. *Credit rationing* may seem a theoretical enigma.

Since George Akerlof's celebrated article on "The Market for Lemons," published in 1970, economists have understood that markets can stop clearing in the presence of asymmetric information. J. Stiglitz and A. Weiss applied this insight to the credit market, where information is clearly asymmetric (Stiglitz and Weiss, 1981; see box 5.11 of Chapter 5). Absent information on the quality of borrowers, a bank will apply the same interest rate to all and add a risk premium to recoup losses on projects that will default. But a high interest rate exceeds the intrinsic return on many good projects and crowds them out of the market. Only risky borrowers will pay that premium. The bank is not fooled and does not finance them.[34]

To avoid such situations, banks structure their credit supply to have borrowers reveal their risk. They can ask borrowers to post collateral (for instance, housing loans are secured by the value of the house and possibly by other assets as well) and adjust the interest rate to the value of the collateral and the level of risk of each borrower, measured in the case of a company or a government by its credit rating. Adverse selection can also be mitigated by government intervention. Laws can force borrowers to disclose information on their balance sheet and projects.[35] Governments can support higher risk projects by issuing guarantees, which lowers the risk for the bank.[36]

c) Liquidity mismatch in banks

One of the raison d'être of banks is to provide liquidity services by pooling and managing households' sight deposits. This crucial social function of banks makes them vulnerable. Households can withdraw their deposits at any time, threatening continuity of operation. Banks can, of course, borrow from capital markets as a "spare tire," but we'll see in the next section that short-term market borrowing is also prone to liquidity crises.

An example borrowed from Jean Tirole helps explain what is at stake (see Holmström and Tirole, 2011, for a full discussion). An entrepreneur projects a 10 million dollar investment yielding a 30 million revenue. She obtains 8 million dollars of equity from a business angel and a 2 million loan from a banker. There are three periods. In period 1, she launches the project using the initial 8 + 2 million. In period 2, there is a 50% chance that costs slip by 20 million. If the entrepreneur cannot cover the cost, the project fails and all money is lost. In period 3, assuming the project has survived, it yields 30 million. We assume for simplicity that the discount rate is zero and the entrepreneur is risk neutral. Whatever happens in period 2, the project's revenue should be enough to reimburse the business angel (8 million), the banker (2 million), and cover the cost slippage of 20 million. But if the cost shock does materialize, the project may stop. It is *ex-ante solvent*, but it can become *illiquid*. The obvious solution is for the entrepreneur to contract a contingent cash line in period 1 and draw it only if the shock materializes.

Assume now that there are many such entrepreneurs. If shocks are uncorrelated, they can still address liquidity shocks with contingency lines. In period 2, half of the entrepreneurs will draw on their lines, the other half won't. However, if a macroeconomic shock (say, higher commodity prices) pushes up costs, entrepreneurs can all become insolvent. In joint work with Bengt Holmström (1998), Tirole calls *inside liquidity* the claims created by the financial system, such as stocks and bonds, which pledge the future stream of income generated in the economy. Faced with an aggregate liquidity shock, inside liquidity may not be enough. The economy needs *outside liquidity* which can be provided by the government, the central bank, or an international organization such as the IMF.

The canonical model of bank liquidity was proposed in 1983 by Douglas Diamond and Philip Dybvig (box 6.8). It shows why banks are useful in an economy where savers are uncertain about their preference for liquidity, and it yields two important results. First, intermediated lending is superior to decentralized lending and borrowing through markets because banks can pool the liquidity risks borne by individual depositors and provide them with liquidity insurance. Second, there are multiple equilibria because an individual depositor's trust in the bank depends on whether the other depositors will withdraw or leave their money. The withdrawal equilibrium is called a *bank run*, and it can topple the bank if its funding relies too much on deposits.

Box 6.8 The Canonical Model of a Bank Run

This presentation is based on Freixas and Rochet (1997; see also Diamond and Dybvig, 1983). Consider an economy inhabited by a continuum of individuals each endowed with one unit of money in period $t = 0$. All individuals are identical *ex ante* but have a probability π of facing a *liquidity shock* which forces them to consume in period $t = 1$ (short run) instead of waiting until period $t = 2$ (long run) when they do not suffer this shock. Their expected utility is written as:

$$U = \pi u(C_1) + \beta(1-\pi)u(C_2) \qquad \text{(B.6.8.1)}$$

$u(C_i)$ represents the utility of consumption C_i in period i ($i = 1, 2$), and β is the discount factor ($0 < \beta < 1$). The deposits received by the bank can either be kept in liquid assets or invested in long-run assets (securities, real estate, bank loans, long-run bonds). It is assumed that only the second type of investment by the bank yields a positive return.

Hence the bank has a clear incentive to invest in long-run assets, the return on which will be transferred to its depositors. The problem is that it must insure itself against the risk that some depositors withdraw their deposits at $t = 1$. The bank can sell long-run assets at $t = 1$, but a penalty is then charged, pushing the return into negative territory. Let $R > 1$ be the return on long-run assets and $r < 1$ the return on long-run assets that are sold before maturity. It is easy to show that the optimal behavior of the bank is to invest a proportion $(1 - \pi)$ of deposits in long-run assets and keep the remaining part in liquid form.

Now let us turn to individual depositors. At $t = 1$, "patient" depositors who do not experience the liquidity shock can leave their money at the bank and consume C_2^* in $t = 2$, or they can withdraw C_1^* to keep it in liquid form until $t = 2$. It can be shown that if $\beta R > 1$, then $C_2^* > C_1^*$: a depositor is better off leaving her money in the bank. The latter therefore prepares for the withdrawal at $t = 1$ of πC_1^*, and it invests the remainder in the illiquid asset. If $\beta R < 1$, all "patient" depositors withdraw their money.

At $t = 1$, however, if a "patient" depositor who does not face a liquidity shock suspects that the others "patient" depositors will withdraw their deposits, she will also want to withdraw hers before the bank itself becomes illiquid. Consequently, the bank needs to liquidate its long-term assets and receives $\pi C_1^* + (1-\pi)rC_1^*$. Since this is lower than C_1^*, the bank goes bankrupt at $t = 1$, which confirms that the "patient, but anxious" depositor was right to walk away. The panic is self-fulfilling.

There are two possible equilibria: a Pareto-efficient equilibrium where individuals trust the bank and leave their deposits until $t = 2$, and a self-fulfilling panic where individuals withdraw their deposits in $t = 1$ and the bank goes bankrupt. Nothing in the model allows us to predict which equilibrium will emerge. In fact, panic can be triggered by a rumor, simply by the news of a first wave of withdrawals, or even by the bankruptcy of another bank.

The risk of a bank run can be mitigated by the banks themselves or through government intervention. Banks can provide incentives to depositors to invest in longer term savings plans (say, one-month or one-year deposits, or invest in equity and bonds with a withdrawal fee at the cost of larger interest payments). Governments can force banks to provide deposit insurance to their clients, usually up to a limited amount per bank account, through a mandatory contribution to a pooled *deposit-guarantee scheme* which indemnifies depositors in case the bank goes bust. Contributions to it should be linked to the bank assets' riskiness to limit moral hazard (i.e., banks engaging in risky loans and investments, knowing that their deposits will be insured anyway). Governments can also force banks to hold sufficient liquidity buffers (through investment in liquid assets such as short-term government bonds) so that they can sell these assets without risk at short notice in case of large deposit withdrawals. Liquidity regulation is further discussed in Section 6.3.1.

Finally, liquidity insurance can be provided by the government itself, either by guaranteeing short-term commercial paper issuance by troubled banks (as governments in advanced economies did on a large scale in 2008–2009) or through the central bank acting as *lender of last resort* (LOLR) and providing emergency lending to cash-strapped banks. The mere prospect of emergency assistance by the central bank can have a powerful impact on depositor confidence and eliminate bank runs. That said, it also creates moral hazard by encouraging banks to take more risk and not build adequate liquidity buffers through their own means. This trade-off was solved in 1873 by British journalist and essayist Walter Bagehot, following the early contribution of banker and politician Henry Thornton (1802):

> In times of financial crisis central banks should lend freely to solvent depository institutions, yet only against sound collateral and at interest rates high enough to dissuade those borrowers that are not genuinely in need. (Bagehot, 1873)

When exposing the *Bagehot principle*, all words matter. If the bank is not *solvent* (i.e., if its liabilities are not matched by its assets and future profits), then liquidity provision by the central bank is futile as it only delays the bank's *resolution* (see Section 6.3.1), which involves a difficult loss-sharing exercise among shareholders, creditors, and possibly taxpayers, which the central bank has no political mandate to conduct. The central bank risks itself making losses if the bank goes bust and collateral proves difficult to repossess. Such central bank losses would be tantamount to a taxpayer subsidy to the bank's shareholders and creditors. Standing ready to lend *freely*, meaning in unlimited amounts (other than by the availability of collateral), is paramount to create depositor confidence. The interest rate being high enough is needed to mitigate moral hazard and make sure that the central bank is a lender of last resort, not first resort, and that banks will normally resort to market funding. The Bagehot principle has remained a reference for modern central bankers (Calomiris, Flandreau, and Laeven, 2016).

d) Liquidity mismatch outside of banks

Liquidity crises don't only hit banks. An important lesson of the global financial crisis is that short-debt debt markets are also prone to runs. The panic of August 2007 is a case in point. On August 9, 2007, concern over the US subprime market, which had been mounting throughout the first half of the year, was at its highest. French bank BNP Paribas froze client withdrawals from three *money market funds* partly invested in troubled assets. Although the bank's intention was to buy time to manage a quickly deteriorating situation, the decision scared investors worldwide, and money markets stopped functioning.

Recent research has underlined the importance of the *information sensitivity* of securities for financial stability (Dang, Gorton, and Holmström, 2012; Gorton and Metrick, 2012). Cash under the form of coins and banknotes is quintessentially information *in*sensitive: its value is constant, at least when prices are stable, which is a key attribute of money as a unit of account and store of value. At the other end of the spectrum are stocks, whose value incorporates in real time incoming information on future cash flows (box 6.4).

Debt (whether materialized as bonds or loans) is in principle not sensitive to information because its payoffs are fixed. As Merton noted in the early 1970s, this, however, assumes that the borrower does not default. When debt is collateralized by securities, it becomes in principle insensitive to the borrower's default, and when it is overcollateralized (say, by applying a large haircut to the value of collateral), it also becomes insensitive to the price of the underlying asset. This is why it has become the norm since the global financial crisis. In the words of Bengt Holmström:

> Collateralized lending obviates the need to discover the exact price of the collateral. A person that runs into a liquidity problem can sell an asset, a watch say, but selling the watch requires that an agreeable price be established. There may be a market for used watches, but it is unlikely to be very efficient at price discovery. . . . The dilemma is solved by pawning the watch. In that case the parties do not have to agree on the value of the watch. . . . The information needed to reach an agreement on the price of the watch (the loan) is relatively small. The broker will offer a price that entails a big enough haircut so that she can recover her money by selling the watch if the owner does not come to redeem it. A safe lower bound is all that is needed. There is no price discovery in the sense that the price is close to what the watch would fetch in an arms-length bargaining process. (Holmström, 2015)

When the borrower's risk of default is low and/or debt is overcollateralized, there is no incentive to produce private information about its value. Debt becomes a sort of private money, and it is in fact largely substitutable with central bank money. The broad money aggregates routinely used by central bankers (Chapter 5, box 5.1) do in fact include short-term commercial debt, and recent theories of monetary policy introduce the concept of *inside money* to describe liquidity created by financial intermediaries (Brunnermeier and Sanikov, 2016). But for large movements of the price of the underlying asset, collateralized debt all of a sudden becomes information-sensitive. Gorton and Holmström have concluded, somewhat paradoxically, that too much information is bad for financial stability

Box 6.9 The Run on Repo: Debt, Collateral, and Information Sensitivity

Collateralized debt is the modern form of pawning. As mentioned in Section 6.1, collateralized loans appeared in the Code of Hammurabi (1750 BCE). Holmström (2015) mentions descriptions of pawn shops under the Tang dynasty in China, around 650 CE. *Repurchase agreements* or *repos*, are short-term loans backed by collateral (see also the description of central bank repo transactions in Chapter 5). Counterparty risk (i.e., the risk that the loan is never recovered) is only residual if the amount of collateral is revised frequently enough to offset any change in the value of collateral. This is usually done through cash or security deposits called *margin calls*. Typically, Bank A borrows X million dollars from Bank B for a given, short period of time and temporarily transfers to Bank B the property of a pool of assets worth the same amount for the life of the loan. Bank B then checks in real time the market value of these assets. If they have depreciated by d%, Bank A transfers to Bank B an additional dX million dollars as margin call. This ensures that Bank B's loss will be limited if Bank A defaults. An alternative, which can be combined with margin calls, is to impose an arbitrary rebate on the value of collateral (a.k.a. a *haircut*), depending on its creditworthiness. This increases the quantity of collateral posted in exchange of a given monetary amount.

Repos involve much less counterparty risk than uncollateralized bank loans and have developed very rapidly. Repos were believed to exceed 10 trillion dollars in 2008, having grown by around 10% a year. This amount was roughly equivalent to the total assets of the banking sector. Repos have long been considered information-insensitive. However, the leveraging and tranching mechanism of asset-based securities (see box 6.1) implied that their price was a highly nonlinear function of the price of the underlying asset—say, a subprime mortgage. In spite of the limited share of subprime bonds in the pool of asset-based securities, the bursting of the

US real estate bubble transformed what was perceived as "informationally insensitive" debt into "informationally sensitive" debt.

The complexity of the chain of structured financial products meant that the information necessary to properly value claims was not accessible. No one could accept structured products as collateral any longer. The subprime crisis thus translated into a collateral crisis and a dash for cash. Average haircuts on repos went to the roof, from zero in the first half of 2007 to 25% by mid-2008, and to more than 45% by the end of 2008. The repo market, which used to be highly deep and liquid, dried up. In the words of Gary Gorton (2010), investors had been "slapped by the invisible hand".

The Merton model of box 6.3 is the right template to understand the panic. The value of a debt security guaranteed by a pool of assets can be compared to the value of the debt of a company which would hold these assets. Figure B6.3.1 shows the value of debt as a function of the value of collateral at the maturity date (dashed line) and at an earlier date (solid line). Toward the right of the figure, when the value of collateral is high, the value of debt is constant and equal to its face value because it will be nearly surely paid back. Toward the left of the figure, the value of collateral goes down (think of a mortgage-backed security in 2007, when concerns over subprime mortgages start mounting). The risk increases that debt will be undercollateralized and not fully paid back—if at all. Its market value gradually departs from its face value. Debt has become information-sensitive.

6.2.4 Financial stability in the general equilibrium

> A micro-prudential approach is one in which regulation is partial equilibrium in its conception and aimed at preventing the costly failure of individual financial institutions. By contrast, a "macroprudential" approach recognizes the importance of general equilibrium effects, and seeks to safeguard the financial system as a whole.
>
> (Hanson, Kashyap, and Stein, 2011, p. 3)

Financial systems connect financial institutions between themselves and with nonfinancial entities. Even when their origin is local, financial crises quickly propagate across institutions and financial market segments. The global financial crisis started in August 2007 as a liquidity crisis in short-term funding markets; then, between 2007 and 2008, it hit large banks, governments, and nonfinancial players. Moreover, feedback loops (or *procyclical* mechanisms) specific to the financial sector can deepen the crises further. Understanding crisis *propagation* and *amplification* has become a policy priority for the academic community after the global financial crisis and has informed the development of macroprudential regulation.

Central banks in advanced and emerging market economies have invested significant resources in developing macroprudential theory and policy. This has given birth to a rich body of theoretical and empirical literature that has roots in earlier thinking on financial crises and financial cycles, notably by the Bank for International Settlements in Basel. That said, the macroprudential literature is far from having reached the level of maturity of monetary economics.

a) Interconnectedness

If the financial system was not interconnected, the default of a financial institution would be an isolated event; shareholders would take a loss, but the system would remain safe and there would be no case for public intervention. Because of interconnections, risks taken by a financial institution create externalities for the financial system and the economy which may warrant public intervention. Interconnectedness can be direct or indirect. Direct interconnectedness is created by financial contracts between participants: loans, equity stakes, derivative contracts, and the like. Indirect interconnectedness is created by common exposures to the same risk, for example, when several banks in the same country finance the housing sector.

A first strand of research on financial stability is empirical and aims at measuring interconnectedness, drawing in particular (but not only) on methods borrowed from network theory (Allen and Gale, 2000). The idea is the following. Any financial system, global or local, can be envisaged as a network of bilateral claims and liabilities. Building a workhorse theoretical network allows one to simulate the propagation of shocks and understand how structures make the network more or less prone to contagion, for instance after the failure of one participant (Eisenberg and Noe, 2010). This line of research, of course, assumes the existence and availability of disaggregated data on banks' balance sheets, which have only recently started to be produced and made available for research.[37]

b) Systemic risk

A challenge facing macroprudential policies is that their objectives are not easy to measure. Systemic risk has been defined as "the risk of threats to financial stability that impair the functioning of the financial system as a whole with significant adverse effects on the broader economy" (Freixas, Laeven and Peydró, 2015, p. 13). But how can it be quantified?[38] A first empirical answer consists in exploring asset price correlations in times of stress (Hartmann, Straetmans, and de Vries, 2004), which also allows one to assess the systemic impact of a single financial institution. This approach relies on the *value-at-risk* (see Chapter 2) of all bank stocks at a given confidence level, conditional on the stock price of one given bank being below its lowest 5% ("contagion value-at-risk"; Adrian and Brunnermeier, 2016). Symmetrically, one can measure the expected losses on a given bank's assets conditional on all stocks reaching their lowest 5% ("marginal expected shortfall"; Acharya, Engle, and Richardson, 2012). A third approach consists in measuring individual banks' contributions to the correction of aggregate market capitalization during a crisis (Browness and Engle, 2012).

All approaches just mentioned face shortcomings. They use market prices and are thus subject to animal spirits and procyclicality: correlation does not imply causation, and observations of tail events may be too scarce to provide for an accurate estimate. Figure 6.8 shows a slightly different approach: the gauge of banking system stress used by the ECB (2007). The indicator measures the probability of default of two or more large banks in the euro area using bank equity returns to estimate the interconnectedness between banks and credit default swaps to extract bank-specific probabilities of default.[39]

c) Procylicality

Theoretical approaches to contagion and shock propagation have identified several *procyclical* mechanisms. One of them features prominently in the

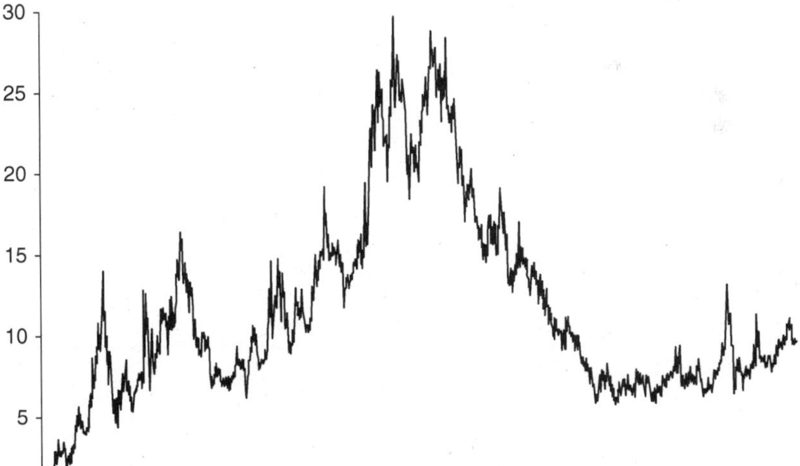

Figure 6.8 Probability of two or more credit events over a two-year horizon for 15 large euro area banks.
Data provided to the authors by the European Central Bank.

literature: credit constraints amplified by falls in asset prices, possibly magnified by fire sales and by a procyclical leverage behavior of banks. Credit constraints arise when the borrowing capacity of private entities is limited by the market value of the assets they can pledge as collateral. Such constraints are sometimes called *Fisherian*, in reference to Irvin Fisher's 1933 theory of debt deflation. Limiting the capacity of nonfinancial entities to raise debt constrains aggregate demand, even more so when consumer prices go down and inflate the real value of debt.[40] The impact of collateral constraints on banks' supply of credit was formalized in the mid-1990s by the financial accelerator literature (Bernanke, Gertler, and Gilchrist, 1996; see also Chapter 5 for a discussion of the consequences for monetary policy). When injected into a general equilibrium model, Fisherian constraints have the potential to generate *credit cycles*, best formalized by the canonical model of Kiyotaki and Moore (1997), the story of which goes as follows (figure 6.9). A negative shock to companies' expected future profits depresses their stock price today, hence the value of the assets they can pledge as collateral. This hampers banks' credit supply and hence firms' capacity to invest, which dents future GDP and validates the initial expectation.

Depending on the structure of the economy, other factors can magnify the global impact of shocks to individual institutions. Some have been described elsewhere in this book, such as exchange rate depreciation in small open economies with large foreign currency–denominated liabilities or the bank–sovereign doom loop. We focus here on two such factors specific to the financial system: *fire sales* and *leverage*.

A *fire sale* is the disposal of illiquid assets (typically, stocks, bonds, and household and corporate loans) by a bank that needs liquid resources to repay its debts.

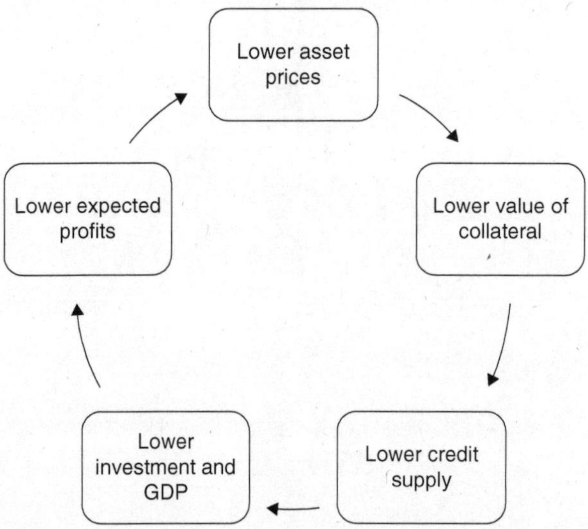

Figure 6.9 The credit cycle according to Kiyotaki and Moore (1997).

Given the urgency, the bank is ready to sell assets at a depressed price. The perspective of an easy profit should be an incentive for other banks to stand ready to purchase them, which should mitigate the price decline. But their ability to raise short-term debt to fund these purchases is constrained by the collateral value of their assets, itself depressed by the fire sales. In short, fire-selling involves a *pecuniary externality*[41] which calls for public intervention (Stein, 2010). Policy answers may consist in having banks internalize the externality say, by forcing them to hold liquidity buffers preventively, or by taxing their short-term debt (Perotti and Suarez, 2011), or by counteracting the fire sale's impact on market prices by having a public authority buying assets as "market maker of last resort."

As indicated earlier, large investment banks borrowed up to 50 times their equity in the runup to the global financial crisis, while the equivalent ratio for nonfinancial companies was typically less than five. Adrian and Shin (2010) have shown how financial institutions increase their leverage in response to higher asset prices (box 6.10). Procyclical leverage also explains why financial crises are almost always associated with high leverage, as explained at the start of this chapter.

Box 6.10 Procyclicality and Leverage

Tobias Adrian and Hyun Song Shin (2008) have used firm-level data to demonstrate the procyclicality of leverage in financial firms. They have shown that financial intermediaries actively adjust their balance sheets to changes in their net worth.

The framework is the same as in box 6.7. Assume a bank with total assets A financed by debt D and equity E (remember that $A = E + D$), and let $\delta = D / E$ be the debt-to-equity ratio. Adrian and Shin first observe that, for a passive investor, the relationship between the value of assets and the leverage ratio is downward-sloping: leverage falls when the value of total assets rises. This is simply because if debt D is held constant, δ and A are negatively related:

$$\delta = \frac{D}{E} = \frac{D}{A - D} \tag{B6.10.1}$$

Data indicate that households follow this type of behavior (figure B6.10.1). However, this is not the case for nonfinancial companies. For commercial banks, the relationship is vertical (figure B6.10.2): commercial banks tend to keep leverage constant, which implies that their debt is procyclical (holding δ constant means that the growth rate of debt D is the same as that of assets A). The relationship even turns positive for investment banks (figure B6.10.3), indicating marked leverage procyclicality. In good times, debt raised by investment banks grows faster than their total assets, and the leverage ratio δ goes up. In other words, investment banks step up their borrowing when market conditions are improving. This explains the high debt-to-equity ratio of investment banks compared to commercial banks and even more to nonfinancial companies, as noted earlier in this chapter.

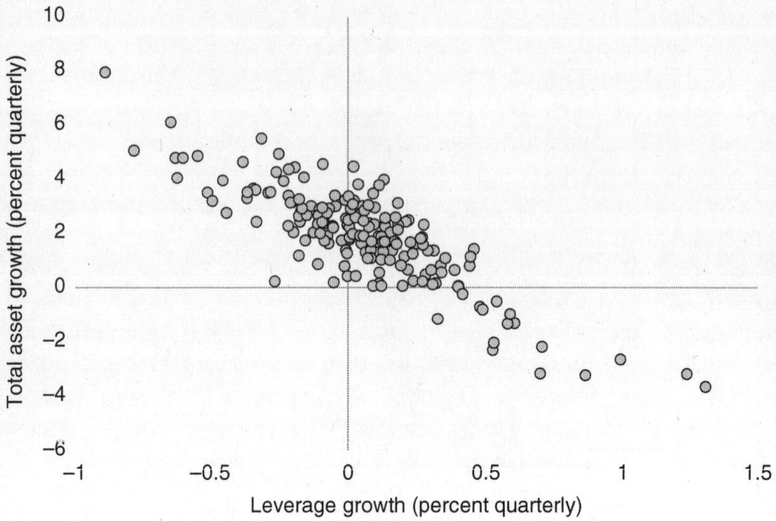

Figure B6.10.1 Asset growth and leverage growth, US households, 1963–2006.
Adrian and Shin (2008, figure 2.2).

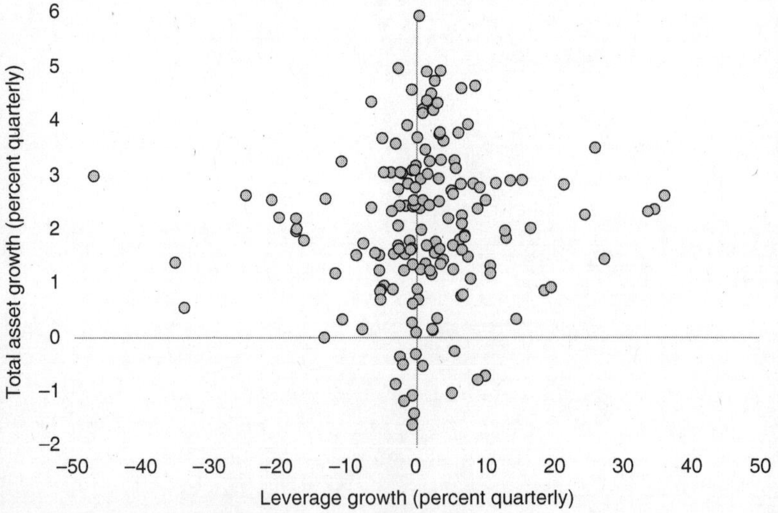

Figure B6.10.2 Asset growth and leverage growth, US commercial banks, 1963–2006.
Adrian and Shin (2008).

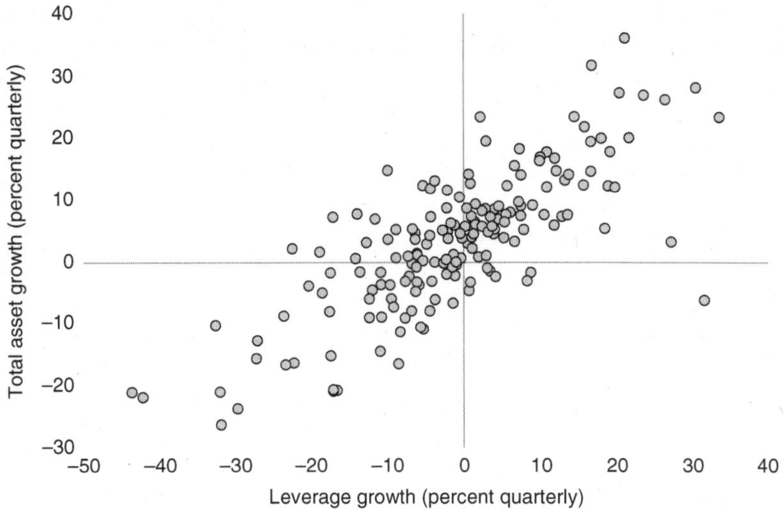

Figure B6.10.3 Asset growth and leverage growth, US investment banks, 1963–2006.
Adrian and Shin (2008).

Adrian and Shin conjecture that banks maintain their equity E proportional to their total value-at-risk ($E = \lambda \times VaR$). Using the same notation as previously, δ can be written as:

$$\delta = \frac{A}{E} - 1 = \frac{1}{\lambda}\frac{A}{VaR} - 1 \qquad \text{(B6.10.2)}$$

It is therefore negatively related to value-at-risk per unit of assets, VaR/A. Adrian and Shin's data confirm the countercyclicality of unit value-at-risk, which implies the procyclicality of leverage. The interpretation is the following: when asset prices increase, financial intermediaries' balance sheets tend to get stronger, creating an incipient situation of surplus capital. The incentive is for intermediaries to find ways to employ this surplus capital through an expansion of balance sheets and an increase in leverage.

d) Black swans

An additional source of systemic risk in the financial system, also evidenced by the global financial crisis, is limited understanding of the global consequences of large, rare shocks.

Before the crisis, the risk management process in financial institutions had been calibrated to "average" shocks (typically, based on a 95% or a 99% value at risk estimated on high-frequency historical data over a limited time span, say the previous two years). This implied that *tail risk* (i.e., the realization of very rare but very large shocks) was typically ignored. Moreover, the possibility that the system would react in a nonlinear way to such very large shocks, through mechanisms such as those just described, was also ignored, if at all understood. This was made worse by lack of granular data describing the network of bilateral exposures between financial institutions, financial market infrastructures, and nonfinancial entities (including governments). Large shocks with unpredictable consequences are often likened to *black swans*, popularized by the writer and epistemologist Nassim Taleb (2007). Black swans are rare, but they do exist, and multiple observations of white swans cannot discard their existence. To answer this criticism, recent models used by policymakers have introduced nonlinearities and the possible default of financial and nonfinancial entities in general equilibrium models with a financial sector (see Hamilton, 2016; Beyer, Cœuré, and Mendicino, 2017, for a survey).

6.3 Policies

After the financial crisis of 2007–2008, financial stability has become a major dimension of economic policy. Until then, this was an issue for sectoral regulators, not for finance ministers and central bank governors. It is now a key policy objective alongside growth, employment, price stability, or fairness. The reason is easy to understand. As shown in Section 6.1, financial crises can be extremely costly for the economy and for public finances. All major central banks now publish financial stability reports. Whereas the pre-crisis international policy discussion tended to be couched in rather deterministic terms, much more attention is being devoted to risk, especially that arising from financial developments. At the Pittsburgh Summit in 2009, G20 leaders committed to an ambitious regulatory agenda, of which most of the reforms detailed in this section are part. This agenda is implemented by the *Financial Stability Board (FSB)*, a body hosted by the Bank of International Settlements which comprises standard setters, central bankers, and government officials coming from the largest advanced and emerging economies. That said, "financial stability" is not (or not yet) an autonomous field of either theory or policy, and there are substantial complementarities and trade-offs with other policy domains such as monetary policy and competition policy.

Financial stability policies are of two sorts. *Microprudential policies* aim at safeguarding the stability and safety of individual institutions and markets. They include banking, insurance, and securities market regulation and supervision. They operate through the setting and enforcement of standards that aim at ensuring the resilience and transparency of individual institutions, as well as through the monitoring of their behavior. *Macroprudential policies* aim at ensuring the stability and efficiency of the financial system *as a whole* over business and credit cycles. In a broad sense, they rely on a diverse set of levers ranging from monetary policy to credit standards to tax policy, and they require coordination across a range of public authorities. In a narrower sense, macroprudential policies rely on a toolbox of specific macroprudential instruments, most of them directed at banks and entrusted to a designated macroprudential authority (which is often, but not always the central bank). We now review these two dimensions in turn, with special attention to the regulatory challenges created by the European monetary union.

6.3.1 Banking regulation and supervision

Banks are subject to specific regulation and monitoring, called *banking supervision*. All large institutions are monitored in real time by dedicated teams of civil servants tasked with making sure that the rules are properly implemented and that risk is properly measured and controlled.

Public authorities in charge of banking supervision are usually (but not always) independent and often (but not always) part of the central bank. In the United States, bank supervision is split between three authorities: the Federal Reserve, the Federal Deposit Insurance Corporation (FDIC), and the Office of the Comptroller of the Currency. In the United Kingdom, it is done by the Prudential Regulation Authority (PRA), a part of the Bank of England (before the crisis, it was assigned to a stand-alone, broad-spectrum entity, the Financial Services Authority). In the euro area, it is done by the ECB for the largest banks and by national authorities for the smaller ones (see box 6.14). In Japan, bank supervision is part of the Financial Service Authority (JFSA), a government agency different from the Bank of Japan. The post-crisis trend has been toward giving supervisory powers to central banks but both models have merits (Cœuré, 2013).

Bank supervisors enforce regulation decided by national governments and parliaments and agreed at a global level in the *Basel Committee for Banking Supervision (BCBS)*, a committee of the Bank for International Settlements. Since the global financial crisis, BCBS membership has been extended to large emerging market economies.

a) Principles

The two pillars of banking regulation are capital and liquidity regulation. Both were considerably strengthened after the global financial crisis. They were complemented by measures aimed at ensuring that the largest banks are not "too big to fail," that is, aimed at addressing the moral hazard created by government bail-outs.

However frustrating for economists, the assignment of instruments to objectives is less clear that what Jan Tinbergen would have advised (see Chapter 1). Capital requirements chase several objectives, and they interact with liquidity regulation. This is because mandating banks to build up liquidity buffers has the ancillary benefit of removing solvency risk from part of their portfolios, whereas mandating banks to build up equity protects their liquidity position by reassuring depositors that they will remain solvent. Using multiple instruments may, however, be justified by the multifold nature of risk and by the uncertainty surrounding the efficiency of each individual instrument (Haldane, 2017). Box 6.11 provides an overview of capital and liquidity ratios, which we then discuss in more detail.

Box 6.11 A Bird's Eye View of Capital and Liquidity Requirements

To take a comprehensive view of capital and liquidity regulation, a simplified bank balance sheet is shown in table B6.11.1. On the asset side, the bank is invested in safe, liquid assets (typically, cash and short-term government bills) and in risky, illiquid assets such as loans, bonds, and equity. On the liability side, it is funded with short-term, runnable liabilities (typically, client deposits and short-term debt) and more stable, long-term liabilities, such as bonds and equity.

Table B6.11.1
A Simplified Bank Balance Sheet

Assets	Liabilities
Safe, liquid assets L	Short-term funding S
Illiquid, risky assets R	Bonds D
	Equity E

Meeting the *capital-adequacy ratio* requires bank equity to exceed a fraction k of *risk-weighted assets* (see box 6.12 for implementation details):

$$E > k(L + wR) \qquad \text{(B6.11.1)}$$

where $w > 1$ is the risk weight on risky assets.

The leverage ratio postulates that bank equity must exceed a fraction λ of non–risk-weighted assets:

$$E > \lambda(L + R) \qquad \text{(B6.11.2)}$$

The leverage ratio being unweighted relative to risks, it can only be a complement, or "backstop" to the risk-weighted capital ratio if one wants to provide banks with the right incentives to limit risks. There are three cases depending on the value of λ:

- If the leverage ratio is small enough ($\lambda < k$), then $\lambda(L + R) < k(L + wR)$ for any level of risky assets R. *Risk-based supervision* always dominates and the leverage ratio never binds.
- If the leverage ratio is high enough ($\lambda > wk$), then $\lambda(L + R) > k(L + wR)$ for any level of risky assets R. Non–risk-based supervision always dominates and the risk-weighted capital ratio never binds. This is shown in figure B6.11.1, where the shaded area indicates admissible levels for E as a function of risky assets.

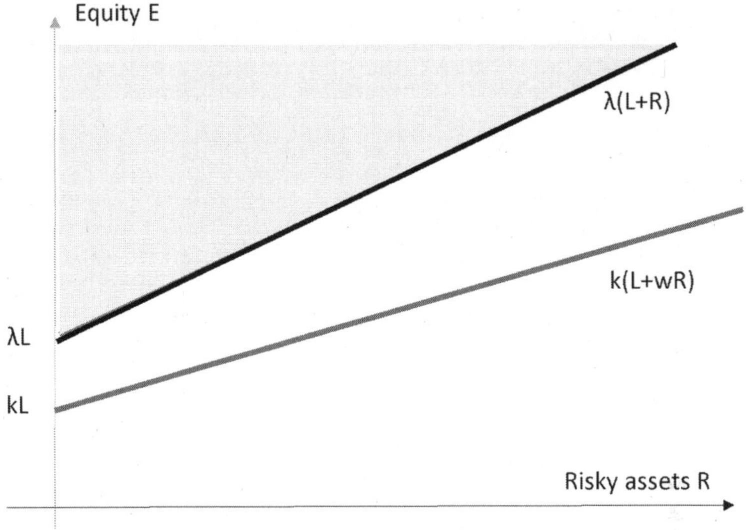

Figure B6.11.1 When a high leverage ratio crowds out risk-based regulation: regulatory capital as a function of risky assets.

- If $k < \lambda < wk$, then risk-based supervision dominates above a certain level of risk; namely, when $\frac{R}{L} > \frac{\lambda - k}{wk - \lambda}$, as shown on figure B6.11.1. This is the most interesting case because it shows that a leverage ratio fosters prudent behavior at risk levels which are too low for risk-based supervision to be effective. Different risk levels can describe banks with different business models (e.g., commercial vs. investment banks).

The same approach allows us to identify liquidity ratios (see box 6.13 for details on implementation). The *liquidity coverage ratio* (LCR) requires banks to hold enough liquid assets to cover a specified fraction ψ of their short-term funding:

$$L > \psi S \tag{B6.11.3}$$

The *net stable funding ratio* (NSFR) requires banks' long-term funding to cover a specified fraction ω of their illiquid assets:

$$D + E > \omega R \tag{B6.11.4}$$

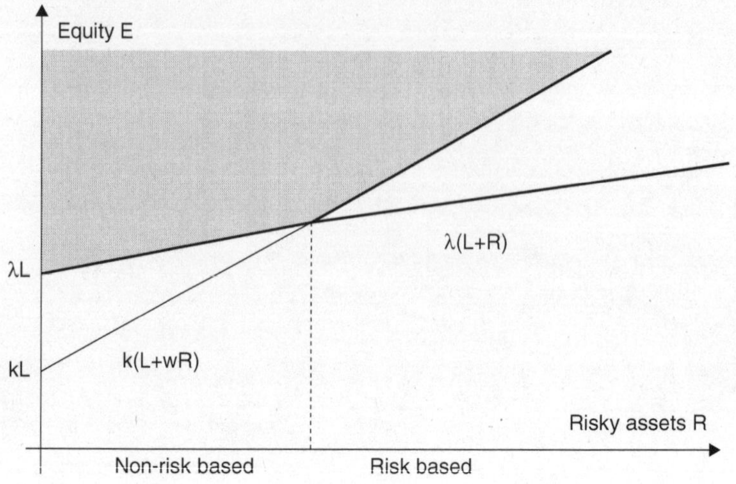

Figure B6.11.2 The leverage ratio as backstop to risk-based regulation: regulatory capital as a function of risky assets.

b) Capital regulation

Capital requirements hit several birds with the same stone. First, they ensure that bank shareholders have "skin in the game" and are incited to run the bank prudently. Second, together with other loss-absorbing liabilities (typically, debt instruments which are converted into equity in case of default), they ensure that depositors are the last to be hurt. Third, they are risk-weighted (i.e., for a given amount of assets, the amount of regulatory capital is larger if assets are riskier), which creates an incentive for shareholders to control the risk profile of the bank and allows for *risk-based supervision.*

Capital requirements were strengthened both quantitatively and qualitatively after the global financial crisis by the BCBS, resulting in 2010 in the Basel III accord (box 6.12). The BCBS only sets indicative standards, leaving implementation to national legislators and regulators (in the European Union, through EU-wide directives and regulations). Implementation by national authorities is monitored through a peer-review process.

Qualitatively, the definition of regulatory capital under Basel III focuses on tangible common equity (i.e., ordinary stocks). Quantitatively, the required core measure of bank capital, the Core Equity Tier 1 (CET1) ratio (see box 6.12) equals 7% of risk-adjusted capital for all banks and between 8% and 10.5% for globally systemic banks. According to Cecchetti and Schoenholtz (2014), this is ten times larger than what would have been the Basel III equivalent of Basel II capital requirements, namely less than 0.75% of risk-weighted assets.

Box 6.12 Bank Capital Requirements

Capital requirements are measured either at the level of a banking group on a consolidated basis or at the level of each participating entity, such as subsidiaries. They are agreed internationally in the BCBS, then implemented into national law. There have been three generations of capital requirements:

- The first Basel accord (Basel I) of 1988 defined *risk-weighted assets* as the sum of a bank's assets each weighted with a specific risk weight set by the regulator depending on the asset class. The *Cooke ratio* (named from the then chairman of the committee) was defined as the bank's equity divided by risk-weighted assets and had to be larger than 8%. Basel I was a first step toward creating an international level playing field for banks but it had several shortcomings. First, it was procyclical because standardized risk weights would force banks to reduce their risk profile in economic downturns. Second, it didn't protect depositors and taxpayers well in case of default because regulatory capital buffers included instruments such as convertible bonds or tax credits which could not really absorb losses. Third, it allowed for regulatory arbitrage because there was no internationally agreed definition of capital. Fourth, there was no liquidity requirement.
- The second Basel accord of 2004 (Basel II) was considerably more complex, based on three "pillars": mandatory risk-based capital requirements (Pillar 1), discretionary capital add-ons triggered upon supervisory judgment (Pillar 2), and market discipline through disclosure by banks (Pillar 3), with a possibility for banks to use their internal models to compute risk weights. With hindsight, it is now understood that the leeway given to supervisors and the unrestricted use of internal models led to a substantial decrease of the quantity of capital and an increase of risks taken by banks (Cecchetti and Schoenholtz, 2014).
- The third Basel accord of 2010 (Basel III) was gradually phased in between 2014 and 2019 and drew lessons from the crisis. It kept the three pillars of the Basel II framework but massively increased both the quantity and quality of capital mandated under Pillar 1 (Basel Committee for Banking Supervision, 2010). The *core equity tier 1* (CET1) ratio focuses on the liability most suited to absorb losses and tangible common equity, and must amount to at least 4.5% of risk-weighted assets (RWA). Total capital must amount to 8% of RWA. A *conservation buffer* of 2.5% of risk-weighted assets ensures that a minimum amount of capital is held after absorbing losses.

The minimum capital requirement therefore amounts to 4.5% + 2.5% = 7% of risk-weighted assets for CET1 and 8% + 2.5% = 10.5% for total capital.

In addition to standard capital requirements, a *countercyclical capital buffer* is set at zero in normal times but can be increased by authorities to up to 2.5% of common equity for macroprudential purposes—say, to curb a system-wide lending boom (see Section 6.3.3). Basel III also introduces a non–risk-based *leverage ratio* requiring CET1 capital to be at least of 3% of total assets. This is equivalent to capping the size of the bank's balance sheet at 33 times its equity.

Last, Basel III includes special provisions for *global systemically important banks* (G-SIB in regulatory jargon), including a surcharge of 1–3.5% of common equity (in practice 2.5%) which pushes the CET1 ratio to possibly as much as 7% + 3.5% = 10.5% of RWA for global banks. The BCBS has developed a common methodology for identifying G-SIBs which are then designated by each jurisdiction. The Financial Stability Board publishes a list of G-SIBs divided into five "buckets" according to their systemic importance (see table B6.12.1 and Passmore and von Haffen, 2017, for an explanation of the methodology).

Table B6.12.1
Global Systemically Important Banks (G-SIBs) in 2017

Bucket	Capital surcharge as % of risk-weighted assets	G-SIBs in alphabetical order
5	3.5	(empty)
4	2.5	JP Morgan Chase
3	2	Bank of America, Citigroup, Deutsche Bank, HSBC
2	1.5	Bank of China, Barclays, BNP Paribas, China Construction Bank, Goldman Sachs, Industrial and Commercial Bank of China, Mitsubishi UFJ, Wells Fargo
1	1	Agricultural Bank of China, Bank of New York Mellon, Credit Suisse, Crédit Agricole, ING Bank, Mizuho, Morgan Stanley, Nordea, Royal Bank of Canada, Royal Bank of Scotland, Santander, Société Générale, Standard Chartered, State Street, Sumitomo Mitsui, UBS, Unicredit

Source: Financial Stability Board, November 2017.

The Basel III capital requirements have been attacked for being both too tight and too loose. Unsurprisingly, banks have claimed that their cost of funding would skyrocket and (given a high degree of competition) would be passed onto their clients, increasing the cost of capital dramatically in the economy with a catastrophic impact on investment and growth. The Institute for International Finance (IIF), which speaks for large international banks, concluded in 2010 that GDP growth would be lower by 0.6 percentage point in the United States, the euro area, and Japan. Were these concerns justified? To start with, it is fair to acknowledge that the conditions of the Modigliani-Miller equivalence theorem (see Section 6.2) are not met for banks. Tilting their funding mix from debt to capital does increase their cost of funding. *Ad absurdum*, if the Modigliani-Miller theorem would hold, there would be no point at all in regulating capital![42] On the other hand, making banks more resilient to shocks reduces their credit risk, lifts their stock price, and decreases the credit spread over the risk-free rate.

All in all, a study coordinated by the Bank for International Settlements had concluded that Basel III would drive lending rates up modestly, loan volumes down a bit, and lower GDP growth by 0.05 percentage points per year during five years, an assessment much more benign than the IIF's (Macroeconomic Assessment Group, 2010). With hindsight, even this estimate appears too pessimistic, although a true counterfactual is, of course, not available. The phasing-in of the Basel III requirements in the 2010s was accompanied by a strong economic recovery in both the United States and the United Kingdom, and later in the euro area. As concluded by Cecchetti (2014), "lending spreads have barely moved, bank interest margins have fallen, and loan volumes are up." Admittedly, a very accommodative monetary environment has kept the cost of capital very low during the period.

Some economists would prefer bank capital requirements to be much higher (see Haldane, 2017, for a discussion). Admati and Hellwig (2013) have pointed out that the reason the Modigliani-Miller equivalence is violated for banks is a double government subsidy. One is explicit: it is the corporate tax relief for debt, which is not specific to banks but benefits them in a disproportionate way given their extraordinary leverage. The other is implicit: banks being too big to fail, the expectation of government support in case of trouble lowers their funding cost. For Admati and Hellwig, capital requirements only offset the distortions created by these two subsidies and are thus socially optimal. This leads them to argue in favor of equity buffers amounting to 20%–30% of banks' non–risk-weighted assets. In the same vein, Minneapolis Fed President Neel Kashkari has proposed initial minimum capital requirements of 23.5–38% of risk-weighted assets (Federal Reserve Bank of Minneapolis, 2016).

Another heated discussion is about the difference between *risk-based* and non–risk-based capital regulation. Risk weights have been considerably improved in the transition from Basel II to Basel III, but they remain in question to the extent that large banks measure them using internal models which are very costly to inspect. The Basel Committee has capped the capital relief allowed by internal models compared to a standardized approach. In addition, the Basel III accord has introduced a non–risk-based leverage ratio relating bank equity to total non–risk-weighted assets.[43] Initially a complement to risk-based requirements, it becomes mandatory as of 2019.

Economists love the leverage ratio because they worry about banks being too big and they don't trust internal models. Bank supervisors are more reluctant because they value risk-based supervision: they use risk-based ratios as a lever to incite banks to better manage their risks. Consistently, they want the leverage ratio to be low enough not to crowd out risk-based regulation, as illustrated in box 6.11.

Shareholders are first in line when banks absorb losses, but this may not suffice in the case of large shocks. Given the negative externalities created by banking crises, a special legal regime exists when banks are likely to fail, called *resolution*. This regime allows a *resolution authority* to force bondholders and, if needed, depositors, to absorb losses once equity has been wiped out—in regulatory parlance, to be "bailed-in," as opposed to being bailed-out by taxpayers (box 6.13).

Box 6.13 Banks' Last Moments: Resolution and Bail-in Rules

Rules governing the winding-down of banks have been considerably strengthened after the global financial crisis to protect taxpayers and limit the moral hazard associated with being "too-big-to-fail." Banks are subject to judiciary insolvency procedures like any other company, but the externalities imposed by bank failures on the financial system and on the rest of the economy, as well as the need to act swiftly to curb financial uncertainty, justify the existence of a special regime to ensure the orderly liquidation of banks, called *resolution.*

When a bank is failing or likely to fail because it is running out of capital and/or liquidity, the resolution authority has the power to decide within a few hours or a few days on the allocation of losses and, based on independent valuation, to adjudicate parts of the bank's assets and liabilities. In most countries, the resolution authority is also the supervisor, while in some, it is separate (in Washington, the *Federal Deposit Insurance Corporation* [FDIC] is separate from the Fed, and, in Brussels, the *Single Resolution Board* is part of the European Commission and separate from the ECB). The objectives of resolution are to ensure continuity of the bank's critical functions, minimize risks to financial stability, and protect taxpayers. The resolution process often results in a "good bank" which can resume lending and a "bad bank" which is gradually wound down. The good bank should be sufficiently well capitalized to inspire market confidence, and the *no-creditor-worse-off principle* ensures in principle consistency between resolution and ordinary insolvency.

The FSB (2014) has approved key attributes of effective resolution regimes for financial institutions, including *bail-in rules*. Bail-in rules clarify the seniority ranking between bank liabilities: Shareholders first cover the losses, then junior bondholders (typically, holders of debt contractually convertible into equity), then senior bondholders, then depositors, depending on jurisdictions and only beyond the amount insured by a mandatory deposit guarantee scheme. In practice, deposits are converted into equity, allowing the bank to resume its operations with a higher level of capital. The *total loss-absorbing capacity* (TLAC), that is the total amount of equity and bail-in-able debt which a bank should maintain in normal times, must be calibrated to avoid depositors and taxpayers contributing unless in extreme circumstances. The FSB (2015*b*) has set global systemically important banks' TLAC at 16% of risk-weighted assets from January 1, 2019, and 18% from January 1, 2025 (emerging market economies benefit from a longer transition period, with deadlines set in 2022 and 2025). In Europe, the *Bank Recovery and Resolution Directive* (BRRD) sets a minimum amount of bail-in-able debt to be issued by banks, called "minimum required eligible liabilities."

Bail-in principles are globally agreed, but their implementation faces pitfalls:

- Wiping out shareholders is not controversial, but bailing in creditors and depositors is. Writing down a bank's senior debt, which is often held by other banks, can create negative spillovers to other parts of the financial system and to the economy at large, threatening financial stability. In Europe, junior debt was sometimes sold by banks to their retail clients, who had no ability to monitor risks taken and sometimes weren't even told that the instruments were convertible. This does not question bail-in as a principle but suggests that "bail-in-able" bank debt should be held neither by other banks (for the former reason) nor by individuals (for the latter reason).
- Concerns are more serious when it comes to uninsured bank deposits, those beyond the amounts insured by deposit guarantee schemes. The insured amount (100,000 euros in Europe) is rather high for an individual but rather low for a small enterprise. Individuals have no capacity to monitor the way banks are run, and, rightly or wrongly, they feel protected by deposit insurance and bank supervision. Inflicting losses on households and small- and medium-size enterprises creates negative externalities to the economy. Moreover, bank deposits constitute the bulk of money in circulation (the M1 aggregate, see Chapter 5), and stable money is essential to a smoothly functioning economy and to maintaining trust in the

currency. In Cyprus in March 2013, direct damage to the economy was limited because a large part of uninsured deposits was held by Russian citizens, but the confidence cost was enormous. Preserving depositor confidence can be a valid reason for committing taxpayers' money. Of course, this needs to be balanced against the moral hazard created in banks and the implicit taxpayer subsidy.

- Finally, resolution faces serious challenges in the case of large and complex cross-border banking groups. Former Governor of the Bank of England Mervyn King famously said that "banks are global in life, but local in death." The risk of conflict is high between national resolution authorities. The FSB is in principle neutral between two approaches: a *single-point-of-entry* approach where resolution takes place at the level of the parent or holding company and is led by the home authority and a multiple-point-of-entry approach where resolution is undertaken in each jurisdiction. The former approach is in principle more effective, but it raises sovereignty and possibly financial stability issues since authorities in one country may not internalize the consequences of their actions for financial stability globally. A worst-case scenario, which would make the two approaches equivalent, would be one where all banking groups would be based on subsidiaries, each of which is building capital and liquidity buffers locally. This would miss entirely the benefits of cross-border risk pooling and economies of scale.

Radical ways to set incentive rights in banks and protect depositors are statutory separation between commercial banking (i.e., deposit-taking) and investment banking activities, and narrow banking. Separation was the rule in the United States between the Glass-Steagall Act of 1933 until the 1990s, and it came back to the fore after the global financial crisis (see also box 6.18). In the United States, former Fed Chair Paul Volcker advocated in 2009 banning deposit-taking banks from engaging in *proprietary trading*; that is, committing their balance sheet to undertake speculative investments. A limited version was adopted as per the Dodd-Frank Act in 2010 and implemented in 2015 after a long and controversial discussion. In Europe, the Vickers and Liikanen reports of 2011 and 2012 advocated statutory separation between commercial and investment banking, with exceptions such as market-making on behalf of clients. A subsequent legislative proposal by the European Commission was never adopted. As for advocates of the long-standing *narrow banking* proposal, they have argued that deposit-taking banks should invest deposits in riskless assets, any other asset (including loans to the economy) being 100% financed by equity.[44] This proposal would make banks ultra-safe, but it would prevent them from performing maturity and liquidity transformation.

c) Liquidity regulation

The purpose of *liquidity regulation* is to address negative externalities created by banks holding insufficient buffers of liquid assets in normal times and being forced to sell more illiquid assets at a discounted price in times of crisis.

Liquidity regulation is not unequivocally good. One drawback relates to the scarcity of *high-quality liquid assets* (HQLA). As also discussed in Chapter 7, several developments have compounded globally to create strong demand for highly rated, liquid securities, such as government bills and bonds.[45] Requiring banks to hold more HQLA crowds out other users and depresses the risk-free interest rate globally. Moreover, it makes banks' intermediation services costlier when they involve liquidity provision or when they involve holding inventories of cash or financial assets.

"Liquid" here means "easily convertible into cash." Two liquidity ratios have been made mandatory by the Basel III agreement: the liquidity coverage

Box 6.14 Bank Liquidity Requirements

The Basel III accord of 2010 (box 6.12) includes rules to ensure that banks maintain adequate liquidity buffers: a 30-day liquidity coverage ratio designed to ensure short-term resilience to liquidity disruptions and a longer term structural liquidity ratio to address liquidity mismatches and promote the use of stable funding sources. The *liquidity coverage ratio* (LCR) has become binding in 2015 and is defined as:

$$LCR = \frac{High\ quality\ liquid\ assets}{Net\ cash\ outflows\ over\ 30\ days\ under\ a\ stress\ scenario} > 100\% \tag{B6.14.1}$$

The stress scenario includes assumptions such as a downgrade of the credit rating of the institution, loss of retail deposits and of wholesale unsecured funding, higher haircuts on secured funding, and margin calls on derivatives. The net stable funding ratio (NSFR) became binding in 2018 and is defined as:

$$NSFR = \frac{Available\ amount\ of\ stable\ funding\ over\ 1\ year}{Required\ amount\ of\ stable\ funding} > 100\% \tag{B6.14.2}$$

Stable funding includes equity and other liabilities which are expected to be available in a reliable way under stress (primarily Tier 1 and Tier 2 capital and stable deposits). The required amount of stable funding reflects the funding of illiquid assets and is calculated as the value of these assets weighted with liquidity risk factors by asset types.

ratio (LCR) controls banks' liquidity at a 30-day horizon, and the net stable funding ratio (NSFR) does so at a one-year horizon (box 6.14).

The LCR and NFSR have been controversial, not least because it is difficult to agree on a definition of HQLA to be used as the numerator of LCR in Equation (B6.14.1). Are residential mortgages highly liquid? Should assets which can be pledged as collateral to obtain liquidity from the central bank count as HQLA? Collateral eligible to ordinary monetary policy operations is fairly liquid in the United States, but it is less so in Europe where loans to small- and medium sized enterprises (SMEs) can be pledged with the ECB—even buildings can be collateral in the case of emergency liquidity assistance provided by national central banks. If an asset is considered HQLA for the sole reason that it can be pledged with the central bank, then the latter becomes a lender of first resort, not of last resort, and liquidity buffers are pointless. This is a reminder of the tension between liquidity regulation and lending of last resort by the central bank, already evidenced in Section 6.2. This tension flared during the global financial crisis, when strained market liquidity led central banks to apply the Bagehot principle in a more flexible way, including by lowering interest rates charged on emergency lending and by accepting lower quality collateral.[46]

A paradox of liquidity buffers is that they are not . . . liquid. Charles Goodhart's parable of the taxi stand says it all:

> There is a story of a traveler arriving at a station late at night, who is overjoyed to see one taxi remaining. She hails it, only for the taxi driver to respond that he cannot help her, since local by-laws require one taxi to be present at the station at all times! (Goodhart 2010, p. 175)

To address this shortcoming, supervisors can request banks to hold more than the LCR or NFSR in normal time and/or to let them deplete buffers in crisis time. But banks may be reluctant, fearing a negative stigma. There is always a risk of coordination failure, in which case the central bank has no choice but to step in.

Among the major central banks, the US Federal Reserve has been the most hesitant to act as LOLR, out of fear of creating moral hazard, pandering to vested interests, and interfering with market mechanisms. It has nevertheless opened its discount window during the global financial crisis, notably by operating the "Term Auction Facility" between December 2007 and April 2010 and by reducing the spread between its primary credit rate and the target federal funds rate from 100 to 50, then to 25 basis points (increased back to 50 when the crisis was over). The Dodd-Frank Act of 2010 mandates the Fed to disclose emergency lending to commercial banks and limits the Fed's authority to lend to other entities (including investment banks) to cases of broad-based liquidity stress, with prior approval of the Secretary of the Treasury. In the euro area, the collateral pool of monetary policy was always broad, and the ECB has been a large-scale provider of *emergency liquidity assistance* (ELA) to banks in crisis-hit countries such as Ireland, Greece, and

Cyprus. ELA is legally extended by national central banks at their own risk (meaning, ultimately, at the risk of their national government), but the ECB Governing Council can object if it would interfere with the objectives of the single monetary policy.[47],[48]

As explained in Section 6.2.3, liquidity is not provided exclusively by banks but also by market participants such as money market funds or investors borrowing securities on repo. Liquidity risk outside banks also creates externalities and calls for public regulation and/or intervention. This will be discussed in Section 6.3.2, which is devoted to capital market regulation.

d) Banking supervision and regulation in the euro area

As explained earlier in this chapter and in Chapter 5, the euro area crisis was amplified by the tight link between sovereigns' and banks' creditworthiness, or the "doom loop," particularly in small economies such as Ireland and Cyprus where banking systems were overextended compared to the domestic tax base. The political decision to launch a *Banking Union* in July 2012 between

Box 6.15 Europe's Weapon Against the Bank–Sovereign Doom Loop: Banking Union

Figure B6.15.1 shows that the correlation between the respective costs of insuring against bank and sovereign defaults is significantly tighter in the euro area than in the rest of the world. This is due to reciprocal exposures of banks to sovereigns and vice-versa. A large fraction of banks' assets are domestic sovereign bonds, which are considered riskless by European regulation, and, until the entry into force of bail-in rules, widespread expectations that banks would be bailed out have created off-balance liabilities for governments.

Steps were taken in 2012 to break the doom loop:

- A *Single Supervisory Mechanism (SSM)* hosted by the ECB in Frankfurt supervises the 130 largest banks in the euro area, harmonizes supervisory definitions and practices for all others, and is gradually removing national options and discretions in bank supervision. The SSM is governed by a 25-member Supervisory Board including a Chair, Vice Chair, 4 members appointed by the ECB, and the 19 heads of the national authorities competent for banking supervision (Schoenmaker and Véron, 2016).
- A *Single Resolution Mechanism (SRM)* approves banks' recovery planning and takes resolution action in case of bank failure. It is governed by a Single Resolution Board hosted by the European Commission in Brussels. A pot of money, the *Single Resolution Fund,* is endowed with 55 billion euros and gradually funded by

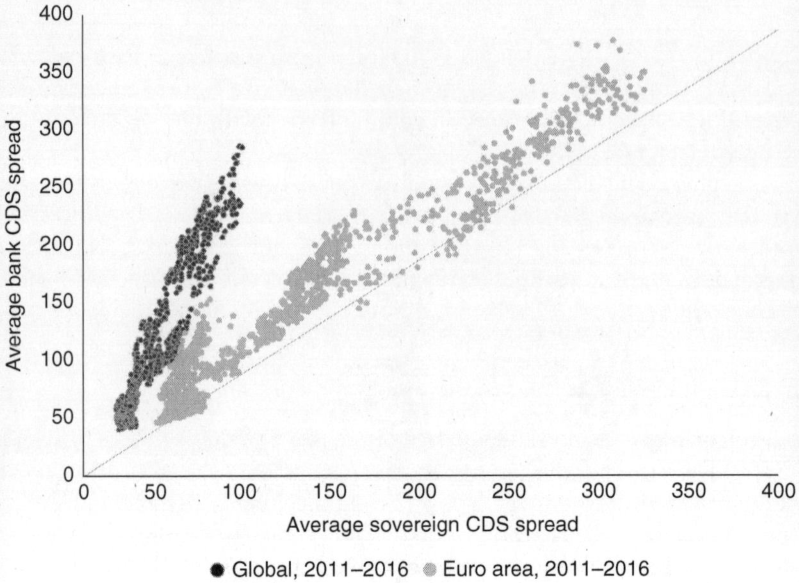

Figure B6.15.1 Correlation between the costs of insuring against bank and sovereign default: average sovereign credit default swap (CDS) spread and bank CDS spread, in percent, 2011–2014.
European Central Bank data, based on spreads of sovereign and bank credit default swaps.

commercial banks and pooled across member states between 2016 and 2023.

- A set of rules were written into European law (in the *Bank Recovery and Resolution Directive* [BRRD]) to organize bank resolution and secure banks' loss-absorption capacity. Bail-in was tested in several countries (Spain, Slovenia, Italy, and, most importantly, Cyprus; see box 6.13), and the European resolution procedure was used for the first time in June 2017 for a Spanish bank, Banco Popular (Philippon and Salord, 2017).
- Macroprudential authority was given to the ECB to supplement decisions taken by national authorities (see Section 6.3.3).

Three measures were, however, postponed to later discussions: a European Deposit Insurance Scheme ensuring that the cost of insuring a bank's deposits (mandatory up to 100,000 euro per bank account under European law) is not all borne by its home government; the possibility for the euro area bailout fund, the European Stability Mechanism, to directly recapitalize banks without going through national governments; and incentives for banks to reduce their sovereign exposures, either through quantitative limits or non-zero capital requirements on nondiversified sovereign exposures.

Absent these measures, the doom loop is not really broken. Bank and sovereign risks remain correlated.

the 19 euro area Member States was largely aimed at breaking the doom loop and mitigating the impact of any future crisis (box 6.15).

e) Banking as an industry: Competition, technical change, and inclusion

Policies addressed at the banking sector are not only prudential (i.e., aimed at avoiding excessive risk-taking and ensuring the stability of the system), but also aim at making the sector efficient, as in any other industry. Given the role of the financial sector in allocating resources across the economy, this is part of the broader set of policies ensuring allocative efficiency (Chapter 9).

Competition issues in the banking sector are closely related to financial stability considerations, and finding the right degree of competition strikes a difficult balance (Vives, 2016). We documented in Section 1 the excessive rent extracted by finance from the economy. We've also seen that large banks tend to consider themselves too big to fail, which creates massive negative externalities. Some degree of monopoly power by banks is nevertheless justified, for at least three reasons. First, economies of scale allow banks to reap the benefits of risk diversification and liquidity pooling. Second, bank capital buffers matter for financial stability. The easiest way for banks to build capital is to retain profits, and thin profit margins therefore pose a risk to their capital position and to financial stability when external sources of capital are scarce.

And third, banks need to generate healthy profits to invest and keep pace with technological change. Banking has become an information-processing industry and relies heavily on digital information. Digital innovations, branded *FinTech,* allow disintermediated, *peer-to-peer lending* and crowdfunding, favoring new non-bank players over incumbent banks. Distributed ledger technologies (such as the Blockchain) may one day allow payment systems and financial market infrastructures to operate without a central counterparty.[49] In many emerging market and low-income economies, retail payments are initiated from mobile phones.[50] Cryptocurrencies such as the Bitcoin already compete, albeit on a small scale, with money issued by central banks and commercial banks.

As shown on figure 6.10, US and Nordic banks have substantially improved their cost-to-assets and cost-to-income ratios between 2010 and 2016, whereas euro area banks have moved in the wrong direction. There are several explanations for this mediocre performance. The first one is not specific to Europe: bank profits have been globally impacted by a low interest rate environment that compresses banks' net interest margin (that is, the difference between lending and borrowing rates). Second, there are too many banks in the euro area, and consolidation has been slowed down by the crisis. Third, as shown by figure 6.10, the cost basis of European banks is too high. And fourth, as explained in box 6.16, in several euro area countries,

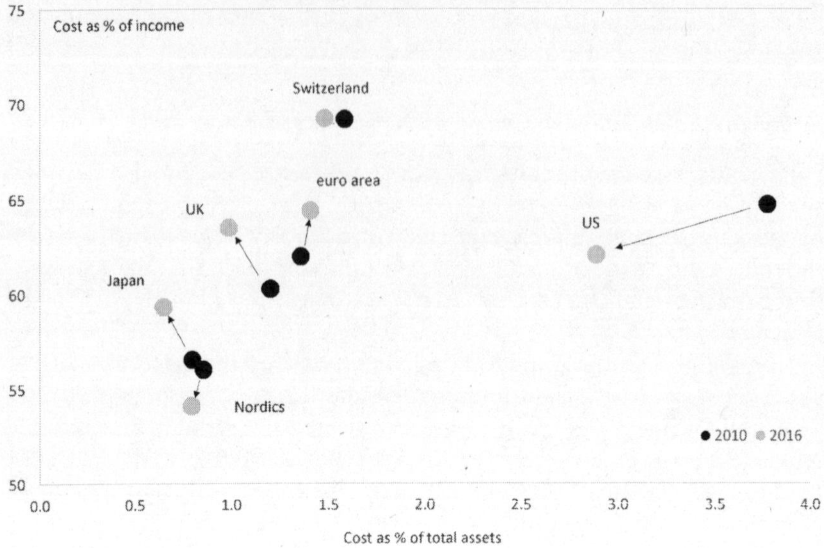

Figure 6.10 Evolution of banks' cost-to-assets and cost-to-income ratios in percent between 2010 and 2016.
Figures refer to the first three quarters of 2016 (for the euro area, the Nordics and the United Kingdom), the full year 2016 (for the United States), and 2015 (for Japan and Switzerland). Figures for the Nordics refer to the simple average of country-level values for Denmark, Finland, and Sweden.
European Central Bank (2017a), chart 3.9, p. 76.

banks are burdened with large amounts of nonperforming loans that require provisioning or write-downs.

Another set of allocative issues raised by finance is more specific to emerging and developing economies, even though some issues arise in advanced economies as well: these are related to financial inclusion. There may be "too much finance" globally, and, at the same time, many households and companies may be excluded from the benefits of accessing financial services. In low-income countries in 2015, according to the IMF, only one out of eight adults held deposit accounts in commercial banks. Digital innovation such as mobile payments can make it easier to provide market solutions to improve financial inclusion, with governments playing a catalytic role (e.g., by distributing special-purpose electronic money, such as prepaid cards to buy first-necessity products, or by making the regulatory environment friendlier to digital payments).[51]

It has also been observed that most households in advanced economies lack financial instruments to diversify their capital: their wealth is often composed of a single human-capital asset (their own skills) and a single real-estate asset (their home), which makes them vulnerable to shocks, especially as local factors, such as the closing down of a factory, may affect these two

Box 6.16 Nonperforming Loans

Loans are *nonperforming* when capital or interest has not been paid for a given time, typically three months. In early 2017, according to the ECB, nonperforming loans (NPLs) amounted to 865 billion euros or 5.9% of euro area bank loans, but this proportion reached 46.2% in Greece, 36.4% in Cyprus, 20.1% in Portugal, 14.8% in Italy, and 14.4% in Slovenia. While US accounting standards force banks to write off these loans (i.e., value them at zero) quickly, this was not the case in Europe until January 2018, when a new international financial reporting standard, IFRS9, forced banks to account for losses in a forward-looking way.

NPLs are a concern both from a prudential and from a macroeconomic perspective. They absorb banks' capital and liquidity without generating profits, and, for a given size of the balance sheet, they crowd out loans to profitable projects. Since part of banks' balance sheets do not respond to changes in financial conditions, they also hamper the transmission of monetary policy. Provisioning or writing down NPLs weighs on banks' profits, and they are tempted to restructure the loans to avoid materializing a loss. Banks then keep lending to "zombie" (i.e., insolvent and nonproductive) companies at the expense of productive ones. Such behavior can uselessly prolong recessions, as was seen in Japan in the 1990s (Caballero, Hoshi, and Kashyap, 2008). Bringing down NPLs requires a combination of actions, not all of which are in the hands of banks:

- First and foremost, banks need to act to identify and value NPLs, provision them, negotiate the payment schedule with the borrower, and/or sell the loan to another institution, such as an asset manager. Governments can empower them legally; for example, by allowing out-of-court settlements with the borrowers and by making it easier to repossess collateral.
- Government-sponsored asset-management companies (or *bad banks*) can be useful for categories of loans (such as loans to commercial real estate) that are homogenous enough to be pooled and generate economies of scale. Bad banks can help set loan prices above prevailing market conditions and closer to their long-term economic value to facilitate the cleaning-up process. This, however, amounts to a transfer from taxpayers to banks' shareholders, which distorts competition and is only justified if the high stock of NPLs creates negative externalities.
- High nominal GDP growth helps since it gradually reduces the relative size of legacy assets in bank balance sheets.

assets simultaneously. In this regard, even advanced societies may suffer from financial underdevelopment (see Badré, 2017; Shiller, 2003). Climate change and the fight against it also raise major intertemporal issues which call for innovative financial solutions.

6.3.2. Capital market regulation and supervision

The rationale for regulating markets is partially identical to that for regulating institutions: make market functioning resilient to shocks. But it also has specific objectives, such as ensuring transparency and equal access to information for all participants. In this section, we discuss the main objectives of capital market regulation before moving to two issues closely related to the previous section: curbing liquidity risk outside of the banking sector and regulating the fast-developing shadow-banking sector.

a) Capital market regulation

Capital markets are supervised and regulated by national *securities regulators*, also called *conduct authorities*, who set global standards in the Madrid-based *International Organization of Securities Commissions* (IOSCO), the equivalent of the BCBS for capital markets. Central banks also have a keen interest in the good functioning of financial market infrastructures.[52]

A first area of interest for capital market regulators is *business conduct* (i.e., possible market manipulation, insider trading, breaches of market disclosure rules, and so on). Regulators coordinate closely with judicial authorities since many breaches of compliance also qualify as criminal offenses. Strict conduct standards help curb risk-taking in the financial industry, where a culture of greed has too often emerged. The United Kingdom has taken this effort one step further with the UK Financial Services (Banking Reform) Act of 2013, making banks' senior managers criminally liable for reckless decision-making leading to a bank failure. This is part of a broader agenda (which also includes compensation rules) to eliminate market inefficiencies created by rent-seeking and distorted personal incentives—in other words, to "save capitalism from the capitalists" (Rajan and Zingales, 2004).

Investor protection more broadly extends to controlling information given to investors to ensure an efficient price discovery process in the market and avoid misselling of complex financial products to financially illiterate investors. *Financial literacy* is an important condition for well-functioning capital markets. The inconvenient truth is that it is usually rather poor, as shown in box 6.17. The importance of financial literacy extends to insurance and retirement savings, which we're not discussing here.

Another objective is to improve market structures and ensure an efficient price discovery process, given the information asymmetry identified in Section 6.2.3. Since the global financial crisis, the priority has been to

Box 6.17 Financial Illiteracy

The Organization for Economic Cooperation and Development (OECD) has surveyed people with different backgrounds in 14 countries, asking simple questions about financial knowledge and financial behavior (Atkinson and Messy, 2012). The findings paint a worrying picture of financial literacy in participating countries. A large proportion of respondents (from 54% in Germany and 64% in the United Kingdom, to as many as 86% in Peru and 90% in Albania) could not calculate simple interest on a savings account over one year and compound it over five years. To a question on risk and return: "Is an investment with a high return likely to be high risk?," the rate of incorrect answers varied from 14% in Hungary to 52% in Poland (the correct answer being yes). To a question on diversification: "Is it usually possible to reduce the risk of investing in the stock market by buying a wide range of stocks and shares?," the rate of incorrect answers varied from 37% in Albania to 53% in Ireland (the correct answer being again yes).

The OECD also found that women have much lower levels of financial knowledge than men in almost all countries studied, Hungary being the exception. Separately, the OECD includes a financial literacy assessment in its Programme for International Student Assessment (PISA), targeting 15-year-old students. In 2015, 22% of students scored below the baseline level of financial proficiency that the OECD considers necessary to participate in society. The number was as high as 38% in Chile and 35% in the Slovak Republic, and as low as 13% in Canada and 11% in Russia.

ensure that securities are traded on *trading venues* (including traditional stock exchanges but also on platforms sponsored by banks) rather than over the counter. A stated objective of G20 leaders has been the migration of bespoke, bilateral derivatives transactions (OTC transactions) to trading platforms and to centralized clearing. The recent strand of market regulation has forced competition among trading venues and among investment firms (see, e.g., Francotte, Lannoo, and Valiante, 2011, in the European case) which has spurred technology investment in platforms and trading.

Regulators have also forced price transparency on stock market transactions, both *pre-trade* (when intentions to buy and sell are registered in an order book) and *post-trade* (after the buyer and seller have met), and they have established rules for the execution of transactions. *Pre-trade transparency* supports the price discovery process, but it can also impair market liquidity. Large-ticket transactions, or transaction on less-liquid financial instruments such as corporate bonds, are likely to have a visible impact on prices when realized, and the prospective buyer or seller doesn't want to reveal valuable private information in advance, which would allow other market participants to anticipate price movements and position against her. This may result in transactions not taking place at all, just as in the Grossman-Stiglitz paradox mentioned in Section 6.2.3. A large part of the policy discussion therefore focuses on exceptions to pre-trade transparency and on the desirability of such transparency for less liquid markets. *Post-trade transparency* has fewer shortcomings and an enormous effort was made since the crisis to improve data reporting and disclosure. Beyond real-time disclosure by trading venues, reporting to databases called *trade repositories* is now mandatory. Trade repositories collect millions of data points every day, and efforts are ongoing to make them usable by authorities and the public at large, which requires harmonizing data formats and allowing aggregation across market segments and jurisdictions.

Another area of market regulation with important consequences for financial stability, and which has been informed by academic research, is the resilience and regulation of clearing houses. Mandatory centralization of clearing for OTC derivatives and the increased use of central clearing for other transactions, such as repos, has made clearing houses grow in size and complexity and become "super systemic" as nodes of the global financial network. This has prompted a reassessment of the regulatory framework (Cœuré, 2017).

Box 6.18 Unifying European Capital Markets

The risk-sharing properties of capital markets (i.e., their ability to stabilize local consumption after an idiosyncratic shock) matter even more in a monetary union. Participating jurisdictions have given up control over monetary policy, hence also over the exchange rate, and more flexibility is needed at a microeconomic level to cushion asymmetric shocks. Moreover, the euro area lacks a system of fiscal transfers, and research has shown that the contribution of capital markets to the smoothing of macroeconomic shocks is much more limited than in the United States (see Chapter 7, Section 7.2.1). In addition, the euro area crisis has evidenced lack of resilience of capital markets to large confidence shocks: cross-border financing was mainly done as interbank lending, which quickly dried up in the crisis, while more resilient forms of finance (such as bond and equity financing) did not have a significant cross-border dimension.

And, finally, the financing mix of nonfinancial companies in Continental Europe is heavily reliant on banks and has exacerbated the impact of the banking crisis on the real economy. As argued by De Fiore and Uhlig (2011), bond and equity financing provide a "spare tire" to companies, which can mitigate the adverse effects of financial crises.

The Capital Markets Union (CMU) project is made even more significant by the UK decision to leave the European Union. Continental Europe has a high saving rate and high investment needs. Having European savings pooled and allocated by financial intermediaries based in London made sense as long as the UK was part of the Single Market. It created economies of scale and scope by pooling transactions in one big financial center, without much friction. London leaving the Single Market will create frictions and regulatory uncertainty and will thus cause questions to arise about the economic relevance of recycling savings in an offshore center. After Brexit, it becomes even more important for the Continent to build an efficient cross-border financial system.

In Europe, the Commission proposed, in 2015, a *Capital Markets Union* (CMU) aiming at the creation of a true single market for capital by encouraging securitization, innovation financing, and cross-border equity and bond flows in the 28 countries of the European Union (European Commission, 2015*a*; 2015*b*). In a nutshell, the CMU consists in nudging Europe's financial structure toward more market-based finance (box 6.18). The project has hit major roadblocks such as the need to unify national contract and insolvency laws.

b) Regulating market-based finance

Tighter bank regulation creates a risk of regulatory arbitrage; that is, of activities migrating to less regulated parts of the industry, leading to either an expansion of the less regulated sector or to a race to the bottom in regulatory standards. And in fact, *market-based finance* has steadily expanded since the global financial crisis. Market-based finance includes different activities, some of which are economically equivalent to banking. Liquidity is provided by money market funds investing in short-term commercial paper issued by financial and nonfinancial players and by repos undertaken by any financial institution. Even the core social role of banks, matching savings and investment in the economy, can be replicated by asset managers when they buy bundles of corporate or housing loans after they have been originated by banks. Hence the generic term of *shadow banking* coined for these activities.

Of course, non-banks do not collect retail deposits but they invest assets on behalf of clients, which justifies why they are regulated more lightly. They can nevertheless create risks to the system. As noted in Section 6.2, a run on a market-based institution (an asset manager or a money market fund) is akin to a bank run. It entails a risk of fire sales of assets with negative externalities to the financial system. The risk is particularly acute for open-ended investment funds, the clients of which can redeem money at any time, just as depositors can withdraw money from their bank account. Securities regulators have responded timidly: they ask funds to monitor and control liquidity risk when fund redemption terms are shorter than the investment horizon,[53] but they have fallen short of intervening directly, even when liquidity mismatches create systemic risk.

Liquidity mismatch in *money market funds* raises even more acute concern. Given their short maturity, shares in money market funds are sold to investors as risk-free alternatives to cash deposits, even though they may be partly invested in illiquid instruments. Concerns are particularly relevant in the case of constant net asset value (CNAV) funds (as opposed to variable net asset value or VNAV). These funds, available in the United States, China, Ireland, and Luxembourg, guarantee the face value of investment. They mimic cash without being as safe, giving investors a false sense of security and creating a risk of run given their sensitivity to information flows on underlying assets (see box 6.9). New EU and US rules for money market funds impose asset disclosure and diversification, create frictions to prevent investors runs, and restrict CNAV funds without banning them altogether.[54]

6.3.3 Macroprudential policies

Macroprudential regulation is recent and still under development, even though it builds on a tradition of research on financial cycles, including (but not only) at the Bank for International Settlements (Borio, Drehmann, and Tsatsaronis, 2012).

a) Objectives and trade-offs

Whether systemic risk in the financial system should be addressed by monetary policy, by microprudential, or by macroprudential policy is a lively debate in the academic and central banking communities.

For long, central bankers have pondered whether financial asset prices should be intermediate targets of monetary policy (see Chapter 5) and whether monetary policy should act *ex post* to revive the economy after a financial bubble has burst or *ex ante* by lifting policy rates and pricking the bubble before it is too late—a choice between *leaning* (against the wind) and *cleaning*. The pre-crisis doctrine strongly emphasized the latter because it avoided central bankers having to form a view on the correct valuation of assets and acting in accordance—in other words, pretending they knew better than the market. The crisis has led some to reconsider the issue, but the answer is not straightforward. On the one hand, it is argued that loose US monetary policy during the "Great Moderation" was a cause of the global financial crisis. The Bank for International Settlements has specialized in warning against the adverse financial stability consequences of expansionary monetary policy and in advocating leaning rather than cleaning (Caruana, 2014). Along the same line, Harvard economist and former Federal Reserve governor Jeremy Stein famously argued that the interest rate policy is a better instrument than targeted macroprudential measures because it shapes the behavior of all economic agents and therefore "gets in all the cracks":

> There is no general separation principle for monetary policy and financial stability. Monetary policy is fundamentally in the business of altering risk premiums such as term premiums and credit spreads. So monetary policymakers cannot wash their hands of what happens when these spreads revert sharply. If these abrupt reversions also turn out to have nontrivial economic consequences, then they are clearly of potential relevance to policymakers. (Stein, 2014)

On the other hand, central banks need narrow mandates to balance their independence, and, having only one instrument, they should not be overburdened with broad financial stability objectives (an argument derived from the Tinbergen principle, see Chapter 1). Moreover, the drivers of financial instability are often sectoral, most importantly originating in the real estate sector (given the importance of housing prices for the financial cycle), which calls for targeted instruments and coordination with nonmonetary authorities. On balance, central banks now accept that they should be "leaning"—but using macroprudential, not monetary instruments (see Constâncio, 2016, for a review of these instruments).

As for the choice between micro- and macroprudential instruments, it is also not straightforward. As we'll see later, most macroprudential instruments are applied to individual banks and thus require close cooperation with bank supervisors. Conflicts can therefore arise. Macroprudential requirements are countercyclical by nature, but, when faced with systemic risk, bank supervisors' instinctive reaction will always be to ask banks to increase their capital and liquidity buffers, with procyclical consequences (Angeloni, 2014). Mark Twain is said to have remarked that "A banker is a fellow who lends you an umbrella when the sun is shining, but wants it back the minute it begins to rain."[55] A way to square this is to design prudential requirements *through the cycle*, so that they avoid the build-up of risk when times are good and don't make things worse when times are bad.

An additional challenge relates to cross-border spillovers arising from macroprudential measures. Macroprudential action in one country can divert excess credit flows toward comparable economies, while lack of action increases the odds of a financial crisis. Moreover, actions on banks can be pointless if they have affiliates in multiple jurisdictions. All of this calls for international coordination of macroprudential frameworks (International Monetary Fund, 2013).

b) The macroprudential toolkit

Macroprudential frameworks differ across countries and notably between advanced and emerging-market economies,[56] but they typically include early warning indicators and a toolkit of macroprudential instruments.

Early warning indicators aim at identifying the build-up of risk and leverage in the system. The simplest indicator is the departure of the credit-to-GDP ratio from its longer term trend, sometimes called the *Basel gap*. More elaborate measures of financial cycles and/or systemic risk have also been developed, such as those discussed in Section 6.2.4.[57] Many central banks now publish Financial Stability Reviews with dashboards and analyses of risks to financial stability. However, identifying financial imbalances in real time remains a challenge.

The macroprudential toolkit mainly includes instruments applied to banks, which can be put in three broad categories:[58]

- *Borrower-oriented instruments* target the asset side of banks' balance sheets. They aim at curbing demand-driven credit expansions in specific sectors. They include caps to loan-to-value and debt-to-income ratios for housing loans and concentration limits to sectoral exposures.
- *Capital-based* and *liquidity-based instruments* are targeted at the liability side of banks' balance sheets. The former, which include the countercyclical capital buffer of the Basel III Accord (box 6.12), aim at curbing supply-driven expansions of credit. The latter address liquidity mismatches in banks insofar as they can create systemic risk.
- Emerging economies have added to this toolkit *capital flow management measures* to curb cross-border flows which can lead to excessive credit supply (see Chapter 7).

Taxes and nonfinancial regulation can be part of the macroprudential toolkit in a broad sense, which also explains why governments are part of macroprudential committees. Take the example of a rise in housing prices. This may be due to banks providing too much credit, in which case raising the countercyclical buffer or capping loan-to-value or loan-to-income is appropriate. But it may also be due to rigid housing supply, in which case construction restrictions should be relaxed and bank supervisors can't do much.

It is too early to conclude on the usefulness of macroprudential policies. Cerutti et al. (Cerutti, Claessens, and Laeven, 2017) have documented their use by a large set of countries and found significant mitigating effects on credit developments, stronger in developing and emerging economies and in closed rather than open economies. A remaining gap in the macroprudential framework is market-based finance, where the prudential approach remains largely directed at individual institutions and almost entirely misses the macroprudential dimension (Constâncio, 2017).

6.3.4 The future of financial regulation

Since the Pittsburgh Summit in 2009, the post-crisis regulatory effort has yielded vastly increased bank capital and liquidity buffers, measures to end too-big-to-fail; centralization and disclosure of previously thinly spread and opaque OTC transactions; and more stringent conduct rules. Commitment to cooperate in the G20 and FSB has produced a reasonable level of cross-border consistency, at least compared to the pre-crisis landscape.[59] When G20 leaders met in Hamburg in 2017, the Pittsburgh agenda was by and large completed. Open questions remain, however.

A first set of questions relates to the consistency and scope of the new regulatory approach. Regulators have invested much effort in improving bank capital and liquidity, but market-based finance remains largely unregulated, and macroprudential thinking, although developing fast, has not come of age. How different policy instruments interact with each other and shape private incentives is not well understood. There are persisting disagreements on the choice between monetary, micro-, and macroprudential instruments to curb the financial cycle. We are still far from a "Tinbergian" world where objectives would be clearly identified and instruments would be clearly assigned. Increasingly complex financial systems have been matched by increasingly complex regulatory frameworks, while decision-making in a complex environment may benefit from the use of simpler decision rules (Haldane and Madouros, 2012). Finally, data availability, although gradually improving, still severely limits policymakers' ability to confront theories with facts and build

Box 6.19 Regulatory Cycles in the United States

The 1929 stock market crash and the Great Depression triggered a strong regulatory reaction in the United States. Commercial (i.e., deposit-taking) and investment banking activities were separated in 1933 by the *Glass-Steagall Act,* and the Securities and Exchange Commission was established to protect investors and ensure fair market functioning. This state of affair lasted until the 1980s but was put under severe pressure in the early 1990s by financial globalization and financial innovation, with commercial banks wanting to join the fray. This culminated in 1999 with the repeal of Glass-Steagall by the Gramm-Leach-Bliley Act and with the unbridled development of derivatives markets.[61] In 2005, the controversy mentioned at the onset of this chapter between two highly respected academics, R. Rajan and L. Summers, was typical of emerging doubts. Rajan was finally right: the global financial crisis erupted and led to another U-turn toward stricter and more intrusive regulation, enshrined in the United States in the "Wall Street Reform and Consumer Protection" or *Dodd-Frank Act* of 2010. The act includes provisions limiting proprietary trading activities of commercial banks, thus constituting, in effect, a modest step back toward Glass-Steagall (figure B6.19.1). In the late 2010s, as this new approach had by and large been implemented, US President Trump was elected on an explicit platform to undo a large part of it—marking perhaps the start of a new cycle.

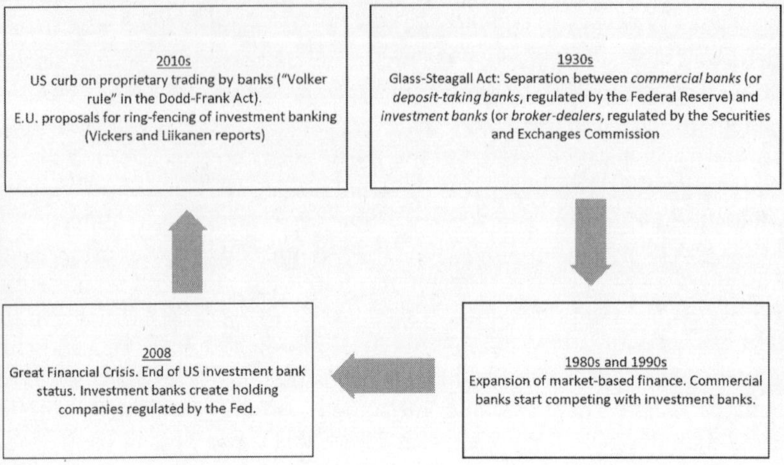

Figure B6.19.1 Regulating banking structures: a never-ending cycle?

models, and to make sense—even after the facts—of a complex network of interactions among financial institutions, markets, and jurisdictions.

A second set of questions relates to the persistence of the global regulatory effort in the face of powerful vested interests and with waning incentives for cross-border cooperation. The history of financial regulation is one of wide pendulum swings between extreme laissez-faire and intrusive regulation. These swings reflect a tension between two opposite forces. On the one hand, financial crises leave the economy and the social fabric deeply scarred and stir popular anger, creating strong demand for regulation. On the other hand, regulation is subject to intense lobbying by a financial industry which keeps cosy links with politicians and bureaucrats and has deep pockets. At times, the former or the latter force have dominated (box 6.19).

A third set of questions relates to the role of technological change. Often in the past, disruptive financial innovation has challenged established business models and prompted new regulatory approaches, but with a significant lag. For instance, derivatives transactions soared in the late 1980s, but it took the global financial crisis, 20 years later, for the regulatory community to address seriously the challenges posed by OTC derivatives and mandate an appropriate degree of centralization and disclosure. The extent to which FinTech will challenge existing regulatory frameworks, at which horizon, and how and when the latter will adjust are an entirely open question.

Pendulum swings between cross-border cooperation and cross-border competition have exacerbated the regulatory cycle. The Basel I Accord was propelled by concerns that US banks had been hurt by the Latin American crisis of 1982. Stricter requirements were needed but would risk shifting business to Japan if Japanese banks would not follow suit (Goodhart, 2010). In the 2000s, in the run-up to the global financial crisis, macroeconomic moderation repressed financial volatility and competition between financial centers and encouraged a race to the bottom of regulatory standards under the guise of "light-touch regulation." In 2009, the Pittsburgh Summit opened a new era of regulatory cooperation, which the 2016 US election and Brexit may eventually challenge. There is no reason to believe that these cycles will stop in the future. This warrants a healthy pessimism on the possibility of ending financial crises.

Notes

1. See Merton (1995) for a functional description.
2. See Ferguson (2008) for a history of finance and Graeber (2011, chapt. 2) for a discussion of the order of appearance of debt and money.
3. See Andreau (1987) and Temin (2004).
4. Option contracts developed in the sixteenth and seventeenth centuries in Amsterdam, Antwerp, and London, but examples are documented in the Antiquity. In his *Politics*, Aristotle tells how Thales of Miletus realized a large sum of money by purchasing the olive presses of Miletus and Chios on a forward basis, betting on favorable future weather (Poitras, 2008; Kairys and Valerio, 1997).
5. On the *commenda* and limited liability, see Carney (2000), Sayous (1929), and Gonzales de Lara (2001).
6. *The Economist* (1999).
7. This also explains the limited role of capital markets in hedging household income against economic shocks in Europe, contrary to the United States; see also Chapter 7.
8. The expansion of derivatives markets was supported by mathematical innovations such as the Black-Scholes formula (which ties the value of an option to the variance of the price of the underlying asset), making the financial industry heavily reliant on mathematical modeling and engineering skills.
9. Such diversification is in fact limited. Savers often invest in companies whose performance is correlated with their own professional prospects, including the one that employs them.
10. Own funds also include reinvested benefits, which belong to shareholders, and other items such as tax credits.
11. See Allen and Gale (2004), Claessens (2016) and Kremer and Popov (2018) for a discussion of financial structures.
12. See European Commission (2015*b*) for a discussion of the pros and cons of bank-based and market-based financial systems.
13. Some market infrastructures (such as typically, RTGS systems) are owned and operated by central banks, while some others are for-profit. In the latter case, they are heavily regulated given their systemic role in the financial system and their nature of natural monopolies.

14. "I always like to think of these [financial] crises as analogous to a power failure. The network would collapse, the connections would go away, and output would of course drop very rapidly. There'd be a set of economists who'd sit around and explain that electricity was only four percent of the economy, and so if you lose eighty percent of electricity you couldn't possibly have lost more than three percent of the economy . . . but it would be stupid" (Summers, 2013).
15. See the studies collected in Claessens et al. (2014).
16. See Chapter 5 for the monetary policy consequences and Section 6.3 for the regulatory consequences.
17. See Velde (2009) for a detailed analysis.
18. See Cœuré (2014) for a discussion.
19. Using instrumental variables helps control the reverse causality from development to finance. Such variables should be correlated with the development of finance but not with current GDP. Variables related to the quality of legal institutions have often been used.
20. According to Goldin and Katz (2008), 15% of Harvard graduates (class of 1990) worked in finance 15 years later, three times more than in the 1970s.
21. See the corporate finance textbook of Brealey, Myers, and Allen (9th edition, 2007).
22. According to a meta-study run by De Mooij (2011), with a corporate income tax rate of 40%, the corporate leverage ratio is 10% higher with interest deductibility than under a system that would be neutral between debt and equity. Interest deductibility also encourages debt-shifting practices by multinationals, consisting in locating debt in high-tax countries.
23. A typical example is the conflict between firm management and shareholders on the use of *free cash flow* (i.e., what remains of the firm's earnings after profitable projects have been financed). See Jensen (1986).
24. The price of debt remains unaffected since it serves a fixed income, assuming that more debt does not increase the firm's probability of default.
25. Signaling models have been used to explain other dimensions of firms' financial choices in the presence of different tax regimes, such as dividend distribution policies when cash dividends are taxed at a higher rate than capital gains (Bhattacharya, 1979; Poterba and Summers, 1985).
26. Financial forecasts are fundamentally different from weather forecasts which have no impact on the weather itself.
27. The random walk can be compared to the course of a drunkard, each step of whom is random and independent from the previous ones.
28. See Biais et al. (Biais, Blosten, and Spatt, 2005) and the textbook by Foucault, Pagano, and Röell (2013). Section 6.3.2 elaborates on the regulatory consequences.
29. Biesenbach and Cipriani (2012) discuss the former event. On the latter, see the joint staff report prepared by US departments and agencies (US Department of the Treasury et al., 2015).
30. See Brunnermeier (2001, chapt. 6) and the accompanying references.
31. Investment banks raise money by issuing bonds and bills and lending out their assets through repurchase agreements. Outside of the United States, most investment

banks are also commercial banks, while not all commercial banks are investment banks. Standalone investment banks are very much a US phenomenon.

32. See Santos (2000) for a survey.
33. See the articles collected by Aoki and Patrick (1994). In his review of the book, Rajan (1996) highlights the institutional underpinnings of the main bank system.
34. Adverse selection is well known in the insurance industry. In a country where health insurance is not compulsory, there is a risk that only individuals with bad health conditions buy insurance. The same is true of credit.
35. An example is the use of positive credit registers of consumer loans which include not only defaulted consumers but also performing ones. This can reduce adverse selection.
36. Note, however, that government intervention in the credit market is justified only if there is a wedge between the social and private returns on the projects (say, because they are innovative or environment-friendly), which justifies the potential cost for taxpayers. Absent such reason, using taxpayer money to subsidize risky projects is just pandering to vested interests.
37. Hale, Kapan, and Minoiu (2014) study the global network of syndicated bank loans. See the Basel Committee on Banking Supervision et al. (2017) study of the network of large clearing houses and their members. Hałaj and Kok (2013) show how missing bilateral data can be inferred from the knowledge of aggregate balance sheets.
38. For a complete discussion, see the book edited by Freixas, Laeven, and Peydró (2015) as well as Hansen (2013).
39. The ECB also produces a composite indicator which aggregates systemic risk measures across different market segments (Holló, Kremer, and Lo Duca, 2012).
40. See Fisher (1933), Eggertsson and Krugman (2012), and the discussion of debt deflation in Chapter 5.
41. A pecuniary externality occurs when the behavior of an economic agent exerts an influence over other agents through its impact on market prices.
42. If the Modigliani-Miller theorem would hold for banks, shareholders' incentives would not depend on their liability structure. When default is possible, the conditions for the Modigliani-Miller theorem are not met. A key reason why bank capital is regulated is to protect taxpayers and bank depositors when the bank goes bust.
43. See Basel Committee for Banking Supervision (2014).
44. See Chamley, Kotlikoff, and Polemarchakis (2012); and Pennacchi (2012) for a review.
45. These developments include the development of collateralized lending, funded pension savings in advanced economies (together with regulatory requirements forcing pension funds to hold safe assets), large-scale asset-purchase programs by advanced economies central banks (Chapter 5), and the build-up of foreign exchange reserves in emerging market economies (largely invested in US and European government bonds; see Chapter 7).
46. On the interrelation between Basel III and ECB monetary policy, see Bucalossi et al. (2016).

47. The agreement on emergency liquidity assistance was published by the ECB in June 2017; see https://www.ecb.europa.eu/mopo/ela/html/index.en.html.
48. The Reserve Bank of Australia has found an original way to square the tension between *ex ante* and *ex post* incentives. A "committed liquidity facility" is available to banks in times of crisis. Access to this facility involves paying an upfront fee to the central bank so as not to distort *ex ante* incentives. See Cœuré (2013) for a discussion.
49. See Financial Stability Board (2017).
50. On the development of digital retail payment and its consequences for financial inclusion, see Committee on Payments and Market Infrastructures and World Bank Group (2016).
51. See Committee on Payments and Market Infrastructures and World Bank Group (2016).
52. Central banks issue their own regulations on payments and set global standards in the Committee on Payments and Market Infrastructures (CPMI) of the Bank for International Settlements. Given possible overlaps, global standards for market infrastructures are produced jointly by the CPMI and IOSCO.
53. See the IOSCO consultation report on open-ended fund liquidity (Board of the International Organization of Securities Commissions, 2017).
54. For Europe, see http://www.consilium.europa.eu/en/press/press-releases/2017/05/16-money-market-fund-rules-adopted/; for the United States, see https://www.sec.gov/spotlight/money-market.shtml.
55. Similar remarks have been attributed to Robert Frost and to Ambrose Bierce.
56. For a review of the international experience, including in emerging-market economies, see International Monetary Fund (2013) and International Monetary Fund, Financial Stability Board and Bank for International Settlements (2016).
57. For an empirical indicator of the financial cycle, different from the business cycle, see Hiebert et al. (2016).
58. Angeloni (2014) reviews European macroprudential policy.
59. There are notable exceptions. Basel III applies to a limited number of internationally active banks in the United States and to all banks in Europe. The leverage ratio is higher in the United States than in Europe. Rules applying to proprietary trading by banks are very different across countries. The "single point of entry" principle for bank resolution is largely theoretical in the case of cross-border banks and even may become implausible in a world where cross-border movement of goods and capital is put into question and national sovereignty has become the highest political value.
60. In particular at shorter maturities, for which Merton's model assumes that the residual default risk converges to zero. The stochastic process driving asset returns can be refined (e.g., by adding jumps to Merton's continuous-time Brownian motion representation). See Huang and Huang (2012) for a discussion of the empirical performance of structural corporate default models.
61. In 1998, worried by the rapid development of CDSs and other OTC derivatives, CFTC Chair Brooksly Born asked to be given authority to regulate them. This was immediately turned down by Treasury Secretary Rubin, Fed Chair

Greenspan, and SEC Chair Arthur Levitt. In 1999, Born stepped down. US authorities concluded that regulating financial derivative would "perpetuate legal uncertainty or impose unnecessary regulatory burdens and constraints upon the development of these markets in the United States" (US Department of the Treasury et al., 1999).

References

Acharya, V., R. Engle, and M. Richardson (2012), "Capital Shortfall: A New Approach to Ranking and Regulating Systemic Risk," *American Economic Review, Proceedings & Papers*, 102 (3), pp. 59–64.

Admati, A., and M. Hellwig (2013), *The Bankers' New Clothes: What's Wrong with Banking and What to Do about It*, Princeton University Press.

Adrian, T., and M. Brunnermeier (2016), "CoVaR," *American Economic Review*, 106(7), pp. 1705–41.

Adrian, T., and H. S. Shin (2010), "Liquidity and Leverage," *Journal of Financial Intermediation*, 19, pp. 418–37.

Aghion, P., Howitt, P., and D. Mayer-Foulkes (2005), "The Effect of Financial Development on Convergence: Theory and Evidence," *Quarterly Journal of Economics*, 120 (1), p. 173–222.

Akerlof, G. (1970), "The Market For 'Lemons': Quality and the Market Mechanism," *Quarterly Journal of Economics*, 84 (3), pp. 488–500.

Allen, F., and D. Gale (2000), "Financial Contagion," *Journal of Political Economy*, 108 (1), pp. 1–33.

Allen, F., and D. Gale (2004), "Comparative Financial Systems: A Survey," in Bhattacharya, S., A. Thakor, and A. Boot, eds., *Credit, Intermediation and the Macroeconomy: Models and Perspectives*. Oxford University Press, pp. 699–770.

Andreau, J. (1987), "La vie financière dans le monde romain: les métiers de manieurs d'argent," École Française de Rome.

Angeloni, I. (2014), "European Macroprudential Policy from Gestation to Infancy," *Banque de France Financial Stability Review*, 18, pp. 71–84.

Aoki, M., and H. Patrick, Eds. (1994), *The Japanese Main Bank System: Its Relevance for Developing and Transforming Economies*, Oxford University Press.

Arcand, J. L., E. Berkes, and U. Panizza (2012), "Too Much Finance?" *IMF Working Paper*, 12/161.

Atkinson, A., and F. Messy (2012), "Measuring Financial Literacy: Results of the OECD/International Network on Financial Education (INFE) Pilot Study," *OECD Working Papers on Finance, Insurance and Private Pensions*, 15.

Avesani, R., A. García Pascual, and J. Li (2006), "A New Risk Indicator and Stress Testing Tool: A Multifactor Nth-to-Default CDS Basket," *IMF Working Paper*, 06/105.

Bachelier, L. (1900/1964), "Théorie de la spéculation," *Annales Scientifiques de l'École Normale Supérieure*, 3(17), pp. 21–86, reprinted in Cootner, P. H. (ed.), *The Random Character of Stock Prices*, MIT Press, pp. 17–78.

Badré, B. (2017), *Can Finance Save the World?* Berrett-Koehler.

Bagehot, W. (1873), *Lombard Street: A Description of the Money Market*, Henry S. King & Co.

Bank of England and European Central Bank (2014), "The Case for a Better Functioning Securitisation Market in the European Union," discussion paper, May.

Basel Committee on Banking Supervision (2010), "Basel III: A Global Regulatory Framework for More Resilient Banks and Banking Systems," October.

Basel Committee on Banking Supervision (2014), "Frequently Asked Questions on the Basel III Leverage Ratio Framework," October.

Basel Committee on Banking Supervision, Committee on Payments and Market Infrastructures, Financial Stability Board and International Organization of Securities Commissioners (2017), "Analysis of Central Clearing Interdependencies," July.

Bernanke, B., M. Gertler, and S. Gilchrist (1996), "The Financial Accelerator and the Flight to Quality," *The Review of Economics and Statistics*, 78(1), pp. 1–15.

Beyer, A., B. Cœuré, and C. Mendicino (2017). "The Crisis, Ten Years After: Lessons Learnt for Monetary and Financial Research," *Economics and Statistics*, 494-495-496, pp. 45–64.

Bhattacharya, S. (1979, "Imperfect Information, Dividend Policy, and the 'Bird in the Hand' Fallacy," *Bell Journal of Economics*, 10(1), pp. 259–70.

Biais, B., T. Glosten, and C. Spatt (2005), "Market Microstructure: A Survey of Microfoundations, Empirical Results and Policy Implications," *Journal of Financial Markets*, 8(2), pp. 217–64.

Biesenbach, A., and M. Cipriani (2012), "The Flash Crash, Two Years On," Federal Reserve Bank of New York, *Liberty Street Economics*, 7 May.

Black, F., and M. Scholes (1973), "The Pricing of Options and Corporate Liabilities," *Journal of Public Economics*, 81(3), 637–54.

Board of the International Organization of Securities Commissions (2017), "Open-ended Fund Liquidity and Risk Management – Good Practices and Issues for Consideration. Consultation Report," CR05/2017, July.

Bordo, M., and L. Rousseau (2011), "Historical Evidence on the Finance-Trade Growth Nexus," *NBER Working Paper*, 17024.

Borio, C., Drehmann, M., and K. Tsatsaronis (2012), "Characterising the Financial Cycle: Don't Lose Sight of the Medium Term!" *Bank for International Settlements Working Paper*, 380.

Braudel, F. (1981), *Civilization and Capitalism*, Collins.

Brealey, R., S. Myers, and F. Allen (2010), *Principles of Corporate Finance*, McGraw Hill.

Brittan, S. (2011), "Good Servants Can Make Bad Masters," *Financial Times*, June 9.

Brunnermeier, M. (2001), *Asset Pricing Under Asymmetric Information: Bubbles, Crashes, Technical Analysis, and Herding*, Oxford University Press.

Brunnermeier, M., and Y. Sannikov (2016), "The I Theory of Money," *CEPR Discussion Paper*, DP11444.

Caballero, R., T. Hoshi, and A. Kashyap (2008), "Zombie Lending and Depressed Restructuring in Japan," *American Economic Review*, 98(5), pp. 1943–77.

Calomiris, C., M. Flandreau, and L. Laeven (2016), "Political Foundations of the Lender of Last Resort: A Global Historical Narrative," *CEPR Discussion Paper*, 11448.

Caruana, J. (2014), "Redesigning the Central Bank for Financial Stability Responsibilities," speech on the occasion of the 135th Anniversary Conference of the Bulgarian National Bank, Sofia, June 6.

Carney, W. J. (2000), "Limited Liability," in Bouckaert, B., and G. De Geest, eds., *Encyclopedia of Law and Economics, Volume I*, Edward Elgar, pp. 659–91.

Cecchetti, S. (2014), "The Jury Is In," *CEPR Policy Insight*, 76.

Cecchetti, S., and E. Kharroubi (2014), "Why Does Financial Sector Growth Crowd Out Real Economic Growth?" *Bank for International Settlements Working Paper*, 490.

Cecchetti, S., and K. Schoenholtz (2014), "Making Finance Safe," October 6, http://www.moneyandbanking.com/.

Cerutti, E., S. Claessens, and L. Laeven (2017), "The Use and Effectiveness of Macroprudential Policies: New Evidence," *Journal of Financial Stability*, 28, pp. 203–24.

Chamley, C., L. Kotlikoff, and H. Polemarchakis (2012), "Limited-Purpose Banking—Moving from 'Trust Me' to 'Show Me' Banking," *American Economic Review: Papers and Proceedings*, 102(3), pp. 1–10.

Cicero, M. T. (66 BCE), "Pro Lege Manilia," §19, English translation by the Perseus Project at Tufts University, http://perseus.uchicago.edu/.

Claessens, S. (2016), "Regulation and Structural Change in Financial Systems," ECB Forum on Central Banking, Sintra, June.

Claessens, S., A. Kose, L. Laeven, and F. Valencia (2014), *Financial Crises: Causes, Consequences, and Policy Responses*, International Monetary Fund.

Cœuré, B. (2013), "Liquidity Regulation and Monetary Policy Implementation: From Theory to Practice," Toulouse School of Economics, October 3.

Cœuré, B. (2014), "On the Optimal Size of the Financial Sector," ECB conference on The Optimal Size of the Financial Sector, Frankfurt-am-Main, September 2.

Cœuré, B. (2017), "Central Clearing: Reaping the Benefits, Controlling the Risks," *Banque de France Financial Stability Review*, 21, pp. 97–110.

Committee on Payments and Market Infrastructures and World Bank Group (2016), *Payment Aspects of Financial Inclusion*, April.

Constâncio, V. (2016), "Principles of Macroprudential Policy," ECB-IMF conference on macroprudential policy, Frankfurt am Main, April 26.

Constâncio, V. (2017), "Macroprudential Policy in a Changing Financial System," Second ECB Macroprudential Policy and Research Conference, Frankfurt am Main, May 11.

Coval, J., J. Jurek, and E. Stratford (2009), "The Economics of Structured Finance," *Journal of Economic Perspectives*, 23(1), pp. 3–25.

Dang, T. V., G. Gorton, and B. Holmström (2012), "Ignorance, Debt and Financial Crises," unpublished manuscript.

De Fiore, F., and H. Uhlig (2011), "Bank Finance Versus Bond Finance," *Journal of Money, Credit and Banking*, 43(7), pp. 1399–421.

Demirgüc-Kunt, A., and B. Levine (1999), "Bank-Based and Market-Based Financial Systems: Cross-Country Comparisons," *World Bank Policy Working Paper*, 2143.

De Mooij (2011), "The Tax Elasticity of Corporate Debt: A Synthesis of Size and Variations," *IMF Working Paper*, 11/95.

Dewatripont, M., and J. Tirole (1994), *The Prudential Regulation of Banks*, MIT Press.
Diamond, D. (1984), "Financial Intermediation and Delegated Monitoring," *Review of Economic Studies*, 51, pp. 393–414.
Diamond, D. (1996), "Financial Intermediation as Delegated Monitoring: A Simple Example," *Federal Reserve Bank of Richmond Economic Quarterly*, 82/3.
Diamond, D., and P. Dybvig (1983),"Bank Runs, Deposit Insurance, and Liquidity," *Journal of Political Economy*, 91(3), pp. 401–19.
Easterly, W., R. Islam, and J. Stiglitz (2000), *Explaining Growth Volatility*, The World Bank.
The Economist (1999), "The Key to Industrial Capitalism: Limited Liability," 23 December.
Eggertsson, G., and P. Krugman (2012), "Debt, Deleveraging and the Liquidity Trap: A Fisher-Minsky-Koo Approach," *Quarterly Journal of Economics*, 127(3), pp. 1469–513.
Eisenberg, L., and T. Noe (2001), "Systemic Risk in Financial Systems," *Management Science*, 47(2), pp. 236–249.
European Central Bank (2007), "A Market-Based Indicator of the Probability of Adverse Systemic Events Involving Large and Complex Banking Groups," *Financial Stability Review*, December, pp. 125–27.
European Central Bank (2017*a*), *Financial Stability Review*, May.
European Central Bank (2017*b*), *Report on Financial Integration*, May.
European Commission (2015*a*), *Action Plan on Building a Capital Markets Union*, communication from the Commission to the European Parliament, the Council, the European Economic and Social Committee and the Committee of the Regions, 30 September.
European Commission (2015*b*), *Economic Analysis Accompanying the Action Plan on Building a Capital Markets Union*, 30 September.
Federal Reserve Bank of Minneapolis (2016), "The Minneapolis Plan to End Too Big to Fail," 16 November.
Ferguson, N. (2008), *The Ascent of Money: A Financial History of the World*, Allen Lane.
Financial Stability Board (2014), "Key Attributes of Effective Resolution Regimes for Financial Institutions," 15 October.
Financial Stability Board (2015*a*), "OTC Derivatives Market Reforms: Tenth Progress Report on Implementation," 4 November.
Financial Stability Board (2015*b*), "Principles on Loss-absorbing and Recapitalisation Capacity of G-SIBs in Resolution," 9 November.
Financial Stability Board (2015*c*), "Transforming Shadow Banking into Resilient Market -based Finance: Regulatory Framework for Haircuts on Non-centrally Cleared Securities Financing Transactions," 12 November.
Financial Stability Board (2017), "Financial Stability Implications from FinTech," Basel, 27 June.
Fisher, I. (1933), "The Debt-Deflation Theory of Great Depressions," *Econometrica*, 1(4), pp. 337–57.
Foucault, Th., M. Pagano, and A. Röell (2013), *Market Liquidity: Theory, Evidence, and Policy*, Oxford University Press.

Francotte, P., Lannoo, K., and D. Valiante (2011), "MiFID Review: What Is Next for European Capital Markets?" CEPS.
Frank, T. (1935), "The Financial Crisis of 33 AD," *American Journal of Philology*, 56(4), pp. 336–41.
Freixas, X., Laeven, L., and J.L. Peydro (2015), *System Risk, Crises, and Macroprudential Regulation*, MIT Press.
Freixas, X., and J.C. Rochet (2008), *Microeconomics of Banking*, 2nd edition, MIT Press.
Garber, P. (1990), "Famous First Bubbles," *Journal of Economic Perspectives*, 4(2), pp. 35–54.
Goldin, C., and L. Katz (2008), "Transitions: Career and Family Lifecycles of the Education Elite," *American Economic Review: Papers and Proceedings*, 98(2), pp. 363–69.Gonzalez de Lara, Y. (2001), "Enforceability and Risk-sharing in Financial Contracts : From the Sea Loan to the Commenda in Late Medieval Venice," *Journal of Economic History*, 61 (2), pp. 500–04.
Goodhart, C. (2010), "How Should We Regulate The Financial Sector?," in Turner, A., A. Haldane and P; Wooley (eds.), *The Future of Finance: The LSE Report*,London Publishing Partnership, pp. 153–76.
Gorton, G. (2010), *Slapped by the Invisible Hand, The Panic of 2007*. Oxford University Press.
Gorton, G., and A. Metrick (2012), "Securitized Banking and the Run on Repo," *Journal of Financial Economics*, 104(3), pp. 425–51.
Graeber, D. (2011), *Debt: The First 5,000 Years*, Melville House.
Grossman, S., and J. Stiglitz (1980), "On the Impossibility of Informationally Efficient Markets," *American Economic Review*, 70(3), pp. 393–408.
Gurley, J., and E. Shaw (1960), *Money in a Theory of Finance*, Brookings.
Hałaj, G., and C. Kok (2013), "Assessing Interbank Contagion Using Simulated Networks," *Computational Management Science*, 10(2), pp. 157–86.
Haldane, A. (2010), "The Contribution of the Financial Sector – Miracle or Mirage?" The Future of Finance conference, London, July 14.
Haldane, A. (2017), "Rethinking financial stability," Rethinking Macroeconomic Policy IV Conference, Peterson Institute of International Economics, Washington, October 12.
Haldane, A., and V. Madouros (2012), "The Dog and the Frisbee," Federal Reserve Bank of Kansas City 36th Economic Policy Symposium, Jackson Hole, August 31.
Hale, G., T. Kapan, and C. Minoiu (2014), "Crisis Transmission in the Global Banking Network," mimeo. Federal Reserve Bank of San Francisco, Fannie Mae and International Monetary Fund.
Hamilton J. D. (2016), "Macroeconomic Regimes and Regime Shifts," in Taylor, J., and H. Uhlig, eds., *Handbook of Macroeconomics, Volume 2*, Elsevier, pp. 163–201.
Hansen, L. P. (2013), "Challenges in Identifying and Measuring Systemic Risk," in Brunnermeier, M., and A. Krishnamurthy, eds., *Risk Topography: Systemic Risk and Macro Modelling*, NBER Books Series.
Hanson, S., A. Kashyap, and J. Stein (2011), "A Macroprudential Approach to Financial Regulation," *Journal of Economic Perspectives*, 25(1), pp. 3–28.

Hartmann, P., S. Straetmans, and C. G. de Vries (2004), "Asset Market Linkages in Crisis Periods," *Review of Economics and Statistics*, 86(1), pp. 313–26.

Hiebert, P., I. Jaccard, T. Peltonen, and Y. Schüler (2016), "Characterising the Financial Cycle: A Multivariate and Time-Varying Approach," ECB-IMF Conference on Macroprudential Policy, Frankfurt am Main, April 26–27.

Holló, D., M. Kremer, and M. Lo Duca (2012), "CISS - A Composite Indicator of Systemic Stress in the Financial System," European Central Bank.

Holmström, B. (2015), "Understanding the Role of Debt in the Financial System," *Bank for International Settlements Working Paper*, 479, January.

Holmström, B., and J. Tirole (1998), "Private and Public Supply of Liquidity," *Journal of Political Economy*, 106(1), pp. 1–40.

Holmström, B., and J. Tirole (2011), *Inside and Outside Liquidity*, MIT Press.

Huang, J. Z., and M. Huang (2012), "How Much of the Corporate-Treasury Yield Spread is Due to Credit Risk?" *Review of Asset Pricing Studies*, 2(2), pp. 153–202.

International Monetary Fund (2013), "Key Aspects of Macroprudential Policy," 10 June.

International Monetary Fund, Financial Stability Board and Bank for International Settlements (2016), "Elements of Effective Macroprudential Policies," 31 August.

Jensen, M. (1986), "Agency Costs of Free Cash Flow, Corporate Finance and Takeovers," *American Economic Review*, 76(2), pp. 323–39.

Jensen, M., and W. Meckling (1976), "Theory of the Firm: Managerial Behavior, Agency Costs, and Capital Structure," *Journal of Financial Economics*, 3, pp. 305–360.

Kairys, J. P., and N. Valerio (1997), "The Market for Equity Options in the 1870s," *Journal of Finance*, 52(4), pp. 1707–23.

Kalemli-Ozcan, S., B. Sorensen, and S. Yesiltas (2012), "Leverage Across Firms, Banks, and Countries," *Journal of International Economics*, 88(2), pp. 284–98.

Keynes, J. M. (1936), *The General Theory of Employment, Interest and Money*, Macmillan.

Kindleberger, C., and R. Aliber (2005), *Manias, Panics, and Crashes: A History of Financial Crises*, 5th edition, J. Wiley & Sons.

King, R., and R. Levine (1993), "Finance and Growth: Schumpeter Might Be Right," *Quarterly Journal of Economics*, 108(3), pp. 717–37.

Kiyotaki, N., and J. Moore (1997), "Credit Cycles," *Journal of Political Economy*, 105(2), pp. 211–48.

Kremer, M., and A. Popov (2018), "Financial development, financial structure and growth: evidence from Europe," in European Central Bank, *Financial Integration in Europe*, pp. 65-97.

Laeven, L., and F. Valencia (2012), "Systemic Banking Crises Database: An Update," *IMF Working Paper*, 12/163.

Langedijk, S., G. Nicodeme, A. Pagano, and A. Rossi (2015), "Debt Bias in Corporate Income Taxation and the Costs of Banking Crises," *VOX, CEPR's Policy Portal.*

Leland, H. (1994), "Corporate Debt Value, Bond Covenants, and Optimal Capital Structure," *Journal of Finance*, 49(4), pp. 1213–52.

Lo, A., and A. Craig MacKinlay (1988), "Stock Market Prices Do Not Follow Random Walks: Evidence From a Simple Specification Test," *Review of Financial Studies*, 1(1), pp. 41–66.

Lo, A., and A. Craig MacKinlay (1999), *A Non-Random Walk Down Wall Street*, Princeton University Press.

MacKay, C. (1841), *Memoirs of Extraordinary Popular Delusions and the Madness of Crowds*, R. Bentley.

Macroeconomic Assessment Group (2010), "Assessing the Macroeconomic Impact of the Transition to Stronger Capital and Liquidity Requirements: Final Report," December.

Malkiel, B. (2003), "The Efficient Market Hypothesis and Its Critics," *Journal of Economic Perspectives*, 17(1), pp. 59–82.

Markowitz, H. (1952), "Portfolio Selection," *Journal of Finance*, 7(1), pp. 77–91.

Merton, R. (1974), "On the Pricing of Corporate Debt: The Risk Structure of Interest Rates," *Journal of Finance*, 29(2), pp. 449–70.

Merton, R. (1995), "A Functional Perspective of Financial Intermediation," *Financial Management*, 24(2), pp. 23–41.

Minsky, H. P. (1986), "Stabilizing an Unstable Economy," Levy Economics Institute of Bard College, *Hyman P. Minsky Archive Paper*, 144.

Minsky, H. P. (1992), "The Financial Instability Hypothesis," *Levy Economics Institute of Bard College Working Paper*, 74.

Modigliani, F., and M. Miller (1958), "The Cost of Capital, Corporation Finance and the Theory of Investment," *American Economic Review*, 48(3), pp. 261–97.

Myers, S., and N. Majluf (1984), "Corporate Financing and Investment Decisions When Firms Have Information that Investors Do Not Have," *Journal of Financial Economics*, 13(2), pp. 187–221.

North, D., and B. Weingast (1989), "Constitutions and Commitment: The Evolution of Institutions Governing Public Choice in Seventeenth-Century England," *Journal of Economic History*, 49(4), pp. 803–32.

Passmore, W., and A. von Haffen (2017), "Are Basel's Capital Surcharges for Global Systemically Important Banks Too Small?" FEDS Notes, Board of Governors of the Federal Reserve System, 27 February.

Pennacchi, G. (2012), "Narrow Banking," *Annual Review of Financial Economics*, 4, pp. 141–59.

Perotti, E., and J. Suarez (2010), "A Pigovian Approach to Liquidity Regulation," *International Journal of Central Banking*, 7(4), pp. 3–41.

Philippon, T. (2015), "Has the US Finance Industry Become Less Efficient? On the Theory and Measurement of Financial Intermediation," *American Economic Review*, 105(4), pp. 1408–38.

Philippon, T., and A. Reshef (2012), "Wages and Human Capital in the US Finance Industry: 1909–2006," *Quarterly Journal of Economics*, 127(4), pp. 1551–609.

Philippon, T., and A. Reshef (2013), "An International Look at the Growth of Modern Finance," *Journal of Economic Perspectives*, 27(2), pp. 73–96.

Philippon, T., and A. Salord (2017), "Bail-ins and Bank Resolution in Europe: A Progress Report," ICMB-CEPR Geneva Reports on the World Economy, 4th Special Report, March.

Poitras, G. (2008), "The Early History of Option Contracts," Simon Fraser University, Faculty of Business Administration, Vancouver.

Poterba, J., and L. Summers (1985), "The Economic Effects of Dividend Taxation," in Altman, E., and M. Subrahmanyam, eds., *Recent Advances in Corporate Finance*. Dow Jones-Irwin Publishing, pp. 227–284.

Poterba, J., and L. Summers (1988), "Mean reversion in stock prices: Evidence and Implications," *Journal of Financial Economics*, 22 (1), pp. 27–59.

Rajan, R. (1996), "Review of Aoki, M., and H. Patrick, The Japanese Main Bank System: Its Relevance for Developing and Transforming Economies," *Journal of Economic Literature*, 34(3), pp. 1363–365.

Rajan, R. (2005), "Has Financial Development Made the World Riskier?" *NBER Working Paper*, 11728.

Rajan, R., and L. Zingales (2004), *Saving Capitalism from Capitalists*, Princeton University Press.

Reinhart, C., and K. Rogoff (2009), "The Aftermath of Financial Crises," *American Economic Review*, 99(2), pp. 466–72.

Reinhart, C., and K. Rogoff (2010), *This Time Is Different: Eight Centuries of Financial Folly*, Princeton University Press.

Robinson, J. (1952), "The Generalization of the General Theory," in Robinson, J. (ed.), *The Rate of Interest and Other Essays*, MacMillan, pp. 67–142.

Ross, S. (1976), "The Arbitrage Theory of Capital Pricing," *Journal of Economic Theory*, 13, pp. 341–60.

Rousseau, P., and R. Sylla (2003), "Financial Systems, Economic Growth, and Globalization," in Bordo, M., A. Taylor, and J. Williamson, eds., *Globalization in Historical Perspective*, University of Chicago Press, pp. 373–415.

Santos, J. (2000), "Bank Capital Regulation in Contemporary Banking Theory: A Review of the Literature," *Bank for International Settlements Working Paper*, 90.

Sayous, A-É (1929), "Les transformations des méthodes commerciales dans l'Italie médiévale," *Annales d'histoire économique et sociale*, 1(2), pp. 161–76.

Schoenmaker, D., and N. Véron (2016), "European Banking Supervision: The First Eighteen Months," *Bruegel Blueprint Series*, 25.

Shiller, R. (2000), *Irrational Exuberance*, Princeton University Press.

Shiller, R. (2003), *The New Financial Order*, Princeton University Press.

Spence, A. (1974), "Competitive and Optimal Responses to Signals: Analysis of Efficiency and Distribution," *Journal of Economic Theory*, 7, 296–332.

Stein, J. (2010), "Securitization, Shadow Banking, and Financial Fragility," *Dædalus*, Fall, pp. 41–51.

Stein, J. (2014), Comments on "Market Tantrums and Monetary Policy," 2014 US Monetary Policy Forum, New York, 28 February.

Stiglitz, J., and A. Weiss (1981), "Credit Rationing in Markets with Imperfect Information," Part I, *American Economic Review*, 71(3), pp. 393–410.

Summers, L. (2013), Mundell-Fleming Lecture, 14th Annual IMF Research Conference, Washington, 8 November.

Taleb, N. (2007), *The Black Swan: The Impact of the Highly Improbable*, Random House.

Temin, P. (2004), "Financial Intermediation in the Early Roman Empire," *Journal of Economic History*, 64(3), pp. 705–33.

Thompson, E. (2007), "The Tulipmania: Fact or Artifact?" *Public Choice*, 130(1–2), pp. 99–114.

Thornton, H. (1802), *An Enquiry Into the Nature and Effects of the Paper Credit of Great Britain*, J. Hatchard.

US Department of the Treasury, Board of Governors of the Federal Reserve System, Securities and Exchange Commission and Commodity and Futures Trading Commission (1999), *Report of the President's Working Group on Financial Markets*, November.

US Department of the Treasury, Board of Governors of the Federal Reserve System, Federal Reserve Bank of New York, US Securities and Exchange Commission, and US Commodity Futures Trading Commission (2015), *Joint Staff Report: The US Treasury Market on October 15, 2014*, 13 July.

Van der Veen, A. M. (2012), "The Dutch Tulip Mania: The Social Foundations of a Financial Bubble," unpublished manuscript, College of William and Mary.

Velde, F. (2009), "Was John Law's System a Bubble? The Mississippi Bubble Revisited," in Atack, J., and L. Neal, eds., *The Origins and Development of Financial Markets and Institutions: From the Seventeenth Century to the Present*, Cambridge University Press, pp. 99–120.

Ventura, J., and H. J. Voth (2015), "Debt into Growth: How Sovereign Debt Accelerated the First Industrial Revolution," *Barcelona GSE Working Paper*, 830, May.

Vives, X. (2016), *Competition and Stability in Banking*, Princeton University Press.

Zingales, L. (2015), "Does Finance Benefit Society?" *Journal of Finance*, 70(4), pp. 1327–63.

7

International Financial Integration and Foreign Exchange Policy

In all areas of economic policy, internationalization is a key factor. For instance, the impact of a fiscal stimulus is more limited in a small, open economy like Ireland, where firms mostly rely on international trade, than in a large country like the United States, where domestic demand is key. Likewise, the international mobility of tax bases affects the optimal level of taxation, while the external channel of monetary policy also depends on trade openness. More generally, economic policy in a given country must take into account cross-country spillovers generated by international trade and financial integration (see Chapter 3).

Although the traditional neo-classical model teaches us that international capital mobility allows a better allocation of global savings, which in turn raises their return through higher growth, the experience of financial integration is plagued with bubbles and crises. Shocks of this sort reduce and sometimes even erase the advantage of international capital mobility. Additionally, international financial integration may involve high exchange rate volatility, which translates into uncertainty on relative prices and relative returns. Many governments consider such uncertainty as detrimental for their economy. In a world of free capital mobility, however, limiting exchange rate volatility involves losing monetary independence.

Hence, exchange rate "regimes" and "policies" need to be studied in close relation to international financial integration. While monetary policy focuses on the internal value of the currency (the purchasing power of money in terms of goods and services produced locally), exchange rate policy is concerned with its external value (the purchasing power of money in terms of goods and services produced abroad). The two are intricately related as the exchange rate is an important channel of transmission of monetary policy (see Chapter 5). In the long term, however, the real value of the domestic currency can hardly be affected by monetary policy. Hence, for many professional economists, the very concept of an "exchange rate policy" is doubtful. Such perplexity contrasts with the passion raised around "currency wars" and, more generally, exchange rate regimes or crises among politicians and in the general public.

7.1 Issues

7.1.1 A brief history of the international monetary system

In medieval Europe, most trade was settled with gold and silver coins.[1] This system evolved gradually, with merchants moving to use paper currency and bills of exchange, but confidence in the currency still depended on the possibility of changing it into precious metal. The *gold standard*, under which the value of each national currency was determined by a given gold weight, was extended to all major economies in the 1880s and lasted until World War I. By construction and arbitrage, the gold standard involved fixed exchange rates between national currencies.[2] In the second half of the nineteenth century, it provided for an unprecedented expansion of trade. The economic dominance of the British Empire allowed the pound sterling to develop as an international currency parallel to gold, even though the gold reserves of the Bank of England did not cover the whole of the currency issued in pounds sterling.[3] An often understated feature of the pre-World War I era was a high degree of capital mobility, especially through the London-based bond market (International Monetary Fund, 1997). Investment needs were concentrated in the railways and government sectors. For sustained periods, Australia, Canada, and Argentina experienced current account deficits of more than 10% of gross domestic product (GDP)—financed by foreign (mostly British) capital inflows.

World War I put a brutal end to this "first globalization" era. Inflationary pressures developed, due to the monetization of military spending and the destruction of part of the production capacity. Between 1920 and 1924, the exchange rates between major currencies were largely left to market forces. But then, the return to the gold standard was carried out with overvalued currencies (especially for the United Kingdom) and insufficient gold reserves, which triggered deflationary pressures. It is considered an ingredient of the Great Depression starting in 1929. The gold standard went bust during the 1930s, with the progressive abandonment of the convertibility in gold of the various currencies involved, starting with the British pound in 1933. These years were marked with many monetary conflicts, with some countries depreciating their currencies in order to stimulate their price competitiveness while others were painfully adjusting their relative prices through deflation.[4]

After World War II, priority was given to exchange-rate stability and the *convertibility* of currencies (i.e., the possibility of exchanging them freely to carry out trade transactions), while capital flows were highly regulated in developed countries (emerging countries remained relatively open to capital inflows and outflows; cf. Ghosh and Qureshi, 2016). The International Monetary Fund (IMF) was created in 1944 at the Bretton Woods Conference. The IMF, an institution of which almost all sovereign States are by now members, is tasked with monitoring world payments and helping countries that experience temporary balance-of-payment difficulties to avoid a crisis.[5] The Bretton Woods Conference also established a *gold exchange standard* whereby all currencies were convertible in US dollars at an almost fixed rate, while official US dollar holdings were convertible into gold at a fixed rate of US$35 per ounce.[6] The US dollar had thus replaced the pound sterling as the anchor of the international monetary system.

The system was inherently fragile, however. There was a contradiction between, on the one hand, the need to supply a rapidly growing world economy with adequate liquidity and, on the other hand, the need to maintain confidence in the dollar, which implied keeping its issuance in line with the gold reserves of the Federal Reserve.[7] During the 1960s, the United States started issuing increasing amounts of short-term debt in US dollar. Hence, the volume of official dollar reserves held by non-US monetary authorities expanded, and there was an increasing risk that any request, or hint of a request, of conversion of official dollar holdings into gold might trigger a currency crisis due to gold shortage. This risk was enhanced by rising inflation. Toward the end of the 1960s and in the early 1970s, speculation accelerated against the dollar and in favor of gold and strong currencies such as the German mark. Eventually, President Nixon unilaterally suspended the convertibility of the dollar on August 15, 1971. The Smithsonian Agreement signed by the G10 countries on December 18, 1971 attempted to safeguard the fixed exchange rate system by choosing a new fixed parity grid, a wider fluctuation margin, and a devaluation of the US dollar. However, the Bretton Woods system was finally abandoned in 1973, and the main currencies had to float—a new environment set by the Jamaica Agreement of January 1976, and incorporated as the second amendment to the IMF Articles of Agreement.[8]

Facing this new environment characterized by increased exchange rate instability, the Europeans created in 1972 the "European Snake," to limit the fluctuation margins between European currencies and between these currencies and the US dollar (the reason why it was dubbed the "snake in the tunnel"). The breakdown of the Bretton Woods system in March 1973 removed the "tunnel," whereas the "snake" was transformed into a fully fledged, stable-but-adjustable exchange rate system in 1979. This *European Monetary System* (EMS) no longer referred to the dollar. In the EMS, all cross-parities were allowed to fluctuate within margins of at most ±2.25% (in some cases ±6%) around a central rate. Europe had created a monetary system of its own on a regional basis, a major breakthrough in monetary history. The evolution of the EMS was not a quiet one, however. Between 1987 and 1992, the member countries of the European Community progressively freed up capital flows, making it increasingly difficult to maintain fixed exchange rates: net capital outflows in one country were causing its currency to be sold and thus exerted a downward pressure on its external value. In 1992, the pound sterling and the Italian lira were forced to exit. In 1993, after a new crisis, the fluctuation margins were widened to ±15%. However, the Maastricht Treaty had set the aim of an Economic and Monetary Union "at the latest" on January 1, 1999, allowing the EMS to survive until a single currency, the euro, was eventually created. In 1999, the European Monetary Union (EMU) was initiated with 11 countries. It was subsequently extended to Greece, Slovenia, Cyprus, Malta, Slovakia, Estonia, Latvia, and Lithuania.

Despite regional monetary cooperation in Europe and, to a much lesser extent, in Asia and in small groupings of countries, the US dollar has remained at the core of the international monetary system. The euro has developed as a reserve currency, with shares amounting in 2016 to 20% of allocated central banks' foreign exchange reserves and 30% of international payments (table 7.1). Since the mid-1990s, China has also taken significant steps toward progressively internationalizing its currency, the *renminbi*, also called the *yuan* (see Eichengreen and Kawai, 2014). However, the US dollar remains the key currency for international transactions as well as the reference currency for the exchange rate policies of most emerging market economies.[9]

During the period of the gold standard, the fixity of bilateral exchange rates was viewed as favorable to international trade and capital integration. Indeed, from 1870 to World War I, capital flows developed to an extent that has hardly been seen again (see figure 7.1). An open question is to what extent the instability of exchange rates following the breakdown of the Bretton Woods system in 1973 has been an impediment to financial globalization. Indeed, despite the spectacular surge of capital flows, the world economy is far from being financially integrated. In a famous paper published in 1980, Martin Feldstein and Charles Horioka regressed the investment rate on the savings rate of 16 countries in the Organization for Economic Cooperation and Development (OECD) over the period 1960–74 (see Fledstein and Horioka, 1980). They found that, on average, a one percentage point increase in the savings rate went hand in hand with a 0.89 percentage point increase in the investment rate.

Table 7.1
International role of the US dollar, the yen, and the euro (percent), 2016

Function	US dollar	Euro	Yen	GBP	Other
Medium of exchange					
Foreign exchange turnover, April 2016[a]	87.6	31.3	21.6	12.8	46.8
Global payments (SWIFT), end-Jan 2016	43.0	29.4	n.a.	8.7	27.6
Unit of account					
Invoicing/settlement of euro area exports of goods to non–euro area, 2016	n.a.	56.1	n.a	n.a.	n.a.
Invoicing/settlement of euro area imports of goods from non–euro area, 2016	n.a.	47.3	n.a.	n.a.	n.a.
Third-country currency peg, April 2016[b]	47.6	30.5	0.0	0.0	22.0
Store of value					
Allocated official reserves, 2016Q4	64.0	19.7	4.2	4.4	7.6
Outstanding international debt securities, narrow measure, 2016Q4[c]	63.0	22.0	2.6	n.a.	12.3
Outstanding cross-border bank loans, narrow measure, 2016Q4[d]	59.1	21.3	3.6	n.a.	16.0

n.a. = Not applicable.
[a]Since a given trade involves two currencies, the percentages sum up to 200% on this line.
[b]Out of 82 pegged or semi-pegged currencies.
[c]Excluding domestic issuance of international debt.
[d]Loans by banks outside the euro area to borrowers outside the euro area.
Sources: BIS, 2016; ECB, 2017; IMF, 2016*b*.

This is a puzzle, because in a world where capital is mobile, the allocation of investment should be determined by rates of return rather than the amount of domestic savings. In fact over this period, international capital flows added little to domestically financed investments. This counterintuitive result was later labeled the *Feldstein–Horioka puzzle*. Subsequent estimations found somewhat lower Feldstein–Horioka coefficients.[10] However, the global financial crisis has led to financial "deglobalization," with a reduction of cross-border flows (see figure 7.1) and a "renationalization" of large banks (with a larger share of domestic assets and liabilities in their balance sheets, see Chapter 6).

The Feldstein-Horioka puzzle has been much discussed in the economic literature, mainly in two respects. First, it has been argued that the close saving–investment relationship is the result of the intertemporal budget constraint: the saving–investment gap cannot accumulate forever. Indeed, a country cannot indefinitely accumulate current account deficits: at some point, its net debt will be so high that international investors will no longer be willing to lend. As for current account surpluses, they may accumulate over time, but since there is no current account surplus in some countries without

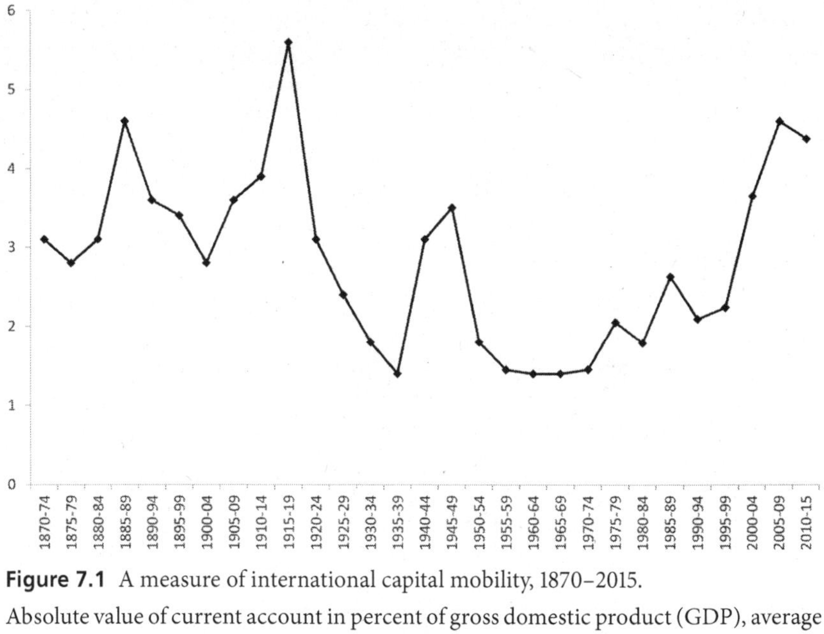

Figure 7.1 A measure of international capital mobility, 1870–2015.
Absolute value of current account in percent of gross domestic product (GDP), average over 11 countries, 5-year averages.[a]
[a]Australia, Canada, Denmark, France, Germany, Italy, Japan, Norway, Sweden, United Kingdom, United States. The current account is the difference between a country's total savings and total investments; hence it is a measure of financial openness.
Taylor (1996), updated by the authors as from 1970 based on OECD data.

deficits in other countries, surpluses also cannot accumulate indefinitely.[11] Second, the Feldstein-Horioka puzzle can be related to the empirical evidence of a strong *home bias* in portfolio choices: savers seem to hold fewer foreign assets than optimal portfolio diversification would suggest.[12] The reason for the home bias is still an open question, but information asymmetries are good candidates: savers have more information on domestic risks than on foreign risk. This reduces their willingness to hold foreign assets, even when such holdings are not limited by national regulations. A major counterexample has however been the willingness of investors all over the world to hold US assets, thus financing huge US current account deficits in the 1990s and 2000s (see Section 7.3).

7.1.2 Currency convertibility and exchange rate regimes

Not all countries participate in the global financial system. Some retain inconvertibility or limited convertibility of their currencies. When the domestic currency is at least partially convertible, its price can either be set freely by the market or managed by the government and the central bank. Governments need to make two crucial decisions in this regard: they must decide on the conditions for exchanging the domestic currency for foreign currencies—*currency convertibility*—and they must decide on the extent of exchange rate flexibility—the *exchange rate regime*. In the words of Chapter 1, the exchange rate regime is the institutional setup with which the exchange rate policy is operated. It is both a legal and an empirical notion. Countries must declare to the IMF the extent of convertibility as well as the nature of the exchange rate regime.

a) Currency convertibility

In most countries, it used to be the case that the administration would decide the value of the *exchange rate* (i.e., the price of the home currency in terms of foreign currencies) and would submit any foreign exchange transaction to prior authorization. The currency was then said to be *not convertible.* This was the case for Western European countries before 1958, of the former Soviet bloc before 1990, and of numerous developing countries until recently.

In some cases, there could be more than one exchange rate: for exports and for imports, or depending on product types, or on individuals. In such cases, one would speak of a *dual* or a *multiple exchange rate system.* In all other cases, the currency is said to be *convertible.* It may, however, be convertible for some transactions and nonconvertible for others. More precisely, it is useful to distinguish:[13]

- *Current account convertibility*: The national currency can be exchanged freely for the purpose of importing goods and services, paying current transfers (e.g., contributions to the European Union's budget or to international organizations), or transferring capital and labor income. This is the case in a majority of countries.
- *Financial account convertibility:*[14] Direct investments, portfolio investments, and bank loans are permitted without restriction. One speaks of *international capital mobility* and *financial openness.* The convertibility may concern some financial transactions, partially or totally, and not others. Capital is actually never fully mobile as there are always valid reasons for control (for example, the fight against money laundering and terrorist finance). However, most advanced economies liberalized capital flows in the 1980s and early 1990s. The movement is more recent and still incomplete in emerging and developing countries (see figure 7.2).

The extent of currency convertibility has important consequences for the determination of exchange rates. When capital does not move freely across countries, foreign exchange transactions arise only as the counterpart of an underlying "real-world" transaction such as exports, imports, or income repatriation. When capital movements are free, foreign exchange transactions also arise from financial asset purchases and sales, which prove to be much larger and more volatile than "real-world" transactions, leading to more exchange rate instability.

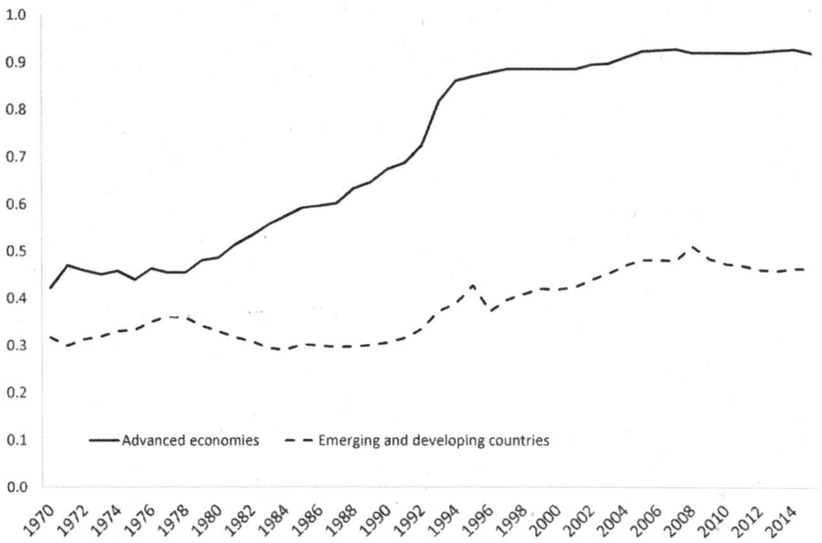

Figure 7.2 Index of financial openness, 1970–2015.
Unweighted averages. Variable number of countries depending on the year. The index is normalized from 0 (financial autarky) to 1 (perfect capital mobility).
Chinn and Ito (2008), based on IMF, Annual Report on Exchange Arrangements and Exchange Restrictions, 2017 update.

b) Exchange rate regimes and currency crises

Large exchange rate fluctuations are a major source of uncertainty for the "real world" because they affect relative prices across countries and between various types of industries within a country. They also influence the relative value of assets and liabilities. In developing countries, foreign liabilities are often denominated in key foreign currencies. Hence, a depreciation of the domestic currency raises the value of the external debt. For all these reasons, governments may wish to control their exchange rate in order to achieve domestic objectives or just to limit exchange rate volatility. Figure 7.3 ranks exchange rate regimes depending on the degree of government or central bank intervention. The highest degree of fixity is obtained when the national currency is abandoned. A first option is to use the currency of another country. Panama and Ecuador have thus "dollarized" their economies, while Kosovo and Montenegro have "euroized" theirs. A dollarized country becomes unable to control the domestic money supply and its central bank is left with only performing technical tasks. Another option is for a group of countries to merge their currencies and create a new one within a *monetary union*. This is the case of the euro area and of the participants in African monetary unions. The difference between dollarization and a monetary union stems from the monetary-decision process: there is no Ecuadorian representative sitting on the Federal

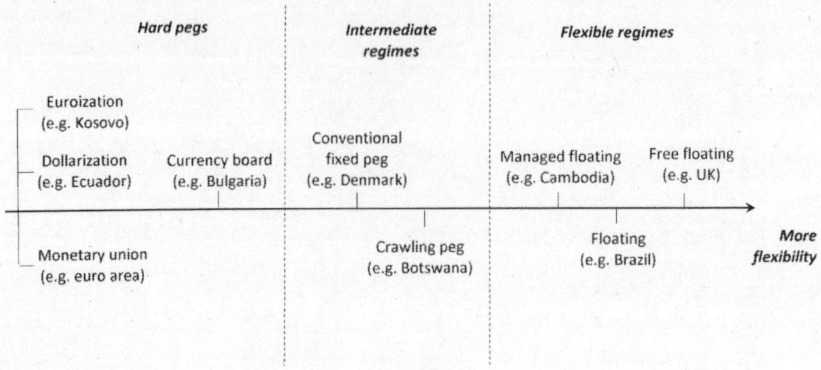

Figure 7.3 Classification of exchange rate regimes.
International Monetary Fund, Annual Report on Exchange Arrangements and Exchange Restrictions, October 2016.

Open Market Committee that sets the US interest rates, nor is there an official from Kosovo on the Governing Council of the European Central Bank (ECB).

A weak form of dollarization is the *currency board*. The national currency continues to circulate, but it can be exchanged at a fixed rate against the currency of some larger country, say, the US dollar, or against a basket of currencies. For this purpose, the issuance of domestic currency by the central bank is backed by foreign assets only. Hence, the domestic monetary base (or at least a substantial and fixed fraction of it) is matched by the corresponding amount of foreign currency held by the central bank. This tight rule allows the fixed exchange rate to be credible. It has been used by countries that had lost their monetary credibility following a period of hyperinflation, such as Argentina in the 1990s. The collapse of the Argentine currency board in January 2002 however illustrates that a currency board does not offer the same guarantee on the fixed exchange rate as that provided by dollarization or a monetary union, although there are also examples of monetary unions coming to an end.[15] More generally, *hard pegs* are exchange rate regimes in which the fixity of the exchange rate is backed by a tight institutional scheme. This clearly includes currency boards, and, by extension since they do not formally involve any "peg," regimes such as dollarization and monetary union in which there is no separate national legal tender.

When the fixed exchange rate is not enshrined in legally binding arrangements such as a currency board, the regime is called *conventional fixed peg*, and its credibility rests primarily on the government will. This is what European countries experienced in the 1980s and 1990s. In the EMS, even though the system had been conceived as a fixed but adjustable peg, a *devaluation* (i.e., downward adjustment of the reference rate around which the market exchange rate was allowed to fluctuate) bore a political cost. The finance minister would return from Brussels, where such decisions were discussed, having impoverished his fellow citizens and having defaulted on a European commitment. Such political incentives, however, are not always effective. In the early 1980s, the EMS experienced numerous devaluations. In 1992 and 1993, after capital flows were fully liberalized in the European single market, the system had to face two major crises. The vulnerability of conventionally fixed exchange rate regimes derives from the strength of speculative attacks when the firmness of the commitment is being questioned by markets and when the scope for official intervention is limited (see Section 7.2.3).

Fixed exchange rate regimes can be given more flexibility by allowing wider fluctuation margins and/or, in the case of *crawling pegs*, by partially adapting the rate of devaluation to the inflation differential with trade partners, so that the resulting real overvaluation promotes domestic disinflation. More generally, *soft pegs* or *intermediate exchange rate regimes* cover conventional pegged exchange rates in a wide sense: fixed or crawling, with or without a fluctuation band. Pegs can be against a single currency (typically, the US dollar or the euro) or against a basket of currencies such as the IMF unit of account, the *special drawing right* (SDR).[16]

Lastly, exchange rates can float more or less freely, without a reference target. In such a *flexible exchange rate regime*, the government may intervene occasionally to control the level or variability of the exchange rate but without setting any nominal objective. Depending on the frequency of such interventions, one will speak of *managed floating, floating,* or *free floating.*

In April 2016, there were four currency unions in the world: the EMU (19 countries), the East Caribbean monetary union (6 countries), the West African Economic and Monetary Union (WAEMU, 8 countries), and the Monetary and Economic Community of Central Africa (CEMAC, 6 countries). Of these four monetary unions, only the European one had a free floating currency. Both WAEMU and CEMAC had their currency (the CFA franc) pegged to the euro, whereas the East Caribbean dollar was pegged to the US dollar with a currency board. At the other end of the spectrum, only 13 currencies were considered in "free floating" in April 2016:[17] the US, Australian, and Canadian dollars; the Chilean and Mexican pesos; the Norwegian and Swedish kronas; the Polish zloty; the British pound; the Japanese yen; the euro; the Somalian shilling; and the Russian ruble. Forty currencies were considered "floating,"[18] 20 in "managed floating," and 61 (excluding the CFA franc) in various forms of conventional pegs. Therefore, the international monetary system is sometimes qualified as a "dirty floating" one, where only a few key currencies are allowed to float freely.

Conventional pegs fell into disgrace after the currency crises of the 1990s, a period when capital flows were progressively liberalized (see figure 7.4). It was then felt that such regimes were unsustainable in a world of perfect capital mobility. In such a world, the only way to keep a stable exchange rate is to surrender monetary independence and adopt a hard peg. If they wished to preserve their monetary independence, countries had to move to some form of floating. However, many countries considered exchange rate instability to

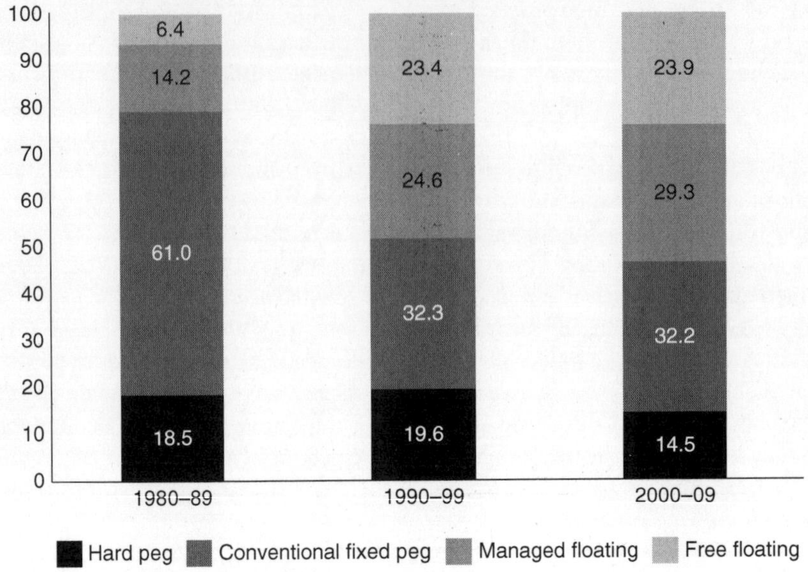

Figure 7.4 Evolution of exchange rate regimes (in percent of the total number of countries, 1980s, 1990s, and 2000s).
Ghosh et al. (2014).

be detrimental for their economies, so they tried to limit the volatility through some barriers to capital mobility in order to make their conventional pegs viable, or they moved to "managed floating" regimes. This behavior was especially widespread in emerging and developing economies due to a "fear of floating" (Calvo and Reinhart, 2002).

7.1.3 The foreign exchange market and the balance of payments

In countries where the financial system is not developed or where convertibility is restrained, the domestic currency is exchanged against foreign currencies either by the public administration or in informal markets, and there can be as many exchange rates as bilateral transactions. In most countries, however, there is a single market where currencies are exchanged, the *foreign exchange market*.

a) The foreign exchange market

The foreign exchange market is a wholesale market where only financial intermediaries, large corporations, and central banks intervene. Operations take the form of transfers between cash accounts expressed in different currencies. The exchanged commodity is indeed money (the "M1" monetary aggregate of Chapter 5).

If the market is sufficiently active, *arbitrage* between currencies ensures at every point in time the uniqueness of the exchange rate and the transitivity between exchange rates. For instance, if a euro is worth 1.2 US dollars and a US dollar worth 110 Japanese yen, then a euro should be worth 1.2 × 110 = 132 yen—otherwise, one could make an easy profit by changing money in all three currencies in a row. Arbitrage is never perfect, due to the difference between the sale price and the purchase price on the market, the *bid–ask spread*, which represents the fee paid to financial intermediaries and depends on the liquidity of the market (i.e., on the frequency and size of transactions). Apart from this fee, there is a single price for a specific currency all around the world at any time, and the matrix of all bilateral prices is consistent.

However, the price of a currency depends on the delivery date: when the currency is delivered within 24 hours, the transaction is called "spot" and the corresponding price is the *spot exchange rate.* When the currency is delivered at a deferred date, the transaction is called "forward" and the corresponding price is the *forward exchange rate.*

On the basis of the spot and forward markets, a large number of foreign exchange *derivatives* have developed. For example, a *foreign exchange swap* is an exchange of cash flows denominated in two different currencies over a certain period of time. A *call option* gives its owner the right, but not the obligation, to purchase foreign currency at a certain date in the future (or, depending on the nature of the option, at any time before this date), for a price agreed upon beforehand. A *put option* gives the right to sell it. Foreign exchange derivatives can be agreed on over the counter, but some of the most standard formats are traded in the marketplace. It can be shown that the value of an option increases with the volatility of the exchange rate over its lifetime (see Garman and Kohlhagen, 1983): the market valuation of options thus provides a way to gauge expected foreign exchange volatility. The corresponding indicator is called *implicit volatility.*

The foreign exchange market went through a considerable expansion in the 1990s as a result of three forces: the development of international trade, capital movement liberalization, and new financial techniques to manage financial risk. The *Bank for International Settlements* (BIS), a public institution based in Basel (Switzerland), is tasked with providing services to central banks and monitoring global financial markets. According to the BIS, foreign exchange transactions amounted to 5,066 billion dollars per day in April 2016, of which 1,652 billion were spot transactions. This roughly represented 18 days of world production and 72 days of international merchandise trade.

The market is highly concentrated, both in terms of location (56% of the turnover is carried out in London or New York) and in terms of the currencies traded (the euro/US dollar, yen/US dollar, and British pound/US dollar pairs together represent more than half of the market, with the former alone representing 23% of all trades in April 2016). The dollar plays a central role as a *vehicle currency* (i.e., as an intermediary for transactions between third currencies): it is easier and less expensive to exchange Korean wons against dollars, then dollars against Mexican pesos, than to trade directly wons for pesos. The dollar also plays a central role as a store of international liquidity. Central banks and commercial banks all over the world hold US dollars in the form of cash or short-term treasury bonds. The latter are considered liquid (easy to sell) and riskless (with negligible risk of default), hence as good as money. Banks also lend in dollars, which makes the dollar a largely extraterritorial funding currency. The extensive presence of dollar assets and liabilities in international banks' balance sheets implies that US monetary policy will affect credit in other countries through the cross-border bank lending channel (Bruno and Shin, 2015): when the Federal Reserve cuts its interest rate, credit conditions are loosened not only in the United States, but also in other countries. This transmission channel of US monetary policy goes in the opposite direction to the exchange rate channel.[19]

b) Balance of payment equilibrium

When the financial account is not convertible, the exchange rate can more easily be fixed by way of administration. However, when companies and households are free to buy and sell foreign assets, the exchange rate has to be constantly consistent with market equilibrium. When it is flexible, it adjusts so as to achieve this equilibrium. When it is fixed, the market cannot be cleared unless the central bank intervenes by selling or buying foreign currency.

In all cases, the relevant instrument to identify supply of and demand for foreign currency is the *balance of payments*, which describes all transactions with the rest of the world. The balance of payments is made up of three sections, or "accounts."

The current transaction account, or *current account*, is the operating account of the country. It describes all earnings from the rest of the world deriving from exports of goods and services, labor and capital income like dividends or remittances, and other current transfers. Symmetrically, it reports all payments made to the rest of the world related to imports of goods and services, labor and capital income, and other current transfers.

The *capital account* tracks capital transfers without a counterpart, like debt forgiveness and investment grants.

The *financial account* nets out all purchases of foreign assets—private and public securities, borrowings, real estate—to the rest of the world (*capital outflows*) with all sales of domestic assets (*capital inflows*). When an equity investment results in a share higher than 10% in a foreign company, which allows the exercise of effective control, the investment is called a *foreign direct investment*. Another example of capital inflows and outflows are sales and purchases of foreign securities by the domestic central bank as part of its *foreign exchange reserves* management. By definition, foreign exchange reserves are made of foreign-denominated securities and deposits (plus gold) held by the central bank. International sales and purchases of securities that are not classified as foreign direct investments or foreign exchange reserves are called *portfolio investments*. The financial account also includes a category called *other investments* that primarily includes bank credit.

Since all transactions have to be financed, any current account imbalance must be compensated by the other two accounts. However, not all items are well measured, and there are usually substantial statistical discrepancies called *errors and omissions*. Table 7.2 summarizes the balance of payments of the United States, the euro area, and China in 2016.[20] The US economy registered a vast current account deficit as it imported more goods and services than it exported. This deficit was financed by foreign purchases of US stocks and bonds (net capital inflows). In the euro area and China, in contrast, the current account was in surplus, compensated by net capital outflows.

Figure 7.5 sketches the balance of payments of an economy which imports more goods and services than it exports. For the sake of simplicity, we assume a balanced capital account, and we also neglect errors and omissions. This country spends more abroad on goods and services than it earns from abroad, and therefore has to borrow from nonresidents or sell them financial assets. Under these conditons, external balance requires the deficit on the current account to be matched by an equivalent net import of capital, i.e. a deficit of the financial account of the same magnitude. In a floating-rate regime, this is achieved by an adjustment of the exchange rate, which affects both the current account and the financial account and brings them into balance with each-other. For instance, if nonresident demand for domestic assets is insufficient *ex ante*, then the exchange rate depreciates, which makes these assets more attractive. In a fixed-exchange rate regime, the exchange rate cannot depreciate, and the central bank has to step in to clear the market. Practically, it has to sell assets out of its foreign exchange reserves. Symmetrically, a net capital inflow mechanically involves a current account deficit.

Central bank interventions and domestic monetary policy are closely interrelated. When the central bank sells foreign exchange reserves, it reduces domestic money supply since the cash it collects in exchange is withdrawn from circulation. Conversely, an increase in foreign reserves expands money supply. This in turn affects the domestic interest rate. In order to offset the impact of foreign reserve movements on money supply, the central bank

Table 7.2
Balance of payments of the United States, the euro area, and China in 2016, in percent of gross domestic product (GDP)

	United States	Euro area	China
Current account	−2.4	3.4	1.7
Capital account	0.0	−0.1	0.0
Financial account (net capital outflows)	−2.0	3.6	0.2
Errors and omissions	0.4	0.3	−1.5
(1) + (2) − (3) + (4)	0.0	0.0	0.0

ECB, BEA, SAFE, and OECD. GDPs in 2016: United States: US$18,625 billion; Euro area: €10,789 billion; China: US$11,232 billion.

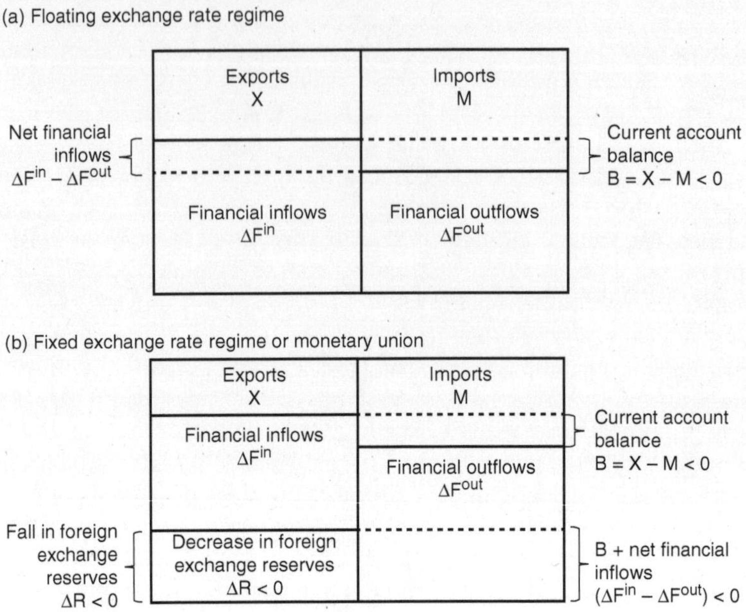

Figure 7.5 Balance of payment equilibrium depending on the exchange-rate regime[a] (capital importing country).

[a]For simplicity, labor and capital income are neglected, as well as the capital account and errors and omissions.
Authors.

can choose to *sterilize* foreign exchange interventions by buying or selling Treasury bills in the open market or choose to issue short-term paper (*sterilization bonds*) for this particular purpose. Intervention sterilization will be discussed further in the last section of this chapter.

Within a monetary union, there is no need to defend the fixed exchange rate through foreign exchange interventions since there is only one currency. An imbalance like the one displayed in figure 7.5 is resolved through flows of financing within the central banks system (box 7.1).

c) The net foreign asset position

When a country accumulates current account deficits, it spends more than it earns one year after another and therefore builds up liabilities toward the rest of the world. Practically, this means that foreigners hold an increasing amount of the country's domestic securities, private and public: They increase their stakes in domestic companies; or they extend more loans to domestic agents. When a country has more external liabilities than external assets, it has a negative *net foreign asset (NFA) position*. This is typically the case of the

Box 7.1 Balance of Payment Equilibrium Within the Euro Area

Within the euro area, a country that suffers a deficit of capital inflows will receive external financing through the Eurosystem,[a] provided local banks are solvent and have enough collateral to pledge with their national central bank (see Chapter 5). Suppose for instance that country A (say, Greece) has to finance some imports from country B (say, Germany), but that neither the German exporter nor a German bank is willing to extend a commercial credit at reasonable interest rate. The importer will ask his local bank (in Greece) for short-term lending. Provided the importer is safe, the bank will extend the credit and then refinance the credit at the central bank of Greece. The bank will thus get the cash necessary to make the payment to the bank of the German exporter. The payment will be processed through the *Target system* (Trans-European Automated Real-time Gross settlement Express Transfer): from the Greek bank to the Greek central bank, then to the ECB, to the Bundesbank, and finally to the commercial bank of the exporter in Germany. The counterpart of this payment will be a negative *Target balance* for the Greek central bank and a positive one for the Bundesbank (figure B7.1.1). It is as if the Greek central bank had contracted a debt vis-à-vis the Eurosystem, making Greece able to receive a capital inflow that fills the gap in the balance of payments. When the importer in Greece reimburses his commercial debt, the whole chain of credit unwinds.

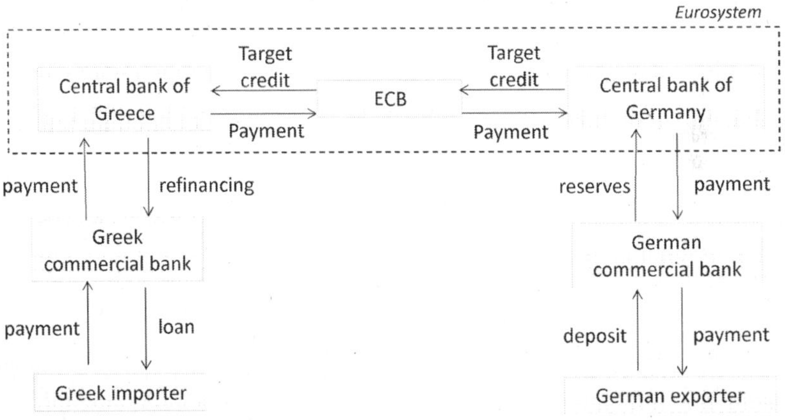

Figure B7.1.1 The target system in the euro area.
Authors.

Target balances played a major role in filling the gap in the balance of payments of Southern euro area countries during the crisis of 2010–17, partly compensating for the sudden stop in private capital inflows to these countries (figure B7.1.2). They have been regarded by some German observers as a hidden financing channel and a major risk for Northern European countries. This is a very disputable interpretation: mutual claims between central banks of the Eurosystem are not hidden, but rather represent an indispensable channel of operation of a monetary union; the Target system provides a guarantee to surplus countries like Germany, as the cost of a possible default of the central bank of a deficit country would be shared among all participating central banks, on the basis of the ECB capital key.

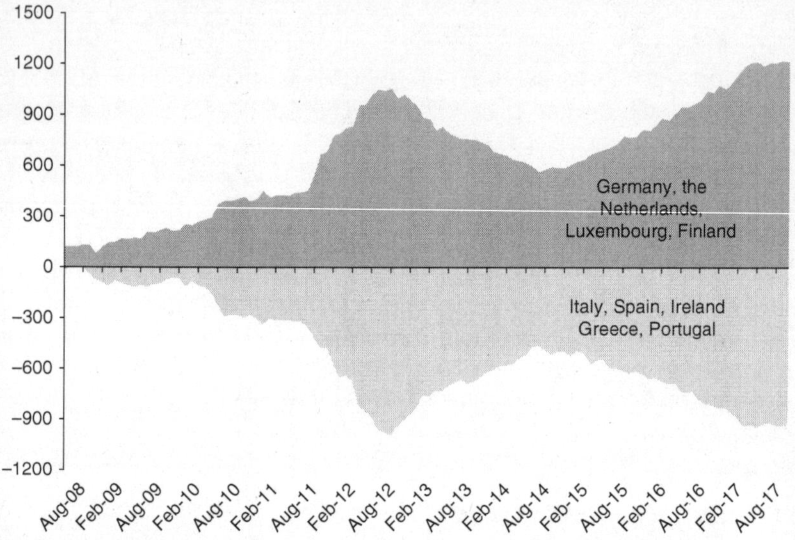

Figure B7.1.2 Target balances in the euro area, 2008–2017, in billion euros. European Central Bank.

[a]The Eurosystem is the combination of the ECB and of the national central banks of the euro area (see Chapter 5).

United States. Figure 7.6 shows how the NFA position of the United States has deteriorated since the mid-1980s while Japan, in contrast, has accumulated assets abroad. However, the NFA of a country results not only from cumulated trade imbalances, but also from return differentials between the asset side and the liability side of the country's aggregate balance sheet and from valuation effects (box 7.2). In particular, the US NFA has deteriorated less than cumulated trade deficits would have suggested thanks to favorable valuation effects and to a higher remuneration of foreign assets than foreign liabilities.[21] According to Gourinchas, Rey, and Govillot (2010), this phenomenon may be related to the international status of the dollar. The latter allows the United States to pay a very low return on its public debt, which provides liquidity services globally. Conversely, investments abroad are better remunerated on

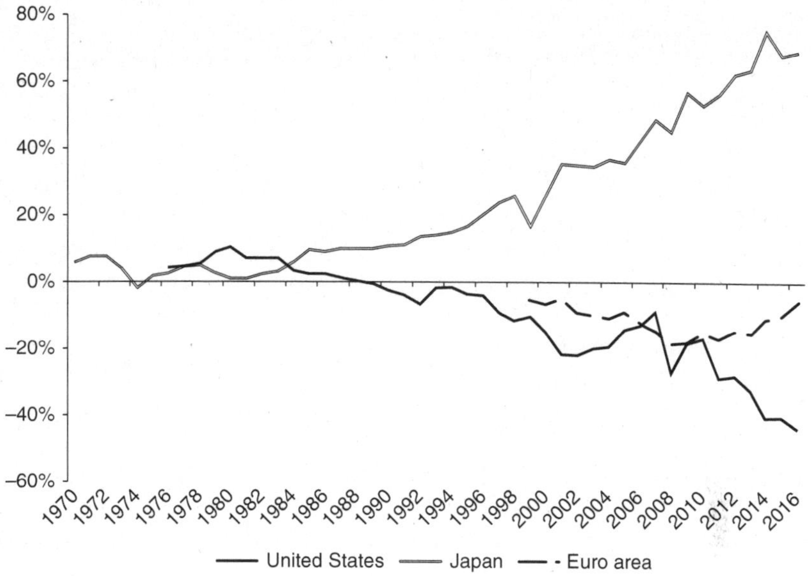

Figure 7.6 Net foreign asset positions of the United States, Japan, and the euro area, 1970–2016, in percent of gross domestic product (GDP).
Updated and extended version of the External Wealth of Nations Mark II database developed by Lane and Milesi-Ferretti (2007).

Box 7.2 The Making of the Net Foreign Asset Position

The net foreign asset position at the end of year t, NFA_t, is the difference between gross assets A_t and gross liabilities L_t, the three aggregates being expressed in the home currency:

$$\text{NFA}_t = A_t - L_t \tag{B7.2.1}$$

At the end of year t+1, the NFA will depend on (i) the revaluation of A_t, given received interests and price variations, (ii) the revaluation of L_t, given interests paid and price variations, and (iii) the trade balance of year $t+1$, TB_{t+1}.

Here we assume that gross assets are entirely denominated in foreign currency, whereas gross liabilities are entirely denominated in the home currency. We neglect changes in local-currency asset prices. Denoting by S_t the nominal exchange rate at the end of year t (units of foreign currency in one unit of home currency), the value of A_t in foreign currency at the end of t is $A_t \times S_t$. Denoting by i_A the nominal interest rates on assets, the value of A_t in the foreign currency at the end of t+1 is $(1+i_A)A_t \times S_t$, and its value in the home currency is $(1+i_A)A_t \times S_t / S_{t+1}$. Since the liabilities are denominated in the home currency, the value of L_t in the home currency at the end of $t+1$ is simply $(1+i_L)L_t$, where i_L is the interest rate on liabilities. The NFA at the end of $t+1$ then is:

$$\text{NFA}_{t+1} = (1+i_A)A_t \times S_t / S_{t+1} - (1+i_L)L_t + \text{TB}_{t+1} \qquad \text{(B7.2.2)}$$

The NFA rises with the accumulation of trade surpluses. It also increases when the interest rate on assets exceeds that on liabilities. Finally, in our setting, a depreciation of the home currency ($S_{t+1} < S_t$) revaluates foreign assets because they are denominated in foreign currency, whereas liabilities stay unaffected.

Conversely, if assets are denominated in the home currency whereas liabilities are in foreign currency, we have:

$$\text{NFA}_{t+1} = (1+i_A)A_t - (1+i_L)L_t \times S_t / S_{t+1} + \text{TB}_{t+1} \qquad \text{(B7.2.3)}$$

In this case, a depreciation of the home currency leads to a revaluation of liabilities but not of assets.

average because they are riskier, in particular through foreign direct investment. In short, the United States plays the role of an international insurer that earns high net returns on sunny days but may suffer large losses on rainy days.[22]

7.1.4 Exchange rates

We have defined the *exchange rate* as the price of the home currency in terms of foreign currencies. It can be defined relative to a single foreign currency (e.g., the euro against the US dollar) or against a basket of foreign currencies (e.g., the euro against the currencies of the major trade partners of the euro area). The former definition corresponds to the *bilateral exchange rate*, whereas the latter is the *effective exchange rate*. In both cases, however, we are measuring the value of a currency against one or several other currencies; in other words, we are concerned with the *nominal exchange rate*.

In fact, policymakers are not concerned chiefly with nominal exchange rates. What matters for consumers' and companies' decisions is the relative price of goods, services, and assets, and any movement of the nominal exchange rate can be offset by a price variation, leaving relative prices unchanged. To assess price competitiveness (or purchasing power in terms of foreign goods), one has therefore to correct the observed exchange rate for relative prices: the resulting indicator is called the *real exchange rate*. For instance, the exchange rate of the dollar against the yen in 2015 was of 121.0 yen per dollar, while the consumer price index was 104.6 in Japan and 108.8 in the United States (based on 100 in 2010).[23] The real exchange rate between the two countries thus was 121 × 108.8 / 104.6 = 125.9.[24] This figure is meaningless until it is compared with the same calculation for another year. In 2010, the nominal exchange rate was of 87.8 yen per dollar, hence the real exchange rate (with price indices again based in 2010) was 87.8 × 100 / 100 = 87.8. Comparing 2015 to 2010, it can be concluded that the relative price of US goods increased by 125.9 / 87.8 – 1 = 43.4%, whereas the relative price of the US currency increased by only 121 / 87.8 – 1 = 38.9%: the US dollar *appreciated* more in real terms than in nominal terms because consumer prices increased more in the United States than in Japan, and the yen *depreciated* more in real terms than in nominal terms.[25]

The preceding example shows that the price competitiveness of US goods deteriorated relative to Japan between 2010 and 2015 or, equivalently, that the purchasing power of US products increased in terms of imported goods from Japan. However, the United States has many other trade partners. During the same period, for instance, the US dollar depreciated in nominal and in real terms against the Chinese currency. To get a comprehensive measure of competitiveness and purchasing power, the real exchange rate must be calculated against a weighted average of foreign partners' currencies. The corresponding indicator is called the *real effective exchange rate*. From 2010 to 2015, the real effective exchange rate of the US dollar appreciated by 17.6%, according to the calculations made by the BIS.[26] There is in fact a series of possible measures of the real effective exchange rate. The different concepts are defined mathematically in box 7.3.

Observing real exchange rates over short and long periods and across countries helps uncover two stylized facts.

Box 7.3 Different Measures of Exchange Rates

Let S_{ij} be the nominal exchange rate between currency *i* and currency *j*, expressed as the price of currency *i* in units of currency *j*. (i.e., S_{ij} rises whenever currency *i* appreciates against currency *j*). P_i is the price index in country *i* and P_j the price index in country *j*. The bilateral real exchange rate is:

$$Q_{ij} = S_{ij}\frac{P_i}{P_j} \qquad \text{(B7.3.1)}$$

A rise of Q_{ij} is called a *real appreciation* of currency *i* and reflects a rise in the relative prices in country *i* vis-à-vis country *j*. Conversely, country *j* experiences a real depreciation vis-à-vis country *i*.

Now let α_{ij} be the share of country *j* in the foreign trade of country *i*, with $\sum_j \alpha_{ij} = 1$. One can define the nominal effective exchange rate of country *i* as a weighted average of its bilateral exchange rates with its trade partners:

$$S_i = \prod_j S_{ij}^{\alpha_{ij}} \qquad \text{(B7.3.2)}$$

Likewise, the real effective exchange rate of country *i* is:

$$Q_i = \prod_j Q_{ij}^{\alpha_{ij}} \qquad \text{(B7.3.3)}$$

A rise of Q_i reflects a rise in the average relative prices of country *i* vis-à-vis its trading partners.

Depending on the purpose of the calculation, different price indices can be used. Price competitiveness can be gauged by deflating the nominal exchange rate with producer prices or export prices. Cost competitiveness can be measured using unit labor costs. Terms of trade are calculated by comparing export prices with import prices. Finally, a measure of the relative purchasing power of one currency unit is obtained through deflating the nominal exchange rate with consumption price indices. Results can differ widely depending on the price index, especially when the nominal exchange rate is fixed.

First, floating currencies tend to display high volatility. It is not rare to see a bilateral nominal exchange rate move upward or downward by more than 10% in just a few months.[27] Since price indices are much more sluggish, in the short run, the real exchange rate evolves very much like the nominal one. In high-inflation countries, however, prices are also very volatile and they tend to evolve in tandem with the nominal exchange rate. In these countries, the real exchange rate is more stable than the nominal one (see Figure 7.7).

The second stylized fact relates to the long-term behavior of the real exchange rate: in advanced economies, the real exchange rate tends to revert to a constant value in the long run, whereas in developing countries, the real exchange rate appreciates as the country develops.

These two stylized facts are illustrated in figure 7.7 for the British pound. During the 1970s, the United Kingdom displayed higher inflation than its main trading partners. This was partly compensated by a depreciation of the British pound, so the real effective exchange rate depreciated much less than the nominal one. Then disinflation made real and nominal effective exchange rates move in sync, with no discernable long-run trend. The next section provides some explanations for these two stylized facts.

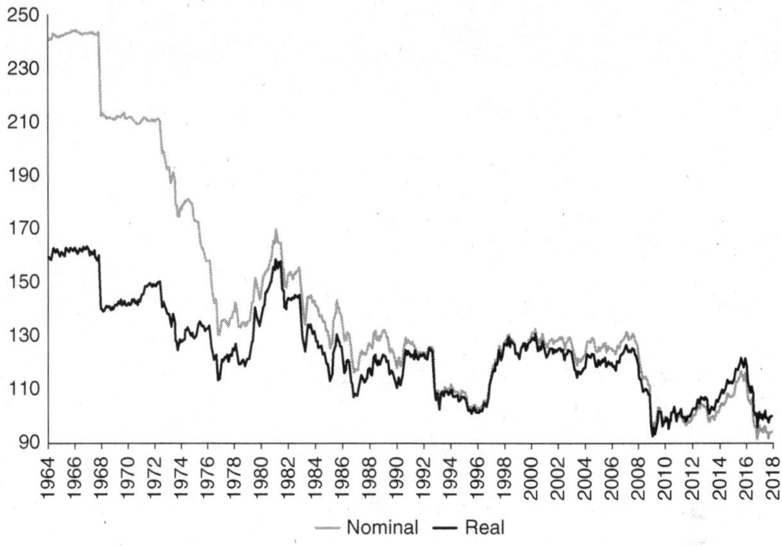

Figure 7.7 Nominal and real effective exchange rate of the British pound, 1964–2015 (100 in 2010).
Bank of International Settlements, narrow index.

7.2 Theories

What are the benefits of financial openness? Why care about the level and volatility of the exchange rate? When can an exchange rate be considered misaligned? How can governments or central banks correct possible misalignments? On all these questions, the theoretical and empirical literature is quite divided. This section provides a toolkit for addressing them.

7.2.1 The joint choice on financial openness and the exchange rate regime

Financial openness and the exchange rate regime cannot be decided one by one in isolation since a country cannot simultaneously enjoy free capital mobility, a stable exchange rate, and monetary independence. There is no single choice, however, as will be discussed herein.

a) The monetary trilemma

According to the Mundell-Fleming model presented in Chapter 4, in a regime with free capital mobility *and* a fixed exchange rate, monetary policy can no longer achieve an internal objective of price stability and/or output stability because the interest rate must be set at a level such that the nominal exchange rate stays constant. For instance, the central bank cannot cut the policy interest rate in order to stimulate aggregate demand because the exchange rate would immediately depreciate. More generally, it is impossible to have at the same time: (i) free capital mobility, (ii) a fixed exchange rate, and (iii) monetary policy independence. This incompatibility is referred to as the *impossible trinity*, or the *international monetary trilemma* (figure 7.8).

Empirical evidence of the impossible trinity can be found by estimating the relation between the variation of each country *i*'s short-term interest rate, Δr_{it}, and that of the "base country" rate, Δr_{bt}:

$$\Delta r_{it} = \alpha + \beta \Delta r_{bt} + u_{it} \tag{7.1}$$

where u_{it} is the error term. In a perfectly credible fixed exchange rate regime, and with perfect capital mobility, we expect $\beta = 1$, consistent with the uncovered interest parity (see Chapter 5). Based on a panel of 155 countries over 1970–2000, Shambaugh (2004) finds that β is positive and significantly higher for peggers than for non-peggers. For countries with pegs and free capital mobility, Shambaugh finds $\beta = 0.67$. For non-peggers with capital controls, β is nonsignificant. Peggers with capital controls and non-peggers with free capital mobility lie in between. The fact that β is positive even for non-peggers may be related to the fact that interest rates react to common shocks or that countries manage their currencies without declaring so. Conversely, the fact that β remains below unity even with a peg and free capital mobility may be explained by domestic shocks that require a reaction of the domestic interest rate in order to maintain the peg. On the whole, such estimates confirm that having a peg and free capital mobility dramatically limits the extent of monetary independence. The result is robust to different country or time samples, to different regime classifications, and to the addition of control variables to the estimation.[28]

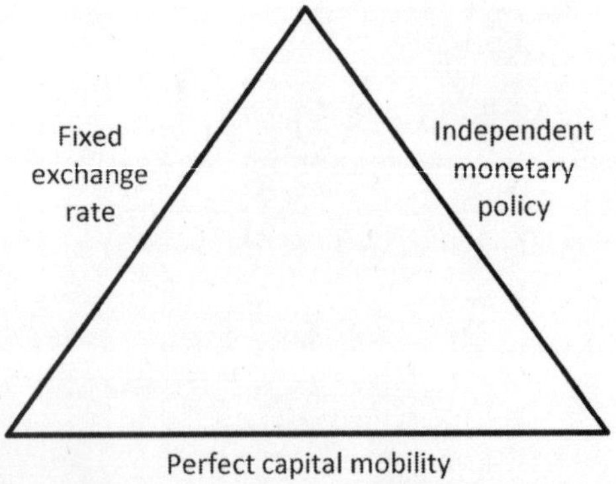

Figure 7.8 The international monetary trilemma.
Authors, based on the Mundell-Fleming model.

The ability of central banks with free floating currencies to retain monetary independence in an environment of free capital mobility has, however, been challenged. Although there is extensive evidence that short-term interest rates are less correlated in a floating regime than in a pegged one (see previous paragraph), this is not a proof of monetary independence. Indeed, as argued by Rey (2013, 2016), the policy of the Federal Reserve influences monetary policy elsewhere in the world not only through policy rates, but also through the global credit channel. For instance, when the Fed cuts its policy rate, the depreciation of the dollar revalues non-dollar assets, hence the collateral of borrowers in non-dollar countries; it also raises the profits of international banks that partially fund themselves in dollar, which raises their willingness to lend; finally, it encourages investors to take more risks and raise their leverage. Rey argues that the trilemma is in fact a dilemma: with capital mobility, an independent monetary policy is possible only if there is an active macroprudential policy as described in Chapter 6.

Another reason why interest-rate shocks are transmitted across countries is that long-term interest rates can be correlated with the "base country," even when short-term ones are not, if exchange rate variations are expected to be reversed and/or if term premia are correlated (Box 7.4). Hence, if loosening monetary policy in the United States reinforces risk appetite globally, then long-term interest rates decline everywhere even if short-term interest rates behave differently. Obstfeld (2015) concludes that countries with free floating currency and free capital mobility do enjoy more independent monetary policies. However, trade-offs also need to be made with financial stability. For instance, a country that wishes to stabilize its currency may not able to avoid "importing" financial instability, unless it restricts capital mobility.

Box 7.4 From Short-Term to Long-Term Interest Rate Correlation

Following Obstfeld (2015), we consider a two-period model, where period t represents the "short term" while period $t+1$ is the "long term." In the home country, the long-term interest rate, i_t^L is the average of the current short-term interest rate i_t and the expected short term interest rate $E_t i_{t+1}$, plus a term premium τ_t (see Chapter 5):

$$i_t^L = \frac{1}{2} i_t + \frac{1}{2} E_t i_{t+1} + \tau_t \quad \text{(B7.4.1)}$$

Similarly, in the United States:

$$i_t^{US,L} = \frac{1}{2} i_t^{US} + \frac{1}{2} E_t i_{t+1}^{US} + \tau_t^{US} \quad \text{(B7.4.2)}$$

The long-term interest-rate differential thus is:

$$i_t^L - i_t^{US,L} = \frac{1}{2}\left(i_t - i_t^{US}\right) + \frac{1}{2}\left(E_t i_{t+1} - E_t i_{t+1}^{US}\right) + \left(\tau_t - \tau_t^{US}\right) \quad \text{(B7.4.3)}$$

Applying the uncovered interest parity with risk premia ρ_t and $E_t\rho_{t+1}$, the short-term interest differentials are

$$i_t - i_t^{US} = E_t e_{t+1} - e_t + \rho_t \quad \text{(B7.7.4)}$$

$$E_t i_{t+1} - E_t i_{t+1}^{US} = E_t e_{t+2} - E_t e_{t+1} + E_t \rho_{t+1} \quad \text{(B7.7.5)}$$

where e_t is the logarithm of the nominal exchange rate at time t (price of the dollar in terms of the home currency) and $E_t e_{t+1}$, $E_t e_{t+2}$ its expected values for $t+1$ and $t+2$. Plugging the short-term differentials into the long-term one, we get:

$$i_t^L - i_t^{US,L} = \frac{1}{2}\left(E_t e_{t+1} - e_t\right) + \frac{1}{2}\left(E_t e_{t+2} - E_t e_{t+1}\right) + \frac{1}{2}\left(\rho_t + E_t \rho_{t+1}\right) + \left(\tau_t - \tau_t^{US}\right) \quad \text{(B7.4.6)}$$

The long-term interest differential (left hand-side of Equation B7.4.6) does not move over time if expected exchange rate variations between t and $t+1$ are expected to be reversed between $t+1$ and $t+2$, and if the term premia τ_t and τ_t^{US} move in tandem.

b) The pros and cons of capital mobility and exchange rate stability

The choice between the different combinations allowed by the impossible trinity depends on the relative value of capital mobility and exchange rate stability.

International capital mobility

International capital mobility has three main virtues in theory. First, it reduces the cost of investment for capital importing countries while raising the return on savings for capital exporting countries. Second, it helps a country to smooth its consumption level over time. Third, it allows for greater portfolio diversification since the pool of assets is larger. In principle, this will reduce the risk for savers for a given return. Investing abroad can also provide a hedge against some shocks on the domestic economy. For instance, a positive shock on domestic prices often comes along with a depreciation of the home currency; the real value (in terms of domestic goods) of holdings in foreign assets stays constant, whereas that of domestic assets falls. These various advantages, however, come with some risks related to the instability of capital inflows and outflows.

While empirical evidence clearly confirms the gains from international trade in goods and services, the evidence is mixed for capital mobility. Gourinchas and Jeanne (2006) evaluate the welfare gain for a "typical" non-OECD country to be equivalent to around 1% of consumption in the long run. Obstfeld (2009) argues that there is a fundamental difference between goods and capital mobility. Only in the latter case is the exchange intertemporal, which involves promises that may or may not be honored, and short-term speculation that reduces the gain from openness. Surveying the empirical literature on this issue, he concludes that financial openness does not reduce consumption instability nor does it systematically boost GDP growth. In fact, financial openness is not a sufficient condition for a country to attract foreign investment, especially long-term inflows. The domestic regulatory and supervisory environment is key.

After World War II, John Maynard Keynes and Harry Dexter White, the Bretton Woods negotiators, viewed free capital mobility as an *impediment* to the development of international trade since destabilizing capital flows would result in calls for protectionism (see Ghosh et al. 2016). Since the 1980s, however, free capital mobility has been increasingly considered as a complement to the mobility of goods and services. In particular, capital mobility allows for the trade balance to be different from zero at any point of time, which raises the scope for gross trade flows. Capital controls have been considered increasingly less feasible except for limited periods of time. Still, a distinction must be made between the controls imposed on inflows and on outflows. Recent IMF research on controls imposed on inflows has shown that, although they have limited impact on the volume of inflows and on exchange rates, they are able to twist their composition in favor of more long-term and more stable inflows (see e.g., De Gregorio, Edwards, and Valdés, 2000; Ostry et al., 2012). On the whole, the recent literature suggests that, although capital mobility should be the rule, some controls on capital inflows can be useful to reduce the risks of financial instability after macroprudential policy tools have been exhausted (Ostry et al., 2010, 2011).[29]

Exchange rate stability

Is exchange rate volatility costly? On the theoretical side, Ethier (1973), Clark (1973), or Hooper and Kohlagen (1978) show that currency risks reduce trade volumes if firms are risk-averse regardless of whether currency hedging is available. Pindyck (1991) and Demers (1991) further argue that the irreversible costs associated with uncertainty reduce investment. But on the empirical side, the link between exchange rate instability and trade, investment, or growth has long been considered ambiguous. However, recent studies that exploit disaggregated data, account for firm heterogeneity, correct for methodological pitfalls, control for financial development, and/or focus on medium to long-term measures of exchange rate uncertainty (that can less easily be hedged) find a negative impact for exchange rate variability on trade (see, e.g., Taglioni, 2002, and the meta-analyses of Ćorić and Pugh, 2010 and Haile and Pugh, 2013), on foreign direct investment (Cavallari and d'Addona, 2013), and on growth (Aghion et al., 2009).

Reciprocally, is nominal exchange rate fixity costly in terms of macroeconomic stability? It is useful to start with two simple ideas. First, if prices and wages are fully flexible, then fixing the nominal exchange rate is costless.

Suppose the economy suffers from a negative foreign demand shock. Domestic prices will fall relative to foreign ones through a decline in home currency prices, a depreciation of the nominal exchange rate, or a combination of the two. If prices are fully flexible, the real exchange rate adjusts no matter the reaction of the nominal one. Second, if prices adjust slowly, exchange rate fixity prevents the optimal relative price adjustment from taking place in the short run. Then, a flexible regime is to be preferred to a fixed peg, except if exchange rate volatility has microeconomic costs (see Friedman, 1953). Clarida, Galí, and Gertler (2002) extend their new-Keynesian modeling of monetary policy (exposed in Chapter 5) to an open economy. Under some restrictive assumptions (notably perfect pass-through of exchange rate variations on the price of imports), they show that optimal monetary policy is basically the same in an open as in a closed economy, although openness may affect the slope of the optimal reaction of the interest rate to inflation: when exchange rate volatility is costless, the best exchange rate regime is a flexible one. Conversely, if exchange rate volatility is costly, it may be optimal to fix the nominal exchange rate.[30]

The final argument is that of central bank credibility. As highlighted by the Barro-Gordon model (see Chapter 5), using a commitment technology helps the central bank to maintain price stability and reduce the cost of disinflation by anchoring inflation expectations at a low level. A fixed exchange rate, which can easily be checked by the private agents, is a powerful commitment technology. The government then needs to make a trade-off between the gains from higher credibility and the losses associated with exchange rate fixity (see Giavazzi and Pagano, 1992; Alesina and Barro, 2002).

All three arguments—cost of exchange rate volatility, cost of exchange rate fixity, and credibility benefit from fixity—are to be evaluated with respect to the anchor currency, which constitutes another dimension of the regime choice specifically studied by the theory of *optimum currency areas* (OCAs).

c) The theory of optimum currency areas

The theory of OCAs was introduced in 1961 by Robert Mundell and developed by Ronald McKinnon (1963) and Peter Kenen (1969). This theory presents the choice of an exchange rate regime within a cost–benefit approach where the cost of fixing the exchange rate results from losing monetary independence (see the discussion in the preceding section), whereas the benefit results from lower exchange rate volatility and possibly (in the case of a monetary union or dollarization) the elimination of currency transaction costs.

The strength of Mundell's argument is that it applies to regions as well as countries, leading to a complete rethinking of monetary geography. In his 1961 paper, Mundell suggested that, due to similarities of regional economies across the US–Canada border, monetary union could make more sense between the Eastern or Western regions of the United States and Canada than within the United States and Canada themselves (box 7.5). Mundell's theory also provided an intellectual ground for Europe's economic and monetary union.

Mundell's cost–benefit approach is illustrated in figure 7.9, inspired by Paul Krugman (1992). The benefits of a fixed exchange rate (or of membership in a monetary union) are an increasing function of integration since exchange rate instability is more detrimental between two countries that have large bilateral exchanges of goods, services, and capital. As for the costs of fixing the exchange rate, they depend on the likelihood of *asymmetric shocks* (i.e., shocks

Box 7.5 Robert Mundell's Optimal Currency Areas

"A Theory of Optimum Currency Areas" is the title of an article published in 1961 by Robert Mundell in the *American Economic Review*. At that time, most currencies had fixed rates under the Bretton Woods arrangement, but the Canadian dollar was floating. A debate was raging between advocates and opponents of floating exchange rates. Mundell, a Canadian economist, cut the Gordian knot by suggesting that this could only be decided on a case-by-case basis. He went further, suggesting that monetary unions would not necessarily coincide with political borders.

Consider the United States and Canada, Mundell said. For the sake of simplicity, suppose the Eastern regions of both Canada and the United States are specialized in car making, while the Western regions of both countries are specialized in lumber products. Suppose also that the labor force cannot move easily from one coast to another.

Mundell then considers a positive productivity shock in the car industry that creates an excess supply of cars and an excess demand for lumber products (because of the higher demand from car industry workers). This is a typical asymmetric shock. It causes a dilemma for the US Federal Reserve and the Bank of Canada. Tightening monetary policy in both countries would curb inflation in the West but increase unemployment in the East. Conversely, cutting interest rates would stimulate employment in the East but lead to overheating in the West. In fact, reorganizing central banks so that there would be an "Eastern dollar" and a "Western dollar" rather than a US dollar and a Canadian dollar would be more suited to this type of economic shock. The central bank of the West could raise interest rates, the central bank of the East could lower them, and the Western dollar would appreciate against the Eastern dollar. Another answer to the dilemma would be labor mobility: workers would move from East to West, and supply would adjust in both regions (see figure B7.5.1). Absent labor mobility, there is a need for a monetary policy that meets the geography of product specialization.

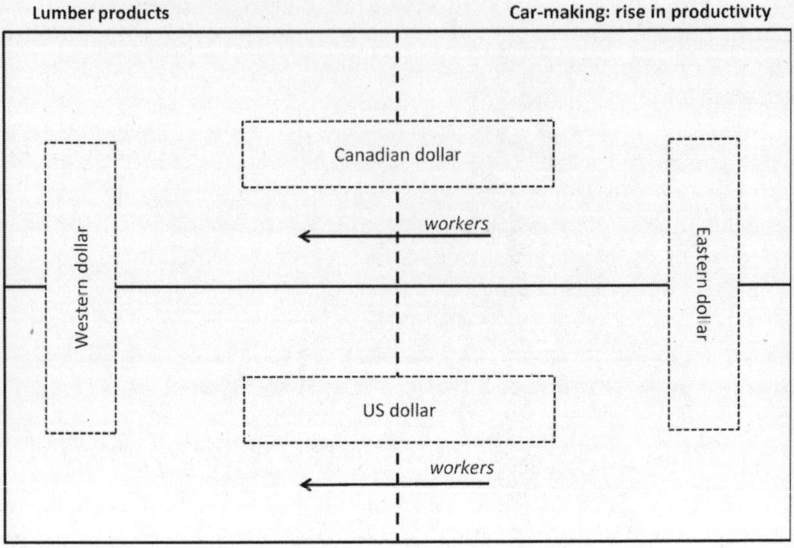

Figure B7.5.1 An asymmetric shock in North America.
Authors, based on Mundell (1961).

Let us now push the reasoning one step further. Since there are also North–South asymmetric shocks, creating four currencies and as many central banks could be justified. At the extreme, in order to face all kinds of asymmetric shocks, it would be appropriate that each company and each household issue their own private currency. This would amount to barter, and this would not be optimal since it would create a lot of transaction costs. Thus, the borders of the optimum currency areas result from a trade-off between the need to mitigate asymmetric shocks and the need to limit transaction costs.

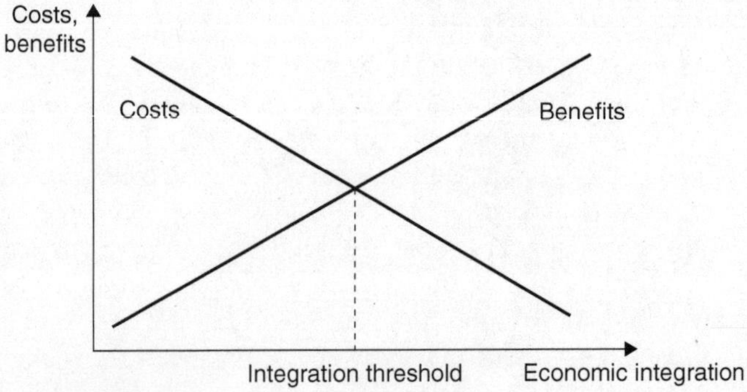

Figure 7.9 Costs and benefits of a monetary union.
Authors, based on Krugman (1992).

that affect in different ways those countries tied to a fixed exchange rate). Indeed, since exchange rate stability involves giving up monetary independence when capital mobility is complete, the central bank of a fixed exchange rate country is unable to stabilize its economy in the event of an asymmetric shock, contrasting with a *symmetric shock* that affects the different countries in the same way.

In principle, more integration between countries raises their exposure to symmetric shocks through supply chains or cross-border capital exposures. However, more integration (including monetary integration) can also reinforce the specialization of countries, leading to more asymmetric shocks.[31] Here we assume that the cost of fixing the exchange rate falls when economic integration rises. The threshold level of integration beyond which fixing the exchange rate is advisable corresponds to the intercept between the "gain" and "cost" schedules, which themselves depend on structural factors such as price flexibility, labor mobility, or the existence of a federal budget that will smooth disposable income by automatically lowering the amount of taxes paid by a country in crisis. In particular, more flexible prices and wages reduce the usefulness of the exchange rate as an adjustment instrument: the "cost" locus moves downward and the threshold level of integration is lower. At the limit, in an economy with perfectly flexible prices and wages, the exchange rate does not matter at all. Interestingly, smaller countries tend to be more specialized than large ones (hence the "cost" locus is higher), but they also benefit more from reduced transaction costs in the event of a monetary union (the "gain" locus is also higher). The position of the threshold is thus uncertain compared to larger countries.

d) Monetary or real shocks?

The theory of OCAs suggests that a country faced with frequent asymmetric shocks should refrain from fixing its nominal exchange rate and, even more, participate in a monetary union unless there are major gains in terms of reduced transaction costs or if its labor and goods markets are very flexible. However, the "shocks" considered in the OCAs theory are *real shocks*, such as productivity or consumption shocks. Some countries may rather face *monetary shocks*. This is the case, for example, if private agents hold liquidities in foreign currency or if the financial system is unstable. In such a case, the "LM" curve of the Mundell-Fleming model (cf. Chapter 4) is highly unstable, and a fixed exchange rate delivers more stability than a flexible one (box 7.6). This result has important implications for emerging economies, especially when the credibility of the central bank is not yet established or the financial system is still in development: during the transition, these countries may be better off with a fixed exchange rate than with a flexible one.

Box 7.6 Monetary Versus Real Shocks

Here we extend the closed-economy reasoning of Poole (1970) to a small, open economy. We use the Mundell-Fleming model presented in Chapter 4. We assume that capital is perfectly mobile and, for the sake of simplicity, that expectations are static. The domestic nominal interest rate i is thus always equal to the world interest rate i^*.

A positive shock to money supply moves the LM curve *ex ante* to the right (see left panel of figure B7.6.1): output increases from its initial value Y_0 and the interest rate declines. In a fixed exchange rate regime, the central bank has to sell foreign currency to clear the foreign exchange market. By so doing, it withdraws domestic currency from circulation and brings domestic money supply down to its initial level. The LM curve goes back to its initial position, and output has eventually not increased: $Y_{fix} = Y_0$. In a flexible exchange rate regime, in contrast, the foreign exchange market is cleared by nominal exchange rate depreciation. Depreciation in turn stimulates net exports, pushing the IS curve to the right: the initial impact of the shock is thus magnified by the exchange rate movement: $Y_{flex} > Y_0$.

In the case of a positive real shock, like a fall in the saving rate, the effect is quite the opposite (right panel of figure B7.6.1). The shock moves *ex ante* the IS curve to the right, pushing both output and the interest rate up. In a flexible exchange rate regime, there is no *ex post* impact on output because the exchange rate appreciates and weighs on foreign trade: $Y_{flex} = Y_0$. In a fixed exchange rate regime, the impact of the shock is magnified by the central bank: the latter buys foreign reserves to counter the appreciation of the currency and thus increases the quantity of money in circulation, which leads to a further output expansion: $Y_{fix} > Y_0$.

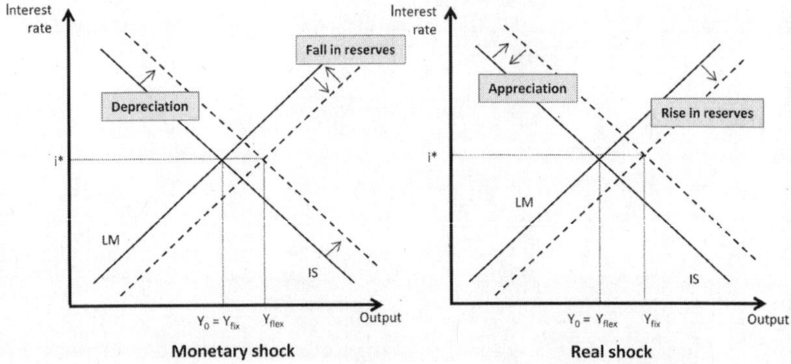

Figure B7.6.1 Exchange rate regime choice with asymmetric monetary and real shocks.
Authors, based on Poole (1970).

e) Risk sharing

In a second paper published in 1973, Robert Mundell argues that a monetary union provides insurance against asymmetric shocks because economic agents share a common pool of money. More generally, international financial integration provides a device to smooth consumption in each country or region due to portfolio diversification: if the domestic economy is hit by, say, a negative, specific productivity shock, then domestic income falls, but households will continue to earn returns from their financial holdings invested abroad. As already mentioned, macroeconomic risk-sharing can also be achieved by means of *fiscal federalism*, that is, temporary transfers of fiscal resources across geographical constituencies, such as regions or countries. If the domestic economy is hit by a negative shock, then its contribution to the federal budget is reduced and it receives transfers from it. On the whole, financial integration as well as the existence of a federal budget are important criteria for forming a currency area.

By decomposing the disposable income of each US state in order to highlight the proportion of its net income originating from other states (dividends, interests, rental income payments across state borders, remittances, federal transfers, and taxes), Asdrubali, Sørensen, and Yosha (1996) found that 39% of shocks to gross state product are smoothed by factor income from other states, 13% by the federal budget, and 23% by saving and borrowing over the 1963–90 period (see box 7.7). Hence, a 10% decrease in the production of a state results in a decline of local consumption of only 2.5%. In contrast,

Box 7.7 Measuring the Extent of Consumption Smoothing

To measure the channels of consumption smoothing in the United States, Asdrubali et al. (1996) rely on the following identity:

$$C_{it} = \frac{C_{it}}{D_{it}} \times \frac{D_{it}}{I_{it}} \times \frac{I_{it}}{Y_{it}} \times Y_{it} \qquad \text{(B7.7.1)}$$

where C_{it} denotes consumption in state i for period t, D_{it} disposable income, I_{it} income, and Y_{it} GDP, all on a per-capita basis. Equation (B7.7.1) states that consumption per capita may be disconnected from GDP per capita thanks to the use of credit (first term), to the federal tax and benefit system (second term), and to factor income from and to other states (third term). Asdrubali et al. regress the log-variation of each of these three terms on the log-variation of GDP per capita. For the third term, for instance:

$$\Delta \log Y_{it} - \Delta \log I_{it} = v_t + \beta \Delta \log Y_{it} + u_{it} \qquad \text{(B7.7.2)}$$

where v_t denotes time-fixed effects and u_{it} is the residual. The coefficient β can be interpreted as the percentage of state i's GDP per capita variations that are *not* passed on to state *i*'s income per capita, thanks to the counteracting impact of factor income from and to other states. Based on real per-capita gross state product in 50 US states over 1963–90, Asdrubali et al. find β to be as high as 0.39; that is, a 1% drop in GDP per capita leads to a fall in income per capita of only (1 – 0.39) × 1% = 0.61%. Similarly, they estimate a β coefficient of 0.13 for smoothing through the federal budget (second term of Equation B7.7.1) and 0.23 for smoothing through state's saving and borrowing (first term).

Sørensen and Yosha (1998) find no evidence of risk-sharing through portfolio diversification across OECD countries nor across EU countries over the same period. Limited portfolio diversification across countries is consistent with the Feldstein-Horioka puzzle discussed in Section 7.1.

For 15 EU countries in 1980–2005, Afonso and Furceri (2008) find that only 43% of shocks to national GDP is smoothed and 39% for EMU countries. The quasi-totality of the smoothing comes from saving and borrowing, not from factor income (not to mention the very small EU budget). For 15 euro area countries over 1979–2010, Furceri and Zdzienicka (2015) find similar results, with a declining degree of smoothing over time. Over a more recent period (2000Q4–2015Q4), Nikolov (2016) confirms the huge discrepancy between the United States (where only 17.6% of the shocks remain unsmoothed) and the euro area (75.7% unsmoothed), with most of the difference coming from cross-border factor income. Other authors have found a smoothing effect of around 80% in Canada and Germany, with a large role for factor income (see Allard et al., 2013).[32]

7.2.2 Exchange rate policy

Assuming that the government has made the choice of a flexible exchange rate, the next question is whether to have an exchange rate policy: should (and can) the central bank intervene to steer the exchange rate towards a different level than the one resulting from market forces?

Until the early 1990s, capital movements were restrained in most countries, so exchange rates were mostly determined by shocks to exports and imports. Since the 1990s, capital movements have become an order of magnitude higher than goods and services transactions, and shocks to capital flows have gained in importance. This evolution has paved the way to a greater disconnect between exchange rate variations and the needs of the "real" economy. For instance, the US dollar failed to adjust downward in the early 2000s despite growing current account deficits in the United States.

Before envisaging interventions on foreign exchange markets, policymakers need analytical tools to disentangle exchange rate variations that correspond to the evolution of economic fundamentals, such as the current account or productivity, from those that consist of temporary deviations from a long-run norm. This distinction, however, is necessarily fragile: any model of *exchange rate misalignments* relies on a normative theory (of where the exchange rate should be) rather than on a positive one (of where the exchange rate actually is). Here we present several ways to determine the exchange rate that is consistent with the fundamentals of the economy.

a) Purchasing power parity and the Balassa-Samuelson effect

In the long run, there is no reason why, when converted into the same currency at market exchange rates, the prices of traded goods should differ across economically integrated countries. Indeed, when a good is tradable, its price should equalize across countries by virtue of the *law of one price*. If some price differentials do survive, this must be due to transportation costs, tariffs, and other trade barriers, or to market imperfections such as imperfect information or monopolistic power. However, if price differentials are structural, they are expected to remain stable or to evolve slowly. Even when they do not, the real exchange rate should revert to a stable level at the aggregate level based on a macroeconomic adjustment mechanism already identified by David Hume in the seventeenth century as the *price–specie flow mechanism*, a self-stabilizing property of the balance of payments. According to Hume, a country enjoying an increase in price competitiveness normally experiences an improvement in its current account. In a fixed nominal exchange rate regime, it accumulates foreign exchange (or gold) reserves. If not sterilized, reserve accumulation inflates the money supply and therefore the general level of prices. The real exchange rate thus appreciates until it is back to its initial level. The price–specie mechanism framed the functioning of the gold standard and led to the recognition of relative price variations as a macroeconomic adjustment mechanism (Cassel, 1921). Transposing to a flexible regime, the accumulation of current account surpluses should progressively lead to both a nominal and a real exchange rate appreciation until the current account is back to balance.

Price level equalization across two countries is called *absolute purchasing power parity* whereas the stability of price differentials is labeled *relative purchasing power parity*. The purchasing power parity level of the exchange rate is the level equalizing prices across two countries. With low inflation, the relative price level moves smoothly over time; hence, the *PPP exchange rate* (i.e., the nominal exchange rate that would allow prices to equalize once expressed in the same currency) moves smoothly and offers a benchmark for the observed exchange rate, which is said to be *overvalued* in terms of PPP if it is stronger than the PPP level and *undervalued* in the opposite case.

As shown as an example in figure 7.7, the real exchange rate of a country like the United Kingdom is not constant in the short run, but it tends to come back to a constant level in the long term, although the adjustment is relatively slow: after an exogenous shock, it takes three to five years on average to close half of the gap between the real exchange rate and its long-term value (Rogoff, 1996), which means that if the exchange rate is overvalued by 10% in one given year, it will still be overvalued by 5% after 3–5 years, absent new shocks.[33]

The problem with the law of one price is that many sectors are shielded from international competition. Hairdressers and restaurants are famous examples, the retail trade and public services are others.[34] In these sectors, the law of one price cannot be expected to hold unless cost and market structures are the same and preferences are identical. *The Economist* regularly publishes a PPP real exchange rate index based on the price of hamburgers—the "Big Mac index." In July 2017, the price of an internationally standardized hamburger, the Big Mac, was 1.70 equivalent US dollars in Ukraine but 6.74 dollars in Switzerland.[35] The law of one price is irrelevant for hamburgers, which cannot be shipped easily abroad and have a high content of nontradable services that do not bear the same cost across countries. Since hamburgers are part of the consumption basket, consumer prices cannot be expected to be equal across countries.

More specifically, the price of nontradable goods tends to be higher in more developed economies. Within the most advanced countries, these differences are limited and PPP still holds in the long run. However, price differentials in nontraded goods sectors are very substantial between countries of different development levels, leading PPP to be invalidated. In 1964, in separate contributions, Bèla Balassa and Paul Samuelson highlighted the role of productivity differentials in explaining such differences in price levels. Their idea goes as follows. Nontradable goods are produced more or less in the same way in all countries, developed or not. In short, a hairdresser has more or less the same number of clients per day in all countries. Productivity in the nontraded goods sectors is thus comparable.[36] In sectors exposed to international competition such as manufacturing, in contrast, labor productivity is higher in developed countries than in developing countries thanks to capital accumulation and technical progress. In developing countries, wages have therefore to be lower, so that prices can be the same and abide by the law of one price. However, since workers can move across industries, low wages in the traded goods sectors will exert downward pressure on wages in the nontraded goods ones. Hence, wages in the nontraded goods sectors are lower than in developed countries even though productivity is comparable: the price of nontraded goods must thus be lower, which feeds a lower level of consumer prices in developing countries than in advanced economies. Figure 7.10 broadly confirms the positive relationship between the level of development (here measured through GDP per capita in PPP) and the real exchange rate (here the bilateral rate against the US dollar).

Now, how do things evolve over time? As productivity in the traded goods sectors converges toward the level in developed countries, wages increase

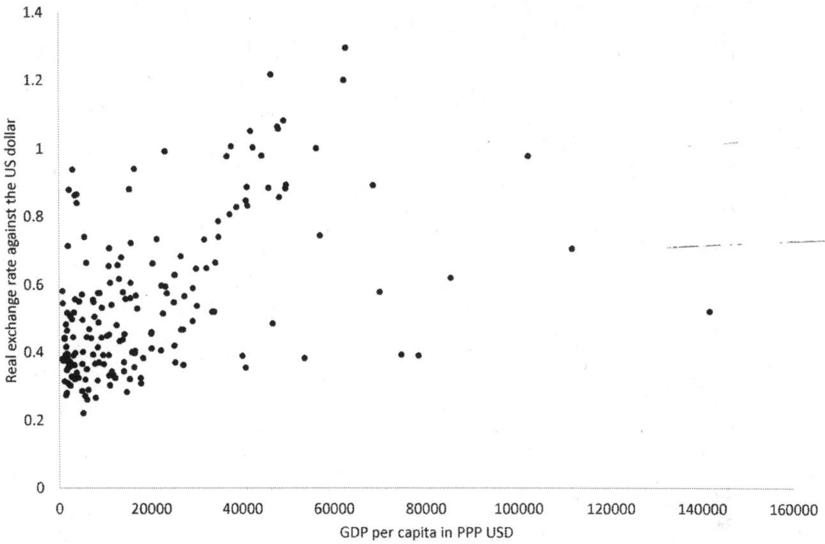

Figure 7.10 The Balassa-Samuelson effect, year 2015 (gross domestic product [GDP] per capita and the real exchange rate).

Based on World Development Indicators, World Bank. A real exchange rate above unity means that consumer prices are above the US level on average, once expressed in US dollar.

gradually both in these sectors and in the nontraded goods sectors (since workers can move from one sector to another). In the nontraded goods sectors, however, wage increases are not compensated by a better productivity and have to be passed to consumers. The aggregate price index therefore increases over time compared to that of advanced economies, implying a real exchange rate appreciation. This is the *Balassa-Samuelson effect* (the math is developed in box 7.8).[37]

This catch-up in prices in developing countries is a natural process which should not be opposed. It does not mean in any respect that competitiveness deteriorates, but it has important policy consequences. For instance, it implies that inflation rates are likely to remain quite dispersed in the euro area between more and less advanced economies, thereby creating a challenge for the ECB until GDP per capita has substantially converged across the member countries. Upstream, it means that there is a contradiction in the convergence criteria European countries have to abide by in order to be allowed into the euro area. According to the Maastricht Treaty, candidate countries are required both to achieve nominal exchange rate stability vis-à-vis the euro and to achieve a rate of inflation close to the inflation rate of the best-performing euro area countries. This is incompatible with the Balassa-Samuelson effect since it amounts to blocking real exchange rate appreciation.[38]

Box 7.8 The Balassa-Samuelson Effect

Consider a small country with two industries: a traded goods sector T, say manufacturing, with weight $0 < \alpha < 1$, and a nontradable goods sector N, say services, with weight $1-\alpha$. The law of one price holds only in the traded goods sector:

$$Q^T = \frac{SP^T}{P^{T*}} = cst = 1 \quad \text{(B7.8.1)}$$

where Q^T is the relative price of traded goods, S is the nominal exchange rate (value of one unit of domestic currency in terms of foreign currency), and P^T, P^{T*} are the price levels of traded goods at home and abroad, respectively. The productivity of the traded goods sector a^T differs from country to country while the productivity of the nontradables sector a^N is identical: $a^T \neq a^{T*}$, $a^N = a^{N*}$.

Suppose that the nominal wage W is the same throughout a given country due to workers' mobility. Profit maximization under perfect competition leads to a real wage equal to productivity so that:

$$P^N = \frac{W}{a^N}, \text{ with } W = a^T P^T \quad \text{(B7.8.2a)}$$

$$P^{N^*} = \frac{W^*}{a^{N^*}}, \text{ with } W^* = a^{T^*} P^{T^*} \quad \text{(B7.8.2b)}$$

Noting that $a^N = a^{N^*}$ and recalling that $SP^T = P^{T^*}$, one obtains the relative price of nontradable goods:

$$Q^N = \frac{SP^N}{P^{N^*}} = \frac{SW}{W^*} = \frac{a^T}{a^{T^*}} \quad \text{(B7.8.3)}$$

Let the aggregate price index P be the weighted average of price indices in both sectors (it is assumed that the share of traded goods α is the same in both countries):

$$P = \left(P^T\right)^{\alpha}\left(P^N\right)^{1-\alpha} \quad P^* = \left(P^{T*}\right)^{\alpha}\left(P^{N*}\right)^{1-\alpha} \quad \text{(B7.8.4)}$$

Combining these equations finally yields the real exchange rate:

$$Q = \frac{SP}{P^*} = \left(\frac{a^T}{a^{T^*}}\right)^{1-\alpha} \quad \text{(B7.8.5)}$$

The real exchange rate depends on the productivity differential in the traded goods sector. If the productivity of the traded goods sector of a country grows more quickly than that of its trading partners, then its real exchange rate appreciates. Depending on the exchange rate regime, this appreciation can materialize through nominal exchange rate appreciation or higher inflation.

b) Real exchange rates and the trade balance

Both PPP and the Balassa-Samuelson effect induce long-term dynamics. In the shorter term, the real exchange rate may depart from both benchmarks due to macroeconomic imbalances. This requires other approaches to the equilibrium exchange rate that link real exchange rate developments to internal and external imbalances.

The exchange rate determines the relative price of goods and services produced in the domestic economy, hence domestic demand for foreign goods, foreign demand for domestic goods, and the price of imported goods in the consumption basket.

Denoting C private consumption, I private investment, G public expenditures, X exports and IM imports, all expressed in units of domestic output, aggregate demand Y^d is written as:

$$Y^d = C + I + G + X - IM \tag{7.2}$$

Denoting Q the relative price of domestic goods in terms of foreign goods (i.e., the real exchange rate of the domestic country), we have $IM = M/Q$, where M is the volume of imports expressed in units of foreign goods and services. The accounting equation can be rewritten accordingly:

$$Y^d = C + I + G + B \tag{7.3}$$

where B is the trade balance expressed in domestic output units:

$$B = X - \frac{M}{Q} \tag{7.4}$$

A real exchange rate depreciation (a decrease in Q) has three distinct effects on the trade balance B, and hence on aggregate demand Y^d: (i) it increases the volume of exports X due to higher price competitiveness, (ii) it reduces the volume of imports M because imported goods and services are more expensive, and (iii) it raises the relative value of each imported unit. The first two are volume effects and they influence positively the trade balance B; the last one is a valuation effect which influences it negatively. The net effect of the real exchange rate depreciation on B is thus ambiguous: B rises if the price elasticities of exports and imports are large enough for volume effects to dominate the valuation effect. This condition is called the *Marshall-Lerner condition* (see box 7.9).

The Marshall-Lerner condition is generally met in the medium term (i.e., after a few quarters). However, as volumes tend to react slowly to relative price variations while the valuation effect is immediate, an exchange rate depreciation triggers an immediate deterioration in the trade balance followed by a gradual improvement. Hence, the shape of the trade balance following an exchange rate depreciation is *J*-shaped: it is called the *J-curve* (see figure 7.11).

Box 7.9 The Marshall-Lerner Condition and the *J*-curve

The Marshall-Lerner condition sets the condition for a currency depreciation to affect the trade balance positively. Denote by X, M, and B exports, imports, and the trade balance, respectively. X and B are expressed in units of domestic production, while imports M are expressed in units of foreign production. To express all flows in units of national production, imports must be divided by the real exchange rate Q. Hence the trade balance in units of national goods is written as:

$$B = X - M / Q \tag{B7.9.1}$$

A real depreciation (fall in Q) leads to a rise in X and a fall in M. Both volume effects have a positive impact on the trade balance B. Now, a real depreciation also revalues every imported good in terms of domestic goods. This relative price effect has a negative impact on B. The net impact of the real exchange rate depreciation on B is positive if volume effects dominate the price effect. Assuming that the trade balance B is small compared to the gross volume of exports X and imports M/Q (hence $X \approx M/Q$ initially) we have:

$$\frac{dB}{X} = \frac{dX}{X} - \frac{dM}{M} + \frac{dQ}{Q} \tag{B7.9.2}$$

Assuming exogenous income in both the domestic economy and in the rest of the world, and denoting by ε_X and ε_M the price elasticities of exports and imports, respectively (ε_X, $\varepsilon_M > 0$), we have $dX/X = -\varepsilon_X \, dQ/Q$ and $dM/M = \varepsilon_M \, dQ/Q$. Plugging this into Equation (B7.9.2), we get the variation in B triggered by a variation of Q:

$$\frac{dB}{X} = -\left(\varepsilon_X + \varepsilon_M - 1\right)\frac{dQ}{Q} \tag{B7.9.3}$$

This relation shows that a depreciation in the real exchange rate ($dQ/Q < 0$) raises the trade balance if and only if:

$$\varepsilon_X + \varepsilon_M > 1 \tag{B7.9.4}$$

that is, if the reaction of trade volumes dominates the revaluation of imported goods. This condition is called the *Marshall-Lerner condition* (see Lerner, 1944).

Whereas the revaluation of the imported goods is immediate, the effect of the real exchange rate on the exported and imported volumes can be slow due to information asymmetries and to long-run contracting. This translates into price elasticities that are lower in the short run than in the long run. Consequently, a real depreciation results in a fall in the trade balance in the short run because the price effect dominates the volume effects; then, the exported and imported quantities adjust and the trade balance increases. This differentiated reaction of the trade balance over time is called the *J-curve*.

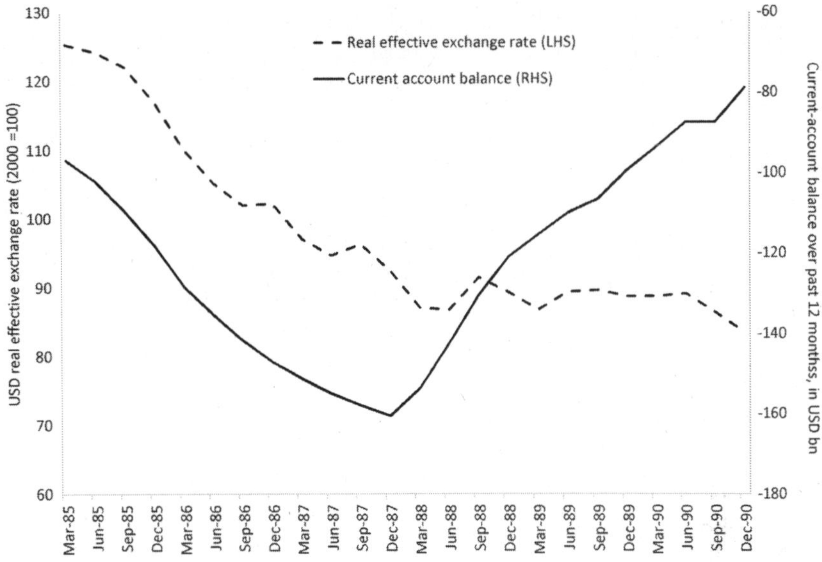

Figure 7.11 The J-curve in the United States, 1985–1990: real effective exchange rate and current account balance.
Ecowin.

Let us temporarily assume that the Marshall-Lerner condition holds. Aggregate demand Y^d is thus a decreasing function of the real exchange rate Q and therefore of both the domestic price index P and the nominal exchange rate S rate.[39] In figure 7.12, aggregate demand is downward-sloping (see the presentation of the AS-AD model in Chapter 1), and it moves to the right when the nominal exchange rate depreciates.

We now turn to the impact of the exchange rate on aggregate supply; that is, on the total volume of goods and services supplied by companies for each general level of prices P or, equivalently, on the price set by the firms for a given level of supply. In the long term, the neutrality of money entails that aggregate supply is vertical; that is, aggregate supply does not depend on the general price level. In the short run, however, to the extent that there are nominal rigidities, the aggregate supply curve is upward-sloping: higher prices temporarily lift aggregate supply. In the very short run, a nominal depreciation of the domestic currency moves the demand curve upward while the supply curve is little affected in presence of nominal rigidities. Hence output increases from point E to point F in figure 7.12. Then, firms tend to raise their prices due to more expensive imported inputs and to the necessity to raise nominal wages in order to compensate workers for losses in purchasing power parity due to the depreciation: the supply curve progressively moves upward. This makes real output progressively come back to its initial level while the general level of prices rises. In the long run (E'), output is back

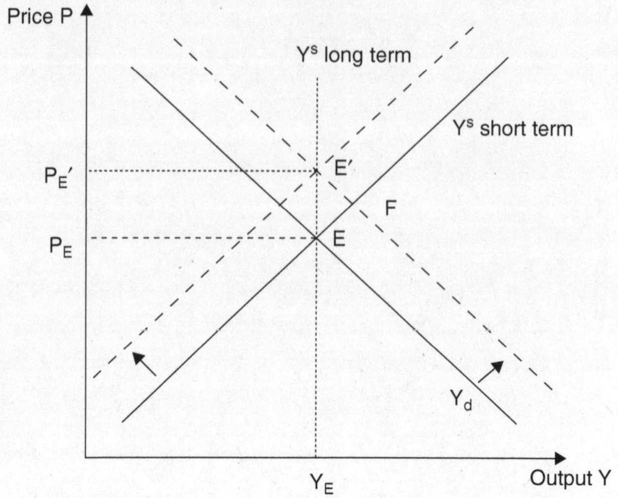

Figure 7.12 Impact of a nominal exchange rate depreciation in the AS-AD model.
Authors.

to its initial level, and all prices have risen in the same proportion as the exchange rate depreciation.

How long does the "short term" last? The answer crucially depends on how the price of exports reacts to changes in the nominal exchange rate. In the standard case, home exporters keep their prices P constant in their home currency whenever the nominal exchange rate S depreciates. Likewise, foreign exporters keep their prices P^* constant in their own currency. Hence the real exchange rate ($Q=SP/P^*$) varies exactly as the nominal exchange rate S. In practice, however, this is often not the case for three reasons. First, as already mentioned, the home exporter may see its costs increase whenever the nominal exchange rate depreciates. This is the case in particular for firms that are closely integrated in global supply chains. In this case, the unit price of exports P incorporates a limited share of domestic value added and a large share of imported inputs. In 2011, for instance, only 58% of the total value added of Korean exports was produced domestically. The rest consisted in foreign value-added incorporated in Korean exports.[40] This part of the unit cost of exports is automatically inflated whenever the won depreciates, translating in an immediate upward movement of the short-run supply curve on figure 7.12: the home price of exports P rises accordingly. Based on panel data for 46 countries over the period 1996–2012, Ahmed, Appendino, and Ruta (2015) calculate that around 40% of the decrease in the reaction of exports to exchange rates over this period can be attributed to rising participation to global supply chains.

The second source of price adjustment following an exchange rate movement is imperfect competition. To the extent that the price elasticity of exports is not constant, home exporters may optimally raise their home currency price *P* in the event of an exchange rate depreciation, thus increasing their margins. Such *pricing-to-market* behavior can take place even when 100% of the value added of exports is produced in the home country. The intuition was initially introduced by Joan Robinson (1947) and later modeled by Paul Krugman (1987). The idea is that grasping more market shares may not be the best response to a depreciation of the home currency. If the price elasticity of exports falls with the price itself, then the exporter will not reduce by 10% his price in the destination country whenever his currency depreciates by 10% because at a lower price the foreign consumer is less sensitive to an additional price cut. According to Gaulier, Lahrèche-Révil, and Méjean (2008), the extent of pricing-to-market varies greatly across countries and products: it tends to be lower for large exporting countries (the United States, Germany, China) and higher for manufactured goods such as food, clothing, firearms, chemicals, or optical goods. On average over all types of goods and exporting countries, a 10% depreciation leads the home currency price of the good to increase by around 2%, which means that the *exchange rate pass-through* is 80%.

Third, the extent of pricing-to-market depends on the invoicing currency of exports. When exports are invoiced in the currency of the destination country, exporters tend to adjust their home currency price *P* so as to maintain their foreign currency price *SP* constant whatever changes in the exchange rate *S*. Based on data on US import prices for the period 1994–2005, Gopinath, Itskhoki, and Rigobon (2010) find that, when imports are priced in dollar, foreign suppliers increase their home currency prices by as much as 7.5% whenever their home currency depreciates by 10% against the dollar. In contrast, when imports are priced in the foreign supplier currency, the corresponding figure is only 5%.[41] Similarly, for countries in the euro area, invoicing exports in euro tends to reduce the extent of pricing-to-market (see Gräb and Lafarguette, 2015).

On the whole, thus, the impact of an exchange rate depreciation on the trade balance and on activity is much less mechanical than a simple Marshall-Lerner calculation would suggest. On average, over a sample of 60 countries from 1980 to 2014, the IMF estimates that a 10% real effective depreciation results in a rise in net exports by 1.5% of GDP, but there is considerable heterogeneity across countries (IMF, 2015).

c) How exchange rates can close external imbalances

The preceding analysis directly yields a first concept of equilibrium exchange rate: assuming that the trade balance reacts positively to a depreciation in the real exchange rate (i.e., that the Marshall-Lerner condition applies), it is possible, based on estimated price elasticities of exports and imports, to calculate the real exchange rate that would be consistent with a certain level of the trade balance.

Assume, for instance, that a 10% depreciation of the real exchange rate raises the current account by 1% of GDP. Then, a 20% depreciation is needed to halve a current account deficit from 4% of GDP to 2% of GDP.

This simple calculation raises the difficult question of the current account level to be targeted. As mentioned in Section 7.1, current account imbalances cannot continue forever since, at some point, savers will be afraid of losing their investments in highly indebted countries. However, the objective need not be zero: aging economies should post surpluses since they need to save, whereas low-income countries should display deficits since they have high investment opportunities. Accordingly, John Williamson's *fundamental equilibrium exchange rate* (FEER) is the real exchange rate that achieves both full employment and a "sustainable" current account level (Williamson, 1983). The methodology consists first in correcting the projected current account for the output gap (i.e., the gap between GDP and its potential level):[42] if the output gap is negative, then imports are depressed; thus, when the economy eventually recovers, the current account balance will diminish. Second, the exchange rate adjustment required to close the gap between this adjusted current account and its target level is calculated depending on the sensitivity of the external balance to the exchange rate.

Table 7.3 presents FEER calculations proposed by Cline (2015) for selected countries. Based on the methodology of Cline and WIlliamson (2012), it provides internationally-consistent estimates of each country's real equilibrium exchange rate and the corresponding exchange rate against the US dollar, assuming a –3/+3% of GDP target for the current account balance. For example, the Turkish lira appears overvalued given the large adjusted current account deficit of the country. To close the projected current account gap, it should depreciate by 8.8% in real effective terms. However, the US current account deficit is also higher than the 3% target, hence the dollar is also overvalued. Accordingly, the equilibrium value of the lira against the US dollar is assessed relatively close to the observed rate in April 2015.

Jerome Stein (1994) suggests a slightly different measure of the FEER that relies on a model of the current account target rather than on ad hoc assumptions about of "sustainable" capital flows. His *natural real exchange rate* (NATREX) relies on fundamentals such as productivity and the rate of time preference (proxied by the ratio of private and public consumption to GDP). The NATREX can be viewed as a dynamic version of the FEER.

A third approach to the equilibrium exchange rate is the *behavioral equilibrium exchange rate* (*BEER*; Clark and MacDonald, 1998). The BEER is the real effective exchange rate that is consistent with current account balance in the long term. It is calculated based on an econometric long-run relationship between the real exchange rate and its macroeconomic determinants, mainly the net foreign asset position, the terms of trade, and the productivity differential (Balassa-Samuelson effect). The BEER is a mere historical regularity which may not apply in the case of a structural break. For instance, the BEER of the US dollar may be estimated for a period where the appetite of world

Table 7.3
An example of fundamental equilibrium exchange rate (FEER) calculations for 2020

Country	Adjusted CA in 2020 (% of GDP)[a]	Target CA (% of GDP)[b]	Necessary change in the REER (%)	Exchange rate against USD, April 2015[c]	FEER against USD[c]
China	2.5	2.5	0.1	6.20	5.69
India	−2.7	−2.7	−0.1	62.7	58.2
Japan	3.4	3.0	2.7	120	107
Korea	4.8	3.0	4.1	1086	961
South Africa	−3.5	−3.0	−2.2	11.99	11.33
Euro area	3.8	3.0	3.1	1.08	1.20
Sweden	6.9	3.0	10.1	8.63	7.26
Turkey	−5.1	−3.0	−8.8	2.65	2.68
UK	−2.3	−2.3	−0.1	1.50	1.63
United States	−4.3	−3.0	−8.0	1.00	1.00

CA: balance of current account; REER: real effective exchange rate. Adjusted CA: current account balance adjusted for the output gap.

[a] Based on IMF forecast in April 2015.

[b] Target set at adjusted CA level if the latter lies in the +/−3% band. Otherwise, the target is set at −3% or +3% depending on the sign of the adjusted CA.

[c] Currency per dollar, except for euro area where it is dollar per euro.

Source: Cline (2015).

investors for the dollar was very high (e.g., due to the lack of an alternative to the dollar as an international store of value). Hence, this "positive" approach is more a complement to rather than a substitute for the FEER approach that is much more normative.

d) The intertemporal approach of the balance of payments

Unlike the previous concepts, which rely on partial equilibrium approaches or on ad-hoc models, the *intertemporal approach of the balance of payments* considers current account imbalances as the result of optimal individual choices (Obstfeld and Rogoff, 1999). Indeed, a model based on household optimization appears appropriate to provide a normative assessment on the exchange rate. A simplified version of the model is sketched in box 7.10.

Box 7.10 The Exchange Rate and Intertemporal Adjustment

Consider a small open economy where households live in two periods. At each period, they consume a tradable good T, which can either be produced locally or imported, and a nontradable good N, which is produced locally and cannot be imported. The consumption level of the representative household is denoted c_t^i, where t denotes the period $(t = 1,2)$ and i the good $(i = N,T)$. All decisions concerning consumption are taken at period 1 and there is no uncertainty. The utility function of the representative household is assumed to be log-linear:

$$u\left(c_t^N, c_t^T\right) = \gamma \log c_t^N + (1-\gamma)\log c_t^N, \quad \text{with } 0<\gamma<1 \quad \text{(B7.10.1)}$$

Let us denote by θ_t the relative price of the nontradable good in terms of the tradable one at period t $(\theta_t = p_t^N / p_t^T)$, R_t the representative household's real income (expressed in terms of the tradable good) at period t, r the real interest rate, and β (with $0 < \beta < 1$) the discount factor (which measures preference for the present). The representative household's program is:

$$\underset{c_t^i}{Max}\; U = u\left(c_1^N, c_1^T\right) + \beta u\left(c_2^N, c_2^T\right)$$

$$s.t.\, \theta_1 c_1^N + c_1^T + \frac{\theta_2 c_2^N + c_2^T}{1+r} \le R_1 + \frac{R_2}{1+r} \quad \text{(B7.10.2)}$$

To solve this program, one writes the Lagrangian $L = U - \lambda(C - R)$, where C denotes intertemporal consumption, $R = R_1 + \dfrac{R_2}{1+r}$ is the intertemporal income, and λ is the Lagrange multiplier. Then, the partial derivative of L relative to each consumption volume c_t^i is calculated, and the Lagrange multiplier can be eliminated by deriving intra and intertemporal consumption ratios as follows:

$$\frac{c_2^T}{c_1^T} = \beta(1+r) \qquad \frac{c_1^T}{c_1^N} = \frac{\gamma}{1+\gamma}\theta_1$$
$$\frac{c_2^N}{c_1^N} = \beta(1+r)\frac{\theta_1}{\theta_2} \qquad \frac{c_2^T}{c_2^N} = \frac{\gamma}{1+\gamma}\theta_2 \tag{B7.10.3}$$

The left-hand column of Equation (B7.10.3) provides the two conditions for the intertemporal optimization of consumption (optimal allocation of consumption for the same good in two different periods), whereas the right-hand column represents the two conditions for intratemporal optimization (optimal allocation of the consumption of two different goods at the same period). From (B7.10.3), the four consumption levels can be recovered as functions of intertemporal income R:

$$c_1^T = \frac{\gamma}{1+\beta}R \qquad c_1^N = \frac{1-\gamma}{1+\beta}\frac{R}{\theta_1}$$
$$c_2^T = \frac{\gamma\beta}{1+\beta}(1+r)R \qquad c_2^N = \frac{(1-\gamma)\beta}{1+\beta}\frac{R}{\theta_2} \tag{B7.10.4}$$

An increase in productivity raises intertemporal income R: consumption increases for both goods at both periods. Note that consumption rises at period 1 even if productivity increases only at period 2, and vice versa. If productivity rises only in the tradable sector, then the production of this sector increases, but not that of the nontradable sector. Market equilibrium then requires an increase in the relative price of nontradables θ_t. The real exchange rate appreciates since it is positively related to θ_t: Denoting by p_t^i the price of home goods (i = N, T), p_t^{i*} the price of foreign goods, Q_t the real exchange rate, and S_t, the nominal one, we have:[a]

$$Q_t = S_t\frac{\left(p_t^T\right)^\gamma\left(p_t^N\right)^{1-\gamma}}{\left(p_t^{T*}\right)^\gamma\left(p_t^{N*}\right)^{1-\gamma}} = \frac{S_t p_t^T}{p_t^{T*}}\left(\frac{p_t^N / p_t^T}{p_t^{N*} / p_t^{T*}}\right)^{1-\gamma} \tag{B7.10.5}$$

Assuming that the law of one price applies to the tradable sector (i.e., $S_t p_t^T = p_t^{T*}$), we get:

$$Q_t = \left(\frac{\theta_t}{\theta_t^*}\right)^{1-\gamma} \tag{B7.10.6}$$

Note that, by definition, we have, at each period, $c_N = y_N$, where y_N denotes the production of nontradables: since N is nontradable, its consumption per inhabitant must equalize its production per inhabitant. From Equations (B7.10.3) and (B7.10.6), a relation between the growth rate of nontradable production and that of the real exchange rate can then be derived:

$$\frac{y_2^N}{y_1^N} = \beta(1+r)\frac{\theta_1}{\theta_2} = \beta(1+r)\left(\frac{Q_1}{Q_2}\right)^{\frac{1}{1-\gamma}}\frac{\theta_1^*}{\theta_2^*} \quad \text{(B7.10.7)}$$

Absent productivity growth in the nontradable sector, y^N is constant and the variation of the real exchange rate only depends on the evolution of the relative price of nontradables abroad and on the discount factor (compared to the real interest rate). Suppose the relative price of nontradables abroad stays constant ($\theta_1^* = \theta_2^*$). If domestic consumers are impatient ($\beta(1 + r) < 1$), they intend to consume more of their intertemporal income during the first period than during the second one. To this purpose, imports of tradables must exceed exports, which amounts to a trade deficit. During the second period, the debt contracted during the first period must be paid back. The real exchange rate appreciates during the first period so as to encourage households to consume more tradables (whose relative price falls); it depreciates in the second period so as to discourage them from consuming tradables (whose relative price then increases).

Similarly, an expected rise in productivity in the tradable sector for period 2 triggers a trade deficit in period 1 and a surplus in period 2. For the same reasons as just described, the real exchange rate needs to appreciate in period 1 and depreciate in period 2. The profile of the exchange rate depends on the transitory or permanent pattern of the productivity shock.

[a]The real exchange rate here refers to the relative price of the consumption basket compared to the price of the same basket abroad. In turn, θ_t represents the relative price of the nontradable good in terms of the tradable one. It is sometime referred to as the *internal real exchange rate.*

The model relies on two key assumptions. First, households are supposed to determine their consumption choices depending on their intertemporal income, assuming full access to financial markets. They borrow or lend freely without being subject to liquidity constraints. Second, two categories of goods are distinguished: tradable goods, whose price is uniform internationally, and nontraded goods. The role of the exchange rate is not to trigger a change in price competitiveness (since the law of one price applies to tradables) but rather to shift the distribution of domestic demand between the two kinds of goods.

A positive, transitory shock to productivity leads to a current account surplus and a depreciation of the real exchange rate in the short run. This is because households save a larger share of their current income since they know that productivity and income will return to their long-run level in the future. Saving more means consuming less, hence imports decline temporarily. On the nontraded good market, there is excess supply, so the price of nontraded goods declines relative to traded ones: the real exchange rate depreciates. This relative price adjustment shifts domestic demand from the traded to the nontraded good, which rebalances the nontraded good market. In the longer run, relative prices come back to their initial levels since the shock considered here is not permanent.

If the rise in productivity is considered permanent, then the current account may adjust downward in the short run because households immediately raise their consumption level, knowing that their income will be higher in the future. There is excess demand of nontraded goods, so the relative price of nontraded goods rises and the real exchange rate appreciates.

The intertemporal model of the balance of payment permits calculation of the real exchange rate path that is consistent with households' intertemporal budget constraint (i.e., with current account sustainability; see, e.g., Obstfeld and Rogoff [2007] on the US case). However, observed variations in the current account balance cannot be explained only through the "permanent income" hypothesis that lies at the core of the intertemporal approach of the balance of payments (Cerrato et al. 2015). Hence this approach is a complement to rather than a substitute for other approaches to the equilibrium exchange rate.

e) The instruments of exchange rate policies

Models of equilibrium exchange rates can be used to assess whether the observed exchange rate is at an appropriate level. Once an exchange rate misalignment has been identified, how can the central bank or the government push the exchange rate toward its equilibrium value? In order to answer this question, we need a model of exchange rate determination.

In Chapter 5, we studied the link between monetary policy and the exchange rate through the uncovered interest parity: to the extent that it has not been anticipated before, a sudden loosening of monetary policy (a cut in the interest rates and/or an increase in money supply) triggers an immediate exchange rate depreciation. The extent of the depreciation depends on the expected monetary policy: if the loosening is expected to be long-lived, then the exchange rate depreciates more in the short run. Alternatively, the central bank may announce a future loosening of monetary policy, in which case the exchange rate may depreciate immediately, even before interest rates are cut or money supply increased.

The monetary framework, however, does not encompass all the tools that may be used by the central bank or the government to influence the exchange rate. In order to depreciate the home currency, the central bank may lower the domestic interest rate or acknowledge it will do so in the near future, communicate its own views about possible exchange rate misalignments, or intervene directly on the foreign exchange market (through raising its reserves in foreign currencies). The government may also introduce obstacles to capital inflows or use the sovereign wealth fund to invest abroad. To understand how foreign exchange interventions or capital controls may affect the exchange rate, a more general model of exchange rate determination is required. By relaxing the assumption of risk neutrality of asset holders, the *portfolio choice model* (box 7.11) provides a comprehensive framework to analyze these various mechanisms. Foreign exchange interventions will only affect the exchange rate to the extent that risk aversion and/or barriers to private capital flows are significant (see Section 7.3).

Box 7.11 The Portfolio Choice Model of Exchange Rate Determination

The portfolio choice model (Branson, Haltunen, and Masson, 1977) highlights the role of financial markets in exchange rate determination. Consider a small, open economy where capital is free to move in and out of the country. The currency of this country is not used internationally, so whereas domestic residents hold foreign-currency assets, foreign residents do not hold domestic-currency assets. The equilibrium of the balance of payments is written as:

$$B = d(SF) + d(SR) \tag{B7.11.1}$$

where S designates the nominal exchange rate, defined as the price of the foreign currency in terms of the home one; that is, S *increases* when the home currency *depreciates*. B is the current account balance in domestic currency, F the net holding of foreign securities by private residents, R the foreign exchange reserves outstanding, and d designates a variation per unit of time. Both F and R are expressed in foreign currency. Equation (B7.11.1) states that the current account balance (left-hand side) should be equal to the financial balance (right-hand side). Over time, this flow equation translates into a relationship between stocks of assets:

$$NFA = S(F + R) \tag{B7.11.2}$$

where NFA is the net foreign asset position; that is, the difference between gross assets and gross liabilities, expressed in the home currency (see box 7.2). NFA can either reflect a net claim on foreign countries ($NFA > 0$) or a net liability ($NFA < 0$).

Let W be total private sector wealth expressed in real terms. It is made of domestic assets D and foreign assets F, deflated by the aggregate price level P:

$$W = (D + SF) / P \tag{B7.11.3}$$

The portfolio approach is based on Tobin's work on optimal portfolio allocation (Tobin, 1958). Portfolio allocation stems from an arbitrage between risk and return. At each moment in time, private agents choose the share of their wealth invested in foreign currency, $f = SF / PW$, that maximizes their utility. As an approximation of a more general concave utility function, utility depends positively on the expected increase in W and negatively on its variance:

$$Max\ U = E\left(\frac{dW}{W}\right) - \frac{\alpha}{2} Var\left(\frac{dW}{W}\right) \qquad \text{(B7.11.4)}$$

where E stands for the expected value, Var for the variance per unit of time, and $\alpha \geq 0$ is the relative risk-aversion coefficient. With risk originating in the exchange rates and in the price level, it can be shown that the solution is:

$$f = \frac{(\alpha - 1)\sigma_{SP}}{\alpha\sigma_S^2} + \frac{i^* + \mu_S - i}{\alpha\sigma_S^2} \qquad \text{(B7.11.5)}$$

where i is the domestic interest rate, i^* the foreign interest rate, $\mu_s = E(dS/S)$ and $\sigma_S^2 = Var(dS/S)$ are the expected variation and the volatility of exchange rate variations, and $\sigma_{SP} = Cov\left(\frac{dS}{S}, \frac{dP}{P}\right)$ is the covariance between inflation and exchange rate variations.

With infinite risk aversion ($\alpha \to \infty$), the share of wealth held in foreign currency is σ_{SP} / σ_S^2. If the home currency depreciates when prices go up ($\sigma_{SP} > 0$), the risk-averse investor will hold part of his or her wealth in foreign assets as a hedge against purchasing power losses due to inflation. At the other extreme, if risk aversion is negligible ($\alpha \to 0$), then Equation (B7.11.5) boils down to a modified version of the uncovered interest parity (see Chapter 5): $i^* + \mu_S - i - \sigma_{SP} = 0$. In between these two polar cases, the share of foreign assets in the domestic investor's portfolio depends positively on the expected yield differential $i^* + \mu_S - i$.

From Equations (B7.11.2) and (B7.11.5), we can write the current exchange rate as a function of the expected one:

$$s = Es + i^* - i - \sigma_{SP} - 2\alpha\left(nfa - \frac{\sigma_{SP}}{\sigma_S^2} - r\right) \qquad \text{(B7.11.6)}$$

where $s = \ln S$, $\mu_s = Es - s$, $nfa = NFA/PW$, and $r = SR/PW$. If investors are risk-averse, the uncovered interest parity must be adjusted for a *risk premium*, the last term in Equation (B7.11.6) that remunerates investors willing to depart from their minimum-risk allocation. A rise in the domestic interest rate i, a fall in the foreign interest rate i^*, an appreciation of the expected exchange rate Es, an increase in the net foreign asset position ratio nfa, or a decrease of foreign exchange reserves r all lead to an appreciation of the domestic currency (s falls). The latter two effects apply only to the extent that private agents are not risk-neutral ($\alpha > 0$).

f) Currency wars

The concept of a "currency war" dates back to the interwar period, when different countries tried to export unemployment through currency devaluation. It was reintroduced in the policy debate in 2010 by Guido Mantega, then Minister of finance of Brazil. At that time, the US Federal Reserve was running a very loose monetary policy, encouraging international investors to borrow liquidity in US dollar in order to invest in those countries still displaying positive returns, among which was Brazil. Absent capital controls, recipient countries then had no other choice than either to let their currency appreciate or to lower their interest rates in order to discourage capital inflows—at the risk of letting financial bubbles develop. G. Mantega (and later, R. Rajan, the governor of the central bank of India) thus accused the United States of destabilizing emerging economies.

Even before the global financial crisis, China had been regularly accused of manipulating its currency in order to maintain its international price competitiveness. Such blame had been nourished by the accumulation of foreign exchange reserves (figure 7.16 in Section 7.3)—a proof that the lack of appreciation of the yuan was not "natural."

Still, the very concept of a "currency war," which echoes that of "trade war," is not well established. First, exchange rates may react to asymmetric shocks. For instance, if a global crisis hits more severely country A than country B, currency A should depreciate with respect to B, even though country B also suffers a crisis. Second, bold reaction by some central banks to a common shock may have positive effects on partner countries through the income channel, although not through the exchange rate one (Cœuré, 2017). It can also be a way to "force" other central bank to also act decisively and therefore act as an implicit coordinating device (Eichengreen, 2013). Finally, it should be remembered that a central bank may (upon some conditions) control the nominal exchange rate. However, the real exchange rate is beyond its reach. Opposing a currency appreciation through unsterilized foreign exchange interventions will inevitably cause prices to increase, as has been the case in China during the 2000s.

Caballero, Farhi, and Gourinchas (2015) have shown how a "currency war" can nevertheless emerge at the zero-lower bound (ZLB; see Chapter 5), when excess savings at the global level can no longer be eliminated through a lower interest rate. In such an environment, the equilibrium of the world capital market is achieved through lower output, and the distribution of the recession across countries depends on exchange rates (see box 7.12).

Box 7.12 Currency Wars at the Zero Lower Bound

Here we present the main intuitions of the model proposed by Caballero, Farhi, and Gourinchas (2015). We consider two countries: home and foreign. In each country, asset demand is an increasing function of the real interest rate, whereas asset supply is a decreasing function of it. We assume that the autarkic, "natural" real interest rate (which equalizes supply and demand for assets in each country) is higher in the home country (r^a) than in the foreign one (r^{a*}). With financial integration, the natural real interest rate (r^w) is the one that equalizes the supply and demand for assets at world level: $r^a > r^w > r^{a*}$.

We start with the standard case where $r^a, r^{a*} > 0$. By definition, in autarky, both countries have a zero net foreign asset position (NFA); see points A and A* in figure B7.12.1. With financial integration, the home country displays a negative NFA (it imports foreign capital) whereas the foreign country displays a positive NFA (it exports capital). Denoting by S the nominal exchange rate (price of the foreign currency in terms of the home currency), we have $\text{NFA} + S\,\text{NFA}^* = 0$.

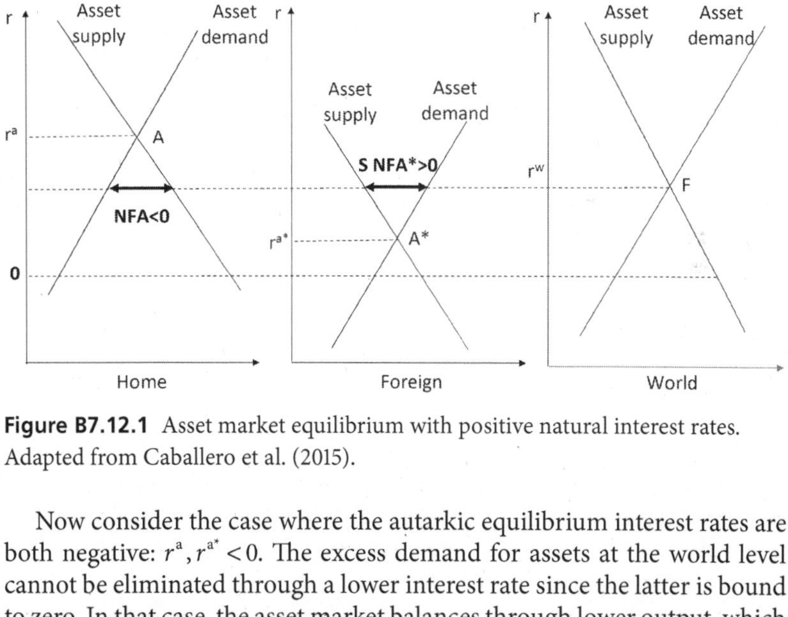

Figure B7.12.1 Asset market equilibrium with positive natural interest rates. Adapted from Caballero et al. (2015).

Now consider the case where the autarkic equilibrium interest rates are both negative: $r^a, r^{a*} < 0$. The excess demand for assets at the world level cannot be eliminated through a lower interest rate since the latter is bound to zero. In that case, the asset market balances through lower output, which reduces both the demand and the supply for assets, but more the former than the latter. Here we assume a fixed asset supply for simplicity. Figure B7.12.2 depicts the constrained autarkic equilibria. For a zero interest rate, asset demand (points B and B*) exceeds asset supply (points A and A*) *ex ante*. As the imbalance cannot be absorbed by a fall in the interest rate, output diminishes, which shifts the demand schedule to the left until it crosses the supply curve at zero interest rate (points A and A*).

With financial integration, the country with the largest excess asset demand in autarky (here the foreign economy) exports its capital. Its currency depreciates, which stabilizes its output level: the asset demand shift backs until it crosses the supply at point C*. Symmetrically, the domestic economy attracts capital, so its currency appreciates and the recession is worse than in autarky (point C). Hence the foreign economy has "exported" part of its recession by accumulating net foreign assets. This effect is even more pronounced if the home country issues a "safe asset." The only way to avoid an aggravation of the recession is for the home country to issue more debt (through a fiscal expansion).

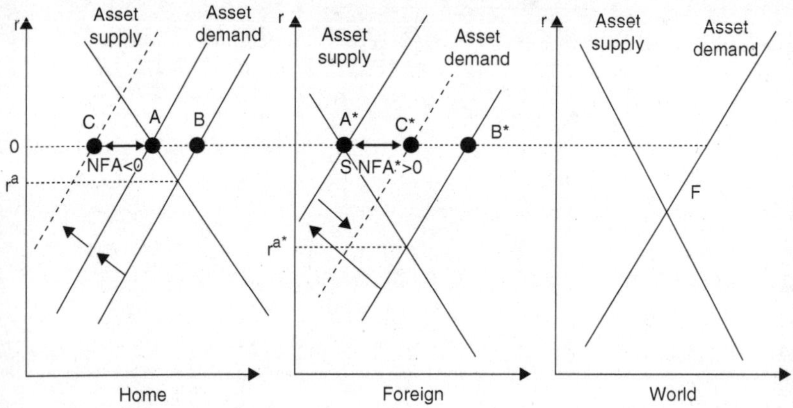

Figure B7.12.2 Asset market equilibrium at the zero lower bound.
Adapted from Caballero et al. (2015).

7.2.3 Models of currency crises

Up to this point, we have focused on steady-state exchange rate regime choice, leaving aside the issue of regime change. But we have seen that what is appropriate for a country at a given point in time may not remain so forever. Governments may have to change exchange rate regimes; or at least they may have to adjust the exchange rate. If they fail to do so, market forces may produce a *currency crisis*, forcing them to modify their exchange rate regime.

Economists are often derided for their facility in providing sophisticated explanations for the latest currency crises while not being able to predict the next one. This occurs because the nature of crises changes over time, consistent with the liberalization of international capital flows throughout the

1990s and the subsequent explosion of gross financial flows and accumulated positions.

a) First-generation currency crisis models

The inconsistency between domestic economic policy and the exchange rate regime is at the core of *first-generation currency crisis models* (Flood and Garber, 1984; Krugman, 1979).[43] Imagine a country with a fixed exchange rate against the US dollar where monetary aggregates grow faster than in the United States. In order to maintain its exchange rate, it has to draw on its foreign exchange reserves. Still, foreign exchange reserves are not infinite. The insight of first-generation models is to show that the crisis will typically occur shortly *before* reserves are exhausted. But the crisis does not start until speculators expect a large enough gain from the break of the fixed exchange rate regime. For this reason, an exchange rate policy can be deemed unsustainable and yet last for some time, until the expectation of capital gains serves as a coordination device among speculators and unleashes the attack on the currency.

The mechanism is comparable to a run on bank deposits (see Chapter 6). In a bank run, depositors rush to the counter to withdraw their deposits because they anticipate that the bank will not be able to refund all of them. Even if they have no prior view on the bank's insolvency, they just *have to* rush because they do not want to be last at the counter. In a currency crisis, it is just about the same: in a speculative attack, financial market participants rush to change their domestic currency holdings into foreign currency because they fear that the central bank may not have enough reserves to convert the whole domestic currency outstanding at the initial fixed rate.[44]

First-generation models thus consider the crisis as the rational reaction of market participants to an inadequate exchange rate policy or regime. A good example is Pakistan in 2008. Monetary growth, fueled by unbridled public spending and direct government borrowing from the central bank, was much faster in Pakistan than in the United States. The only way to sustain the fixed US dollar–Pakistani rupiah exchange rate was for the State Bank of Pakistan to sell US dollars and buy rupiahs. As a consequence, foreign exchange reserves were gradually depleted, and, in the summer of 2008, market participants triggered the crisis by selling in a rush their remaining rupiahs. The exchange rate stabilized only when the IMF and Asian Development Bank extended foreign currency–denominated loans to the government and reserves could then be gradually replenished.

b) Second-generation currency crisis models

The mechanism described in the first-generation models is well fitted to countries with high inflation or an unsustainable current account deficit. However, consider the European exchange rate crises of 1992–93 which forced the UK and Italy out of the European exchange-rate mechanism and threatened the continued participation of France and Spain in it. At that time, European countries were in a fixed exchange rate regime where Germany served as the de facto anchor. But the Bundesbank was undertaking restrictive monetary policies in the wake of German unification, which had caused an expansion of aggregate demand; some of them registered current account *surpluses* and none of them was lacking foreign exchange reserves. First-generation currency crisis models fall short of explaining what happened in Europe. What is needed here is not a monetary model, but a model with short-term nominal rigidities linking the exchange rate and the real economy. What is also needed is an explanation of why a crisis can occur even in the absence of unsustainable trends. The contribution of *second-generation currency crisis models* is to show that devaluation expectations can be triggered by the sub-optimal character of the exchange rate policy. The rationale for speculation is not that the current policy cannot be sustained (as in the first generation models), but that it may not be desirable to sustain it. In some cases, devaluation expectations can even be self-fulfilling: the mere expectation that the government will devalue can force it to do so.

There may be several unrelated reasons why financial market expectations can feed back onto the real economy. Inflationary expectations provide a first explanation (Jeanne, 1996): if private agents expect a devaluation, they will ask for higher wages to compensate for their expected loss of purchasing power. In a supply-driven economy, this pushes unemployment up unless the government actually devalues to restore competitiveness. This is the open-economy version of the Barro-Gordon time-consistency dilemma (see Chapter 5). Box 7.13 presents a simplified model along these lines. Another explanation, probably more relevant to the European experience, is demand-driven (Obstfeld, 1994). Under uncovered interest rate parity, devaluation expectations push nominal interest rates up. This penalizes aggregate demand and induces the government to devalue to revert to the initial output level. In short, expectations of a crisis may be enough to cause it: such crises are *self-fulfilling currency crises*.

Box 7.13 A Self-Fulfilling Currency Crisis

This model was proposed by Jeanne (1996) as an attempt to explain the European currency crises of the early 1990s. We consider a small economy. Domestic prices are determined by purchasing power parity. The exchange rate is fixed but can be devalued by a fixed percentage δ. A surprise devaluation would cause a short-term decrease in unemployment through lower real wages (as in the Barro-Gordon model presented in Chapter 5). However, it would impair the reputation of the central bank. The government thus faces a dilemma.

To simplify, the central bank is supposed to choose the inflation rate directly. It minimizes the quadratic loss function: $L = u^2 + cz$, where u designates the unemployment rate, c the (fixed) political cost of a devaluation, and z is equal to 1 in the event of a devaluation and 0 otherwise.

The unemployment rate is sluggish and is negatively affected by unexpected inflation (i.e., the difference between realized inflation π and expected inflation π^e):

$$u = \rho u_{t-1} - \lambda(\pi - \pi^e) \quad \text{with } 0 < \rho < 1,\ \lambda > 0 \qquad \text{(B7.13.1)}$$

Under purchasing power parity, expected inflation is equal to the expected rate of exchange rate devaluation. The expected inflation rate is thus either 0 (no devaluation) or δ (devaluation). Optimal monetary policy depends on expectations:

- If private agents do not expect any devaluation, then expected inflation is zero and realized inflation is either 0 or δ depending on whether or not there has been a devaluation. The loss function is either $L_0^0 = (\rho u_{t-1})^2$ (no devaluation) or $L_0^d = (\rho u_{t-1} - \lambda\delta)^2 + c$ (devaluation). The government rationally chooses to devalue if $L_0^d < L_0^0$ (i.e., if: $\Phi < -\lambda\delta$, where $\Phi = \frac{c}{\lambda\delta} - 2\rho u_{t-1}$ represents the "fundamentals" of the economy).
- If private agents expect a devaluation, then expected inflation is δ. The loss function is either $L_d^0 = (\rho u_{-1} + \lambda\delta)^2$ (no devaluation) or $L_d^d = (\rho u_{-1})^2 + c$ (devaluation). The government chooses rationally to devalue if $L_d^d < L_d^0$ (i.e., if $\Phi < \lambda\delta$).

Figure B7.13.1 summarizes the results. If fundamentals are very good ($\Phi > \lambda\delta$), there is no devaluation even if agents expect it to happen. If fundamentals are poor ($\Phi < -\lambda\delta$), there is a devaluation even if agents do not expect it to happen. For intermediate fundamentals ($-\lambda\delta < \Phi < \lambda\delta$), there are two possible equilibriums, and expectations are self-fulfilling: the economy can shift from one to another (e.g., the government can be forced to devalue) if there is a shift in private expectations.

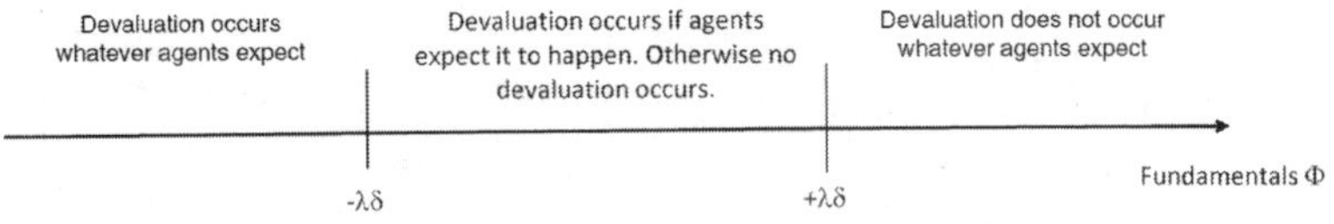

Figure B7.13.1 Fundamentals and expectations in a second generation currency crisis.
Authors, based on Jeanne (1996).

According to second-generation models, countries vulnerable to a currency crisis can be identified by the conjunction of a relatively weak economy and adverse market expectations. The best example is the crisis of the pound sterling in 1992. The pound sterling had joined the European Exchange Rate Mechanism (ERM) a year earlier, at a central rate against the Deutsche mark that many observers deemed too high. In 1992, the economy was weak and speculative attacks began to materialize. The Bank of England then raised its interest rate only moderately, sending the signal that the government was not ready to worsen the recession to defend the currency. After massive foreign reserve losses, participation in the ERM was suspended and the pound began to float. The Chancellor of the Exchequer, Norman Lamont, subsequently declared that he had been "singing in his bath" that evening. Change of the exchange rate regime, prompted by the currency crisis, had lifted a burden from the government's shoulders.

c) Third-generation currency crisis models

Starting from July 1997, Thailand, then other East Asian economies, Brazil, and Russia had to give up their fixed exchange rate. Once again, the prevailing currency crisis model had not helped anticipate crisis. The main channel of transmission of an exchange rate devaluation to the real economy was now financial (Corsetti, 1998). All these countries had in common US dollar–denominated short-maturity external debt (as an example, foreign banks had granted loans to their Thai subsidiaries to invest in the then-booming domestic housing sector). Any devaluation of the currency would increase the burden of foreign currency–denominated debt, raise solvency concerns and cause a "sudden stop" of capital inflows. A similar mechanism was at play in 2008 in several non–euro area European economies such as Hungary, Iceland, and Latvia (which could eventually maintain its fixed exchange rate) that were heavily dependent on short-term, euro-denominated external financing.

A banking crisis can cause a currency crisis: worries about the solvency of the borrowers triggers a *sudden stop* of capital inflows. A currency crisis can also cause a banking crisis when banks' debts are denominated in foreign currency. A vulnerable banking sector (due to a high proportion of nonperforming loans, for example) reinforces risks in both directions. *Third-generation currency crisis models* (Krugman, 1999) have focused on the "twin" banking and currency crises.

Models have also sought to explain *contagion effects* at work in the late 1990s and again in the late 2000s, particularly at the regional level in Europe and in Asia. Contagion stems from regional integration: if the currency of a country is devalued, then neighboring countries see their price competitiveness temporarily reduced. Knowing this regional dependency, market participants may find it optimal to attack the currency in a preemptive way. But contagion can also result from a change in investor sentiment following an unexpected event in a given country. In July 1997, the Thai baht crisis was a wake-up call to investors who had forgotten that investment in emerging market economies was inherently risky. The upward revision in the price of risk was immediately built into the risk premiums paid by *all* emerging market economies, not only Thailand. Finally, an additional channel of contagion stems from the international investors' budget constraint: in order to offset losses in a given country, they sell assets that have not depreciated yet, throwing other countries into the crisis.

Currency crisis models can be tested both "in sample" (through probit or logit econometric estimation over a period $[t_1, t_2]$) and "out-of-sample" (by testing the ability of a model estimated over $[t_1, t_2]$ to predict crises beyond t_2). The typical model of *early warning indicators* proceeds in three steps: (i) define the event "currency crisis," (ii) estimate (or calibrate) a model over past crisis and noncrisis events and set a threshold above which the model will send an alarm, and (iii) test the model out-of-sample. Forecast accuracy can be measured through the *noise-to-signal ratio*; that is, the proportion of false alarms over accurate ones (Kaminsky, Lizondo and Reinhart, 1998). Based on 83 studies covering crises spanning the 1950s to the 2000s, Frankel and Saravelos (2012) conclude that the most important variables to predict currency crises are official reserves, the real exchange rate, the growth rate of credit, the level of GDP, and the current account. Catão and Milesi-Ferretti (2014) find similar determinants on a more recent period. In all cases, however, the models perform relatively poorly in predicting crises; when they correctly predict crises that did take place (signal), they also predict many crises that did not (noise).

7.3 Policies

The first policy choice when it comes to exchange rates and financial integration is the joint choice of an exchange rate regime and a degree of capital mobility. Even in a flexible regime, though, policymakers may want to smooth exchange rate variations or correct large misalignments, which raises a second question: which instruments can be used to do so? Finally, national policy choices are taken in the context of an international monetary system that may evolve over time, especially given the multipolarization of the global economy.

7.3.1 Capital mobility and the choice of an exchange rate regime

We know from Section 7.2 that not all combinations of exchange rate regime, capital mobility regime, and monetary policy regime are feasible: if capital is highly mobile internationally, then a government must choose between (i) a fixed exchange rate with no monetary independence or (ii) a flexible exchange rate with monetary independence: policymakers need to choose one of the two summits of the triangle represented in figure 7.8 that involve free capital mobility, or find an appropriate trade-off between the two (e.g., some monetary independence and some exchange rate stability).

The triangle sheds a useful light on the many contradictions of twentieth-century exchange rate policies. In the 1930s, European countries faced a contradiction between the gold standard fixed exchange rates, capital mobility, and the economic consequences of the war, which called for different monetary policies in different countries. In the late 1990s, East Asian and Latin American countries faced the same kind of contradiction. Eventually, most of them chose to let their exchange rate float. However, some of them preferred to move to other summits of the triangle. Malaysia retained its fixed rate against the dollar and installed capital controls, while Ecuador gave up monetary independence and dollarized its economy. China, which had not yet liberalized its financial account, did not have to change its policies significantly and resisted the crisis. In the global financial crisis, once again, countries like Latvia temporary experienced the difficulty of maintaining a fixed exchange rate vis-à-vis the euro when ailing Western European banks could withdraw their financial support overnight.

In the remainder of this section, we discuss the criteria that policymakers can use when deciding between the three vertices of Mundell's triangle.

a) The pros and cons of capital openness

Since the 1980s, liberalization of capital movements has been encouraged by the IMF to allow for an optimal allocation of world savings and to let money flow from rich capital-abundant countries to poor capital-scarce countries. Throughout the 1990s, capital movement liberalization was part of the *Washington consensus* (see Chapters 1 and 9). It was even imposed by the G7, OECD, and IMF to several emerging nations.[45] This resulted in an unprecedented development of international capital flows.

The currency crises of the late 1990s in emerging markets dealt a blow to the consensus on free capital mobility. Capital liberalization in Asia had unleashed short-term, dollar-denominated capital inflows which had inflated asset prices and bank lending and had led ultimately to "twin" banking and currency crises. Furthermore, the contribution of capital mobility to long-term economic development was increasingly put into question. In a 1990 paper, Robert Lucas noted that most capital flows were "North–North" flows between rich countries rather than "North–South" flows from rich to poor countries, as standard growth theory would have predicted. Two explanations for the *Lucas paradox* are information asymmetry and weak institutions in low-income countries that prevent capital from being invested there. Modern capital flows are "diversification finance" rather than "development finance": they seek lower risk as much as higher return.[46] Moreover, the welfare gains of financial openness have been found to be much lower than previously thought (see section 7.2.1).

After the Mexican and then the Asian, crises of the 1990s, it did not come as a surprise that emerging countries reconsidered the merits of capital openness.[47] The IMF itself adopted a more benign approach to capital controls, and its then chief economist, Michael Mussa, recognized that:

> The experience in recent financial crises could cause reasonable people to question whether liberal policies toward international capital flows are wise for all countries in all circumstances. The answer, I believe, is probably not. . . . high openness to international capital flows, especially to short-term credit flows, can be dangerous for countries with weak or inconsistent macroeconomic policies or inadequately capitalized and regulated financial systems. (Mussa, 2000, pp. 43–44)

Several types of capital controls exist. A first option is administrative control of foreign exchange operations, with different restrictions depending on the type of operations that can be undertaken (most restrictions being related to financial transactions other than trade finance). A second option is to rely on incentives rather than controls. The aim is to "throw sand in the wheels" of financial globalization by discouraging short-term capital flows, which are deemed to generate exchange rate volatility. In the 1990s, the Chilean government forced foreign investors to leave a minimum reserve (*encaje*) at the central bank as an interest-free deposit. This was an application of the tax on foreign exchange transactions initially proposed by James Tobin (1974). Proponents of the *Tobin tax* usually advocate a 0.05% levy on transactions unrelated to a current account transaction or foreign direct investment. The Tobin tax follows from a remark by John Maynard Keynes on the impact of taxes on stock market liquidity:

> It is usually agreed that casinos should, in the public interest, be inaccessible and expensive. And perhaps the same is true of stock exchanges. . . . The introduction of a substantial Government transfer tax on all transactions might prove the most serviceable reform available, with a view to mitigating the predominance of speculation over enterprise in the United States. (Keynes, 1936, pp. 159–160)

Building on the Asian experience of 1997–98, the IMF has moved to advising a sequencing of financial account liberalization in emerging countries, where full liberalization should only come after a sound financial system has developed domestically with well-managed and supervised banks and a low level of nonperforming loans. After the global financial crisis, the IMF's doctrine has further evolved (IMF, 2012), stating that "Capital flow measures are a part of the toolkit and their use is appropriate under certain conditions, but they should not substitute for warranted macroeconomic adjustment" (p. 16).

In an econometric estimation for a panel of emerging market economies over 1995–2008, Ostry et al. (2012) find that controls on capital inflows, together with prudential measures aiming at limiting foreign exchange exposures or more generally limiting credit bubbles, are indeed powerful instruments to reduce the vulnerability of a country to "sudden stops" (of capital inflows). As a matter of fact, several emerging economies reintroduced temporary controls on capital inflows after the global financial crisis, when international capital movements returned massively to emerging market in a search for yield in the context of very loose monetary policies in advanced economies. In 2010, for instance, Peru imposed a 60% reserve requirement for new foreign holders of debt with maturity up to three years, while Thailand restored a 15% withholding tax on nonresidents' interest earnings and capital gains on new purchases of government bonds (see Ghosh and Qureshi, 2016).

Maintaining foreign exchange controls, however, is not advisable in the long run for three reasons. First, Chilean-type reserves or a Tobin tax are not enough to discourage capital outflows when the expected depreciation of the domestic currency are significant (see Eichengreen, Tobin, and Wyplosz, 1995, for a discussion). Second, and more importantly, taxes as well as administrative controls can be circumvented through financial innovation or off-shoring to countries that do not impose them. Third, it is very hard to distinguish "good" and "bad" capital inflows a priori: most likely, "good" inflows will be penalized as well as "bad" ones (Garber and Taylor, 1995).

b) Criteria for exchange rate regime choice

As explained in Section 7.2, the choice of an exchange rate regime should result from a cost–benefit approach. The benefits and costs of three exchange rate regimes are summarized in table 7.4. Net results largely differ across countries. For instance, a smaller, more open economy will reap larger gains from lower exchange rate volatility (fixed exchange rate regime) or the elimination of currency transactions (monetary union); a country whose central bank has a poor record in terms of price stability will benefit from the nominal anchor provided by a fixed exchange rate, but, at the same time, it will encounter important risks of currency crisis.

A major issue for choosing an exchange rate regime based on these criteria is to measure the potential for asymmetric shocks. Various methodologies can be used, ranging from calculating business cycle correlations across countries to more sophisticated econometric methods aimed at measuring shock asymmetry, or more structural measures such as openness, industry diversification, or intra-industry trade (see box 7.14).

In the event of an asymmetric shock, the question is whether prices and wages are flexible enough to substitute for a nominal exchange rate adjustment. The global financial crisis and the subsequent euro area crisis have offered a "natural experiment" of price flexibility across euro area member states. As shown in figure 7.13, Irish wages and prices adjusted very quickly

Table 7.4
Benefits and costs of three exchange rate regimes

	Benefits	Costs
Flexible exchange rate	Independent instrument of macroeconomic adjustment in case of an asymmetric shock	Instability of relative prices related to nominal exchange rate volatility
	Effectiveness of monetary policy (cf. Mundell-Fleming model)	Risk of "currency war" in case of a symmetric shock
Conventional fixed peg	Limited instability of relative prices due to low exchange rate volatility	Loss of an instrument of adjustment in case of an asymmetric shock, risk of inadequate monetary policy
	Nominal anchor for price expectations	Risk of currency crisis
	Effectiveness of fiscal policy (cf. Mundell-Fleming model)	
Monetary union	Elimination of transaction costs related to currency exchanges	Irrevocable loss of an instrument of adjustment in case of an asymmetric shock, risk of inadequate monetary policy
	Limited instability of relative prices	
	Nominal anchor for price expectations	
	Effectiveness of fiscal policy (limited crowding out)	
	Coordinated monetary policy in case of a symmetric shock	

Source: Authors.

after 2008, while Greek prices continued to rise for three years before the adjustment started.

If prices and wages are sluggish, then an asymmetric shock in a monetary union cannot be absorbed by relative price adjustment in the short term. The question is whether workers can easily move from depressed regions to better-off ones. Based on an indirect methodology, Blanchard and Katz (1992) showed that in the 1970s and the 1980s, labor mobility played a substantial role in absorbing asymmetric shocks in the United States but much less so in the European Union. More recent studies (Dao, Furceri, and Loungani, 2014; Beyer and Smets, 2015) find some convergence between the United States and the EU, with less labor mobility in the former and more in the latter. Yet,

Box 7.14 Identifying Asymmetric Shocks

Descriptive Methods

To identify the need for a flexible exchange rate, a simple way is to calculate observed *real* exchange rate volatility: whatever the exchange rate regime, a volatile real exchange rate suggests that there is a need for relative price adjustments, which are easier if the nominal exchange rate is allowed to adjust. The problem with this method is that real exchange rate volatility can be driven by speculative movements in a floating regime, whereas, in a fixed exchange rate, nominal exchange rate rigidity can be an obstacle to real exchange rate adjustment. Hence, this first measure of shock asymmetry is not independent from the exchange rate regime itself.

A more popular measure of shock asymmetry relies on cross-country correlation of variables such as industrial production, GDP, or employment: The higher the cross-country correlation, the less the need for real exchange rate adjustment. Figure B7.14.1 shows the correlation of real GDP per capita growth rates between a number of countries and the euro area aggregate for two periods: 1999–2007 and 2008–2015. The graph illustrates the convergence of Central and Eastern European countries to the core EU average. Among EU countries, only Greece displays very low correlation over the two subperiods. The correlation is very high for "core" euro area countries (Germany, France, Italy, Benelux, Austria), but also for some countries outside the euro area (Denmark, Sweden) or even outside the EU (Switzerland) or outside Europe (Canada).

The problem with this method is that a high correlation between two countries can come either from symmetric shocks to output or from strong policy reactions, including monetary policy reactions, to asymmetric shocks. In order to isolate shock asymmetry, econometric estimations must be carried out.

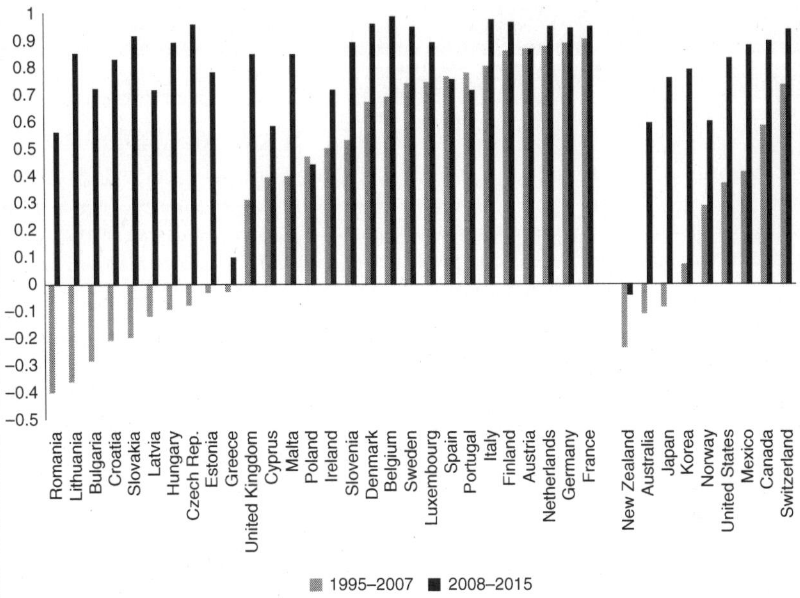

Figure B7.14.1 Correlation of growth rate of gross domestic product (GDP) per capita with euro area aggregate.
Authors, based on European Commission, Ameco database.

Econometric Methods

In econometric terms, exogenous shocks can be identified using the residuals of estimated equations. In order to account for interdependence between variables and/or countries, vector autoregressive models (VAR) methodologies have been developed. Blanchard and Quah (1989) suggest estimating a VAR model with two variables (the logarithm of output and the logarithm of the price level) and identifying demand shocks and supply shocks by applying an identification matrix to the residuals of the VAR model. The identification matrix is based on the assumptions that demand and supply shocks are orthogonal, and that demand shocks have no long-run impact on output, consistent with the aggregate supply–aggregate demand model (see Chapter 1). This exercise can be performed for each country successively, after which cross-country correlations of the shocks can be derived. Using this methodology, Bayoumi and Eichengreen (1994) found that only a core group of European countries exhibited a correlation of shocks comparable to US regions over the 1963-1988 period. However, the result could be attributable to the exchange rate regime itself since only a core group around Germany experienced stable exchange rates over the sample period. For the 1990-2014 period, Bayoumi and Eichengreen (2017) found relatively large correlations between Germany and peripheral countries such as Italy, Spain, Portugal and Ireland – a result they interpreted as the outcome of large capital flowing from Germany to these countries during the boom period.

Another avenue consists in estimating the common factor in the evolution of GDP per capita for a group of countries. Along this line, Cavallo and Ribba (2015) estimate a "near-VAR" model based on a vector of six variables containing two blocks: a euro area block with inflation, the cyclical component of industrial production, the overnight interest rate differential with the United States, and the nominal exchange rate of the euro against the US dollar; and a country-specific block with the inflation rate and the cyclical component of industrial production of each country, successively. This six-variable vector is regressed on its own lagged values, and the authors impose a "small country" hypothesis in which country variables cannot affect euro area variables on impact. The model is estimated with monthly variables between January 1999 and December 2011, and the variance decomposition allows to calculate the share of national output variations that can be attributed to euro-wide shocks at different horizons. Figure 7.14.2 reports the results at the horizons of 1, 12, and 24 months for six countries. The share of common shocks in national output variations is very high for Germany, France, Italy, Spain, and Belgium; it is much lower for Greece, Ireland, and Portugal. These findings are consistent with those of Bayoumi and Eichengreen. Such calculations are, however, backward-looking, based on past statistical evidence. They need to be complemented with more structural analysis.

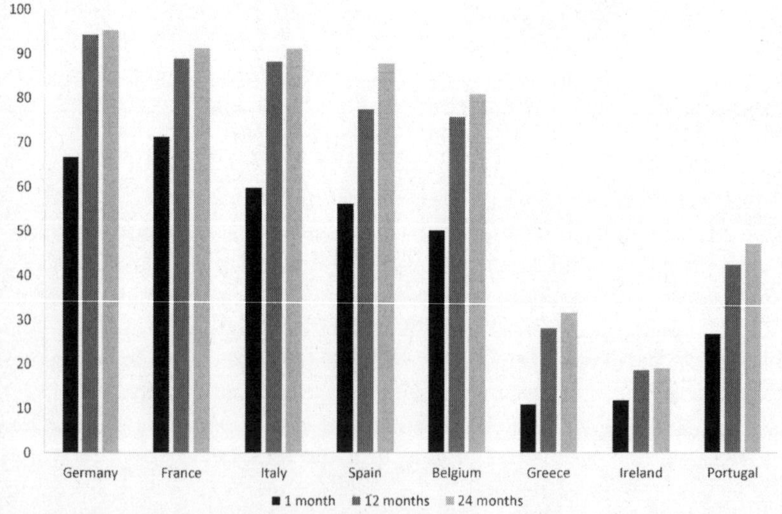

Figure B7.14.2 Fraction of the forecast error variance of national output attributable to common euro-area shocks at different horizons, in percent.
Based on Cavallo and Ribba (2015), table 4.

Measures of Trade Specialization

A more structural way to measure the scope of asymmetric shocks is to look at the extent of industry specialization. A synthetic measure of specialization is given by the Herfindhal index:

$$H = \sum_{i=1}^{n} \left(\frac{Y_i}{Y} \right)^2 \tag{B7.14.1}$$

where Y_i is output (or employment, or value added) in industry *i*, Y is total output, and n is the number of industries. $H = 1$ if the country is specialized in a single industry. It is lower, the more diversified the economy. An alternative measure of specialization is the extent of interindustry trade. For instance, the Finger-Kreinin index can be calculated as follows:

$$FK = \sum_{i=1}^{n} Min\left(\frac{X_i}{X}; \frac{M_i}{M} \right) \tag{B7.14.2}$$

where X_i and M_i denote exports and imports of product *i*, respectively. *FK* varies from zero (only interindustry trade) to one (only intraindustry trade). Another measure of intraindustry trade is the Grubel-Lloyd index:

$$GL = \sum_{i=1}^{n} \left(\frac{X_i + M_i}{X + M} \right) \left(\frac{(X_i + M_i) - |X_i - M_i|}{X_i + M_i} \right) \tag{B7.14.3}$$

This index also varies from zero (only interindustry trade) to one (only intraindustry trade). The advantage of relying on trade data is that it is available at a detailed level, allowing for a precise measure of specialization. Figure B7.14.3 ranks a few countries depending on the share of intraindustry trade, measured through the Grubel-Lloyd index. In most countries of the euro area, the index is very high, meaning that intraindustry trade forms the bulk of trade in these countries, thus limiting the scope for asymmetric shocks. However, some smaller countries like Greece, Finland, or Ireland display a relatively low share of intraindustry trade.

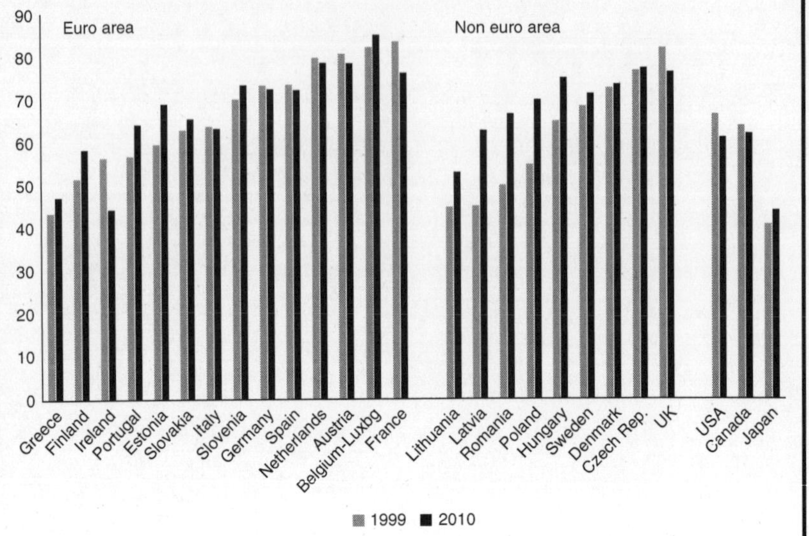

Figure B7.14.3 Grubel-Lyoyd index of intraindustry trade, in percent. CEPII-CHELEM.

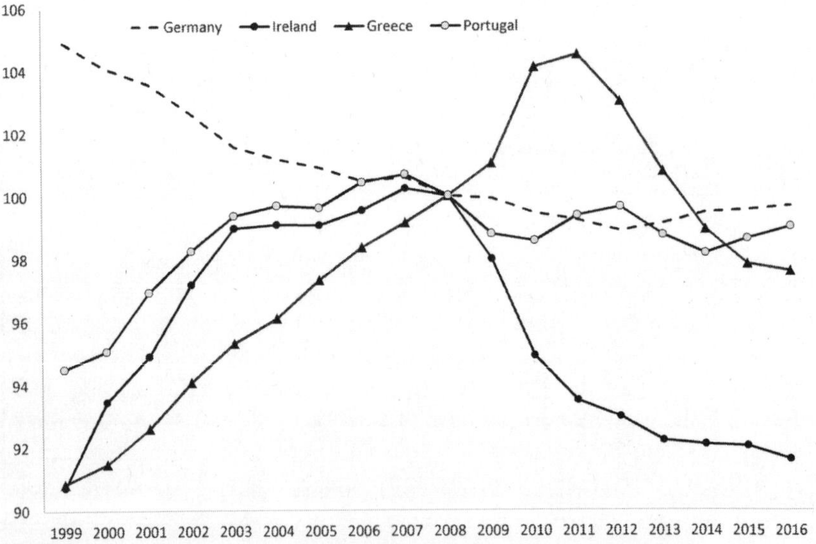

Figure 7.13 Consumer price index relative to Euro area, 1999–2016 (2008 = 100). European Commission, Ameco database.

the adjustment through labor mobility remains slower in the EU than in the United States.

In practice, the theory of optimum currency areas has seldom been used to decide whether or not to proceed to monetary union. In the European case, monetary union has been a final goal for several decades as a way to promote political integration and to avoid beggar-thy-neighbor monetary policies. Policymakers in Continental Europe were also convinced that monetary union was a necessary complement to the single market. Irrevocably fixed exchange rates and lower conversion costs would enhance price transparency and favor cross-border investment.

A number of studies have attempted to measure the impact of the euro since its inception, especially on trade and prices—a difficult exercise since euro area countries need to be compared to a control group (see Chapter 1). According to Baldwin (2006), the euro itself has increased intra-euro area trade by 5–10%, while Fontagné, Mayer, and Ottaviano (2009) and Martin and Méjean (2010) find evidence of a pro-competitive effect leading to a significant convergence of trade prices.

However, prices have not converged within the euro area to an extent comparable to the United States. In fact, monetary union cannot foster price convergence if goods and services markets stay segmented as they have remained (especially for services) in the European Union, despite the single market agenda. Indeed, lack of international competition in services sectors contributed to the build-up of large real exchange rate misalignments in the 2000s.

An important criterion for the choice of an exchange rate regime is the size of the economy: a small economy is mechanically more open to trade; the content of imported inputs in its production is larger, which reduces the impact of exchange rate variations on external competitiveness while raising the scope for home currency price volatility. Additionally, a small economy will rely more than a large one on foreign currency pricing and invoicing for goods and services, but also for assets and liabilities. Hence the trade-off between shock absorption and price stability is tilted in favor of a fixed exchange rate in a small economy. Figure 7.14 confirms that larger countries (as measured through GDP in purchasing power parity) tend to display more exchange rate flexibility, although country size is clearly not the only factor of exchange rate regime choice.

Based on a panel of 137 countries over 1999–2011 and a classification of exchange rate regimes in three categories (flexible, intermediate, and fixed), Ghosh (2014) estimates that a larger country has a lower probability of choosing a fixed exchange rate regime. Consistent with the impossible trinity, he also shows that countries with capital controls have a higher probability of fixing their exchange rate. For low-income countries, higher GDP per capita (in purchasing power parity), higher foreign liability to GDP ratio, and high official reserves to import ratio all raise the probability of fixed (or

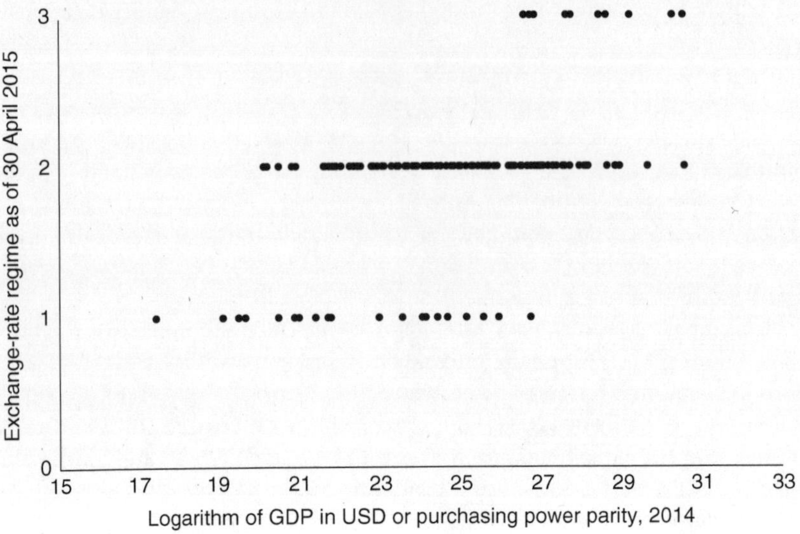

Figure 7.14 Country size and exchange-rate regime.[a]

[a]1: hard peg; 2: intermediate regime; 3: free floating regime. For the definition of the regimes, see section 7.1.

World Bank (World Development Indicators, July 2016) for GDP, IMF (Annual Report on Exchange Arrangements and Exchange Restrictions, 2015). Sample of 166 countries where euro-area countries are considered as one single country with a free floating regime.

intermediate) regimes. For advanced economies, high export concentration (in terms of sectors) tends to favor a fixed exchange rate regime.

c) Credible exchange rate regimes

While economists generally put forward the shock-absorbing properties of an exchange rate regime, policymakers often emphasize its contribution to the credibility of economic policy.

As discussed in Chapter 5, monetary policy is not always credible. This can be due to a track record of economic policy mistakes (e.g., in Latin America in the 1980s) or to the absence of a track record at all (e.g., in countries in transition, such as Eastern European countries in the 1990s, or in newly established countries, such as Timor-Leste or Kosovo). External anchoring can then be used to import credibility. By announcing that the exchange rate will not move, the central bank achieves a double end: it gives incentives to firms and employees to ask for moderate price and wage increases, and it ties its own hands to make monetary surprises impossible. This justifies *ex post* the fixed exchange rate. In short, it helps the economy settle on the right equilibrium.

A number of case studies seem to confirm that an exchange rate peg can curb inflation efficiently. On average, over 1980–2010, Ghosh, Qureshi, and Tsangarides (2014) find that countries with a hard or conventional peg display an inflation rate of about half the inflation observed in countries with more flexible regimes. The relationship between a stable exchange rate and stable prices works, of course, two ways, since fixing the nominal exchange rate is not sustainable when inflation is high. Case studies (Argentina in March 1991, Bulgaria in June 1997, Zimbabwe in February 2009), however, show that a shift in the exchange rate regime can have a dramatic impact on the domestic inflation rate. Figure 7.15 illustrates this feature in the case of Argentina, after a currency board was put in place in 1991.[48] A more modest case is that of the French policy of "franc fort" in the late 1980s and early 1990s, when policy authorities strove to keep the peg to the Deutsche mark despite rising unemployment and successfully brought the inflation rate below the German level in the 1990s. However, external anchoring cannot be a durable substitute for internal credibility. Even a hard peg is vulnerable, as shown again in the case of Argentina, when the currency board had to be abandoned at the end of 2001 in the midst of a political and social crisis.

Credibility was a strong argument for some European countries when considering membership to the euro area. For instance, Italy had a poor nominal stability record before being a founding member of the euro area: its inflation rate was systematically higher than that of Germany, with regular devaluations of the Italian lira. Being part of the monetary union helped Italy to gain credibility and enjoy low interest rates. But strong monetary credibility also had

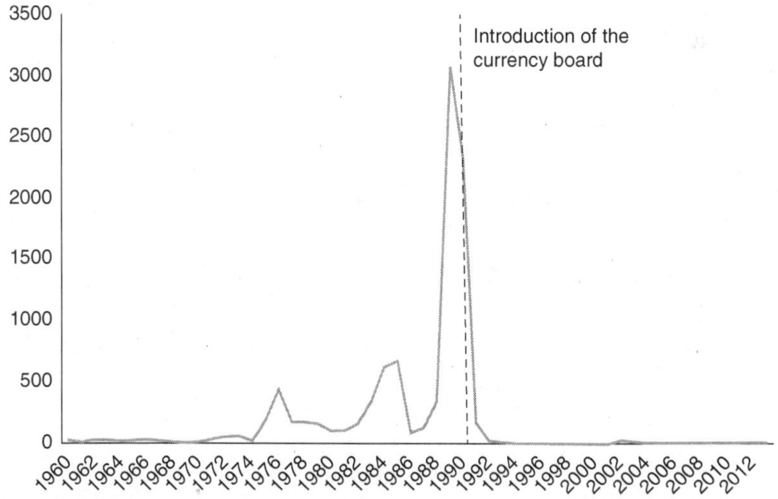

Figure 7.15 Consumer price inflation in Argentina, in percent per year, 1960–2013.
International Monetary Fund, World Economic Outlook Database, July 2016.

perverse effects: in several countries, it contributed to a precipitous fall in long-term rates which in turn fuelled a credit bubble.

7.3.2 Managing exchange rates

In a floating exchange rate regime, the exchange rate moves in order to equalize the supply and demand for the currency. Why should governments try to influence this process? There are three reasons. First, they may wish to bring the exchange rate back toward a level in line with *fundamental values*; that is, a value they deem consistent with macroeconomic equilibrium (the equilibrium exchange rate of Section 7.2). Given the uncertainty surrounding estimates of equilibrium exchange rates, there is much credibility to lose in the exercise and governments usually step in only when market rates have departed very substantially from equilibrium values. Second, they can aim at using the exchange rate as a policy instrument to bring the whole economy to a different equilibrium point. Third, without reference to a particular level of the exchange rate, they can aim at reducing its volatility because they regard it as costly for economic welfare.

Governments affect the exchange rate through their conventional and unconventional monetary policies (see Chapter 5), foreign exchange interventions, and communication policies (*oral interventions*). Foreign exchange interventions are mainly used in countries applying intermediate exchange rate regimes, but they can be used in exceptional times in countries with floating currencies. The effectiveness of the interventions mainly depends on their consistency with monetary policy, on the extent of international capital mobility, and on possible coordination between various central banks.

a) Who is in charge?

In all countries, choosing the exchange rate *regime* is a political decision, responsibility for which rests on the government. But, depending on countries, exchange rate *policy* is decided either by the central bank or the ministry of finance. In the United States, Japan, the United Kingdom, and Canada, the exchange rate policy is solely the responsibility of the finance minister, with the central bank acting as his or her agent. In the US federal framework, the Federal Reserve Bank of New York undertakes all market operations, including foreign exchange interventions.

Whether the Maastricht Treaty provides for an effective exchange rate policy is unclear. Unlike in the United States, the United Kingdom, or Japan, the responsibility for exchange rate policy is legally shared between ministers of finance and the ECB, and de facto it is largely in the hands of the latter. "I am Mr. Euro," Wim Duisenberg, the ECB's first president, once famously said. The ECB and national central banks manage foreign exchange reserves without government interference and are solely responsible for market interventions (the decision to intervene is taken by the ECB, and the interventions are implemented by the ECB and national central banks). Ministers can only negotiate formal monetary agreements with third countries[49] and formulate "general orientations for exchange rate policy" on a proposal from the Commission or the ECB, and provided these do not endanger price stability (Treaty on the Functionning of the European Union, Article 2).[50] Hence, any deliberate weakening of the euro to prop up output is possible only in total absence of inflationary pressures and if consistent with the monetary policy orientation.

Exchange rate policy raises an obvious problem of international coordination since not all countries can depreciate (or appreciate) their currencies simultaneously. The institution responsible for monitoring exchange rate regimes and exchange rate policies in relation to global current account imbalances is the IMF. According to Article IV of the IMF Articles of Agreement, "Each member shall notify the Fund . . . of the exchange rate arrangements it intends to apply," and the Fund "shall exercise firm surveillance over the exchange rate policies of members." This was detailed in a 1977 decision on surveillance over exchange rate policies of member countries, which was not changed until June 2007, when it was decided to account for monetary unions but also for spillovers of the exchange rate regime of a given country to other countries and to financial markets at large. At the insistence of the United States, the revised 1977 decision also stresses the need to avoid "exchange rate manipulation," a clear allusion to China's exchange rate policy.[51]

However, there is not much the Fund can do to "exercise firm surveillance over exchange rate policies." It cannot twist the arms of its members, except for those seeking financial assistance, in which case foreign exchange policy can be included in the conditions attached to the loan. As a result, the Fund has shied away from pointing out which are the misaligned currencies.

Before the *G20* (see Chapter 3, p. 125) was chosen in 2009 as the "premier forum for international economic cooperation," exchange rates between major economies, and more generally in the global economy, were mostly discussed by G7 ministers of finance and central bank governors. Statements released after G7 finance minister meetings include a section on exchange rates, usually written in arcane language (a wording such as: "We agreed to monitor the exchange rate situation carefully and act as appropriate" is meant to send the signal that the G7 is ready to intervene on foreign exchange markets). In the 2000s, this has increasingly gone along with bilateral policy dialogue with large emerging-market economies, in particular with China, but the result was not much different from what the G7 had delivered. Coordinating exchange rate policies is constrained by a context of independent central banks that have a purely domestic mandate (low domestic inflation, low domestic unemployment, domestic financial stability, etc.). There is an agreement in the G7 and G20 that "excessive" exchange-rate variations should be avoided: the exchange rate should play its role of shock absorber (as a channel of domestic monetary policies) but not be manipulated for competitiveness purpose (see the Communiqué of the G20 Finance ministers and Central bank governors meeting in Buenos Aires on 20 March 2018).

b) The intervention toolkit

As presented in box 7.11 in Section 7.2, there are three ways for monetary authorities to influence (or try to influence) the exchange rate: official interventions, interest rate variations, and communication. When they want to avoid a depreciation of the domestic currency, monetary authorities can (i) sell foreign currencies on the international money market, (ii) raise the domestic interest rate (to attract foreign investors), or (iii) publicize some private information on exchange rate fundamentals or simply signal their willingness to defend a certain level of the exchange rate. If investors are risk-neutral, the exchange rate follows the uncovered interest rate parity. In this case, official interventions cannot affect the exchange rate unless they are accompanied by monetary policy and/or communication. If investors are risk-averse, an intervention can be powerful, even with unchanged monetary policy. This was the case in China in the 2000s, as evidence in figure 7.16: despite growing current account surpluses and net inflows of foreign direct investment, the People's Bank of China was able to delay the nominal appreciation of the yuan (fall

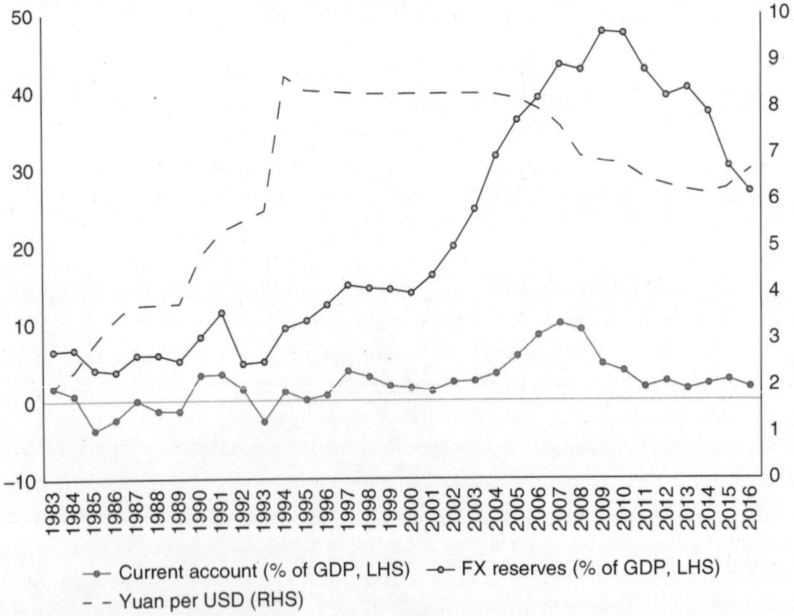

Figure 7.16 Foreign exchange reserves and the exchange rate in China, 1983-2016. World Bank, World Development Indicators (July 2017).

in the number of yuan per US dollar). The ratio of foreign exchange reserves to GDP peaked at 47% of GDP in 2010, before receding with the diminishing current account surplus and the reversal of private capital flows in relation to the weakening of China's GDP growth prospects.

As already discussed, purchasing foreign currency implies creating money. To offset this impact on monetary aggregates, the central bank can sterilize its interventions by reducing by the same amount its claims on the domestic economy (e.g., by selling securities to domestic agents). These can be government or corporate securities taken from the central bank's portfolio or bills issued by the bank for that specific purpose and called *sterilization bonds*. Monetary policy is then immunized from the impact of exchange rate policy. However, sterilized interventions are less effective than nonsterilized ones, precisely because they do not change the supply of money (box 7.15). They affect the exchange rate only to the extent that the central bank is able to buy or sell large amounts of foreign currency compared to the daily turnover or because they signal new information on future intentions of the central bank.

Box 7.15 Are Foreign Exchange Interventions Effective?

One usually identifies three channels through which foreign exchange interventions can affect the exchange rate (Dominguez and Frankel, 1993).

- *The monetary channel.* Suppose that a central bank opposes the appreciation of its currency. It purchases foreign currency in exchange for central bank money. This increases simultaneously the assets of the central bank, of which official reserves are part, and its liabilities, through currency in circulation. The increase of money supply is magnified by a multiplier effect through the banking system. The overall monetary expansion results in a lower interest rate, which discourages capital inflows and halts the appreciation of the currency. In fact, the foreign exchange intervention amounts to a loosening of monetary policy.
- *The portfolio channel.* If assets denominated in various currencies are imperfect substitutes, then a change in the relative supply of domestic and foreign assets will affect their relative price (i.e., the exchange rate). Again, consider a central bank that opposes the appreciation of its currency. To this end, it purchases foreign currency against domestic currency, which increases the relative supply of the latter and causes the exchange rate to drop. The effectiveness of this channel relies on imperfect capital mobility and/or investors' risk-aversion (see box 7.11 in Section 7.2). Empirical studies tend to downplay this channel when capital is mobile since the amounts

under consideration are insufficient to alter the balance of the foreign exchange market. For the same reasons, capital controls can enhance the effectiveness of the portfolio channel. The typical example is China in the early 2000s, when massive official interventions could halt the appreciation of the renminbi in spite of the doubling of the current account surplus and massive foreign direct investment inflows (figure 7.16).

- *The signaling channel.* When intervening, the central bank changes the structure of its own balance sheet in a way that aligns its incentives with the signal that is being sent to the markets. For example, if it sells foreign currency in exchange for domestic currency, it is in its own interest that the domestic currency does not depreciate; otherwise, it will take a loss on this operation. By intervening, the central bank reveals either that it holds private information on economic fundamentals that backs a scenario of appreciation or that the government is politically committed to having this scenario materialize. This signaling effect is particularly important when market participants do not have a precise idea of the equilibrium value of the exchange rate.

Empirical studies (Frenkel, Pierdzioch, and Stadtmann, 2001; Sarno and Taylor, 2001) cast a doubt on the effectiveness of interventions, at least when they are sterilized, which is routinely the case in advanced economies.[52] Based on historical data, they find that the impact is counterintuitive: the domestic currency depreciates following foreign currency sales. One possible explanation is reverse causality: the central bank sells foreign currency when its domestic currency depreciates. However, empirical work confirms that, in general, interventions have weak effects on the exchange rate in advanced economies. Similarly, interventions seem to increase rather than reduce exchange rate volatility. Econometric studies should be taken with a grain of salt since they do not account for the economic and political context. There seems to be a consensus among policymakers on the fact that interventions are effective when they support decisions or public announcements related to exchange rate fundamentals (i.e., monetary and fiscal policy), but this is only partially backed by empirical studies.

As noted by Menkhoff (2013), however, the bulk of the literature on the effects of foreign exchange interventions has focused on advanced economies which not only sterilize their interventions, but also face a very large foreign exchange turnover where interventions are necessarily small compared to daily private transactions. Foreign exchange interventions are widespread in emerging countries, which totalized 73% of global foreign exchange reserves at end-2015, up from 27% in 1990. Figure 7.17 reports the ratio of foreign exchange

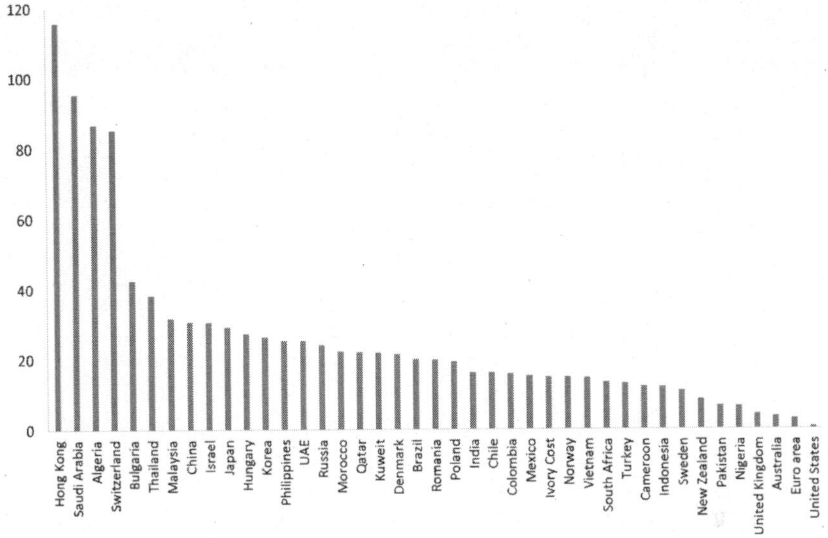

Figure 7.17 Foreign exchange official reserves in percent of gross domestic product (GDP), end of 2015.
World Bank, World Development Indicators (July 2017).

reserves to GDP for a sample of countries at end 2015. The highest ratios can be found in countries operating a currency board (Hong Kong, Bulgaria), oil exporting countries (Saudi Arabia), or countries which have heavily intervened to limit the appreciation of their currencies either during the Global financial crisis (Switzerland) or in the 2000s (Malaysia, China, Japan). At the other end of the spectrum, countries or currency areas with free floating currencies (United Kingdom, Australia, Euro area, United States) display low reserve-to-GDP ratios.

Hence, central banks in emerging economies have much larger "fire power" than their counterparts in advanced economies when they want to influence their exchange rate. They also less often sterilize their interventions due to less active domestic bonds markets and to the cost of sterilization (see next paragraph). Consequently, they are more likely to affect exchange rates. Based on panel data for a panel of 18 emerging market economies over 2003–2011, Daude, Levy Yeyati, and Nagengast (2016) find that foreign exchange interventions do have an impact on exchange rates once the other determinants of exchange rates are accounted for.

However, foreign reserve accumulation in developing and emerging economies comes with a cost since foreign assets in the balance sheet of the central bank typically yield a lower interest rate than domestic assets. The cost is magnified for sterilized interventions since then the central bank needs to sell high-yield securities to buy low-yield ones. The cost of carrying foreign assets weighs on the benefit of the central bank, hence indirectly on the government budget. In the 2000s, the budgetary cost of sterilization in emerging countries was nevertheless limited thanks to low-risk premiums, reaching at most 1% of GDP in Indonesia based on market interest rates (Mohanty and Turner, 2006). The People's Bank of China was even earning a positive carry, the one-year Chinese interest rate being less than half the comparable US Treasury rate.

Turning to "oral interventions," Fratzscher (2008) finds that public statements on the exchange rate by monetary policy committee members in the United States, euro area, and Japan do affect exchange rates in the short term and that they reduce their volatility. Interestingly, this effect is independent from "effective" interventions on the foreign exchange market.

Foreign exchange interventions are more effective when they are coordinated internationally. The paragon example is the Plaza accord on September 22, 1985, between the United States, Japan, and three European countries (Germany, France, and the United Kingdom). Gathered in a hotel in New York, the G5 countries decided to coordinate interventions of the foreign exchange market in order to curb the dollar, which had dramatically appreciated since 1979. Upon announcement (hence, before any intervention was actually carried out), the dollar depreciated heavily. It depreciated by around 50% against the yen in only two years. Similar international coordination on the exchange rate has not been reiterated since then, except in 1987 to stop the weakening of the dollar. In the early 2000s, the G7 tried several times to trigger an appreciation of the yuan. However, China was not a member of the group and did not listen to the call until it actually decided to let its currency appreciate.

c) Is free floating really stabilizing?

The main rationale for a free float regime is the ability of the exchange rate to adjust endogenously to the economic cycle: in a downturn, the home currency depreciates both because the home central bank cuts its interest rates and because investors expect lower yields due to slower growth. The depreciation temporarily stimulates aggregate demand through higher exports and lower imports. In an upturn, the home currency appreciates, which limits the inflationary risk.

In practice, do exchange rate variations fulfill their roles as macroeconomic shock absorbers in free floating areas? Figure 7.18 plots the real effective exchange rate against the output gap for the United States and the euro area from 1995 to 2015. We expect a positive correlation between the two variables; that is, a strong currency when the output gap is positive and a weak currency when the output gap is negative. This is what is observed for the United States but not for the euro area. In particular, the output gap pick of 2000 corresponds to a strong dollar and a weak euro,[53] and the depression of 2009 is accompanied by a weak dollar and a strong euro.

Why did the euro play such a pro-cyclical role? A first answer has to do with monetary policy reaction functions on both sides of the Atlantic. Over the business cycle, the figure suggests that the US Federal Reserve reacted more

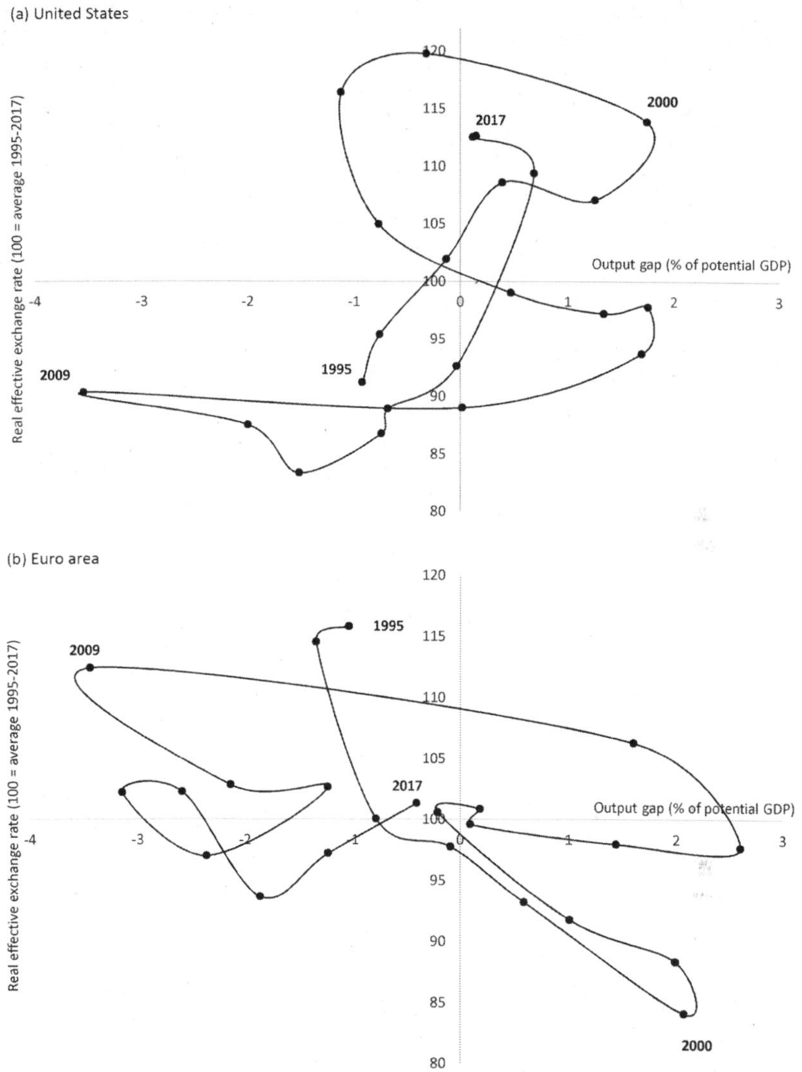

Figure 7.18 Output gaps and real effective exchange rates in the United States and the euro area.[a]

[a]Euro area with 12 countries, synthetic euro before 1999.
European Commission, Ameco database (November 2017).

swiftly to demand shocks than did the ECB. Another answer has to do with the role of the dollar in the international monetary system, especially its role as a funding currency. In an economic downturn, the Federal Reserve lowers its interest rate, which encourages banks in the United States, but also in Europe, to borrow more in US dollars. This additional borrowing weighs on the dollar. In the upturn, the interest rate increases, with the opposite outcome.

7.3.3 The future of the international monetary system

The international monetary system (IMS) has changed substantially since the Bretton Woods conference of 1944. Since 1972, industrialized countries have lived with floating exchange rates, and, since the 1990s, they have lived with freely mobile capital. However, the US dollar has remained the main international currency (see table 7.1 in Section 7.1).

This asymmetric arrangement has proved resilient: it has cushioned major shocks such as the emerging-market crises of the late 1990s, the global liquidity crisis following the collapse of LTCM in 1998, the geopolitical risk arising from the terrorist attacks of 9/11, and the global financial crisis in 2008. The Fed has played a key role by supplying liquidity in reaction to these shocks. Furthermore, the dollar has played the role of a *safe asset*[54] and the United States the role of a "global insurer" related to the structure of its aggregate balance sheet, with riskless liabilities in the form of treasury bills and more risky assets in the form of equity and long-run investments in foreign currencies. In normal times, this structure produces a positive net income due to higher remuneration on the asset side than on the liability side; in times of crisis, however, the asset side endures a sharp loss (Gourinchas and Rey, 2007; Gourinchas et al., 2010).[55] Gourinchas and Rey (2016) estimate that, between 2007Q4 and 2015Q3, the US balance sheet suffered a loss of approximately US$4.13 trillion (i.e., 22.9% of 2015 US GDP or 5.6% of world GDP). They argue that this loss absorption by the United States has de facto participated in the required deleveraging process in other parts of the world. Finally, the international monetary system has been resilient to *global imbalances* (i.e., large and persistent current account imbalances around the world).[56]

Still, the IMS may appear increasingly less adequate in the context of a multipolar economy.

a) Toward a multipolar monetary system

As long as the United States dominated the global economy, exchange rate distortions or financial imbalances in other countries were benign. For instance, the fact that China kept its currency pegged on the US dollar and accumulated official reserves in dollars was benign as long as China remained a minor global player. However, the share of China in world GDP rose from 1.6% in 1990 to 14.8% in 2015, at current exchange rates. Table 7.5 reports different measures of country or currency area "size." In 2015, the US economy remained the largest in terms of GDP at current exchange rates. In terms of population, however, China was by far the largest country, whereas for trade, the euro area was the largest.

Historical experience suggests that, although the incumbent international currency benefits economies of scale and network effects, this advantage should not be overblown: there is room for more than one international currency (see, e.g., Chițu, Eichengreen, and Mehl 2014). The theoretical literature highlights five main conditions for a currency to play a major international role (see the survey by Bénassy-Quéré 2016):

Table 7.5
Comparative size of for countries or currency areas, 2015

Item	Euro area[a]	United States	China
Population (million)	339	321	1,374
GDP (EUR bn at current exchange rates)	10,454	16,083	9,688
Exports of goods and services (EUR bn at current exchange rates, excluding exports within the European Union and the euro area)[b]	2,380	1,717	1,780

[a]Austria, Belgium, Cyprus, Estonia, Finland, France, Germany, Greece, Ireland, Italy, Latvia, Lithuania, Luxembourg, Malta, the Netherlands, Portugal, the Slovak Republic, Slovenia, and Spain.
[b]Data are for 2013. The share of intra-EU and euro zone exports is estimated based on CEPII-CHELEM bilateral trade data for goods in 2012.
Sources: World Bank, European Commission and CEPII-CHELEM databases.

- Be issued by a large country or monetary area;
- Be used to denominate assets that are traded in deep and liquid markets;
- Provide nominal stability both internally (low inflation) and externally (a stable or at least not depreciating exchange rate);
- Enjoy financial stability and a safe regulatory environment;
- Be backed by some attributes of noneconomic power (military force, voice in international forums).

Table 7.6 summarizes the strengths and weaknesses of the euro and the yuan in terms of various determinants of currency internationalization. A static view suggests that the euro has more strengths than the yuan, and the euro is already playing a significant role as an international currency. Depending on the capacity of China to reform its economy and enforce rule of law, however, the dynamic view may be more favorable to the yuan, thanks to the size effect and the backing of the currency by a single sovereign state.

Since the mid-1990s, China has taken significant steps toward progressively internationalizing the renminbi as a means of payment and store of value. In September 2016, the renminbi was incorporated into the *Special Drawing Right* (SDR) basket, joining the US dollar, the Japanese yen, the British pound, and the euro.[57] Although there is still a long way toward full internationalization, particularly because of to legal uncertainties and government hesitations concerning the liberalization of capital flows, in the long run it is difficult to imagine that the renminbi would not play a very significant role in international exchanges (see, e.g., Eichengreen and Kawai, 2014; Yiping, Wang, and Fan, 2015). Concerning the euro, it has already developed as a regional currency and meets several conditions for internationalization (see ECB, 2015; Bénassy-Quéré, 2016). Yet its capital markets lack the depth and liquidity of the dollar-denominated one and it is not backed by a single sovereign state.

Table 7.6
Strengths and weaknesses of the euro and the yuan as international currencies

Requirement	Euro	Yuan
Size of country or monetary area	Strength	Strength
Deep and liquid financial markets	Strength	Weakness
Nominal stability	Strength	Strength
Financial stability and rule of law	Strength	Weakness
Noneconomic power	Weakness	Strength

Source: Bénassy-Quéré (2016).

b) The implications of a multipolar monetary system

The mismatch between a unipolar IMS and a multipolar real economy has at times been singled out as a key ingredient of the macroeconomic environment that led to the global financial crisis (see, e.g., Ivashina, Scharfstein, and Stein, 2015) and on the long-lasting shortage of aggregate demand at the global level (Gourinchas and Rey, 2016): the IMS would have contributed both to financial instability and economic slack at the global level.[58]

Financial instability

In 1960, Robert Triffin predicted that the Bretton Woods system was self-defeating since it relied on continuous issuance of US dollar (to fund growing international trade), which would inevitably clash with the slow-growing stock of gold in Federal Reserve vaults. The system would end up with a dollar crash, which in fact happened in 1971. Zhou (2009) and Farhi, Gourinchas, and Rey (2011) have revived the concept of the *Triffin dilemma* in the context of the post–Bretton Woods system. According to Farhi, Gourinchas, and Rey, the growth of emerging economies and their appetite for liquid, riskless assets increases demand for international liquidity, putting downward pressure on US interest rates and the US current account. At some stage, international investors will either lose confidence in US solvency or fear massive monetization of US bonds, which could trigger a crash of the dollar. To avoid such an outcome, it would be advisable to develop alternative sources of international liquidity, either through the internationalization of other currencies or through regular allocations of SDRs, that would contribute to developing its role (Mateos y Lago, Duttagupta, and Goyal 2009). A multipolar monetary system could alleviate the Triffin dilemma by diversifying the sources of international liquidity. Multipolarity could also act as a disciplinary device: because they would be offered a choice between several currencies with equivalent liquidity features but issued by countries with varying depths of imbalances, international investors would no longer invest in a country displaying long-lasting deficits (Kwan 2001; Eichengreen 2010).

Economic slack

The global financial crisis and the euro area crisis have reduced the supply of high-quality government bonds (safe assets), while the demand for these bonds was simultaneously increasing as a result of higher risk aversion, stricter financial regulation, and the willingness to self-insure against balance-of-payment crises (see box 7.16). Consequently, the remuneration of these safe assets fell to very low levels. In the context of low inflation, the nominal interest rate on safe assets became very low or even negative, but not strongly negative: it could not fall to its equilibrium level (see Chapter 5). As explained in box 7.12 in Section 7.2, if surplus countries refrain from issuing more safe assets (e.g., because they follow strict fiscal rules), then the only way to rebalance the market of safe assets is through a lower global income that will reduce the demand for safe assets more than its supply. In brief, the shortage of safe assets contributes to the slack of aggregate demand at the global level.

Box 7.16 Global Financial Safety Net and Self-Insurance

The *global financial safety net* (GFSN) covers all national, bilateral, regional, and multilateral mechanisms and provides insurance against crises (i.e., ways to compensate possible reversals of private capital flows). The need for a strong GFSN is an increasing function of gross financial exposures, which have rocketed since the 1990s, and the related financial interconnectedness, which increases the risk of liquidity crises (see Chapter 6). In 2014, official reserves held by central banks totaled US$12 trillion, and the other elements of financial safety amounted to around US$4 trillion. Hence, the GFSN totaled US$16 trillion or 22% of world GDP (IMF, 2016*a*).

At multilateral level, the IMF may provide its member countries with emergency financing in proportion of their quotas. However, there are costs attached to this first safety net. First, these financings are senior to any other form of debt: in case of insolvency, private creditors will not be reimbursed until the IMF is repaid in full. Consequently, an IMF program will mechanically lead to downgrading regular debts, hence increase the interest rate attached to them. The Fund may even ask for debt restructuring before it can lend to the crisis country, if its debt is deemed nonsustainable. Second, and most important, the IMF financing is conditional on an adjustment program that the IMF regards as necessary to restore market access. The program generally involves cuts in public spending, increases in taxation, privatizations, or product market deregulations, which are highly unpopular, not to mention a currency devaluation. Hence there is a high political cost attached to IMF programs. Consequently, governments are unwilling to rely on the IMF, and they prefer to self-insure through reserve accumulation. This has especially been the case since the Asian crisis of 1997.

As already mentioned (see Section 7.3.2), reserve accumulation at the national level involves a cost related to the gap between the remuneration of domestic and foreign assets in the central bank's balance sheet. More importantly, reserve accumulation produces negative spillovers on the global economy since it raises the demand for safe assets that are in short supply. In order to reduce the scope of reserve accumulation at national level, the IMF has introduced different facilities that involve a prequalification of countries, with no further conditionality when the facilities are actually used. However, countries are reluctant to ask for these precautionary lines due to a "stigma" effect.

At European level, the European Stability Mechanism (ESM), which was introduced in reaction to the euro area financial crises, works very much like the IMF. In East Asia, the Chiang Mai initiative covering the ASEAN+3 grouping[a] comprises a multilateral currency swap arrangement aiming to provide short-term liquidity, address balance-of-payments difficulties, and supplement existing international arrangements, although its capacity has remained largely untested.

Bilateral swap lines between central banks expanded dramatically during the global financial crisis, with 40 arrangements at end-2009 (IMF, 2016*b*). In 2013, the network of swap lines among advanced economies' central banks was made permanent. These unconditional credit lines are aimed at maintaining financial stability (through avoiding liquidity crises in the banking sector) rather than avoiding balance-of-payment crises. China has developed its own network of swap lines in renminbi, mainly to protect foreign users of the Chinese currency, with the objective of expanding its international role.

[a]The ASEAN+3 group brings the ten ASEAN countries (Brunei, Burma, Cambodia, Indonesia, Laos, Malaysia, Philippines, Singapore, Thailand, and Vietnam) together with China, Korea, and Japan. It is the main cooperation forum in East Asia.

A multipolarization of the IMS would be consistent with the multipolarization of the real economy. It could alleviate some of the flaws of the existing system, especially through a diversification of the sources of global liquidity. Whether the IMS can evolve toward multipolarity, however, will depend on the capacity of both China and the euro area to introduce the necessary reforms so that they can effectively issue liquid, safe assets.

Notes

1. For a more detailed history, see Eichengreen (1997).
2. In reality, transport and transaction costs introduced a small wedge between bilateral exchange rates and the ratio of the gold values of currencies.

3. The foreign exchange reserves of the Bank of England were only disclosed in 1931.
4. See, notably, Eichengreen (1992).
5. On the IMF, its role, and its early development, see Dam (1982).
6. More precisely, all member countries submitted a par value of their currency expressed in terms of gold or in terms of the US dollar using the gold weight of the dollar effective on July 1, 1944 ($35 per Troy ounce). All exchange transactions between member countries had to take place at a rate that could not diverge by more than 1% from the par value. A member could modify the par value of its currency only to correct a "fundamental disequilibrium" in its balance of payment and after consultation with the IMF. Canada left the Bretton Woods monetary system in 1951. Other countries remained part of it until its breakdown in March 1973.
7. Robert Triffin (1960) and Jacques Rueff (1965) were the first to note this contradiction.
8. Amendments to the IMF Articles of Agreement must be approved by the Board of Governors and become effective when three-fifths of the members, having 85% of the total voting power, have accepted the proposed amendment. There have been three such amendments. The first amendment (adopted in 1968 and ratified in 1969) created the SDR in an attempt at increasing world liquidity. The second amendment (the Jamaica agreement) was adopted in 1976 and ratified in 1978. The third amendment, adopted in 1990 and ratified in 1992, enables the IMF to suspend the voting rights of member countries that violate the Articles. A fourth amendment, decided in 1997 to double the liquidity available to the Fund through SDRs, was ratified by the US Congress only in 2009. A fifth amendment was decided in 2010 to reform the Executive board of the Fund and raise the weight of emerging countries. It was ratified by the US Congress in 2016.
9. The future of the IMS is discussed in Section 7.3.3.
10. For instance, Kumar and Rao (2011) find a lower coefficient for 13 OECD countries over the 1975–2007 period than over 1960–1974. Interestingly, they show the coefficient to be lower and declining in the euro area (up to 2007).
11. For some authors (Summers, 1988), public authorities can themselves avoid unsustainable paths through adjusting fiscal policy.
12. Optimal portfolio choice is discussed in Section 7.2.
13. For a simple presentation of balance-of-payment accounting, see Section 7.1.3 or the more comprehensive presentation in Feenstra and Taylor (2015).
14. Formerly called capital account convertibility.
15. E.g., the nineteenth-century Latin Union in Europe and the former Soviet Union. In summer 2015, Greece came close to being obliged to leave the European monetary union.
16. Following the inclusion of the Chinese yuan on September 30, 2016, the SDR basket contains five currencies: the US dollar (41.73% of the basket), the euro (30.93%), the yuan (10.92%), the yen (8.33%), and the British pound (8.09%).
17. Free floating is a regime where interventions are exceptional ("at most three instances in the previous six months, each lasting no more than three business days," cf. IMF Annual report on Exchange Rate Arrangements and Exchange Restrictions, October 2016, p. 48).

18. That is, "mostly market determined," where interventions may be carried by the central bank to moderate exchange rate fluctuations but not to target a specific level (see IMF 2016*b*, p. 48).
19. A cut in US interest rates triggers a depreciation of the dollar, hence an appreciation of the other countries, which has a negative impact on aggregate demand in the short run in these countries (see Chapter 5).
20. The presentation of the balance of payment here follows the Sixth Edition of the IMF's *Balance of Payments and International Investment Position Manual* (2013). Earlier presentations used to record the balance of the financial account as net capital inflows, so that the sum of the current account, capital account, and errors and omissions would be zero.
21. See Gourinchas and Rey (2007) and Lane and Milesi-Ferretti (2007, 2009). Conversely, the NFA of Switzerland increased less than the accumulation of its trade surpluses due to losses on its gross foreign assets, notably due to the appreciation of the Swiss franc (Stoffels and Tille, 2007).
22. Indeed, the US NFA suffered a sudden fall during the global financial crisis.
23. The data are from the OECD Economic Outlook of June 2016, available at https://stats.oecd.org/.
24. When calculating a real exchange rate, is it useful to check that the numerator and the denominator are expressed in the same currency. Here, the numerator is the US price index expressed in yen, whereas the denominator is the Japanese price index expressed in yen. Hence both are in yen, and the ratio is the relative price of US goods in terms of Japanese ones.
25. From this example, it can be seen that nominal and real exchange rates vary almost in parallel when inflation is very low.
26. See https://www.bis.org/statistics/eer.htm.
27. Or even in a few days. For instance, the British pound depreciated by 11.3% between June 23, 2016 (the day of the referendum on Brexit) and June 27, 2016.
28. See Obstfeld, Shambaugh, and Taylor (2005), Klein and Shambaugh (2015), or Obstfeld (2015).
29. Macroprudential policies are studied in Chapter 6.
30. If prices are set in a foreign currency, then exchange rate flexibility is less powerful for macroeconomic adjustment. See the discussion in Gopinath (2017).
31. According to Krugman (1993), monetary union tends to reinforce the specialization of its member states since companies can locate freely to exploit agglomeration spillovers such as a specialized labor force, infrastructures, or subcontractor networks. Being more specialized, the members of a monetary union are more prone to asymmetric shocks. However, monetary union may raise intra- rather than interindustry trade, in which case an industry-specific shock will not be asymmetric (see Fontagné and Freudenberg, 1999). Frankel and Rose (1998) argue that being part of a monetary union may by itself raise the correlation of business cycles. Empirical evidence is relatively weak. The European monetary union does not seem to have raised the level of interindustry specialization among its member states. However the (asymmetric) 2010 crisis was largely endogenous to the monetary union itself (see De Grauwe, 2014; Bénassy-Quéré and Cœuré, 2014).
32. For an application to West Africa, see Tapsoba (2009).

33. Such calculation derives from estimating the mean-reverting coefficient ρ in the following panel regression, where Q_{it} is the real exchange rate of country i at time t and u_{it} is the residual of the regression: $\Delta \ln Q_{i,t} = \rho \ln Q_{i,t-1} + \sum_{k=1}^{p} a_k \Delta \ln Q_{i,t-1} + u_{i,t}$.
34. In fact, even in traded goods sectors prices may diverge across countries during long periods, see Rogoff, Froot, and Kim (2001).
35. Source: *The Economist*, The Big Mac index, July 13, 2017.
36. This is only partly true since technical progress also enhances productivity in nontraded goods sectors. US and European shopkeepers benefit from highly advanced payment and supply chain management schemes, which most Indian shopkeepers do not have.
37. Note that, in the very long run, when productivity is equalized internationally, the price of both traded and nontraded goods should equalize, and PPP should apply across all countries.
38. Assuming that the nontraded goods sectors represent half of the economy and that the productivity of these sectors catches up with the level of the euro area at a rate of 4% a year, the Balassa-Samuelson effect implies a real exchange rate appreciation of 2% a year, which may be achieved through nominal exchange rate appreciation, inflation differentials, or a combination of the two.
39. The impact of a depreciation of the exchange rate on aggregate demand can, however, be negative in a strongly indebted country because the depreciation revalues the net debt, causing a negative wealth effect.
40. See the Trade in Value-Added (TiVA) database, available from the OECD's statistical website.
41. Based on bilateral trade data over 1989–2015, Boz et al. (2017) confirm that exchange-rate pass-through is highly dependent on whether exports are denominated in dollar or not. In all cases, there is more pricing to market for those exports directed to the United States than for those directed to smaller countries.
42. See the definition of the output gap in Chapter 1.
43. The model draws on an article by Salant and Henderson (1978) on the exhaustion of gold reserves.
44. The only way to make sure the run cannot happen is for the central bank to hold in its vault as much foreign currency as the total domestic currency in circulation: this is the basis of the currency board system, presented earlier in Section 7.1.
45. The G7 is defined in Chapter 3, p. 125. Financial account convertibility was famously set as a precondition to the Republic of Korea's OECD accession in 1996. One year later, the economy collapsed in a financial crisis.
46. On the Lucas paradox, see Alfaro, Kalemii-Ozcan, and Volosovych (2008), Obstfeld and Taylor (2004), Cohen and Soto (2004).
47. For instance, Malaysia reinstalled capital controls: compulsory transaction through authorized intermediaries to sell ringgit-denominated assets, a 12-month ban on repatriation of ringgit proceeds obtained by foreigners, forced repatriation of ringgits held abroad, and more.
48. Other examples include Bulgaria in June 1997 and Zimbabwe in February 2009.
49. This provision was used only to negotiate on euro adoption by small, non-EU countries such as the Republic of San Marino.

50. This possibility has never been used as of the time of this publication.
51. *Review of the 1977 Decision on Surveillance over Exchange Rate Policies*, available on the IMF website.
52. An important exception being nonsterilized interventions carried out by Japan in the 1990s and early 2000s to avoid excessive yen appreciation. Interventions reached unprecedented amounts in the early 2000s. For instance, the Bank of Japan sold 1,284 billion yen (around US$10 billion) in one trading day on December 10, 2003. Japan stopped intervening in March 2004, as GDP growth had materialized.
53. Despite a coordinated intervention of central banks in 2000 to strengthen the euro.
54. A safe asset is a financial asset whose value stays constant or even increases in cases of market stress. Following the terminology of Chapter 6, a safe asset is relatively information-insensitive.
55. Hence the "exorbitant privilege" of the dollar comes along with an "exorbitant duty" in crisis times.
56. On causes and consequences of global imbalances, see e.g., Bernanke (2005) or Blanchard and Milesi-Ferretti (2011).
57. SDRs were created in 1969 to supplement other reserve instruments. It is a credit on the IMF, which is allocated depending on the quota of each country at the IMF. Countries can convert their SDRs into key currencies in order to finance an external deficit. However, SDRs represent a small share of global reserves: only 1.8% of total foreign exchange reserves in September 2017.
58. Contrasting with the "hegemonic stability" theory of Charles Kindleberger (1981), stating that a unipolar system is more stable because the "hegemon" is ready to pay for global stability.

References

Afonso, A., and D. Furceri (2008), "EMU Enlargement, Stabilization Costs and Insurance Mechanisms," *Journal of International Money and Finance*, 27(2), pp. 169–87.

Aghion, P., P. Bacchetta, R. Rancière, and K. Rogoff (2009), "Exchange Rate Volatility and Productivity Growth: The Role of Financial Development," *Journal of Monetary Economics*, 56, pp. 494–513.

Ahmed, S., M. A. Appendino, and M. Ruta (2015), "Depreciations Without Exports? Global Value Chains and the Exchange Rate Elasticity of Exports," *World Bank Policy Research Working Paper* No. 7390.

Alesina, A., and R. J. Barro (2002), "Currency Unions," *The Quarterly Journal of Economics*, 117(2), pp. 409–36.

Alfaro L., S. Kalemli-Ozcan, and V. Volosovych (2008), "Why Doesn't Capital Flow from Rich to Poor Countries? An Empirical Investigation," *Review of Economics and Statistics*, 90(2), pp. 347–68.

Allard, C., P. K. Brooks, J. C. Bluedorn, F. Bornhorst, F. Ohnsorge, and K. M. Christopherson Puh (2013), "Toward a Fiscal Union for the Euro Area," *IMF Staff Discussion Note*, No.13/9.

Asdrubali, P., B. E. Sørensen, and O. Yosha (1996), "Channels of Interstate Risk Sharing: United States 1963–1990," *Quarterly Journal of Economics*, 111, pp. 1081–110.

Balassa, B. (1964), "The Purchasing Power Doctrine: A Reappraisal," *Journal of Political Economy*, 72, pp. 584–96.

Baldwin, R. (2006), "The Euro's Trade Effects," *ECB Working Paper* No.594, March.

Bank of International Settlements (BIS) (2016), *Triennal Survey of Foreign Exchange and Derivatives Market Activity*.

Bayoumi, T., and B. Eichengreen (1994), "Shocking Aspects of EMU," in Torres, F., and F. Giavazzi, eds., *Adjustment and Growth in the European Monetary Union*, Cambridge University Press, pp. 193–235.

Bayoumi, T., and B. Eichengreen (2017), "Aftershocks of Monetary Unification: Hysteresis with a Financial Twist," *IMF Working Paper* WP/17/55.

Bénassy-Quéré, A. (2016), "The Euro as an International Currency," in Badinger, H., and V. Nitsch, eds., *Handbook of the Economics of European Integration*, Routledge, pp. 82–100.

Bénassy-Quéré, A., and B. Cœuré (2014), *Economie de l'Euro*, 2nd edition, La Découverte.

Bernanke, B. (2005), "The Global Saving Glut and the US Current Account Deficit," Sandridge Lecture, Virginia Association of Economists, Richmond, 10 March.

Beyer, R. C. M., and F. Smets (2015), "Labour Market Adjustments and Migration in Europe and the United States: How Different," *Economic Policy*, October, pp. 643–82

Blanchard, O., and L. Katz (1992), "Regional Evolutions," *Brookings Papers on Economic Activity*, 1992-1, pp. 1–75.

Blanchard, O., and G-M. Milesi-Ferretti (2011), "(Why) Should Current Account Balances Be Reduced?" *IMF Staff Discussion Note* 11/03.

Blanchard, O., and D. Quah (1989), "The Dynamic Effect of Aggregate Demand and Supply Disturbances," *American Economic Review*, 79, pp. 655–73.

Boz, E., G. Gopinath, and M. Plagborg-Møller (2017), "Global Trade and the Dollar," *NBER Working Paper*, 23988.

Branson, W., H. Haltunen, and P. Masson (1977), "Exchange Rates in the Short Run," *European Economic Review*, 10, pp. 395–402.

Bruno, V., and H. S. Shin (2015), "Capital Flows and the Risk-Taking Channel of Monetary Policy," *Journal of Monetary Economics*, 71, pp. 119–32.

Caballero, R. J., E. Farhi, and P.-O. Gourinchas (2015), "Global Imbalances and Currency Wars at the ZLB," *NBER Working Paper*, 21670.

Calvo, G., and C. Reinhart (2002), "Fear of Floating," *Quarterly Journal of Economics*, 117, pp. 379–408.

Cassel, G. (1921), *The World's Monetary Problems*, Constable and Co.

Catão, L. A. V., and G.-M. Milesi-Ferretti (2014), "External Liabilities and Crises," *Journal of International Economics*, 94, 18–32.

Cavallari, L., and S. d'Addona (2013), "Nominal and Real Volatility as Determinants of FDI," *Applied Economics*, 45, pp. 2603–2610.

Cavallo, A., and A. Ribba (2015), "Common Macroeconomic Shocks and Business Cycle Fluctuations in Euro Area Countries," *International Review of Economics and Finance*, 38, pp. 377–392.

Cerrato, M., H. Kalyoncu, N. H. Naqvi, and C. Tsoukis (2015), "Current Accounts in the Long Run and the Intertemporal Approach: A Panel Data Investigation," *The World Economy*, 38(2), 340–59.

Chinn, M., and H. Ito (2008), "A New Measure of Financial Openness," *Journal of Comparative Policy Analysis*, 10, pp. 309–22.

Chițu, L., B. Eichengreen, B., and A. Mehl (2014), "When Did the Dollar Overtake Sterling as the Leading International Currency? Evidence from the Bonds Markets," *Journal of Development Economics*, 111(2014), 225–45.

Clarida, R., J. Galí, and M. Gertler (2002), "A Simple Framework for International Monetary Policy Analysis," *Journal of Monetary Economics*, 49, pp. 879–904.

Clark, P. B. (1973), "Uncertainty, Exchange Risk, and the Level of International Trade," *Western Economic Journal*, 11(3), pp. 302–313.

Clark, P., and R. MacDonald (1998), "Exchange Rate and Economic Fundamentals: A Methodological Comparison of BEERs and FEERs," *IMF Working Paper*, No. 98/00.

Cline, W. R. (2015), "Estimates of Fundamental Equilibrium Exchange Rates May 2015," *Peterson Institute for International Economics Policy Brief*, PB 15-8, May.

Cline, W. R., and J. Williamson (2012), "Estimates of Fundamental Equilibrium Exchange Rates, May 2012", *Peterson Institute for International Economics Policy Brief*, 12–14, May.

Cœuré, B. (2017), "The International Dimension of the ECB's Asset Purchase Programme," speech at the Foreign Exchange Contact Group meeting, 11 July.

Cohen, D., and M. Soto (2004), "Why Are Poor Countries Poor?" *CEPR Discussion Paper*, DP 3528.

Ćorić, B., and G. Pugh (2010), "The Effects of Exchange Rate Variability on International Trade: A Meta-Regression Analysis," *Applied Economics*, 42, pp. 2631–2644.

Corsetti, G. (1998), "Interpreting the Asian Financial Crisis: Open Issues in Theory and Policy," *Asian Development Review*,16, pp. 1–47.

Dam, K. (1982), *The Rules of the Game: Reform and Evolution of the International Monetary System*, University of Chicago Press.

Dao, M., Furceri, D., and P. Loungani (2014), "Regional Labor Market Adjustments in the United States and Europe," *IMF Working Paper*, No. 14/26.

Daude, C., E. Levy Yeyati, and A. J. Nagengast (2016), "On the Effectiveness of Exchange Rate Interventions in Emerging Markets," *Journal of International Money and Finance*, 64, pp. 239–261.

De Grauwe, P. (2014), *Economics of the Monetary Union*, 11th edition, Oxford University Press.

De Gregorio, J., S. Edwards, and R. Valdés (2000), "Controls on Capital Inflows: Do They Work?" *Journal of Development Economics*, 63(1), 59–83, October.

Demers, M. (1991), "Investment Under Uncertainty, Irreversibility and the Arrival of Information over Time," *Review of Economic Studies*, 58, pp. 333–350.

Dominguez, K., and J. Frankel (1993), *Does Foreign Exchange Intervention Work?* Institute for International Economics.

Eichengreen, B. (1992), *Golden Fetters: The Gold Standard and the Great Depression, 1919–39*, Oxford University Press.

Eichengreen B. (1997), *Globalizing Capital: A History of the International Monetary System*, Princeton University Press.

Eichengreen, B. (2010), "Managing a Multiple Reserve Currency World," *Insights*, 8, 29–33.
Eichengreen, B. (2013), "Currency War or International Policy Coordination?" *Journal of Policy Modeling*, vol. 35(3), pp. 425–433 .
Eichengreen, B., and M. Kawai (2014), "Issues for Renminbi Internationalization: An Overview," *ADBI Working Paper* 454.
Eichengreen, B., J. Tobin, and C. Wyplosz (1995), "Two Cases for Sand in the Wheels of International Finance, Editorial Note," *The Economic Journal*, 105, pp. 162–72.
Ethier, W. (1973), "International Trade and the Forward Exchange Market," *American Economic Review*, 63(3), 494–503.
European Central Bank (2015), *The International Role of the Euro*, Biennial Report, July.
European Central Bank (2017), *The International Role of the Euro*, Biennial Report, July.
Farhi, E., P.-O. Gourinchas, and H. Rey (2011), "Reforming the International Monetary System," *CEPR Report*.
Feenstra, R. C., and A. M. Taylor (2015), *International Macroeconomics*, MacMillan.
Feldstein, M., and C. Horioka (1980), "Domestic Saving and International Capital Flows," *Economic Journal*, 90, pp. 314–29.
Flood, R., and P. Garber (1984), "Collapsing Exchange Rate Regimes: Some Linear Examples," *Journal of International Economics*, 17, pp. 1–13.
Fontagné, L., and M. Freudenberg (1999), "Endogenous Symmetry of Shocks in a Monetary Union," *Open Economies Review*, 10, pp. 263–87.
Fontagné, L., T. Mayer, and G. Ottaviano (2009), "Of Markets, Products and Prices: The Effects of the Euro on European Firms," EFIGE Report, Bruegel Blueprint, January.
Frankel, J., and A. Rose (1998), "The Endogeneity of the Optimum Currency Area Criteria," *Economic Journal*, 108, pp. 1009–26.
Frankel, J. A., and G. Saravelos (2012), "Can Leading Indicators Assess Country Vulnerability? Evidence from the 2008–09 Global Financial Crisis," *Journal of International Economics*, 87(2), pp. 216–31.
Fratzscher, M. (2008), "Communication and Exchange Rate Policy," *Journal of Macroeconomics*, 30(4), pp. 1651–72.
Frenkel, M., Pierdzioch, C., and G. Stadtmann (2001), "The Interventions of the European Central Bank: Effects, Effectiveness and Policy Implications," working paper, Koblenz University.
Friedman, M. (1953), "The Case for Flexible Exchange Rates," in *Essays in Positive Economics*, University of Chicago Press, pp. 157–203.
Furceri, D., and A. Zdzienicka (2015), "The Euro Area Crisis: Need for a Supranational Fiscal Risk Sharing Mechanism?" *Open Economies Review*, 26, pp. 683–710.
Garber, P., and M. Taylor (1995), "Sand in the Wheels of Foreign Exchange Markets: A Sceptical Note," *Economic Journal*, 105, pp. 173–80.
Garman, M., and S. Kohlhagen (1983), "Foreign Currency Option Values," *Journal of International Money and Finance*, 2, pp. 231–37.
Gaulier, G., A. Lahrèche-Révil, and I. Méjean (2008), "Exchange Rate Pass Through at the Product Level," *Canadian Journal of Economics*, 41, pp. 425–49.
Ghosh, A. R. (2014), "A Comparison of Exchange Rate Regime Choice in Emerging Markets with Advanced and Low Income Nations for 1999–2011," *International Review of Economics and Finance*, 33, 358–370.

Ghosh, A. R., and M. S. Qureshi (2016), "What's In a Name? That Which We Call Capital Controls," *IMF Working Paper* WP/16/25.

Ghosh, A. R., M. S. Qureshi, and C. G. Tsangarides (2014), "On the Value of Words: Inflation and Fixed Exchange Rate Regimes," *IMF Economic Review*, 62(2), pp. 288–322.

Giavazzi, F., and M. Pagano (1992), "The Advantage of Tying One's Hands: EMS Discipline and Central Bank Credibility," *European Economic Review*, 32 (5), pp. 1055–75.

Gopinath, G. (2017), "Rethinking Macroeconomic Policy: International Economy Issues," Perterson Institute for International Economics, 10 October.

Gopinath, G., O. Itskhoki, and R. Rigobon (2010), "Currency Choice and Exchange Rate Pass-Through," *American Economic Review*, 100(1), pp. 304–36.

Gourinchas, P.-O., and O. Jeanne (2006), "The Elusive Gains from International Financial Integration," *Review of Economic Studies*, 73, pp. 715–41.

Gourinchas, P.-O., and H. Rey (2007), "From World Banker to World Venture Capitalist: US External Adjustment and the Exorbitant Privilege," in Clarida, R., ed., *G-7 Current Account Imbalances: Sustainability and Adjustment*. University of Chicago Press, pp. 11–55.

Gourinchas, P.-O., and H. Rey (2016), "Real Interest Rates, Imbalances and the Curse of Regional Safe Asset Providers at the Zero Lower Bound," paper prepared for the ECB Forum on Central Banking, Sintra, June.

Gourinchas P.-O., H. Rey, and N. Govillot (2010), "Exorbitant Privilege and Exorbitant Duty," Discussion Paper No. 10-E-20, Institute for Monetary and Economic Studies, Bank of Japan.

Gräb, J., and F. Lafarguette (2015), "The Role of Currency Invoicing for the International Transmission of Exchange Rate Movements," in *The International Role of the Euro*, European Central Bank, pp. 44–54.

Haile, M. G., and G. Pugh (2013), "The Effects of Exchange Rate Variability on International Trade: A Meta-regression Analysis," *The Journal of International Trade and Economic Development*, 22(3), pp. 321–350.

Hooper, P., and S. W. Kohlagen (1978), "The Effects of Exchange Rate Uncertainty on the Prices and Volume of International Trade," *Journal of International Economics*, 8, pp. 43–511.

International Monetary Fund (1997), "Capital Flows to Emerging Countries: A Historical Perspective," in *International Capital Markets: Developments, Prospects and Key Policy Issues*, September.

International Monetary Fund (2012), *The Liberalization and Management of Capital Flows: An Institutional View*.

International Monetary Fund (2015), "Exchange Rates and Trade Flows: Disconnected?" *World Economic Outlook*, pp. 105-142.

International Monetary Fund (2016a), "Adequacy of the Global Financial Safety Net," IMF Staff report, March.

International Monetary Fund (2016b). *Annual Report on Exchange Arrangements and Exchange* Restrictions, October.

Ivashina, V., D. S. Scharfstein, and J. C. Stein (2015), "Dollar Funding and the Lending Behavior of Global Banks," *Quarterly Journal of Economics*, 130 (3), 1241–81.

Jeanne, O. (1996), "Les modèles de crises de change: un essai de synthèse en relation avec la crise du franc de 1992–1993," *Économie et Prévision*, no. 123–124.

Kaminsky, G., S. Lizondo, and C. Reinhart (1998), "Leading Indicators of Currency Crises," *IMF Staff Papers*, no. 45, pp. 1–48.

Kenen, P. (1969), "The Optimum Currency Area: An Eclectic View," in Mundell, R., and A. Swoboda, eds., *Monetary Problems of the International Economy*, University of Chicago Press, pp. 41–60.

Keynes, J. M. (1936/2007), *The General Theory of Employment, Interest and Money*. Macmillan.

Kindleberger, C. (1981), "Dominance and Leadership in the International Economy," *International Studies Quarterly*, 25(2), pp. 242–54.

Klein, M. W., and J. C. Shambaugh (2015), "Rounding the Corners of the Policy Trilemma: Sources of Monetary Policy Autonomy," *American Economic Journal: Macroeconomics*, 7(4), pp. 33–66.

Krugman, P. (1979), "A Model of Balance of Payments Crises," *Journal of Money, Credit and Banking*, 11, pp. 311–24.

Krugman, P. (1987), "Pricing to Market when the Exchange Rate Changes," in Arndt, A., and J. Richardson, eds., *Real Financial Linkages Among Open Economies*, MIT Press, pp. 49–70.

Krugman, P. (1992), *Currencies and Crises*, MIT Press.

Krugman, P. (1993), "Lessons of Massachusetts for EMU," in Torres, F., and F. Giavazzi, eds., *Adjustment and Growth in the European Monetary Union*, Cambridge University Press, pp. 241–61.

Krugman, P. (1999), "Balance Sheets, the Transfer Problem and Financial Crises," *International Tax and Public Finance*, 6, pp. 459–472.

Kumar, S., and B. B. Rao (2011), "A Time-series Approach to the Feldstein–Horioka Puzzle with Panel Data from the OECD Countries," *The World Economy*, 34(3), pp. 473–85.

Kwan, C. H. (2001), *Yen Bloc: Towards Economic Integration in Asia*, Brookings Institution Press.

Lane, P., and G. M. Milesi-Ferretti (2007), "The External Wealth of Nations Mark II: Revised and Extended Estimates of Foreign Assets and Liabilities, 1970–2004," *Journal of International Economics*, 73, pp. 223–50.

Lane, P., and G.-M. Milesi-Ferretti (2009), "Where Did All the Borrowing Go? A Forensic Analysis of the US External Position," *Journal of the Japanese and International Economies*, 23(2), 177–99.

Lerner, A. P. (1944), *Economics of Control: Principle of Welfare Economics*, Macmillan.

Lucas, R. (1990), "Why Doesn't Capital Flow from Rich to Poor Countries?" *American Economic Review*, 80, pp. 92–96.

Martin, J., and I. Méjean (2010), "Euro et dispersion des prix à l'exportation," *Economie et Statistique*, 435–36, p. 49–64.

Mateos y Lago, I., R. Duttagupta, and R. Goyal (2009), "The Debate on the International Monetary System," *IMF Staff Position Note* 09/26.

McKinnon, R. (1963), "Optimum Currency Areas," *American Economic Review*, 53, pp. 717–25.

Menkhoff, L. (2013), "Foreign Exchange Intervention in Emerging Markets: A Survey of Empirical Studies," *The World Economy*, 36(9), pp. 1187–208.

Mohanty, M. S., and P. Turner (2006), "Foreign Exchange Reserve Accumulation in Emerging Markets: What are the Domestic Implications?" *BIS Quarterly Review*, September, pp. 39–52.

Mundell, R. (1961), "A Theory of Optimum Currency Areas," *American Economic Review*, 51, pp. 657–65.

Mundell, R. (1973), "Uncommon Arguments for Common Currencies," in Johnson, H., and A. Swoboda, eds., *The Economics of Common Currencies*, George Allen & Unwin, pp.114–32.

Mussa, M. (2000), "Factors Driving Global Economic Integration," *Federal Reserve Bank of Kansas City Proceedings*, pp. 9–55.

Nikolov, P. (2016), "Cross-border Risk Sharing after Asymmetric Shocks: Evidence from the Euro Area and the United States," *Quarterly Report on the Euro Area* 15(2), pp. 7–15.

Obstfeld, M. (1994), "The Logic of Currency Crises," Banque de France, *Cahiers économiques et monétaires*, 43, pp. 189–213, and *NBER Working Paper*, 4640.

Obstfeld M. (2009), "International Finance and Growth in Developing Countries: What Have we Learned?" *NBER Working Paper,* 14691.

Obstfeld, M. (2015), "Trilemma and Trade-offs: Living with Financial Globalization," *BIS Working Paper* No. 480, January.

Obstfeld, M., and K. Rogoff (1999), *Foundations of International Macroeconomics*, MIT Press.

Obstfeld, M., and K. Rogoff (2007), "The Unsustainable US Current Account Position Revisited," in Clarida, R., ed., *G7 Current Account Imbalances: Sustainability and Adjustment*, University of Chicago Press, chapter 9.

Obstfeld, M., J. C. Shambaugh, A. M. Taylor (2005), "The Trilemma in History: Tradeoffs Among Exchange Rates, Monetary Policies, and Capital Mobility," *Review of Economics and Statistics*, 87(3), pp. 423–38.

Obstfeld, M., and A. Taylor (2004), *Global Capital Markets: Integration, Crisis, and Growth,* Cambridge University Press.

Ostry, J. D., A. R. Ghosh, M. Chamon, and M. S. Qureshi (2012), "Tools for Managing Financial-Stability Risks from Capital Inflows," *Journal of International Economics*, 88(2): 407–21.

Ostry, J. D., A. R. Ghosh, K. Habermeier, M. Chamon, M. S. Qureshi, and D. B. S. Reinhardt (2010), "Capital Inflows: The Role of Controls," *IMF Staff Position Note* SPN/10/04, February 19.

Ostry, J. D., A. R. Ghosh, K. Habermeier, L. Laeven, M. Chamon, A. Kokenyne, and M. S. Qureshi (2011), "Managing Capital Inflows: What Tools to Use?" *IMF Staff Position Note* SPN/11/06, April 5.

Pindyck, R. (1991), "Irreversibility, Uncertainty, and Investment," *Journal of Economic Literature*, 29, 1110–48.

Poole, W. (1970), "Optimal Choice of Monetary Policy Instruments in a Simple Stochastic Macro Model," *Quarterly Journal of Economics*, 84, pp. 197–216.

Rey, H. (2013), "Dilemma not Trilemma: The Global Financial Cycle and Monetary Policy Independence," *Proceedings - Economic Policy Symposium - Jackson Hole, Federal Reserve of Kansas City Economic Symposium*, pp. 285–333.

Rey, H. (2016), "International Channels of Transmission of Monetary Policy and the Mundellian Trilemma," *IMF Economic Review*, 64(1), pp. 6–35.

Robinson, J. (1947), *Essays in the Theory of Employment*, Part III, "The Foreign Exchanges," Blackwell.

Rogoff, K. (1996), "The Purchasing Power Parity Puzzle," *Journal of Economic Literature*, 34, pp. 647–68.

Rogoff, K., K. A. Froot, and M. Kim (2001), "The Law of One Price over 700 Years," *IMF Working Paper* 01/174, November.

Rueff, J. (1965), "The Role and the Rule of Gold: An Argument," Interview by F. Hirsch, *Essays in International Finance*, No. 47, Princeton University, June.

Salant, S., and D. Henderson (1978), "Market Anticipation of Government Policies and the Price of Gold," *Journal of Political Economy*, 86, pp. 627–48.

Samuelson, P. (1964), "Theoretical Notes on Trade Problems," *The Review of Economics and Statistics*, 46, February, pp. 145–54.

Sarno, L., and M. Taylor (2001), "Official Intervention in the Foreign Exchange Market: Is It Effective and, If So, How Does It Work?" *Journal of Economic Literature*, 39, pp. 839–68.

Shambaugh, J. C. (2004), "The Effects of Fixed Exchange Rates on Monetary Policy," *Quarterly Journal of Economics*, 119(1), pp. 300–51.

Sørensen, B. E., and O. Yosha (1998), "International Risk-Sharing and European Monetary Unification," *Journal of International Economics* 45(2), pp. 211–38.

Stein, J. (1994), "The Natural Real Exchange Rate of the US Dollar and Determinants of Capital Flows," in Williamson, J., ed., *Estimating Equilibrium Exchange Rates*, Peterson Institute for International Economics, pp. 133–176.

Stoffels, N., and C. Tille (2007), "Why Are Switzerland's Foreign Assets so Low? The Growing Financial Exposure of a Small Open Economy," *Federal Reserve Board of New York Staff Reports*, 283.

Summers, L. (1988), "Tax policy and International Competitiveness," in Frenkel, J., ed., *International Aspects of Fiscal Policy*, University of Chicago Press, pp. 349–375.

Taglioni, D. (2002), "Exchange Rate Volatility as a Barrier to Trade: New Methodologies and Recent Evidence," *Economie Internationale*, 89–90, pp. 227–59.

Tapsoba, S. (2009), "West African Monetary Integration and Interstates Risk-Sharing," *Journal of Economic and Monetary Integration*, 9(1), pp. 31–50.

Tobin, J. (1958), "Liquidity Preference as Behaviour Towards Risk," *Review of Economic Studies*, 25, pp. 65–86.

Tobin, J. (1974), *The New Economics One Decade Older*, Princeton University Press.

Triffin, R. (1960), *Gold and Dollar Crisis*, Yale University Press.

Williamson, J. (1983), *The Exchange Rate System*, Institute for International Economics.

Yiping, H., D. Wang, and G. Fan (2015), "Paths to a Reserve Currency: Renminbi Internationalization and Its Implications," in Eichengreen, B., and M. Kawai, eds., *Renminbi Internationalization: Achievements, Prospects, and Challenges*, Asian Development Bank Institute, and Brookings Institution.

Zhou, X. (2009), "Reform of the International Monetary System," essay posted on the website of the People's Bank of China, 9 April.

8

Tax Policy

> Taxation without representation is tyranny.
>
> James Otis (1725–83), US lawyer and politician at the time of the American Revolution

> A common contribution is essential for the maintenance of the public forces and for the cost of administration. This should be equitably distributed among all the citizens in proportion to their means.
>
> French Declaration of the Rights of Man and of the Citizen, Article 13, 1789

Governments seldom charge for their services. Except in specific areas such as museums, swimming pools, or universities, these services are generally provided free of charge. Think about scientific research, defense, or diplomacy.

Those are public goods (see Chapter 2); it is therefore impossible to identify precisely which citizens benefit from them and to let them pay for their consumption. Such *government services*[1] have to be financed through *taxation* (i.e., compulsory contributions by households or corporations).

Not all tax-financed government services are public goods. Think of schooling: it would be possible for the government to charge for its provision, but the common practice is to finance it at least partly through taxation. It is by their vote that citizens can express preferences regarding the level and quality of public services provision and the corresponding level of taxes.

The problem is that taxes generally distort relative prices. For instance, the personal income tax (PIT) is paid by households on their labor income. This increases the relative price of labor as compared to leisure and may therefore change the labor supply. Such distortions may affect welfare and gross domestic product (GDP) growth. Consequently, there is a trade-off between the provision of public goods (which in many cases, such as education, security, or infrastructure building, is expected to have a positive impact on welfare and growth) and the desire to reduce taxation in order to limit price distortions.

From a pure efficiency standpoint, public services should be financed through *lump sum taxes* (i.e., taxes that are levied in equal amounts on every citizen independently of their activity, consumption, or income) because such taxes do not distort work, saving, and consumption decisions. However, such taxation (experimented with by Margaret Thatcher's government in 1979 through the so-called *poll tax*[2]) is questionable from an equity standpoint since the poor pay relatively more as a percentage of their income than the wealthy. In order for the burden of taxation to be distributed in an equitable way, and even more so when income redistribution is a policy objective, taxes have to be proportional or more than proportional to income, which inevitably introduces economic distortions.

Because it is at the heart of the efficiency–equity trade-off, and because it is the simplest way to redistribute wealth among citizens, tax policy has always and everywhere been hotly politicized, often at the cost of overlooking essential economic considerations. Tax policy is a matter for political decision and is in all democracies a prerogative of parliaments. As we shall show in this chapter, though, economic analysis can greatly contribute to the design of efficient taxation systems.

8.1. Issues

8.1.1. What is taxation about?

Tax policy consists in setting, within the annual budget, the *rate* and the *base* of each tax. For instance, the government can decide to increase the consumption tax by one percentage point (a decision on the rate) or to exempt some items from this tax (a decision on the base). *Tax revenues* depend on the combination of rates and bases. It is possible to maintain a given level of revenues through simultaneously cutting the rate and broadening the base (this has been the general trend recently, as we shall see). In most cases, choices on the rate and on the base interact: a higher tax rate tends to reduce the tax base. Additionally, tax bases generally depend on economic activity: for instance, for a given definition of rates and bases, a downturn in, say, consumption spending will automatically reduce the income accruing to consumption taxes. Hence, tax revenues are often difficult to predict.

a) Why do governments tax?

Tax policy is at the crossroads between the three functions of economic policy identified by Richard Musgrave and listed in Chapter 1:

- *Allocation*. Taxation affects relative prices between goods and services, labor and leisure, labor and capital, and the like. In so doing, it creates *price distortions*: for example, a tax on imports increases the price of foreign goods relative to the domestic ones. Only lump sum taxes are nondistortionary, but they are few. In a perfect market economy (i.e., where relative price adjustments maintain an optimum allocation of resources; cf. the first theorem of welfare discussed in Chapter 1), taxes would typically be detrimental to economic efficiency. However, the presence of market imperfections modifies this diagnosis. For instance, taxation makes it possible to correct externalities such as air pollution: without taxation, industries would pollute more than what is socially optimal. Taxation also makes it possible to finance public goods that would not be spontaneously produced by the markets. Last, it can play a *paternalistic* role by protecting private agents from their own errors. Taxes on alcohol and cigarettes are examples of such paternalist taxes, sometimes referred to as *sin taxes*.
- *Distribution*. Income taxation modifies the distribution of income between rich and poor, between families and single individuals, or between generations. Capital taxation (either at the firm or at the household level) and *social insurance contributions* (or *social security contributions*)[3] (levied on labor) affect the relative returns of capital and labor. Distributional effects can be involuntary but are also sought by governments when the market equilibrium is regarded as contrary to equity. Since the French revolution of 1789, it has been increasingly admitted that taxation should be either *proportional* to income or *progressive* (more than proportional, meaning that the rich pay relatively more in proportion of their income) but not *regressive* (less than proportional, meaning that the rich pay relatively less), as was often the case previously.[4]

- *Stabilization*: As shown in Chapter 4, a lower tax burden during a cyclical downturn helps sustain the demand for goods and services, and, conversely, higher taxes during a boom slow down demand, alleviating upward pressures on prices. Automatic stabilization (i.e., stabilization performed at constant tax rates through the endogenous adjustment of tax bases) is usually distinguished from discretionary stabilization through decisions to change tax rates and bases countercyclically. However, constraints on public finances as well as political pressures can lead the government to raise tax rates during economic downturns and reduce them when the economy is booming. Such procyclical policies accentuate, rather than dampen, business cycles. The stabilization role of tax policy, already discussed in Chapter 4, will not be further addressed in this chapter.

These three functions of taxation are closely interconnected and often give rise to trade-offs. For instance, automatic stabilizers (stabilization function) are larger in countries that have higher levels of taxation designed to redistribute more income among the residents (redistribution function) or to produce more government services (allocation). Typically, automatic stabilizers are larger in the euro area than in the United States. A progressive income tax reduces income inequalities across households (redistribution), but it also reduces the incentive to work and therefore affects economic efficiency (allocation). A tax on cigarettes reduces diseases and increases tax revenues (allocation) but generally has regressive effects, meaning that the poor pay relatively more.

b) How much?

During earlier historical periods, taxation was almost exclusively determined by wars: in peacetime, taxes would represent a very low share of national income, whereas kings and emperors would raise taxes to finance wars, whatever the social consequences. The beginning of the twentieth century still followed this pattern, with taxation representing less than 10% of GDP before World War I but reaching or even exceeding 50% of GDP for some belligerents during each of the two world wars. In the United States, the top marginal income tax rate reached 77% in 1918 and 94% in 1945, and the tax base was greatly extended, whereas only 2% of the population paid this tax in 1915.[5]

Between World Wars I and II, the decline in taxation was contradicted by the birth of the *welfare state* (i.e., the system of social protection). Compulsory health and old-age insurance had started to develop in Germany in the late nineteenth century under Chancellor Bismarck and had spread to other European countries (but not to the United States). Coverage was extended in the twentieth century. In the United States, the New Deal of Franklin Delano Roosevelt introduced federal social programs that contributed to a significant rise in federal taxes. The trend accelerated after World War II with the introduction of comprehensive social insurance regimes covering unemployment, aging, health, and poverty risks. These systems involved a steady increase in *total taxation* (i.e., in the aggregate burden of taxes in a broad sense, i.e. including social insurance contributions).

In the 1980s, a divide emerged between, on the one hand, the further development of social protection in continental Europe, and on the other hand, a rollback on welfare development in the United States and several other English-speaking countries. Consistently, total taxation continued to rise in continental Europe, while it stabilized around a constant level in the United States and decreased in the United Kingdom. In the late 1990s and in the 2000s, however, some governments such as Canada or Sweden made substantial efforts to stabilize or even curb total taxation, while it rose again in the UK. In several countries, the 2009 global crisis led to an increase in taxation in percent of GDP, both due to the fall in the denominator (GDP) and to the rise in the numerator in an attempt to limit the public deficit (figure 8.1).

Within the European Union, total taxation varies from 25% of GDP in Ireland to 45% in France and 47% in Denmark (figure 8.2). With a few

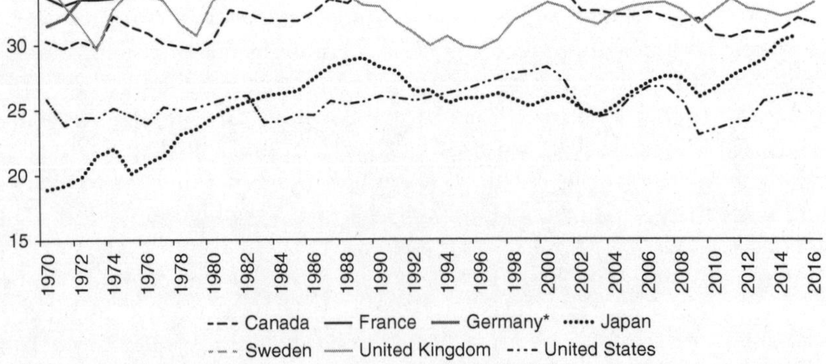

Figure 8.1 Total taxation in percent of gross domestic product (GDP), 1970–2016.
*West Germany before 1991.
OECD Tax Revenue Statistics.

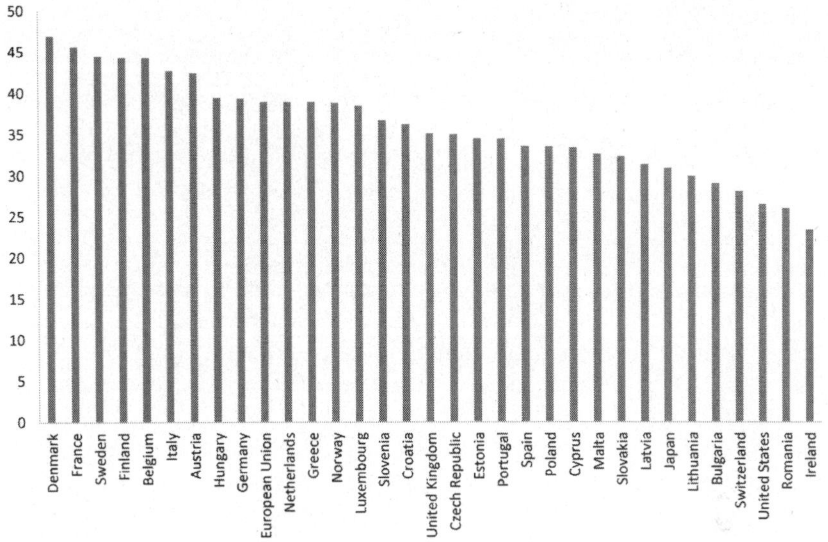

Figure 8.2 Total tax revenues in percent of gross domestic product (GDP), 2016.[a]
[a] Excluding imputed social contributions.
European Commission, Ameco database.

exceptions, Central and Eastern European countries display lower levels of taxation than western countries, while Scandinavian economies display relatively high levels.

The wide dispersion of total taxation rates across countries of similar development levels, even within the EU, points to significant differences in national preferences for the provision of government services: taxation is high in Scandinavian countries where a large range of educational, health, and social services are available for free and financed by taxes, and it is low in Ireland where similar services are provided by the private sector. An indication that this difference can be ascribed to preferences is that differences in total taxation levels have not narrowed over the past decades in spite of the much tighter integration of product and capital markets. Thus, the widespread expectation that globalization would force convergence does not seem to be supported by the data. We will return to this issue when examining the consequences of openness for tax policies.

8.1.2. Typologies of tax systems

Taxes can be classified along three dimensions depending on (i) who collects them, (ii) how they are collected, and (iii) who pays.

a) Who collects taxes?

Taxes can be levied by the central government, state governments (especially in federal countries, e.g., *Länder* in Germany, *cantons* in Switzerland, *provinces* in Argentina), local governments, and social insurance administrations. However, the administration that levies the tax may not be the one that decides on it or benefits from it. For instance, local taxes can be levied by the central tax administration on behalf of local authorities.

Figure 8.3 shows the diversity of tax structures among the countries of the Organization for Economic Cooperation and Development (OECD). In federal countries (like Germany, Switzerland, Spain, or Canada), the central government often receives less than half of total tax receipts. In France, the largest part of the revenue is received by social security funds, whereas in Denmark or in the United Kingdom, social security is managed by the central government, along the lines of the "Beveridgian" system (where social security benefits are funded by general taxation; see later discussion).

The distribution of taxes between the central and local governments raises issues of *tax autonomy* and *tax competition*, in the context of Oates's equivalence discussed in Chapter 3. On the one hand, it is desirable that taxes be raised at the local level to make local governments financially responsible and

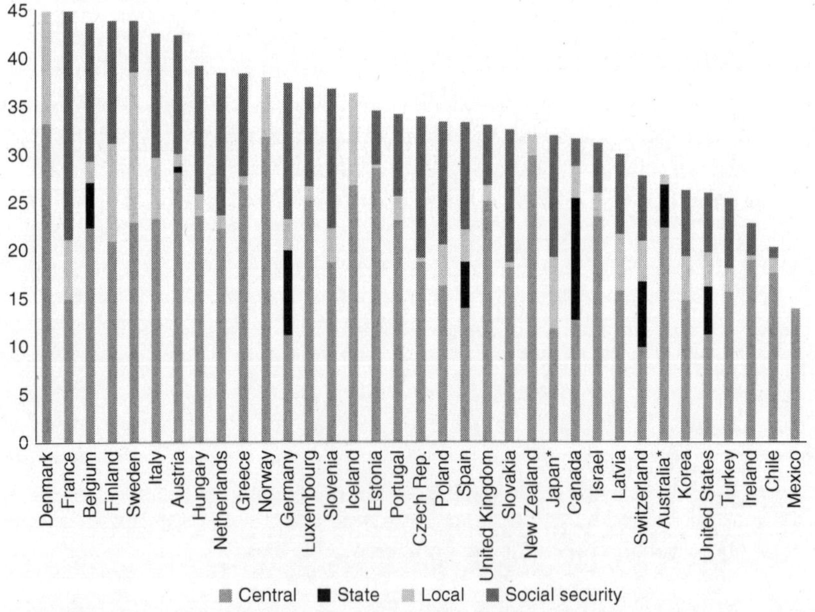

Figure 8.3 Tax revenue received by administrative level, in percent of gross domestic product (GDP), 2016.
* 2015.
OECD Tax revenue Statistics.

to allow them to develop policies that are consistent with local preferences (tax autonomy). On the other hand, there is a risk that autonomy would allow wealthy localities to become even wealthier because they are able to attract more individuals and companies through cutting taxes (tax competition), whereas poor localities would need to raise tax rates because the tax base is limited and because they have higher social expenditures. Central governments therefore frequently organize redistribution across localities. The level of this redistribution is a contentious issue since it affects the trade-off between efficiency (of local public choices) and equity (between localities).

b) How are taxes collected?

Another classification of taxes relies on the way they are collected.

A *direct tax* is a tax levied on income (or wealth) whatever the use of this income (or wealth). Direct taxes include:

- For households, the *personal income tax* (a tax on labor and capital income that can be paid directly by the households or levied by the employers), *inheritance taxes, property taxes,*[6] and *wealth taxes*;
- For companies, the *corporate income tax,*[7] and local business taxes such as the German *Gewerbesteuer*, the French *Contribution économique territoriale* or the Italian *Imposta regionale sulle attività produttive* (IRAP).

In contrast, an *indirect tax* is levied on the use of income, mainly on consumption. Typical examples include taxes levied on imports of goods and services (*import duties*), the US sales tax and the European *value-added tax* (*VAT*),[8] both of which are borne by consumers when they buy a good or a service. *Excise taxes* (i.e., taxes on specific products such as cigarettes or alcohol) are other examples of indirect taxes. Finally, environmental taxes (including energy, transport, and pollution taxes) are also indirect taxes.

The third category of taxes covers *social insurance contributions* that are paid both by employers and employees on the basis of the wage bill. Although they can be considered as direct taxes, social insurance contributions are generally treated separately due to the link between individual contributions and benefits.

Figure 8.4 shows the 2014 structure of taxation in the OECD countries according to this second classification. In Denmark, Australia, New Zealand, and Canada, direct taxes represent 60% or more of taxation. Conversely, Central and Eastern European countries, Greece, and Turkey rely more heavily on indirect taxes.

The disparity of tax systems illustrated by figure 8.4 embodies a differentiation between *Bismarckian systems* (Germany, Austria, France, the Netherlands) and *Beveridgian systems* (the UK, Denmark, Ireland). In

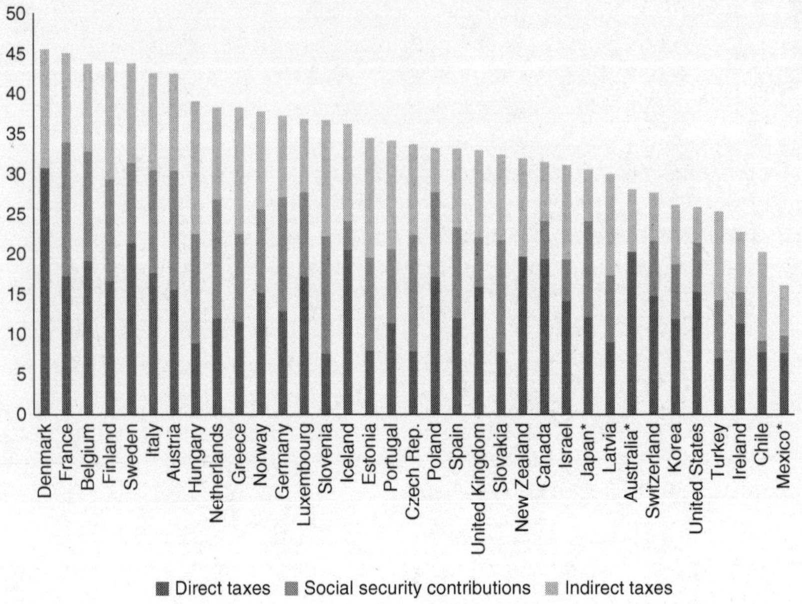

Figure 8.4 Direct[a] and indirect taxes, in percent of gross domestic product (GDP), 2016.

* 2015.

[a] Direct taxes include taxes on payroll and workforce.

OECD.

the first ones, inspired by the scheme introduced by German Chancellor Bismarck in the 1880s, social insurance benefits are treated as deferred wages; they are therefore financed primarily by social contributions based on wages, and each employee knows that what he or she will receive when unemployed or retired will be proportional to his or her contribution. In the second system, introduced in the United Kingdom after William Beveridge's 1941 report, social benefits are viewed as public transfers whose objective is to ensure that the most deprived receive a minimum level of income; they are financed primarily through taxes and there is little link, at the individual level, between contributions and benefits. With time, the contrast between the two schemes has tended to fade away: Beveridgian systems have introduced some insurance schemes, whereas Bismarckian ones have been altered by the capping of unemployment benefits or complemented with redistributive transfers. In some countries, there has also been a shift from social insurance contributions to indirect taxes, notably environmental taxes (Denmark, Sweden), and VAT (Denmark, Germany).

Since the mid-1960s, the share of indirect taxes in total tax revenues has tended to decline in advanced countries, but this aggregate evolution results from the opposite trends of declining excise taxes and rising VAT revenues (figure 8.5). In fact, in a world of mobile capital and labor income bases, VAT has been increasingly regarded as an efficient, nondistortionary way to raise revenues. Another evolution since the 1980s has been a fall in the share of PIT revenues (over total tax revenues) from 30% in 1985 to 24% in 2015. Governments in many countries have reduced politically sensitive personal income taxes while increasing both social insurance contributions and VAT rates.

As highlighted by Tony Atkinson (1977), unlike indirect taxes, direct taxes can be personalized (i.e., adapted to the taxpayer's characteristics). For instance, the PIT depends on the household's characteristics and on the nature of income received (labor income, capital income, pensions, or social transfers). Similarly, the corporate income tax (CIT) depends on taxable profit that takes into account recent investment or R&D expenditures; in some countries, the tax rate is also different depending on the size of the company or on the use of profit (whether it is distributed as dividends or reinvested in the company). In contrast, indirect taxes are levied on anonymous transactions: any taxpayer

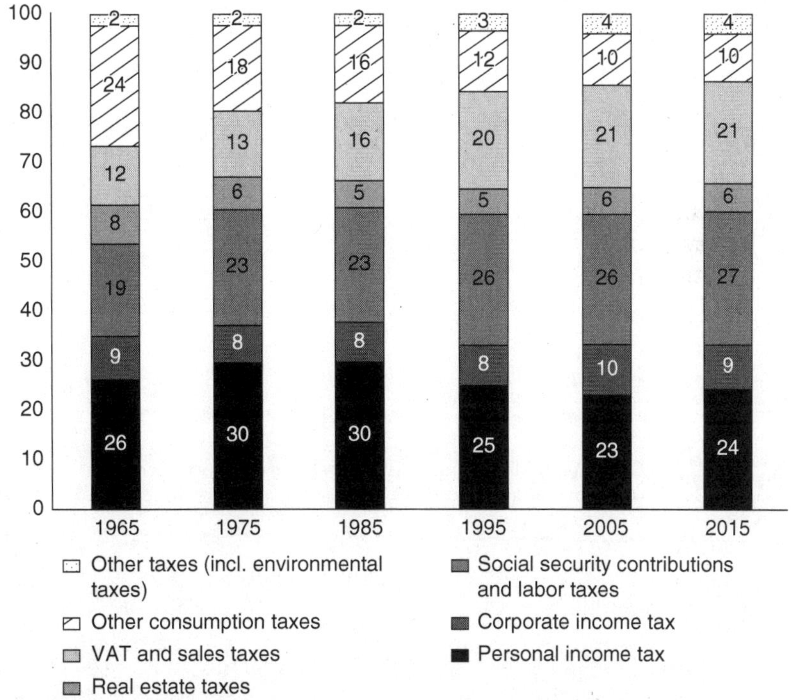

Figure 8.5 Structure of taxation in OECD countries (unweighted average), in percent of total tax revenue, 1965–2015.
OECD Tax Revenue Statistics.

thus faces the same tax rate. It follows that only the direct taxes should be used for redistribution purposes.

Indirect taxes are devoted to allocation functions, which consist both in financing the provision of public goods and in correcting market distortions. Note that these two objectives are largely incompatible because what is aimed at is a stable tax base in the first case and a shrinking one in the second. This calls for using distinct instruments: on the one hand, a broad, inelastic base from which revenues can be raised without too many distortions; on the other, an elastic tax base to which a high tax rate can be applied.

c) Who pays?

Economists are generally reluctant to classify taxes according to the person who administratively pays the tax and makes the transfer to the tax administration—the *taxpayer*. For instance, they are not at ease with adding up employers' social contributions and CIT on the grounds that both are paid by corporations. Similarly, they prefer not to aggregate personal income taxes raised on labor income and those raised on capital income. They prefer to attach each tax to its tax base. Accordingly, a third classification of taxes distinguishes three categories: labor, capital and consumption. For instance, labor taxation covers social insurance contributions paid both by employers and employees and lumps them together with the part of personal income taxes paid on labor income.[9]

Figure 8.6 shows the 2015 structure of EU countries' taxation systems across the three tax bases just mentioned. Taxes on labor account for the bulk of between-country differences in total taxation: those countries with the highest total tax burden are also those where labor taxation is the heaviest. The distribution of taxation among the three tax bases also depends on development levels. Developing countries tend to rely more heavily on indirect taxation (see box 8.1).

The question of who pays taxes raises the twin question of who does *not* pay taxes (i.e., that of *tax avoidance*). For 2015, the European Commission estimated the gap between expected and effective revenues from the VAT (the "VAT gap") to be close to 13% of net VAT receipts on average, with large variations across the Member States (up to 37% in Romania, but close to zero in Sweden; see European Commission, 2017a). Part of the VAT gap is related to corporate insolvency or bankruptcy (i.e., companies that are in fact unable to transfer the VAT they have collected from their customers to the tax administration). Part of the gap, however, comes from fraud through unreported sales, failure to register (small businesses), misclassification of commodities (when different rates are applicable), omission of self-deliveries, nonremittance of tax collected (for instance, through strategic bankruptcy), and imported goods not brought into tax.[10]

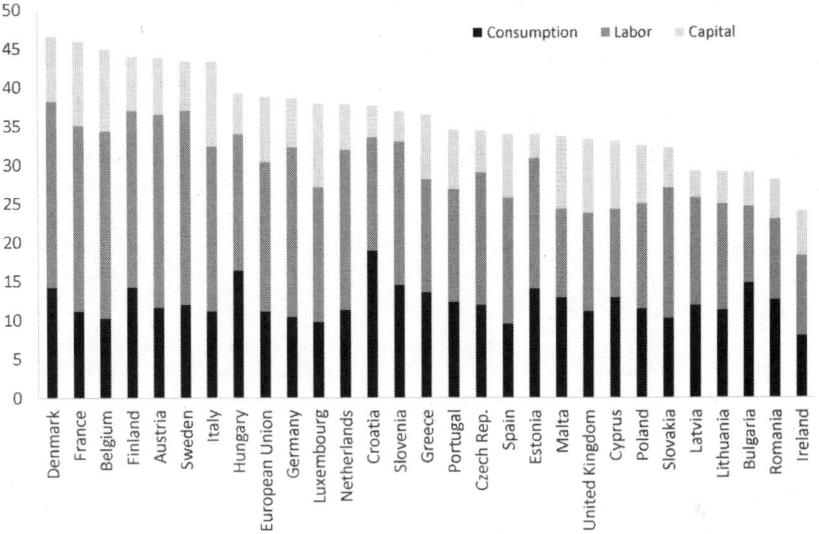

Figure 8.6 Implicit taxation of consumption, labor, and capital in the EU, in percent of gross domestic product (GDP), 2015.
European Commission, *Taxation trends in the European Union*, 2017.

Box 8.1 Taxation in Developing Economies

Developing countries generally display a lower level of total taxation than advanced economies. In West Africa, for instance, total taxation varies from 7% of GDP in Nigeria to 25% in Senegal (IMF figures for year 2015), against 30–50% of GDP in advanced economies. This is in part because taxation in developing countries encounters difficulties arising from low institutional development, corruption, and the large size of the informal sector. Those who hold political power and control natural resources often have the ability to escape taxation.[a] Second, the demand for public services, like education, health, and infrastructure, increases with the level of income, thereby giving rise to higher public spending and taxation. Third, Besley and Persson (2014) have shown that ethnic fractionalization has a significant, negative impact on the ratio of tax revenues to GDP: a poor sense of national identity reduces the ability of the national government to raise taxes.

These weaknesses especially affect direct taxes, in particular the personal income tax (PIT), which barely exists in developing countries. Social insurance contributions are also very limited, which reflects the low development of social protection systems, but also of wage-earning. Correspondingly, indirect taxes, especially import tariffs, often play a central role in tax collection (see figure B8.1.1).

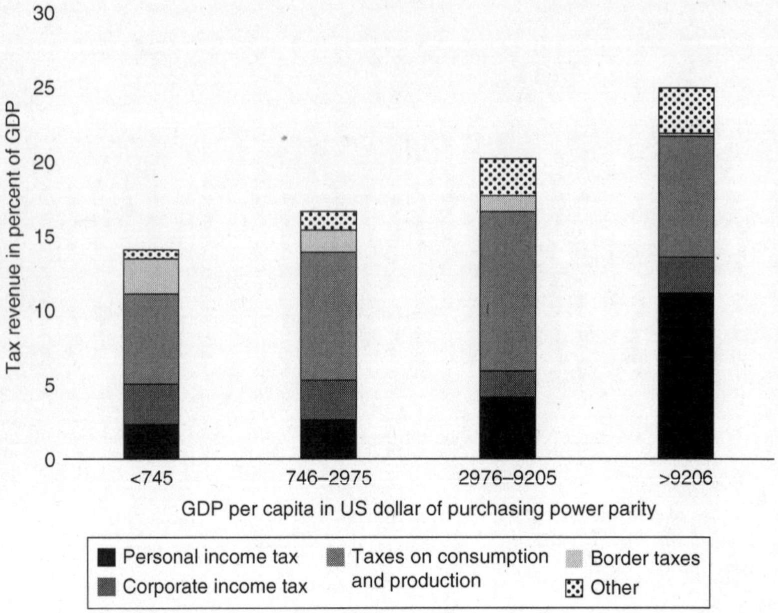

Figure B8.1.1 The tax structure depending on average income per capita, based on years 1996–2001.

Authors, based on Gordon and Li (2009).

a See Fjeldstad and Rakner (2003).

Avoidance also concerns the taxation of wealth and of its returns in relation with tax "havens." For instance, Zucman (2014) estimates that more than 60% of foreign-owned deposits in Switzerland "belong" to the British Virgin Islands, Jersey, and Panama and largely escape residence-based taxation in the country of the ultimate beneficiary. He estimates the tax revenue loss to be US$190 billion globally, and US$75 billion in Europe for 2013. In the area of corporate taxation, too, there is ample empirical evidence that multinational companies organize their legal and financial structures with a view to reducing their tax bill through complex corporate structures involving tax havens and special tax regimes (such as the "double Irish Dutch sandwich" or patent boxes; see, e.g., Fuest et al., 2013). Contrasting with the off-shoring of private wealth, these tax avoidance activities are usually perfectly legal, and some countries actively create loopholes for multinational companies with the objective of attracting tax bases from other countries.

8.1.3 The main trade-offs

As already mentioned, taxation plays a central role along two dimensions of public intervention: it involves a trade-off between redistribution and allocation. The infranational and international mobility of tax bases also raises the question of the extent to which taxation may differ across jurisdictions: there is a second trade-off between differentiation and harmonization.

a) The efficiency–equity trade-off

The first tax policy trade-off is between efficiency and redistribution. It arises because more redistribution requires more taxes that, in turn, are the source of additional distortions.

As presented in Chapter 1, the extent of redistribution through taxes and transfers can be assessed by comparing the Lorenz curve or Gini coefficients based on market income (earnings) to that based on gross income (including social transfers) or disposable income (after tax and transfers). Figure 8.7 shows the evolution of the corresponding Gini coefficients for Finland and the United Kingdom between 2002 and 2015. Market income is somewhat less

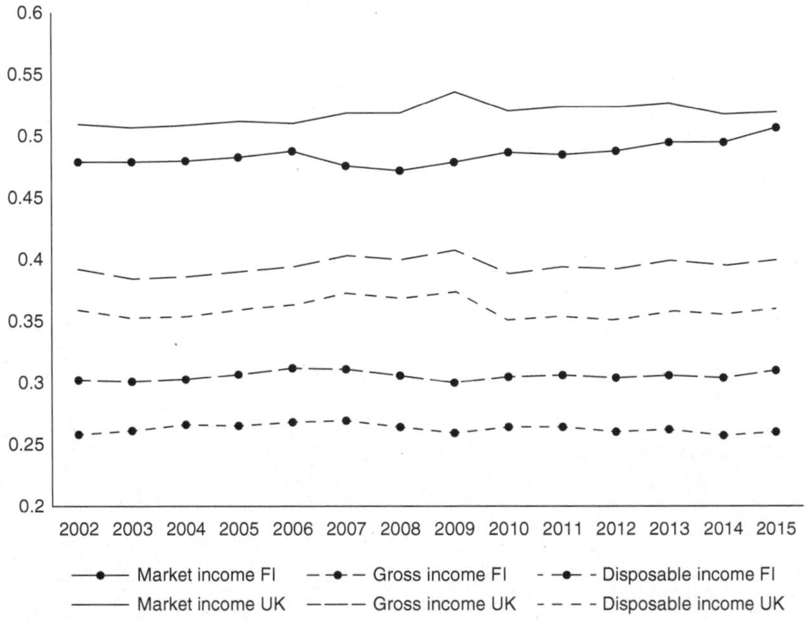

Figure 8.7 Inequalities in Finland and in the United Kingdom, 2002–2015 (Gini coefficient on market income, gross income, and disposable income, see text for definitions).
OECD database, 2017.

equally distributed (the Gini coefficient is higher) in the UK than in Finland, although the inequality in market income in Finland tends to converge to the British level. As expected, in both countries, the distribution of gross income is less unequal than that of market income, and that of disposable income is less unequal than that of gross income. However, the income redistribution is much more important in Finland than in the UK: in 2015, the inequality in disposable income is 48.7% less than that of market income in Finland, while the corresponding figure is only 30.8% in the UK. The graph shows that, over the 2002–2015 period, Finland managed to absorb rising market inequalities through more redistribution.[11]

The degree of redistribution across income deciles depends on two key elements. The first one is the profile of the *average tax rate* (i.e., the ratio between tax payments and income across income deciles): if the average tax rate increases with income, the tax system is deemed *progressive*; if it declines, it is said to be *regressive*; finally, if it is stable, the tax system is simply called *neutral*. The second key element for redistribution is the extent of social benefits, especially *mean-tested transfers* (i.e., conditional on primary income being under a certain threshold).

Redistribution does not occur solely across income levels (vertical redistribution) but also between categories of households; for instance, between single persons and families or between two-parent and single-parent families. This horizontal redistribution aims at correcting income inequalities *per consumption unit*.[12] Targeting redistribution on the poorest families allows the system to combine vertical and horizontal redistribution.

Redistribution through taxation involves an efficiency loss: taxing richer taxpayers more heavily in order to finance transfers to poorer ones may discourage efforts to earn a higher income through participation in the labor force and through longer working hours. In an open economy, heavy taxation may also encourage wealthy households and companies to relocate their tax residence abroad.

In contrast with redistribution, the appropriate variable to assess incentives to work is not the average tax rate, but the *marginal tax rate* (i.e., the fraction of a marginal increase in income that is captured by the tax system). Formally, if $T(R)$ is the tax bill T as a function of pre-tax income R, the marginal rate is $T'(R)$ while the average rate is $T(R)/R$. Most PIT schedules directly specify marginal tax rates per income bracket.

Strikingly, a tax system with a constant marginal rate can be progressive if there is a *basic allowance* (i.e., if the first R_0 units of income are exempted from taxation), which is generally the case for the PIT. Figure 8.8 illustrates this possibility in the case of a flat marginal tax rate of 20% combined with a basic allowance of 1,000 euros. However, it is difficult to achieve significant degree of redistribution through the tax system with a single marginal tax rate, as will be illustrated in Section 8.3.

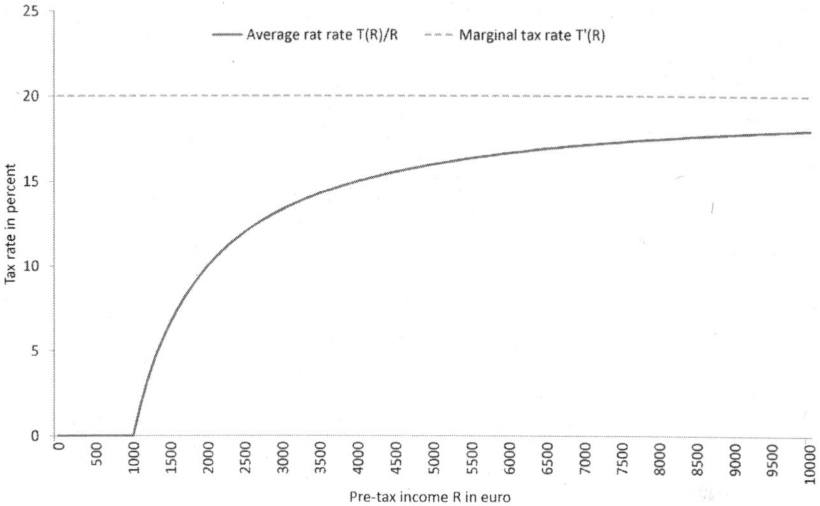

Figure 8.8 Redistribution with a flat marginal tax rate combined with basic allowance.[a]
[a] Flat marginal tax rate of 20% combined with basic allowance of 1,000 euros.
Authors.

In most advanced economies, the combination of increasing PIT rates as a function of income and means-tested transfers at the low end of the income distribution results in *net marginal tax rates*[13] being a U-shaped function of income: very-low-income households receive social transfers (minimum income, housing, and family benefits) that fall when their income rises, resulting in high marginal net tax rates for incomes immediately above the ceilings of means-tested transfers; the marginal rate also increases at the higher end of the income scale due to PIT progressiveness. The net marginal tax rate is often higher for low incomes than for the higher ones: the discouraging effect of the tax and transfer system is more marked for low-income households, thus creating *poverty traps*. This feature is illustrated in figure 8.9 in the case of France in 2010. The graph shows the net marginal tax rate of a single-worker couple with two children. The net marginal rate is close to 70% for households earning one full-time minimum wage. It falls dramatically to 6% at around three times the minimum wage before rising gradually as the income reaches successive income brackets to arrive at a maximum of 41% for the highest income bracket.

There is a consensus among economists that high net marginal rates for low incomes have a negative impact on work incentives and lead to poverty traps. At the other end of the income scale, the debate on the impact of high marginal tax rates on economic efficiency is more open. The direct impact of taxes on the labor supply of the resident labor force is probably limited. The risks of discouraging investment in human capital and of encouraging highly qualified workers to move abroad are more significant.

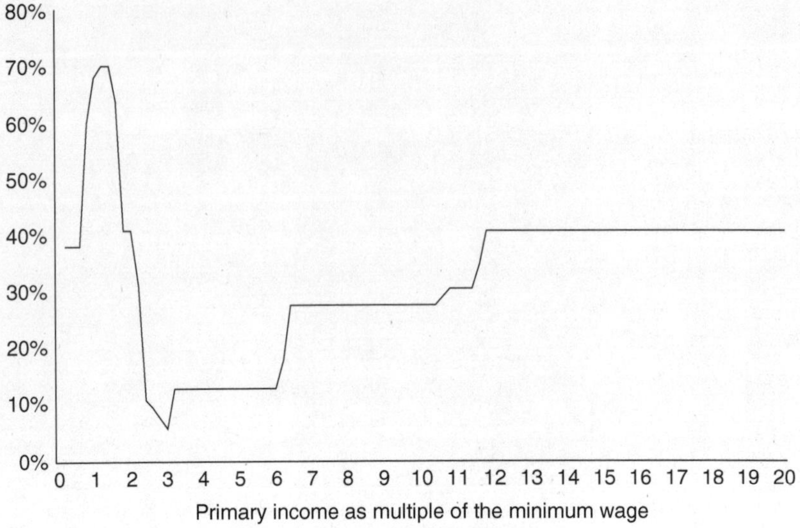

Figure 8.9 The U-shape of the net marginal income tax rate in France, 2010, in percent (single-worker couple with two children).
French Treasury.

b) The differentiation–harmonization trade-off

As evidenced in figures 8.1 and 8.2, the total tax burden varies greatly across advanced economies. Within each country, taxation also varies across jurisdictions (municipalities, states, cantons, provinces, Länder, etc.). These differences reflect differences in preferences in terms of public good provision and of equity. However, the mobility of certain tax bases such as capital or skilled labor makes it difficult for a given jurisdiction to impose a higher tax rate on these bases. Taxation then falls more heavily on less mobile bases such as unskilled labor or consumption. Figure 8.10 illustrates this phenomenon in the EU, where both capital and (skilled) labor are allowed to move freely: from 1995 to 2015, the average top PIT rate fell by 8 percentage points while the top CIT rate fell by 12 percentage points. During the same period, the standard VAT rate rose by 2.4 percentage points.[14]

The question then is whether EU countries should coordinate their tax policies in order to limit the downward trend in the taxation of mobile bases and allow the design of more equitable tax systems or whether each country should remain free to express its own preferences in terms of taxation (e.g., through light taxation on high incomes). This trade-off points to the difference between formal tax sovereignty, which is enshrined in national parliaments, and actual or "genuine" sovereignty, which depends on the ability of each parliament to depart from international standards.[15] It also points to the theory of federalism, according to which tax coordination

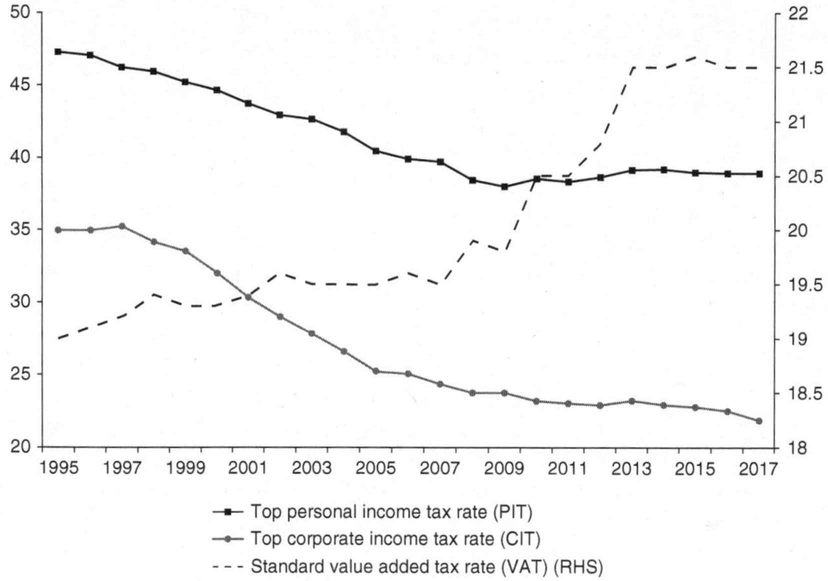

Figure 8.10 Trends in three tax rates in the European Union (simple EU28 average, in percent).
European Commission *Taxation trends in the European Union*, 2017.

should aim at making the best trade-off between respecting local preferences and internalizing the externalities across jurisdictions coming from base mobility and/or economies of scale (see Chapter 3).

8.2 Theories

Like in other policy areas, the theory of tax policy covers both a positive and a normative dimension. The positive dimension consists primarily in providing tools to identify which tax base will finally bear the burden of taxation, to measure the loss of economic efficiency due to distortionary taxes, or to assess the welfare gain due to targeted taxes (such as environmental taxes). In turn, the normative dimension of tax theory involves laying down guidelines for designing the tax system in an optimal way, given the primary distribution of income, social preferences and international constraints.

8.2.1. Tax incidence and efficiency losses

A first major insight from tax theory is that taxation is rarely borne by the particular taxpayer that orders the bank transfer to the tax administration. For instance, suppose that the labor supply is strictly fixed in a specific place or for a specific skill: the quantity of hours supplied by workers is constant whatever the wage offered by (competitive) firms. In this particular case, a cut in employers' social insurance contributions will ultimately benefit the employees through higher wages since employers will compete among themselves to hire the fixed stock of labor. Reciprocally, higher employers' contributions will be passed on the employees through lower wages. Although employers pay the contributions, they do not bear the tax burden. This simple reasoning applies both in partial equilibrium (i.e., considering only one market in isolation) and in general equilibrium (i.e., accounting for the interaction between several markets).[16]

a) Tax incidence in partial equilibrium

Consider a standard market with a positively-sloped supply curve and a negatively-sloped demand curve. This is represented in figure 8.11, where quantities are noted *Q* and prices *P*. Market equilibrium is obtained when the supply and demand schedules intersect. In the absence of taxes, this corresponds to point *E* in both the left and the right panels.

Let us now introduce a proportional tax *t*. The tax can be either a *specific tax* (a fixed amount per volume unit, for instance per ton or gallon) or an *ad-valorem tax* (a fixed percentage of the unit price). Energy taxes are generally of the former type, whereas VAT or social contributions are of the latter type. Both types of taxes have similar effects in perfect competition but react differently to inflation. Here we consider a specific tax, which is easier to tackle graphically.

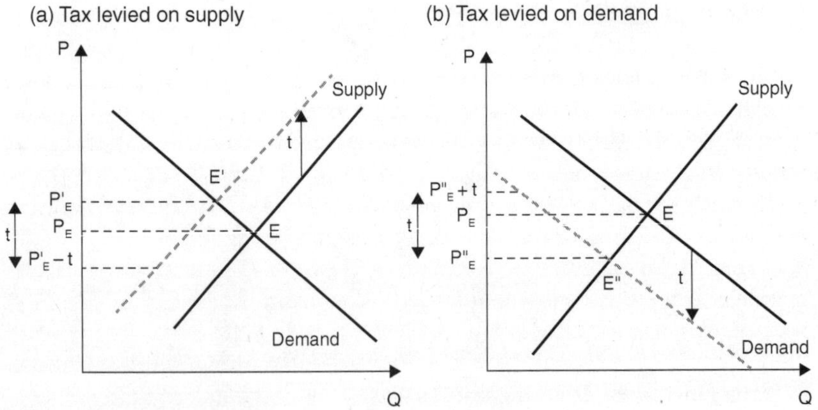

Figure 8.11 Tax incidence in partial equilibrium.
Authors.

On the left panel of figure 8.11, the tax *t* is formally levied on supply. In order to compensate for the tax they have to pay, suppliers require a higher price for any level of production: The supply curve moves upward by *t*. At the initial before-tax equilibrium price P_E, there is now excess demand since suppliers are no longer willing to supply the same quantity at this initial price. The market equilibrium moves from *E* to *E*′, where the quantity is lower and the price paid by consumers is $P_E' > P_E$, whereas the price received by suppliers (after the tax has been paid) is $P_E' - t < P_E$. Both sides therefore suffer a loss. As is apparent in figure 8.11, the tax is partly borne by the demand side since the market price has increased due to the tax. The steeper the demand curve, the stronger the price increase, hence the greater the share of the tax that is eventually borne by the demand side. In the extreme case where demand is totally rigid (a vertical demand curve), the tax levied on supply is entirely borne by the demand side since the price received by suppliers remains constant at P_E: the effective tax burden falls on the demand side. This is what is called *tax incidence.*

Now, if the tax is levied on the demand (figure 8.11, right-hand side, it shifts the demand curve downward, and the incidence of the tax again depends on the relative slopes of the demand and supply curves. For instance, because of a low price elasticity of fuel demand in the short run, taxes on gas are mostly paid by consumers. Conversely, taxes on manufactured goods are more likely to be shared between consumers and producers because demand for these items is more elastic to the price. Price elasticities are crucial, for instance, when an increase in VAT rates is at stake. If demand is weakly elastic to prices, the VAT increase will be quickly passed on to consumer prices.

These results have far-reaching practical implications for labor taxation since the labor supply curve is frequently kinked: at the lower end of the wage scale, there is often a minimum wage (or, equivalently, a backstop provided by social benefits to the unemployed), and labor supply is perfectly flexible at this wage level. Any increase in employers' contributions will then be borne by employers since they are unable to reduce net wages paid to employees. Symmetrically, a cut in social contributions for low-paid jobs is not passed on to net wages, which indeed creates an incentive for employers to hire more workers (rise in *L* on figure 8.12). For higher wages, labor supply becomes an increasing function of the net wage. For instance, a higher wage may persuade the partner of an already-working person to take a job. The scarcity of some skills can also make labor supply steeper. The burden of social contributions is then shared between employers and employees, and the distinction between employers' and employees' contributions is not relevant (except in the short term where there may be some wage rigidity).

Finally, tax incidence analysis can be applied to external tariffs. Protectionist governments impose tariffs on imports as a way of protecting local production and hence— or so they think—the jobs and purchasing power of local workers. But economists view tariffs on imports as a tax on consumption. If

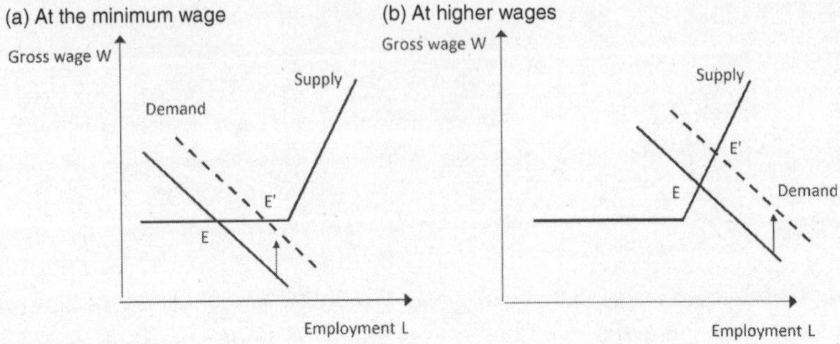

Figure 8.12 Effect of a cut in employers' social contributions depending on the wage level.
Authors.

the price of a product is given internationally (i.e., if the supply curve is horizontal), a *t*% tax on imports raises by *t*% the local price for producers and consumers alike: it is fully passed on to consumption prices, which reduces households' purchasing power. Reciprocally, even a unilateral tariff cut is beneficial to the households' welfare, a result that some policymakers find hard to believe.

b) Distortions and social losses

The second policy lesson from tax theory is that, except if it is lump-sum, introducing a tax within a "perfect" market involves a social loss[17] because relative prices are changed by the tax, hence they no longer carry the correct information on relative scarcity. For instance, a tax on consumption raises the price paid by the consumer. Accordingly, she reduces her consumption, and her utility declines. The fall in consumption triggers a fall in the before-tax market price. Since both the unit price and the quantity sold decline, the producer's profit is reduced. There is tax revenue that could be used to compensate both consumers and producers through lump sum transfers, but it can be shown (see box 8.2) that the tax revenue does not cover their respective losses, leading to a net social loss.

The size of this loss depends positively on the price elasticities of supply and demand and is quadratic on the tax rate, which has two practical implications: (i) except if taxation aims at correcting specific market distortions (such as pollution externalities), one should avoid, on efficiency grounds, taxing elastic bases; and (ii) a large tax has proportionally more impact on welfare than a small one. This implies that it is preferable to rely on a range of small taxes rather than on a single large tax. However, tax collection generally entails a fixed cost, and this is an argument against a proliferation of small taxes.

Box 8.2 Computing the Social Loss

In the previous section, we have seen that taxation introduces a discrepancy between the price paid by consumers and the price received by suppliers. If demand and supply are not rigid, taxation also reduces the quantity produced and exchanged on the market, irrespective of whether the tax is actually paid by the demand side or by the supply side. Using a simple surplus analysis, figure B8.2.1 measures the resulting social loss. In the absence of a tax, the quantity produced and exchanged is Q_0 and the market price is P_0. In the presence of a tax, output falls to Q_1 and there is now a difference between the price paid by the demand side (here, consumers) $P_1^{\,d}$ and that received by the supply side (producers) P_1^s. Table B8.2.1 derives the surplus of consumers, producers, and the government. The tax induces a social loss because the quantity produced and consumed decreases. Even if the tax proceeds are redistributed in a lump-sum way (to avoid additional distortions), this is not enough to compensate for the loss incurred by both consumers and producers. The social loss or *deadweight loss* is represented in the figure B8.2.1 by the $C + E$ triangle, called the *Harberger triangle.*[a] The deadweight loss L hence can be measured by the surface of the $C + E$ triangle. It is equal to the base of the triangle (i.e., the tax rate t) multiplied by the height of the triangle ($Q_0 - Q_1$) and then divided by two:

$$L = -\frac{t}{2}(Q_1 - Q_0) \qquad \text{(B8.2.1)}$$

The $(Q_1 - Q_0)$ quantity can be derived from the price elasticities of supply and demand, ε^s and ε^d:

$$\frac{Q_1 - Q_0}{Q_0} = -\varepsilon^d \frac{P_1^d - P_0}{P_0} = \varepsilon^s \frac{P_1^s - P_0}{P_0} < 0$$

with ε^s, $\varepsilon^d > 0$, and $\left(P_1^d - P_0\right) - \left(P_1^s - P_0\right) = t$

These two relations imply:

$$\frac{Q_1 - Q_0}{Q_0} = -\frac{t}{P_0} \times \frac{1}{\frac{1}{\varepsilon^d} + \frac{1}{\varepsilon^s}} \qquad \text{(B8.2.2)}$$

Hence the loss L is:

$$L = \frac{1}{2} t^2 \left(\frac{\varepsilon^d \varepsilon^s}{\varepsilon^d + \varepsilon^s} \right) \frac{Q_0}{P_0} \qquad \text{(B8.2.3)}$$

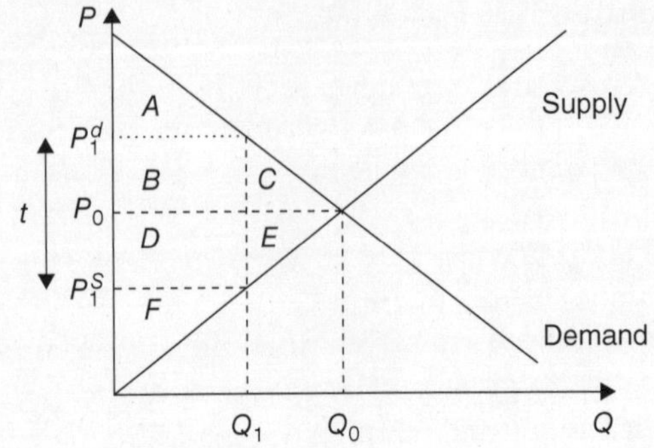

Figure B8.2.1 Taxation and surpluses.

Table B8.2.1
Social loss related to taxation

Surplus	Without tax (1)	With tax (2)	Difference (2)–(1)
Consumers	A + B + C	A	−(B + C)
Producers	D + E + F	F	−(D + E)
Government	0	B + D	+(B + D)
Total	A + B + C + D + E + F	A + B + D + F	−(C + E)

This methodology can be used to compute the deadweight loss resulting from virtually any kind of tax. For instance, Hufbauer and Elliott (1994) have assessed the cost of protection on orange juice in the United States. In 1990, the import duty on orange juice was 20% in *ad valorem* equivalent. They have found the deadweight loss to amount to US$70 million, equivalent to 13% of domestic orange juice consumption. When moving away from a single good, however, a partial equilibrium analysis may no longer be appropriate since income effects, with possible spillovers across markets and intertemporal effects, should be accounted for.

[a]For a historical perspective on the Harberger triangle, see Hines (1999*a*).

The *Ramsey rule* (1927) more precisely states that for the government to minimize deadweight losses while raising a given amount of tax revenue, the tax rate on each market needs to be inversely proportional to the *compensated price elasticities* of supply and demand. A compensated price elasticity is the variation of supply or demand resulting from a 1% variation in the price level, holding income constant (i.e., compensating for the variation of income due to the price variation). This rule can be written as[18]

$$t = k\left(\frac{1}{\varepsilon^s} + \frac{1}{\varepsilon^s}\right) \tag{8.1}$$

where t is the *ad-valorem* tax rate, k refers to the total amount of taxes to be collected, $\varepsilon^d > 0$ the compensated price-elasticity of demand, and $\varepsilon^s > 0$ the compensated price elasticity of supply. Note that the Ramsey rule aims at levying taxes while minimizing distortions. Hence, it concentrates on the allocation function, neglecting the redistribution function of tax policy. Indeed, applying the Ramsey rule can lead to unfair policies. For instance, it would imply taxing unskilled labor rather than capital or skilled labor, bread rather than perfumes, and health expenditures rather than theater tickets.

c) "Too much taxes kill taxes": The Laffer curve

Another consequence of the surplus analysis developed in box 8.2 is that the tax revenue is not a monotonous function of the tax rate, because a tax rate increase has two opposite effects on tax receipts. On the one hand, each unit of the tax base is taxed more heavily, which raises revenues. On the other hand, the tax base is reduced by the tax increase, which cuts revenues. The net effect depends on the elasticity of the tax base (see box 8.3). Starting from no taxation at all, a tax increase raises tax revenues, but less and less so as the tax rate increases. After a certain threshold, called the *revenue-maximizing tax rate*, a further rise in the tax rate *reduces* tax receipts because the positive impact of the tax increase is overcompensated by the reduction in the tax base. The revenue-maximizing tax rate can be low for elastic tax bases (e.g., internationally mobile tax bases).

Figure 8.13 illustrates the inverted U-shaped relationship between the tax rate and the tax revenue for two different values of the semi-elasticity[19] of the tax base to the tax rate (see the calculation in box 8.3).

This inverted-U-shaped curve was popularized in the 1970s by Arthur Laffer after he had supposedly sketched it on a napkin at a December 1974 working lunch (Wanniski, 2005). The idea was not new (it had already been hinted at by David Hume and by John Maynard Keynes), but Laffer surprised his contemporaries by declaring that, in view of the high tax pressure in the United States at that time, a cut in the income tax rate was likely to increase tax revenues (Laffer, 2004). Put differently, he was supposing that the income tax rate was lying on the downward-sloping section of the *Laffer curve*. His argument had a strong influence on President Ronald Reagan's tax policy. However, the legislated tax cuts led to steady increases in the budget deficit,

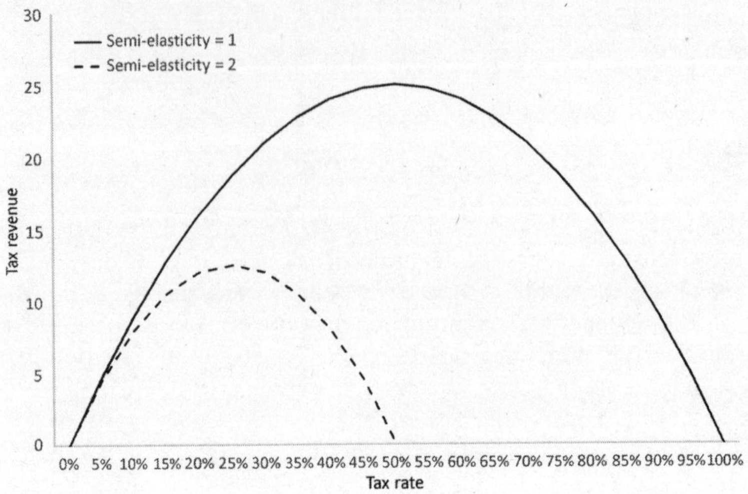

Figure 8.13 The Laffer curve: tax revenue as a function of the tax rate.
We use the calculation of Box 8.3 with $B_0 = 100$. For a unitary semi-elasticity, the tax revenue rises from 0 for a zero tax rate to 25 for a tax rate of 50%. For higher tax rates, the revenue falls, and it is zero for a tax rate of 100%. For a semi-elasticity of 2, the maximum revenue is reached with a tax rate of 25%.
Authors.

Box 8.3 Tax Rates and Revenues

Let us denote by $B(t)$ the tax base as a function of the tax rate t:

$$B(t) = B_0(1 - \varepsilon t) \qquad \text{(B8.3.1)}$$

with B_0, $\varepsilon > 0$. The tax revenue then is:

$$R(t) = tB(t) = tB_0\left(1 - \varepsilon t\right) \qquad \text{(B8.3.2)}$$

Raising the tax rate t from zero increases the tax receipt up to a level where the shrinkage of the tax base equals the rise in the tax rate. The rate t^* that maximizes the tax revenue is given by derivating the revenue $R(t)$ with respect to the tax rate:

$$t^* = \frac{1}{2\varepsilon} \qquad \text{(B8.3.3)}$$

This rate is lower, the higher ε. For instance, for $\varepsilon = 1$, we have $t^* = 50\%$, whereas for $\varepsilon = 2$ we have $t^* = 25\%$ (see figure 8.13).

showing that the economy was not in the downward-sloping section, but rather on the upward-sloping section of the Laffer curve.

A compelling illustration of the Laffer curve is provided by the Russian PIT reform of 2001, which involved a sharp fall in the top marginal tax rate, from 30% to 13%. Related tax receipts eventually rose by 25% in real terms. However, it is not clear whether tax revenues increased as a result of the reform itself or due to to accompanying enforcement measures (see Ivanova, Keen, and Klemm, 2005).[20]

Whatever its empirical relevance, the Laffer curve acts as a warning device for decision-makers, because of the threat of reduced tax revenues if they raise rates beyond a certain threshold. However, the Laffer curve does not constitute any fiscal "theory," which would need detailed modeling of microeconomic behaviors in each area of taxation. Neither does it provide any operational guide: in the absence of a precise specification of individual behaviors, one cannot determine whether the average tax rate of the economy is higher or lower than its revenue-maximizing level and therefore whether a tax rise would lead to higher or lower tax revenues.

d) Tax incidence in general equilibrium

Up to now, we have focused on a single specific market and used a partial equilibrium approach. This is obviously a limitation since the behavior of, say, consumers, depends on the variation of all relative prices (including consumption prices, but also wages, interest rates, etc.), as well as on the variation of their income. Hence, taxation on one specific market alters behaviors on other markets by modifying relative prices (substitution effects) and purchasing power (income effects).

Figure 8.14 illustrates the need for general equilibrium reasoning on the specific case of a consumer who allocates her nominal income R between two goods in quantities C_1 and C_2, respectively, in order to maximize her utility $U(C_1,C_2)$. On the graph, the choice of the consumer is represented by point E, where the budget constraint is tangent to a utility (or indifference) curve. *Ex ante* (i.e., before price adjustments occur), the introduction of a tax on good 1 moves the budget constraint downward and clockwise (around the point corresponding to zero consumption of good 1), as shown on the left panel of Figure 8.14. Utility maximization then leads the consumer to substitute good 2 for good 1 in her consumption basket because the relative price of good 1 has increased. However, the purchasing power of her income R is reduced by the tax increase, which leads to a fall in the consumption of both goods. The net effect on the consumption of good 2 is ambiguous. Suppose that demand for both goods decreases. Their prices will fall from P_1 to P'_1 and P_2 to P'_2 (right panel of Figure 8.14), which eventually will shift the budget constraint upward. By ignoring these effects, one would overestimate the impact of the tax on the market for good 1.

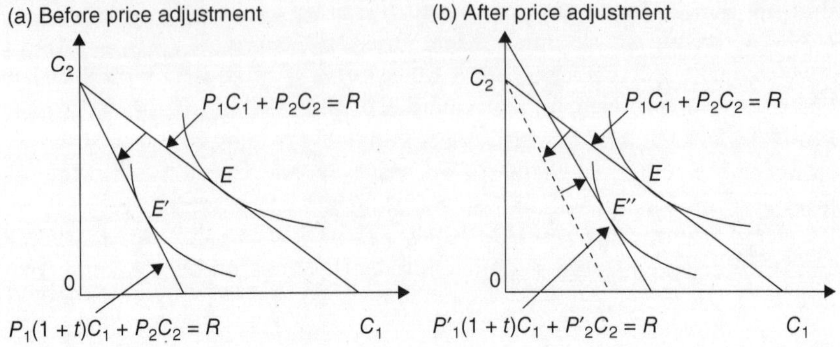

Figure 8.14 Effect of a consumption tax in a two-good model.
Authors.

This simple example has multiple applications. For instance, taxing capital income amounts to raising the price of deferred consumption (good 1) relative to immediate consumption (good 2). If the substitution effect dominates (households prefer consuming immediately because it is less expensive than consuming tomorrow), the saving rate falls; conversely, if the income effect dominates (households need to save more today in order to maintain a given level of consumption tomorrow), the saving rate increases, see box 8.4. Suppose the saving rate falls. In a closed economy, the before-tax return will

Box 8.4 The Impact of Taxes on Households' Capital Income

Consider an individual who lives two periods. In period 1, he is young: He works and receives a wage w that is used to pay social insurance contributions and a PIT at rate t_w, to consume a quantity c_1 of a representative good that we take as the numeraire (which means that its price is equal to 1), to pay a consumption tax t_c and to save an amount s. In period 2, he is old, no longer works but consumes the product of his savings after paying a tax t_s on capital income and a consumption tax t_c. For simplicity, we assume that there is no bequest. The real interest rate is noted r. The budget constraints for each period are:

$$\text{Period 1: } (1+t_c)c_1 = (1-t_w)w - s \tag{B8.4.1}$$

$$\text{Period 2: } (1+t_c)c_2 = (1+(1-t_s)r)s \tag{B8.4.2}$$

Assume that the individual maximizes an intertemporal, CES-type utility function[a]:

$$\underset{s}{Max}\, U(c_1, c_2) = \left(c_1^{\frac{\sigma-1}{\sigma}} + \beta c_2^{\frac{\sigma-1}{\sigma}} \right)^{\frac{\sigma-1}{\sigma}} \tag{B8.4.3}$$

where $\sigma > 0$ is the intertemporal elasticity of substitution and β the preference rate for future consumption ($0 < \beta < 1$). The resolution of the optimization program leads to the following level of saving:

$$s = \frac{(1-t_w)w}{1+\beta^{-\sigma}\left(1+r\left(1-t_s\right)\right)^{1-\sigma}} \tag{B8.4.4}$$

The level of saving depends positively on disposable income in period 1, $(1 - t_w)w$. Note that the income tax t_w has a proportional impact on saving by lowering period 1 disposable income. The impact of the after-tax return on saving $r(1 - t_s)$, however, depends on whether the intertemporal elasticity of substitution σ is higher or lower than unity. If $\sigma > 1$, then a rise in the capital income tax, by reducing the relative price of current consumption in terms of the future one, reduces the level of saving. If $\sigma < 1$, we get the opposite effect as the individual will save more for his or her old age in order to spread the consumption loss over the two periods. Lastly, the consumption tax t_c plays no role insofar as it affects consumption in the two periods in the same way.

[a] CES stands for Constant Elasticity of Substitution: the elasticity of substitution does not depend on the amounts consumed at the two periods.

increase in order to equalize savings with investments. The upward adjustment of the real interest rate then wipes out the impact of the tax increase for savers, but the tax is at least partially passed on to companies, which suffer from the rising cost of investment.

The distribution of the tax burden between households (savers) and firms (investors) depends on the elasticity of both savings and investments to the real interest rate. Instead of investing (directly or indirectly) in companies, households may buy government bonds or foreign assets. Hence, they are generally considered highly responsive to the return offered by corporate investment. In contrast, physical investment by companies is relatively rigid: it depends more on market prospects than on the real interest rate. Consequently, both taxes on savers and on investors are likely to be borne mainly by firms: the before-tax return on capital has to increase to ensure unchanged after-tax return for savers.

To raise the before-tax return on capital, a firm must reduce its capital stock (assuming, typically, that marginal productivity is a decreasing function of the capital stock). Because the capital stock per worker falls, labor productivity also falls, which leads to a reduction either in wages or (if and when wages hit the minimum wage floor) in employment (cf. box 8.5). On the whole, the incidence of a tax on savings depends on the relative elasticities of supply and demand, not only on the capital market, but also on the labor market. The more rigid the labor supply relative to capital supply, the higher is the share of the tax eventually borne by workers (through lower wages) rather than capital owners (through reduced after-tax return). Empirically, Arulampalam, Devereux, and Maffini (2012) find that at least 54% of an additional corporate tax is passed through to lower wages and that this proportion even exceeds 100% in the long run.[21] Only general equilibrium reasoning allows one to understand why.

This discussion qualifies the traditional debates on the burden-sharing of taxes between labor and capital: although a tax on capital raises the price of capital relative to labor, which can involve favorable substitution effects for employment, it also reduces labor income. Thus, a tax on savings can ultimately have the opposite impact from what is generally believed.

Box 8.5 The General Equilibrium Effect of Capital Taxes

Here we build on the savings model presented in box 8.4. Suppose that period 1 savings are used to acquire productive capital that the old generation sells to the young one. For simplicity, we assume that there is neither capital depreciation nor demographic growth. As there are only two generations, the young generation must buy the entire capital stock of the economy. The supply of capital by each young person is (see box 8.4):

$$k^s = \frac{(1-t_w)w}{1+\beta^{-\sigma}\left(1+r\left(1-t_s\right)\right)^{1-\sigma}} \tag{B8.5.1}$$

Here we assume that $\sigma > 1$, so that capital supply is an increasing function of the after-tax return. We assume a Cobb-Douglas production function,

$$Y = K^{\alpha}L^{1-\alpha} \tag{B8.5.2}$$

where K represents the capital stock, L employment and $0 < \alpha < 1$. Let us call $y = Y/L$ the output per worker and $k = K/L$ the capital stock per worker. The per capita level of output and income is $y = k^{\alpha}$. The marginal productivity of capital is $\alpha k^{\alpha-1}$ and that of labor is $(1-\alpha)k^{\alpha}$. Profit maximization in perfect competition involves equalizing each of these marginal productivities to the corresponding factor cost. If t_{ssc} designates the employers' social contribution rate and t_{cit} the corporate income tax (CIT) rate, and if capital depreciation is ignored, profit maximization leads to:

$$\text{Capital: } \left(1-t_{cit}\right)\alpha k^{\alpha-1} = r \tag{B8.5.3}$$

$$\text{Labor: } (1-\alpha)k^{\alpha} = \left(1+t_{ssc}\right)w \tag{B8.5.4}$$

From Equation (B8.5.3), it is possible to recover capital demand as a decreasing function of the real interest rate and of the CIT rate:

$$k^d = \left(\frac{r}{\alpha\left(1-t_{cit}\right)}\right)^{1/(\alpha-1)} \tag{B8.5.5}$$

Then, Equation (B8.5.4) shows how the wage that firms are prepared to pay depends positively on capital per worker. Together with Equation (B8.5.5), this leads to the following negative relation between the CIT and the wage that firms are prepared to pay for a given interest rate:

$$w = \frac{1-\alpha}{1+t_{ssc}} \left(\frac{r}{\alpha(1-t_{cit})} \right)^{\alpha/(\alpha-1)} \quad \text{(B8.5.6)}$$

The negative impact of the CIT on the wage rate is moderated by its positive impact on the cost of capital, which triggers substitution from capital to labor. The final impact depends on the reactions of supply and demand on both the capital and the labor markets.

Figure B8.5.1 represents the supply and demand for capital as functions of the real interest rate. A rise in the PIT rate (or in employees' social insurance contributions) or a rise of the tax on capital income shifts the capital supply curve k^s to the left. In a closed economy, the interest rate rises to restore the balance between supply and demand. Conversely, a rise in the corporate tax rate shifts the capital–demand curve k^d to the left: the real interest rate decreases to restore equilibrium. In both cases, capital per worker falls. The result is a reduction in the marginal productivity of labor. Symmetrically, a rise in employers' social insurance contributions (t_{ssc}) reduces employment and therefore both the productivity of capital and its return. The relative impact of taxation on wages and on capital returns depends on the relative slopes of the supply and demand curves in both markets.

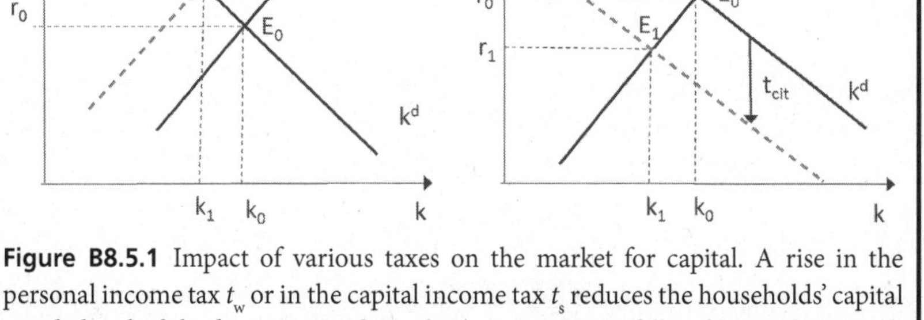

Figure B8.5.1 Impact of various taxes on the market for capital. A rise in the personal income tax t_w or in the capital income tax t_s reduces the households' capital supply k^s, which leads to a rise in the real interest rate r, to a fall in the per capita stock of capital k and, ultimately, to a fall in labor income; a rise in the corporate income tax t_{cit} lowers capital demand k^d from the firms, which leads to a decline in the real interest rate but also lowers the capital stock and therefore labor productivity.
Authors.

8.2.2 Redistribution

The theory of income redistribution is enshrined in the theory of welfare, which was briefly presented in Chapter 1 but is beyond the ambition of this book. Here, we restrict ourselves to the difficult problem of combining efficiency and equity, which is the purpose of the literature on *optimum taxation*.[22]

A first approach consists in minimizing the efficiency cost of taxation for a given amount of public revenue. This leads to the *Ramsey rule*, which recommends taxing the various tax bases in inverse proportion of the compensated elasticities of supply and of demand. However, as already mentioned, the Ramsey rule can lead to an inequitable distribution of the fiscal burden. A more elaborate approach, which has inspired most of the literature on optimum taxation, consists in introducing an equity objective alongside the efficiency one. In consequence, for example, the optimum tax rate on luxury goods will be higher than implied by the Ramsey rule, whereas the optimum tax on necessity goods will be lower.

Through James Mirrlees's pioneering work (1971), the optimum taxation literature first addressed personal income taxation, which may encapsulate means-tested transfers (considered as negative taxes). Mirrlees defines the social utility function as a weighted sum of individual utilities, with weights inversely proportional to individual incomes, which amounts to giving more consideration to the poorest. This social utility function is maximized under two constraints: a public *income constraint* (i.e., the tax revenue to be collected) and an *incentive constraint* that recognizes the impact of taxation on the incentive to work.

Assuming that individuals can be characterized by their productivity and that each individual's income is equal to his or her marginal productivity, redistribution requires taxing higher productivity individuals more heavily, but this is likely to discourage them from working and therefore to reduce tax revenues by shrinking the tax base. The marginal tax rate needs to be relatively small for the middle class because it is numerous, hence the disincentive effect is large. This approach, which does not account for labor market imbalances, justifies higher marginal tax rates at the lower end of the income. An optimum income tax profile can be derived from this trade-off between equity and efficiency (cf. box 8.6).

On the whole, optimum taxation theory offers a better understanding of the efficiency–equity trade-off but hardly provides operational guidance to governments contemplating a tax reform. As underlined by Slemrod (1990), measuring the elasticity of labor supply or the degree of substitution between consumption and leisure is particularly difficult, and optimum taxation models rarely argue for strongly progressive tax profiles except when they assume very low elasticities of substitution between consumption and leisure. Furthermore, these models are highly stylized. For instance, they do not distinguish between the individual and the household, even though the composition of a household is crucial for the elasticity of the individual labor supply and for the individual's utility.

Box 8.6 Optimum Taxation

Assume that there is a continuum of individuals, each characterized by his or her labor productivity w. Mirrlees's general result (1971) can be summarized in the following way (see Salanié, 1998).[a] The optimum marginal tax rate for an individual with potential wage or productivity w is $T'(w)$ such that:

$$\frac{T'(w)}{1-T'(w)} = E(w)R(w)H(w) \qquad \text{(B8.6.1)}$$

$E(w)$ measures the inverse of the elasticity of labor supply for each productivity level w. Assuming more productive labor is more elastic to taxation, E is a decreasing function of w: consistent with the Ramsey principle—other things equal, higher-productivity workers should be less heavily taxed: $E'(w)<0$.

In turn, $R(w)$ is the weight allocated by the government to individuals with productivity w in the social utility function: the government may want to give more consideration to the poorest by alleviating their net tax burden: $R'(w)>0$.

Last, $H(w)$ reflects the primary income distribution. It is a decreasing function of the number of individuals with productivity w and an increasing function of the number of individuals with productivity higher than w:

$$H(w) = \frac{1-F(w)}{wf(w)} \qquad \text{(B8.6.2)}$$

where f is the statistical distribution of w and F its cumulated distribution: the marginal rate of taxation of individuals with productivity w must not be too high if there are many such individuals (a high $f(w)$) in order to dampen what could be a massive discouraging effect on labor supply; conversely, a rise in the marginal tax rate of individuals with productivity w is appropriate if there are many individuals with a productivity higher than w ($1 - F(w)$ is high) because these individuals then contribute significantly to the budget without facing a disincentive to work.

Combining $E(w)$, $R(w)$, and $H(w)$ yields a roughly flat or moderately U-shaped optimum tax rate. However, the marginal tax shape strongly depends on assumptions regarding the social utility function or the elasticity of labor supply. Refined versions of the Mirrlees model have introduced a lower substitutability between consumption and leisure at the lower end of the income scale, which justifies higher marginal rates for low-income individuals often observed in advanced economies. Accounting for the clustering of labor productivities in the middle of the income scale also helps in recovering a U-shaped curve since it is optimal to reduce taxation on the most numerous groups of individuals in order to limit the tax-induced fall in labor supply.

8.2.3 Corrective taxation

The efficiency–equity trade-off misses the point that, in some cases, taxation may actually improve economic efficiency if it corrects existing market failures such as imperfect competition, externalities, asymmetrical information, and the like. In such cases, taxation can substitute for other policies—regulations, codes of conduct, or the creation of new markets.

The idea goes back to the 1920s, when Arthur Pigou (1920) proposed to introduce a tax on London chimney emissions in order to fight the infamous "smog." This involved bridging the gap between the *private cost* of emissions, incurred by the agents who were responsible for them, and their *social cost*, which includes the damage caused to other agents (*polluter–payer principle*).[23] This principle can be applied to any activity that causes negative externalities to other producers or consumers (e.g., carbon taxes or congestion charges, such as the one introduced in London in 2003 for motorists willing to enter the city center). The effectiveness of so-called *Pigovian taxes* hinges on equalizing the marginal cost of emission reduction for polluters to the social cost of the emission (see box 8.7). All polluters will reduce their emissions up to the point where the marginal cost of a further reduction is equal to the tax, hence to the social benefit of an additional reduction. Beyond that point, they will prefer paying the tax rather than incurring the costs of further reducing their emissions. This behavior is economically efficient and socially optimal, because the firm that faces the lowest marginal cost of cutting emissions will reduce its emissions more than a firm facing a higher marginal cost, unlike what happens with the imposition of a uniform emission limit for any firm.

However, Pigovian taxes affect emissions only indirectly, through changes in marginal costs. Their success relies on adequately assessing the social cost of damage and the economic agents' response to price variations. If these parameters are known, then it is possible, using a tax, to reach the desired quantity objective (for example, a given reduction of pollution). But if these parameters are uncertain, the quantitative results from a tax will also be uncertain. In brief, setting a price for pollution allows one to internalize the externality in an efficient way, but the outcome in terms of the volume of pollution may be uncertain.

Another solution for correcting externalities is to rely on regulations. In the London case, for instance, it could have been decided that only cars with even plate numbers would be allowed to enter inner London on even days and odd-plated cars on odd days.[24] The quantity of vehicles entering the city would then have been certain (in our case, a 50% drop in traffic could have been expected), but the social cost of the regulation would have been higher because, on even days, some owners of odd-plated cars would suffer a cost while some owners of even-plated cars would be granted a benefit that they cannot value. As mentioned earlier, this would not have been a cost-efficient way of reducing the traffic.

A way to combine economic efficiency with a better control on the volume of pollution is to consider the externality as the result of a missing market

Box 8.7 The Principle of a Pigovian Tax

The idea behind the Pigovian tax is to let polluters internalize the cost of pollution. Assume for instance that households consume a good in quantity q, the production of which releases an amount e of pollution that deteriorates households' welfare. Let $U(q, e)$ be their utility function, we have:

$$\frac{dU(q,e)}{dq} = \frac{\partial U}{\partial q} + \frac{\partial U}{\partial e}\frac{de}{dq} < \frac{\partial U(q,e)}{\partial q} \qquad \text{(B8.7.1)}$$

The marginal utility of consuming the good is reduced due to the associated pollution de/dq. In turn, the production cost, $C(q, e)$ is an increasing function of the quantity produced and a decreasing function of the pollution released. Hence the marginal cost of production is reduced thanks to the associated emissions:

$$\frac{dC(q,e)}{dq} = \frac{\partial C(q,e)}{\partial q} + \frac{\partial C(q,e)}{\partial e}\frac{de}{dq} < \frac{\partial C(q,e)}{\partial q} \qquad \text{(B8.7.2)}$$

In the decentralized, perfect competition equilibrium, this marginal cost determines the price of the good. This price is, however, too low in terms of social welfare: a central planner would rather choose a price that equalizes the marginal cost of production (Equation B8.7.2) to the total marginal utility of consumption (including associated pollution disutility, Equation B8.7.1). A way to reach the social optimum is to impose a tax t on each unit of production, with:

$$t = -\frac{\partial U(q,e)}{\partial e}\frac{de}{dq} > 0 \qquad \text{(B8.7.3)}$$

The marginal cost of production then is inflated by the tax, which makes the firm internalize the negative externality of pollution:

$$\frac{\partial C(q,e)}{\partial q} + \frac{\partial C(q,e)}{\partial e}\frac{de}{dq} + t = \frac{\partial C(q,e)}{\partial q} + \left(\frac{\partial C(q,e)}{\partial e} - \frac{\partial U(q,e)}{\partial e}\right)\frac{de}{dq} \qquad \text{(B8.7.4)}$$

Note here that the tax is imposed on production rather than on the emissions themselves. Although it is preferable to target the pollution itself, it is often impossible to do so due to information problems.

(for instance, a market for clean air or for smooth-flowing traffic). Public intervention then consists in establishing this new market. Issuing *tradable emission permits* or *tradable traffic permits* makes it possible to limit the total quantity of pollution (or of traffic) to the volume of available permits and to minimize the cost of pollution (or traffic) reduction by concentrating reduction efforts on those who will suffer less. For instance, the transport authority of a big city could allocate a given volume of inner-city traffic permits to residents for one semester corresponding to, say, a 25% reduction in traffic compared to past figures. Those who use public transportation would have the opportunity to sell their permits on a market, and those who did not have enough permits (or did not live in this area) could buy these permits at market price. One advantage of this system is that the transport authority would not need preliminary knowledge on the relationship between price and traffic; a second advantage is that those individuals who are able to use public transport would gain from selling their permits, which would reduce the private welfare cost of the tax.

Such tradable permit schemes with an initial allowance are called *cap-and-trade* systems. Prominent examples are the US sulfur dioxide trading system established under the 1990 Clean Air Act to combat acid rain and the EU Greenhouse Gas Emission Trading System (ETS) launched in 2005 for carbon dioxide emissions. A cap-and-trade system sets an overall pollution quantity and lets the price be set at a decentralized level, while a Pigovian tax sets an overall price and lets the pollution level vary. Absent uncertainty, the two systems are equivalent. However, uncertainty may lead to instability either on the side of quantities (with a Pigovian tax) or on the side of prices (with a market). The high instability of the ETS prices observed since 2005 is however an impediment to long-term investments in energy-saving production processes.

In theory, any problem of externalities can be resolved through negotiation. For example, smokers can be forbidden from smoking, or they can be required to negotiate with nonsmokers the right to smoke in exchange for some compensation. In 1937, in his article "The Nature of the Firm," Ronald Coase, a British economist and 1991 Nobel Prize winner, stated what has subsequently been called the *Coase theorem*: as long as all parties are free to bargain, negotiation will deliver an efficient outcome irrespective of legal entitlements. If the law forbids smoking, it is up to the smokers to buy the nonsmokers' indulgence, whereas if smoking is allowed, it is up to the victims to buy pure air from smokers. However, the Coase theorem is valid only in the absence of (or with limited) transaction costs; that is, it can fix neighborhood disputes, but it cannot solve the global warming problem. Furthermore, the outcome of the negotiation depends on the initial allocation of property rights. In the case of industrial pollution, the difficulty is precisely to establish property rights: Do firms have the right to pollute when they produce, in which case the firm has to be subsidized to reduce its emissions, or is the planet entitled to preserve its climate, in which case firms have to pay for the pollution they generate? The Pigovian tax adopts the latter viewpoint, whereas the market for tradable emissions permits is more flexible depending on the initial allocation of permits.

What should be done with tax revenues? There are three possibilities. The first consists in compensating polluters through a lump sum transfer in order not to penalize them unduly or, from a more political-economy perspective, to make the tax more acceptable to them. For example, the Swedish power stations are taxed proportionally to their nitrogen dioxide emissions, but they receive a transfer proportional to their electricity production. This taxation-cum-redistribution scheme allows behavior to be directed toward a reduction of emissions without modifying the net tax burden for the sector as a whole. The second possibility is to use tax revenues to produce public goods, in particular to finance environmental expenditures. This is the option chosen in London, where congestion charge receipts are invested in the city's transportation infrastructure. Finally, the tax revenue can be used to cut other taxes considered as distorting, especially taxes on labor: this allows a *double dividend* to be reaped since social welfare rises both because of the Pigovian tax itself (which corrects an externality) and because of the cut in tax-induced distortions on the labor market. Germany and the Netherlands thus have substituted eco-taxes for social insurance contributions (see Section 8.3). The very existence of a double dividend is, however, debated since (i) under perfect competition on the goods market, the incidence of green taxes is likely to fall on labor, (ii) the success of a Pigovian tax means that the tax base will shrink, which makes cuts in social security contributions unsustainable, and (iii) Pigovian taxes are generally regressive.

8.2.4 Taxation in open economies

Taxation in open economies raises two distinct issues: (i) the use of taxation to protect national suppliers against international competition or to carry out a "fiscal" devaluation and (ii) the taxation of mobile tax bases and subsequent issue of tax competition.

a) Taxing foreign suppliers

Since the introduction of the General Agreements on Tariffs and Trade in 1947, followed by the creation of the World Trade Organization in 1994, reducing tariffs on imports and exports has been a long-lasting objective of the international community. At the top of the international agreements, regional and bilateral agreements have proliferated, reducing trade barriers even further. Taxing imports is admitted by international rules in very specific cases of verifiable dumping or illegal state aid, or if a major internal objective (e.g., an environmental objective) is at stake. The political economy of international tariffs is, however, favorable to well-organized groups of local suppliers, especially when consumers are uncoordinated and when their price elasticity is relatively low (Grossman and Helpman, 1994).

A uniform tax on imports is equivalent (when associated with a uniform export subsidy) to a real depreciation of the domestic currency. Theoretically, in the long run, it is absorbed by the adjustment of the real exchange rate (Lerner, 1936; Lindé and Pescatori, 2017). For example, if the trade balance is in surplus thanks to barriers on imports, the real exchange rate will appreciate. In practice, however, tax rates applied to various goods and services differ widely. They are generally much higher for agriculture than for manufactured goods, and, among the latter, they can be very low—with exceptions (tariff peaks). Hence the macroeconomic logic does not really apply.

At a microeconomic level, the dynamics of tariffs is subject to two opposite forces. On the one hand, the development of intraindustry trade implies that domestic and foreign goods are close substitutes, which reinforces demands for protection. On the other hand, the fragmentation of international supply chains reduces the demand for protection since tariffs on intermediate goods will inflate the cost of domestically produced final goods.

More generally, the issue of tariff protection arises when domestic companies consider domestic taxation (or environmental standards) as a disadvantage in world competition. One way to address their concern, then, is to move domestic taxation from source-based to destination-based (box 8.8). For instance, raising the VAT rate while cutting social insurance contributions will reduce the unit cost of home suppliers since both imported and local goods are subject to the VAT while only domestic suppliers will enjoy the cut in social contributions. Like the monetary devaluation, such *fiscal devaluation*, however, has only a transitory effect. In the long term, to the extent that local wages are indexed on the consumer price index, the unit cost of labor will increase following the VAT hike.[25]

Box 8.8 Source, Residence, and Destination

Consider a company whose legal residence is in country R. As a simplification, assume that the company is owned by residents of R. The company has a subsidiary in country S, which exports all its production to country D where its consumers are located.[a] The income produced by the subsidiary may be taxed at the source country S, at the residence country R, or at the destination country D. It is actually taxed in the three countries: The *source country* S raises a CIT on the profit made by the subsidiary, on the top of social insurance contributions and local taxes related to real estate and public services. The *residence country* R may raise a tax on repatriated profits (after crediting the mother company for the CIT already paid by the subsidiary).[b] More importantly, it will raise an income tax on the dividends perceived by the shareholders of the company. Finally, the *destination country* D raises a VAT or a general sales tax on the value of the goods sold on its market. The trend over the past decades has been a shift away from *source-based taxation* in favor of *destination-based taxation*.

[a]This box borrows from the *Mirrlees Review* (2011), chapt. 18.
[b]In many countries, though, repatriated profits are exempted at the residence, while the CIT paid at the source is not credited.

Likewise, it has been proposed in the US tax policy debate to replace the standard CIT (which is raised on the profit of a company in the source country) by a *destination-based cash flow tax* (DBCFT; see Auerbach 2010).[26] A *cash flow tax* would allow a company to deduct the entire value of its investments immediately in the year of the investment rather than progressively through depreciation allowances. Furthermore, new borrowing would be taxable, but debt repayments would be deductible. A *destination-based* cash flow tax would exempt sales to foreign customers while purchases from foreign suppliers would not be deductible. The problem with the DBCFT is that, unlike the VAT, which is also destination-based, it involves a discrimination between foreign and domestic inputs because the total value of foreign inputs (not just the share corresponding to the profit of foreign suppliers) is taxed under the DBCFT whereas domestic inputs are deductible (see Cline, 2017). A destination-based cash flow tax can therefore be regarded as a protectionist measure.

b) Taxing mobile bases

It was argued in Section 8.2.1 that taxes are ultimately borne by the least flexible bases. In an open economy, capital is generally more mobile than goods and especially labor. Hence, the burden of taxation tends to fall on labor and consumption, two relatively immobile tax bases.

The seminal model of tax competition (Zodrow and Mieszkowski, 1986; Bucovetsky and Wilson, 1991) relies on the international arbitrage condition: if capital is internationally mobile, the after-tax returns on capital are equalized. If a country increases the tax rate on capital, some capital will flow out; since the marginal productivity of capital is decreasing, the the pre-tax return will rise. In practice, the least productive investments are delocalized so that, on average, the pre-tax marginal return is higher, equalizing the after-tax return to its international level (see box 8.9). As the government can tax an immobile tax bases (land, consumption, or low-skilled labor), the burden of taxation will fall on them, while no levy will be imposed on the mobile bases.[27]

These traditional results of the literature on tax competition, which predict a *race to the bottom* in corporate tax rates, have been questioned since the late 1990s by the "new economic geography" literature (see Baldwin et al., 2003, and Chapter 9 of this book). According to this research avenue, large, geographically connected countries benefit from *agglomeration rents*[28] allowing them to maintain higher tax rates without suffering from a relocation of their activities. These agglomeration effects are related to economies of scale, which create an incentive for firms to concentrate their activities in a small number of places, provided that transport costs between production and markets are not too high (Andersson and Forslid, 2003). Government services themselves can contribute to this dynamics. The presence of firms in a location generates resources that can be used to provide local amenities such as infrastructure or education which, in turn, will attract new firms—the "bright lights, big city" effect.

Box 8.9 Tax Competition According to Zodrow and Mieszkowski

Consider a representative household that consumes both a private good (in quantity x) and a public one g. The household's utility function is $U(x, g)$, with positive and decreasing marginal utilities in each of the two goods (and zero marginal cross-utilities).[a] The private good is produced by a representative firm through the production function: $y = f(k)$, where k is the amount of productive capital, $f'(k) > 0$ and $f''(k) < 0$. In turn, the public good is delivered by the government by taxing private capital at a proportional rate t: $g = tk$. The public budget is balanced. The problem of the (benevolent) government is to set t so that the household's utility is maximized.

The household is endowed with an amount of wealth K that is invested in shares of productive capital. In a *closed economy*, the representative household holds the domestic productive capital stock: $K = k$. Its budget constraint is $x = f(k) - tk$. The first-order condition of profit maximization involves equal marginal utility for the public as for the private good:

$$\frac{u_g}{u_x} = 1 \qquad \text{(B8.9.1)}$$

where u_g, u_x denote the marginal utilities of the public and the private good, respectively.

In a *small, open economy*, the representative household chooses between investing in domestic or in foreign capital. The arbitrage condition is the equality between the domestic, after-tax return $f'(k) - t$, and the exogenous world real interest rate, r^*: $f'(k) - t = r^*$. The first-order condition becomes:

$$\frac{u_g}{u_x} = \frac{1}{1-\varepsilon_k} > 1 \qquad \text{(B8.9.2)}$$

where $\varepsilon_k > 0$ is the elasticity of the capital to the tax rate. Because u_g is a decreasing function of g, Equation (B8.9.2) implies a lower public good provision, hence lower equilibrium taxation than in the closed economy case (Equation B8.9.1).

Allowing the public good to be productive, or considering two large economies (that together determine the world interest rate), reduces the impact of capital mobility on the optimal tax rate without eliminating it. Finally, it can be shown that smaller economies are more prone to lowering their tax rates because the world capital return is more exogenous for them than for large economies.

Figure 8.10 in Section 8.1 confirms the downward trend of marginal tax rates for mobile bases (the CIT and, to a lesser extent, the PIT) and the upward trend of marginal tax rates for immobile bases (the VAT) in the European Union.

[a]This box is derived from Krogstrup (2002).

Empirical studies[29] confirm that location choices are primarily driven by the breadth of local demand. Cost factors, including taxation, also have an impact, but they are mainly secondary factors, especially in advanced economies. This means that tax differentials can be maintained to the extent that they compensate for geographic or size differences.

Competition across jurisdictions to attract productive investment through lower taxation should be distinguished from the mere facilitation of tax avoidance through schemes that allow assigning profits to entities located in tax havens or low-tax jurisdictions. Whereas there is a valid discussion to be held on the degree to which lower taxation can compensate locational disadvantages, there is no economic argument for tax avoidance (apart from the hypothesis that government taxation is predatory). Tørsløv, Wier and Zucman (2018) estimate that close to 40% of multinational profits are shifted to tax havens globally.

8.3 Policies

As mentioned in Section 8.1, tax policies aim at (i) collecting resources without introducing too many market distortions, (ii) redistributing incomes without discouraging labor supply or saving, and (iii) correcting specific market imperfections. The availability of a wide range of instruments makes these various objectives less contradictory than might appear at first glance. If taxation is so much debated, it is, of course, because of its impact on the various agents' disposable income, but also because tax incidence is generally poorly understood, because the agents' horizons may differ, because the model used to understand its effects can vary (depending on whether it assumes perfect or imperfect competition, open or closed economy, etc.), and, of course, because of differences in the relative weights of the efficiency and redistribution objectives. Here we focus on how the theories presented in Section 8.2 can be called on to address concrete tax policy issues.

8.3.1. Distributing the tax burden efficiently

Economic theory suggests that the amount of public goods provided by the government should be determined trhough comparing their marginal benefit to the marginal efficiency cost of raising taxes. Beyond this principle, however, theory fails to provide any reliable tool for determining the optimum level of the total tax burden. As already mentioned, the Laffer curve does not provide useful guidance to identify this level: absent tax collection problems, an economy as a whole generally lies on the left part of the curve, where a higher tax rate increases tax revenues. Although high taxes mechanically translate into large price distortions in the economy, there is hardly a correlation between total tax pressure and long-term growth, as illustrated in figure 8.15.

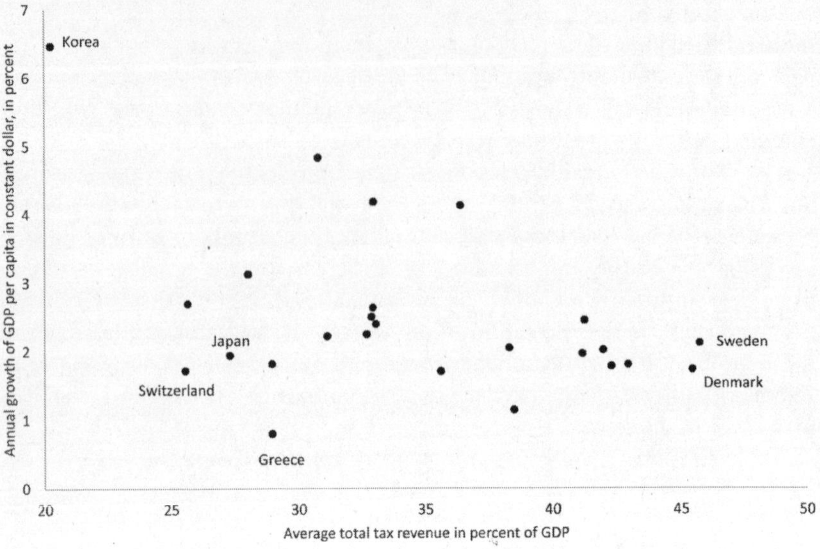

Figure 8.15 Total tax pressure and gross domestic product (GDP) growth in OECD countries, 1980–2015.
OECD.

Korea appears as an outlier, with both low taxation and high growth of GDP per capita over 1980–2015. However, Denmark and Sweden display similar growth rates as Switzerland or Japan, with much higher tax pressure. The level of tax pressure is mostly determined by social preferences and especially by the desired generosity of the welfare state. Furthermore, the link between taxation and growth is not univocal, since more public education, health services, or infrastructure may actually increase the growth potential of a country (see Chapter 9), while less inequality is also growth-enhancing (see Ostry, Berg, and Tsangarides, 2014).

Theory is more prolix on how to distribute the tax burden in an efficient way (i.e., so as to raise taxes without introducing too many market distortions): public resources should be raised through low tax rates applied on large, relatively inelastic tax bases. However, several tax bases can be used: consumption, payrolls, personal income, corporate income, and more. A first question is, which of them should be favored.

a) The long-run equivalence between different taxes

It is safe to start from the long-run equivalence between social insurance contributions, personal income taxation, and general consumption taxes.[30] With W denoting the nominal cost of one unit of labor for the employer and Ω the purchasing power of the corresponding remuneration for the employee, we have:

$$\Omega = \frac{(1-t_{sc2})(1-t_{PIT})}{(1+t_{sc1})(1+t_{VAT})}\frac{W}{P} \tag{8.2}$$

where t_{SC1}, t_{SC2}, t_{PIT}, t_{VAT} denote the rates of employers' social contributions, employees' social contributions, the PIT, and VAT (or any general consumption tax), respectively, and P represents the before-tax consumption price index. Equation (8.2) states that the four taxes and contributions have approximately the same impact on workers' purchasing power.[31] The distribution of these taxes between employers (who pay W/P in real terms) and employees (who receive Ω, also in real terms) only depends on the relative slopes of labor supply and labor demand, as detailed in Section 8.2.1. If labor supply is steeper (less flexible) than labor demand, then W/P will remain unchanged whatever the taxes, and a tax increase will result in a fall in purchasing power Ω.

An important exception to this equivalence between taxes occurs at the minimum wage level because the latter is generally defined as net of social contributions but gross of VAT.[32] In this case, a rise in social insurance contributions mechanically raises the cost of labor W because the net wage received by employees cannot fall; on the other hand, VAT rise causes a drop in the employees' purchasing power (unless the minimum wage is adjusted). Policies aimed at encouraging the demand for low-skilled labor can use cuts in social contributions because they lower labor costs while preserving purchasing power. Since the 1990s, European countries have extensively used targeted cuts in social security contributions to reduce the cost of low-skilled workers while maintaining their purchasing power relative to the median worker. For instance, in France, the net minimum wage received by the workers was 67% of the median wage in 2011, but the labor cost at the minimum wage was only 50% of that at the median wage. In Belgium, the corresponding figures were 66% and 46% (see Groupe d'experts du SMIC, 2014).

Another exception to tax equivalence occurs in the short run, before wage negotiations take place: A rise in employers' social insurance contributions increases labor costs because nominal wages are rigid. In contrast, a rise in the employees' social contributions, PIT, or VAT reduces their purchasing power (since wages are not indexed in the short run). Hence, these various taxes have different stabilization properties. In 2007, Germany raised its standard VAT rate by three percentage points while cutting employers' social contributions by one percentage point. This tax package had a negative impact on consumption in the short run due to its detrimental impact on purchasing power. Later in 2007, German unions asked for wage increases to compensate for the rise in VAT.

Finally, the preceding reasoning does not account for capital income or pensions, which are taxed through VAT and PIT (or withholding taxes), but are not subject to social insurance contributions, which are generally based on payrolls.[33] Cutting labor taxes by one percentage point may be financed by an increase in a broad-based PIT by less than one percentage point.[34]

b) The value-added tax

Since its introduction in France in 1954, the value-added tax has been adopted in most countries in the world. In December 2016, more than 140 countries had a VAT, with standard rates ranging from 8% to 25%. VAT is a prerequisite for EU membership. About 20 countries, like the United States, Canada, Australia, New Zealand, Singapore, or Japan, do not use VAT but a retail sales tax (RST). The latter is raised only on final consumption, whereas VAT is raised at each stage of the value-added chain (with appropriate tax credit for intermediate consumption). As detailed in box 8.10, VAT and the RST are equivalent from an economic point of view, but VAT is generally viewed as more resilient to tax evasion.

Most developing countries have also adopted VAT systems. However, some sectors are often left out, which significantly reduces VAT receipts. Enforcing VAT in developing countries, where a large part of the economy is informal, is

Box 8.10 VAT Versus Sales Tax

Let us assume that a single producer of intermediate goods sells for 100 euros to a single producer of a final good; and that the latter is sold for 150 euros to final consumers.[a]

- Under a 20% VAT rate, the producer of intermediate goods charges 20 euros (20% × 100) VAT to his or her customer and transfers this amount to the tax administration; the producer of the final good charges his or her customers 30 euros (20% × 150) VAT and transfers 10 euros (30 – 20, the VAT he or she already paid for the intermediate good) to the tax administration. The total tax revenue is therefore 30 euros.
- Under a 20% retail sales tax (RST), the producer of intermediate goods charges no tax and pays no amount to the tax administration. The final good producer charges 30 euros (20% × 150) to his or her customers and transfers this amount to the tax administration.

Hence, the same rate of VAT and of RST produces the same tax revenue. However, the VAT is generally viewed as preferable because it spreads the risk of noncompliance over a larger number of agents: if one firm within the supply chain fails to comply with VAT, the corresponding tax will be levied at the next stage of the chain; furthermore, suppliers have an incentive to register to charge the VAT since this will allow them to receive a refund for the VAT paid on the expenditure side; finally, there is no incentive under VAT to cheat on the nature of sales and declare a final sale as a business-to-business transaction.

[a] This box partly draws on Keen and Smith (2006).

a crucial issue especially since import tariffs are being cut as a result of membership in the World Trade Organization.

If the advantage of the VAT is to be used to raise revenues in a minimally distortive way, it is important to resist the temptation to use it for targeted actions, such as promoting employment in selected sectors. Multiple rates tend to create loopholes and to distort relative prices. Furthermore, playing with a consumption tax is a very indirect way to stimulate employment. Suppose, for instance, that the VAT rate is reduced for restaurants in order to stimulate employment. There is no guarantee that the tax cut will be passed on to the consumers and that the consumers will react by raising their demand. Even if both conditions are fulfilled, the gain may be captured by the landowners through higher rents. To encourage demand for labor, it is therefore preferable to act directly on labor costs through cuts in social insurance contributions.

8.3.2. Distributing the tax burden equitably

Although it is generally considered an efficient way to raise public revenues, the VAT is a regressive tax: despite lower rates on necessity goods, low-income household tend to pay more in percent of their income than do high-income ones just because they consume a larger share of their income. There is a need to at least counterbalance this regressive feature through a progressive income tax (*vertical equity*). However, tax equity also involves taxing all sources of income the same way (*horizontal equity*). We start with this horizontal dimension of equity before studying vertical equity.

a) Horizontal equity

Taxing all sources of income equally is a necessity to avoid creating tax loopholes. For instance, failing to raise a CIT could lead some households to "incorporate" so as to declare their revenues as corporate income. It is also a necessity to avoid creating price distortions (e.g., between labor and capital). Finally, it is a requirement in terms of equity. For instance, rentiers, self-employed, and wage earners should be taxed the same way.

Taxing all types of income equally is, however, a very complicated task because several taxes interact. For instance, should the same PIT rate apply to dividends as to labor income? The problem with taxing the dividends is that they have already been taxed as profit at the source through the CIT. Therefore, dividends are often taxed at a lower rate than labor income. However, if the incidence of the CIT falls partially on labor, there is no reason to tax dividends and labor income differently.

Restricting the problem to the CIT does not make it easier, though: should interest payments be deductible from the taxable profit, as it is generally at least partially the case? Doing so introduces a distortion between debt and equity financing of the firm and also incentivizes multinational companies to shift profit to low-tax countries through intracompany loans (box 8.11).

Box 8.11 The Search for a Nondistortionary Corporate Tax

The relevance of taxing corporate income may be questioned since capital is internationally mobile, which tends to shift the burden of a CIT on to immobile tax bases.[a] The corresponding income may be taxed at the less-mobile shareholder level (i.e., as a personal capital income). Still, the CIT may be justified on several grounds: (i) the corresponding income may be easier to trace at the corporate level than at the individual one; (ii) the tax base is easier to measure at the corporate level, especially when the purpose is to tax rents rather than total profit[b]; (iii) the CIT may be used as an (imperfect) substitute for missing fees for the use of government services by corporations; (iv) the CIT is the only way to tax foreign shareholders; (v) the CIT acts as a backstop for the PIT; and (vi) from a political point of view, it may be less difficult to directly tax corporations than actual voters—workers or capital owners.

Still, taxing corporate income raises two series of questions:

- Should the tax be raised in the country where the activity takes place (*source principle*), in the country where capital owners (either individuals, headquarters, or institutional investors) are located (*residence principle*), or in the country where the goods and services are finally consumed (*destination principle*)?
- Should the tax fall on the full return on equity (including both normal return and rents), on the full return on capital (including debt-financed capital), or only on rents (excluding "normal" return by exempting interest payments and "normal" dividends)?

In most countries, the CIT is raised under the source principle, and repatriated profits from foreign affiliates are exempted from any taxation. However, in some countries (the United Kingdom, Ireland), there is a credit for taxes paid abroad on the affiliates' profits so that the residence principle *de facto* applies to the multinationals headquartered in the country (unless taxes paid abroad exceed the domestic tax bill, since there is no refund). Due to this tax credit scheme, foreign affiliates of, say, UK multinationals do not receive the same tax treatment as local firms abroad or as affiliates of multinationals headquartered in exemption countries.

In most countries, the tax base is the full return on equity. In particular, interest payments are at least partially deductible from taxable profit. This tax base, combined with the source principle, is especially vulnerable to tax optimization by multinationals. Indeed, multinationals can shift profit from one country to another through transfer pricing (e.g., overpricing intermediate goods or services sold by those affiliates located in low-tax countries) and intrafirm finance (e.g., loans from affiliates located in low-tax countries to those located in high-tax ones), which has led governments and international organizations (especially the OECD) to try to impose codes of conduct.

To remove some of these distortions, several tax reforms have been proposed and sometimes adopted. One of them aims at taxing only rents, not the "normal return," by introducing an allowance for the cost of equity finance. Such a system, which was introduced in Belgium in 2006,[c] reduces the distortions related to the CIT since debt and equity finance are treated equally and only extra profits ("rents") are taxed, and tax optimization through intrafirm loans is reduced. The main disadvantage of this system is that it amounts to narrowing the tax base, which leads to a rise in the statutory tax rate if constant receipts are needed. This reintroduces the risk of more distortions as well as profit-shifting.

Another proposal consists, on the contrary, in removing interest payment deductibility. Again, debt and equity finance would be treated equally so that both would be taxed, which means a broadening of the tax base and a lower statutory tax rate. Such a *Comprehensive Business Income Tax* (CBIT) was proposed by the US Treasury in 1992. Countries such as Germany or France have moved significantly in this direction by limiting the deductibility of interest payments from taxable profit. This is also the direction taken by the European Union through the Anti-Tax Avoidance directive of 2016 (see box 8.15).

[a]This box relies on Devereux and Sørensen (2006) and Auerbach, Devereux, and Simpson (2007).

[b]The taxation of economic rents is theoretically nondistortionary since the normal return generated by the marginal investment project is exempted.

[c]The interest deduction for risk capital (a.k.a. *notional interest deduction*) was introduced in Belgium in 2006 to replace the special tax regime for "coordination centers"—a system that was banned as discriminatory by the European code of conduct. The interest deduction is calculated as a notional interest rate (itself a moving average of past 10-year interest rates on government bonds) multiplied by the company's equity.

The CIT may also affect differently the same income depending on corporate ownership. In some countries, such as Germany or France, all companies are taxed the same way whatever the ownership, but income from foreign affiliates is exempted. In other countries, such as the United Kingdom, the tax paid by affiliates in foreign jurisdictions is credited on the mother's tax bill, meaning that, unless taxes paid abroad exceed the domestic tax bill, foreign affiliates *de facto* pay the British CIT (Box 8.11).

Aside from the interaction between different taxes and tax systems, the taxation of all income sources along the same rates is also impaired by the temptation of national governments to grant exemptions. For instance, companies may deduct part of their R&D expenditures from the CIT base or households may deduct part of their child care expenditures or charitable donations from the PIT base. The notion of *tax expenditure* refers to the loss in tax revenues related to these specific provisions: it can be interpreted as equivalent to subsidies in favor of various purposes or interest groups. According to the Tax Policy Center of the Brookings Institution, the 13 top tax expenditures in the United States totaled US$972.9 billion in 2016, hence around 5% of US GDP. The call for simplification and base broadening (through reduced exemptions) of the tax system is a leitmotiv of newly elected governments but generally does not resist the pressure from lobbies and the pursuit of reelection.

Finally, the ability of governments to tax equally all sources of income is also impaired by the unequal mobility of tax bases. Following the theoretical model of tax competition (see Section 8.2.4), the higher mobility of capital compared with labor and especially consumption induces a shift of taxation from the former to the latter. When consumption is mobile, as is the case for digital trade, it becomes more difficult to tax it (box 8.12). In a sense, the *race-to-the bottom* related to base mobility is consistent with the Ramsey rule, which suggests that highly elastic tax bases should be taxed less. However, such rate differentiation introduces a distortion between different activities—here with traditional retail and new business models.

Box 8.12 Taxing the Digital Economy

The digital economy differs from the traditional economy by three key characteristics that affect the ability of a government to tax both sectors the same way. First, the nonphysical location of digital activities (and the intermediation carried out by digital platforms) makes it easy for digital companies to register their headquarters in countries where the rules concerning taxation and data use are most advantageous. Second, the digital economy heavily relies on data. These *de facto* constitute an untaxed production factor substituting for sometimes heavily taxed labor. Consumers also often exchange their data for free services, in a sort of barter economy that escapes VAT or sales taxes and therefore benefits from a distortion vis-à-vis traditional services. Third, the principles governing transfer pricing between subsidiaries of the same group hardly apply to the digital economy. The general principle of "arm's-length pricing" stipulates that trade between firms of the same group should be charged at the same price as though those were independent from each other (i.e., at market price). The problem here is that the services traded are very specific (e.g., royalties paid in exchange for using a brand or algorithm), so there is no market benchmark.

These specificities involve distorted competition between companies of the same sector (for instance between the GAFAs[a] and smaller firms) and between governments (through profit-shifting by multinational companies). Taxing the digital economy therefore calls for reforming existing taxation frameworks while at the same time preserving the incentives for innovation.

The OECD BEPS[b] working group has identified four key domains along which to tax the digital economy: (i) the territoriality of digital companies needs to be restored (this implies, e.g., to redefine permanent establishment requirements, to develop the concept of significant digital presence, or to use source taxation); (ii) for tax purposes, value the data and the provision of "free" services to users; (iii) define international digital transactions (e.g., sales, rental, royalties) on which to ground differentiated taxes; and (iv) collect VAT or destination-based consumption taxes.

Other proposals include, for example, taxing royalties at the source and crediting the corresponding tax in the country of the firm receiving the royalties. For instance, if royalties paid to other EU Member States and royalties paid to third countries were both taxed at source, widely used tax-planning strategies based on the location of intellectual property in tax havens would become ineffective. Introducing such source taxation would, however, necessitate a revision of the Interest and Royalties Directive, or at least a coordination of double taxation agreements with third countries, to make sure that royalties or interest paid to tax havens outside the EU do not go untaxed.[c]

Another possibility would be the adoption by a club of countries of an *ad valorem* tax on advertising revenues or revenues from personal data collection. Collecting taxes on these revenues would be effective as both are easily imputable to a national territory. In order to preserve the incentives for innovation, the tax rates would need to be low, and a lump-sum allowance would be introduced to exempt smaller companies.[d]

[a]Google, Amazon, Facebook, and Apple and, more generally, the giants of the digital economy.
[b]Base Erosion and Profit Shifting.
[c]See Finke et al. (2014).
[d]See Charrié, J. and L. Janin (2015), "Taxation of the digital economy," France Stratégie, Policy Brief n°26, March.

Finally, horizontal equity raises the question of identifying the taxpayer: is she an individual or a household? The same individual income provides a different standard of living depending on whether the individual shares some fixed costs with another income earner living in the same household or whether he or she is the only income earner of a household with several children. In many countries, the PIT is raised on the total income of the household rather than on each individual income.[35] However, family-based taxation may reduce the incentive of the second income earner (often a female) to work if the PIT is progressive since the marginal tax rate of the second income earner will, by construction, be higher than with individual taxation. This is a clear example of efficiency–equity trade-off, where individual taxation is to be preferred for efficiency purpose, but family taxation is more equitable. Empirical research confirms that a more neutral tax treatment of second earners (relative to single individuals) has a positive impact on female labor participation (Jaumotte, 2003), while, conversely, family-based taxation negatively affects female labor supply (Dingeldey, 2001).

b) Vertical equity

PIT and wealth taxes are the traditional instruments of income redistribution through the tax system. However, as evidenced through the marked fall in the top marginal rate of the PIT in the United States (figure 8.16), there is a tendency toward reduced progressivity of the PIT.[36] In some countries (such as France), the progressivity of the tax system results in large part from relatively generous means-tested transfers. Hence the whole tax system needs to be considered when measuring the progressivity of taxes in any given country.

The redistribution motive raises the traditional trade-off between efficiency and equity. As underlined by the optimum taxation theory, distortions induced by progressive income taxation carry an economic cost. In some cases, it is possible to raise both efficiency and equity by redesigning taxes. For instance, when a high statutory tax rate is levied on a narrow tax base (due to the multiplicity of exemptions), it can be more efficient and more equitable to reduce the rate while broadening the base. This was the case with the US PIT reform in 1986, which combined tax rate cuts and base-broadening. After the

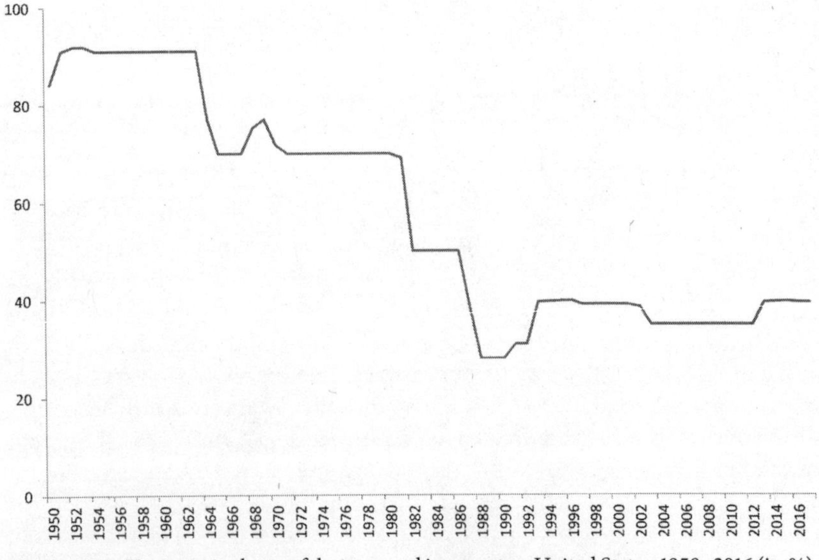

Figure 8.16 Top marginal rate of the personal income tax, United States, 1950–2016 (in %). http://federal-tax-rates.insidegov.com/ and Tax foundation.

reform, fewer individuals were able to escape the tax, whereas those who already complied with it benefited from lower rates. However, most tax reforms of the 1990s and 2000s have resulted in a flattening of the marginal tax rate curve, with rates falling more markedly for high-income brackets. The most radical examples are provided by countries having implemented *flat tax* systems (i.e., tax systems with constant marginal tax rates). In its purest form, the flat tax system applies the same flat rate to personal income, corporate income, and consumption. In 2016, however, of all EU countries, only Estonia had the same rate for the three bases (table 8.1).

In theory, a flat tax system may achieve both efficiency and redistribution when combined with a generous *basic allowance* (i.e., a fixed income level that is not taxed): taxpayers are exempted on their first units of income. In practice, however, a flat tax system generally leads to much flatter average tax rates because, for high levels of income, the basic allowance becomes negligible. Figure 8.8 in Section 8.1 illustrates this phenomenon, with a flat tax at 20% and a basic allowance of 1,000 euros. The personal tax appears highly progressive for relatively low incomes (between 1,000 and 3,000 euros), but much less for higher levels of income where the average tax rate converges to the flat marginal rate.

Another problem with the flat tax system is the absence of progressivity below the basic allowance threshold (in our example, the minimum wage). In figure 8.8, households (or individuals) whose income is below the basic allowance do not pay any tax, but they do not receive any transfer. Hence their average tax rate (zero) is the same as for individuals receiving the minimum wage.

One way to extend tax progressiveness to the very-low-income population is to combine a flat tax with *means-tested transfers* (i.e., transfers that are granted to households below certain thresholds of primary income).

Table 8.1
European Union countries with a flat tax system, 2016

	PIT rate (%)	CIT rate (%)	Standard VAT rate (%)
Bulgaria	10	10	20
Czech Rep.	15	19	21
Estonia	20	20	20
Cyprus	35	12.5	19
Hungary	15	20.6	27
Latvia	23	15	21
Lithuania	15	15	21
Romania	16	16	20

CIT, corporate income tax; PIT, personal income tax; VAT, value-added tax.
Source: European Commission, *Taxation Trends in the European Union*, 2017.

Means-tested transfers are a form of *negative taxation*, and they are widely used in advanced economies. However, they raise a number of difficulties. First, they involve bureaucratic costs for both the social administrations and the households concerned. Second, it has been observed that a significant proportion of the potential beneficiaries fail to apply for the transfers due to a mixture of information problems and worry of a stigma effect.[37] Finally, means-tested transfers involve high marginal net tax rates as moving above the income thresholds triggers a loss of the transfers (see figure 8.9 in Section 8.1). In turn, high marginal rates reduce the incentives to work, hence they may lock the individuals in *poverty traps*.

As an alternative to means-tested transfers, it has been proposed to introduce a *universal transfer* or *basic income* system, where a transfer would be given to any individual or household, regardless of their income, and financed through an income tax applied from the first unit of income (box 8.13). Such a system would address the three weaknesses of means-tested transfers at the same time since it would (i) dramatically reduce the administrative costs, (ii) eliminate the problem of nonrecourse, and (iii) erase the high net marginal tax rates observed at the lower end of the income scale.

The advocates of the basic income scheme further argue that it would provide "real freedom" to the individuals by allowing them to discriminate between "attractive (or promising)" jobs and "lousy" ones (Van Parijs, 1995). The availability of a basic income may also increase the willingness of individuals to take more risks (e.g., through innovating and starting new businesses).

On figure 8.17, we simulate a basic income of half the minimum wage financed through a flat marginal tax rate of 20% that tops up the initial flat tax of 20% that is supposed to cover the other government costs. Individuals (or households) whose income is lower than 1.25 times the minimum wage receive a net transfer, the amount of which reaches 60% of their primary income for half the minimum wage and even more below this threshold (not shown on the graph). In contrast, with a more traditional basic allowance system, the average tax rate is never negative (see figure 8.8 in Section 8.1). In both cases, though, at the other end of the income scale, the average tax rate is rather flat as it converges toward the marginal rate. Of course, a universal transfer system may be combined with a progressive marginal tax schedule. The problem, however, is that the marginal tax rate may reach very high levels for high incomes, which raises the question of tax acceptability and avoidance.

The basic income proposal encounters two key constraints. The first is its affordability, already illustrated in figure 8.17. Indeed, if extending a universal transfer to all taxpayers costs x% of GDP, it would require levying a tax worth x% of GDP on the top of what is already required to finance the provision of public goods (Atkinson, 2015). Even without any change in the net tax paid by taxpayers, a universal income would raise both tax pressure and government spending. In some countries, such perspective is hardly implementable given initial tax burdens. The second problem concerns the net beneficiaries

Box 8.13 The Different Objectives of a Universal Transfer System

The idea of a universal transfer paid to any individual independently of his or her income goes back to the sixteenth century when it is said to have been (unsuccessfully) proposed to the mayor of Bruges. At the beginning of the nineteenth century, the *Speenhamland system* was the first natural—and unhappy—experience of universal allocation: in Speenhamland, a district located in southern England, magistrates decided that the parish would supplement peasants' income up to a certain subsistence level based on the price of bread and the number of children. This system spread quickly in the south of England. But Thomas Malthus criticized this encouragement to have children without being able to provide for their needs. The idea, nevertheless, was taken up by the utopians of the late nineteenth century, then again in the 1930s and 1940s in the UK by the economist James Meade, and finally in the twentieth century by Lady Juliet Rhys-Williams, who proposed this system as an alternative to the Beveridge report. Contrasting to the Malthusian view, she argued that a universal transfer would maintain the incentives to actively seek for work.

The welfare systems put in place after the World War II, however, relied on unconditional transfers in kind (e.g., the British National Health Service) and means-tested transfers (e.g., family allowances, or social assistance), in combination with progressive income tax schedules. The limitations of these systems emerged in the early years of the twenty-first century in relation with (i) flattening tax schedules in relation to rising capital and skilled labor mobility, (ii) the incomplete recourse and heavy administrative burden of means-tested transfers, and (iii) the fragmentation of labor and of family patterns. The idea of a universal transfer then reemerged as a way to address the three problems at the same time through a "basic income" given to all individuals, whatever their market income, and financed through an income tax paid on all market income (with no allowance). Additionally, an unconditional transfer would better protect individuals against the instability of their professional careers and family patterns. It would even provide "real freedom" to individuals (Van Parijs, 1995) since they would no longer be obliged to accept any job to survive. Rather than an unconditional transfer, Atkinson (2015) envisages a condition of "participation" in society: work, education, training, active job search, home care for young children or elderly people, or else voluntary work in a recognized association (with special provisions for illness and disability). In practice, few individuals would be excluded from the scheme, but, according to him, a form of reciprocity is required.

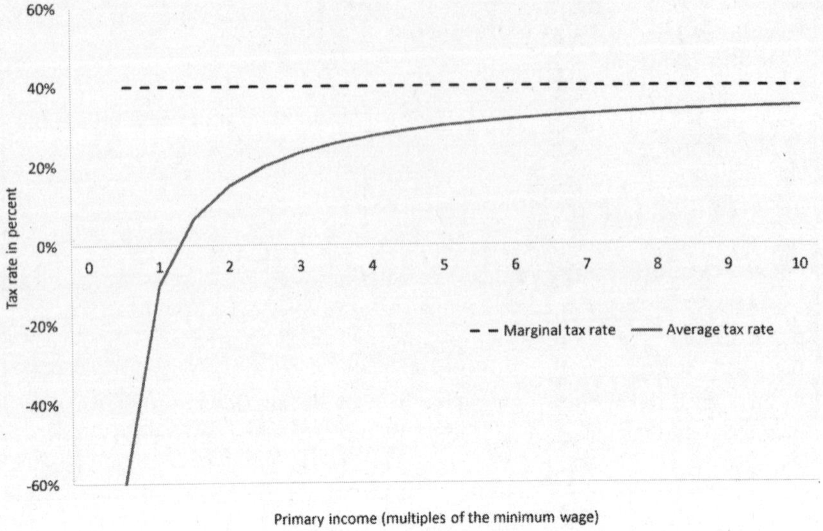

Figure 8.17 The average tax rate under a universal transfer system.[a]
[a]Universal transfer corresponding to half of the minimum wage combined with a flat marginal rate of 40%. The graph is truncated at 0.5 times the minimum wage for readability.
Authors.

of the transfer at the lower end of the income schedule. In most free-market versions of the basic income proposal, the transfer would replace all forms of social benefits, including any form of health care or public education. The idea is to empower the individual who will then take care of herself. However, most authors consider that the basic income is not meant to satisfy the totality of a beneficiary's basic needs, nor should it be a single benefit (i.e., replacing all other cash benefits). For instance, disability allowances will still need to be provided. The problem then is whether the basic income really simplifies the social transfer system. An intermediate solution would be to offer a universal child benefit, paid by the PIT. Such universal benefit would be complementary to public investments in health care and education, and it would help address the child poverty that is widespread in many countries. The benefit would replace means-tested family benefits (Atkinson, 2015).

Vertical equity concerns also have a dynamic, intergenerational dimension. Indeed, progressive income taxation limits wealth accumulation. Combined with inheritance taxes, it reduces inherited inequalities across individuals while also limiting individual incentives to climb the social ladder. In the case of France, Piketty (2001*a*, 2001*b*) showed that this mechanism has been powerful in limiting the increase of inequalities. The problem arises again if wealthy households can escape taxation, for instance, by relocating their income or wealth.

As shown in figure 8.18, the distribution of personal wealth was very unequal in Europe at the end of the nineteenth century. In the United Kingdom, as much as 70% of personal net wealth was owned by only 1% of the population (which means that the other 99% had to share a mere 30% of total wealth). The top 1% share fell during most of the twentieth century, down to 15% in the UK during the 1980s. However, wealth inequalities increased again in the 1990s and in the beginning of the twenty-first century—a feature that may be related to flattening PIT schedules, reduced inheritance taxes, and the scrapping of wealth taxation in most advanced economies. Not only is wealth concentrated in a small number of hands, but, thanks to longer life, these hands tend to belong to the elder part of the population. Individuals increasingly tend to inherit when they are close to retirement, if not already retired. The wealth received cannot be used to help in acquiring a first home or starting a business.

A reform of inheritance taxation was proposed by Anthony Atkinson (2015), following an old idea of John Stuart Mill. The idea would be to introduce a progressive taxation of the cumulated donations and inherited wealth received over the entire lifetime of the heir: the rate would depend upon donations and inheritance received in the past. Hence there would be an incentive for the donor to spread his or her donations more evenly across various receivers.

One step further would be the introduction of a minimum or universal inheritance, equivalent to a negative wealth tax (Atkinson, 2015). The idea comes from the philosopher and revolutionary Thomas Paine (1797/1999) who had proposed that, at the age of 21, each individual would receive lump-sum capital from a fund while losing his or her "natural" inheritance. The idea of

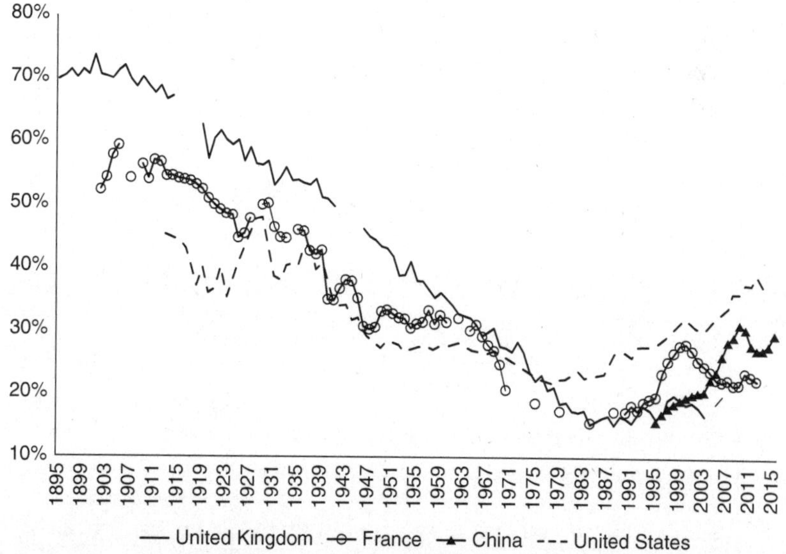

Figure 8.18 Top 1% share in personal net wealth, 1895–2015, in percent. World Wealth and Income Database, February 2017.

"asset-based egalitarianism" was taken up by several authors in the twentieth century. From 2003 to 2010, the British government ran a Child Trust Scheme where a lump-sum endowment of £250 was invested by the government for each newborn, with further payment for poor families and the possibility for families to top up the investment. These sums were to be made available at the age of 18, with no restriction on use. Anthony Atkinson (2015) has proposed a slightly revised version of the scheme named "inheritance for all": a capital endowment financed by the lifetime capital tax described earlier. Universal inheritances would be paid at birth into "capital endowment accounts" as a minimum endowment to every individual, thus reducing wealth inequalities between and within generations.

8.3.3 Correcting market failures

As illustrated earlier, it is difficult in practice to design a tax system that would reconcile neutrality and redistribution. However, in some cases, neutrality is not searched for—just the opposite, as the tax is then designed to correct market imperfections. Introducing nonneutral taxes may contribute to making markets more efficient.

a) Paternalist taxation

What is the difference between a social insurance contribution and a private contribution to a pension fund or a health insurance scheme? Both aim at protecting the individual against the risk of getting old without resources or of having to support costly medical care. The only difference is the compulsory nature of social contributions as opposed to free contributions to private schemes (and the choice between various schemes). Why, then, impose a public social insurance system financed through taxation? Two reasons may be put forward: equity, and individual myopia (or lack of rationality).

- *Equity*: A compulsory system allows for redistribution across individuals and better risk mutualization. For instance, the cost of a given illness is basically the same whether the patient is rich or poor. Leaving each individual responsible for his or her own insurance through the private system is therefore anti-redistributive, since the poor will pay relatively more, in proportion to their income. Some households may even not be able to pay for the insurance scheme. Having a single, compulsory system allows for cross-subsidization from the richer contributors to the poorer. It can also create incentives for the poorer to take costly preventive measures such as vaccination and consulting a doctor when sick, which has positive externalities on other individuals (lower risk of contagion) and on public finance (lower pressure on public-funded hospitals).

- *Myopia or lack of rationality*: If individuals are myopic, then they may not correctly insure against the various risks they incur. For instance, they may be overoptimistic concerning their ability to work during their old age or not well-informed about their life expectancy. Also, *financial illiteracy* is well-documented: most households do not master the basics of risk, return, and portfolio choice (Lusardi and Mitchell, 2007). In addition, it is well-known from behavioral economics that people exhibit dynamic inconsistency (see, e.g., Kahneman and Tversky, 2000, and Chapter 2 of this book). For this reason, the government may wish to force, or at least incentivize individuals to hedge against some risks. The same idea can justify policies aimed at encouraging households to save, for instance, through a tax exemption on voluntary contributions into pension funds or in some popular savings vehicles (e.g., life insurance) or through owning their house (exemption of mortgage interest payments).

These targeted tax exemptions, however, introduce distortions insofar as they modify the relative yield of the various savings vehicles, for instance, between investing in housing, bonds, or equity. Hence, a specific distortion (excessive preference for the present) is replaced by another one (distortion across savings vehicles).

In advanced economies, tobacco and alcohol are heavily taxed, notably on grounds of public health since individuals may not properly assess the risks involved in consuming too much of these items. Taxes are designed to make individual behaviors fit a "safe" behavior defined by the government.[38] In the same vein, the British government introduced a tax on soda drinks in 2016 in order to fight child obesity. Opponents of "fat taxes" argue that it is anti-redistributive; since sodas and fatty products are cheaper than healthy fruits and vegetables, they are consumed in larger quantities by the less wealthy households. Another way to encourage poor households to consume healthier food could be to reduce tariffs on agricultural imports because this would lower the consumer prices of farm products. More radically, some economists consider paternalism to be contrary to the freedom of choice, which is at the heart of free markets. Milton Friedman was the herald of this approach, as exemplified in the case of Social Security, in the following judgment:

> I believe that it is not the business of government to tell people what fraction of their incomes they should devote to providing for their own or someone else's old age. (Milton Friedman, "Social Security: The General and the Personal," *Wall Street Journal*, March 15, 1988)

It can be objected that paternalism does not go against individual freedom as long as it does not involve coercion (Thaler and Sunstein, 2003). Tax policy is well suited for this purpose, as long as the tax level is not confiscatory. Thaler and Sunstein refer to *nudges* (i.e., small incentives to help individuals take the "right" decisions without, however, forcing them).

b) Environmental taxes

Whereas paternalist taxation aims at responding to households' lack of information or to their too-short horizons, environmental taxes implement the polluter-payer principle and aim to have polluters internalize the externalities they produce, along the lines of box 8.7. *Energy taxes,* which mainly aim at raising public revenue from a relatively less-elastic demand, need to be distinguished from *environmental taxes,* or *green taxes,* intended to curb the behavior of taxpayers. The former have traditionally been much higher than the latter, with wide differences across OECD countries (see figure 8.19). It should be noted, however, that, as discussed in Section 8.2.3, taxation is not the only way of having private agents internalize the cost related to their polluting emissions. In the European Union, the industry is covered by the Emission Trading System (ETS), which means that, rather than paying a tax for their carbon emissions, firms need to buy carbon emission on the cap-and-trade market. Some sectors (such as construction or vehicles) are

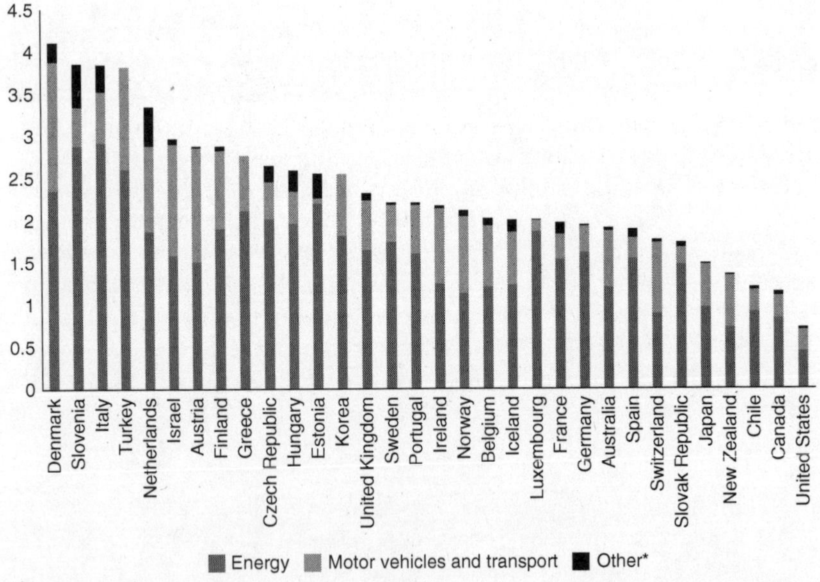

* Ozone depleting, water and wastewater, waste management, mining and quarrying, unallocated.

Figure 8.19 Environmentally related tax revenues in 2014 (% of gross domestic product [GDP]).
OECD.

covered by environmental standards. The coexistence of taxes, markets, and technical standards generates a wide variety of explicit and implicit carbon prices that make the reduction in carbon emissions especially inefficient (OECD, 2013).

How should the proceeds to environmental taxes be used? To the extent that their incidence is significantly on the producers (and not just on the consumers), environmental taxes will increase the costs of the polluting companies. Those in competition with foreign firms that do not support similar taxes will then need to be compensated for the sake of their competitiveness and the establishment of a level playing field. More generally, the political economy of green taxation suggests that the revenue of these taxes should be redistributed to the polluters themselves. Otherwise they will oppose the tax or propose voluntary contributions in order to rule out regulation or taxation (see Wilson, 1980). For instance, a carbon tax may be imposed on passenger transportation companies in proportion to their carbon emissions and returned to them in proportion to their passenger traffic. Individual companies would then be incentivized to reduce their carbon emissions, while the sector as a whole would not be submitted to higher taxes. Another way of compensating the polluting industries is through cutting taxes on labor, in order to reap a *double dividend* (see Section 8.2.3). Finland (1990), Sweden (1990), Norway (1991), Denmark (1992), the Netherlands (1996), Slovenia (1997), Germany (1998), and the United Kingdom (2000) have introduced simultaneously green taxation and a reduction of income taxes. These joint measures were revenue-neutral on average. In Germany, Denmark, and Sweden, the tax shift amounted to up to 1.1% of GDP (Andersen, 2010). However, empirical evidence on the double dividend is weak, especially since the welfare loss related to green taxes (e.g., through increased inequalities[39]) is not always accounted for (Mirrlees, 2011).

Environmental taxes can be extremely effective provided the tax rate is high enough. In 2002, for instance, Ireland introduced a heavy levy on plastic bags (0.15 euros per bag). By the end of the year, the consumption of these bags had fallen by 90% (OECD, 2007).[40] In 1991, a heavy tax on carbon dioxide and sulfur dioxide emissions was introduced in Sweden. The subsequent reduction in emissions exceeded 50%. In Norway, the carbon emission tax introduced in 1991 led to a reduction in corresponding emissions by 21% the same year.

By construction, however, success with a Pigovian tax reduces the revenue that can be expected from this tax. An emblematic example outside the environmental sphere is that of the *Tobin tax*, a small tax on capital flows inspired by Nobel Laureate James Tobin (1978)[41] that has been advocated by a number of nongovernmental organizations to limit the scope for speculation and, at the same time, raise revenues for less-developed countries. The two objectives are somewhat contradictory. Additionally, since financial turnover is highly mobile, imposing a tax on financial transactions in one country (or in a group of countries) is likely to move the activity to another country. We'll come back to these coordination problems in the next section.

On the whole, the capacity of various countries to raise environmental taxes depends on the structure of the economy, the ability of the government to redistribute the proceeds appropriately, and social preferences, but also geographic factors. For instance, the size of the United States and its relatively low population density may explain why its citizens, confronted with large transportation needs, are attached to cheap energy and oppose energy taxes.

8.3.4 Tax cooperation

a) From competition to cooperation

The debate on tax competition opposes those who praise its positive effect on budget discipline and those who accuse it of distorting public choices and inducing inequality. The underlying paradigm behind the first argument is that of the *Leviathan government,* namely a partisan government moved by electoral objectives or dominated by an administration plagued by its own logic; the opponents, in contrast, believe in a *benevolent government* whose objectives coincide with social ones and are not taken hostage by the administration.

The European Union offers an instructive case due to the full mobility of goods, services, capital, and labor across the different Member States. Tax coordination within the EU is impeded by strong disagreements regarding the degree of desirable tax competition and by the unanimity rule governing tax issues. Somewhat paradoxically, the only example of strong coordination in the EU concerns VAT, even though it mostly affects immobile tax bases (see box 8.14). VAT harmonization has been viewed as a useful complement to the single market in goods and services, whereas capital tax harmonization was not initially viewed as a useful complement to the single capital market.

Cooperation on capital taxation has proved a long and painful process in the EU. A "tax package" was adopted in January 2003 that includes a "code of conduct" regarding detrimental practices on corporate taxation (for instance, tax rebates for foreign-owned companies) and full exchange of information across Member States on capital income after a transitory period. However, it took more than a decade and a financial crisis for the automatic exchange of information to become effective. Simultaneously, some initiatives have been taken in the area of corporate taxation, but again the discussions have proved difficult (box 8.15).

At international level, the OECD and G20 have launched the Base Erosion and Profit Shifting (BEPS) initiative, gathering more than 100 countries and jurisdictions. The BEPS initiative aims at setting an international tax framework to tax profits at the source of value creation. The initiative has developed

Box 8.14 VAT in the European Union

VAT is the only tax subject to harmonization in the EU, as a complement to the single market. According to a 1977 directive, three different VAT rates are applicable in the EU: a standard rate (minimum 15%) and two reduced rates (minimum 5%). Some "super-reduced" rates (2–4%) can be seen as inheritances from the past to be progressively phased out, and some activities, such as financial services, are exempted from VAT. Reduced rates can be applied only to a limited list of subsistence items such as food or drugs. In 1999, the European Council extended the right to use reduced VAT rates for a strict list of labor-intensive services (small repairs, house renovation, house cleaning, domestic care, hairdressing) for an experimental period of three years in order to boost job creation in these sectors. The experiment was then extended several times, and, in May 2009, the Council allowed these exceptions to remain permanent. It is easy for Member States to argue that, because those services are mostly immobile across EU countries, cutting VAT on them is not harmful to other Member States, so the subsidiarity principle (see Chapter 3) should apply to them.

Within the EU, and with few exceptions, VAT is raised according to the destination principle; that is, it is raised in the country where final consumption takes place, at that country's prevailing rate. To reduce compliance costs for companies active in different countries, and to limit cross-border fraud, the European Commission has proposed a reform whereby the tax will be collected only in one Member State for each European company: goods will be taxed in the source country but at the rate of the destination country (the tax administration in each country will therefore collect the VAT for all EU countries and transfer the proceeds).

targeted measures in 15 key domains such as the digital economy, controlled foreign companies (CFC) rules, interest deductions, and permanent establishment status.

b) Global taxation

When common public goods are identified (see Chapter 3), a common tax would appear appropriate. However, levying a tax at the international level would require adequate representation of the citizens. Three examples are developed here.

- *A European tax?* The EU budget, whose purpose is to finance common policies, is funded through Member States' contributions,

Box 8.15 Coordination on the Corporate Income Tax Within the European Union

In 1990, the "mother-affiliate" European directive tackled the double taxation of repatriated profits by a mother company from its subsidiaries. Member States are requested either to exempt repatriated profits or to deduct taxes already paid by the affiliates from the mother's tax bill (partial credit system). The objective was to avoid discriminating against foreign subsidiaries (taxed twice) in relation to local firms (taxed only once).

In 2001, the European Commission proposed a two-step strategy to remove remaining corporate tax distortions in the EU: on the one hand, to suppress specific distortions (for example, by extending the scope of the mother-affiliate directive); on the other hand, to harmonize and consolidate the corporate tax base across Member States through a *Common Consolidated Corporate Tax Base (CCCTB)* system (i.e., through consolidation and apportionment of the tax base).

Such an apportionment system is used in Canada and the United States. The European Commission has proposed to introduce it in the EU. According to the CCCTB, each Member State would be allocated a share of the single consolidated tax base of each multinational firm, according to an apportionment formula, based on physical capital, payrolls, employment, and sales. It could then tax this base at its own statutory rate.

In 2016, the Commission made a new proposal of a CCCTB, now organized in two steps: first, the harmonization of the tax base across the Member States; second, the consolidation and apportionment of the base. The first step will, however, make tax competition more transparent, hence more vigorous, which raises the question of coordinating not only the bases but also the rates. As for the second stage of CCCTB, the elimination of intragroup tax avoidance will be conditional on a proper definition of "permanent establishment" and of group structure (to avoid a group with intensive activities in a country avoiding the CIT thanks to its legal structure).

The Anti-Tax Avoidance Directive adopted in 2016 has introduced a number of anti-avoidance measures. For instance, a Member State is allowed to tax the profits parked in a low-tax country, the transfer of assets, and a share of interest payments (based on a fixed ratio of its earnings); it is also possible to tax some hybrid schemes that exploit national mismatches to avoid taxation. A *general anti-abuse rule* allows states to counteract aggressive tax planning in all other cases.

transfers of VAT revenues, and import tariffs. Even though the EU budget finances common policies, each Member State is tempted to calculate its net contribution (i.e., the difference between what it gives to and what it gets from the EU budget). This blocks any discussion on the characteristics of the budget in terms of allocation and of redistribution (Tabellini, 2003). If, as the Sapir report recommended in 2004, the European budget had to develop toward more redistribution (between rich and poor regions, between expanding regions and regions in conversion) and higher provision of government services (infrastructures, R&D), then it would be advisable to back the budget with a genuine European tax, paid by citizens or companies and not by states. In all logic, this tax should replace some existing taxes (because Member States would reduce their direct contribution to the EU budget, or companies would be permitted to credit the European tax on the national tax), and it should rest on a mobile base within the EU such as corporate income (because it would allow internalizing tax externalities). Along these lines, the "Monti group" presented nine reform proposals in January 2017, aiming at overhauling EU financing without increasing the contribution of Member States. In particular, they recommended replacing the current contributions based on national income with resources based on a European carbon tax, a common environmental tax (e.g., on fuel or other energy), a common CIT, a common reformed VAT, or a tax on the financial sector. The Report, however, specifies that the revenues forming the EU budget are unanimously agreed upon between Member States and can therefore not be qualified as "EU taxes."

- *A global wealth tax?* In 2013, Thomas Piketty proposed to introduce a progressive global wealth tax in order to limit the concentration of wealth in the world. The rate would start small but rise up to 10% annually for net worth in billions. The tax would incentivize the net wealth holders to make valuable use of their assets. Implementing such a tax would require international cooperation. For instance, countries accounting for the largest share of world output could establish a global registry of financial assets or impose sanctions on tax havens refusing to cooperate. Such cooperation could, however, be difficult to reach.
- *A Nordhaus tax?* Ambitious actions on climate change are undermined by the issue of free-riding since all countries will benefit from the efforts of a subset of countries. A Climate Club (Nordhaus, 2015) could provide an effective solution to this

problem and contribute to reach global climate targets. The idea is to establish a Club upon agreement of a few countries (the main polluters) to undertake harmonized emissions reductions centered on an international target carbon price. The target price could be met using a carbon-tax, cap-and-trade, or hybrid mechanism. The novelty of the Club scenario is the penalization of nonparticipants through a uniform *ad valorem* tariff on their exports into the Club region. According to Nordhaus, a relatively low tariff rate (e.g., 2%) would be sufficient to induce participation as long as the international target carbon price is not too high.

Notes

1. In this chapter, we speak of *government services* to designate all goods produced or services provided by governments (or, in some cases, public enterprises) whatever the justification (or the lack of it) for their public character. We reserve the expression *public goods* to goods and services whose consumption is neither excludable nor rivalrous, as defined in Chapter 2.
2. The "poll tax" was a flat community charge decided in the 1980s to replace a tax based on property values. The project was abandoned after the resignation of the Prime Minister. It was, however, replaced by a council tax based on property values but with regressive structure (Atkinson, 2015).
3. In Europe, contributions to health, old-age, and unemployment insurance are often called *social security contributions*, but, in the United States, the federal old-age insurance program is called *social security*. To avoid confusion, we speak of *social insurance contributions* rather than social security contributions.
4. In the Middle Ages, serfs would pay contributions in money and kind to finance the expenditures of the lords. The French Revolution introduced the notion of proportional taxes, but progressive taxation only appeared at the beginning of the twentieth century.
5. See Salanié (2003).
6. Property taxes are based on the market value of land and housing held by households, with a tax rate generally decided at the local level.
7. The CIT is levied on companies' profits, after tax allowances (such as accelerated capital depreciation, or R&D allowances) have been deducted.
8. As detailed in Section 8.3, the VAT is a tax on final consumption. Unlike a general sales tax, the VAT is paid at each stage of the value chain and then recovered on intermediate consumptions and investments. The fact that intermediate consumption is not taxed ensures that the same good is not taxed several times (as an intermediate consumption, then as a final consumption) and explains why this tax is named "value-added."

9. In some countries, personal income taxes on labor income are raised by the employers and transferred by them to the tax administration. Although the employer then pays the entire package of labor taxes, these taxes in fact bear on labor supplied by the workers.
10. The VAT is also subject to false claims for credit or refund, fictitious "invoice mills" (companies that are set up solely to generate invoices that allow for VAT credit or refund, whether the corresponding VAT has been paid or not), "carousel fraud" (within the EU, where company A imports goods from another member state and sells the goods to company B; the latter is refunded for VAT paid on its domestic purchases, while company A did not pay any VAT on imported goods and disappears before the tax administration can ask it for VAT received on its sales to B).
11. Similar analysis can be conducted on net wealth rather than income, generally showing more extensive and rising inequalities.
12. To compare income across households, statisticians take into account the number of persons within a household as well as their relative consumption levels. According to an equivalence established by the OECD, the first adult aged 18 and older represents one consumption unit, each subsequent adult aged 18 and older represents 0.7 consumption units, and each person younger than 18 accounts for 0.5 consumption units. A family composed of two adults and two children younger than 18 therefore represents 2.7 consumption units.
13. The net marginal tax rate is the marginal fall of net income (including the loss of means-tested transfers) following a marginal rise in primary income.
14. The quasi elimination of wealth taxes in the EU is consistent with these trends. In 2017, only France, Luxembourg, and the Netherlands still retained a wealth tax.
15. Hence, tax policy has common features with monetary policy where international capital mobility reduces the leeway for an independent monetary policy (see Chapter 7).
16. Partial and general equilibrium settings are explained in Chapter 1.
17. The concept of social loss is discussed in Chapter 1. A social loss appears when there is a fall in social welfare. In this section, social welfare is approximated by the sum of agents' surpluses. Producers' surplus is equal to aggregate profit. Consumers' surplus is the difference between the disposition to pay and the actual market price, for each unit of good. Last, the surplus of the public sector is equal to its tax revenue.
18. See Salanié (2003).
19. Consider two variables x and y. The elasticity of y to x is $(\mathrm{d}y/y)/(\mathrm{d}x/x)$, whereas the semi-elasticity is $(\mathrm{d}y/y)/\mathrm{d}x$. The concept of semi-elasticity is often preferred to that of elasticity when x may be close to zero (tax rate, interest rate).
20. There is also some evidence of a Laffer curve for corporate income tax, especially since multinational firms may shift profit abroad as the tax rate increases relative to the foreign one. See Clausing (2007) and Devereux (2006).
21. This striking result is based on data for 23,000 companies located in 10 countries over the period 1993–2003 (i.e., during a period of high capital mobility). In a

closed economy, Auerbach (2005) argues that capital owners may bear a large part of a corporate tax increase in the short run because the price of their shares is immediately reduced. In the longer run, the tax is borne by both corporate and noncorporate capital owners, as shown by Harberger (1962).

22. For a review, see Slemrod (1990). See also Auerbach and Hines (2002).
23. The polluter-payer principle is enshrined in the Rio declaration on environment and development by the United Nations in 1992. It is in fact very old. From the Middle Ages to the French Revolution, a so-called *pulverage charge* existed in Dauphiné and in Provence (France). This tax was charged by villages crossed by transhumant herds to compensate for the dust raised by their passage.
24. Other schemes are, of course, possible for regulating traffic in cities, such as granting access only to emergency vehicles and to buses and delivery vehicles during certain hours.
25. See IMF (2011), Farhi, Gopinath, and Itskhoki (2011).
26. The proposal was endorsed in 2016 by two Republican members of the US Congress, Paul Ryan and Kevin Brady.
27. This result contrasts with the "happy" tax competition theory (Tiebout, 1956), according to which each individual will relocate to the jurisdiction offering the combination of taxes and government services that are closest to his or her preferred basket: individuals "vote with their feet." Hence, tax competition will just eliminate ineffective jurisdictions.
28. *Rents* are excess profit related to limited competition or economies of scale. Taxing rents theoretically does not involve any efficiency loss, unlike taxing "normal" profit.
29. Surveyed by Hines (1999*b*, 2007), de Mooij and Ederveen (2001), Devereux and Griffith (2002), and Devereux (2006).
30. See, e.g., Malinvaud (1998), Sterdyniak et al. (1991).
31. For relatively high tax rates, $1/(1 + t) > 1 - t$, so t_{VAT} or t_{SC1} have a slightly larger impact on purchasing power.
32. As for PIT, households at the minimum wage are generally exempted.
33. This should be qualified, however. As suggested by the theory of tax incidence, capital income may *de facto* escape any form of taxation due to its high elasticity compared to other tax bases.
34. Conversely, the VAT base, which is limited to consumption, is generally not broad enough to finance a cut in social charges on a less than one-to-one rate variation basis.
35. See OECD (2016). For instance, the PIT in France is based on a family quotient, while Germany applies joint taxation and decreasing-in-income child allowances. Other countries with joint taxation or options for joint taxation are the United States (optional, married couples), Estonia (for married couples), Luxembourg (spouses and partners), Switzerland (married couples), Ireland (optional, married couples), Norway (optional), Poland (optional, married couples), Portugal (families), and Spain (optional, families). The individual tax systems of Denmark

and the Netherlands also include "joint" elements such as transferrable tax reliefs and allowances between partners.

36. See Piketty and Saez (2007).
37. See, for instance, Riphahn (2001) or Currie (2004).
38. The corresponding tax revenues are, of course, welcomed by the government. However, it should be noted that there is some contradiction between using such a tax to curb private consumption (which relies on high elasticity of consumption) and the wish to raise public revenue (which necessitates low elasticity).
39. A poorer household spends a larger share of its income on heating and transportation.
40. In the Irish case, retailers were obliged to fully pass on the tax to their customers.
41. After an old suggestion by Keynes (1936): "The introduction of a substantial Government transfer tax on all transactions might prove the most serviceable reform available, with a view to mitigating the predominance of speculation over enterprise in the United States" (Keynes 1936, chapt. 12, VI).

References

Andersen, S. M. (2010), "Europe's Experience with Carbon-Energy Taxation," *Sapiens*, 3(2), pp. 1–11.

Arulampalam, W., M. P. Devereux, and G. Maffini (2012), "The Direct Incidence of Corporate Income Tax on Wages," *European Economic Review*, 56(6), pp. 1038–1054.

Andersson, F., and R. Forslid (2003), "Tax Competition and Economic Geography," *Journal of Public Economic Theory*, 5, pp. 279–304.

Atkinson, A. (1977), "Optimal Taxation and the Direct Versus Indirect Tax Controversy," *Canadian Journal of Economics*, 10, pp. 590–606.

Atkinson, A. (2015), *Inequality, What Can Be Done?* Harvard University Press.

Auerbach, A. (2005), "Who Bears the Corporate Tax? A Review of What We Know," *NBER Working Paper*, no. 11686, October.

Auerbach, A. (2010), "A Modern Corporate Tax," Center for American Progress and The Hamilton Project, December.

Auerbach, A., M. P. Devereux, and H. Simpson (2007), "Taxing Corporate Income," *CESifo Working Paper*, no. 2139, November.

Auerbach, A., and J. Hines (2002), "Taxation and Economic Efficiency," in Auerbach, A., and M. Feldstein, eds., *Handbook of Public Economics*, vol. 3, North Holland,pp. 1347–1421.

Baldwin, R., R. Forslid, P. Martin, G. Ottaviano, and F. Robert-Nicoud (2003), *Economic Geography and Public Policy*, Princeton University Press.

Besley, T., and T. Persson (2014), "Why Do Developing Countries Tax So Little?" *Journal of Economic Perspectives*, 8(4), pp. 99–120.

Bucovetsky S., and J. D. Wilson (1991), "Tax Competition with Two Tax Instruments," *Regional Science and Urban Economics,* 21(3), pp. 333–50.

Charrié, J., and L. Janin (2015), "Taxation of the Digital Economy," *France Stratégie, Policy Brief,* no. 26, March.

Clausing, K. A. (2007) "Corporate Tax Revenues in OECD Countries," *International Tax and Public Finance*, 4, pp. 115–33.

Cline, W. (2017), "The Ryan-Brady Cash-flow Tax: Disguised Protection, Exaggerated Revenue, and Increased Inequality," Peterson Institute of International Economics, Policy Brief 17-4, January.

Coase, R. H. (1937), "The Nature of the Firm," *Economica*, 4, pp. 386–405.

Currie, J. (2004), "The Take Up of Social Benefits," *NBER Working Paper,* no. 104888.

De Mooij, R. A., and S. Ederveen (2001), "Taxation and Foreign Direct Investment: A Synthesis of Empirical Research," *International Tax and Public Finance*, 10, pp. 673–93.

Devereux, M. P. (2006), "The Impact of Taxation on the Location of Capital, Firms and Profit: Survey of Empirical Evidence," *Oxford University Centre for Business Taxation Working Paper* 07/02.

Devereux, M. P., and R. Griffith (2002), "The Impact of Corporate Taxation on the Location of Capital: A Review," *Swedish Economic Policy Review*, 9, pp. 79–102.

Devereux, M. P., and P. B. Sørensen (2006), "The Corporate Income Tax: International Trends and Options for Fundamental Reform," *European Economy, Economic Papers*, 264, December.

Dingeldey, I. (2001), "European Tax Systems and their Impact on Family Employment Patterns," *Journal of Social Policy*, 30(4), pp. 653–72, October.

European Commission (2017a), *VAT Gap Report*, September.

European Commission (2017b), *Taxation Trends in the European Union* (annual report).

Farhi, E., G. Gopinath, and O. Itskhoki (2011), "Fiscal Devaluations," *NBER Working Paper*, No. 17662, December.

Finke, K., C. Fuest, H. Nusser, and C. Spengel (2014), "Extending Taxation of Interest and Royalty Income at Source: An Option to Limit Base Erosion and Profit Shifting?" *ZEW Discussion Paper*, 14-073.

Fjeldstad, O.-H., and L. Rakner (2003), "Taxation and Tax Reforms in Developing countries: Illustrations from sub-Saharan Africa," *CMI Report*, R 2003:6, Chr. Michelsen Institute.

Fuest, C., C. Spengel, K. Finke, J. H. Heckemeyer, and H. Nusser (2013), "Profit Shifting and 'Aggressive' Tax Planning by Multinational Firms: Issues and Options for Reform," *World Tax Journal,* 5(3), 307–24.

Gordon, R., and W. Li (2009), "Tax Structures in Developing Countries: Many Puzzles and a Possible Explanation," *Journal of Public Economics*, 93(7), 855–66.

Grossman G., and H. Helpman (1994), "Protection for Sale," *American Economic Review*, 84, pp. 833–50.

Groupe d'experts du SMIC (2014), "Salaire minimum interprofessionnel de croissance," *Rapport annuel*, 2 décembre.

Harberger, A. (1962), "The Incidence of the Corporate Income Tax," *Journal of Political Economy*, 70, pp. 215–40.

Hines, J. R. (1999*a*), "Three Sides of Harberger Triangle," *Journal of Economic Perspectives*, 13, pp. 167–88.

Hines, J. R. (1999*b*). "Lessons from Behavioral Responses to International Taxation," *National Tax Journal*, 2, pp. 305–23.

Hines, J. R. (2007), "Corporate Taxation and International Competition," in Auerbach, A. J., J. Hines, and J. Slemrod, eds., *Taxing Corporate Income in the 21st Century*, Cambridge University Press, pp. 268–95.

Hufbauer, G., and K. Elliott (1994), *Measuring the Cost of Protection in the United States*, Institute for International Economics.

International Monetary Fund (2011), "Fiscal Devaluation: What Is It—and Does It Work?" *Fiscal Monitor: Addressing Fiscal Challenges to Reduce Economic Risks*, Annex 1, pp. 37–42, September.

Ivanova, A., M. Keen, and A. Klemm (2005), "The Russian Flat Tax Reform," *IMF Working Paper*, no. 05/16.

Jaumotte, F. (2003), "Female Labour Force Participation: Past Trends and Main Determinants in OECD Countries," *OECD Working Paper*, No. 376.

Kahneman, D., and A. Tversky (2000), *Choices, Values and Frames*, Cambridge University Press.

Keen, M., and S. Smith (2006), "VAT Fraud and Evasion: What Do We Know, and What Can Be Done?" *National Tax Journal*, 59, pp. 861–87.

Keynes, J. M. (1936), *The General Theory of Employment, Interest and Money*, Macmillan and Co, London, p. 160.

Krogstrup, S. (2002), "What Do Theories of Tax Competition Predict of Capital Taxes in EU Countries? A Review of the Literature," *HEI Working Paper*, no. 05/2002.

Laffer, A. (2004), "The Laffer Curve: Past, and Present Future," Backgrounder no. 1765, The Heritage Foundation, www.heritage.org.

Lerner, A. P. (1936). "The symmetry between import and export taxes." *Economica*, 3 (11), pp. 306–313.

Lindé, J., and A. Pescatori (2017). "The macroeconomic effects of trade tariffs: Revisiting the lerner symmetry result." *IMF Working Paper*, 17 (151).

Lusardi, A., and O. Mitchell (2007), "Baby Boomer Retirement Security: The Roles of Planning, Financial Literacy, and Housing Wealth," *Journal of Monetary Economics*, 54, pp. 205–24.

Malinvaud, E. (1998), "Les cotisations sociales à la charge des employeurs: analyse économique," Report du Conseil d'Analyse Economique no.33, La Documentation Française.

Mirrlees, J. (1971), "An Exploration of the Theory of Optimal Income Taxation," *Review of Economic Studies*, 38, pp. 175–208.

Mirrlees, J. (2011), "Reforming the Tax System for the 21st Century: The Mirrlees Review," Oxford University Press.

Nordhaus, W. (2015), "Climate Clubs: Overcoming Free-Riding in International Climate Policy," *American Economic Review*, 105(4), pp. 1339–70.

OECD (2007), "The Political Economy of Environmentally Related Taxes," February.
OECD (2013), *Effective Carbon Prices*, November 4.
OECD (2016), "Neutrality of Tax-Benefit Systems," Social Policy Division - Directorate of Employment, Labour and Social Affairs.
Ostry, J. D., A. Berg, and C. G. Tsangarides (2014), "Redistribution, Inequality, and Growth," *IMF Staff Discussion Note*, SDN/14/02, February.
Paine, T. (1797/1999), *Agrarian Justice*, Digital edition, www.grundskyld.dk.
Pigou, A. C. (1920), *The Economics of Welfare*, Macmillan.
Piketty, T. (2001*a*/2016), *Les Hauts Revenus en France au 20ème siècle: inégalités et redistribution (1901–1998)*, Le Seuil, 928 p.
Piketty, T. (2001*b*), "Les inégalités dans le long terme," in *Inégalités économiques*, Rapport du Conseil d'Analyse économique, no. 33, La Documentation Française, pp. 137–204, available on www.cae.gouv.fr.
Piketty, T. (2013), *Capital in the Twenty-First Century*, Harvard University Press.
Piketty, T., and E. Saez (2007), "How Progressive is the US Federal Tax System? A Historical and International Perspective," *Journal of Economic Perspectives*, 21, pp. 3–24.
Ramsey, F. P. (1927), "A Contribution to the Theory of Taxation," *Economic Journal*, 37, pp. 47–61.
Riphahn, R. T. (2001), "Rational Poverty or Poor Rationality? The Take-Up of Social Assistance Benefits," *Review of Income and Wealth*, 47(3), 379–98.
Salanié, B. (1998), "Un exemple de taxation optimale," in Bourguignon, F., ed., *Fiscalité et reduistribution*, Rapport du Conseil d'Analyse Economique, no. 11, pp. 87–90, la Documentation Française.
Salanié, B. (2003), *The Economics of Taxation*, MIT Press.
Slemrod, J. (1990), "Optimal Taxation and Optimal Tax Systems," *Newspaper of Economic Perspectives*, 4, pp. 157–78.
Sterdyniak, H., M. H. Blonde, G. Cornilleau, J. Le Cacheux, and J. Le Dem (1991), *Vers une Fiscalité Européenne*, Economica.
Tabellini, G. (2003), "Principle of Policymaking in the European Union," *CESifo Economic Studies*, 49, pp. 75–102.
Thaler, R., and C. Sunstein (2003), "Libertarian Paternalism," *American Economic Review*, 93, pp. 175–79.
Tiebout, C. (1956), "A Pure Theory of Local Expenditures," *Journal of Political Economy*, 64, pp. 416–24.
Tobin, J. (1978), "A Proposal for International Monetary Reform," *Eastern Economic Journal*, 3, pp. 153–59.
Tørsløv, T., Wier, L., and G. Zucman (2018), "The Missing Profits of Nations", mimeo, July.
Van Parijs, P. (1995), *Real Freedom for All. What (if Anything) Can Justify Capitalism?* Oxford University Press.
Wanniski, J. (2005), "Sketching the Laffer Curve," *Yorktown Patriot*, 14 June.
Wilson, J. (1980), *The Politics of Regulation*, Basic Books.

Zodrow, G., and P. Mieszkowski (1986), "Pigou, Tiebout, Property Taxation, and the Underprovision of Local Public Goods," *Journal of Urban Economics*, 19, pp. 356–70.

Zucman, G. (2014), "Taxing Across Borders: Tracking Personal Wealth and Corporate Profits," *Journal of Economic Perspectives*, 28(4), pp. 121–48.

9

Growth Policies

The "Great Recession" generated by the 2007–2008 economic and financial crisis and the subsequent long period of mediocre growth in the developed world have again put long-term growth at the forefront of economic policy debates. While demand policies may be effective in the short term to dampen cyclical fluctuations and even though they may have a longer term impact through hysteresis effects, they cannot be relied on to trigger lasting growth. Long-term production of goods and services is essentially determined by potential supply, whose rate of growth conditions the increase in wealth and welfare.

Economic growth is by no means a given. In 1913, Argentina's gross domestic product (GDP) per person was 70% higher than Spain's.[1] In the aftermath of World War II, that of Ghana exceeded that of South Korea by almost 50%. In 1970, Italy's GDP per person was more than 60% higher than

Ireland's. Yet, in 2016, Spain's GDP per person was almost 80% higher than Argentina's, Korea's was close to nine times higher than Ghana's, and Ireland's was almost twice Italy's.[2] Prosperity and underdevelopment result from persistent growth divergences over decades. For example, a growth differential of a single percentage point per year (as compared to a 2% trend) cumulated over 50 years results in a 63% income gap; for a differential of two percentage points, the gap after 50 years reaches 164%; and for three percentage points, it is 326%.[3]

People benefit from long-term growth directly through higher incomes or indirectly through wider access to public goods such as health, education, safety, and infrastructures. Their capacity to reap these benefits depends on income distribution: rising concerns about inequalities have made *inclusive growth* a priority objective. People also suffer from some of the consequences of growth, such as damage to the environment, which may in turn make growth unsustainable. It is thus important to address measurement issues through defining and adopting indicators that provide better estimates of living standards than GDP, considering not only material, but also ethical, social, environmental, and even philosophical dimensions.

Yet, growth is the only mechanism that makes it possible to increase the living standards of some individuals without decreasing those of others, and this is why this chapter focuses on growth and growth policies. We recognize the importance of the issues raised by proponents of no-growth and "*degrowth.*"[4] The interest of the discussion they have initiated is to propel noneconomic and nonmonetary concerns to the fore. They also have a point in arguing that sensible environmental goals are not compatible with the current growth models or in challenging the idea that "more is better." However, the assumed contradiction between economic growth and other objectives is misleading. Concerns about sustainability and equity call for better economics of growth and better growth policies, not for disregarding them altogether.

The quest for the determinants of growth is similar to opening successively, and with increasing difficulty, a set of Russian dolls. A first step consists in documenting the trajectories of various countries' economies over long periods of time. A number of stylized facts emerge from this exercise. A second step consists in uncovering the determinants of economic growth by introducing *production factors*; namely, labor and capital, and by calling on what is known as *growth accounting*, which identifies their contribution to economic growth.

To proceed beyond this descriptive approach, however, it is necessary to turn to growth models. So-called *neo-classical growth models* explain human and physical capital accumulation and its impact on income per person. They relate growth to the behavior of savings or to investment in education. These models are useful representations of reality—they help explain, for instance, why growth rates in Europe and Japan slowed down at the end of the twentieth century when income per person in those economies got closer to the

US level—and help address economic policy choices. However, they remain frustrating in that a significant part of the determinants of long-term growth comes out as an unexplained residual. To unearth what is behind that residual, later models, based on explicit microeconomic underpinnings, focus on *endogenous growth* mechanisms that explain how growth can persist over time, and how and why some countries use their production factors more effectively than others and achieve better growth performances. In turn, these models point to deeper determinants such as economic institutions and their adequacy for a given level of development. The last stage of the analysis therefore consists in determining in what context (in terms of education and research systems, of intellectual property protection, of competition, of corporate finance, of taxation, etc.) innovation and endogenous growth are most likely to flourish,[5] with the remaining caveat that growth itself is likely to influence the context.

Moving to a deeper level of analysis does not deprive the previous one of relevance, and the various approaches we have outlined are to a large extent complementary. Basic models go a long way toward explaining growth differences: for example, the largest part of the stellar East Asian growth performance in the last quarter of the twentieth century is accounted for by high saving and investment rates, which, given decreasing returns to capital, cannot produce sustainable growth. As economists move away from the well-charted approaches based on measuring growth and its components toward understanding its deeper determinants, their knowledge and recommendations become less assertive. Informed by past errors, they realize the limits of their science.[6] However, the challenges of economic policymaking underline how essential such investigations are. To find out how to jump-start European growth, for example, it is not enough to observe that it has been diverging from that of the United States or even that investment has slowed down or that innovation has lagged: what matters is to determine whether European countries should, as a priority, devote additional resources to education and research, whether they should enforce tighter competition in product markets, or whether they should embark on tax reforms, among other possible policy measures.

Growth economics therefore relies on a combination of mechanics and alchemy. The former is necessary to isolate and quantify the proximate determinants of output development along a growth trajectory. The latter is called for to understand what makes countries take off and move from one growth trajectory to a higher one. Beyond the obvious laundry list—the recommendation to fix all the major deficiencies that hinder labor market participation, the acquisition of knowledge, capital accumulation, innovation, and productivity improvements—there is therefore no such thing as a growth recipe. This makes the search for successful growth strategies especially arduous. To borrow from the title of a book by a famous development scholar (Easterly, 2001), the quest for growth is likely to remain somewhat elusive.

9.1 Concepts and Issues

9.1.1 Measuring growth and development

"A rising tide lifts all boats," John F. Kennedy once famously said.[7] But all boats are not lifted equally. Aggregate measures of the level of development require aggregating the standards of living of many individuals, and such aggregation involves ethical choices: the utilitarian, or "Benthamian" (cf. Chapter 1) observer will assess development using the well-being of the community as a whole as a criterion and therefore focus on the evolution of average income, while the "Rawlsian" observer will focus on the poorest individual and will therefore be concerned with absolute poverty reduction.[8]

Macroeconomists typically adopt a utilitarian approach, as they have been chiefly concerned with the progression of average income per person and have only come recently to focusing on inequality in income distributions and on absolute poverty reduction. Development economists often blend the two approaches by looking both at average income and at some measure of absolute poverty, such as the proportion of the population living on less than a given daily threshold.[9]

GDP per person, or *per capita GDP*, corresponds to the average value added per person created within a given constituency and is therefore relevant to measuring the average standard of living, however inequitable its distribution may be.[10] Of course, the "average person" is fictitious, so that GDP per person is not a satisfactory representation of any individual's income, not to even mention standard of living.

Comparing countries' incomes at various points in time requires several technical and complex corrections. Across time, GDP needs to be measured *in constant prices*, that is, to be adjusted for the evolution of prices. Across countries, adjustments are also needed to account for variations in exchange rates. The common practice is to use exchange rates adjusted for price differences: *purchasing power parity exchange rates* or *PPP exchange rates* are the nominal exchange rates that would equalize prices across countries (see Chapter 7).[11] These can be computed, but they are fraught with uncertainty and this uncertainty significantly affects comparisons. A major difficulty is the choice of a basket of goods and services that can be similar enough across countries (from a welfare perspective) to compare real incomes and stable enough over time to assess the evolution of real GDP for each country.

It is increasingly recognized that GDP is beset by several shortcomings.[12]

First, it does not include nonmarket and nonmonetary activities that impact on well-being and is therefore a poor measure of the latter (see also Chapter 1). Individual welfare also depends on life expectancy, access to public services, the length and quality of leisure, and more. It is misleading and misguided (Sen, 2000) to reduce the various dimensions of human development to a single measure. Such considerations and Sen's contributions led to the introduction by the United Nations Development Program (UNDP) in the 1970s of a multidimensional human development indicator to provide a more comprehensive measure of well-being (the Human Development Index [HDI], described in Chapter 1).

More generally, improvements in livelihoods brought by technical progress and economic growth play a decisive role in the long-term evolution of income and living standards. Angus Deaton, who received the Nobel Prize in economics in 2015, has shown how the Scientific Revolution and Enlightenment generated improvements in health and well-being that had been largely underestimated by analyses based on income figures (Deaton, 2013) and how this progress also generated inequalities because not everyone benefitted from it.

Second, GDP sums up individual expenditures and does not consider positive or negative externalities. For example, the value-added generated by polluting industries adds to GDP, but the damage these industries cause to the environment is ignored—on the contrary, expenditures incurred to correct this damage contribute to GDP. Conventional GDP does not consider the depletion of natural resources. The concept of *sustainable development* aims at correcting this shortcoming through the introduction of intertemporal concerns and the consideration of how current patterns of production and consumption will affect those of tomorrow. However, while various efforts have been made to develop integrated so-called environmental-economic or "green" national accounts,[13] no single headline indicator is yet available that adequately captures this intertemporal dimension within national accounts. Instead, the General Assembly of the United Nations unanimously adopted in September 2015 a set of 14 *Sustainable Development Goals*, monitored through a framework of 169 targets and a list of 244 indicators, which partially address the two shortcomings just highlighted—if not by a single indicator, then by mainstreaming objectives other than the growth in monetary income.

Third, per capita GDP is not relevant for studying the efficiency of production because a large part of the national residents do not work. Productive efficiency is better captured by *labor productivity* (see box 9.1). This difference is particularly relevant when comparing economic performance between Europe and the United States. Table B9.1.1 indicates that, in 2013, while the population of the euro area (data available for 11 countries) was 2% lower than the US population, the total number of hours worked in the euro area was 14% lower. This 12% gap chiefly came from the number of hours worked by employees and from the lower proportion of persons in the labor force. Consequently, the comparative judgment differs depending on whether GDP per person or labor productivity is considered. The euro area's GDP per person is 26% lower than that of the United States (see also figure 9.5a), but labor productivity is only 4% lower. Olivier Blanchard (2004) has argued that the gap in GDP per person should therefore not be ascribed to uneven economic performance, but rather to a European "preference for leisure." The accuracy of this diagnosis has, however, been questioned. Productivity in the euro area may be overestimated because a large proportion of low-skill workers whose potential productivity is below average are excluded from the labor force.[14]

Box 9.1 From Per Capita GDP to Labor Productivity

Per capita GDP is the ratio of the value-added Y created during a given year in a country (the gross domestic product) to the country's total population *Pop*. It depends on labor productivity but also on participation, employment and hours worked:

- A fraction $(1 - w)$ of the population does not participate in the labor market because it is too young or too old: w is the proportion of the working-age population (often defined as 15–64 years old) to the total population.
- A faction $(1 - x)$ of the working age population $wPop$ (early retirees, but also adults excluded from the labor market such as invalids, housewives, etc.) does not participate in the labor market. x is called the *participation rate.*
- The *labor force* is therefore $L = xwPop$. Within it, however, a fraction u is unemployed (where u is the *unemployment rate*) and *employment* is $N = (1 - u)xwPop$.
- Last, each employee works on average d hours per year. The total number of hours worked is therefore $H = d(1 - u)xwPop$.

Finally, hourly labor productivity can be written as:

$$\frac{Y}{H} = \frac{1}{1-u}\frac{1}{d}\frac{1}{x}\frac{1}{w}\left(\frac{Y}{Pop}\right) \quad \text{(B9.1.1)}$$

This is sometimes adjusted for labor quality to account for divergences in skills.

Table B9.1.1 decomposes the gap between the number of hours worked in 11 countries of the euro area (for which data are readily available) and in the United States in 2013. While the euro-area population (thus defined) was 2% smaller, the quantity of labor supplied was 13% lower—and this gap was even larger in previous years. This divergence stemmed from differences in the average number of hours worked d (1,788 hours a year in the United States, 1,540 in the euro area), in the participation rates x, and in the unemployment rates u. Consequently, in the comparison between the euro area and the United States, there is a factor of (1788/1540) × (0.94/0.89) × (0.74/0.73) × (0.67/0.65) = 1.26 between the gap in per capita GDP and the gap in GDP per hour worked.

Table B9.1.1
Comparison of working hours between the United States and the euro area

2013	Variable	US	Euro area (11)	Euro area vs. US
Total population in millions	*Pop*	316.50	308.69	−2%
Proportion of the working age population	*w*	0.67	0.65	−2 pp
Participation rate of those 15–64 years old	*x*	0.74	0.73	−1 pp
Employment rate	$1-u$	0.94	0.89	−5 pp
Average number of hours worked per worker	*d*	1788	1540	−14%
Total number of hours worked (billion)	*H*	260.34	226.70	−13%

Difference in relative terms (%) or in absolute terms (percentage points).
Source: Authors calculations with OECD. Stat data

9.1.2 Growth accounting

The renowned scholar of the quantitative history of growth, Angus Maddison (1997) distinguishes four major determinants of long-term per capita GDP growth: (a) technical progress; (b) the accumulation of productive capital (i.e., of infrastructures and machines that are used for producing goods and services), which in various respects incorporates technical progress; (c) the improvement of know-how, of the level of education, and of the general organization of labor; and (d) the increasing integration of nations through trade, investment, and economic and intellectual exchange.[15] *Growth theory* aims to understand the role, interactions, and characteristics of these determinants based on rational welfare-maximizing individual behaviors (see Section 9.2). *Growth accounting* aims at providing a quantitative account of the role of the various determinants of growth.

The starting point of growth accounting is the *production function*, which connects real GDP Y_t in period t (a *flow variable* over a quarter or a year) to factors of production, typically the *capital stock* K (equipment and buildings available for production), *labor* N (hours worked), and *technology* A:

$$Y_t = f\left(K_t, N_t, A_t\right) \tag{9.1}$$

Capital K_t is a *stock variable* because it is transmitted from one period to another: at time *t*, the economy inherits machines bought and buildings built during previous periods, and its production capacity is primarily determined by them. Each generation thus stands on the shoulders of the previous ones; this goes a long way toward explaining differences in income between countries at any point in time: except for natural resources producers, rich countries are primarily those with a large capital stock. The evolution of the capital stock is generally described by an equation such as $\dot{K}_t = -\delta K_t + I_t$ where δ is the rate of capital depreciation and *I* stands for capital expenditures (a.k.a. gross fixed capital formation). Part of the capital stock thus disappears at each period (through discard or obsolescence), and part is renewed or augmented by the acquisition of new capital. Empirically, *K* is generally computed through the so-called permanent inventory method; that is, by cumulating past investment flows deflated by the replacement cost of capital and by discarding obsolete equipment and buildings after a given lifetime. This may be misleading when a large fraction of the capital stock is being discarded (for example, because of overcapacities) or when obsolescence accelerates (because of technical progress). But most countries do not have better ways to measure the capital stock.

N, the labor input, is generally best measured by the number of hours worked, which is the product of the working-age population, the activity rate, the employment rate, and the working time (see box 9.1).

A, the stock of technologies, depends on past inventions that serve in the production process before they become obsolete. Technology may affect production in various ways. *Solow neutrality*, assumes that technical progress is equivalent to an augmentation of the quantity of labor used in production (and therefore increases the marginal productivity of capital). Alternatively, *Harrod neutrality* is based on the opposite assumption that technical progress is equivalent to an augmentation of the quantity of capital used in production. With Solow-neutral technical progress the production function can be written as $Y_t = F(K_t, A_t N_t)$, while with Harrod-neutral technical progress the production function will be written as $Y_t = F(A_t K_t, N_t)$. Finally, under *Hicks neutrality*—the standard assumption—, technical progress affects the productivity of capital and labor symmetrically. The production function can then be written as $Y_t = A_t F(K_t, N_t)$.

The contribution of technology is more difficult to measure than that of other inputs. It depends not only on technology but also on the functioning of the markets and on the organization of production. It is typically measured as the part of growth that cannot be explained by capital accumulation or by the growth of worked hours (box 9.2). It is therefore a residual, named the *Solow residual* after Robert Solow (1987 Nobel Prize in economics), who introduced this decomposition (Solow, 1956). It represents the increase in the effectiveness of the combination of the two production factors—labor and capital, and it is also called *total factor productivity* (*TFP*).

Box 9.2 Growth Accounting

With constant returns to scale, and under Hicks neutrality of technical progress, the production function can then be written as:

$$Y_t = A_t F(K_t, N_t) \qquad \text{(B9.2.1)}$$

where A_t represents total factor productivity (TFP); that is, the effect of technical progress (in the broad sense, encompassing institutional factors) on the productivity of capital and labor.

The growth rate of income can be decomposed into the growth rates of each factor:

$$\frac{\dot{Y}}{Y} = \frac{\dot{A}}{A} + \frac{AK}{Y}\frac{\partial F}{\partial K}\frac{\dot{K}}{K} + \frac{AL}{Y}\frac{\partial F}{\partial L}\frac{\dot{N}}{N} \qquad \text{(B9.2.2)}$$

where $\dot{X}$ represents the variation of the X variable, measured either as $(X_t - X_{t-1})$ under discrete time between two consecutive periods, or as a time-derivative dX/dt under continuous time.

Defining

$$\omega_k = \frac{AK}{Y}\frac{\partial F}{\partial K}, \omega_N = \frac{AN}{Y}\frac{\partial F}{\partial N} \text{ and } g = \frac{\dot{A}}{A}$$

the decomposition becomes:

$$\frac{\dot{Y}}{Y} = \omega_K \frac{\dot{K}}{K} + \omega_N \frac{\dot{N}}{N} + g \qquad \text{(B9.2.3)}$$

The growth rate of TFP is not directly observable, but it is deduced from the preceding equation once the growth rates of Y, K, and N are known. It is the so-called Solow residual. Several methods can be used to calculate the Solow residual.

Method 1. Let us denote by c^K the *user cost of capital*, which represents the real cost of using of a unit of capital during the period of production (equal to the real interest rate plus the rate of capital depreciation); and w the real wage (i.e., the nominal wage divided by the price level). In a competitive economy, the factors' costs are equal to their *marginal product* (equal to the additional output that an additional unit of this factor produces) so that $c^K = A\partial F/\partial K$ and $w = A\partial F/\partial N$. ω_K and ω_N are, therefore, the respective shares of capital and labor earnings, $c^K K$ and wN respectively, in the firms' income. They can be observed from national accounts (roughly, at a country level, $\omega_N \sim 0.6$ and $\omega_K \sim 0,4$). In a competitive economy and under constant returns to scale,

$$c^K K + wN = Y \qquad \text{(B9.2.4)}$$

$$\text{and } \omega_K + \omega_N = 1 \qquad \text{(B9.2.5)}$$

The "Solow residual" g is then deduced from Equation (B9.2.3).

Method 2. An econometric rather than accounting method consists in regressing $\frac{\dot{Y}}{Y}$ on $\frac{\dot{K}}{K}$ and $\frac{\dot{N}}{N}$ and in extracting the residual g. Coefficients ω_N and ω_K are thus estimated, rather than calibrated. This method is delicate to implement because K and N are measured with an error and because they are correlated in the short run with the dependent variable Y, which requires the use of instrumental variables.

Method 3. From the preceding equations, and under the hypothesis that factor incomes are equal to their marginal product, it can be shown (by differentiating Equation B9.2.4) that:

$$g = \omega_K \frac{\dot{c}^K}{c^K} + \omega_N \frac{\dot{w}}{w} \tag{B9.2.6}$$

The marginal increase of TFP is therefore given back to workers and capital owners.

These methods can be generalized when more than two factors are used in production; for example, when energy consumption is taken into account or when capital and labor are broken down into several categories. Such a breakdown is useful to limit biases in the calculation of g. Indeed, the categories of capital and of labor that develop fastest are also those whose return increases fastest, as illustrated by high stock market yields of new technologies or by the fast wage increases enjoyed by skilled professionals. If the corresponding rise of the volume of K or of N were weighted by the average return or the average wage in the economy, their contribution to g would be underestimated.

The first and the third approaches are valid only if the factor returns are equal to their marginal products. This is the case neither in the presence of distortions nor in the presence of externalities because the private marginal product then differs from the social marginal product.

TFP should not be confused with labor productivity Y/N: TPF measures the combined effectiveness of labor and capital, while labor productivity measures the sole effectiveness of labor. Capital accumulation mechanically raises labor productivity (each worker is better equipped and therefore more productive). Noting per capita capital $k = K/N$, and under constant returns to scale (box 9.2), the growth rate of labor productivity over time can be decomposed into two components simply derived from Equation B9.2.3:

$$\frac{\dot{Y}}{Y} - \frac{\dot{N}}{N} = g + \omega_K \dot{k} \tag{9.2}$$

The first term of the right-hand side, *g*, represents TFP growth. The second term relates to the growth rate of the capital stock per person (i.e., the growth rate of the *capital intensity* of the production process). This decomposition helps explain that labor productivity growth can come either from an acceleration of TFP or from an increase in capital intensity (also called *capital deepening*).

Let us, for example, look at the origin of the growth gap between the euro area and the United States (table 9.1). They somehow traded places between the 1990s and the 2000s. In the early 1990s (as in the previous decade), the United States was a slow-labor productivity, high-employment growth economy while the growth pattern in the euro area was the opposite. By 2000, the United States had become a high-productivity growth, slow-employment growth economy while the euro area had adopted a growth pattern resembling that of the United States in the 1980s. The 2007–09 economic crisis had a big and lasting impact on growth and productivity in both regions. Labor productivity growth was almost halved in the United States, while in the euro area, TFP declined at a rate of 0.5% per year. TFP also slowed down in the United States (to a rate of growth of 0.6% per year on average), but in a much more limited way. This drop in TFP since the 2000s is one of the stylized facts discussed in the next section. Beyond TFP, the negative impact of the crisis has been stronger in Europe and been mainly borne by labor.

Measures of labor productivity components are of course statistical constructs, and it remains difficult to quantify the respective roles of technical

Table 9.1
Growth accounting in the United States and in the euro area (average annual growth rates, in percent per year)

	United States				Euro area			
	1990–1995	1995–2000	2000–2008	2008–2014	1990–1995	1995–2000	2000–2008	2008–2014
GDP (1)	2.6	4.3	2.1	1.2	1.5	2.9	1.9	−0.2
Total hours worked: (2) = (3) + (4)	1.1	2.0	0.1	0.1	−1.0	1.1	0.8	−1.1
Employment (3)	0.7	1.7	0.7	0.1	−0.6	1.5	1.1	−0.5
Working time (4)	0.3	0.3	−0.6	0.0	−0.5	−0.4	−0.2	−0.6
Labor productivity (5) = (1) − (2)	1.6	2.3	2.0	1.1	2.5	1.8	1.0	0.9
Contrib. of capital/labor ratio (6)	0.8	0.7	1.2	0.5	1.8	1.0	1.0	1.4
TFP: (7) = (5) − (6)	0.8	1.6	0.8	0.6	0.7	0.8	0.0	−0.5

Source: Authors calculations from *Penn World Tables* 9.0 (Feenstra, Inklaar, and Timmer, 2015), available for download at www.ggdc.net/pwt

progress and of capital intensity. A telling debate took place in the 1990s on the sources of the Asian "miracle"—the growth, at that time, of small East Asian economies. According to Alwyn Young (1992), their astonishingly strong growth since the 1960s involved nothing miraculous, but was due to massive capital accumulation encouraged by "Colbertist" policies[16] (very low rates of interest, proactive industrial policy, etc.) rather than total factor productivity (see box 9.3). In short, as Paul Krugman later wrote (1994*b*), the Asian miracle was "the fruit of perspiration, not of inspiration." Given decreasing returns to capital and labor, growth ineluctably had to slow down. The 1997–98 financial crises partially validated if not the diagnosis, at least the concerns of Young and Krugman since they were *inter alia* a consequence of overinvestment. Similar debates have developed about the sources of China's growth in the 2000s.

Box 9.3 A Tale of Two Cities: Asian Growth According to Alwyn Young

In 1992, MIT economist Alwyn Young compared the economic models of Hong Kong and Singapore. Both cities had similar histories as UK enclaves in the Chinese world with large commercial ports, having developed their manufacturing industry after World War II and then financial services. The levels of their per capita GDP were identical in the 1960s, and their rates of growth were comparable between 1960 and 1990. But the resemblance stopped there. After a careful growth-accounting study, Young concluded that the growth in Singapore came primarily from the accumulation of productive capital, while total factor productivity slowed down. Singapore was a "victim of its own targeting policies, which are increasingly driving the economy ahead of its learning maturity into the production of goods in which it has lower and lower productivity" (Young, 1992, p. 16). In 1994, Paul Krugman (1994*b*) insisted that: "There is no sign at all of increased efficiency. In this sense, the growth of Lee Kuan Yew's Singapore is an economic twin of Stalin's Soviet Union growth achieved purely through mobilization of resources." In contrast, Hong Kong could maintain a rapid progression of total factor productivity. Young explained this contrast by very different growth models: free market in Hong Kong, central planning in Singapore. In another article, Young (1995) extended his conclusions to other Asian "dragons": growth there was due to capital accumulation, the labor force, and education, but not to technical progress.

Both the figures and the diagnosis were sharply criticized by other economists who, building on different measures of the share of factors in value added, constructed a rate of TFP growth in Singapore higher than Young's (see notably Iwata, Khan, and Murao, 2003, for a synthesis of this debate).

9.1.3 Stylized facts

Four stylized facts emerge from the observation of historical and recent trends:

- By secular standards, fast growth in income per person is a recent phenomenon
- Since the turn of the 21st century, productivity has been on a declining trend
- The "Great Divergence" across nations has given way to (partial and incomplete) convergence
- While remaining high (mainly due to country divergences), global income inequality has somewhat subsided while inequality within nations has deepened.

a) Growth: A recent phenomenon

Figure 9.1 shows the average world GDP per person (in 1990 PPP dollars) since the start of the first millennium and projected to 2030, as estimated by Angus Maddison (Maddison, 2007). Four major periods can be distinguished.

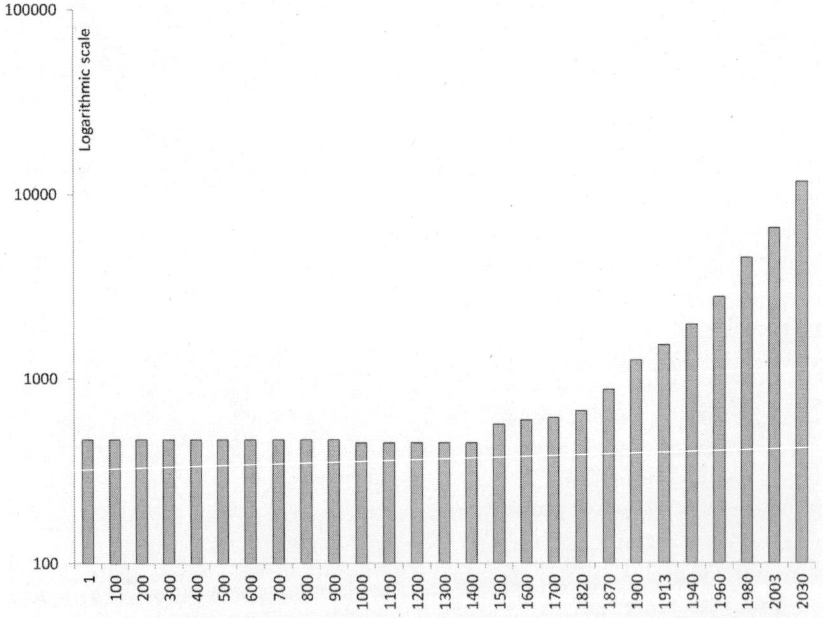

Figure 9.1 Long-term evolution of world gross domestic product (GDP) per person, in 1990 International Geary-Khamis dollars.
The Geary-Khamis dollar (or international dollar) is a current purchasing parity dollar equivalent.
Data from Maddison (2007) and http://www.ggdc.net/maddison/.

From prehistory through the Middle Ages, yearly income remains at around \$450 per person (in fact, it declines throughout the first millennium). It then increases to about \$600 between 1400 and 1800. The true "take-off" comes with the Industrial Revolution in the nineteenth century, and GDP per person exceeds \$1500 on the eve of World War I. By 2003 it reaches \$6,500, having multiplied by more than five over the course of the century. Maddison expected it to reach \$11,700 by 2030. While there were innovations before the Industrial Revolution, they produced one-off effects and did not lead to the kind of sustained dynamics of accumulation of knowledge and innovation that emerged since that time. Sustained growth of income per person in the world is thus a recent phenomenon. The historically exceptional performance of growth over the past century (in the United States, within the "special century" from 1870 to 1970, as studied by Gordon, 2016) casts a shadow on future growth prospects: Is this exceptional performance to be considered as the new normal, or should we expect a return to the relative stability of the past? How can policies support the first scenario (and should they)?

The historical emergence of the growth phenomenon[17] can be related to changes in the world economic system and especially to breakthroughs that have been conducive to productivity and international trade: improvements in agricultural productivity; the "discovery" of America in the fifteenth and sixteenth centuries; the emergence and expansion of the so-called European world-economy;[18] major technological innovations, such as the steam engine and the railways in the nineteenth century; electricity in the twentieth century; and urbanization on a large scale. However, technology and trade alone hardly account for the recent dramatic increase in world GDP. They cannot explain why the standard of living did not increase until the Middle Ages despite a string of technological innovations (fire, the wheel, metals, and later navigation). Understanding these turning points involves the study of history as much as economics.[19] Mokyr (2017) explores cultural explanations that relate the growth explosion to the European Enlightenment and its twofold foundation: understanding that nature (which is what technological change is about) should be used to advance the well-being of humanity and that power and government should serve society at large. He concludes that the powerful synergy between these two ideas unleashed and sustained the growth explosion.

b) A decline in productivity

Since the 2008 financial crisis at least, TFP growth has significantly slowed (figure 9.2) in most developed and developing countries (see, e.g., Adler et al., 2017), compounding fears of "secular stagnation" (see box 9.4). While the slowdown has been prolonged for the countries of the Organization for Economic Cooperation and Development (OECD) as a group, with negative productivity growth since 2009, TFP growth seems to have started declining in emerging countries (as a group and with the notable exception of India) right after the financial crisis. This is questioning the long-term

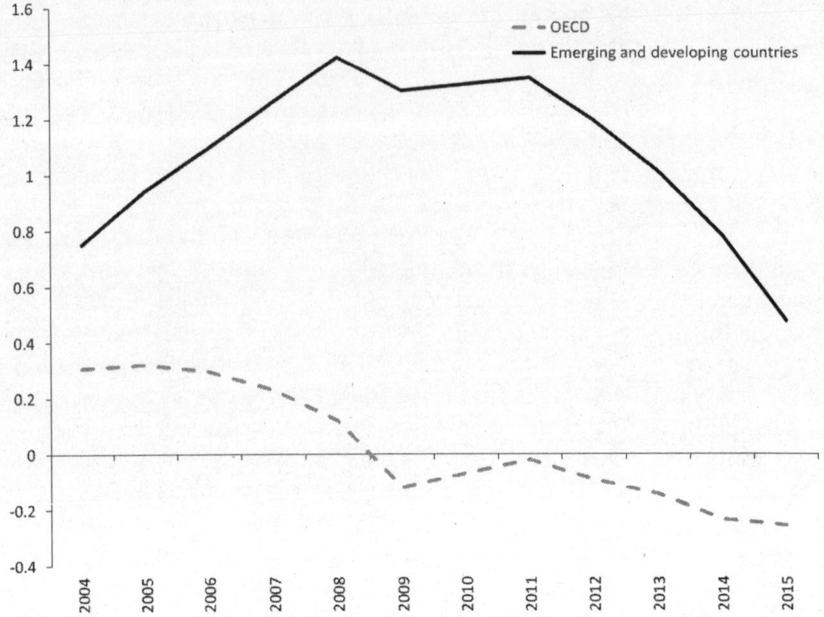

Figure 9.2 Total factor productivity growth in % per year (ten-year moving average, in percent per year).

TFP figures are adjusted by the Conference Board for the rapid price declines in the IT sector.

The Conference Board, 2016. The Conference Board Total Economy Database, Regional Aggregates, adjusted version, November 2016, http://www.conference-board.org/data.economydatabase/.

Box 9.4 Secular Stagnation and Solow's Paradox

The concept of *secular stagnation*, introduced by Alvin Hansen in 1939, was revived by Larry Summers (2014) in the aftermath of the 2008 crisis. According to Summers, it stems chiefly from a supply/demand imbalance: In normal situations, an excess supply of goods and services over aggregate demand can be addressed by a decline in real interest rates which raises aggregate demand to the full employment level. The fallout from the 2008–2009 crisis resulted in aggregate demand remaining lastingly depressed and the zero lower bound (see Chapter 5) prevented a decline of the real interest rate to the level necessary to restore full employment.[a] Output was therefore constrained by insufficient aggregate demand.

The supply-side version of the secular stagnation hypothesis starts from the same observation but puts the blame on a slowdown of technical progress. This may seem paradoxical in view of the spreading of digital technologies.

Indeed, the rebound of TFP in the 1990s owed much to ICTs: through substituting capital for labor, managing inventories, and making better use of inputs, ICT contributed to accelarating the growth of TFP. Yet its contribution to long-term TFP growth is difficult to measure for two main reasons.

First, the ICT volume is poorly apprehended by national accounts because equipment and software prices have been decreasing rapidly. Economists and national accountants have developed *hedonic price indices* that take account of the quality improvements brought by the new generations of products. Instead of focusing on the price of the product itself, hedonic prices are based on the services delivered through the product (for example, in the case of computers, the hedonic price would account for the memory capacity, processing speed, screen resolution, etc.).

Second, TFP is more about the diffusion of innovation than on technical progress per se. Yet, the diffusion of technologies is difficult to track. Robert Gordon (2000), a renowned specialist in productivity and growth, first claimed that the acceleration of TFP in the United States was circumscribed in the computer sector and, apart from that sector, was primarily cyclical (because it corresponded to a period of expanding demand), before revising his assessment.[b] Jorgenson, Ho, and Stiroh (2008) find that between 1995 and 2000, investments in ICT contributed to 37% of labor productivity growth in the United States, and ICT industries contributed to 58% of TFP's. However, the impact of new technologies can be delayed, particularly because the full effect on productivity requires complementary investments in other forms of capital (for example, firms need to reorganize to use the new ICT equipment as much and as efficiently as possible). Such effects have been notably documented Yang and Brynjolfsson (2001), or, in France, by Askenazy (2001).

This result echoes the so-called *Solow paradox*: for a long time, computers were seen everywhere—except in the productivity figures (to paraphrase Robert Solow's famous 1987 statement).[c] In his work on the diffusion of innovation, the economic historian Paul David (1990) notably highlighted that it had taken a long time for the invention of electricity to affect productivity and questioned the very existence of a modern paradox of productivity from a historical perspective.

Productivity pessimists, however, question the analogy between ICT and past generic innovations such as electricity and argue that ICT benefits have now been reaped. Gordon (2016), for example, argues that the kind of innovation that ICT unleashed is unlikely to make contributions to productivity and standards of living that match those that earlier waves of innovation (such as electricity) brought. Others disagree, referring to the capacity of successive waves of innovation to overcome pessimistic expectations in the past and pointing to the promises of new innovations in the areas of artificial intelligence, biotechnologies, and nanotechnologies. Gordon has a point, however, when he emphasizes the exceptional character of the period between 1870 and 1970 and the dangers of deriving historical lessons from just that period.

TFP, an accounting residual, is clearly not independent from capital and human investments (that are needed to benefit from innovations) and a more granular approach is needed to analyze and understand processes. Jorgenson and Vu (2016) further challenge the priority given to innovation. They argue that it played in fact a relatively modest role that does not justify the weight it has in modern growth theory. Nonetheless, the recent weakness of TFP raises crucial questions about growth patterns.

[a]The corresponding "savings glut" echoes the global savings glut hypothesis formulated by Ben Bernanke (2005). See notably Teulings and Baldwin (2014). A review of the debate is provided by Jaubertie and Shimi (2016).

[b]See Gordon (2000, 2003), Oliner and Sichel (2002), and, in the French case, Cette, Mairesse, and Kocoglu (2004).

[c]"You can see the computer age everywhere but in the productivity statistics," *New York Review of Books*, 12 July 1987.

growth prospects of a group of countries that had been driving global growth.

Figure 9.3 illustrates the different dynamics for the United States and the euro area, already suggested by table 9.1. While TFP growth has been

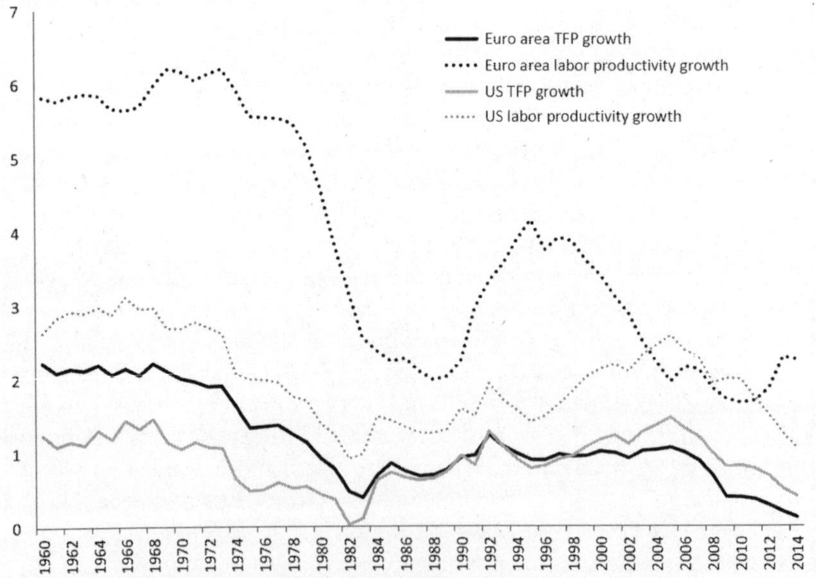

Figure 9.3 Total factor and labor productivity growth 1960–2014, in percent per year. United States and euro area.
PWT 9.0 (Feenstra et al., 2015).

fluctuating in the United States since the 1960s, it did so within a narrow range of between 0% and 1.5% a year. Europe's experience was that of a nearly consistent decline, from more than 2% in 1960 to close to zero in 2014. Its higher productivity growth in the 1960s and 1970s was linked to the catching-up dynamics discussed earlier. In turn, the US total factor (and labor) productivity acceleration in the 1980s and 1990s, which lasted until the mid-2000s, echoed the liberalization of factor markets in the 1980s and the emergence of the "new economy" in the 2000s. Figure 9.3 also suggests that the recent turning point toward renewed deceleration happened in 2005, well before the emergence of the global financial crisis.

c) The end of the "Great Divergence"

In a globalized world where the same technology is accessible everywhere, income levels might be expected to converge across countries. Overall, a positive correlation can be observed between initial and final GDP per person (figure 9.4), with a positive Y-axis intercept indicating that poorer countries have, on average, grown faster over the 1870–2010 period. The dispersion of GDP per person expressed in current PPP dollars, however, was still as high in 2010 as in 1870, with a coefficient of variation of about 65% for both dates.[20]

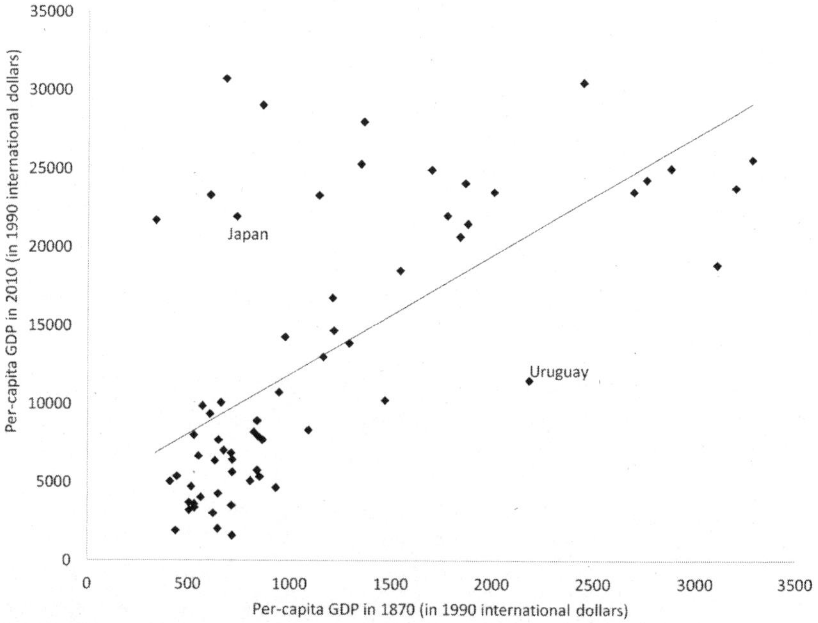

Figure 9.4 Gross domestic product (GDP) per person in 1870 and 2010 (in 1990 International Geary-Khamis Dollars).
Data from Maddison, http://www.ggdc.net/maddison.

These two observations are not incompatible: some countries were poor in 1870 but rich in 2010, and vice versa. For example, Uruguay was three times richer than Japan in 1870 but almost three times poorer in 2010.

These evolutions result from the end of the *Great Divergence,* brought on by the emergence of the Western World by the nineteenth century and by the domination of the US economy in the twentieth century. Growth and income divergence between the West and the rest of the world had characterized the growth explosion from the Industrial Revolution until World War II. Since the second half of the twentieth century, however, the movement of divergence has stopped and given rise to reversal.

In the 1950s and 1960s, Europe and Japan rapidly caught up with the US economy (figure 9.5a). In the 1970s and 1980s, the three major economies slowed down in the aftermath of the oil shocks, but the US economy accelerated again in the 1990s, with the result that catch-up by Europe and Japan came to an end and even started to reverse. Convergence stopped below 80% of US income per person. In the last quarter of the twentieth century, the newly industrialized countries of Asia (Hong Kong, Singapore, South Korea, and Taiwan) also caught up at an impressive pace (figure 9.5b). In turn, China and, to a lesser extent, India experienced stellar growth from the end of the twentieth century. In Europe, Central and Eastern Europe have been converging toward Western Europe.

The picture has remained different in Africa. Many African countries have progressed in absolute terms but little if at all in relative terms (figure 9.5c). The promising resumption of economic growth in Sub-Saharan Africa from 1995 on may signal the start of a slow catching-up process for Sub-Saharan Africa as well.

Economists have approached convergence in two main, complementary ways. The first one is the reduction in the dispersion in income levels across countries. This is called *σ-convergence* because it involves a change in the standard deviation (σ) of cross-country incomes over time. The second one investigates whether poorer countries grow faster than richer ones. This is called *β-convergence* because it can be measured through a positive β coefficient in the following estimation:

$$\frac{1}{T-1}\ln\frac{Y_{iT}}{Y_{i1}} = \alpha - \beta \ln Y_{i1} + \varepsilon_{iT} \qquad (9.3)$$

where Y_{i1} is the initial level of per capita GDP of country i and Y_{iT} the final level at date T, α and β are the coefficients to be estimated, and ε_{iT} is an error term. A positive β means that the lower the initial GDP per capita, the higher the growth rate. β-convergence is a necessary condition for σ-convergence. However, the reverse does not apply[21]. β-convergence does not imply that all countries will end up with the same GDP per capita.

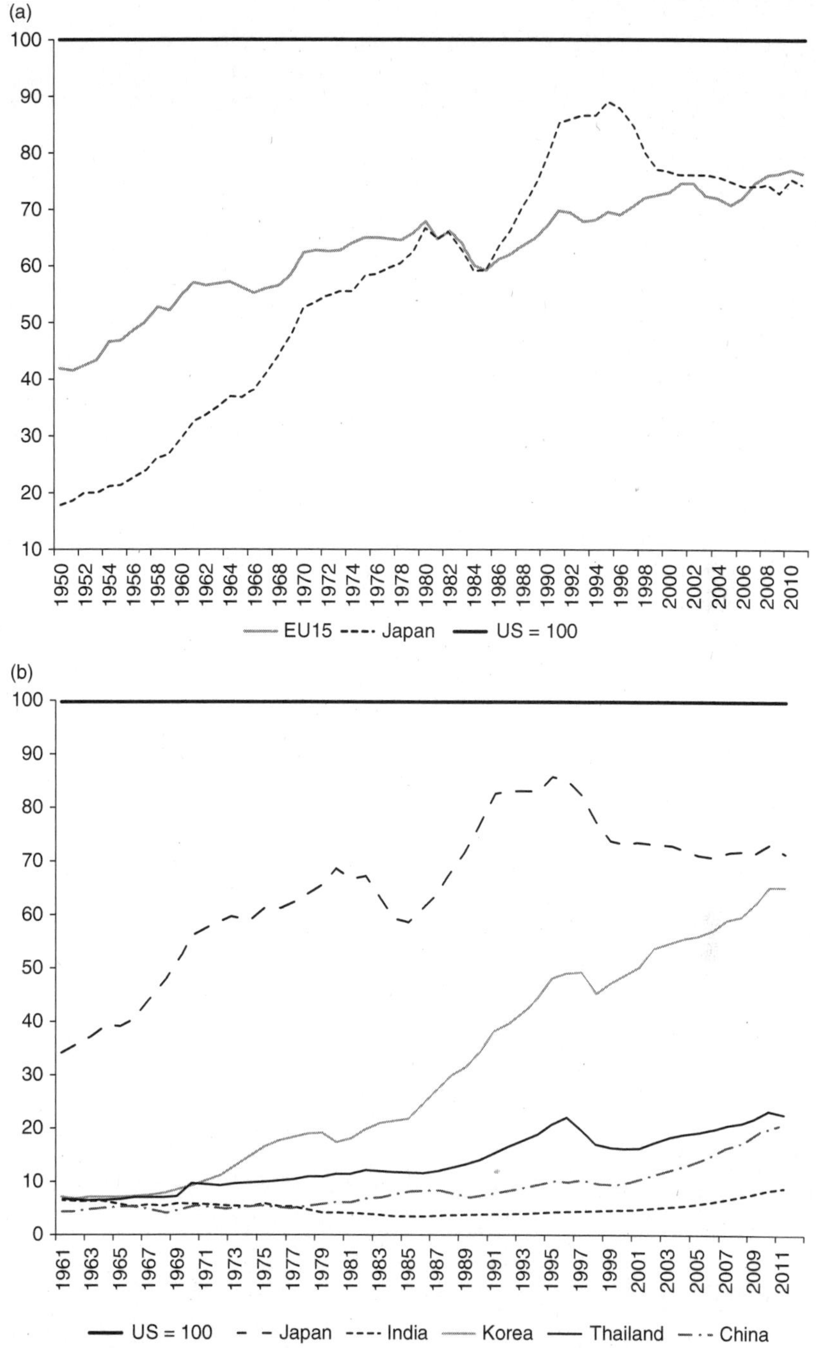

Figure 9.5 (9.5a, 9.5b and 9.5c) Per capita gross domestic product (GDP) in percent of the US level.
GDP is measured in purchasing power parity 2005 dollars.
Penn World Tables PWT 8.1 (Feenstra et al., 2015), available for download at www.ggdc.net/pwt.

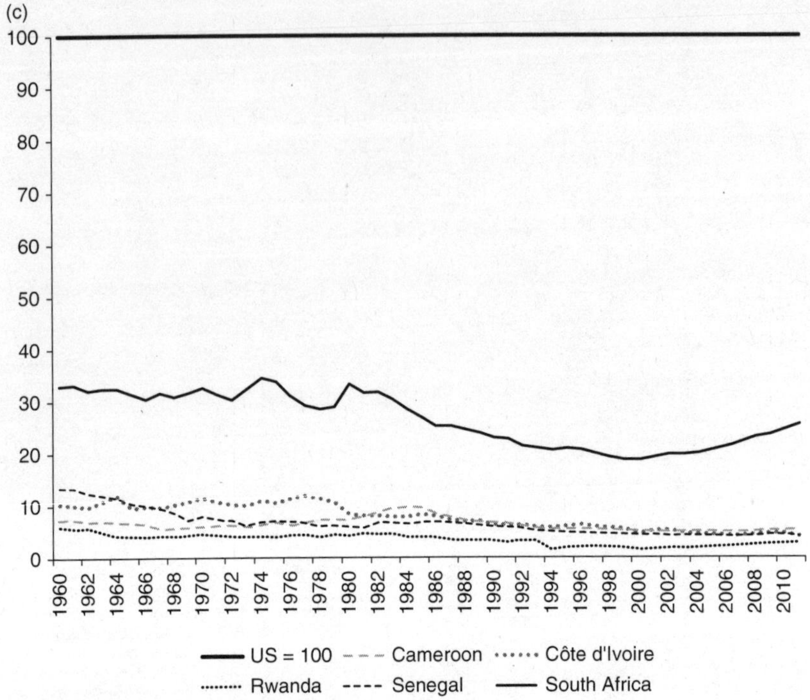

Figure 9.5 (9.5a, 9.5b and 9.5c) Continued

Figure 9.6 shows the link between the average growth rate of countries' per capita GDP between 1950 and 2014 and its 1950 level. There is no worldwide β-convergence (in plain English, poorer countries do not grow faster over that period), but there is clearly convergence within the OECD.

The failure of poor countries convergence may be due to structural factors independent from the initial income level. If this holds *conditional convergence* (as opposed to *absolute convergence*, or *unconditional convergence*) can be uncovered by conditioning Equation (9.1) on structural variables Z_{iT}:

$$\frac{1}{T-1}\ln\frac{Y_{iT}}{Y_{i1}} = \alpha - \beta \ln Y_{i1} + \gamma Z_{i1} + \varepsilon_{iT} \quad (9.4)$$

Conditioning factors may be of various nature: geographic, institutional, legal, political or cultural. Conditional convergence means that two countries sharing the same conditioning factors converge in the long run. It suggests, for example, that Serbia's GDP per person may not be able to converge toward that of Germany or France, but that of Slovenia is more likely to reach that goal because Slovenia benefits from the EU legal and institutional framework while Serbia currently does not.

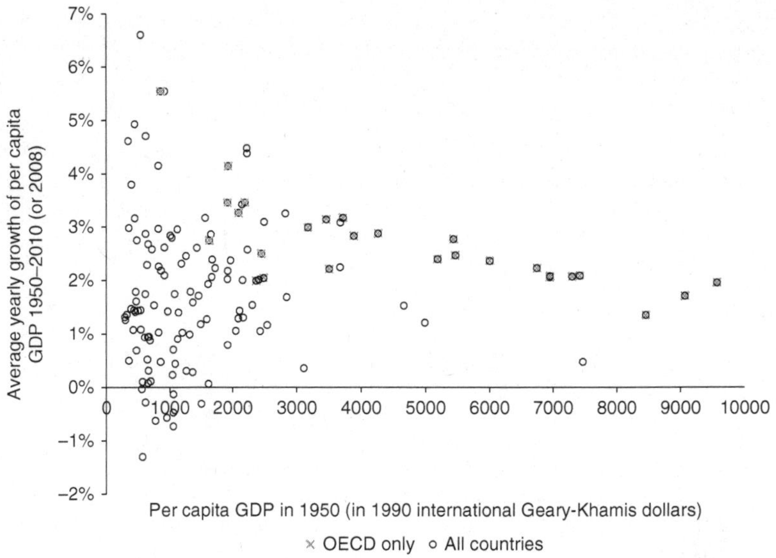

Figure 9.6 Convergence in the world and within the Organization for Economic Cooperation and Development (OECD) (β-convergence).
Penn World Tables PWT 9.0 (Feenstra et al., 2015), available for download at www.ggdc.net/pwt.

Groups of comparable countries within which β-convergence is at play (here, the group of OECD countries) are called *convergence clubs*. A crucial issue for development-aid policies consists in understanding how any country can "join the club." Conditioning variables that are usually found to have a significant long-term impact on per capita GDP are (see Barro and Sala-ì-Martin, 1995, chapt. 12, for a survey):

- The quality of human capital (level of education, life expectancy);
- The functioning of markets (degree of competition, distortions introduced by state interventions, corruption);
- Macroeconomic stability (and, in particular, price stability);
- Political stability (absence of wars, coups, or frequent power shifts between opposite camps).

One problem with this approach, however, is that it implicitly assumes that the capacity to reform institutions is independent of the level of wealth. Recent research on growth has carefully tackled the reverse-causality problem (i.e., fact that better institutions may be an outcome of growth).

Empirical studies show that convergence is often *unconditional* between regions of the same country—be they US states (Barro and Sala-ì-Martin, 1991), Canadian provinces (Coulombe 2007; Coulombe and Lee, 1995), or Japanese prefectures. In such a case, convergence tends to be unconditional because many "Z" factors are identical, and convergence is, moreover, encouraged by cultural homogeneity, factor mobility, and fiscal redistribution mechanisms specific to each country. However, persistent gaps in income per head can be found within countries. Underdevelopment in southern Italy is a case in point, as is the very slow pace of convergence of the East German regions. Those can be, in part, attributed to outward migration of skilled labor. *A fortiori*, convergence between different countries is generally conditional. However, the catching-up of Asia suggests that globalization may lead to the alignment of conditioning factors (access to technology, strengthening of institutions, etc.) that favor convergence across countries.

d) Less inequality across nations, more within nations

How are growth and globalization benefits distributed across individuals? There are many ways to define and measure *inequality*. One may want to study the income distribution that results from the play of market forces and thus focus on incomes before taxes and transfers. An alternative approach will consist of documenting incomes after taxes and transfers. Instead of incomes, one may observe consumption expenditures, more closely related to living standards. At world level, redistribution through taxes and transfers has a limited impact on income inequalities, which are essentially driven by the returns to capital and labor and by the cumulative political and economic impact of income concentration and of wealth inequalities, notably studied by Piketty's (2014) seminal work. Milanovic (2016), in particular, argues that "deconcentration" of capital and interventions before taxes and transfers is a more promising way to reduce inequalities than is redistribution, especially given the difficulty of increasing taxes on capital income in a globalized world.

Up until the end of the twentieth century, most of the attention was about inequality within the borders of countries, and differences between countries were approached from the perspective of convergence (or the lack of it). In order to assess the distributional consequences of globalization, recent studies have started to focus on global inequalities.[22] After the pioneering work of Bourguignon and Morrisson (2002), the generalization of household surveys has allowed researchers to build richer and more accurate datasets (see notably the work conducted by Branko Milanovic at the World Bank). The calculation of global inequalities requires that similar methodologies govern the household surveys that are used and that incomes can be compared between different currencies, which points to the use of PPP exchange rates.[23]

Global inequality (i.e., inequality among world households irrespective of their country of location) increased considerably during the nineteenth and twentieth centuries, due to the unequal participation in the Industrial Revolution. As figure 9.7 indicates, the Lorenz curve describing the global distribution of income (cf. Chapter 1) departed more and more from the 45-degree line, which indicates a larger concentration of income among the richest individuals.

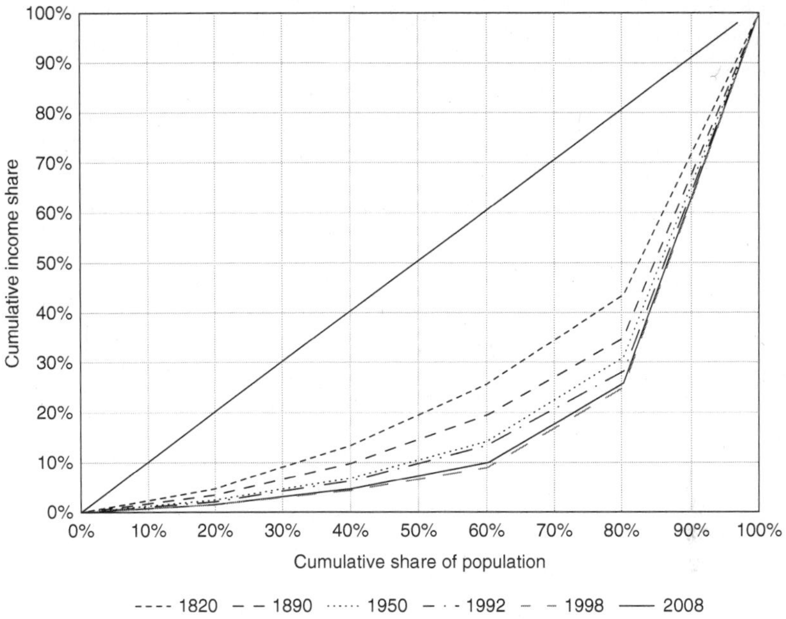

Figure 9.7 Lorenz curve of global income distribution.
Bourguignon and Morrison (2002), Lakner and Milanovic (2015).

Bourguignon and Morrisson (2002) document that the Gini index of world income distribution[24] increased from 0.5 in 1820 to 0.64 in 1950 and 0.66 in 1992. Further work by Bourguignon (2015) and Milanovic (2005, 2012, 2016) suggests that it finally stabilized in the 2000s and afterward started to decline.[25] A major reason is the increase in the standard of living of hundreds of millions of individuals living in fast-growing countries in Southeast Asia and China.

The picture suggested by the Lorenz curve and the evolution of the Gini, however, tells us that growth benefits have been distributed unequally, but it does not tell much about who reaped these benefits. Figure 9.8 introduces a simplified version of the so-called elephant curve (or "growth incidence curve," Lakner and Milanovic, 2015). It shows how the average income of various percentiles (from the 10% poorest to the 1% richest) of the global income distribution grew between 1988 and 2008.[26] The curve confirms the emergence of a global middle class, which typically corresponds to the well-off households in emerging countries. A substantial fraction of the Chinese and Indian populations has attained middle-class status. The upper middle-class in developed countries did relatively poorly, possibly feeding into the growing discontent that surfaced in the elections in these countries in the second-half of the 2010s.

While the lowest decile did not do as well as the global middle class, it still experienced on average a 25% growth over the 20-year period: these latter

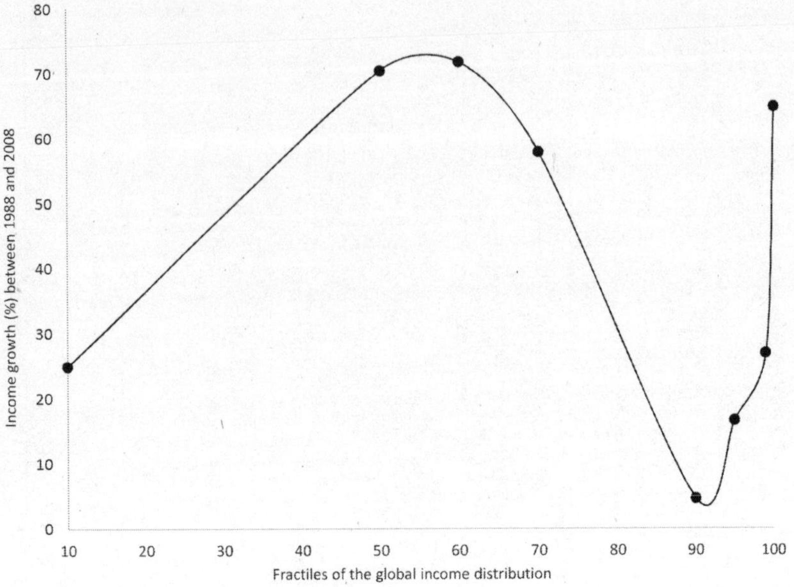

Figure 9.8 The elephant curve: growth incidence on world income distribution (1988–2008). This curve shows the average income growth between 1998 and 2008 for eight percentile points (artificially connected): below 10%, 40–50%, 50–60%, 60–70%, 80–90%, 90–95%, 95–99%, and top 1%
Data from Lakner and Milanovic (2016), table 3, p. 10.

results attest to some success of the global fight against extreme poverty. The global poverty headcount ratio (individuals leaving with less than US$1.90 [2011 PPP] as a percentage of the world population) has declined from 41% in 1981 to 11% in 2013.[27]

Global income inequality combines inequality within countries and inequality across countries (i.e., between average incomes per capita). It is consequently significantly higher than any of its two components. The main force behind global income inequality since the early twentieth century has been inequality between countries (figure 9.9), leading Milanovic (2016) to claim the existence of a rent attached to the country of birth, which he calls the "citizenship premium." That premium seems to have been ebbing toward the end of the 2000s (a movement strengthened by the impact of the financial crisis).

Our earlier discussion of convergence suggests that inequality between countries has been on a declining trend, even though it has still deepened for some countries. However, such convergence amounted to comparing average incomes per head between countries without accounting for the size of their populations and corresponds to what François Bourguignon (2015) labels the "international income scale." A different measure consists in

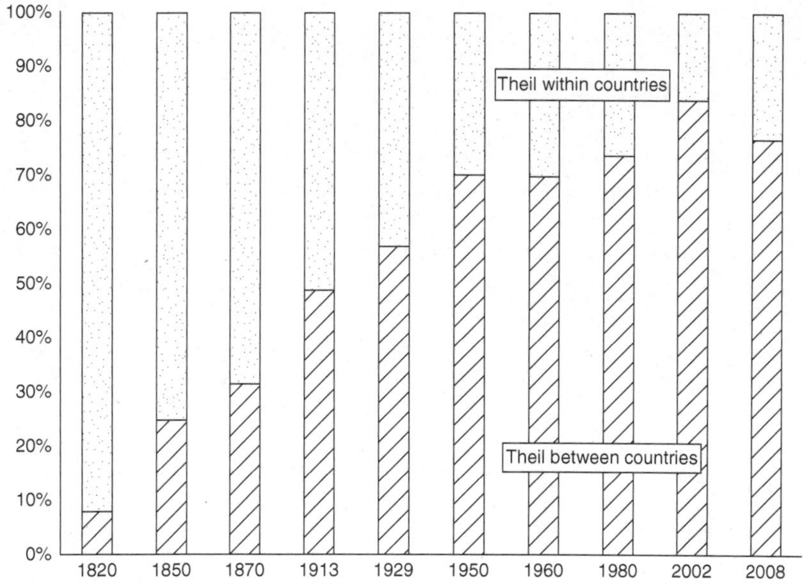

Figure 9.9 Decomposition of global inequality between and within countries, shares of the total Theil (L) index, 1820–2008, in percent.
The Theil index is a measure of generalized entropy that is decomposable (here between inequality within countries and inequality between countries). The inequality indicator used here is the Theil index, a measure of generalized entropy. The indicator used here is Theil (L), the mean log deviation of the sample. For more details, see for example http://siteresources.worldbank.org/PGLP/Resources/PMch6.pdf
Milanovic (2012) and Lakner and Milanovic (2016).

weighing countries according to their populations. The population-weighted intercountry Gini has been declining constantly since 1950, slowly until the early 1990s and much faster since (Milanovic, 2012, figure 2), notably due to the acceleration of economic growth in China and other populous countries such as Brazil, India, Indonesia, Vietnam, and South Africa (Milanovic, 2016, chapt. 4).

Against this change in international inequality patterns, the major recent evolution has been the increase of within-country inequality in a very large number of countries and in a majority of OECD countries. A notable exception is Latin America, where social policies (notably conditional cash transfer programs) and investments in education leading to a narrowing of wage gaps played a major role (Lopez Calva and Lustig, 2010). The two-way relationship between economic growth and inequalities will be further discussed in Section 9.2.3.

9.2 Theories

"Growth accounting" is a description, not an explanation of economic growth. In order to understand the mechanisms of the latter and assess the role of economic policy in fostering it, we need to turn to theory and investigate the determinants of labor force growth, capital accumulation, and technological innovation.

In preindustrial theories like those of Thomas Malthus (1798), fertility was regarded as the fundamental determinant of growth. According to Malthus, fertility adjusted to technological shocks so that the standard of living remained constant. Subsequent theories generally included demography as an important, but exogenous phenomenon, except sometimes for migrations (cf. Barro and Sala-ì-Martin, 1995, chapt. 9). They focused mainly on capital accumulation. In the 1980s, they had reached, however, a somewhat frustrating conclusion: under decreasing marginal returns to capital, incentives to accumulate capital fade over time so that the capital/labor ratio reaches a steady state. Growth in GDP per person can only stem from a constant flow of technological innovation. In the 1960s and 1970s, very few economists remained interested in growth theory, and, in their review of the literature, Hahn and Matthews (1964, p. 890) concluded that it might have reached the point of diminishing returns.

A renewal started in the late 1980s with the advent of the so-called endogenous growth theory, which focuses on the determinants of total factor productivity. In this context, economists revisited Joseph Schumpeter's seminal ideas on what drives innovation and ventured into new areas such as the interaction between growth and geography or between growth and the quality of institutions. Standard models were also revisited to shed light on economic development. This renewal turned growth theory into one of the most active branches of economic analysis.

In what follows, we first present the standard models of growth through capital accumulation with exogenous technical progress; we then turn to models with endogenous technical progress; finally, we discuss the role of deep growth determinants such as geography, income distribution, and institutions.

9.2.1 Growth through capital accumulation

The basic tool for the analysis of growth is the production function already introduced in Section 9.1, which we assume can be written:

$$Y_t = A_t F(K_t, N_t) \tag{9.5}$$

where Y denotes output, A technical progress (total factor productivity), K the capital stock, and N the employed labor force (or the total number of hours worked), all dated at time t. As growth analysis deals with medium to long-term horizons, it is generally assumed that the economy is at full employment. Therefore, employment N is equal to the labor force L, so that:

$$Y_t = A_t F(K_t, L_t) \tag{9.6}$$

The assumption of full employment may seem to run counter to experience. However, it also accounts for situations of persistent unemployment. Let us suppose that there is a rate of structural unemployment u that cannot be permanently reduced whatever the level of aggregate demand. The preceding formulation can be adapted by replacing L by $L(1 - u)$.[28]

a) First steps: Growth and disequilibrium

Theories of the accumulation of productive capital in a closed economy take as a starting point the equilibrium between the supply of capital (i.e., the flow of savings) and the demand for capital (i.e., the flow of investment desired by profit-maximizing companies).

A first intuition was developed independently by economists Roy Harrod in 1939 and Evsey Domar in 1946, who highlighted the risk of economic instability in the growth process. They pointed out that the growth rate of the capital stock determined by investment (and therefore by the savings rate) does not spontaneously correspond to the growth rate that is necessary to maintain full employment. They therefore saw a risk either of a shortage of labor (leading to inflation) or of a shortage of capital (leading to unemployment): balanced growth was possible only if, by sheer coincidence, the economy remained on the "razor's edge" in which the savings–investment balance corresponds to the full employment equilibrium (box 9.5).

Box 9.5 The Harrod-Domar Model

The model developed by Harrod (1939) and Domar (1946) assumes that technology is given and that efficient production requires capital and labor inputs to be in a constant proportion. It is thus based on a production function with *complementary inputs*:

$$Y_t = min(AK_t, BL_t) \tag{B9.5.1}$$

where Y_t is output, K_t is the stock of capital, A and B are constant parameters, and the labor force L_t grows at a constant rate n.

As inputs are complementary, full employment requires a sufficient capital stock to employ all the labor force. Conversely, if the capital stock is higher than this level, production capacity will not be fully employed due to a shortage of labor. Labor growth and the growth of the capital stock are determined independently. Full employment equilibrium therefore hinges on a stroke of luck.

The evolution of the capital stock over time is:

$$\dot{K}_t = -\delta K_t + I_t \qquad \text{(B9.5.2)}$$

where δ is the rate of capital depreciation and I_t is gross fixed capital formation (investment). Investment is financed by available savings: $I_t = \sigma Y_t$ where σ is the constant savings rate. As long as the capital stock remains the binding constraint on production, $Y = AK$ and the evolution of K is given by:

$$\dot{K}_t = (\sigma A - \delta) K_t \qquad \text{(B9.5.3)}$$

The trajectory of the economy depends on the level of the savings rate: If $\sigma > \delta / A$, then the capital stock and output grow at the constant rate $\sigma A - \delta$, until $AK_t = BL_t$, after which output growth is limited by the availability of labor. Below a certain threshold for the capital–labor ratio, a policy favorable to saving increases the growth rate.

The *Harrod-Domar model* does not provide a realistic description of long-term growth. Domar himself considered it instead as a study of the interaction between temporary shortages of demand and investment in the context of the consequences of the 1929 crisis and then of the war economy characterized by a shortage of capital. A model which predicts that growth is constrained by a shortage of capital also provided an accurate description of Europe in the immediate post–World War II period and a theoretical justification for the reconstruction aid policies meant to compensate for the European countries' insufficient savings and fill their "financing gap." This approach was explicit in the June 1947 *Marshall plan*,[29] and even more so in the "national assessment" simultaneously prepared in France by Planning Commissioner Jean Monnet.

b) Saving, investment, and balanced growth

Firms do not invest to make use of available savings but to make profits: the return to capital is the main engine of investment. In the mid-1950s, recognition of this microeconomic incentive led Robert Solow (1956) and Trevor Swan (1956) to separately develop a model that has carried considerable intellectual influence and still provides a reference framework for the analysis of economic growth.

Unlike Harrod and Domar, Solow and Swan describe a growth path where markets are in balance. Production factors are *substitutable* —therefore, there are no more "razor's edge" equilibriums—and the marginal return to capital is decreasing: The more capital is accumulated, the less profitable it is at the margin. As a consequence, the incentive to invest vanishes when the marginal return on capital is equal to the user cost of capital (i.e., when adding to the capital stock costs exactly the value of the additional production it brings). At this stage, the per capita level of the capital stock, and therefore also (under constant returns to scale) per capita GDP, are stable over time (see the detailed model in box 9.6). The corresponding growth path is called the *steady state*.

In the basic *Solow-Swan model* the savings rate is exogenous, production exhibits constant returns to scale, labor and capital are substitutes, population and technology are constant, and each exhibits decreasing marginal returns. There is an equilibrium value of the per capita level of the capital stock k that only depends on the savings rate and on the rate of capital depreciation. In a more complete version where population and TFP grow over time at respective exogenous and constant rates n and g, it is the TFP-adjusted level of per capita GDP that is stable in the long run, and its value also depends on g. The capital stock and GDP both grow at a constant rate $n + g$, and, under this specification, the model is fully consistent with growth accounting as introduced earlier.

In this category of models, when the capital stock reaches its equilibrium value, the *growth rate* of GDP only depends on demography and on exogenous technical progress (but *not* on the savings rate, which determines the

Box 9.6 The Solow-Swan Model

The production function is of the Cobb-Douglas type: $Y_t = AK_t^{\alpha} L_t^{1-\alpha}$ with $0 < \alpha < 1$, which implies both decreasing returns to each production factor taken separately and constant returns to scale (output is multiplied by two if capital and labor are multiplied by two). Labor and capital are substitutes.

Assume first that total factor productivity A is constant. Labor supply grows at a constant rate n. The capital stock is augmented every year by the volume of investment I, but each year a fraction δ of it is discarded. In a closed economy, output Y is equal to the income distributed to economic agents. A fraction σ of this income is saved and invested domestically every year. Thus:

$$\dot{L}_t = nL_t \qquad \dot{K}_t = -\delta K_t + I_t \qquad I_t = S_t = \sigma Y_t \tag{B9.6.1}$$

Let lower case letters represent variables per person:

$$k_t = K_t / L_t \qquad y_t = Y_t / L_t \qquad s_t = \sigma Y_t / L_t$$

The dynamics of k_t are given by:

$$\frac{\dot{k}_t}{k_t} = \frac{\dot{K}_t}{K_t} - \frac{\dot{L}_t}{L_t} = -\delta + \sigma \frac{y_t}{k_t} - n \tag{B9.6.2}$$

On the steady-state trajectory where variables per person y, k, and s are constant, capital accumulation is determined by the following equation:

$$\sigma y^* = (n + \delta) k^* \quad \text{with} \quad y^* = k^{*\alpha} \tag{B9.6.3}$$

This means that, in the steady state, the savings of each period exactly finance the capital expenditure necessary to replace the depreciated capital and to equip the new workers with additional capital. The capital stock per person thus remains constant. The steady state levels of per person output, capital, and savings are:

$$y^* = \sigma^{\frac{\alpha}{1-\alpha}} (n+\delta)^{-\frac{\alpha}{1-\alpha}} \; ; \; k^* = \sigma^{\frac{1}{1-\alpha}} (n+\delta)^{-\frac{1}{1-\alpha}} \; ; \; s^* = \sigma^{\frac{\alpha}{1-\alpha}} (n+\delta)^{-\frac{\alpha}{1-\alpha}} \quad \text{(B9.6.4)}$$

In figure B9.6.1, where the *X*-axis represents the level of the capital stock per person and the *Y*-axis represents savings and investments per person, the steady-state equilibrium corresponds to the intersection of the curve $s_t = \sigma k_t^\alpha$ (representing savings) and of the straight line $(n + \delta)k_t$, which represents the investment per person necessary to keep k_t constant.

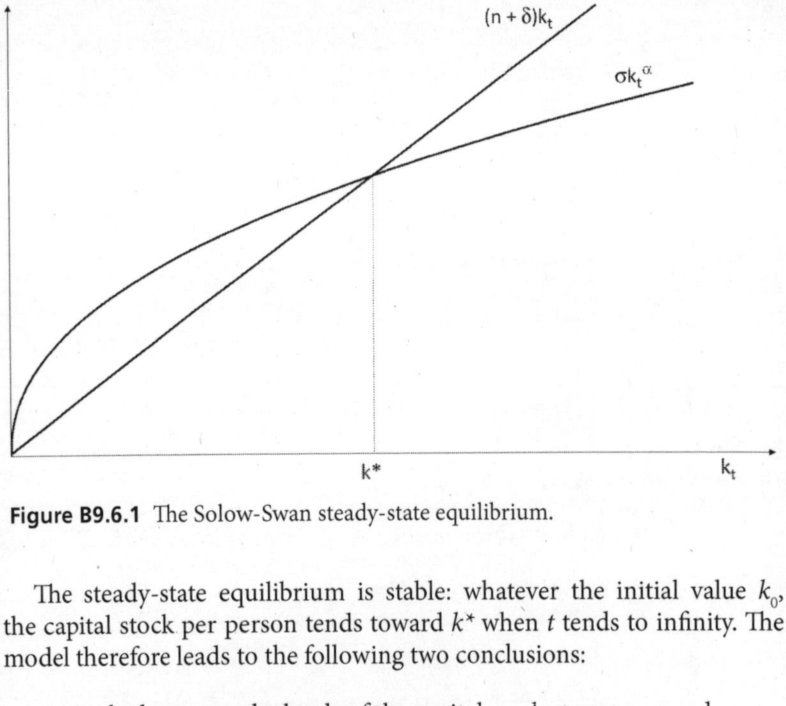

Figure B9.6.1 The Solow-Swan steady-state equilibrium.

The steady-state equilibrium is stable: whatever the initial value k_0, the capital stock per person tends toward k^* when t tends to infinity. The model therefore leads to the following two conclusions:

- In the long run, the levels of the capital stock per person and of income per person are constant. Income grows at a constant rate that depends only on demography.
- In the long run, income per person depends positively on the savings rate, all the more that capital plays an important role in the production function (in a competitive economy, α represents the share of capital income and $(1 - \alpha)$ the share of labor income in output).

The first conclusion is disappointing: the model does not account for the fact that income per person grows over time. The only possible explanation for growth in this model is that total factor productivity increases exogenously. Let us indeed suppose that total factor productivity A grows at rate g:

$$\dot{A}_t = gA_t \qquad \text{(B9.6.5)}$$

and let us again solve the model for the steady state. Results obtained are similar, but for the inclusion of trend growth rate. We find:

$$y^* = \sigma^{\frac{\alpha}{1-\alpha}}(n+g+\delta)^{-\frac{\alpha}{1-\alpha}};\ k^* = \sigma^{\frac{1}{1-\alpha}}(n+g+\delta)^{-\frac{1}{1-\alpha}};\ s^* = \sigma^{\frac{\alpha}{1-\alpha}}(n+g+\delta)^{-\frac{\alpha}{1-\alpha}} \qquad \text{(B9.6.6)}$$

where lowercase letters now represent variables per "effective labor unit": $y = Y/AL$, $k = K/AL$, and $s = S/AL$.

The model predicts that, all other things being equal, a 1% increase of the savings rate leads to an $\alpha/(1-\alpha)$% increase of steady-state per capita GDP. Per capita income y and the per capita capital k grow at rate g, and income grows at rate $(n+g)$ over time. The parameter g can be interpreted as the pace of technical progress. But it is assumed to be exogenous: The model is silent about its origin.

level of GDP per person but not its rate of growth along the stationary path). Growth is temporarily faster when the economy starts from an initial situation of capital shortage (which explains accelerated catching up by developing economies), but it sooner or later adjusts to the (lower) steady state. Hence a first, disappointing, conclusion for economic policy: under decreasing marginal returns to capital, policies aimed at encouraging saving or investment are not able to influence the long-term *growth rate*, but only the long-run *GDP-per capita level*.

Up to now, we have not introduced any normative assumption, but simply drawn logical consequences from the assumption of a decreasing marginal return to capital. We can now use the model for a normative purpose. The social objective cannot be to reach the highest possible level of per capita GDP. Indeed, as box 9.6 explains, this requires maintaining a high per capita capital stock, which necessitates allocating to capital accumulation a large fraction of income that is, therefore, not available for consumption and does not contribute to the individuals' immediate well-being. From a normative standpoint, GDP per person should therefore be high enough to make resources available, but not too high, otherwise replacement investment would absorb too large a share of GDP.[30]

This suggests that there might be an "optimum" level of the per capita capital stock and therefore of per capita GDP, a question addressed as early as in

1928 by Frank Ramsey. He assumed that the social objective was to maximize *per capita consumption* on a sustainable basis. Let us suppose that a benevolent planner (cf. Chapter 1) can choose the households' savings rate. The *Ramsey model* shows (box 9.7) that there is a savings rate that maximizes per capita consumption at the steady state. With a Cobb-Douglas production function, this optimal savings rate is exactly equal to the weight of capital in the production function. It is as if capital income (i.e., dividends paid by firms) were entirely reinvested in the economy, while labor income was consumed. At the optimum, the model shows that the marginal return to capital (i.e., the real interest rate) is exactly equal to the GDP growth rate, $n + g$: this relation is called the *golden rule* of capital accumulation. When it is verified, a marginal increase of the capital stock generates an additional income that exactly covers the additional expenditure needed to maintain that additional unit of capital so that per capita consumption remains unchanged.

Box 9.7 The Ramsey Model and the Golden Rule

Let us start with the model of box 9.6 without technical progress ($g = 0$). The government is assumed to choose the savings rate (for example, by means of tax measures) so as to maximize long-term per capita consumption $c^* = (1 - \sigma)k^\alpha$. The optimal savings rate comes out as:

$$\hat{\sigma} = Arg\max c^*(\sigma) = Arg\max\left[(1-\sigma)\sigma^{\frac{\alpha}{1-\alpha}}(n+\delta)^{-\frac{\alpha}{1-\alpha}}\right] \quad \text{(B9.7.1)}$$

Caps on per capita variables designate variables along the optimal growth trajectory. Simple calculations show that $\hat{\sigma} = \alpha$ (beware that this simple result holds only when the production function is a Cobb-Douglas). The optimal growth trajectory has an interesting property. From the results of box 9.6, the marginal productivity of capital on this trajectory is:

$$\frac{\partial y}{\partial k} = \alpha \hat{k}^{\alpha-1} = \frac{\alpha \hat{y}}{\hat{k}} = n + \delta \quad \text{(B9.7.2)}$$

However, profit maximization in a competitive environment implies that this marginal productivity is exactly equal to the user cost capital K so that:

$$\frac{\partial y}{\partial k} = c^K = r + \delta \quad \text{(B9.7.3)}$$

where r is the real interest rate. These two relations imply that on the steady-state path that maximizes per capita consumption, the real interest r rate is equal to the growth rate of the economy n. This is the so-called *golden rule*. This result also applies when $g \neq 0$, $r = n + g$.

The result can be also represented in figure B9.7.1, which, as in box 9.6, represents per capita income and per capita savings (equal to per capita investment) as functions of the stock of capital per person. At the steady state, and whatever the value of σ, investment σk^{α} is exactly equal to the increase in the capital stock needed to maintain the stock of capital constant, namely $(n + \delta)k$, which leads to the value of the steady-state per capita capital stock k^*. Per capita consumption is represented in the figure by the distance between the two curves k^{α} and σk^{α}. The figure shows that this distance is maximum for $k = \hat{k}$ where the tangent to the production function $y = k^{\alpha}$ is parallel to the line $(n + \delta)k$. This leads to the golden rule $r = n$, since the marginal productivity of capital $\frac{\partial y}{\partial k}$ is equal to the user cost of capital $r + \delta$. In figure B9.7.1, $\sigma > \alpha$ and therefore $k^* > \hat{k}$: there is "too much" savings, "too much" capital, and the real interest rate (measured by the tangent in k to the curve $y = k^{\alpha}$) is lower than the growth rate (measured by the tangent in $\hat{k}$, $n + \delta$).

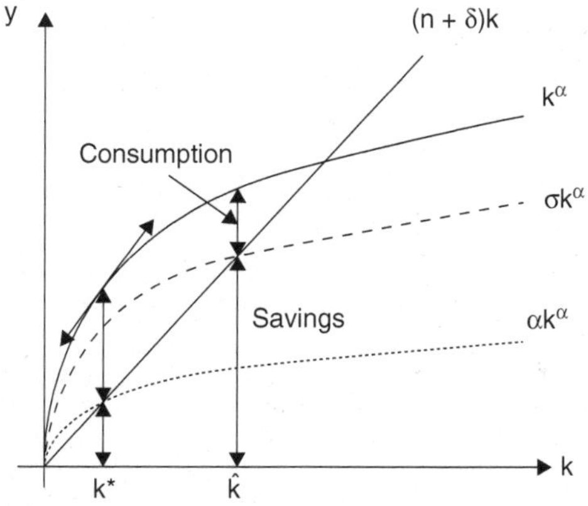

Figure B9.7.1 The Ramsey optimum.

The golden rule provides a simple means for identifying optimal growth trajectories: if the interest rate is durably higher than the growth rate, there is "not enough" capital, and a higher savings rate would allow raising consumption (consumption would have first to decrease to give way to an increase in savings, but it would eventually benefit from the consecutive rise in per capita GDP); if the rate of interest is durably lower than the growth rate, there is "too much" capital and citizens would be better off using the income from it for consumption rather than investment. The former situation can be found in developing economies where too much of the income is consumed, while the latter is called *dynamic inefficiency* and is found in economies where incentives are distorted in favor of investment, such as present-day China or the East

Asian "Tigers" in the late 20th century (box 9.3). Such considerations play an important role in deciding whether pension schemes should be funded and invested in the economy, as explained in Section 9.3.

c) Growth and catching-up

The Solow-Swan model provides a theoretical framework for growth accounting whose empirical importance was emphasized in a previous section. But are its assumptions realistic? With a Cobb-Douglas production function, the model predicts that a one percentage point increase of the savings rate, other things being equal, leads to a $\alpha/(1-\alpha)\%$ increase in per capita GDP, where α is the weight of capital in the production function (box 9.6). In 1992, N. G. Mankiw, D. Romer, and D. N. Weil tested this relation on a panel of countries and found an elasticity of per capita GDP to the savings rate of approximately 1.5, consistent with a value α of 0.6: in a closed economy under constant returns to scale, capital income would thus absorb 60% of the value added! In reality, α is known to be close to 30–40%.

Mankiw et al. propose an explanation: TFP is not exogenous and rather depends on the accumulation of a second type of capital, namely *human capital.* Indeed, part of national savings is invested in education and training and used to finance the accumulation of human capital. Education expenditures have to be treated as investment and not as consumption; they durably improve the individuals' productive capacities. In this "augmented Solow model," the elasticity of per capita GDP to the savings rate is no longer $\alpha/(1-\alpha)$ but $\alpha/(1-\alpha-\gamma)$ where γ is the share of human capital in the production function. For a value of γ close to 0.5, the model becomes realistic.[31] The model therefore predicts that convergence of per capita GDP is conditional on the proportions of income invested in physical and human capital. Countries that do not invest in education cannot converge toward developed countries whatever their physical investment. Moreover, Mankiw et al. find that the predictions of the standard Solow model without human capital are plausible (they lead to $\alpha = 0.36$) when the sample is limited to the (then) OECD member countries. This suggests that there is unconditional convergence among industrialised economies but not globally. The three authors explain this by the fact that the levels of accumulated human capital are comparable among industrialised countries.

Yet the Mankiw et al. model shows that a simple extension of the standard Solow-Swan model makes it capable of accounting for the complexity of the catching-up process and of explaining an important part of growth divergences between countries. It suggests that the absence of unconditional convergence among all countries in the world illustrated by figure 9.6 might be mainly explained by differences in the rate of accumulation of human capital. But it does not provide a fully satisfactory explanation of growth. Like in the Solow-Swan model, of which it is only an extension, growth in the steady state depends on exogenous factors (demography and technical progress) only.

9.2.2 External effects, innovation, and growth

The Mankiw et al. approach suggests that to better understand the origins of growth, the TFP "black box" must be opened. The corresponding theories were born in the 1980s and 1990s and are known as *endogenous growth theories*.

There are at least two good reasons to suppose that TFP is not an exogenous phenomenon:

1. Productive efficiency does not rely on the sole efforts of each firm but also on the interaction between them: the accumulation of "know-how" and the benefits from agglomeration, such as the attraction of skills, the development of specialized suppliers, and the like. These external effects explain why geographical clusters such as Silicon Valley or (thanks to governement intervention) the Pearl River delta emerge and grow. They need to be incorporated into the theory in order to understand how the organization of markets affects growth and when public intervention is necessary.
2. Technical progress results from major inventions and from innovations that naturally depend on the overall scientific context[32]—and perhaps also on luck—but inventions and their application in industry also respond to economic constraints and incentives: Firms invest in Research and Development (R&D) to create new products that will give them a competitive edge; consequently, the pace of innovation cannot be regarded as given, and it should be incorporated into utility-maximizing economic models.

The common feature of endogenous growth models is to relax the hypothesis of a decreasing return to capital at the aggregate level. Growth can, therefore, be self-sustained even in the absence of exogenous technical progress.

a) Externalities

External effects are at the root of the first type of endogenous growth models, pioneered by Paul Romer (1986). Romer's initial model is presented in a simplified version in box 9.8. The key idea is that in the presence of external effects, the *social* return to capital is higher than the *private* return because investment has positive effects beyond those the investing company can appropriate. Hence, the return to capital may be decreasing at the firm level but be constant economy-wide.

Telecommunication networks provide a good example of such mechanisms. To each user, connection to a network (either for voice communication or, for example, for exchanging music) gives access to transactions with all other connected users. Such access represents for each individual the *private* profit of being connected. However, the connection of an additional user increases the usefulness of the network for each already connected user.[33] Every additional

Box 9.8 Learning-by-Doing and Growth in the Romer Model

In Paul Romer's (1986) "learning-by-doing" model, the economy is made of *N* identical firms under perfect competition. Each individual firm operates with a Cobb-Douglas production function so that the production of firm *i* at time *t* is:

$$Y_{it} = A_t K_{it}^{\alpha} L_{it}^{1-\alpha} \tag{B9.8.1}$$

Total factor productivity A_t is not exogenous but depends on the economy's total capital stock: Romer considers that the size of the productive sector creates a positive externality through the exchange of know-how, which he designates under the generic term of *learning-by-doing* and which improves productivity. Accordingly, he uses the following specification for TFP:

$$A_t = AK_t^{\beta} \tag{B9.8.2}$$

where A > 0, $K_t = \sum_{i=1}^{N} K_{it}$ and, since firms are identical, $K_{it} = K_t / N$ for all *i*.

In the specific case of $\alpha + \beta = 1$ and if all firms are identical, we have $Y_{it} = AN^{\beta} K_{it} L_{it}^{1-\alpha}$. The production function is of the generic form known as *AK*, with constant returns to capital. Unlike in the Solow–Swan model, growth is self-sustained, even in the absence of exogenous technical progress.

connection therefore produces a positive externality, which means that the *social return* it generates is higher than the private return to the new user. This is known as a *network externality*.

More generally, investment carried out by a specific firm often generates positive spillovers onto other firms. For instance, the investing firm needs to train its employees in the new technologies embodied in the new generation of capital. This "know-how" will later be available to other firms through labor mobility and contacts along the supply chain. This *learning-by-doing* process, already formalized by Kenneth Arrow in 1962, forms the basis for Paul Romer's model. Romer's "know-how" resembles the "human capital" of Mankiw et al. A crucial difference, however, is the presence of externalities that allow the economy to escape the curse of a decreasing return to capital.[34] As a result, GDP growth can be sustained even in the absence of exogenous TFP growth.

In Romer's model, since each firm remunerates capital at its marginal productivity, the share of capital income in total income is α, as in the Solow model. Network externalities and know-how are not remunerated: these are public goods freely accessible to all. As a consequence, there are no private incentives to develop them, and public policies play an important role in allowing them to fully come into play. This will be discussed in Section 9.3.

The difference of treatment of human capital in the augmented Solow-Swan model à la Mankiw et al. and in endogenous growth models lends itself to empirical investigations. Does it contribute to growth only transitorily (as the former model would suggest) or permanently (as the latter models would imply)? According to Arnold et al. (2007), growth in OECD countries seems to support the latter rather than the former. This has significant implications for policy as it suggests that spending on research and education can have a lasting impact on economic growth (rather than on the sole level of per capita income).

A variant of endogenous growth models, illustrated in box 9.9, considers public infrastructures (or, more generally, public expenditures on education and public services) as a source of *production externalities* able to prevent marginal returns to private capital from falling. Public infrastructure plays the role of "know-how" described in box 9.8. It is a factor in long-term growth, but through its impact on supply rather than on demand—unlike in the Keynesian models studied in Chapter 4. As we shall see in Section 9.3, such models provide a rationale for infrastructure policies, public investment in research, and official development assistance to poor countries.

There is a limit, however, to the ability of public investment to support long-term growth. Any public expenditure is financed by a tax on (present or future) privately created wealth; this tax reduces the net return on investment and slows down private capital accumulation. Hence, there is a trade-off between, on the one hand, the provision of productivity-enhancing public infrastructures and, on the other hand, the introduction of a distortion likely to lower production. Box 9.9 illustrates this trade-off. At the optimum, a rise in public expenditure increases output by a quantity that is exactly sufficient to finance this additional expenditure.

Box 9.9 Public Intervention and Long-Term Growth

The model, based on Barro and Sala-ì-Martin (1995, chapt. 4), highlights the trade-off between positive externalities generated by public expenditures and taxation-induced distortions. It features an economy where public R&D and education expenditures G financed by a value-added tax τ raise total factor productivity:

$$G = \tau Y \qquad \text{(B9.9.1)}$$

$$Y = \left(AG^{1-\alpha}\right)K^{\alpha} \qquad \text{(B9.9.2)}$$

where K is the physical capital stock, and A is exogenous. To simplify, the labor force is supposed constant and equal to unity. From these two equations, the aggregate relationship between K and Y can be written as:

$$Y = \tau^{\frac{1-\alpha}{\alpha}} A^{1/\alpha} K \qquad \text{(B9.9.3)}$$

Production exhibits constant returns to the physical capital stock: as in box 9.8, it is an AK-type model in which long-term growth is possible even without technical progress.

Equation (B9.9.3) says that, for a given level of private capital K, an increase in the tax rate τ raises output Y. However, K cannot be assumed constant when τ increases, because a rise in τ reduces the marginal return on capital. Indeed, under profit maximization, K is set at a level that allows the after-tax marginal return on capital to be equal to the cost of capital (i.e., to the sum of the interest rate r and of the depreciation rate δ):

$$r+\delta=(1-\tau)\frac{\partial Y}{\partial K}=(1-\tau)\tau^{\frac{1-\alpha}{\alpha}}A^{\frac{1}{\alpha}} \qquad \text{(B9.9.4)}$$

In a closed economy, the interest rate is given by Equation (B9.9.4). It is a hump-shaped function of the tax rate τ: For $\tau > 1-\alpha$, the interest rate increases with τ; beyond $1-\alpha$, r decreases when τ rises further. Assuming the savings rate σ to be a monotonic, increasing function of r, capital accumulation is given by:

$$\dot{K}=\sigma(\tau)Y-\delta K \qquad \text{(B9.9.5)}$$

where $\sigma(\tau)$ follows the same hump shape as $r(\tau)$. Assuming a constant value for both A and τ, the growth rate of K and of Y is the same (see Equation (B9.9.3)), equal to:

$$g=\frac{\dot{K}}{K}=\sigma(\tau)\tau^{\frac{1-\alpha}{\alpha}}A^{\frac{1}{\alpha}}-\delta \qquad \text{(B9.9.6)}$$

Even without any exogenous technological trend, growth can still be positive in the long run in the presence of public intervention. The relation between the tax rate, τ, and the growth rate, g, is, however, nonlinear. Growth is maximum when $\tau = 1-\alpha$ because, in this case, the savings rate is maximum.

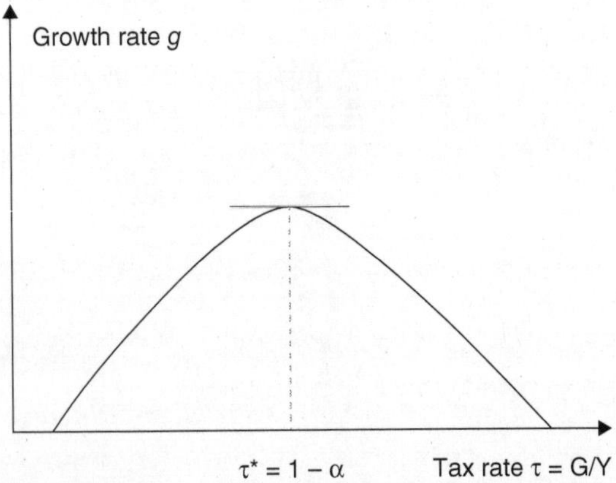

Figure B9.9.1 Growth rate as a function of taxation.

A number of empirical studies have estimated the impact of the accumulation of public capital on GDP per person and found it to be significant. In the US case, a 10% rise in the stock of public capital was found to translate over the long run into a 4% increase of per capita GDP (Munnell, 1992). This elasticity, however, is lower—around 0.2—for regions or municipalities.

Overall, this first type of endogenous growth models justifies public intervention on two conceptually different grounds: on the one hand, to coordinate private decisions and exploit externalities among economic agents and, on the other hand, to produce public goods—infrastructures, education, public research—which enhance private productivity. A model like the one presented in box 9.9, however, suggests that state intervention can either be favorable or detrimental to growth depending on the level of taxation.

b) Creative destruction

The Austrian-born economist Joseph Schumpeter—who had a huge influence on the economics of innovation—identified five types of innovation: (i) on products, (ii) on methods, (iii) on demand, (iv) on raw materials, and, finally (v) on firms' organization. In his 1942 book *Capitalism, Socialism and Democracy*, Schumpeter analyzed the process of *creative destruction* through which a major innovation leads to the disappearance of a previous generation of products. Entrepreneurs engage pecuniary and human resources to find and develop new technologies that will give them an edge over competitors - an innovation rent, as economists call it. But they themselves are constantly challenged by other innovators who aim at destroying their rents and appropriating new ones. The expectation of profit creates an incentive to innovate. Since profit is built on the elimination of the previous generation of innovations, Schumpeter called this process "creative destruction."[35]

> These revolutions periodically reshape the existing structure of industry by introducing new methods of production—the mechanized factory, the electrified factory, chemical synthesis and the like; new commodities, such as railroad service, motorcars, electrical appliances; new forms of organization—the merger movement; new sources of supply—La Plata wool, American cotton, Katanga copper; new trade routes and markets to sell in and so on. . . . Thus, there are prolonged periods of rising and of falling prices, interest rates, employment and so on, which phenomena constitute parts of the mechanism of this process of recurrent rejuvenation of the productive apparatus.
>
> Now these results each time consist in an avalanche of consumers' goods that permanently deepens and widens the stream of real income although in the first instance they spell disturbance, losses and unemployment. [T]he capitalist process, not by coincidence but by virtue of its mechanism, progressively raises the standard of life of the masses. It does

> so through a sequence of vicissitudes, the severity of which is proportional to the speed of the advance. But it does so effectively. (Schumpeter, 1942/1976, p. 68)

Creative destruction has major policy consequences. It implies that declining industries should not be protected. On the contrary, the displacement of existing firms and industries by newcomers should be encouraged as an engine of innovation and economic growth. Implementing such a philosophy has proved difficult, however, since it relies on the adjustment mechanism by which redundant employees in declining industries will find jobs in the new industries. In continental Europe, labor mobility (both geographically and between sectors) is limited, and labor force reallocations are generally accompanied by substantial wage losses. Moreover, job destruction is immediate while "job creation" is slow to materialize. This makes such adjustment socially painful and politically controversial.

The recognition of the creative destruction process at the microeconomic level also sheds light on the sources of productivity divergences between countries. For example, research conducted at the OECD (Bartelsman, Scarpetta, and Schivardi, 2003) has highlighted three salient facts:

- In the developed economies, about one-third of labor productivity gains come from *churning* (i.e., from the creative destruction of firms); the remaining two-thirds being achieved within existing firms. Firms' demography therefore appears as an important determinant of economic growth. With several co-authors, Philippe Aghion provides a theoretical background for such results and notably emphasizes the innovation-promoting role of free entry and product market competition (e.g., Aghion, 2011): increased competition and the threat of entry compel firms to invest more to address the competitive threat.
- New and old firms do not equally contribute to productivity gains. Old firms increase labor productivity through investing and substituting capital for labor. New firms typically raise TFP. The renewal of firms therefore in itself contributes to TFP gains.
- There is a major difference between Europe and the United States. The firms' birth and mortality rates are broadly similar, but surviving firms grow much faster in the United States: they are born small but those that survive have more than doubled their labor force over their first two years. In Europe, they grow by 10–20% only. In other words, the US economy "tests" new firms and enables them to grow very fast when they introduce innovative products or efficient technologies.

In the mechanism of innovation, competition on the goods market and the protection of intellectual property play a decisive role. Innovation can be seen first as widening the range of products available through so-called *horizontal differentiation.* This mechanism is related to trade liberalization and is further described in the next section. According to a second approach, very close to the original Schumpeterian vision, innovation consists in improving product quality through what is known as *vertical differentiation.* Every new product moves the technological frontier and eventually completely displaces the previous one while squeezing the rents accruing to their producers and opening new profit prospects to innovators. An example is the development of digital photography and the resulting displacement of film photography. In this spirit, a model by Aghion and Howitt (1992) shows how the R&D effort—and therefore eventually the growth rate of the economy—depends on the expected gains from innovation (box 9.10). The *Aghion-Howitt model* predicts that the innovation effort is less when innovation is more easily replicated or when competition on the goods market is fierce (because the innovation rent decreases). Section 9.3 further elaborates on these two conclusions and discusses their consequences for public policy.

Box 9.10 The Economics of Innovation in the Aghion-Howitt Model of 1992

The model focuses on the determinants of the research and development effort and on its effects on growth. This box provides a simplified version (kindly shared by Philippe Aghion).

Labor is the only factor of production and it can be used either in the production of consumer goods or in research, the latter producing innovations that increase productivity.

The total supply of working hours L is therefore allocated either to production, for a quantity X, or to research, for a quantity N. Hence:

$$X + N = L \qquad \text{(B9.10.1)}$$

Consumer goods are produced by firms under perfect competition according to the following technology:

$$Y = AX^{\alpha} \quad \text{with } A > 0,\ 0 < \alpha < 1 \qquad \text{(B9.10.2)}$$

where Y is output.

Productivity is represented by the variable A and is endogenous: it can be raised by innovations, which stem from research. However, research results are random: a unit of labor employed in research produces, with probability $\lambda < 1$, an innovation that improves productivity by a factor $\gamma > 1$. The parameter γ therefore measures the size of innovations and λ their frequency.

Labor–market equilibrium requires that the expected return to research equals the hourly real wage w. If $\pi(\gamma)$ represents the expected profit from innovation (λ being the probability to achieve it) we thus have:

$$w = \lambda\pi(\gamma) \quad \text{(B9.10.3)}$$

If the research effort is successful in producing an innovation, the innovator is then the sole person to command a superior technology. He or she benefits from it by eliminating existing firms and immediately deriving a profit π:

$$\pi(\gamma) = \gamma A X^{\alpha} - wX \quad \text{(B9.10.4)}$$

However, this gain is temporary. At the next period, innovation is fully disseminated, and the rent from innovation disappears.

If the research effort was unsuccessful in the first place, the quantity of labor devoted to it brings no return.

Profit maximization leads to:

$$\frac{d\pi}{dX} = \alpha\gamma A X^{\alpha-1} - w = 0 \quad \text{(B9.10.5)}$$

If each firm considers w as given, Equation (B9.10.5) provides the optimum level of A. Profit then is written as:

$$\pi = \frac{1-\alpha}{\alpha} wX \quad \text{(B9.10.6)}$$

Combined with Equation (B9.10.3), this equation leads to the optimum allocation of labor:

$$X = \frac{1}{\lambda}\frac{\alpha}{1-\alpha} \quad \text{and} \quad N = L - \frac{1}{\lambda}\frac{\alpha}{1-\alpha} \quad \text{(B9.10.7)}$$

The amount of labor allocated to research logically depends positively on the probability of success λ (it does not depend, however, on the size of innovations γ since, in equilibrium, productivity earnings are passed to employees; the innovator's profit only comes from displacing the existing producers and appropriating their profits).

In this simple economy without demography or capital, the rate of growth of output is simply the growth rate of productivity resulting from the innovation process. Since N units of labor employed in research will produce a productivity gain of Nlambda(gamma-1) on average, we have:

$$g = \lambda(\gamma-1) = \left(\lambda L - \frac{\alpha}{1-\alpha}\right)(\gamma-1) \quad \text{(B9.10.8)}$$

The growth rate eventually depends on the probability and on the size of innovations, as well as on the size of the economy (the larger the economy, the higher the return to innovation) and on the share of profits in value added (a higher share encourages innovation because the corresponding rent is larger). The model can easily be extended to a situation where the innovator captures the rent only partially, instead of totally displacing existing producers.

There is an important theoretical literature on intellectual property which underlines the difficult trade-off between patent protection (to encourage innovation) and the dissemination of innovation (to promote its adoption throughout the economy). *Ex ante*, policymakers are tempted to promise rents to innovators; *ex post* they are tempted to expropriate them. This problem illustrates the time inconsistency dilemma analyzed in Chapter 2.[36]

Finally, innovation and growth models describe the incentives to innovate, but they ignore the way in which innovations are received and disseminated. However, the dissemination of an innovation requires a "critical mass" of users. Paul David, the historian of innovation, explains how the QWERTY keyboard became a standard on American typewriters (David, 1985). When adopted in the 1870s by one of the first typewriter manufacturers, Remington, this keyboard minimized the risk of keys overlapping each other when the user had to type fast. All competitors eventually adopted it. Yet studies showed that the Dvorak Simplified Keyboard (DSK), a system patented in 1932, allowed much faster typing. Despite its superiority, however, DSK was not able to prevail. The QWERTY system was extended to computer keyboards even though the initial reason (the overlapping of keys) had since long become irrelevant. Paul David uses this example to stress the importance of history in economic choices and the fact that the actual destination often depends on the trajectory (this is called *path dependency*), while economists too often describe equilibrium situations without taking either the initial situation or the trajectory into account. Path dependency generally characterizes any innovation that involves network externalities.

9.2.3 Beyond the production function

a) International trade

For a long time, growth theory and trade theory developed as two separate branches of economic analysis. Growth models were initially developed in a closed-economy framework and trade models hardly addressed growth beyond Bhagwati's (1958) insights on *immiserizing growth*.[37] It is only recently that models have been developed that explore the relationship between growth and trade.

Beyond the traditional efficiency gains from trade due to specialization captured in the classical trade models, the relationship between trade and economic growth can be analyzed along four main dimensions. First, there are productivity gains to be expected from heightened competition through trade liberalization. Not only does competition increase the pressure for firms to innovate in order to stay ahead of new foreign competitors, but it also sustains a Darwinian process through which only the fittest (i.e., the most productive) firms survive and expand. Second, international trade fosters knowledge spillovers that enhance productivity in the less-advanced countries and sectors. Third, international trade increases the size of markets, which both allows domestic firms to exploit economies of scale (notably through learning by doing) and increases the potential rent accruing to successful innovators (see the model in box 9.10). Finally, trade (boosted by the collapse of costs of communication) allows participants to unbundle or reorganize the production process into subcomponents that can be globally and geographically scattered, thus globalizing competition (as opposed to seeing competition as taking place among nations) and boosting the sharing of know-how (Baldwin, 2016).

The influence of international trade on product innovation is readily understood within the framework of models of trade in varieties of similar products. In those models (introduced by Paul Krugman and others in the 1980s), consumers choose between products (say, cars or restaurant meals) according to their preferences and relative prices, but they also choose between varieties of the same products (say, Toyotas or Volkswagens and sushis or sashimis). The larger the range of varieties available, the greater the consumers' utility: consumers are said to have *taste for variety*.

Taste for variety can result from an exogenous preference of the consumer for a diversified consumption basket (for example, as regards food or cultural products) or from a trial-and-error research into the ideal variety (for example, for the purchase of a car).

Formally, the consumers' utility is often assumed to be represented by a *Dixit-Stiglitz*[38] function which makes utility dependent on both the overall quantity consumed and the number of products available to consumers. Assuming there is a continuum of goods indexed on [0, 1], and calling C_i the consumption of good *i*, consumer utility *U* (*C*) is written as:

$$U(C) = \left[\int_{i=0}^{1} \alpha_i C_i^{(\sigma-1)/\sigma} di \right]^{\sigma/(\sigma-1)} \quad \text{where} \quad \int_{i=0}^{1} \alpha_i \, di = 1 \qquad (9.7)$$

$\sigma > 1$ represents the elasticity of substitution between products and α_i the weight of good *i* in the consumer's utility.

Innovation can be regarded as consisting in widening the range of varieties available to consumers. A good example is the food industry where a large part of innovation consists in extending the variety of goods available to consumers (e.g. new yoghurt flavors).

In a closed economy, the expansion of varieties is bound by a trade-off between efficiency in production and the number of varieties produced. A simple way to represent this is to assume that the production of each variety involves a fixed as well as a variable cost. Producing more varieties is then detrimental to productivity.

Under free trade, however, each country produces fewer varieties, while consumers have access to more of them. International trade allows reaping of the benefits from economies of scale in the production process without restraining consumer choice.

Now, let us assume that the producer of each variety enjoys some monopoly power because his or her output is not perfectly substitutable for other products. This provides both an incentive for product innovation, which is then guided by the quest for the rents generated from such monopoly power. Combined with fixed costs, the model delivers an endogenous mechanism for growth, since the return to capital is now increasing. The model thus describes a self-sustained growth process driven by the specialization of the labor force in a constantly increasing range of goods exhibiting increasing returns. The intuition for the mechanism goes back to a 1928 article by Alwyn Young; Romer (1990) and Grossman and Helpman (1989) provide examples of such models.[39]

This approach highlights the importance of *demand externalities* (as opposed to the previously described production externalities): a wider market generates a larger solvent demand for each product variety, which stimulates output and distributed income. The existence of this "virtuous circle" also sheds some light on the reasons why some countries may remain trapped in underdevelopment: their domestic market is simply too small to generate the necessary investments.

b) Geography and history

Growth theory studies the evolution of wealth over time. Its distribution across space was long ignored by classical economists but, following Hotelling's (1929) seminal work on spatial competition, it has elicited a growing interest since the 1950s. Starting in the 1990s, research has explored the interactions between growth and geography.[40]

The supply and demand externalities highlighted by endogenous growth models explain why growth rates differ across countries and regions: firms choose their location according to geographical (access to transportation infrastructures, to natural resources, to drinking water, etc.), cultural (language, political system), and industrial (proximity to suppliers, access to final consumers, know-how externalities) criteria. Understanding such mechanisms has been the focus of the *new economic geography* after Paul Krugman (1991*a*, 1991*c*) outlined this research program in the early 1990s.

The toolkit of the new economic geography resembles that of endogenous growth theory: the assumptions of monopolistic competition, fixed costs, and/or externalities open the way to increasing returns and to the notion that a "critical mass" of activities and product differentiation gives an important role to the size of markets. The specific feature of economic geography is the introduction of transport and congestion costs that may offset the incentives for concentration. Firms face a trade-off between concentrating their activities in a single location to take advantage of economies of scale and disseminating them to reduce transport costs and get closer to end-consumers. Overall, the spatial location of economic activities results from a balance between forces of agglomeration and forces of dispersion.[41]

As a consequence, there is no single growth trajectory, unlike in the Solow-Swan model, but growth paths exhibit multiple equilibriums and path dependency: *history matters*. The *core/periphery model*, revisited by Krugman (1991*b*), provides an example of such thinking. The model formalizes the tension between *dispersion forces* resulting from transport costs and possibly congestion costs (such as traffic jams or water pollution in big cities) and *agglomeration forces* (also known as *polarization forces*) resulting from positive spatial spillovers between economic activities (such as access to suppliers, a pool of skilled workers and research laboratories). When transport costs are high, the former dominate and production remains scattered. When transport costs are small the latter prevail and production concentrates in one place. The equilibrium is discontinuous, even *catastrophic* in mathematical terms:[42] a small change in transport costs can lead to a brutal relocation of firms. Although highly stylized, the core–periphery model captures one of the deep insights of the new economic geography: location is determined by both deterministic and random factors. The reason why the US movie industry is based in Hollywood is that it migrated there from New York in the 1910s after Thomas Edison and a few other companies had liaised to exploit their technological monopoly and had established a centralized patenting system. Independent companies unwilling to abide by the rules set by what had become known as *The Trust* migrated west and soon settled in Hollywood, where D. W. Griffith had shot a movie in 1910. Los Angeles's climate was certainly a factor in the choice of this location, but many other places could have been chosen. However, after the agglomeration effects had been set in motion, the industry quickly concentrated there and the dissolution of the patent oligopoly in 1918 did not reverse the trend. Likewise, cities were initially founded on the basis of geographical criteria such as access to rivers or elevated watch points, which have become less relevant over time.

These mechanisms shed light on past economic history. Why are Hong Kong and Singapore major financial centers? Because both cities developed around their harbors and warehouses and had both a "critical mass" of capital and skilled labor accumulated throughout the twentieth century that they could shift toward new activities in the 1970s and 1980s. Why could peripheral countries like Finland and New Zealand develop in the late twentieth century? The answer is that transport and communication costs decreased dramatically. Why is Sub-Saharan Africa so poor? In large part because of the legacy of colonialism, but also because many African countries are landlocked and too far from dominant markets to be competitive in spite of abundant natural resources and low labor costs. Looking forward, if commodity prices become higher as resources are depleted, the associated rise of transport costs may weaken agglomeration forces in the world economy.

Economic geography also has prescriptive implications. The public sector can influence firms' location decisions; this is why European governments compete to attract company headquarters and regularly quarrel over the location of regulatory authorities: every country hopes that by so doing it will increase its attractiveness.

c) Income distribution

The two-way relationship between income distribution and development has been the subject of intense debate.[43] In 1955, Simon Kuznets suggested that there was an inverted U-shaped relationship between the level of development and within-country income inequality: inequality would be low in poor countries (like African countries) and in rich countries (like Europe) but high in those in between (like Latin American countries). As a consequence, development came together with a temporary rise in inequality. The *Kuznets curve* was influential in shaping views on the trade-offs implied by development, but it has been empirically disputed (Deininger and Squire, 1996) and rests on unclear theoretical foundations. It provides at best a weak empirical regularity (Barro, 2000). Kuznets explained it by the reallocations of labor during the industrial transition phase. In an agrarian economy, income inequalities are weak; in the first phase of the transition, polarization between the agricultural sector and the manufacturing/urban sector increases inequalities; after manufacturing and urban workers have started to adapt, organize and fight for their share of income, however, inequalities decrease. The very sharp increase in inequality experienced by China in the first phases of its capitalist development and the gradual pick-up in wages that has followed after a significant lag seem to validate this explanation.

Modern thinking emphasizes the income effects of within-sector technological innovation, rather than intersectoral dimensions, as innovation creates temporary but unequally distributed rents (Galor and Tsiddon, 1997). The initial rise in inequality comes as a corollary to the creative destruction process explained earlier. OECD work (Causa, de Serres, and Ruiz, 2014; OECD 2015) finds that technological change that encourages the hiring of skilled labor and forces job cuts in the declining sectors played a significant role in the increase in income disparities in advanced economies. Milanovic (2016) sees such skill-biased technological change as a determinant of a new, possibly lasting, cycle of rising domestic inequalities. Biased technological change is not universal: for example, the strong growth and high productivity gains of the post-World War II period benefited unskilled labor. However, it is not without precedent: the technological innovations brought by the Industrial Revolution provoked desperate reactions, such as the revolt of the Luddites against the new wool and cotton mills in 1811–12 in England, or the uprising of the Lyons *canuts* (silk workers) in 1831 in France. Early 21st century's technological progress, notably information and communication technologies and the advent of artificial intelligence, does put a high premium on skilled labor.

The impact of inequality on growth is also complex and ambiguous. The classic argument is that inequality may result from the normal play of a market economy, in which the returns to individual efforts, innovation, and risk-taking act as incentives to invest. Moreover, inequality leads to an increase in the savings rate because the rich save more than the poor. In the absence of redistributive taxation, an increase in inequality can then be favorable to growth if wealth accumulated by the richest fraction of the population is invested in the industries that generate productivity gains (Kuznets, 1955; Kaldor, 1957). In turn, those gains may "trickle down" to the less wealthy. This story is consistent with the Kuznets curve, but there is little empirical support for any automatic trickle-down mechanism. Deaton (2013) also argues that wage inequality, stemming from inequalities in returns to education, promotes the supply of skills and, although not desirable per se, can raise living standards for all.

However, inequalities may also negatively affect growth through several channels that economic theory has attempted to clarify:

- Income inequality often translates into an inequality of opportunities. In particular, less-developed countries have underdeveloped financial markets. Exclusion from credit markets prevents the poorest individuals from investing, whether in physical or in human capital (education), which in turns locks them in *poverty traps*—hence the interest in micro-credit pioneered by Muhammad Yunus as a way to relax the credit constraint on the poor.[44]
- There may be a temptation for government policy to react to increased inequality by easing credit conditions for poorer households (see Rajan, 2010). Cynamon and Fazzari (2016) show how the slow income growth for the bottom 95% of the US income distribution since the 1980s could not be compatible with both a stable debt-to-income ratio and a stable consumption ratio. The debt ratio increased dramatically and fed into unsustainable growth dynamics. Moreover, the need for households to deleverage then acted as a powerful drag on domestic demand, affecting the capacity of the economy to bounce back after the crisis.
- Income inequalities may lead to political instability or political deadlock. The risk of misery-based riots or revolutions creates a climate of uncertainty that discourages investment.
- In a democracy, inequality may tilt the political balance toward redistribution rather than toward incentives to wealth creation. For example, Benabou (1996) presents a theoretical model in which income dispersion increases the risk of conflict between social groups over the distribution of profits and creates a "prisoner's dilemma" in which none of these groups wishes to contribute to wealth creation. Alesina and Rodrik (1994) emphasize another mechanism based on tax incentives: the more uneven the primary distribution of income, the more the median voter will vote for a redistributive taxation. However, an excessively high marginal tax rate on high incomes is a barrier to capital accumulation and therefore to growth.

- Inequality may also weaken support for growth-enhancing institutions and systems such as economic openness, open international trade, or even the foundations of the market economy. This interaction, in the context of the rise of populist debates in the 2010s in developed countries, is notably further explored by Rodrik (2017).

In many countries, those issues are a matter for fierce policy debates without conclusive theoretical guidance. Early empirical work suggested that that inequalities may have a negative influence on growth in underdeveloped economies but a positive one in developed countries: having built a very rich dataset, Deininger and Squire (1996) conclude that the relation between inequality (measured by the Gini index of income distribution) and the growth rate depends on the development level; in accordance with the Kuznets model, they find a negative influence of inequalities on growth for either low or high GDP per capita and a positive influence in between.[45] However, they find that the inequalities that hamper growth are not income inequalities but rather factor endowment inequality, especially as regards land distribution. Recent work at the International Monetary Fund (IMF), however, has led to the more general conclusion that inequalities are detrimental to the long-term level and duration of growth. Ostry et al. (2014) find that a 5-point pre-tax and transfers Gini increase (i.e., the difference in the 2010s between Sweden and France, or China and Chile) reduces average annual growth by half a percentage point (holding redistribution and initial income constant). They also empirically document that, for a given redistribution, a 1-point Gini increase in inequality reduces the average expected duration of growth spells by 7%. Moreover, their study does not find any evidence of any adverse direct effect on growth from nonextreme fiscal redistribution, so that the total effects of redistribution, including the growth-enhancing effects of reduced inequality, are on average favorable to growth.

A new frontier for research may be to better relate inequality to the determinants of economic growth, such as innovation. Aghion et al. (2016) for example shows that innovation is positively associated with both top income inequality and upward social mobility, but not with Gini inequality. Innovation may thus spur mobility (because it opens opportunities to innovators) and increase top income inequality (because the innovators get rich) without affecting the broader distribution of income in a major way.

The relationship between growth and inequality thus ultimately depends on both the sources and the nature of growth, as well as on the kind of inequality that is considered.

d) Institutions

So far, we have primarily associated TFP growth with technical progress. However, TFP depends, in a much more general way, on all factors that contribute to raising the effectiveness of labor, capital, and their combination. Important dimensions here are the legal and regulatory environment of production, the nature of the relationship between employers and employees, and the enforceability of laws and contracts, all factors that can be summarized under the generic term of *institutions*. Douglass North, who was awarded the Nobel Prize in 1993 with Robert Fogel, has defined institutions as "the humanly devised constraints that structure human interaction. They are made up of formal constraints (rules, laws, constitutions), informal constraints (norms of behavior, conventions, and self-imposed codes of conduct), and their enforcement characteristics" (North, 1990). Following Ronald Coase, the emphasis here is on the transaction costs implied by a low-quality institutional environment and on the importance of the security of contracts.[46] Thus, the more uncertain the legal, tax, and social environments are, the larger the precautions that any given investment requires.

In an influential contribution, La Porta et al. (1999) have stressed the importance of *legal origins*. In their view, countries such as France and the former French colonies with a civil law tradition suffer from an overextended government and regulations hampering private initiative, while the UK and its colonies operating under common law benefit from more flexible institutions and a better protection of property rights. According to the authors, such difference can be traced back to the different contexts of France and England in the twelfth and thirteenth centuries, the former being prone to rebellion while the latter was calmer and more industrious. La Porta et al. (1998) have also suggested that civil law is more likely to be associated with intermediated finance, while common law better underpins market finance since it better protects minority shareholders

One can object that countries like China and India have developed original models which cannot be reduced to civil law or common law and that there is always a gap between formal legal principles and on-the-ground experience, as confirmed by Dani Rodrik (2004) in the comparison between China and Russia: investors felt better protected in China even though the country provided no legal protection while they had the full formal protection of a private property rights regime in Russia.

Daran Acemoglu, Philippe Aghion, and Fabrizio Zilibotti (2002) have proposed an interesting framework of analysis by introducing the concept of *distance to the frontier*: for countries farthest away from the technological frontier, technical progress mainly takes place through the adoption of existing technologies, and the institutions favorable to growth are those that encourage this imitation process. But the closer one gets to the frontier, the more important it is to encourage innovation and to develop specific institutions capable of protecting intellectual property, fostering project finance, or giving incentive to risk-taking.

This analytical framework can easily be transposed to other fields. The 1997–98 financial crises in emerging market economies provided a reminder that the opening of the financial account should not be recommended to all countries, as the OECD and the IMF tended to believe before the crises, but only to countries equipped with robust financial institutions (Kose et al.,

2006). The main contribution of Acemoglu et al. (2002) is finally to show the importance of flexible institutions. Institutions matter at all stages of development, but they must adapt to each stage. This is an invitation for international institutions to refine their recommendations to developing countries.[47] Together with J. Wallis and B. Weingast, D. North has developed a theory of development as a transition process between institutions (North, Wallis, and Weingast, 2009; see box 9.11).

Box 9.11 Douglas North's Approach to the Social Development Process

North et al. (2009) emphasize the necessary connection between economics and politics within a "social order." The authors consider that only three generic social orders have existed in history:

- The *primitive social order* that dominated prerecorded human history
- The *limited access social order,* in which violence is contained and order and stability maintained through political manipulation based on rent generation through limited entry and rent distribution. This order rests on the logic of the "natural State." In response to endemic violence, warlords agree on controlling and sharing property rights and rents, which creates a common interest in pacifying relations. Access to all functions is limited and constitutes privileges for those who receive them and share an interest in stability. The limited access order is based on cronyism, personalization, and corruption, but the "natural State" is neither fragile nor failing. It simply corresponds to the first stages of social development of societies prone to natural violence. As such, the limited access social order is stable.
- The *open access social order* emerged over the past 300 years and was adopted by the few countries that successfully developed. It rests on political and economic competition and on the contestability of rents. Rents do exist, but they result from dynamism and innovation, are fundamentally impersonal (rather than attached to a person), and can be contested. They cannot be appropriated forever, and their contestability (through elections or competition) makes their distribution at any point in time acceptable for all, including those who do not benefit from them. Organizations rest on membership and contract. The open access social order is also stable.

For North et al., development really means the transition from a limited access to an open access social order. Preconditions for this transition are the emergence of a legal framework that protects the elites' property rights (and that can, over time, expand beyond the elites), the emergence of impersonal organizations able to survive individuals, and the political control of the military. In order for the transition to take place successfully, changes must be small, mutually reinforcing, and cumulative. They must also be supported by the ruling elites, so they need to be compatible with the elites' perceived interests, even though the final outcome might not be supported by them.

This taxonomy may be oversimplifying (developed countries retain many features of limited access social orders, such as the reproduction of social elites and resistance to the elimination of rents), but it has important implications for policy reform in developing countries. For example, attempts to introduce elements of an open access social order into limited access order societies are bound to fail if the necessary coherence between economics and politics is ignored. Also, a limited access political system is incompatible with economic deregulation and liberalization, and it makes no sense to try to reform it using economic means only. This analysis reinforces North's earlier claim (1994, pp. 4–5) that "it is adaptive rather than allocative efficiency which should be the guide to policy. Allocative efficiency is a static concept with a given set of institutions; the key to continuing good economic performance is a flexible institutional matrix that will adjust in the context of evolving technological and demographic changes as well as shocks to the system. . . . It is doubtful if the policies that will produce allocative efficiency are always the proper medicine for ailing economies."

Empirical studies have endeavored to build indicators of the quality of institutions and to relate them to GDP per person. The World Bank publishes a *Worldwide Governance Indicators* database with five variables: voice and accountability, political stability and absence of violence, government effectiveness, regulatory quality, rule of law and control of corruption (Kaufman, Kray, and Mastruzzi, 2008). Such variables are based on an array of rankings and surveys, and their reliability is therefore debated.

Building on these indicators, the IMF (2003) has uncovered a strong positive correlation between the quality of the institutions and GDP per person—which in turn suggests that institutional improvements can foster growth. Coeuré (2017, slide 6) also finds a very strong correlation within the euro area between 2015 GDP per capita and 2008 world governance indicator ranks. Figure 9.10 illustrates the correlation across countries between the level of GDP per capita, the respect for the rule of law (panel a), and the quality of regulation (panel b).

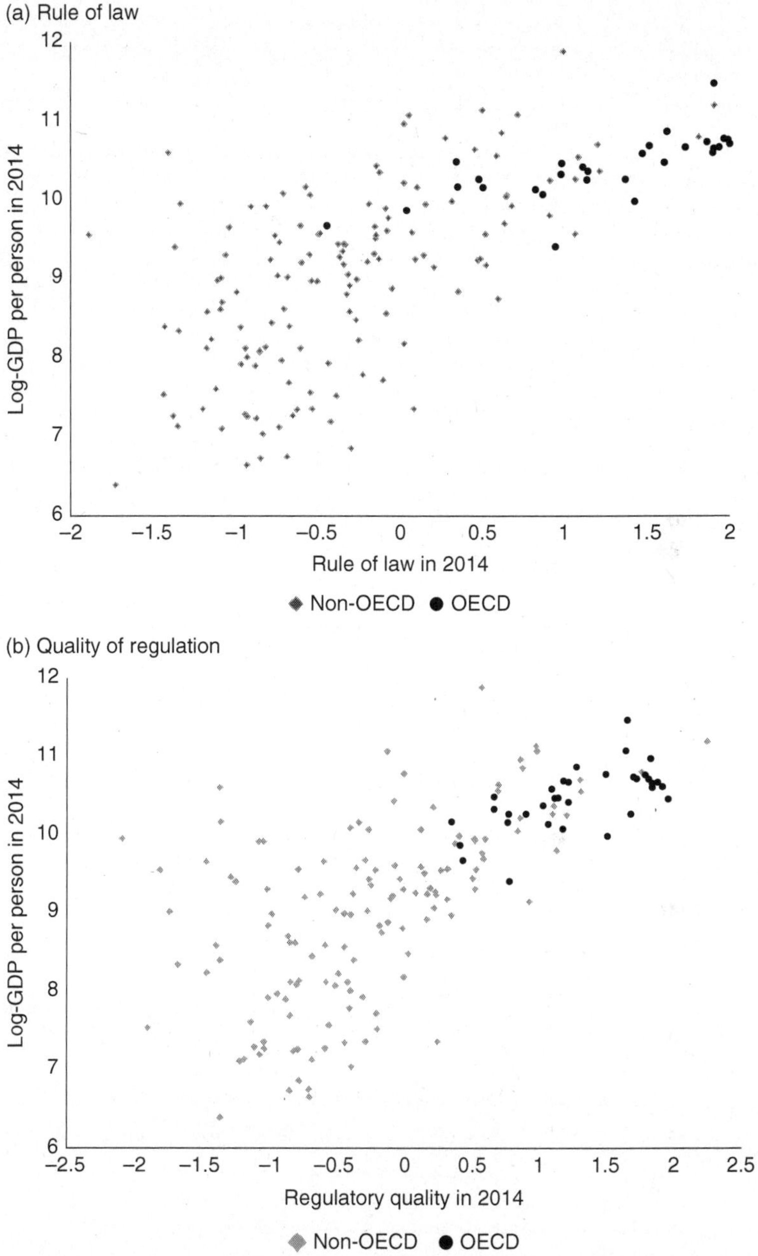

Figure 9.10 (9.10a and 9.10b) Institutions and gross domestic product (GDP) per capita in 2014.
World Bank Worldwide Governance Indicators, and Penn World Table 9.0 (per capita GDP in constant PPP 1991 dollars).

Correlation does not imply causality. Are institutions causing development or vice-versa? It is admittedly easier to convince people to shed their informal protections and networks and trust the rule of law when they can rely on a tax-financed social safety net. This suggests that it may be difficult to find out whether good institutions are conducive to growth or the other way around. Econometric techniques can be used to sort this out with the use of well-chosen instrumental variables, but only up to a point.

The Pandora's box of the origins of institutions will not be closed anytime soon. There is also another dimension to the debate; namely, the nature of the dependent variable: Is institutional quality correlated with the level of income or with the process of economic growth? Meisel and Ould Aoudia (2008) claim that the quality of institutions as measured through the World Bank Worldwide Governance Indicators is strongly correlated with the level of income but not with the speed of development over a medium to long-term horizon. They discuss the specific institutional variables that facilitate economic take-off and those that help sustain economic growth over the long term and make economic catch-up possible.

The emphasis on the role of institutions is both an opportunity and a danger for growth theory. The opportunity is to reach a deeper understanding of the determinants of economic performance and to recognize that there cannot be a single institutional template for all countries and at all times. This makes room for much richer policy conclusions. However, if mechanisms are excessively context-dependent, there is a risk of ending up with "soft" theories which produce neither general testable propositions nor clear policy recommendations. Minimal structure must therefore be imposed on the theoretical description of the links among institutions, organizations, and growth. North's research suggests that these links are complex and nonlinear. This message is increasingly being heard by policymakers (Commission on Growth and Development, 2008). Section 9.3 explores the resulting policy recommendations.

9.3 Policies

Unlike, say, price stability, for which most countries rely on a single instrument (monetary policy), the quest for growth requires playing on several keyboards at the same time, with the risk that any policy recommendation ends up reading like a laundry list of a wide number of measures that should be implemented but among which policy priority is hard to determine. Even when this is avoided, any growth policy package will have to draw on several domains and target several objectives and may end up as a wishful list of objectives that sound like potentially empty promises. As a technocratic rather than political institution, the OECD may be immune from grand promises. However, in recent years, its annual *Going for Growth* report has altogether addressed education, labor markets, pensions, product market regulation, competition policy, and international trade. This is, in fact, hardly surprising in view of the determinants of growth identified in the previous section. The 10-year growth strategy formulated in March 2010 by the European Union, called the Europe 2020 Strategy (box 9.12), furthermore illustrates the multipronged nature of the notion of economic performance well beyond the growth of GDP.

Box 9.12 Europe 2020

In March 2010, the European heads of state and government agreed on the Europe 2020 strategy, designed to help Europe emerge stronger from the economic and financial crisis and turn it into a "smart, sustainable and inclusive delivering high levels of employment, productivity and social cohesion." Europe 2020 is a common reference framework that serves as a soft coordination device: Member States have set national targets accordingly and report on them in their annual reform programs. The strategy pursues five interrelated goals and their corresponding measurable targets:

- Employment: 75% of the population aged 20–64 should be employed;
- Research and innovation: 3% of GDP should be invested in R&D;
- Climate change and energy: Meeting the so-called 20/20/20 climate/energy targets (specifying that the emissions of greenhouse gases should be reduced by 20% from their 1990 levels, that renewables should represent 20% of energy use, and that energy efficiency should increase by 20%);
- Education: The share of early school leavers should be under 10%, and at least 40% of the younger generation should have a tertiary degree;
- Combating poverty: Reduction by 20 million of the number of people at risk of poverty;

The progress report published in 2016 shows that targets are likely to be reached or exceeded by 2020 for climate change, energy, and education, but that difficulties remain in the areas of employment, R&D, and poverty reduction.

The overriding problem for any government that wishes to promote growth is not to find out what needs to be fixed. It is to select priorities. The economist's role is to make the best use of theory to help it.

9.3.1 A roadmap

To put some order in the discussion, we can start from the theories introduced in Section 9.2 and sort out policies accordingly (figure 9.11):

- The time horizon for effectiveness ranges from a few quarters to a few years. In the short term, governments can stimulate labor supply through policies that favor participation in the labor force. Corresponding measures can be regulations (e.g., on the retirement age) and changes to tax and benefits rules (as, e.g., with the introduction of in-work benefits).
- In the medium run, governments can stimulate capital accumulation through tax incentives (such as accelerated depreciation or cuts to the corporate income tax), competition, and reforms of financial markets. They can also invest in public capital. The time horizon here is a few years.
- In the long run (up to a few decades), the capital stock is endogenous and only total factor productivity and labor supply matter. Public policies affect the quality of the labor force through education and training; they also have a bearing on total factor productivity through the funding of research, investments in infrastructure and improvements to institutions.

The public discussion is less clear-cut as it often confuses long-term and short-term determinants of growth. For example, politicians and voters frequently attribute long-term economic performance to monetary and fiscal policies. Technocrats tend to hold the opposite view and maintain that macroeconomic policies have no bearing on long-term growth. Both views are equally untrue. Before addressing the levers of a growth program one by one, we first discuss the link between short-run and long-run policies.

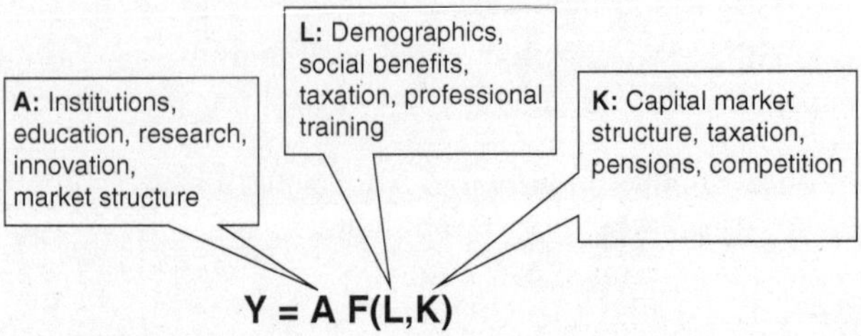

Figure 9.11 Using theory to design growth policies.

Economists usually assume a clear separation between stabilization and allocation policies. The former policies focus on short-term fluctuations and are tasked with maintaining production close to its potential level, while the latter focus on long-term trends and aim at raising this potential level. This is, among others, the underpinning of Europe's economic policy framework described in Chapter 2. Such a sharp distinction may not be entirely correct, and several arguments point to the existence of an interrelation between long-term trends and short-term fluctuations. These are:

- *Precautionary behavior*. Macroeconomic instability leads companies and households to engage in *precautionary behavior*.[48] We saw in Chapter 2 that uncertainty about the return on investment projects raises their break-even return and delays their implementation. Similarly, increased uncertainty over household income makes individuals consume less and invest more in risk-free (hence unproductive) securities such as Treasury bonds. However, negative-growth consequences of macroeconomic instability may only materialize at high levels of uncertainty—say, two-digit inflation.
- *Unemployment hysteresis*.[49] When employees having lost their jobs in an economic downturn remain lastingly unemployed, their skills deteriorate, and they become (and are perceived) as less employable (Blanchard and Summers, 1986). As time goes by, finding a job becomes increasingly difficult and sometimes even impossible. At the macroeconomic level, persistent unemployment, even of a cyclical nature, is not easily reverted (Ball, 1999). Negative demand shocks raise the nonaccelerating inflation rate of unemployment (NAIRU), and the employment rate does not revert to a long-term level. Although empirical evidence on unemployment hysteresis remains weak, the extent of the 2007-09 crisis has raised concern that part of the unemployed would de facto be excluded from the labor market, which would permanently reduce the level of potential output (OECD, 2010).
- *Creative destruction*. The impact of recessions on the demographics of firms and their innovation behavior is disputed. The Schumpeterian tradition sees recessions as productive because they hasten the attrition of the least efficient firms and contribute to creative destruction. Labor and capital freed up by bankruptcies are directed to more productive firms, which raises overall productivity. Governments should therefore not oppose the "cleansing" effect of recessions (Caballero and Hammour, 1994) by attempting to stabilize the economy. In contrast, another line of thinking stresses irreversible losses caused by recessions: companies that go bust are not necessarily the least effective ones and can simply be the most fragile or those which took more risks (Aghion et al., 2008*b*). Furthermore, their disappearance induces a social loss because of

the depreciation of capital goods and of firm-specific skills and knowledge. Far from being stimulated, the productive fabric could thus be hampered by recessions.

Each of these arguments is theoretically relevant, and the jury is out on whether output volatility is good or bad for long-term growth. Ramey and Ramey (1995) look at a sample of 92 countries and find a negative effect of GDP volatility on long-term GDP growth. For example, the "stop-and-go" policies carried out in the UK in the 1980s and 1990s are generally thought to have slowed down UK productivity growth (Barrell and Weale, 2003). Beyond this simple evidence there are, however, good reasons to believe that the sign of the relationship depends on the structure of markets. Recessions are costlier in a country where the labor market is rigid and the probability of exiting unemployment is low or where accessing credit is difficult (so that firms cannot borrow to avoid going bust). Aghion and Banerjee (2005) have shown that the impact of GDP volatility on growth is more negative when financial markets are less developed.

Hence, the dichotomy between stabilization and allocation holds only as a first approximation. Macroeconomic policy is likely to have long-term effects when fluctuations are wide and market institutions do not allow economic agents to weather recessions.[50] Symmetrically, it is increasingly recognized that policies favoring long-term growth are likely to increase resilience to cyclical fluctuations.[51]

When designing a growth program, however, the interaction between short- and long-term policies is generally ignored. Here, we follow the production function sketched in figure 9.11. We start from labor supply (L) and capital (K) accumulation, and then focus on the TFP (A), which is at the core of growth policies. We add a discussion on the spatial dimension of policies and conclude with a discussion on the choice of priorities.

9.3.2 Increasing labor supply

The *participation rate* (the ratio between the population in the labor force and the population of active age) varied in 2015 in the OECD from less than 60% in Turkey and South Africa to more than 80% in Sweden, Switzerland, and Iceland. In other words, if participation in the labor force (and employment) were at the Icelandic level, Turkey's and South Africa's incomes per head could be significantly higher. This is quite an extreme example, but the variance of participation rates is nevertheless striking, especially for women, young workers, and older workers.

As for working hours (box 9.1), genuine preferences may account for some part of observed differences. But a large part of them can be ascribed to the involuntary effects of public policies. Women may be discouraged from working full time by taxation or because of the lack of child care infrastructure. Students may find it difficult to combine study and work because regulations do not favor part-time work. Older workers may give up working part-time because retirement rules make it difficult to combine with a pensioners' status. So, even though some differences may be genuine, in most countries there is room for improving public policies.

Increasing labor-force participation is an important objective in developing and developed countries for different reasons. In the former, the priority is to deal effectively with the informal sector, where jobs are unprotected and have low productivity, and to raise participation in the formal sector of the economy (which calls for institutional reforms as well). In industrial countries, the population of working age is frequently stagnant or declining while the number of pensioners is rising. In the medium term, at least, a higher participation rate can help offset the effect of aging and contribute to growth. Two main instruments have recently been used to this end: in-work benefits and pension reforms.

Policies of this sort can help maintain a positive rate of growth of the labor force for several years. In the short term, and beyond the medium-term horizon, however, they are bound to have limited impact. The only policies that can contribute to sustaining the growth rate of the labor force in the long run are measures aimed at increasing the fertility rate and/or immigration. The fertility rate is often considered an extraeconomic variable, but it can be raised by providing childcare facilities for young working families so that labor-market participation is not an obstacle to raising children. France and Northern European countries provide examples of such policies. As for the importance of immigration, it has been understood by countries like the United States, Ireland, Sweden, and the United Kingdom, where inward migration has contributed to significant increases of the labor force and correspondingly to higher growth. But the political environment in the mid-2010s and the ensuing backlash against migration put such understanding to a test.

9.3.3 Developing and regulating financial systems

Many growth strategies tend to overlook the role of financial markets even though that role is crucial for growth since they transform households' savings into productive capital accumulation. Financial markets thus fulfil a key allocation function in the sense given in Chapter 1.[52] Three channels of influence on long-term growth can be identified (Pagano, 1993):

- *Lower cost of capital.* Collecting household savings entails transaction costs, which reflect the costs of production of financial services, but also the taxes and regulations in force and oligopoly rents. Competition in the financial sector increases the effectiveness of the intermediation process and lowers the cost of capital.

- *Higher savings.* By giving confidence to savers, a robust financial system makes it possible to increase the saving rate, thus GDP per person (this is again the Solow-Swan model of Section 6.2).
- *Better allocation of capital.* The financial system makes it possible to collect and share information on investment projects, to diversify risk, and to finance innovation: in a nutshell, to direct saving toward the most productive projects.

a) Lower the cost of capital

Firms' investment decisions depend on the difference between the marginal productivity of capital and its cost, which is equal to the interest rate plus the rate of capital depreciation. Public policies can theoretically affect the cost of capital through monetary, regulatory, and tax policies. Monetary policy directly affects short-term interest rates and indirectly influences (see Chapter 5) medium and long-term interest rates (which are relevant for business fixed investment). As for regulatory policies, in advanced countries they have lost the impact they had when governments could direct household savings to the financing of priority investment or to specific sectors, but bank and capital market regulation do have an impact on the cost of capital (Chapter 6). Finally, taxation enters into play through the tax on corporate earnings (and various tax rebates) and through taxes on capital assets, notably real estate, generally raised locally. Taxation also changes the relative return to various savings instruments—public or private, risk-free or risky, short-term or long-term.

The situation is different in emerging economies. East Asia's economies maintained until the early 1990s a system of *financial repression* (i.e., interest rates maintained at low levels by governments to encourage investment), and this remains the case in China.[53] Such policies may stimulate growth in the short to medium run, but they involve the risk of triggering a misallocation of capital that is detrimental to longer-term economic performance. And many governments still extend subsidized loans to help some sectors, such as agriculture. The European Union generally views such interventions, deemed *state aids*, as obstacles to free competition which should be prohibited unless for the sake of general interest.

Turning to taxes, temporary tax exemptions have a limited effect on capital expenditures save for their timing, but the permanent features of corporate taxation such as amortization schemes, the definition of the tax base, and headline tax rates do play a role as incentives or disincentives to invest (see Chapter 8).

b) Stimulate savings

In the Solow-Swan model of box 9.6, steady-state GDP per capita depends positively on the savings rate. If capital moves freely across countries, capital expenditures are not constrained by the availability of domestic savings, and there is no point in inciting households to save more. But, for various reasons discussed in Chapter 7, savings and investment remain correlated and governments continue to have recourse to policies aimed at encouraging savings. An example is pension reform. Funded pensions are a form of forced savings and help increase GDP per person, provided that pension money is invested in corporate bonds or stocks (but they can encourage excessive investment if savings are already high).

Policies aimed at encouraging savings suffer from several drawbacks. An obvious one is the short time horizon of policymakers, who are bound by the political cycle. Impatient policymakers prioritize consumption at the expense of savings. Ignorant ones prioritize both. Another drawback is the difficulty of judging the adequate level of capital: at an aggregate level, this is about dynamic inefficiency (i.e., over- or undercapitalization) in the sense of the Ramsey model, whereas at the industry level, this is about whether companies are constrained by insufficient capital supply or rather by a poor demand outlook or bad functioning of the labor market.

The relation between financial development and the level of savings is more ambiguous than it may seem. In developed countries, households access insurance through financial markets, and portfolio diversification reduces their precautionary saving. It also lifts their financing constraint by giving them access to financing instruments such as residential mortgages. The low level of household savings in the United States and in the United Kingdom is a case in point. It has been argued that the wave of financial innovation of the 2000s, which ended with the global financial crisis, was encouraged by politicians who supported residential investment, in particular by the less wealthy households, absent the corresponding income streams (Rajan, 2010).

Likewise, in low-income and emerging-market economies with limited social safety nets, households need high levels of savings as self-insurance, but this does not necessarily require a developed financial system as savings can be invested in simple ways such as land, cash, or gold. However, a well-functioning financial system provides additional and better diversified stores of value. Public policies primarily aim to promote *financial inclusion* by encouraging or forcing financial firms to expand cheap access to bank accounts and payment and savings instruments.[54] More recently, digital innovations such as payments via mobile phones have supported market-based solutions, with governments only playing a catalytic role (e.g., by distributing special-purpose electronic money, such as prepaid cards to buy first-necessity products, or by making the regulatory environment friendlier to digital payments).[55] One particular area of interest for public policy in emerging market economies, and for support by multilateral institutions, has been the development of local-currency capital markets, for example, by facilitating the issuance of local-currency bonds. This allows savings to match investment locally without being recycled through US dollar–denominated capital markets.

c) Influence savings allocation

Finally, governments can also influence the allocation of savings between various supports—mortgages, public bonds, stocks, and the like—to direct savings to the productive economy. *Credit rationing*, which was in place until the 1980s in many developed economies, amounted to a central planning of capital allocation to individual companies. Fiscal incentives can nowadays still channel savings—for example, to finance innovation through R&D tax credits (see earlier discussion) or to favor small- and medium-size enterprises (SMEs). Tax policy and regulatory policies influence decisions to invest in equity, bonds, or housing.

The role of the financial system in technological innovation has been a constant feature in history and was recognized by Schumpeter (1911). In eighteenth-century Britain, the rise of government debt allowed savers to switch out of low-return sectors and lifted profits in rising industries such as textiles and iron (Ventura and Voth, 2015). The ability of the US financial market to innovate and channel funds to the most productive uses has been regarded as a major competitive advantage of the US economy in comparison to Europe and Japan. The rise of US corporate finance, together with a fluid labor market, has contributed to the emergence of a growth model that relies on the entry and fast rise of new players that, bringing to the market new products and productivity-enhancing technologies, are able to challenge the incumbents (Philippon and Véron, 2008).

In Europe, the introduction of the euro in 1999 accelerated cross-border integration of financial markets. It created a unified monetary market and, until the 2010-2012 crisis at least, better integrated markets for government and corporate bonds and wholesale financial services. Asset management, retail banking, venture capital, and SME financing have however remained fragmented along national lines. This fragmentation precludes competition, prevents economies of scale from materializing in the financial industry, hurts SMEs that do not have access to global capital markets, holds back innovation, and hampers the diversification of risks. In short, it favors rent-seeking by financial institutions at the expense of European households and companies. Integrating financial services ranks high on the EU agenda since the European Commission and EU Member States have drafted a "Financial Service Action Plan" (European Commission, 2005) aimed at harmonizing the regulation on financial products, consumer protection, and the functioning of the markets. The EU regulatory and supervisory framework has been further streamlined after the financial crisis, with unified bank supervision and resolution within the euro area, and the EU has put forward a plan for a "Capital Markets Union" as a complement.

The financial crisis has led to reconsideration of the usefulness and dangers of the financial innovations of the 1990s and 2000s, beginning with securitization and leverage. Former Federal Reserve Chairman Alan Greenspan's diagnosis that: "clearly, our high financial returns on investment are a symptom that our physical capital is being allocated to produce products and services that consumers particularly value" (Greenspan, 1998) was, clearly, too benign. This makes the case for a strong regulatory framework and stringent supervision of financial activities, as discussed in Chapter 6, but it does not question the importance of a well-functioning financial system for long-term growth.

9.3.4 Encourage TFP growth

In the long term, the growth of per capita GDP depends on TFP growth, which therefore lies at the very heart of growth policies along three complementary dimensions: (i) improve the institutional environment; (ii) invest in education, research, and infrastructures; and (iii) improve the functioning of markets.

a) Improving institutions

Imperfect as it may seem, research on institutions has produced useful policy recommendations: it suggests that governements should, first, ensure that the legal framework in which the economy operates is conducive to private initiative (through creating an independent judiciary to enforce private contracts, fighting corruption, limiting red tape, ensuring transparent information, etc.); second, that they should put in place effective market regulation (through creating an anti-trust authority, developing proper banking regulation, ensuring consumer protection, etc.); and, third, that they should achieve macroeconomic stability (through, e.g., an independent central bank and appropriate fiscal rules and institutions, as described in Chapters 3 and 4).

Such recommendations form the backbone of the agenda set out by international institutions. These institutions, such as the OECD for economic policy, the IMF for international monetary management, the World Bank for development, or the World Trade Organization (WTO) for trade, have therefore become the guardians of a world policy order. For emerging countries, becoming a member of the OECD or the WTO goes well beyond formally adopting sound institutional principles. It is part of a process of domestic reform and results in tying the hand of current and future policymakers. It is also a strong signal sent to foreign investors and contributes to the credibility and reputation of a country. EU membership, or the prospect of it, has played a similar role for economies in transition after the fall of the Berlin Wall. The importance of "good governance" for economic development has also been recognized by the lower income countries, as illustrated for example by the New Partnership for the Development of Africa (NEPAD), set up by the African Union in 2001, which includes national commitments and peer-country reviews. Likewise, when lending to low-income countries, the IMF and the World Bank take their governance into account.

Beyond first principles, however, it is difficult to identify a set of precise recommendations that could be used as roadmaps by governments and international organizations. Different countries rely on different institutional setups—about, for example, the role of the state in the economy—without clear impact on economic performance. In short, no single policy recipe is right for all countries and at all times.

Williamson (1990) had summarized the growth policy priorities recognized at the end of the 1980s under the name of "Washington consensus" as including 10 priorities: (i) fiscal discipline, (ii) reorientation of public expenditures, (iii) tax reform, (iv) financial liberalization, (v) unified and competitive exchange rates, (vi) trade liberalization, (vii) openness to foreign direct investment, (viii) privatization, (ix) deregulation, and (x) secure property rights. Rodrik (2006) has argued that the "augmented Washington consensus" in the early 2000s included 10 additional priorities—and some confusion: (xi) corporate governance, (xii) anti-corruption, (xiii) flexible labor markets, (xiv) WTO agreements, (xv) financial codes and standards, (xvi) "prudent" capital-account opening, (xvii) nonintermediate exchange-rate regimes, (xviii) independent central banks/inflation targeting, (xix) social safety nets, and (xx) targeted poverty reduction. Since then, the financial crisis dramatically illustrated the importance of sound regulation. But while significant efforts have been devoted to better understanding the sequencing of reforms, the syndrome of the laundry list remains inescapable.

b) Investing in education, innovation, and infrastructures

Governments everywhere have an essential role in human capital accumulation, research, and infrastructure building because all three involve significant externalities. The modalities of government intervention differ across countries—some intervene directly in their financing, some indirectly through giving incentives to private agents to make growth-enhancing investments.

Education

The rate of return to education is hard to measure, since education does not play a direct role in production.[56] More precisely, it is difficult to know which part of the supplementary wage income generated by an additional year of higher education measures the marginal yield of study, preexisting talent, or rent accruing to belonging to a given social, ethnic, or gender group. Moreover, returns to education should not be assessed from a solely monetary perspective.

At a macroeconomic level, however, the link between the education level and GDP per person has been well documented since the seminal study of Nelson and Phelps (1966). After controlling for other factors, Barro (2001) finds that an additional year of schooling raises medium-term growth by 0.44 percentage points. Other studies, in particular those undertaken under the aegis of the World Bank, have confirmed that (i) primary education exhibits the highest social profitability in developing countries, while tertiary education is more relevant in OECD countries; (ii) the private return to education is higher than the social return because of the opportunity cost of public subsidies; and (iii) the return to female education is higher than to male education (see, e.g., Sianesi and Van Reenen, 2002, for a survey).

Education is an ideal playground for the "distance-to-the frontier" approach to economic growth outlined in the previous section. When an economy is far from the technological frontier, investment in primary and secondary education is enough to make the workforce able to imitate innovations found elsewhere. But countries approaching this frontier must invest in tertiary education to develop their own innovation capacity. Aghion et al. (2008*a*) find that tertiary education has a strong effect on growth in countries close to the technological frontier (whereas it does not affect growth in countries that are distant from it): a one percentage point increase in the proportion of university graduates in the labor force increases medium-term TFP growth by about 0.1 percentage points. This suggests that higher education is a very profitable investment in developed countries.[57]

Against this background, countries exhibit surprising disparity in their investment in human capital accumulation. Some developing countries are known for putting considerable effort into primary and secondary education (as reflected in the Human Development Index presented in Chapter 1), others remain characterized by a high incidence of illiteracy. According to World Bank data, the adult literacy rate was 69% in Morocco and 80% in Tunisia in 2012. Disparity can be found also among developed countries, this time in tertiary education attainment and resources invested in higher education. According to 2016 OECD statistics, in 2015 only 18% of the population aged 25–64 had reached tertiary education in Italy—against 35% in Spain, a country of similar development level. In 2013, total expenditure on tertiary education was 1.2% of GDP (of which 0.2% comes from private funds) in Germany—against 2.6% of GDP (of which 1.7% comes from private funds) in the United States; and 1.6% of GDP (of which 1.0% comes from private funds) in Japan. The large discrepancy between Europe and the United States is one of the key factors behind the lower European TFP performance documented in table 9.1.

To improve the performance of European higher education, however, money will not be enough. Research indicates that both the size of the budget and the quality of governance contribute to determining the research output of universities (Aghion et al., 2008). Stronger incentives for quality teaching and research and increased competition between universities are needed in Europe. These incentives, however, do not need to imply convergence on a single template for the financing or the governance of universities.

Research and innovation

Two groups of indicators are frequently used to measure research and innovation. The first group covers the effort of each country in terms of R&D spending or personnel. It portrays Europe as a laggard behind Japan and the United States (hence the objective of bringing R&D expenditures to 3% of GDP in the Europe 2020 strategy), notwithstanding very large discrepancies among European countries. Specifically, total (public and private) expenditure on R&D amounts to around 3.5% of GDP in Japan in 2014, about 2.75% of GDP in the United States, and slightly above 2% of GDP in the EU, with a large variance within the region (from 0.38% in Romania to 3.17% in Finland and Sweden in 2014; Eurostat, 2016). In spite of the the stated 3% target, however, the ratio of gross domestic expenditure on R&D for the EU has modestly increased from 1.81% of GDP in 2002 to 2.03% in 2014.

A significant difference between Europe on the one hand and the United States and Japan on the other is the contribution of privately funded R&D: it amounts to 1.3% of GDP in the EU against about 2% in both the United States and Japan. The difference between the two sides of the Atlantic, therefore, does not come from government-funded but rather from private-sector research. The reason why European companies invest less than their European counterparts has primarily to do with the industrial structure (the United States is more specialized in research- and technology-intensive sectors), but also with market imperfections such as the relative underdevelopment of risk capital (Philippon and Véron, 2008), or the lack of a unified digital market.

In addition to market imperfections, there is a broader reason for government intervention in the field of research, which is that the social return on research spending generally exceeds its private return. Many countries have introduced tax incentives for spending on R&D by companies or individuals. In the United States, R&D tax credits exist both at the federal and state levels (Wilson, 2005). The same applies in Europe, although some tax schemes have been challenged by the European Commission because they are deemed to distort markets ("State aids" in EU parlance).[58]

The second group of R&D indicators relates to outcomes, namely published articles and registered patents. As shown in figure 9.12, the EU performs relatively well compared to its R&D efforts: its share of world scientific articles is slightly higher than that of the United States, although its share of *triadic patents*[59] is lower. In turn, Japan performs exceptionally well in terms of patents, although not in terms of publications. Finally, China appears as an impressive newcomer making a substantial effort.

Companies invest in research to develop new products that will give them a competitive edge or new processes that will reduce costs and improve product quality. However, every innovation is soon copied by competitors. This highlights the importance of intellectual property protection in the

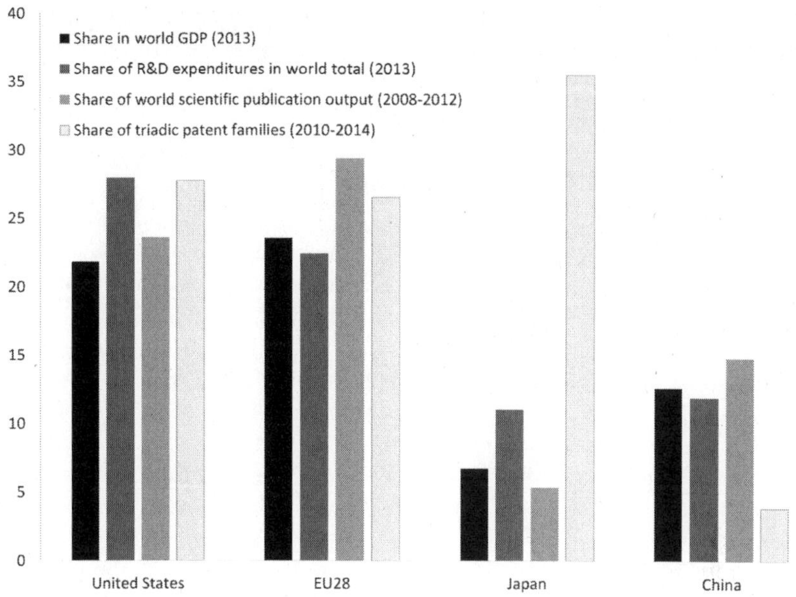

Figure 9.12 Indicators of research achievements (shares of world total), US, EU, Japan and China.
In the share of World Scientific Publication Output, EU data only include Belgium, France, Germany, Italy, the Netherlands, Poland, Spain, Sweden, and the United Kingdom. That indicator is thus underestimating the EU-28 true figure (though it comes out as the highest). Triadic patents are those registred simultaneously in the US, the EU and Japan.
Authors calculations from OECD and Scimago Research Group (CSIS), *Compendium of Bibliometric Science Indicators 2014*; Eurostat; and IMF Economic Outlook.

incentive to innovate. If a new product or a new process remains forever the exclusive property of its inventor, companies have a strong incentive to invest massively in research and development. However, the reward of innovation is appropriated by companies and their shareholders, not by consumers or the society at large. Productivity gains in other companies or sectors may be slowed down by limitations to the dissemination of the invention. Conversely, if companies cannot appropriate the revenue of innovation because it can be accessed freely by competitors, they have little incentive to innovate. Innovation becomes a public good, and it is up to taxpayers to finance it. The case of software patents illustrates this dilemma (box 9.13).

What is the best regime can only be assessed on a domain-by-domain basis. Some inventions are essentially nonrival, such as mathematical formulas and, more generally, ideas.[60] It would be absurd to hinder their dissemination. Others are essentially rival, such as manufacturing processes. Some can be replicated at low cost, such as software (box 9.13), while others cannot, such as

Box 9.13 Software Patents

Without patents, there is little incentive to innovate since any new software can be easily copied. But generalized patenting would also discourage innovation since developers would have to pay fees on every bit and part of their new software and for any algorithm needed to compile the code. Also, it is difficult to prove the "newness" of a software and to distinguish between genuine technical progress and new business methods (such as the "single click" purchase patented by Amazon in the United States). Smaller software producers also fear that large companies would tend to license any line of code as a defense against competition. Substantial litigation costs incurred in disputing software patents should not be ignored. The Economics Nobel Prize winner Gary Becker (2013), writing on the patenting of software, claims that "their exclusion from the patent system would discourage some software innovations, but the saving from litigation costs over disputed patent rights would more than compensate the economy for that cost."

This economic dilemma is reflected by international law. The WTO agreement on *trade-related aspects of intellectual property rights* (TRIPs) states that "patents shall be available for any inventions, whether products or processes, in all fields of technology, provided that they are new, involve an inventive step and are capable of industrial application." Whether software is "technology" and an "invention" is open to discussion.

In 2002–05, a highly contentious discussion developed in the EU along these lines. Software is protected by copyright but not patented as such under European law, contrary to the United States and Japan. The European Patent Office case law nevertheless views as patentable software that solves "technical problems" (as opposed to introducing new business methods). In 2002, the European Commission sought to incorporate this practice into EU law. Unsurprisingly, the proposal was supported by large firms such as Microsoft or IBM and opposed by free software and open source programmers. It was endorsed by the Council of Ministers, but rejected by 648 votes to 14 in the European Parliament in July 2005 and therefore abandoned.

nuclear technologies. The social value of innovation also has to be considered. Drugs are a case in point (box 9.14).

The upshot is that TFP-enhancing innovation depends on a fine balance between (i) government support and private initiative and (ii) patent protection and the dissemination of inventions. Creating a climate that is conducive to innovation and thereby growth is the result of an elaborate chemistry.

Box 9.14 Fighting HIV/AIDS in Poor Countries: Public Health and Intellectual Property

Public health is a major concern in poor countries which suffer from a high prevalence of pandemics such as HIV/AIDS, tuberculosis, and malaria. Medicines to fight these diseases have been developed at a high cost by pharmaceutical companies and are, rightly, protected by patents. Such patents grant the company exclusive rights to produce and sell medicines for a long period of time, generally 20 years. As a result, the cost of therapy makes it inaccessible to many. According to the joint United Nations program on HIV/AIDS, HIV programs in low-and middle-income countries have cost US$13.7 billion in 2008.

Low-income countries have therefore sought to grant so-called *compulsory licenses* so that generic antiretroviral therapy could be produced locally without the consent of the patent holder (which is, nevertheless, entitled to an adequate compensation). The WTO TRIPS agreement (see www.wto.org) originally restricted generic copies to being produced mainly for the domestic market. It was amended in 2003 to allow exportation of a limited list of medicines to countries that cannot produce them themselves. Under this provision, as an example, Indian pharmaceutical firms have exported generic antiretroviral drugs to African countries. In some instances, the mere threat of granting a compulsory license has led pharmaceutical companies to offer significant discounts in the local market.

The new TRIPS agreement strikes a balance between providing incentives for future inventions and disseminating more broadly existing inventions. It has been instrumental in fighting HIV/AIDS in Africa and has thus contributed to lowering mortality rates and supporting long-term GDP growth on the continent. There is, however, wide acknowledgment that intellectual property rights should remain adequately protected to allow private investment in medical research.

Public infrastructures

Why produce goods if there is no way to bring them to the market? Economic development requires proper infrastructures such as schools, hospitals, roads, railways, airports, dams, electricity grids, telecommunication and broadband networks, and water supply and sanitation. Such infrastructures are often financed by governments—or by foreign aid when countries are less developed—and by private money as countries grow richer and develop sophisticated financial markets.

In all cases, however, there is a need for government intervention:

- First, many infrastructures are natural monopolies (see Chapter 1). If in private hands, the government (directly or through a dedicated agency) has to check that owners do not appropriate an excessive share of the rent they generate and may sometimes decide that the services should be provided for free. Designing appropriate regulatory frameworks that at the same time favor competition and foster investment in infrastructure is a delicate task, especially in network industries such as telecoms, electricity, and railroads.

- Second, infrastructures involve externalities: they are used by the public at large, but they can also damage the environment. There is, therefore, a need for adequate compensation (to subsidize the gap between the private cost and the social benefit) or taxation (to compensate for damages). Dams are often controversial because they offer country-wide social benefits but cause local damage.
- Finally, there are instances in which the market cannot finance infrastructure by itself, in particular because of the lack of financial instruments to manage the risks or time horizon they are associated with. Raising money for long-term investment requires the existence of a market for very-long-term loans and bonds and for the hedging of inflation risk.

Such market imperfections may be a reason for the government to step in, but they should not be an excuse to undertake projects that have political appeal but a negative net social value—so-called white elephants. These remarks underline the crucial role of careful evaluations of public investments, both in making decisions or in assessing their results and impact. Most of the time, evaluations are neglected, and, when they are undertaken, they are often perceived as conditions to be fulfilled rather than a method to guide decision-making, to protect decisions from various interest groups, to manage public debt, to monitor the quality of resource allocation, and to reorient projects. The considerable development during the 2000s and 2010s of impact evaluation techniques has significantly contributed to mainstreaming this necessary interaction between public decisions and the evaluative approach.

From the mid-2000s on, the focus has shifted to a greater attention to *public–private partnerships*[61] to crowd-in significantly higher private investment in infrastructure. Governments have tried to appear as catalysts more than as primary funders of public infrastructure investment. An example of a government-sponsored, PPP-based infrastructure scheme is the Trans-European networks program launched by the European Union in 1994 in the fields of transport, energy, and telecommunications. It is funded by European governments, the EU, and the European Investment Bank (the regional development bank). In the same vein, the Juncker Plan launched in 2015 promised to unlock public and private investments of €315 billion over three years. This plan, however, also came as a response to several years of post-Great Recession mediocre growth. Indeed, infrastructure investments often appear as politically attractive policy measures that can both stabilize the economy (Keynesian motive) and raise long-term potential growth. Increasingly, priority is given to communication infrastructures such as broadband Internet or satellite networks. These are deemed to generate a higher social return by benefiting sectors with higher productivity gains, but there is a lack of compelling evidence.

c) Making labor and product markets work better

Finally, a proper functioning of markets contributes to TFP growth by improving the quality of resource allocation. The allocation role of markets is by no means a recent discovery, but it is fair to say that the importance of properly functioning markets has gained increasing recognition in the past two or three decades in relation to the growing needs for factor reallocation across sectors and across firms of the same sector (see Comin and Philippon, 2005). We discussed the importance of the market for capital earlier (see also Chapter 6); here, we review labor and product markets.

Labor markets

In an economy where labor is permanently reallocated across firms and sectors, the quality of the match between workers and jobs becomes an important determinant of productivity and growth. First, the shorter the period during which labor remains idle after a lay-off or quitting, the higher the aggregate labor input and production. Second, the better the match between labor supply and labor demand, the higher the productivity level. Conversely, an economy where university graduates end up serving pizzas is unable to attain the productivity level that would be expected from the existing level of human capital.

The two objectives can be contradictory: a quick match is not necessarily a good match. Thus, the performance of labor market institutions matters. In the United States, there is little government involvement in the labor market, and the short duration of unemployment insurance acts as a strong incentive for the unemployed to take up a new job. There is a risk that this could lead to deterioration in the quality of the match. The magnitude of reallocations (as measured by gross flows) ensures that many opportunities exist at each point in time.

In Europe, the traditional pattern is one of job security (for those on regular contracts), but it has been undermined by changes in the structure and dynamics of firms. It is in the Scandinavian countries that labor market institutions have undergone the deepest reforms; this has led to the emergence of a new model generally called *flexsecurity*. Workers are no longer offered job security, but, if unemployed, they benefit from generous unemployment benefits and personalized training and placement services. Benefits are conditional on active search behavior, but they can be extended for a long period if necessary. The model is costly (expenditures on labor market policies amount to more than 4% of GDP in Denmark and 2.5% in Sweden, against 0.5% in the United States) but effective in fostering quality matching. It has been adopted as a reference by the EU. Yet, in practice, on-the-job protection of employees on regular contracts remains widespread in continental Europe.

Product markets

The functioning of markets for products and services has become increasingly prominent in the evaluation of economic performance, especially by international institutions such as the OECD.[62] Empirical studies have demonstrated the positive impact on productivity growth of suppressing rents created by heavy-handed regulation and/or barriers to entry. Nicoletti and Scarpetta (2005) of the OECD have built synthetic indicators measuring the intensity of regulation. They showed that the variance of these indicators between countries helped explain the different dynamics of labor productivity. However, economic reform in OECD countries led to substantial reduction in regulatory pressure between 1998 and 2013 and to a relative convergence of the aggregate indicator of product market regulation toward low levels (figure 9.13).

Liberalization, however, involves trade-offs. Incentives to invest in research depend on the degree and nature of competition on product markets, and the latter's role as a driver of or an obstacle to innovation is fiercely debated. Economists view competition as the engine of efficient resource allocation, while industrialists often accuse it of weakening industrial champions.

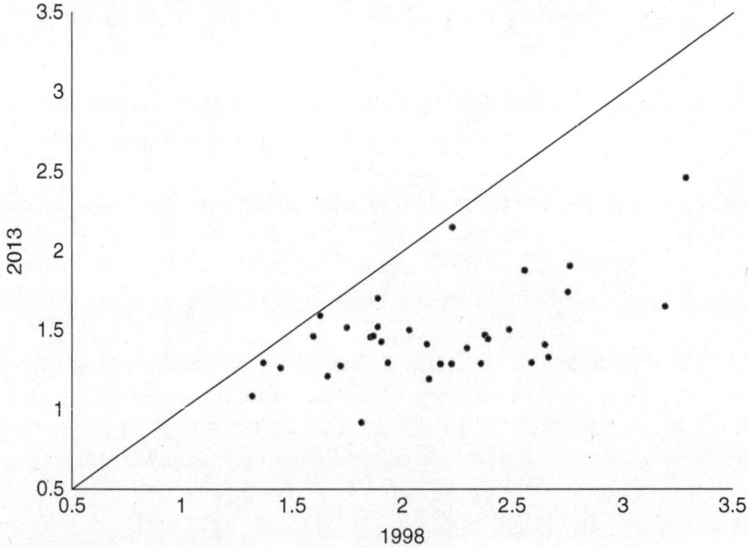

Figure 9.13 Evolution of product market regulation indicator, 1998–2013. Data are for 1998 and 2013 except for Estonia, Israel and Slovenia (2008 and 2013), and for Luxemburg and Slovakia (2003 and 2013).
OECD.

In early models of Schumpeterian innovation, such as the canonic model of Aghion and Howitt (1992, see Section 9.2), too much competition in product markets discourages innovation since it reduces the monopoly rent that rewards it (for the same reasons, in that model, patent protection is unambiguously good for innovation). However, the case can also be made that there should be *enough* competition so that incumbent firms are challenged by new entrants. Put together, this suggests an inverted-U relationship between competition and innovation. Aghion, Bloom et al. (2005) have provided a theoretical underpinning for this trade-off and have uncovered this inverted-U pattern in industry-level data by relating the number of patents submitted by UK companies to a measure of competition based on operational margins.

More generally, Griffith and Harrison (2004) have shown that reforms which have facilitated market entry and reduced administrative costs in Europe have led to lower profit margins and have supported investment and employment. Gutierrez and Philippon (2016) also confirm the role of competition in sustaining investment. Governments have to make sure that markets deliver appropriate price and quality signals and that competition is not stifled by collusion among existing players. This is what market regulation is about. Depending on the legal system, it is enforced by independent anti-trust agencies and/or by courts, and by specialized, technical agencies (such as the Federal Communication Commission and Food and Drug Administration in the United States). The debate is especially acute about network industries. In the telecoms sector, for example, liberalization has led to the entry of new players who have challenged the former monopolies. However, as competition developed, there was a need to ensure that incentives to innovate remained strong enough to invest and innovate, which requires profitability.[63]

Another example is the Microsoft case in the 2000s. Competitors filed cases against Microsoft, complaining that the company was attempting to obstruct them[64] and that this would penalize innovation. Some economists argued that Microsoft stifled its competitors, others countered that the domination of one company did not imply that the market was not contestable and that Microsoft was investing its profits into R&D. The European Commission followed the first and fined Microsoft, which lost its appeal in 2007.

9.3.5 Countering the effects of distance and history

So far, we have envisaged growth policies mostly at the level of a country. However, countries or supranational entities like the EU also implement *regional development policies* with the aim of fostering growth. Those are, in principle, distinct from mere redistribution policies. Regions (and cities) specialize dynamically according to their comparative advantages with capital and, to a lesser extent labor, being permanently relocated across regions. The combination of history, geography, and market forces usually results in a very uneven distribution of income and wealth.[65] Inequality can to some extent be corrected through tax-based redistribution, but the real issue is whether policy can foster growth in the less-developed regions. This is the aim of regional policies. In Europe, for example, *structural funds* top-up country-level redistribution schemes and focus on growth-enhancing investments, with an aim to equalize GDP per person across European regions. In the EU federal budget for 2017, structural funds (or funds for economic, social and territorial cohesiveness), which are cashed in by regions,[66] amounted to €53.6 billion or 34% of the total.

Are such policies economically efficient? Neo-classical growth theory envisages the convergence of regional income per person conditional to their level of human capital or to the quality of their institutions. European data do not exhibit unconditional convergence: before the financial crisis, convergence was a fact among EU countries but not among EU regions (OECD, 2004, part 2), and fast-converging regions had been rich regions in poorer countries, such as Catalonia.

Economic geography has shed a new light on the discussion of regional policies.[67] As seen in Section 9.2 (and illustrated with the "core/periphery" model), there is a tension between agglomeration and dispersion forces. Agglomeration forces have proved to be powerful. Most of the EU's richest regions lie along a central axis which goes from Northern Italy to Germany, and to the Netherlands. Most of the United States' richest states lie along the nation's coasts and borders. Le Gallo and Dall'erba (2006) have studied the time dynamics of regional wealth in Europe and uncovered a strong dependence of the convergence process of a region's GDP per person on the wealth of its neighbors, leading to the formation of a "nonconvergence club" of peripheral regions.

Agglomeration forces create policy dilemmas. Economic concentration is the outcome of an economically efficient process which leads to a higher GDP growth *at the aggregate level* by exploiting the positive spillovers which arise when activities are clustered, and this higher income can be shared across regions through (preferably lump-sum) tax transfers. In that sense, governments should accept rather than oppose agglomeration, especially in new and R&D-intensive industries where existing capital plays a less important role and network externalities are high. However, the risk is that this will create industrial desertification and feed the resentment of the local populations.

How to promote the development of poor regions without stifling the agglomeration process? A first option might be to lower transport costs (through subsidies or through the improvement of transport infrastructures). However, reduced transportation costs can, at least in a first stage, encourage concentration by easing the relocation of the labor force. In France, high-speed trains have encouraged concentration of economic activity in the Paris region by making it easier to live in remote places and work in the capital. This is economically efficient (because it increases GDP in the aggregate) but it creates geographic inequalities.

Another option is to let agglomeration happen and to increase fiscal transfers to peripheral regions. This is, to a large extent, what has developed within nations, sometimes in an indirect way when laggard regions welcome rich retirees from richer ones. The Sapir report to the president of the EU Commission (Sapir et al., 2004) has advocated in that spirit to distinguish between the allocation and redistribution functions of the EU budget by setting up a "growth fund" at an EU level and a "convergence fund" devoted to less-advanced regions.

A more forward-looking and ambitious way to tackle geographical inequalities and combine economic efficiency with regional equity, however, is to encourage the diffusion of ideas and knowledge so that peripheral regions can "jump" to a more human capital–intensive, less physical capital–intensive development regime (Martin, 1999). This implies, for instance, investing in mobile phone and broadband Internet access. The rise of the Indian information and communication technology (ICT) industry can be understood in that context: fast development of electronic communication infrastructures has supplemented largely defective transport infrastructures. As network coverage expands and the price of Internet access goes down, social and banking services can be provided to poor countries and regions over mobile networks and increase total factor productivity.

As seen in Section 9.2, endogenous growth models also highlight the possibility of multiple equilibriums and the role of history in shaping growth trajectories. As a result, many countries or regions face the challenge of devising policies to escape low-development traps. There are two kinds of complementary remedies:

- Open the domestic economy to international markets to reap the productivity benefits of specialization without constraining the consumers' choice. Such strategies were inaugurated by Britain's repeal of the protectionist Corn Laws and embracing free trade in the 1830s, which proved vastly beneficial to its growth. Yet the empirical literature on trade opening and economic growth does not reach firm conclusions (Rodriguez and Rodrik, 2001). In short, no country has reached a sustainable high-growth path without opening up to trade, yet trade opening does not suffice to generate growth. A reason for this result is that trade opening may also push an economy in the direction of specializing in traditional sectors in which it has comparative advantage, such as agriculture, which may hamper long-term productivity growth. While nineteenth-century Britain was embracing free trade, it was also benefiting from the Industrial Revolution.
- Convince economic agents that future development justifies investing today. Krugman (1991*a*) and Murphy et al. (1989) have modeled situations where industrial development is not deterministic because it depends on demand expectations. Both take-off

and stagnation are possible depending on initial expectations. Underdevelopment as a coordination failure was the dominant model in the postwar years[68] and echoes the "big-push" theory of development that was very popular in the 1950s and 1960s. In this context of multiple equilibriums, the capacity of governments or international institutions to influence expectations and help move the economy from a particular equilibrium to another one becomes crucial. In this coordination role, governments need to be credible (in the same way as they need credibility for the management of short-term demand, as discussed in Chapters 4 and 5). Their credibility can be backed by kick-starting productivity-enhancing investment with public money, by engaging in an overhaul of the regulatory and tax systems, or by seeking public support of international organizations such as the OECD and the IMF for their reform strategy.

- However forceful, "big-push" strategies crucially depend on expectations and are therefore inherently fragile. This was illustrated by the failure of the forced industrialization strategies of many developing countries in the 1960s. Once in place, newly created industries have to generate lasting TFP gains, which brings us back to the preceding set of recommendations. It was not the 1950s "Great Leap Forward" that ensured China's economic take-off, but its transition to a market economy and its opening to international trade in the 1990s.

9.3.6 Choosing priorities

After squeezing theory as hard as we could to extract its policy consequences, we still do not have a recipe for long-term growth. The report produced by the Spence Commission on long-term growth in developing countries (Commission on Growth and Development, 2008) has concluded that growth trajectories are largely idiosyncratic beyond the common features that link recorded experiences of high and sustained growth. The renewal of growth theory in the 1990s has made the latter much richer and has improved its ability to match empirical data. However, the link between policies and outcomes is more tenuous than for the policies outlined in the previous chapters, if only because the timescale is much more extended, objectives are more diverse, and mechanisms are much more complex. Governments should not take these difficulties as an excuse to focus on short-term growth only. They are already all too tempted to do so, given their short political tenures. For developing countries as well as for Europe, investing in growth is crucial.

Successful growth strategies require the identification of priorities. Among the many factors bearing on long-term growth, governments need to choose a few on which to focus—because political capital is always scarce. Are there robust methods to do so? In its series of "Going for Growth" reports, the OECD intends to help policymakers set their agenda for reform to achieve "strong, sustainable, balanced and inclusive growth." The 2017 report notes that the pace of structural reforms within the OECD has slowed, notably in the areas of education and innovation, and that governments tend to focus on specific policy areas and miss gains from synergies and reform complementarities. The report proposes the following priorities: facilitating entry and growth of innovative firms, promoting equal access to high-quality education and the inclusion of women and migrants in the labor market, boosting investment in infrastructure, and improving the training of workers and labor market activation policies.

Hausmann, Rodrik, and Velasco (2008) propose a country-specific method for deciding on priorities. They analyze obstacles to growth as a series of distortions that introduce wedges between the private and social values of a series of activities (e.g., investment, labor supply, human capital accumulation, etc.). Removing any of those distortions through structural reforms has both direct effects and general equilibrium effects on all activities. They recommend ranking reforms according to their direct effect and start with those having the strongest direct effects. For example, high private returns on education suggest that lack of education is likely to be a severe constraint on growth.

The best strategy would clearly be to remove all distortions at once, but this is neither realistic politically nor practically. In practice, governments also consider political constraints, such as the distribution of winners and losers from the reforms and their prospective voting behavior. In effect, the political economy is key to understanding why growth-enhancing reforms are often not implemented, despite their potential effects on welfare. Policy design and the quality of the policymaking process, therefore, play a crucial role.

Notes

1. The relevance of GDP as a measure of a country's standard of living is discussed in the first section of this chapter.
2. These comparisons are drawn from Angus Maddison's work (2001) on growth in the long term and updated with IMF March 2017 data.
3. The exact figures, of course, depend on the rate of growth used as a benchmark.
4. For a presentation and discussion, see D'Alișa, Demaria, and Kallis (2014). Drews and Antal (2016) question the term "degrowth" (which is coined from the French word "décroissance"), and argue that effective communication instead calls for a more positive word that suggests welfare improvements.
5. Among the explanatory factors of growth, some are beyond the economists' realm because they are truly exogenous. For example, landlocked countries face

significant challenges—which does not mean they cannot develop, depending on the natural resources they have and how well they and their neighbors perform (just compare Switzerland and Rwanda).

6. In the 1950s, there was widespread pessimism with respect to Asian development prospects. In the 1960s, the idea that the Soviet Union was on its way to catching up with the United States was commonly accepted. In the 1970s, European countries seemed to have entered a high growth path. In the 1980s, Japan was regarded as a model, while the US economy was feared to be plagued by deindustrialization and declining productivity. The 2007–2009 financial and economic crisis may lead in retrospect to a more critical diagnosis of economic policies in the 1990s and 2000s and of the underlying health of the US economy in these decades of rapid growth.
7. Remarks in Heber Springs, Arkansas, at the Dedication of Greers Ferry Dam, October 3, 1963.
8. An observer who would be concerned with the distribution of welfare would stand between the two. On these issues, see Amartya Sen's Nobel lecture (Sen, 1999).
9. The World Bank thus uses an international poverty line of PPP US$1.90 (at 2011 prices), updated in October 2015 from the earlier line of PPP US$1.25 in 2005 (at 2005 prices) and PPP US$1 in 1990 (at 1990 prices).
10. We do not discuss here the difference between GDP per person—which measures the average output per person produced by the residents of a given territory within that territory—and gross national product per person (*GNP per person*)—which measures the *residents'* average income. Both measures can differ appreciably when residents own income-producing external assets (or conversely when they are indebted to nonresidents), when they receive private transfers from foreign countries (notably from emigrants working abroad), or when they benefit from international development assistance. Our purpose here is not to analyze these differences, and we shall therefore use income per person and per capita GDP interchangeably.
11. PPP rates are published by the World Bank, which now coordinates an international comparison program (ICP), started in 1968, based on price and expenditure surveys now conducted every six years, as well as estimations for some countries. One of the notable innovations in the 2005 ICP program was the full participation of China, which provided price surveys yielding a more accurate estimate of the country's PPP exchange rate–based GDP. Because of prices being higher than previously thought, China's real GDP was revised downward by about 40%, which in turn affected the measurement of world growth by half a percentage point over the 2005–2008 period. This episode is a strong reminder of the fragility of international comparisons. As of May 2016, the latest available ICP survey had been conducted in 2011 and involved 199 countries.
12. See notably Stiglitz, Sen, and Fitoussi, 2009 (Commission on the Measurement of Economic Performance and Social Progress, chapt. 1). See also Deaton (2013) and Gordon (2016) for discussion and examples and for the argument that the past evolution of per capita GDP underestimated actual gains in welfare.

13. For example, the United Nations Statistical Commission established in 2005 a Committee of Experts on Environmental-Economic Accounting (UNCEEA) to mainstream environmental-economic accounting and establish a system of integrated environmental and economic accounting as an international standard. See also Hamilton (2006) for estimates of produced, natural, and intangible capital as well as "genuine" savings rate that take environmental degradation into account.
14. See Cette (2004, p. 24, table 4).
15. This assumes constant labor market participation and working time.
16. Jean-Baptiste Colbert was in the seventeenth-century a minister under French King Louis XIV and the architect of its economic policy. What became known as "Colbertism" involves systematic state intervention in the development of supply and the promotion of exports.
17. The rise of Europe played a major role. US physiologist Jared Diamond (1997) has proposed a pioneering explanation that opened a lively debate. He has assigned the European successes to the development of agriculture and of livestock farming, themselves due to the local abundance of seeds and the availability of animals which could be domesticated, allowing the growth of productivity and the greater concentration of people. Europe's East–West geography facilitated migration within a constant climatic environment and therefore innovation and technological diffusion. Also, proximity to domesticated animals could have allowed the immunization of local people against microbial germs. When major explorations led to physical contact between the Europeans and indigenous populations in other continents, the latter suffered from imported pandemics while the former were immune from them.
18. On the world economy concept, see Braudel (1981–84, vol. 3, chapt. 1) and Wallerstein (1979).
19. For a synthetic presentation, see Braudel (1985).
20. Levels of per capita GDP ranged in 2015 from 1 to 241 between the Central African Republic (US$597 per person and per year) and Qatar (US$143,788). The five richest countries in the World were four European countries and a country of European immigration: Luxembourg, the United States, Norway, Ireland, and Iceland. The five poorest countries were all African (Malawi, Burundi, Democratic Republic of Congo, Tanzania, and Niger).
21. For a discussion, see Quah (1993) and Sala-i-Martin (1996).
22. For recent work and data, see notably Piketty (2014), Atkinson (2015), Milanovic (2008, 2012, 2016), Deaton (2013), Bourguignon (2015), Alvaredo et al. (2017), and the World Wealth & Income Database (www.wid.world).
23. Even so, the calculation is fraught with problems. Rich individuals, for example, underreport in household surveys, and the poorest countries are unlikely to have developed household surveys. This may lead to underestimating global inequality.
24. The Gini index is equal to twice the area located between the Lorenz curve and the 45-degree line (cf. Chapter 1). It is equal to 0 when income distribution is uniform and to 1 if all income is concentrated on only one individual.
25. Global inequality indicators should of course be interpreted with caution as their calculation is fraught with various types of errors, notably sampling errors.

26. Caution is needed. The chart does not depict how individuals and households within a given percentile fared over time: they may have changed percentiles, these percentiles may include households of different countries for different periods, the country coverage is smaller in 1988, differences in population growth rates shift percentile composition across countries, and the like. Any tempting causality between globalization and the growth incidence curve should accordingly be treated with much caution (for a critique, see, for example, Freund, 2016). But the curve shows how the world income distribution shifted over time, with a top 1% percentile made of comparatively even richer people, for example.
27. Source: World Bank Poverty and Income Database, April 2017. Results for Sub-Saharan Africa have been more sobering, however. The poverty headcount ratio has declined from 54% in 1999 to only 41% in 2013. Moreover, given the fast rate of population growth, the number of extremely poor individuals has in fact increased from 258 million to 378 million over the same period.
28. However, this formulation ignores any interdependence between short-term fluctuations and long-term growth, such as hysteresis in the rate of unemployment. This is a point to which we return at the beginning of the Section 9.3.
29. The European Recovery Program, better known as the "Marshall plan" (after the American Secretary of State George C. Marshall) was a program of financial assistance by the United States for rebuilding the countries of Europe; it cost overall US$13 billion over four years, which represented 5.3% of the 1947 US GDP. The USSR was invited to take part but refused. The institution set up to implement the plan, called the Organization for European Economic Cooperation (OEEC), later became in 1960 the Organization for Economic Cooperation and Development (OECD).
30. Incidentally, this shows why GDP maximization cannot be taken as a criterion for evaluating policies.
31. This is because $0.3/(1 - 0.3 - 0.5) \sim 1.5$.
32. See, for example, Kuhn (1962).
33. Congestion costs are ignored.
34. Mankiw et al.'s model in fact becomes an endogenous growth model when the sum of the shares of both factors—physical capital α and human capital γ in the production function is equal to unity.
35. The central role assigned by Schumpeter to the entrepreneur was criticized by the French historian Fernand Braudel, who advocated a more systemic approach (prefiguring the importance that economists would give to institutions in the 1990s and 2000s; see Braudel, 1985, and the discussion in Section 9.3).
36. See, for example, Guellec (1999) or Tirole (2003).
37. Jagdish Bhagwati, a trade economist, pointed out in 1958 that growth in a country's export supply could result in a deterioration of the relative price of those exports and that this terms-of-trade effect could in turn affect income negatively.
38. Named after the seminal contribution by Avinash Dixit and Joseph Stiglitz (1977), which expands on a monopolistic competition framework initiated in 1933 by Chamberlin. See Krugman (1995) and Combes, Mayer, and Thisse (2006) for a history of these ideas.

39. See Gancia and Zilibotti (2004) for a detailed review.
40. See Combes et al. (2006) for a history of the relations between economics and geography.
41. The handbook by Baldwin et al. (2003) presents these models. Krugman (1995) reviews the history of the theory of development in the light of these mechanisms.
42. A catastrophe, or bifurcation, is a noncontinuous jump from one path to another in a nonlinear dynamic model with several possible paths.
43. See the Kanbur (2000) synthesis.
44. Rajan and Zingales (2003) highlight that the lack of access to finance is a key determinant of the persistence of poverty.
45. Also see Banerjee and Duflo (2003) for a discussion of the methods used.
46. See North (1990) and the literature review in Borner, Bodmer, and Kobler (2003).
47. See Acemoglu, Johnson, and Robinson (2004) for a general synthesis on the role of institutions in growth.
48. Aversion to risk and precautionary behaviors are explained in Chapter 2.
49. The expression was popularized in macroeconomics by Blanchard and Summers (1986). It is borrowed from physics. One speaks of "hysteresis" when the transformation of a material under the effect of temperature and/or pressure is irreversible: The material bears the memory of its last transformations.
50. In this respect, it is ironic that the United States, where the labor market is very fluid and financial markets are deep, has more active stabilization policies than Europe (see Chapters 4 and 5), where labor markets are more rigid and financial markets provide less insurance against macroeconomic risk.
51. The OECD has devoted a lot of attention to this issue. See notably the analysis by Drew et al. (2004) on how labor- and product-market rigidities affect the resilience of countries to temporary economic shocks.
52. See, for example, Greenwood and Jovanovic (1990), Levine (2005), and the pioneering works of Schumpeter (1911) and of Gurley and Shaw (1955).
53. This policy indeed contributed to promoting domestic investment, but may also have led to overinvestment rather than total factor productivity (see Young, 1992). In their seminal works, McKinnon (1973) and Shaw (1973) argue that financial repression is altogether a barrier to successful economic development. Both the theoretical and the empirical literatures, notably in the wake of severe financial crises, have subsequently qualified the McKinnon and Shaw hypothesis.
54. The development of micro-credit also allows households and small enterprises to borrow even in the absence of collateral.
55. On the development of digital retail payments and its consequences for financial inclusion, see Committee on Payments and Market Infrastructures and World Bank Group (2016).
56. We do not intend here to discuss the economics of education as this is beyond the scope of this book. One can refer to the works of Gary Becker, Jacob Mincer, James Heckman, and others. We focus here on the link between education and the level of GDP per person.
57. Aghion, Boustan et al. (2005) find a similar result for US states.

58. To know more about the Commission's attitude to innovation-related tax schemes, see the Frequently Asked Questions section on "Tax incentives to promote R&D" on the EU website.
59. Triadic patents are those filed simultaneously with the US, European, and Japanese patent offices.
60. On the economics of knowledge and the "nonrivalry" of ideas, see Jones (2005).
61. Public–private partnerships are projects that are funded and operated through a partnership between the government and one or several private companies.
62. See, for example, the annual study of the OECD on the euro area. As part of the Lisbon process, European countries also produce "'structural" indicators measuring the degree of integration of markets for goods and services, openness to competition, creation and destruction of companies, and the like. These indicators are available on Eurostat's website.
63. Griffith and Harrison also find that insufficient profits would be unfavorable to R&D, but they take this result with a grain of salt. See Schiantarelli (2005) for a survey.
64. For example, by bundling its Windows operating system and Internet browser with other software such as Windows Media Player and by abusing its dominant position. The complete record is available at www.usdoj.gov.
65. As an example, in 2005, individual income in European regions ranged between €2,519 per year on average in northeastern Romania and €76,053 per year on average in Inner London, a 1:30 ratio.
66. One-tenth of it, known as the "Cohesion Fund," is distributed at a country level.
67. See Martin (1999) and Baldwin et al. (2003, chapt. 17) for a detailed discussion.
68. See, for example, Ray (2001) and Krugman (1994*a*). Initial work on the subject can be traced to Young (1928) and especially to Rosenstein-Rodan (1943).

References

Acemoglu, D., P. Aghion, and F. Zilibotti (2002), "Distance to Frontier, Selection, and Economic Growth," *Journal of the European Economic Association*, 4, pp. 37–74.

Acemoglu, D., S. Johnson, and J. Robinson (2004), "Institutions as the Fundamental Causes of Long-Run Growth," in Aghion, P., and S. Durlauf, eds., *Handbook of Economic Growth*, Elsevier, pp. 385–472.

Adler, G., R. Duval, D. Furceri, S. Kiliç Celik, K. Koloskova, and M. Poplawski-Ribeiro (2017), "Gone with the Headwinds: Global Productivity," *IMF Staff Discussion Notes* No. 17/04.

Aghion, P. (2011), "Industrial Policy, Entrepreneurship and Growth," in Audretsch, D. B., O. Falck, S. Heblich, and A. Lederer, eds., *Handbook of Research on Innovation and Entrepreneurship*, Edward Elgar.

Aghion, P., U. Afcigit, A. Bergeaud, R. Blundell, and D. Hémous (2016), "Innovation and Top Income Inequality," mimeo, Harvard University.

Aghion, P., P. Askenazy, N. Berman, G. Cette, and L. Eymard (2008*b*), "Credit Constraints and the Cyclicality of R&D Investment: Evidence from France," *Banque de France Working Paper*, no. 198.

Aghion, P., P. Askenazy, R. Bourlès, G. Cette, and N. Dromel (2008*a*), "Éducation supérieure, rigidités de marché et croissance," in Aghion, P., G. Cette, E. Cohen, and J. Pisani-Ferry, eds., *Les leviers de la croissance française*, Report to the French Council of Economic Analysis no. 72.

Aghion, P., and A. Banerjee (2005), *Volatility and Growth*, Clarendon Lectures in Economics, Oxford University Press.

Aghion, P., B. Bloom, R. Blundell, R. Griffith, and P. Howitt (2005), "Competition and Innovation: An Inverted-U Relationship," *The Quarterly Journal of Economics*, 120, pp. 701–28.

Aghion, P., L. Boustan, C. Hoxby, and J. Vandenbussche (2005), "Exploiting States' Mistakes to Identify the Causal Impact of Higher Education on Growth," mimeo, Harvard University.

Aghion, P., L. Boustan, C. Hoxby, and J. Vandenbussche (2009), "The Causal Impact of Education on Economic Growth: Evidence from US." mimeo, Harvard University.

Aghion, P., M. Dewatripont, C. Hoxby, A. Mas-Colell, and A. Sapir (2008), *An Agenda for Reforming European Universities*, Bruegel.

Aghion, P., and P. Howitt (1992), "A Model of Growth Through Creative Destruction," *Econometrica*, 60, pp. 323–51.

Alesina, A., and D. Rodrik (1994), "Distributive Politics and Economic Growth," *The Quarterly Journal of Economics*, 109, pp. 465–90.

Alvaredo, F., L. Chancel, T. Piketty, E. Saez and G. Zucman (2018), *World Inequality Report*, World Inequality Lab.

Arnold, J. M., A. Bassanini, and S. Scarpetta (2007), "Solow or Lucas? Testing Growth Models Using Panel Data from OECD Countries," *OECD Working Paper*, no. 592.

Arrow, K. (1962), "The Economic Implications of Learning by Doing," *Review of Economic Studies*, 29, pp. 155–73.

Askenazy, P. (2001), *Des 35 heures à la nouvelle economie. Changements organisationnels et diffusion de l'innovation.* Notes de l'Ifri 27, La Documentation Française for the French Institute of International Relations (Ifri).

Atkinson, A. (2015), *Inequality: What Can Be Done?* Harvard University Press.

Baldwin, R. (2016), *The Great Convergence*, Belknap Press.

Baldwin, R., R. Forslid, P. Martin, G. Ottaviano, and F. Robert-Nicoud (2003), *Economic Geography and Public Policy*, Princeton University Press.

Ball, L. (1999), "Aggregate Demand and Long-Run Unemployment," *Brookings Papers on Economic Activity*, 2, pp. 189–251.

Banerjee, A., and E. Duflo (2003), "Inequality and Growth: What Can the Data Say?" *Journal of Economic Growth*, 8, pp. 267–99.

Barrell, R., and M. Weale (2003), "Designing and Choosing Macroeconomic Frameworks: The Position of the UK after Four Years of the Euro," *Oxford Review of Economic Policy*, 19, pp. 132–48.

Barro, R. (2001), "Human Capital and Growth," *The American Economic Review*, 91, pp. 12–17.

Barro, R. (2000), "Inequality and Growth in a Panel of Countries", *Journal of Economic Growth*, 5, pp. 5–32.

Barro, R., and X. Sala-ì-Martin (1995), *Economic Growth*, McGraw-Hill.

Barro, R., and X. Sala-ì-Martin (1991), "Convergence Across States and Regions," *Brookings Papers on Economic Activity*, 1, pp. 107–82.

Bartelsman, E., S. Scarpetta, and F. Schivardi (2003), "Comparative Analysis of Firm Demographics and Survival: Micro-Level Evidence for the OECD Countries," *OECD Economics Department Working Papers*, no. 348.

Becker, G. (2013), "On Reforming the Patent System," The Becker-Posner Blog, 21 July, http://www.becker-posner-blog.com.

Bernanke, B. (2005), "The Global Saving Glut and the US Current Account Deficit," speech at the Sandridge Lecture, Virginia Association of Economics, March 10, 2005 and the Homer Jones Lecture, St. Louis, Missouri, April 14, 2005.

Benabou, R. (1996), "Inequality and Growth," in Bernanke, B., and J. Rotemberg, eds., *NBER Macroeconomics Annual 1996*, 11, MIT Press, pp. 11–74.

Bhagwati, J. (1958), "Immiserizing Growth: A Geometrical Note," *Review of Economic Studies* 25(June), pp. 201–205.

Blanchard, O. (2004), "The Economic Future of Europe," *Journal of Economic Perspectives*, 18, pp. 3–26.

Blanchard, O., and L. Summers (1986), "Hysteresis and the European Unemployment Problem," in Fischer, S., ed., *NBER Macroeconomic Annual 1986*, 1, pp. 15–90.

Borner, S., Bodmer, F., and M. Kobler (2003), *Institutional Efficiency and its Determinants: The Role of Political Factors in Economic Growth*, OECD Development Centre Studies.

Bourguignon, F. (2015), *The Globalization of Inequality*, Princeton University Press.

Bourguignon, F., and C. Morrisson (2002), "Inequality Among World Citizens: 1820 – 1992," *American Economic Review*, 92, pp. 727–44.

Braudel, F. (1981–84), *Civilization and Capitalism, 15th–18th Centuries*, 3 vols. (The Structures of Everyday Life; The Wheels of Commerce; The Perspective of the World), Harper & Row, original editions in French (1979).

Braudel, F. (1985), *La dynamique du capitalisme*, Arthaud.

Caballero, R., and M. Hammour (1994), "The Cleansing Effect of Recessions," *American Economic Review*, 84, pp. 1350–68.

Causa, O., A. de Serres, and N. Ruiz (2014), "Can Growth-Enhancing Policies Lift All Boats? An Analysis Based on Household Disposable Incomes," OECD *Economics Department Working Papers*, No. 1180.

Cette, G. (2004), "Productivité et croissance: diagnostic macroéconomique et lecture historique," in Cette, G., and P. Artus, eds., *Productivité et croissance*, Rapport au Conseil d'Analyse Economique 48, La Documentation Française.

Cette, G., J. Mairesse, and Y. Kocoglu (2004), "Diffusion des TIC et croissance potentielle," *Revue d'Économie Politique*, 114, janvier–février, pp. 77–97.

Chamberlin, E. (1933), *Theory of Monopolistic Competition*, Harvard University Press.

Coeuré, B. (2017), "Convergence Matters for Monetary Policy," speech at the Competitiveness Research Network (CompNet) conference on "Innovation, Firm Size, Productivity and Imbalances in the Age of De-globalization" in Brussels, 30 June 2017.

Combes, P. P., T. Mayer, and J. F. Thisse (2006), *Economie géographique—L'intégration des régions et des nations*, Economica.

Comin, D., and T. Philippon (2005), "The Rise in Firm-level Volatility: Causes and Consequences," *NBER Macroeconomics Annual*, 20, MIT Press, pp. 167–228.

Commission on Growth and Development (2008), *The Growth Report. Strategies for Sustained Growth and Development*, The World Bank.

Committee on Payments and Market Infrastructures and World Bank Group (2016), *Payment Aspects of Financial Inclusion*, April.

Coulombe, S. (2007), "Globalization and Regional Disparity: A Canadian Case Study," *Regional Studies*, 41, pp. 1–17.

Coulombe, S., and F. C. Lee (1995), "Convergence Across Canadian provinces, 1961 to 1991," *Canadian Journal of Economics*, 28, pp.155–78.

Cynamon, B. Z., and S. M. Fazzari (2016), "Inequality, the Great Recession, and Slow Recovery," *Cambridge Journal of Economics*, 40(2), 373–99.

D'Alisa, G., F. Demaria, and G. Kallis (eds.) (2014), *Degrowth: A Vocabulary for a New Era*, Routledge.

David, P. (1985), "Clio and the Economics of QWERTY: The Constraints of History," *American Economic Association Papers and Proceedings*, 75, pp. 333–37.

David, P. (1990), "The Dynamo and the Computer: An Historical Perspective on the Modern Productivity Paradox," *American Economic Review*, 80, pp. 355–61.

Deaton, A. (2013), *The Great Escape: Health, Wealth, and the Origins of Inequality*, Princeton University Press.

Deininger, K., and L. Squire (1996), "A New Data Set Measuring Income Inequality," *World Bank Economic Review*, 10, pp. 565–91.

Diamond, J. (1997), *Guns, Germs and Steel: The Fate of Human Societies*, W. W. Norton and Company.

Dixit, A., and J. Stiglitz (1977), "Monopolistic Competition and Optimum Product Diversity," *American Economic Review*, 67, pp. 297–308.

Domar, H. (1946), "Capital Expansion, Rate of Growth and Employment," *Econometrica*, 14, pp. 137–47.

Drew, A., M. Kennedy, and T. Sløk (2004), "Differences in Resilience between the Euro-area and US Economies," *OECD Working Paper*, no. 382.

Drews, S., and M. Antal (2016), "Degrowth: A 'Missile Word' that Backfires?" *Ecological Economics*, 126(July), pp. 182–87.

Easterly, W. (2001), *The Elusive Quest for Growth*, MIT Press.

Edquist, H., and M. Henreskon (2016), "Do R&D and ICT Affect Total Factor Productivity Growth Differently?" *Telecommunications Policy*, http://dx.doi.org/10.1016/j.telpol2016.11.010.

European Commission (2005), "Financial Services Policy, 2005–2010," White Paper, European Commission.

Eurostat (2016), *Smarter, Greener, More Inclusive? Indicators to Support the Europe 2020 Strategy*, 2016 edition, The European Union.

Feenstra, R., R, Inklaar, and M. Timmer (2015), "The Next Generation of the Penn World Table," *American Economic Review*, 105(10), 3150–82.

Freund, C. (2016), "Deconstructing Branko Milanovic's 'Elephant Chart': Does It Show What Everyone Thinks?" Real Economic Issues Watch, Peterson Institute for International Economics (https:/piie.com/blogs/realtime-economics-issues-watch/deconstructing-branko-milanovics-elephant-chart-does-it-show.

Galor, O., and D. Tsiddon (1997), "Technological Progress, Mobility and Economic Growth," *American Economic Review*, 87, pp. 363–82.

Gancia, G., and F. Zilibotti (2004), "Horizontal Innovation in the Theory of Growth and Development," in Aghion, P., and S. Durlauf, eds., *Handbook of Economic Growth*, Elsevier, pp. 111–70.

Gordon, R. (2000), "Does the 'New Economy' Measure up to the Great Inventions of the Past?" *Journal of Economic Perspectives*, 14, pp. 49–74.

Gordon, R. (2003), "Exploding Productivity Growth: Context, Clauses, and Implications," *Brookings Papers on Economic Activity*, 34, pp. 207–98.

Gordon, R. (2016), *The Rise and Fall of American Growth: The US Standard of Living Since the Civil War*, Princeton University Press.

Greenspan, A. (1998), "Is There a New Economy?" remarks at the Haas Annual Business Faculty Research Dialogue, University of California, Berkeley, 4 September.

Greenwood, J., and B. Jovanovic (1990), "Financial Development, Growth, and the Distribution of Income," *Journal of Political Economy*, 98, pp. 1076–106.

Griffith, R., and R. Harrison (2004), "The Link Between Product Market Reform and Macro-Economic Performance," *European Commission Economic Papers*, no. 209.

Grossman, G., and E. Helpman (1989), "Product Development and International Trade," *Journal of Political Economy*, 97, pp.1261–83.

Guellec, D. (1999), *Economie de l'innovation*, La Découverte.

Gurley, J., and E. Shaw (1955), "Financial Aspects of Economic Development," *American Economic Review*, 45, pp. 515–38.

Gutierrez, G., and T. Philippon (2016), "Investment-Less Growth: An Empirical Investigation," *NBER Working Paper*, no. 22987.

Hahn, F., and R. Matthews (1964), "The Theory of Economic Growth: A Survey," *Economic Journal*, 74, pp. 779–902.

Hamilton, K. (2006), *Where Is the Wealth of Nations? Measuring Capital for the 21st Century*, World Bank.

Hansen, A. (1939), "Economic Progress and Declining Population Growth," *The American Economic Review*, 29(1), pp. 1–15.

Harrod, R. (1939), "An Essay in Dynamic Theory," *Economic Journal*, 49, pp. 14–33.

Hausmann, R., D. Rodrik, and A. Velasco (2008), "Growth Diagnostics," in Serra, N., and J. Stiglitz (eds.), *The Washington Consensus Reconsidered: Towards a New Global Governance*, Oxford University Press, pp. 324–56.

Hotelling, H. (1929), "Stability in Competition," *Economic Journal*, 39, pp. 41–57.

International Monetary Fund (2003), *World Economic Outlook*.

Iwata, S., Khan, M., and H. Murao (2003), "Sources of Economic Growth in East Asia: A Nonparametric Assessment," *IMF Staff Papers*, 50, pp.157–76.

Jaubertie, A., and L. Shimi (2016), "The Debate on Secular Stagnation: A Status Report," *Trésor-Economics*, No. 182, October 2016, Ministère de l'Economie et des Finances.

Jones, C. (2005), "Growth and Ideas," in Aghion, P., and S. Durlauf (eds.), *Handbook of Economic Growth*, Elsevier, pp. 1063–111.

Jorgenson, D. W., M. S. Ho, and K. J. Stiroh (2008), "A Retrospective Look at the US Productivity Growth Resurgence," *The Journal of Economic Perspectives*, 22(1), pp. 3–24.

Jorgenson, D. W., and K. M. Vu (2016), "The ICT Revolution, World Economic Growth and Policy Issues," *Telecommunications Policy*, http://dx.doi.org/10.1016/j.telpol2016.01.002.

Kanbur, R. (2000), "Income Distribution and Development," in Atkinson, A., and F. Bourguignon, eds., *Handbook of Income Distribution*, Elsevier, pp. 791–841.

Kaldor, N. (1957), "A Model of Economic Growth," *The Economic Journal*, 67(268), pp. 591–624.

Kaufman, D., A. Kraay, and M. Mastruzzi (2008), "Governance Matters VII: Aggregate and Individual Governance Indicators, 1996–2007," *World Bank Policy Research Working Paper*, no. 4654.

Kose, M. A., E. Prasad, K. Rogoff, and S.-J. Wei (2006), "Financial Globalization: A Reappraisal," *IMF Working Paper*, no. 06/189, August.

Krugman, P. (1995), *Development, Geography, and Economic Theory*, MIT Press.

Krugman, P. (1994*b*), "The Myth of Asia's Miracle," *Foreign Affairs*, November–December, pp. 62–78.

Krugman, P. (1994*a*), "The Fall and Rise of Development Economics," in Rodwin, L., and D. A. Schön, eds., *Rethinking the Development Experience: Essays Provoked by the World of Albert Hirschman*, The Brookings Institution Press, pp. 39–58.

Krugman, P. (1991*c*), *Geography and Trade*, MIT Press.

Krugman, P. (1991*b*), "History Versus Expectations," *Quarterly Journal of Economics*, 106, pp. 651–67.

Krugman, P. (1991*a*), "Increasing Returns and Economic Geography," *Journal of Political Economy*, 99, pp. 483–99.

Kuhn, T. (1962), *The Structure of Scientific Revolutions*, University of Chicago Press.

Kuznets, S. (1955), "Economic Growth and Income Inequality," *American Economic Review*, 65, pp.1–29.

Lakner, C., and B. Milanovic (2015), "Global Income Distribution: From the Fall of the Berlin Wall to the Great Recession," *World Bank Economic Review*, 30(2), pp. 203–32.

La Porta, R., F. Lopez-de-Silanes, A. Schleifer, and R. Vishny (1998). "Law and Finance," *Journal of Political Economy*, 106, pp. 1113–55.

La Porta, R., F. Lopez-de-Silanes, A. Schleifer, and R. Vishny (1999), "The Quality of Government," *Journal of Law, Economics and Organization*, 15, pp. 222–79.

Le Gallo, S., and S. Dall'erba (2006), "Evaluating the Temporal and Spatial Heterogeneity of the European Convergence Process, 1980–1999," *Journal of Regional Science*, 46, pp. 269–88.

Levine, R. (2005), "Finance and Growth: Theory and Evidence," in Aghion, P., and S. Durlauf, eds., *Handbook of Economic Growth*, Elsevier, pp. 865–934.

Lopez Calva, L. F., and N. Lustig (2010), *Declining Inequality in Latin America: A Decade of Progress?* Brookings Institution Press and UNDP.

Lucas, R. (2004), "Industrial Revolution, Past and Future," *Annual Report 2003*, Federal Reserve Bank of Minneapolis, http://minneapolisfed.org/pubs/region/04-05/essay.cfm.

Maddison, A. (1997), "Causal Influences on Productivity Performance 1820–1992," *Journal of Productivity Analysis*, November, pp. 325–60.

Maddison, A. (2001), *The World Economy: A Millennial Perspective*, OECD Development Centre, Organization for Economic Cooperation and Development.

Maddison, A. (2007), *Contours of the World Economy 1–2030 AD*, Oxford University Press.

Malthus, T. (1798), "An Essay on the Principle of Population, as It Affects the Future Improvement of Society with Remarks on the Speculations of Mr. Godwin, M. Condorcet, and Other Writers," J. Johnson.

Mankiw, N. G., D. Romer, and D. N. Weil (1992), "A Contribution to the Empirics of Economic Growth," *The Quarterly Journal of Economics*, 107, 407–37.

Martin, P. (1999), "Public Policies, Regional Inequalities and Growth," *Journal of Public Economics*, 73, pp. 85–105.

McKinnon, R. (1973), *Money and Capital in Economic Development*, The Brookings Institution.

Meisel, N., and J. Ould Aoudia (2008), "Is 'Good Governance' a Good Development Strategy?" *Working Paper*, no. 58, Agence française de développement.

Milanovic, B. (2005), *Worlds Apart: Measuring International and Global Inequality*, Princeton University Press.

Milanovic, B. (2012), "Global Income Inequality by the Numbers: In History and Now – An Overview," *Policy Research Working Paper*, WPS 6259, The World Bank.

Milanovic, B. (2016), *Global Inequality. A New Approach for the Age of Globalization*, Belknap Press.

Mokyr, J. (2017), *A Culture of Growth. The Origins of the Modern Economy*, The Graz Schumpeter Lectures, Princeton University Press.

Munnell, A. (1992), "Infrastructure, Investment and Economic Growth," *Journal of Economic Perspectives*, 6, pp. 189–98.

Murphy, K., A. Schleifer, and R. Vishny (1989), "Industrialization and the Big Push," *Journal of Political Economy*, 97, pp. 1003–26.

Nelson, R., and E. Phelps (1966), "Investment in Humans, Technological Diffusion, and Economic Growth," *American Economic Review: Papers and Proceedings* 51, pp. 69–75.

Nicoletti, G., and S. Scarpetta (2005), "Regulation and Economic Performance. Product Market Reforms and Productivity in the OECD," *OECD Economics Department Working Paper*, no. 460.

North, D. (1990), Institutions, Institutional Change and Economic Performance, Cambridge University Press.

North, D. (1994), "Institutions Matter," revision of 28/03/94, http://129.3.20.41/econ-wp/eh/papers/9411/9411004.pdf.

North, D., J. Wallis, and B. Weingast (2009), *Violence and Social Orders. A Conceptual Framework for Interpreting Recorded Human History*, Cambridge University Press.

OECD (2015), "Growth and Income Inequality: Trends and Policy Implications," OECD *Economics Department Policy Note*, No. 26, April.

OECD (2010), "The Impact of the Economic Crisis on Potential Output," *OECD Working Paper*, forthcoming.

OECD (2004), *Economic Survey of the Euro Area*, Organisation for Economic Cooperation and Development.

Oliner, S., and D. Sichel (2002), "Information Technology and Productivity: Where Are We Now and Where Are We Going?" *Federal Reserve Bank of Atlanta Economic Review*, third quarter.

Ostry, J. D., A. Berg, and C. G. Tsangarides (2014), "Redistribution, Inequality, and Growth," *IMF Staff Discussion Note*, SDN/14/02.

Pagano, M. (1993), "Financial Markets and Growth: An Overview," *European Economic Review*, 37, pp. 613–22.

Philippon, T., and N. Véron (2008), "Financing Europe's Fast Movers," *Bruegel Policy Brief*, no. 2008/01.

Piketty, T. (2014), *Capital in the Twenty-First Century*, Harvard University Press.

Quah, D. (1993), "Galton's Fallacy and Tests of the Convergence Hypothesis," *The Scandinavian Journal of Economics*, 95(4), pp. 427–43.

Rajan, R. (2010), *Fault Lines: How Hidden Fractures Still Threaten the World Economy*, Princeton University Press.

Rajan, R., and L. Zingales (2003), *Saving Capitalism from the Capitalists*, Random House.

Ramey, G., and A. Ramey (1995), "Cross-Country Evidence on the Link between Volatility and Growth," *American Economic Review*, 85(5), pp. 1138–51.

Ramsey, F. (1928), "A Mathematical Theory of Saving," *Economic Journal*, 28, pp. 543–59.

Ray, D. (2001), "What's New in Development Economics," *American Economist*, 44, pp. 3–16.

Rodriguez, F., and D. Rodrik (2001), "Trade Policy and Economic Growth: A Skeptic's Guide to the Cross-National Evidence," in Bernanke, B., and K. Rogoff, eds., *Macroeconomics Annual 2000*, MIT Press, pp. 261–338.

Rodrik, D. (2004), "Getting Institutions Right," *CESifo DICE Report*, No. 2.

Rodrik, D. (2006), "Goodbye Washington Consensus, Hello Washington Confusion? A Review of the World Bank's Economic Growth in the 1990s: Learning from a Decade of Reform," *Journal of Economic Literature*, 64, pp. 973–87.

Rodrik, D. (2017), "Populism and the Economics of Globalization," mimeo, Harvard University.

Romer, P. (1986), "Increasing Returns and Long-run Growth," *Journal of Political Economy*, 94, pp. 1002–36.

Romer, P. (1990), "Endogenous Technological Change," *Journal of Political Economy*, 98, pp. 71–102.

Rosenstein-Rodan, P. (1943), "Problems of Industrialization of Eastern and Southeastern Europe," *Economic Journal*, 53, pp. 202–11.

Sala-ì-Martin, X. (1996), "The Classical Approach to Convergence Analysis," *Economic Journal*, 106:437, pp. 1019–36.

Sapir, A., P. Aghion, G. Bertola, M. Hellwig, J. Pisani-Ferry, D. Rosati, J. Viñals, H. Wallace, M. Buti, M. Nava, and P. M. Smith (2004), *An Agenda for a Growing Europe*, report to the President of the European Commission, Oxford University Press.

Schiantarelli, F. (2005), "Product Market Regulation and Macroeconomic Performance: A Review of Cross Country Evidence," *IZA Discussion Paper*, no. 1791.

Schumpeter, J. (1942/1976), *Capitalism, Socialism and Democracy*, Harper & Row (reprinted 1976 George Allen & Unwin).

Schumpeter, J. (1911), *The Theory of Economic Development*, Harvard University Press.

Sen, A. (2000), "A Decade of Human Development," *Journal of Human Development*, 1, pp. 17–23.

Sen, A. (1999), "The Possibility of Social Choice" (Nobel Lecture), *American Economic Review*, 89(3), July, pp. 349–78.

Shackleton, R. (2013), "Total Factor Productivity Growth in Historical Perspective," working paper 2013-01, Working Papers Series, Congressional Budget Office.

Shaw, E. (1973), *Financial Deepening in Economic Development*, Oxford University Press.

Sianesi, B., and J. Van Reenen (2002), "The Returns to Education: A Review of the Empirical Macro-Economic Literature," Institute for Fiscal Studies, WP 02/05.

Solow, R. (1956), "A Contribution to the Theory of Economic Growth," *Quarterly Newspaper of Economics*, 70, pp. 65–94.

Stiglitz, J., A. Sen, and J. P. Fitoussi (2009), *Report by the Commission on the Measurement of Economic Performance and Social Progress.*

Summers, L. (2014), "US Economic Prospects: Secular Stagnation, Hysteresis, and the Zero Lower Bound," keynote address at the NABE Policy Conference, 24 February 2014, *Business Economics*, 49(2), pp. 65–73.

Swan, T. (1956), "Economic Growth and Capital Accumulation," *Economic Record*, 32, pp. 334–61.

Teulings, C., and R. Baldwin (2014) (eds.), *Secular Stagnation: Facts, Causes and Cures*, A VoxEU.org book, CEPR Press.

Tirole, J. (2003), "Protection de la propriété intellectuelle: une introduction et quelques pistes de réflexion," in *Propriété intellectuelle*, rapport du Conseil d'Analyse Economique 41, La Documentation Française, pp. 9–48.

Ventura, J., and H. J. Voth (2015), "Debt into Growth: How Sovereign Debt Accelerated the First Industrial Revolution," *Barcelona GSE Working Paper*, no. 830, May.

Wallerstein, I. (1979), *The Capitalist World-Economy*, Cambridge University Press.

Wilson, D. (2005), "The Rise and Spread of State R&D Tax Credits," *Federal Reserve Bank of San Francisco Economic Letter*, no. 2005–26.

Williamson, J. (1990), "What Washington Means by Policy Reform," in Williamson, J. (ed.), *Latin American Readjustment: How Much Has Happened*, Peterson Institute for International Economics, pp. 7–20.

Yang, S., and E. Brynjolfsson (2001). "Intangible Assets and Growth Accounting: Evidence from Computer Investments," working paper, Massachusetts Institute of Technology, May, available as Paper 136 at the Center for eBusiness@MIT (http://ebusiness.mit.edu).

Young, A. (1928), "Increasing Returns and Economic Progress," *Economic Newspaper*, 38, pp. 527–42.

Young, A. (1992), "A Tale of Two Cities: Factor Accumulation and Technical Change in Hong Kong and Singapore," in Blanchard, O., and Fischer, S., eds., *NBER Annual Macroeconomics*, MIT Press, pp. 13–54.

Young, A. (1995), "The Tyranny of Numbers: Confronting the Statistical Realities of the East Asian Growth Experiment," *The Quarterly Journal of Economics*, 110, pp. 641–80.

Index